With loving memories to our nice friends — Geneva & John from Alma in behalf of Zhearl — deceased 10-13-82

1

# American
# DIARIES
# of
# WORLD WAR II

# American
# DIARIES
# of
# WORLD WAR II

Edited
and with introductions by

**DONALD VINING**

THE PEPYS PRESS
1270 Fifth Ave.
New York, N.Y. 10029

Copyright 1982 by Donald Vining

Excerpts from PACIFIC WAR DIARY © 1963 by James J. Fahey reprinted by permission of Mr. Fahey and Houghton Mifflin Co., Boston.

Excerpts from TIN CAN DUTY IN THE PACIFIC © 1980 by Joseph McNamara used by permission of Mr. McNamara.

Library of Congress Catalog Card Number: 82-60613

ISBN 0-9602270-6-7 Hard Cover
ISBN 0-9602270-7-5 Paperback

# TO
# THOSE WHO DID NOT RETURN

# TABLE OF CONTENTS

PREFACE .................................................... ix

ON LAND
Neal Barton ................................................... 3
Keith Christensen ............................................ 28
Frank Lovell ................................................. 49
Max B. Siegel ................................................ 63
Otto V. Petr ................................................. 75
Anne McCaughey .............................................. 82
Desiderio J. Sais ........................................... 107
Edward Robb Ellis ........................................... 122

AT SEA
Francis H. Brummer .......................................... 133
Joseph McNamara ............................................. 144
Casimir Bielik .............................................. 180
James J. Fahey .............................................. 196
Paul Goldman ................................................ 216
Walter L. Rhinehart ......................................... 242
William D. Askin ............................................ 251

IN THE AIR
Harry Schloss ............................................... 269
Kenneth E. Booke ............................................ 286
Ralph G. Edwards ............................................ 308
Carroll A. Lewis, Jr. ....................................... 319
William J. Sullivan ......................................... 329

PRISONERS OF WAR
Thearl Mesecher ............................................. 343
Michael Mazza ............................................... 374
Michael Harkovich ........................................... 381
Bernard Epstein ............................................. 416

GLOSSARY . . . . . . . . . . . . . . . . . . . . . . . . . . . . . . . . . . . . . . . . . . . . . . 425
INDEX . . . . . . . . . . . . . . . . . . . . . . . . . . . . . . . . . . . . . . . . . . . . . . . . . 427

# PREFACE

People who keep diaries at no other time in their lives may keep one in wartime. Even those who take a humble view of the importance of their life feel it acquire weight that makes it suddenly worth recording. There is also that urge to leave some record of one's existence in case life is cut short—in World War I this led to much poetry as well as many diaries and in most wars it leads to many children whose fathering might otherwise have been postponed.

Following the first World War many diaries kept in the trenches of France were published, especially in England, where there was such a need to understand what a decimated generation of young men had gone through, and where at any rate diaries have always had more readership than they have in the United States. After World War II, however, only a few were published. Perhaps this is partly accounted for by the fact that in the prior world conflict there was more in the way of a common denominator in the experiences of the soldiers and sailors. The war was more geographically limited and the experience of one sailor or soldier could be taken to be more or less representative of all. In World War II this was by no means the case, for fighting in jungles is quite different from fighting in the desert or in the streets of major cities of Europe, war in the air is very different from war on the ground, and a sailor's life in the typhoons of the Pacific is quite different from that of a seaman penned in by the ice of the Baltic.

An additional reason for the scarcity of diaries from World War II may well be that the fighting men and women in that conflict were inhibited by rumors that the top brass disapproved of the keeping of diaries, viewing them as potential aids to the enemy if captured. Direct orders against diary-keeping seem seldom to have been issued but an understanding circulated, more in some branches of service than in others, more under certain overzealous officers with little comprehension of what diaries tend to deal with than under others.

The diaries of top commanders might indeed be of use to the enemy for in these matters of strategy, of troop strength, of available material could conceivably appear, as could evaluations of the strengths and weaknesses of fellow commanding officers. Yet diaries by Generals Alexander and Eisenhower were written and eventually published. If an official injunction against the keeping of diaries truly existed, the generals were either as unaware of it as most of those who kept the diaries here published or chose to disregard it.

As to diaries kept by the ordinary man or woman in service, their potential usefulness to the enemy is hard to discern. Purely personal concerns and physical discomfort are the most common themes; it can be no news to any enemy that military food would get no stars in the Michelin Guide or that conscripts long for home and loved ones. The getting or non-getting of mail, the pleasures of furlough and shore leave, the oppressiveness of heat or constant rain loom large in wartime diaries; discussion of the technology of even the diarist's own duties seldom figures, and the larger strategies are unknown to him. Rumor is rampant and if taken seriously by the enemy would prove more often damaging than helpful. Spies have far more effective ways of getting information than by rummaging for useful crumbs in the diaries of pawns in the war game. Loose lips in bars and brothels, carbon copies of the endless official reports and orders would clearly be more productive.

Many stationery companies actually published thousands of small diary books entitled MY LIFE IN SERVICE or something similar, the pages interspersed with patriotic and inspirational quotations. These provided special pages on which could be recorded the units assigned to, the advances in rank, the citations received, etc. and often there were pages for snapshots and/or autographs of buddies. A number of the diaries in this book were kept in just such volumes. Other diarists used small pocket diaries or whatever notebook came to hand. One soldier wrote his account of battle in a notebook found on a hill just taken from retreating Germans in Sicily and prisoners of war sometimes had to scrounge for paper on which to record their experiences, using cigarette paper, cardboard, or the backs of can labels.

The same reasons that make diaries of service personnel of small use to spies at the time make them of only minor use to historians whose concern is cause, strategy, weaponry, and effect. The value of the diaries is in giving a sense of what war is like to the millions. Memoirs written by those in command, even when they are not primarily concerned with staking a claim to personal glory and second-guessing the strategy of allies and foes, have a distanced overview which is perfectly proper to the station of those writing them. One will seldom get from them, however, much feeling for the smell, sound, temperature or taste of the ordinary warrior's life. It is not something the generals know a lot about, to begin with, since their food, accommodations, transportation, and privileges have throughout history been understandably on a higher level. Concerned with larger issues, small human touches are not something their books will much deal with.

World War II was extremely well documented by journalists and photographers both in and out of service. Fine histories of the war have also been written as the passing of years put matters in perspective. The aim of this book was therefore not to produce even an ancillary book of history. Though it may not be without historical value, no war ever being quite like the one that preceded it or the one that followed, the real focus of the book is on the human dimension.

There can be no pretense that these twenty-four diaries encompass the range of human experience in World War II. Despite wide publicity in military and veterans' magazines, no submissions were made by many categories of service personnel. Nothing was forthcoming from nurses, military surgeons, submariners, Seabees (Construction Battalions), military engineers, Coast Guard, among others. Even more regrettably, no diaries came in from blacks, Nisei, or women who served in the auxiliary forces. As groups low on the totem pole, viewed with some suspicion and disgruntlement by many officers, these three groups probably tended to heed even rumored regulations more than those who had the security of general acceptance. As far as women in service are concerned, it may be that Arthur Ponsonby was right when he wrote in the introduction to his 1922 book ENGLISH DIARIES, "Women, if they write at all, write a great deal..the idea of noting regularly insignificant details of daily life does not seem to appeal to the female mind." Though much has happened to women since that was written, I believe it still holds true today. The tiny diaries kept by so many men simply do not give women a scope that interests them. If we want to know what their reaction was to their pioneering service in World War II, we will have to get it from their recollections or their letters, though the latter are circumscribed both by official censorship and, as letters always are, by regard for the prejudices and sensibilities and interests of the recipient.

In view of the fact that these many gaps exist, some may find the book distorted by the inclusion of more than one diary by members of bombing crews, by ordinary sailors, by prisoners of war. The justification I offer for this is the clear evidence they give of the persistence of individuality even while undergoing roughly similar experiences. This individuality can be troublesome to command when it results in breaches of discipline which impede the war effort or in serious errors of judgement (both of which surface in these diaries) but on the other hand it is reassuring to find that it is never quite possible, even for the best of reasons, to reduce all human beings to cogs in a machine, neither under our system of government nor in the totalitarian systems we were opposing.

Literary polish is seldom present in diaries kept in the Anglo-Saxon tradition (French or continental diaries are something else). Subject matter, not style, is the concern of most diaries in English. Most of these diaries were written, furthermore, by very young men who had not yet had time to get the education some later pursued. The hectic conditions under which the diaries were kept must also be taken into account by pedants upset by the grammar, punctuation and spelling. As long as these errors did not obscure meaning, and I found they seldom did, I chose to preserve them. I had no desire to make the men seem homogenized by copy editing, to erase all traces of their humble origins, their youth, the stress they were under, the weariness, the unselfconsciousness, the linguistic frailty. If generals who became President (Eisenhower) and Secretary of State (Haig) can survive reputations for mangling the English language, why expect more from the very young far lower on the military ladder?

Some "diaries" were submitted which had, quite clearly, been subjected by their own authors to a great deal of post-war editorial attention. Not only was the language corrected and smoothed to an unconvincing and unlikely gloss but incidents not originally recorded were inserted, others amplified far beyond what the diarist could have known at the time, ruminations full of hindsight were indulged in, and often the diary format was totally jettisoned in favor of a continuing narrative. Interesting as these often were, I felt they were too adulterated to include and unfortunately the diary on which they were based had been lost. Though lenient on lapses in grammar and spelling, I played the purist as regards the diary form. We have many sources for recollection and reconstruction of war experience at a remove of time; what was wanted here was the feel of the moment as recorded soon after. This includes an abundance of rumor, of not knowing, of wondering what the future holds. It also includes evidence of the lack of time, energy, and privacy to record in full and to write smooth prose.

Many people do not find the reading of diaries, even at their smoothest, a comfortable pastime. Like the reading of plays, diary-reading calls for a type of mind that is challenged by the need to fill in the interstices where matters are not spelled out as they would be in a novel or biography. I have chosen not to clutter the diaries with editorial notes which fill the gaps at the expense of constant disturbance of the rhythm of the diarist and the reader. I have provided a brief glossary to explain some military terms which might puzzle those who did not serve in World War II but for elucidation of the point, strategy and outcome of military engagements the reader will have to consult the many historical source books available. It is no part of the purpose of this book to provide that sort of illumination. My focus has been strictly on the human experience. I trust that readers will find these diaries moving documents, provocative of thought about humanity and about war. I certainly have found them so in the process of selecting and editing.

I want to thank the editors of the many magazines of military branches which ran notices about my search for World War II diaries kept by men or women of any rank, any branch of service, any geographic sector. These included ARMY RESERVE MAGAZINE, MARINE CORPS GAZETTE, U.S. NAVAL INSTITUTE PROCEEDINGS, and SEA POWER. Thanks also go to the editors of the magazines or bulletins put out by the various veterans' organizations. Among these were THE RETIRED OFFICER, THE JEWISH VETERAN, THE DISABLED VETERAN, VFW (Veterans of Foreign Wars), the 8TH AIR FORCE NEWS, THE OVERSEA'R (Overseas Red Cross Workers), GOLD STAR MOTHER, and perhaps others of which I am not aware since some subgroups of veterans picked up the notice in the publications of larger circulation and reprinted it.

Thanks must also go to Mary Jo Pugh of the Bentley Historical Library, University of Michigan, and Michael Plunkett of the Manuscripts Department of the Alderman Library, University of Virginia, who were kind enough to give me detailed information about World War II diaries included in their holdings, which I had learned about from William Matthews' bibliography AMERICAN DIARIES IN MANUSCRIPT. As the publication rights to diaries belong to the writer or his heirs rather than to the one possessing the manuscript, I was unable to use these diaries though the librarians in question did their best to help me locate nearest of kin, the diarists themselves being deceased. This was particularly regrettable since these university libraries contain diaries by prisoners of war in the Pacific, one of the categories in which there were no submissions by living diarists. In time, of course, these will pass into the public domain. These are not the first diaries of World War II to be published and I am sure they will not be the last.

# ON LAND

# NEAL BARTON

The diary kept by Cornelius W. "Neal" Barton during his days of basic training probably does not reflect the experiences or feelings of most draftees having their initiation into the armed services. Past service in the Home Guards prepared him for much that the ordinary recruit found strange and trying. A chemical engineer born in 1910, Barton had the good fortune to be given a congenial assignment in the 53rd Medical Battalion, Co. D, 1st Platoon. His background plus his natural gifts for leadership also enabled him to advance quickly from Private to positions of responsibility and, after a fairly brief tour of duty in Ireland, to be sent back to the States to attend Officers Candidate School.

Neal Barton, in fact, chose to remain in the Army after World War II and on his retirement in 1961 held the rank of Lt. Colonel. Subsequently he worked in Sales Service Management for a commercial chemical firm. Now, as then, he is a resident of Staten Island, New York.

Like several other diaries in this book, Barton's was kept in one of the small MY LIFE IN SERVICE books, produced by stationers in great quantities. Kept as available time allowed rather than daily, the diary does document such common experiences of basic training as the chafing at command foulups, the search for some diversion in the small towns lying adjacent to army camps, and the informal conditions of wartime marriage.

*******

## May 5th INDUCTION DAY

Had to get up at 6 o'clock to be ready at 6:40. Reported at Great Kills Station and we (11) left for 7th Armory in Manhattan. After a torturous morning we were herded into P.R.R. trains for Fort Dix.

The week at Dix was spent with pick and shovel. We learned how to stand reveille and retreat, do a few simple facings and how to get accustomed to people you wouldn't think of associating with. This might sound snobbish but fall in the same situation and then reach a conclusion.

On Tuesday the 13th we (those selected) entrained for Camp Claiborne, La. A continuous 2 day train ride brought us in and I began my training on May 15th, 1941 as a member of Company D, 53rd Medical Battalion, Corps Troops, Unattached.

First impressions are lasting and I'll always remember Claiborne. A vast sea of tents and one story buildings standing on light brown sticky clay, vegetation sparse, weather sultry and an air of utter strangeness with no hint of whether life for the next year would be interesting. I had no mental attitude whatever, was resigned to the circumstances which put me in this spot and felt I had to put up with it.

Right away I got a taste of how inefficient the army can be when a mistake is made somewhere along the line of an order. I entrained as a member of Headquarters Detachment, was shifted to Company A on the way down and on arrival in camp found no tent or cot set out for me. No one knew where the hell I was to go and so for an hour I wandered around. Finally found I was assigned to Company D and since it was near supper time and no provision for the night had been made for me a cot, blanket, pillow and sheets were thrust at me and I followed a sergeant from one tent to another looking for a place to set it. Wound up in tent five after going thru it twice (two men had been shifted in the interim). Again I felt strange and only lost it after I noticed the other 3 fellows were trying their damndest to make me feel at home.

Supper was a treat. We ate out of crockery and the meal was corned beef and cabbage, the mess hall was spotless, the food excellent and everyone was in good spirits.

The next morn and the several following were spent by the company in getting and spreading gravel atop the ubiquitous mud. As for myself, I had done a chore for Sgt. Mulgrew, who told me to go to my tent and await further orders. When I reported it finished I awaited further orders for two days, only emerging from my tent for meals, latrine, and after 4:30 each afternoon.

I got my further orders that Saturday. It was Kitchen Police and I bent to it with a will. My helpmate was Tony Diana, a strapping fellow who I immediately liked for his willingness to pitch in. Our job was to scrub down the mess tables after each meal. Also to mop the floor. Monday began our 13 week training period. After breakfast we were given calisthenics by Sgt. Mulgrew. Then a drill by 1st Sergeant Dorondo. We were terrible and I said so to the orderly, Abe Baker. He asked if I knew how to drill and I said yes, home guard training. A few days later I asked Sgt. Mulgrew in the presence of Abe if he knew that a certain rule about inhaling while flexing or bending the body was correct, he said yes and I proved by the book he was wrong. Abe took notice.

On May 19th I was called before the captain, who asked me about the home guard, then informed me that he needed acting sergeants and was ready to appoint me. Next day it was a company order.

Life changed from that day. I got both respect and resentment. I sat at the noncommissioned officers table and stopped grabbing for food. I stood aside at drill and corrected individuals. Called the roll at reveille and reported the platoon "ready or accounted for". In class the duty was to maintain order.

Each day during the first few weeks of the basic training schedule was more or less alike. After ½ hr. of calisthenics and drill we went to class under a hospital tent. At first the officers took charge of the classes. Gradually the privates who knew something about the subjects took over. Our basic training consisted of the following:

  12  hours Materia Medica (Pharmacy)
   5  "    Field Medical Records
  10  "    Litter Drill
  67  "    Medical Aid, Splinting and Bandaging
  21  "    Elementary Anatomy & Physiology
  16  "    Medical, Surgical Nursing
   8  "    Treatment of Gas Casualties
   9  "    Organization, Function Medical Units
122  "    Unit Training, Medical Units
  16  "    Battalion, Tactical Training

And in addition all the training that an infantryman would get. The whole business is stretched over a thirteen week period. Classes are interesting and informative. I've taught some myself on Military Sanitation, Discipline, and Personal Hygiene.

As Acting Sergeant I performed many duties and details. One of the most satisfying jobs I received was to see that tents were in order every morning. We were required to have beds made before 7, tent flaps rolled, floors swept and everything in place. "No loose ends" is the expression used.

After several weeks of constant pounding the only thing that beats me was the sudden storms that broke from the skies. It seemed a pity to make a bunch of fellows roll their tent flaps after a hard night at the beer cans and a storm brewing. Yet they did it. Thru these days it never occurred to me that I was bunking with the three steadiest, cleanest, and cooperative members of the outfit. We never had an argument as to care of the tent. If one left something out of place, another would replace it. It was always clean, only disorderly when to be so would not come to the attention of an officer. I've already mentioned that they did their best to put me at ease and I've tried to appreciate them.

Nick Russi came out of Rochester, was put in the company probably because of his knowledge of restaurant work. Short, quiet, well mannered and always busy with paper and pencil for Mildred.

Vic Aeselback was yanked out of a Buffalo steel company to do his hitch. Older than myself, well bred, college education and has a liking for the same things I have. He'd give you the shirt off his back.

Joe Fisk, also out of Buffalo (wishing he were back) came out of Canisius College. Neat, methodical, and quiet except for crooning. These three I come in contact with every day. There are probably others I'd like as well under the same conditions. These pages will decide that.

The first taste I really got of army life for which I didn't care was on June 14th. Sergeant of the Guard they called me. My duty was to change the men every two hours, which necessitated my keeping awake. The men walk their posts for two hours then have four hours off. At 4 a.m. (last change of the guard) I headed for the kitchen for breakfast. Filled in on French toast, Karo syrup and butter then went to bed. Arose at 7 sick to my stomach and staggered to the latrine in boots and raincoat. Had to be helped back to the tent. Slept until 10 when I arose and felt better. Didn't eat hearty until that evening. A lieutenant passed it off as the change reaction of coming to a different climate. Everyone else had their weeks earlier. I still think it was the Karo syrup.

On Monday 16th of June, after an energetic morning, the boys sat down to a dinner of roast pork. Half of them never received any. I had to rob the cooks of what they had put aside for themselves to tell how it tasted. We had had it previously, all you could eat, but the meals up to this were short and incomplete and the boys were disappointed. There was talk about not coming into mess at supper nor did they.

At 4:45 I was notified to prepare to go on maneuvers. Hastily I grabbed a bite with the other 6 who attended mess and left in command car with Sergeant Samuels of Company A and a motorcycle escort. Sgt. Decker drove. It had rained, was chilly, and I had my raincoat on, hiding my shoulders, so the Military Police took me for an officer and saluted when we asked directions. We drove 83 miles ending at Leesville, headquarters for the Red invading army (3rd).

Arriving at 10, the Capt. was in bed so we slept in an ambulance, using litters for beds and a good night's sleep I had. Awoke at 6:15 a.m. Smelled food and headed for it with mess gear. Wheatcakes, blackberries, milk and flakes tasted good. While shaving from canteen cup, the Capt. put in an appearance.

At 7 a.m. we were busy establishing a prophylaxis station, six blocks from the center of town on the school grounds where the invaders had headquarters. At 8:15 we were set up and waiting for business. At nine a major, 2 cpts. and lt. walked up and asked for the commander, for whom I sent. He was notified, released from the assignment and a more disappointed man I never did see. We felt sure we would be stationed there for at least two weeks as a change.

Nothing to do but gather all ends and await return of second in command who had gone back to Claiborne to pick up missing items. The cpt. in the meantime had cleared out to his former bivouac at Boyce leaving instructions to follow on return of Capt. Endris.

Dinner of corn on the cob, corned beef hash, lettuce, peaches and jam was well digested when Capt. Endris arrived. We finally pulled out for Boyce at 3:30. Arriving there, we were shuttled back to Claiborne, arriving in time for evening mess. The short-lived taste of maneuvers was over.

Action in regard to the mess hall incident had gotten under way. Bulletin confined us to the camp area until return of the Capt., who explained the mess situation as one beyond the control of the battalion command. The articles of war were read. The words mutiny, insubordination, overt act were thrown around and everybody quaked in their shoes. To my way of thinking mutiny and insubordination were not present, no orders were given to be disobeyed. It couldn't have been an overt act, as the men themselves suffered in not eating, or would at some subsequent meal—if a man wants to rob his stomach, that's his business.

The first sgt. had a fear that he would be responsible, and out of that fear he called a meeting of non-coms for instructions before standing to the inquiry that formed. The outcome was that the board got him on perjury. They busted him to buck private.

On the 22nd the entire company set out at 8 p.m. on a night march in which we were to learn the principles of orientation (know where you are). When we arrived deep in the woods we gathered for instruction and the captain sent Sgt. Baker and myself out with 8 men each to establish a clearing and aid station. The instructions were, clearing ½ mile on 250° azimuth and aid on 180° azimuth ½ mile further. I had the latter group. We established stations and sent back messengers who guided the rest of the company to us without benefit of lights.

Of all the phases of training that we go thru the most interesting to me and the men is the class on heavy tent pitching. We are so advanced in it now that in these classes we lay out our entire clearing unit. It takes eight men to erect or pitch a four pole tent (48' long). When each man knows his job the tent can be pitched in 8 minutes. My squad to date has done it in 13 minutes. There is bound to be a camera cocked as the tent goes up and the thrill of the builder is on the face of every man who helped pitch it.

On Monday July 7th the entire battalion set out to establish service stations. Our company erected four hospital tents and stood by waiting for patients. Any clearing station unit erects at least four tents. They are known as Administration, Admission, Supply & Evacuation. As the number of sick or wounded increases more tents are erected and they are designated as Surgical, Shock, Walking Wounded, Gas, Epidemic, etc.

I was in charge of the admission tent. Joe Fisk acted as clerk. As the patient came in I read the tag off to him then designated the tent he was to be taken to. It worked out very nicely.

Again we went out on bivouac July 9th. This time we left at 1:30 with full field packs, gas masks and medical kits. After hiking 4 miles we set up tents while Pete the cook prepared a good meal on his new equipment. The adjutant had the presence of mind to pick a spot near a temporary road stand where beer and soda was sold, as well as near a farmer's garden. Between beer and watermelon the boys forgot the snakes. They did ferret out a harmless field snake and did him in.

After dark we were required to set up our hospital tents without benefit of lights. The major was surprised to see them go up and be prepared for action in 45 minutes.

Asked the lieutenant for, and got, a ten minute break. Found Vic and went for a beer. On the way back we were hailed by two girls who wanted to know if it was in order for them to have the road as they were told to pull over. Didn't know how Vic felt about it so I went up the road to ask the M.P. about it and to give Vic a chance to figure them out.

Saw their plates were Minnesota on the way back and would like to have struck up an acquaintance. The girls gave us up as a bad job and went upon their way. This incident is registered as typical of everyday life for a soldier. He is seldom stopped for info by older people and never stopped by civilian men. Whether the girls are just being pleasant or looking for business I wouldn't know. I'm not a hardened soldier as yet. But the girls sure do go for uniforms.

Our morale officer arranged a weekend stay at Lake Charles, 80 miles away, for the battalion on July 11th. We left in convoy at 1:30 Sat. afternoon and arrived in pouring rain at 4:30. The trip down was pleasant for me since I rode in the rear guard jeep. Some of us had the presence of mind to bring our raincoats so we wandered about town. Lake Charles is an oil depot, connected with the Gulf by a canal and ocean-going oil tankers load up for Phila. & NY. It is therefore prosperous and the homes certainly show it. I walked block after block admiring spacious grounds planted with specimen palms and all the flowers I sold as house or conservatory plants. At seven I was hungry so went back to the jeep to rob some sandwiches. Then shaved and stood by for the dance arranged to be held in the high school gym. Rode to the gym in a private car ahead of the convoy and enjoyed the evening. There until 12 when we broke it up. The girls were well chaperoned but Mac managed to get a date with one who roomed with two others. We had to phone her to find if it was okay and did. Had rye highballs until 4 when the girls took me back to grammar school where we were bivouaced. Slept on a table. Awoke at 8:30 and headed for cafeteria, mainly to get a cup of civilian coffee. It sure tasted good after 70 days of Army mud.

Heard the Masonic Lodge was giving out meal tickets so I headed for it. Was the first in. I asked if a Lutheran Church was in town and they finally found it. Services were at 10:45 and they told me I should come back then or stay around and they'd see that I got there. The ladies supplied me with writing paper and I finished three letters, read the papers and started to play ping-pong when a hostess came over to take me to church.

The church was small, belonging to the Missouri synod which is highly evangelical. Heard blood & fire and then stood on the sidewalk waiting to be taken to dinner. It came in the person of a little quiet German by name of Stehr who took me in the meanest looking car to a modest home for a fine German meal. It developed later that he owned the super gas station across from his home and the car repair & upholstering establishment next it; not to mention 3 acres of ground behind his house, which was on the main stem only three blocks from the center of town.

After dinner Mr. Stehr took me to see the estate of his friend. Was amazed to see a monkey menage and a deer reservation where the does came up to feed from your hand. Bamboo, thirty foot palms, hundreds of lotus blooms, and a pear orchard (they require special attention in hot climate).

I missed the convoy and Mr. Stehr took me two miles out assuring me that I would get a lift, which I did. Missed the convoy by half an hour but beat them back by a half hour. My benefactor happened to be a contractor erecting buildings in our camp and he dropped me off in front of the mess hall in time to eat. Turned into bed at 8:30 and had trouble arising for reveille at 5.

Come Sunday the 27th Tony, Vic and Ford went awalking with me. Walked 2 ½ miles down west road then turned off south thru the woods. Soon railroad embankment appeared so we stood on the woods' edge rather than in the sun. Tony walked over to the embankment and called me. When I arrived he asked if I would like to take a picture of a snake. Sure, I said, and he answered, one foot from where you were standing. Went back with the camera cocked and took a snap of a four foot gray runner which isn't poisonous. Even if he was our puttees would have been ample protection. We continued along the embankment until we struck a north road and wound up at a former bivouac where a farmyard was stacked with melons. Went in and purchased a 35 center and the four of us gorged ourselves. Tony wanted to buy one of the chickens which was gobbling up the pits as we spewed them out, so he could try his hand at roasting it but found he and we had 40 cts. among us.

The proprietor was the thin emaciated type with a high pitched voice. We questioned him on living the land and found that one could buy an acre for $2.50 and up. His father bought land at 25 cts. an acre and heavily wooded at that. The ground yields well, planting of vegetables starts April 1st. Two crops of tomatoes can be harvested a year.

On Tuesday August 5th the battalion set out to establish for maneuvers. Payday was the 4th so we had lots of amusement with the drunks. The battalion moved out going south on Route 165, ending two miles east of the junction of 190 & 171.

We immediately pitched hospital tents and the first platoon went into operation. Among the first patients we took in was a case of gonorrhea and acute appendicitis. All the officers had a gleam in their eyes and it looked for a while like a cutting would be done. Finally decided to evacuate the patient to the 43rd Evacuation Hospital. In the eve a corpse came in that once housed the spirit of a negro. He had gone down for the third time and it left him. Since the Q.M. wasn't prepared to deal with this kind of situation, we had to evacuate the corpse also.

In the evening a convoy was granted to take off duty soldiers to town. Had a good cup of coffee and a highball with people introduced by Corporal Asona. Expect to go back on future occasions.

After 16 days at this location the second platoon moved up to within one mile of the town of DeRidder. The first sgt. stayed with us and that almost stopped my future well-being in the Army.

The circumstances leading up to the event was the mass of confusion we've been going thru. To my way of thinking there are two distinct echelons in any army service, that of company administration and that of the technical function. One deals with the operation of the company and the morale of its personnel. It includes the records of it and its proper discipline. The second echelon is that relating to service. This is what sets the company apart from the rest of the army. We are medicals and it takes one trained in its principles to properly run the service. All this was the basis for the following.

No latrine orderly had been assigned thruout our stay and on this particular morning we were busy packing equipment preparatory to moving. The 1st Sgt. had been absent over night and Lieutenant Koepp had gone over the method of preparing to leave. Everything was scheduled.

A detail was wanted by him to strike tents. It was a little ahead of schedule but it was furnished by Sgt. Vaughan. A bit later when every man was busy he calls for four men. I answer all are busy. He insists so I go to Sgt. Johnson and go over his list of men. None available. 1st Sgt. in the meantime disappears so I go back to my duty. In a few minutes he comes back bellowing for me. Wants his four men. I suggest taking them off the tent striking detail. He says no. Insists, saying the captain wants them. I tell him to tell the captain when I have 4 men available I'll send them.

Well, the captain called me. I told him I was dead wrong, having lost my head over the interference. I took two men off the tent striking detail (there were ten men on it and it only takes eight to strike a tent) walked them down to the latrine, ordered soap, water, brushes and creosote for one to use and the other went on the business end of a shovel.

We arrive at the site where the second platoon had set up the station and the following morning I was instructed to report to the C.O.

The article of war pertaining to the offense was read and then the action that could be taken. The captain chose to admonish and reprimand. The first sgt. couldn't understand this type of punishment and in the first non-com meeting railed about the captain's decision. It was too bad that the old army had to give way to a new composed of officers and men who did not know how to run things. He was going to transfer to headquarters company where a few oldtimers were left.

I wasn't vindictive because the captain had given me a break. I too know the workings of the old army. I tried to convince him that he shouldn't question the captain's decision. Later the non-coms told me I was a dope in giving him advice.

We stayed in this new location one day and promptly moved out to a position one mile west of Dry Creek, La., in a field of cutover timber.

We arrived at 5:20 after moving 52 miles. The ground was bumpy and full of stumps, many of which had been blasted out, leaving gaping holes. It did look like a war torn field what with burnt tree butts all over. Markers and tents were set out and pitched. Right in the middle of erecting tent number 2 the first sgt. called my detail to unload trucks so they could return for the 2nd platoon. In the meantime nine chauffeurs laid around idle. They did start to unload a truck ten minutes after we set to work but laid it down when my detail had the other trucks unloaded, which was 3 minutes after they set to work. All tents were pitched at 7:10 and we went to mess. It sure tasted good after a day of hard work. It consisted of macaroni and cold water.

Labor Day weekend went on until the night of Labor Day itself without event worth noting. Then after an amusing evening chewing the rag and incidentally taking time out to catch an armadillo we went to bed. At 3 a.m. one of those Gulf squalls came in to annoy us. Every now & then a gust of wind and buckets of water came down thru and under the tent. It began to look like we would be buried under our cover. I was lucky in that I had a bed composed of 3 bales of linen and mosquito bars with a fly tent as a mattress and a leakproof part of the tent above me. However, I got up during the storm and fastened down the skirt ends, burying a pickaxe in them. Each man did some kind of tightening to secure the tent. However no other soldier managed to keep from getting wet. Cots and equipment were soaked. Upon inspecting the next morning I found that records in the administration & admission tents were soaked. Thank heaven my platoon wasn't on duty.

3 times on Tuesday morning the first sgt. tried to call reveille and three times a squall answered him. We finally did get the men lined up, dispensed with roll call and had them go half-heartedly over the grounds policing it.

.....

I made a momentous decision yesterday. Orders were to obtain answers from all men over 28 in regard to release. I was the first called before the commander. After being assured that present law says I will be released after one year of service I put my answer in the form of a question thusly, "If the captain considers me valuable in my present position I'm willing to stay the year out." His answer was that I was good first sergeant material. If I minded myself there was no reason that I wouldn't be chosen. I gave answer to stay. 26 of 28 men applied for release and I don't blame them one iota. A private would have no reason to stay in our present situation to my way of thinking.

I'm conceited enough to believe I can do this army some good. I firmly believe it can be made to function a lot better. I get that way thru reading the ARA's and the various manuals available on the different subjects. I'm conceited also in believing that I can judge character—I've done it for years getting a pleasant surprise in finding my deductions to be correct. With these aims I feel I can do more than the average man can do for his colors.

We moved again Sept. 8th to a position one mile east of Oberlin, La. Our area turned out to be a former rice meadow, low, damp and infested with mosquitoes, something we hadn't had anywhere else. It took only one night to convince us that mosquito bars were necessary and that came thru as a battalion order. Arriving, we promptly set to work erecting hospital tentage by tent peg markers. It was apparent that the tents weren't going to line up on the square and much confusion resulted from the change of position. Trucks had been unloaded and supplies lay in the path of the new line of tents. They had to be moved. Finally the first three tents were up in complete darkness and we turned in for a night's rest. In the morning we had to complete our unit even while we cared for sick call.

That evening we had opportunity to visit the town of Oberlin. We caught the townsmen unprepared for the business they could have done in food. Beer and soda is easily supplied as bottling plants are in most towns of 5000 people or over. At 8 o'clock all desirable food had vanished. The business area consists of one story frame boxes built mainly of second-hand lumber. You can buy most anything necessary to meager living at the same counter in any one of a half dozen stores. Prices are low. I obtained two yards of cheesecloth to protect against mosquitoes for 10 cts. That neatly disposed of the necessity of putting up a bar every night.

Noticed an imposing looking building at the end of the pavement and headed for it. Turned out to be the county seat and District Attorney's office for five counties. I walked thru it and would have gone in to see the county clerk about Louisiana law re: marriage and land if he had been on duty. Incidentally the building was almost an exact copy of our boro hall in Staten Island on a smaller scale.

All the older people (or at least a great many) in these parts speak French to the exclusion of English. It is an understandable provincial (south) French. They evidently refuse to learn the English for they have lived here all their lives and yet understand no English. Since Huey Long introduced a schooling system their children are compelled to learn and they act as go-betweens for parents and others.

.....

Mike Frankel managed to get most of the Staten Island boys together so we took the picture on the preceding page to forward to the Staten Island Advance, who had asked for it.

.....

We left Oberlin as a platoon on Monday afternoon the 16th for a position one mile south of Forest Hills on state highway.

We moved again on Friday for a point 19 miles out of Alexandria, near Boyce. This move was evidently made to throw the red army off guard for it was nowhere near where the action was to take place.

Sunday afternoon saw us moving South and East towards Opelousas, which is near Longfellow's Evangeline country. The territory we previously have been in has been cut-over timberland, stark and naked for twenty years or more, so it really was a thrill to see towering pine, dense underbrush or open wet woodland heavy with Spanish moss and dead tree butts.

Five days we spent at Point Blue, during which we experienced the side winds of a hurricane. Officially the wind was blowing at a ten mile per hour intensity but in between there were some powerful gusts. Folding my cot one morning I suddenly found myself buried in canvas. After groping around clumsily I finally located a pole and howled for others to do so. It took mighty effort to raise and then hold it until all pegs were redriven. All that morning we were in constant fear that the tents we were in would come down. As for the rain, it came right thru the canvas, overflowed the ditches, making us all uncomfortable.

All day Sunday we lay around expecting to move. The order came at 7 p.m. and the boys, now having an incentive to move, went at it with a will for they knew if they didn't beat the 34th Division to the road they would be out another 3 days waiting for them to pass by. We were on our way to Claiborne 30 minutes after the order to move, and we left the place in apple pie order, too.

My first night back in camp was very uncomfortable—I couldn't get used to the mattress on such short order.

.....

MANEUVER MEMORANDUM

The background of an individual is always reflected in any observations he makes. Now I don't claim to be a complete soldier as yet so if a civilian point of view creeps into my narrative it is because I haven't been fully schooled in army administration. Yes, we have a manual, but so many changes occur which haven't been recorded, or so many AR's are missing that complete knowledge of a possible procedure is very often lacking. To inquire brings varying ideas as to how the problem is to be handled. Administration therefore hasn't been all that it should be. To use common sense often leads to difficulty in that the higher echelon sees the problem in a different light. He in turn is often embarrassed by higher command also. The result is extra labor or loss of time.

Before setting out for the field we were given a mimeographed list indicating the articles we were to take along. The list apparently had been made for infantry as several items down were not part of our equipment. Each soldier was allowed one barracks bag and the idea was for two to double up—e.g., one barracks bag inside another to facilitate handling. It developed that the equipment we were to carry practically filled the bag. We therefore had few comply.

In addition to the clothing packed in these bags we were to bring along our shelter halves, 2 blankets and mosquito netting. This was a separate bundle and very necessary. Our haversacks slung over our backs contained mess gear, raincoat and toilet articles, web belts around the hips with canteen and aid packet, gas mask slung to the left side and medical pouches on either side completed the soldier.

At the time I raised a question about the cooks carrying first aid pouches and the full compliment of clothing along with their four kitchen uniforms. I hesitated to raise the question whether as a clearing company we should have them as all of our medical chests duplicate their contents. I don't believe offiers carried theirs altho several did have their little black personal bags with them. Only one soldier ever carried them on his person thruout maneuvers. The rest of the company seemed to insist on using their pouches to keep their barracks bags off of wet ground. That is, if they hadn't lost them.

As for clothing we were required to carry four uniforms and three sets of fatigues. Seldom did a soldier wear the latter and then only because his uniforms were dirty or he was saving it to go to town. As a non-com I had no occasion to wear them other than once and that was to construct dish racks. The other two were excess baggage available for collecting mildew. I don't say that fatigues shouldn't go with a medical soldier but I do say that one pair would have sufficed. They to be worn only when performing kitchen police, latrine or other dirtying work. To take along six pair of underclothes was sheer nonsense. Two uppers and three lowers were all I ever used, washing them as I took them off. Seven pair of socks were allowed and necessary seeing the condition of most soldiers feet. They should be changed every day and washed immediately. A certain corporal I know slept for days without removing puttees.

Company supplies were handled admirably. The few shortages that occurred were in the main faults of the Q.M. However, none of them had any bearing on the immediate discomfort of the patients.

The most important of all army services is the variety and quantity of food the men receive. Personally I had little fault with it and that was in the variety. Still, you do get hungry and must eat. Quality of food was always good.

In moving from bivouac to bivouac no definite scheme of accounting for men or equipment was ever followed. Sometimes personal equipment was loaded separately or was until I insisted it stay with the men. I've been taught that a soldier's equipment is part of him and must always be close by. In this respect it indicates that he must take care of it, and the best way is to get it under cover as soon as he arrives in a new area. The books allow 15 minutes to set up shelter halves and 15 minutes to strike and pack. As for the latter, the procedure is to get all government equipment packed first and then personals as they are less likely to be overlooked.

Sanitary procedures turned out to be one of the worst managed details of the army. Trained men fresh from school were lacking in the aggressiveness that gets things done. This led to interference from sources not familiar with methods the army lays down. The kitchen lacked proper incineration on many a day. Waste pits were overfilled, no allowance being made for that one foot of soil to ground level.

Latrines lacked guards the first half of maneuvers. They were never properly dug, nor adequate for the men to be served by them. Again lack of aggressiveness led to improper contruction and the men were confronted with a straddle trench 20 or more inches in width, the ground on which they stood well oiled and a six foot drop below them.

Standard latrine boxes weren't available so a two-holer board was placed between horses for the men to sit on. If comment was made about washing them down daily the answer was "the sun keeps it sanitary".

Why an epidemic of pediculous something or other didn't break out is a miracle. From the mobile laundry which did our work on two occasions I received a woolen undershirt in error. It was full of the bodies of steamed lice. After picking them out I turned the shirt over to a soldier who had lost one in the Q.M. laundry.

Patients come in from the field with filthy clothes and bodies, not all, but a few. They were perfectly capable of spreading lice if they harbored them. How we escaped is beyond my poor ken. In two incidents I ordered able patients to wash their clothes. Lt. Benz made a practice of having others do their underclothes.

In leaving an area our company did its best to leave the surface as clean as we found it. We were never lax in that matter.

Last but most important comes the matter of discipline and its relation to morale. When we left for the field we were fairly well trained and on our way to being soldiers army style. Morale was high, the rigors of the field were unknown and therefore not hard to look forward to.

After a few weeks in the field during which time the men familiarized themselves with the snake bogey boo, had opportunity to go to town of an evening, morale was excellent. When the order came to move and the unit moved, morale started to sink, only rising slightly with each chance to go to some town or other.

Even tho spirits were low the men never neglected their mission in the field. Patients marveled at the kind considerate treatment they received, one even going so far as to write the commander on the merits of some of the men. It was observed that contrary to general army tho't the older men gave the better service in most instances. Yes, it was difficult on occasion to require a man to empty a diarrhoea patient's pan without him losing his stomach or to have a festering pussy wound treated, but they hardened to it.

Maneuvers proved that we got the men & the will. All we need now is for those at home to produce the material.

.....

We've been back in camp for 16 days now and have spent that time in housecleaning, taking inventory and such. As for myself, I've kept me busy on a simple landscaping scheme for our area.

The whole company at some time or other has been out cutting sod so we could hold back the erosion that goes on constantly down here. There isn't a stone in the soil and the heavy rains cut troughs in the most level of land quickly. After sodding banks we continued to lay more around our new recreation hall. I then secured Eupatorium (annual aquatum, I should have said) buck and slash pines and some shrubs of the Daphne family from the woods and scattered them about. They look pretty good. The first sergeant tho't it would be a good idea to spell out our organization in the grassy bank facing the road and to that end I set out looking for bricks to lay out "Co. D, 53rd Medical Battalion". Believe it or not, I found some! This country is totally devoid of any kind of masonry material so far as general observation goes, but I tho't I had seen a ruin on one of my jeep trips out of camp for something or other so I investigated and sure enough—bricks galore. After finishing these projects the company went into a month's "refresher" course in how to be a medical soldier. The program calls for officers to attend classes in the morning at battalion headquarters and the non-coms to teach other soldiers in their respective recreation halls during the morn. In the afternoon it's reversed.

After attending classes for four days I was put on a detail to build a boxing ring. Six men were picked to help me and we went looking for instructions. After beating around for an hour looking for the officer in charge, took matters in my own hands and got the battalion tool chest.

Were you ever confronted with an order to do something entirely foreign to your usual type of work? Well, this was one of those incidents. Here I had six men, only one of which ever swung a hammer as a carpenter and that as a helper.

After making an inventory of the lumber supplied I decided to build the ring in 4 sections as Nick Rubino, the boxing instructor, informed me it should be 24 by 24 feet. Such a proposition took on the proportions of a housebuilding project and frankly I was flabbergasted.

Well, to make a long story short I had lumber cut and nailed together. I think it's damn good considering the fact that none of us are carpenters. When the four sections are completed we will bolt them together and prop the legs to level.

The next thing that happened was that I found myself on "Battalion Sod Detail". The Sanitation & Improvement Officer liked the manner in which the different companies were beautifying their areas and instigated the detail to carry on in the adjacent areas such as the motor pool where the battalion's rolling equipment was stored and the Headquarters Office. I was put in charge and each company furnished men daily—30 in all. We set to work on the ditches at the motor pool, squaring them off, banking the sides and sodding them. I had put in 4 days at this and then on the 20th October I went on furlough but not before I had laid out another week's work for the crew.

I got a break for my furlough in being allowed to leave a day ahead of time. However I lost most of the time because of a washout along the Missouri Pacific lines.

Vic and Nick had been given their release and I rode the distance home with them, taking the New York Central instead of the Pennsy. Both of them were stuffed with money, the government having given them 5 cts a mile for 1428 of 'em. That, added to accrued pay and travel allowance came well over a hundred bucks. We ate like kings and stayed awake for fear of being 'rolled' (taken for your money). Vic went so far as to put it in his shoe and it had him limping all the way.

The washout brought me into Grand Central late and I almost missed Kat. For once she was late also.

After a bite we decided to stop in Dad's office before going home. He had to show me around and was he proud!

Furlough days were thoroughly enjoyed. No time was wasted on those things that I could do in camp. I lunched as a guest of Mr. Gandy's at the Lions' Club, was wined and dined at various homes and in general used every waking hour on some pleasant task or mission.

The 51st Regiment Company L, of which I was a member before draft gave me a review. The captain insisting that as guest of honor I should walk on his right, which I did, uniform and all—who am I to tell a captain whether he's right or wrong?

The Corinthian Club failed to have their usual Hallowe'en party, the event I especially had in mind for coming home on the 20th. So instead a few got together and gave me a dinner at the Old Mill. We had to stop at Key's for cocktails first then after the dinner visited with People's & Jackson's. It was then that my engagement to Kat was announced.

Leaving New York was hard on me. It wasn't because the taste of civilian life had gotten me, but the distance. I pray to God that the distance between me and all I hold dear will shorten so that visits home will be more frequent.

.....

I walked into camp on November 4th just in time to fall in the pay line. When I came out the bankroll was heavy but by the time I reached my tent it was low. Men going on furlough needed cash and they knew I had it—Oh, well, being more fortunate than they I feel that I'm only doing my part to make their stays at home as enjoyable as possible.

Before the day was out the captain had seen me & published an order appointing me Acting First Sergeant in the absence of Sgt. Bedwell, going on furlough.

The succeeding two weeks were hectic but I got plenty done and picked up a lot of knowledge. I got in the master sergeant's hair, as he says, on three occasions. The result in each instance being that while I wasn't right according to the way things have been running, I was sufficiently correct in my way of thinking to warrant annoying him. I think the major backed me up in the first instance. In the other two I stood up to him and talked.

I always wanted to see a uniform arrangement in everything a soldier does within his own community. If one man puts his shoes at the head of his bed, why, everybody does it. If we are going to hang clothes on a rack everybody is going to hang the same thing first, last, and in between. And all racks will be in the same tent corner. All this makes for an understanding of discipline and it surely will help a man to obtain a habit of orderliness. Well, I drew an order and got the captain to sign in approval. I drew other orders from bulletin announcements that previously had gone unnoticed and then threatened. On inspection tour I found almost all had complied to the letter.

During this period the men were agitating for recreational amusements and I took the subject up with the captain. Found I couldn't get a ping-pong board or the material to make it with so got around it by getting the material for another purpose. However, when it isn't being used for the purpose it was intended for, the boys use it for a ping-pong table. The first night we had it every company in the battalion had a representative on hand. Officers came to investigate later.

During the two weeks I headed the enlisted men of Company D, 53rd Medical Battalion I can point with pride at one thing in particular. The recreational facilities were brought to a head and we have the best equipped hall in the battalion and surely one of the best in the entire camp. I've investigated.

.....

The army has a highly systematized method of feeding its soldiers. They call it Ration Strength. For every soldier available for duty each day the Army allows between 40 & 44 cents to feed him. There are two ways in which this allowance is used. Under one plan the company buys their food where they will and they eat what they want. Under the other system, and that is practiced in all large concentrations of troops, the Quartermaster buys the food and apportions it dollar for dollar. Under this system there is a saving and 2 cents per day per man goes into a company mess fund. It mounts up fast and is always there when you want a beer party or such.

There is another way in which our company swells its mess fund. Being a collecting company or rather a clearing company which hospitalizes patients, we get under Army rules a ration plus 50 per cent in cash for each patient we care for. On maneuvers we had plenty and our mess fund went way over $600. The object in getting the 50 per cent in cash is to furnish our patients with special food, if diagnoses warrant it, and we did.

However we spent from time to time on beer, watermelon, etc. and never dented the fund. It grew in spite of ourselves then on Thanksgiving Day we had a blowout equal to any feast I've ever had. The opposite page is a cutout from the folder menu commemorating the event, showing who attended.

215 pounds of turkey, 20 pumpkins, 10 mince pies, 60 pounds mixed nuts, 100 apples, 100 oranges, stringbeans, mashed & sweet potatoes, punch, (We had Tokay wine on the menu but weren't allowed to serve it), creamed onions, peas, stuffing, grape jam instead of cranberries, grapes and candy. All this was set on our tables, we all dressed for the occasion, the captain offered thanks and then we stuffed ourselves.

All day long the boys visited the mess hall. Seemed as tho they would eat, go walk it off then start the process all over. Nothing was removed from the tables but dirty or empty dishes.

Thanksgiving was my last day as acting first sergeant and on Friday I went back to my usual duties.

The battalion sod detail was put in my care and I started to map the area for ditching. The previous ditching had to do with road edges. One morning Capt. Endres advised that a nabor of his had offered some shrubbery if we would dig them out.

I formed a detail of 8 men and we rode 20 miles to Oakdale. We secured 9 liquista hedges 6 feet in height and a few odds & ends of crepe myrtle & hedging. They dressed up our buildings very nicely.

Guess the boys made a hit with the daughter and she's invited us back another day. Said she would hunt up some more shrubbery from the nabors. A few days later I again put in appearance with only four men. It took us an entire morning to load up and when I found I couldn't get the detail back in time for chow why I went to town and bought pork chops, bread & butter after Mrs. Burkholter said she would fix for us, and she did. The Burkholters have their own cow. That means milk & butter of which we had all we could swallow. Hot biscuits & syrup, tomatoes, preserved fruit, beans & pickles made up the meal. Everybody ate heartily. We had a full load going back. The "take" contained 6 holly trees, 2 ft. 3 tamarack, more crepe myrtle, more liquista, plenty of hedging, 4 fan palms, Lantana, rose bushes, silver leaved maples, canna roots and some vine-like bushes which arch gracefully against a wall.

We "washed up" the plants amongst the four companies. Needless to say, we got the best.

.....

We learned that the proposed furloughs to be granted over the holidays were cancelled two days after the Japs had run wild. We were all downhearted at the news and a few turned heaven and hell in order to secure a few days leave. I managed to squeeze in on it as I had the money to go home. On December 11th I received furlough papers for 7 days, was told I would have to travel by car, that no extension of time would be granted and to be ready for recall immediately.

I managed to get passage home from a Company C man—his car was the heaviest of all those going North and he looked the most sensible of the bunch.

Good time was made to Perth Amboy. We were on the road 41 hours, traveling a distance of 1581 miles. I arrived home at 7:30 of a Sunday morning to find Mother sick and wasted but happy to see me. She insisted I rest a few hours, which I did.

The whole point of this furlough was to pick up Kat and bring her back with me to live in Alexandria. The government grants quarters allowance to enlisted men of the first three grades and I felt I should take advantage of it. After an hour's rest I had to get up and tell Mother what we were doing in camp since I came home last.

After dinner I went down for Kat and chatted with her parents for an hour or so.

.....

We were on our way at 5 o'clock, destination for the first night was Collingswood, N.J. at June's.

At 7:30 the next morning we started on the first phase of our 1500 mile trip. At 1 p.m. we arrived in Maryland and called on Dick, who thought we might be married there.

The trip we took to the county seat turned out to be a failure so we went on thru Washington, ending at Warrenton, Va. for the night.

Again we were up early as we subsequently were for the remainder of the trip. Finally we arrived in Alexandria at 5 p.m. 4 days after leaving Staten Island.

There was lots to do. Kat would get information during the day and pass it on to me in the evening. I'd finish it up from there.

At the Lutheran Service Center Kat made the acquaintance of Pastor Mehl who secured lodging for her and finally married us come Sunday. I'll always remember the wedding party and the fun we had. Harry McCollum & Bill McAndrews of the Signal Battalion and Les Bedwell, our First Sgt., besides me & my bride were the principals.

I found that in spite of my marriage I still had to be in camp at 11:45 each night. Kat took it good-naturedly but was ever suspicious of what it meant.

Finally the restriction was lifted somewhat. Married men were allowed one night home and one night in—I managed to squeeze in only one and then came the great change.

I had sat up late my first full night in camp—chewing the fat in the orderly tent and had just been in bed a little over an hour when I was awakened and told we were to get ready to move out of camp. This occurred at 1:30 a.m. At 2 a.m. every man in the company was working to get things in order. Loose equipment had to be boxed and crated, mattresses, sheets and all other things with two ends were in process of being accounted for.

It was 5 p.m. the next evening before we let down and then only for a few hours. We had to mount our trucks and other mobile equipment on flat cars at the railroad yard. In bitterly cold weather (for Louisiana).

.....

From this point on my narrative must falter from loss of memory. I take my pen up again after nine months of enforced silence.

It would be needless to say that I was dazed by events directly after the New Year. Kathie had been with me only eighteen days and only a few hours daily at that when I was packed off to a point nearer home (and the ocean).

Left in Alexandria with the car. Kathie decided to drive home rather than sell it. After 10 days she had found her way to June's. The marvel of it all was that she had driven 1580 miles without license.

.....

The company entrained at Bringhurst with many other troops. We traveled in first class in pullman cars. Due to the amount of freight being hauled along our route it took four days to make the trip and we finally arrived at Ft. Dix in New Jersey.

The East was in the grip of a cold snap and we felt it. Due to the speed in which we arrived quarters weren't ready for us and we were assigned to tents. Most of them were without stoves and we rushed around taking them out of other tents in the area.

For two weeks we kept our stoves red hot and still felt cold if we moved a few feet from them. In the meantime our officers had been busy looking for other quarters.

After a week's quarantine we were allowed passes, and when Kat arrived a few days later I was allowed out but had to be back for 6 a.m. reveille. We subsequently moved into barracks adjacent to the service club. Kat secured a room in a farmhouse only 1½ miles down the road and even went so far as to get work in Pemberton.

Just when all this had settled us the army decided that we were to ship out.

The order arrived at 4 p.m. the 17th of February and we were again ready to move. A few days later we were well at sea in a 6000 ton ship, part of a convoy heading toward Ireland as we later found out.

The crossing was one of fears and discomfort to every soldier. The hot stuffy holds contributed to mass seasickness aboard. After the first three days meals fell off and a good many refused to eat, relying on candy for subsistence.

We awakened on the morning of March 1st to the sight of land. It was quite a thrill realizing that this was an outpost of the old world and that we would soon set foot on soil once more—unharmed.

It wasn't until the next evening that we docked. Some volunteer organization had prepared coffee and sandwiches for us. The military wanted to get us out of Belfast in a hurry so we had only ten minutes in which to refresh ourselves. Needless to say lots of soldiers never came near the food.

After struggling thru five blocks with two barracks bags and our field equipment on our backs (much to the amusement of the populace) we arrived at the railroad. We were amused at the toy freight trains and engines. All around us were signs of the blitz they had received eight months previous and as we pulled out of the station (in coaches) we saw whole blocks that had been wiped out and they were dwelling places, too.

The ride took us to the town of Ballymoney. We were broken down to lots of 50 men or so and marched to different parts of town. We won trademan's hall for the first night. The next day my men were shifted to St. Patrick's Hall. This we occupied for two months.

Of course we soon settled down to a training program—the dominant feature being a march of about eight miles a day. I became very adept at missing a great many, especially after I developed blisters.

.....

Came the day when our company was given the assignment of operating a small hospital at Kilrea. Everyone was sick of the training program and anxious to do something constructive.

For six weeks we were charged with the hospital—the work getting heavier daily as patients came in. Every man soon found that he was busy at least 12 of the 24 hours in the day.

.....

Just when we had reached a saturation point in work we were relieved by an English contingent and packed off to a new area.

We were sorry to leave as Kilrea was a lovely spot. The site was an old monastery of 400 years ago. We had our best weather at this location and most important of all, rationing wasn't thorough, which meant that we could buy thick steaks, plenty cakes and other foods without endangering civilian supplies.

It was in this town that I picked up two antique silver vases at the cost of only one pound.

.....

Our new area proved to be famous as the one time home of Lily Langtry, the actress. Drummabaragh House it is called, being the hunting lodge of Sir Something or Other. It nestles in a valley about a mile from the village of Doagh.

Again we settled down to a training program which continued in intensity until we got around to devoting a full day to marching (19 miles). There was much complaining and as a means to tighten down on the boys pass restrictions were limited.

Ordinarily pass restrictions would mean little for a soldier could sneak out. But this place is completely surrounded by a stone wall, very ancient and high. It couldn't be climbed as the stones were loose.

It wasn't long before someone dubbed the place "the Rock" and substituted "Warden" for Major. Later on when our company was fortunate in leaving the place to work in Waringsfield our captain would tell us that if we didn't do a good job we'd probably go back to the Doagh House (pronounced "Dog"—Doagh is the name of the village). To us that was the same as a boogey man to a child and we worked like Trojans to keep out of it.

Again came the day when we were given an assignment to prepare a hospital. We were carried off to Waringsfield, an estate about eight miles south of Lisburn. Here the British had almost completed a hospital on the American plan of architecture. Nissen huts of corrugated steel were connected by the usual long corridors. It was a distinct improvement over our construction in that it was built of brick and steel—fireproof.

It was a lovely bit of country. The river ran peacefully by at the bottom of the hill we occupied. Pretty Mary's fort, an historical earthwork affair lay nearby and the estate house was one of those massive stone mansions built in the early 1800's and protected by high stone walls around the courtyard.

The hospital consisted of 26 wards, could accommodate 900 patients. We were to operate it as a convalescent section of a nearby General Hospital.

There was lots of work to be accomplished. At first we equipped the hospital from our clearing station materials, drew on the British for beds, etc., meanwhile receiving an average of 50 patients a day.

Soon a flow of our own American equipment came thru and we started to substitute it for the English materials. Finally a trainload of material arrived and we did the same procedure all over again, the earlier American equipment being taken up and the most modern available replaced it. Aluminum and stainless steel operating tables, surgical racks, serving and steam tables, wheel chairs, desks, etc.

After the first three weeks the work became so heavy that 30 men from Company A were sent in to help. These were soon absorbed and authority decided to send us 200 men out of England. These men turned out to be a "green" hospital crew and our commander was given jurisdiction over this detachment in which there were 16 officers who outranked our C.O. When I was called out of the company we were caring for 900 patients with a total hospital unit strength of 309 enlisted men, 37 officers and 40 nurses.

My duties allowed me contact with civilians and I made the most of this contact. I especially enjoyed visiting with Mr. Henderson of the Northern Bank Limited in Lisburn. He lives over the bank as manager.

Mr. Henderson was a member of the cricket club, the tennis club & the country club. I had the privilege of using them all and certainly was shown deference. If he wasn't available on any of my frequent calls at the bank I had the run of the house. The maid served tea and I usually was around for lunch and dinner. The Madam was slightly deaf and I got in her good graces by sending home for some batteries for her audiphone. Nothing was too good for me from then on. One Saturday I had in mind going to Portadown as I was in the habit of picking up souvenirs in a different town each week. While waiting for a bus Frank Benner the fruit grocer picked me up. I decided to "walk orchards" with him that afternoon. We visited the apple country below Portadown and I watched while he bought each farmer's coming apple crop, still a month from ripeness. He wrote out checks totalling 4800 pounds that afternoon and pledged another 18000 when his pickers walked in.

Earlier in Ballymoney I spent a few evenings with Rev. Armstrong (Church of Ireland). A very learned and righteous man, he was a staunch Irishman and had written a history of Ireland. An Episcopal minister in our understanding but nevertheless fair to all religion. Others I met in Ireland were narrow.

.....

In the conversations that often took place the boys would often talk about going back to the USA and their eyes would light up. The day Joe Fisk, Jake Hempel and myself received that word brought no elation. It was too momentous to fathom. The rest of the company tho was quite happy about it for it indicated that it could happen and they were genuinely happy for our sake too.

We were packed off to await available transfer (with others) to the USA to attend Officers Training Schools. We had won Medical Administration Corps at Camp Barkley in Texas.

After a week of expectations we finally moved. Out of Ireland, into Scotland and finally aboard HMS X-1, the largest ship afloat. In peaceful days she was called the Queen Elizabeth.

Quite a few Royal Airmen, Canadian soldiers on furlough and Royal Navy sailors and officers were making the trip.

The ship needed guards and the airmen were put to that distasteful job. One could find them posted at the bottom of stairways and passageways not used in the boat's trips East to West.

As for us officer candidates, we mounted machine and anti-aircraft guns as well as the heavy hardware to deal with subs or other warcraft. I found that if action was imminent the English gun crews were to rush to these various turrets and throw us out—we were only performing the tiring job of watching. They did, however, take pains in showing us how to operate our gun (Jake was my partner).

I'm glad I didn't end up in the Navy. Night watches are the most trying job I ever attended to—even if they only last 4 hours.

In the free time I had I explored the boat and hadn't quite nosed over it all when we reached New York, six days out of Scotland.

The sight of the hills of Staten Island brought joy to my heart. We tied anchor only 200 yards from the shoreline for 2 hours until the Hudson River was clear of certain traffic before moving to a pier adjacent to that housing the submerged Normandie.

An Army tug then took us down harbor again to Fort Hamilton. As it was late I made no attempt to call Kathie or my folks. When I did, I'm afraid the shock of having me back had something to do with their dazed condition when I finally came home.

I was given eight days on detached service and ten days delay en route to Camp Barkley and enjoyed every minute of it.

.....

The days spent at OCS Camp Barkley were ones of nervous strain. Studies came easy and I and a few others had plenty of time for card playing. However, the strain was occasioned by what is termed "ATTITUDE". Indescribable and vague since many a man well ahead in studies, neat in appearance and command personality was washed out. I came to the opinion after graduating that how well you get along with those around you carries qreat weight in determining whether you are officer material.

Great stress was placed on personal cleanliness and orderliness.

Demerits were given for laxity in these departments as well as any infringement of school orders—and there were many. I was proud of the fact that I was one of the 19 out of 287 men who finished the course as "virgins".

On December 19th, by Act of Congress and the hand of Brigadier General Hefflebower, I was commissioned 2nd Lt. MAC.

My commissioning orders were to report to the Seventh Medical Supply Depot at Fort Sam Houston and I was allowed ten days en route. Naturally I went home for five days.

In the few weeks that the unit was at Fort Sam I familiarized myself with the men by accompanying them to the medical warehouse, watching them at drill and adding comments in classroom.

At this point was informed that diaries were considered good sources of information to enemies and it would be better to send this record home.

# KEITH CHRISTENSEN

Many people keep diaries only during brief periods of their lives which they feel are extraordinary—while traveling abroad or while involved in war. Keith Christensen, of Rapid City, South Dakota, felt that even Army life was too routine to be interesting, not realizing that the routine of one war acquires antiquarian interest by the time the next war comes along with new weaponry, new means of transportation, new strategies dictated by different geographic settings. What he did feel might be of interest was an account of 60 days when he was involved in a test of Army rations.

Using a staccato style very different from that of Neal Barton, whose diary precedes it in this volume, Christensen kept his meticulous record daily rather than at leisure as Barton did. Using a commercially published book not unlike the MY LIFE IN SERVICE series but actually titled A DIARY OF THE TRAVELS OF___, Christensen at one point expresses frustration at the limitations of the allotted space. This, as much as the daily fatigue and the frequent lack of proper light accounts in large measure, no doubt, for the fragmented sentences. However that may be, the diary gives a very vivid account of what transpired in the mountains during the rations test. Not by any means the least interesting thing it reveals is the way in which human nature resists all attempts to control it tightly.

Born in 1921, Keith Christensen had had two years of study at North Dakota State University when he entered the Army and became a member of H Co., 201st Regt., Fort Carson, Colo. He completed his work for his BS in 1949, was recalled to duty in the Korean War, 1950-1952, took a Master's Degree in Guidance and Counseling in 1955 and has subsequently been teacher and counselor. In 1981 he retired from the U.S. Army Reserve with the rank of Major (Infantry).

*******

June 9, 1944 Friday Camp Carson, Colo.

Mon.-Tues.-Wed. on range for record firing. Up at 3:30 all three mornings. I fired Wed. for record. Windy as hell. Fired 188 out of possible 210. Leave next week (Thurs.) for the 2 mos. experiment.

JUNE 10, 1944

Close order drill & manual of arms all morning. Makes one disgusted. Kid stuff. Inspection of rifle & equipment.

## JUNE 11, 1944

Letter from furlough date & one from Wilber at mail call. Into Colorado Springs tonight. Some joint on edge of town for a couple hrs, then to "Hogen's" for rest of evening. Never again! I hate the Springs. Waited until 2:00 A.M. for bus to camp.

## JUNE 12, 13, 1944

Mon. 12 pitched tents and had a review of squad tactics, arm signals until 10:00. Cleaned rifles from 10-12. Laid around all afternoon. Walked over to 89th after supper. They were out on bivouac. Came back and wrote Edna a long letter, 12 pages. Like to see her before I go over.

Tues. 13 Took a 4 hr. hike in morning, 8-12. Feet dam hot in wool socks and boots. Washed feet and put on cotton socks. Went to a show after chow. Bing Crosby in "Going My Way". Excellent!

## JUNE 14, 1944

Up at 5:15. Start of physical checkup for mts. Weighed in at 6:00. 175 lbs. Scale a bit low, I figure. From 8-11 we took tests. 5 min. up & down on box-alternate foot-Pulse 60 Chinning 9; sit-ups 51, 300 yd. dash round flags, 52 sec. Back to barracks at 11:00. Check on reactions—skin, eyes, gums, reflexes, this afternoon. Cleaned weapons from 3-5.

## THURSDAY, 15

Up at 6:00 We rolled our full field in the morning. Sleeping bag, jacket, etc. in barracks bag. No blankets. Slept all afternoon. In the evening-show with Ed. "Adventures of Mark Twain". Service club for sundae on way back. All this ends tonight. Hit the hay after my last warm shower & shave.

## FRIDAY, JUNE 16, 1944

The purpose behind these two months in the mts.

The Army at the present time has a variety of rations, "C", "K" and now this new 10 in 1. All have been used both on this side and in combat areas. All have been lacking in food value under certain conditions, topographical or climatical. We are to test all under adverse conditions. We will be pushed to our physical utmost. Medical check-ups will be made daily to determine the effect both pro and con. Urine specimens will show whether the body is absorbing the vitamins or is at capacity. These tests have never been tried so we are privileged in a way. The going will be dam tough but if in any way we benefit the rest of the services or ourselves we feel justified and compensated for our efforts.

ADDED NOTE: July 4, 1944

The above literary masterpiece was written before the mind was attacked and overcome by the "canned vitamins" the Army terms rations. Oh, for a strawberry shortcake and a T-bone steak.

Up at 5:30. Chow at 6:00. Cleaned barracks, rolled up bedding. Covered sun tans & O.D.s. Fell out at 9:00. Police call. Platoon Leader inspected for candy, etc. 10:00 Entrucked at 11:00 and on our way. Our truck hit another in Manatou. Knocked wench cable loose. We fell behind. Caught up while others were on piss call. Dusty as hell after we left highway. Reached area about 4:00P.M. E. Co. still conducting tests so we laid around. Chow at 5:30. Pitched tents. Bed rolls covered with dust. Talks by doctors after chow. Took off on a 2 mi. hike then. Back to tents at 8:15. I washed in stream before chow so ready to turn in. Cold as hell. Tomorrow to be a full & busy day. A.G.F. tests & examinations. Getting dark so close & hit the sack.

JUNE 17, 1944 Bivouac area-Tarryall Lake

7:30 P.M. Still haven't eaten. Dead tired. One hell of a full day.

Up at 4:30. Entire platoon urinated at 5:05 A.M. Drank one mess cup full of water at 5:30 (Primer). Struck tents. At 6:30 the medics took our urine samples. ½ platoon then took some vitamin "C" in solution. Ate chow at 7:00. At 8:00 they took 1 oz. of blood from our arms.

Then the tests began. Same as before while at Carson in morning. Afternoon started the A.G.F. Chow at 11:30. 0ur last cooked food. Start rations for supper. We finished the tests at 4:00. Dog tired. Went down to stream, stripped & bathed. A car full of girls had quite a laugh. The hell with them. Too tired to think of loving. Left for permanent camp area at 5:15. Dusty as hell. No sense in taking a bath. Pitched tents—laid out sleeping bags. No rations as yet. 7:45-rations. "K" & 1 can pork and egg yolks & 4 crackers. Hitting the hay after I finished chow (canned). Woe befall the guy who wakes me. Mail call at 8:45. Hit the sack at 9:00. Called us out at 9:15. Related entire set-up as far as rations go.

JUNE 18, 1944

Up at 5:30. Ate at 6:45. Filled out paper on reaction towards rations. Hiked 2 mi. Cleaned rifles until 11:00. Back at 11:20. Ate chow at 11:30. "K" rations. Hope to have afternoon off—washing to do. Policed area about 2:00. Just loafed till then. Rifle inspection at 3:30.

JUNE 19, 1944

Up at 5:30. Thru eating by 6:45. Moved out at 7:00. Rifles and combat packs. Over to range. Fired 24 rounds at targets. Left range on 25 mile hike. Break every 50 mins. Ate rations at 11:30. 1 hr. off. Started again at 12:30. Tried short cut over mt. Wrong hunch. It took 3 hrs. to get to the top. No water since noon. Dry as hell. Another guy and I left down a valley. Picked up road we came down on. Met up with 4 more. Nearly in camp when captain caught us. Slightly peeved. We fired 24 more rds. and then went in to eat. Washed up a bit, washed sox and then ate. Cleaned rifle after chow 8:00-8:20. Called us out at 9:00. Fire warden gave us a talk on fire prevention. No time for ourselves. Only interesting remark. Elev. here 8500. Mt. tops 9-10 thousand. (We should know. We climbed one today.) No rattlesnakes. They never go higher

than 6000. Mail call now. See if I have any and then hit the hay. Sleep until 6:30 tomorrow. They must feel sorry for us. Ain't that a lick?
JUNE 20, 1944
   Up at 6:30. No duty until 9:00. Shaved, ate, hung sleeping bags up to air. Walked out to transition range. Fired 16 rds. Thru at 11:00. Ate at 11:30. "K" rations. Chocolate made me run. Laxative, I guess. Platoon fell out at 12:00 for bayonet practice. I helped around area. Filled G.I. cans with water. 55 gals. Dug a latrine 1'-7'-3½'. Co back at 2:00. Afternoon off. Night problem coming up. Just finished washing a few clothes, hair & body. Helmet a far cry from a tub or shower. Laid down from 4:15-5:10. Ate chow. Cut off hair in front. Let it lay flat. No combing. Some guys have scalp locks. Look exactly like Indians. Ed rubbed my back with vinegar. A little sore & red from too much sun. Want a tan in too much of a hurry. Called out at 9:00 for night vision test. Took about 1½ hrs. Got to bed at 10:30. Eyes sore from the red goggles we had to wear. Saw dial at 7 ft. Not too good.
   Going to start conserving pages. These lengthy discussions of a day's experiences take up too much paper. Never have enough pages at this rate. (ADDED JUNE 28, 1944-) Rescinded!
JUNE 21, 1944 First day of summer 25 mile hike
   Up at 5:30. Ate chow & fell out at 7:00. Walked to range. Combat packs & M-1. Fired 12 rds. Took off on march. Walked until 11:30. Stopped for chow. 1 hr. (Tarryall River) Washed up a bit—soaked feet. Started back at 12:30. Hot, dusty & windy. Tired as hell. Back at 4:45. Fired 12 rds. & into area. Ate chow 5:30. 3 letters for mail call. Tomorrow off. 4 hr. hike tomorrow night. Turn in early. Exhausted. They're trying to kill us, it seems. B.S'd until 10:30.
JUNE 22, 1944
   Up at 11:30. Just dozed from 6:00 on. Ate chow at 12:00. Inspection at 12:20 or soon after. A spot check—missed me. Took off for creek after insp. Shaved-left mustache. We're growing them. Boiled fatigues in tub. ½ bar of G.I. Wrote letters while clothes were boiling. Get letters off while I'm free. Wrung out fatigues and hung them up to dry. Ate chow at 5:30. B.S.d around until 8:30. Fell in at 8:30. Combat packs & M-1s. 3 breaks until 11:50. Followed road-thank God! A different route. Ate "K" rations 11:50-12:34. Started back.
JUNE 23, 1944
   Reached area at 4:10 a.m. Stayed up until 5:00. Made coffee. Hit the sack at 5:00. Slept until 10:00. Laid in sack until 1:00. Tent hot as hell. Two letters for mail. Edna and Mother. Write them both on finishing this. Ate at 2:00. "K" rations. Walked into hills with Ed. Write letters. Discussed pro and con of marriage. Ate chow at 5:30. John and I took a bath. 5 gals. $H^2O$ in a tub. He washed me and then vice versa. Held

church at 8:00. J & I didn't go. Going to a show as it is dark. Ann Sheridan in "Winter Carnival". Looks like rain. Hope it holds off. Hit the sack at 10:30. Had seen show.

JUNE 24, 1944

Up at 5:00. Weighed in at 5:30 (175). Ate chow at 6:00. Put toilet articles in pack. Mounted trucks at 7:45. Back to area—same as June 16, 17. Went thru A.A.F. and A.G.F. tests same as before. Results on table in rear of book. Ate "K" at noon. John had some illegal jam, peanuts & butter. Had a feed. Chased a weasel in out of the rocks for about 1 hr. after chow. Fell in at 12:45—had pack weighed. 26 ½ lbs. and rifle. John and I took it easy on 4 mi. march. Salt tablets made me sick to stomach. Lt. Moore gave us a royal ass chewing on return to camp. Claimed we laid down on the job. Had warm showers before returning. Really felt good.

JUNE 25, 1944

Entire company overslept. Up at 6:30. Ate chow cold & fell out at 7:15. Over to range. Fired 12 rds. Took off on hike. Rifles & C packs. About 11:00 the 3rd & 4th platoons became separated. We were following the side of a mt. About 500 ft. up. Quit at 12:00 & ate. Chased cattle, filled canteens at spring—3 halazone pills, and finally left at 1:30. Took flat country back—i.e., small hills. Followed roads a bit. Heard firing at 3:30 so we hurried back. 3rd & 4th were back & firing. Fired 12 rds. more. Back to area. Ate at 5:00. Shaved, washed a few clothes & bathed after chow. (In tub). When John gets back (sq. ldrs. meeting) we'll have another pow wow. Last night until 10:30. Fire, Indian dances, songs.

JUNE 26, 1944

Overslept. Missed reveille, 5:45. Ate chow. Hung sleeping bag out to air. Fell out at 7:30. Hand infantry training all morning. Creeping and crawling, cover & concealment, and rushing & falling. Back to area at 11:00. Ate chow 11:30. "K" rations. John & I B.S.d by lean-to until 12:30. Security all afternoon. Up on Mt. Rolled rocks over cliffs, etc. Back at 4:00. Ate chow & then worked on lean-to. Russian & I went down to old lumber mill. Tore tin off roof—nailed on lean-to. Just got back from niqht training—vision. Night field glasses excellent. 6 power. To bed 10:30.

JUNE 27, 1944 ½ mile from area in fox hole 8:30 p.m. Weighed. 171, down 8 lbs in 12 days.

Up at 6:00. Ate at 6:30. Fell out at 7:00 for police call. Inspector general coming. Out for training at 8:00. 1 hr. talk by Lt. Moore on scouting & patroling. Blacked our faces to show daytime camouflage. At 10:00 John & I took off on scouting mission to find a platoon-3rd. Climbed a mt. & observed them. Found a radio & messed up the air a bit. Back to camp at noon. Ate chow at 11:30. "K" rations. Worked on lean-to, sewed rip in canvas. Fell out 12:30. Squall tactics until 3:00. Marched to present area. Dug fox hole 3:30-5:30. Back to area at 7:00. Washed all mess equip. Mosquitoes thick now. Hit sack after I heat coffee by candle. 3 lumps of sugar. Energy.

JUNE 28, 1944 First night in lean-to

Miserable night. Awake every hour. Legs cold. 3:30 put mt. jacket over them. Cramped as hell. Neck stiff. Rained during night. Raincoat over top helped. Ate chow 7:30. Dirty as hell. Hands, face, hair, etc. "K" ration given out 9:00. Eating candy and chocolate. Slept from 10:30-12:30. Ate "K" rations at 12:30. Legs stiff at knees. Filled up fox holes at 2:00. At 3:00 we hiked to area. Mounted trucks and went to shower area. Back at 5:00. Ate chow and 5:30 started working on lean-to. Down to old lumber mill—tin and sawed wood. Took down tents. Patchwork effect on lean-to. Semi-finished. Now 9:10. Start fire and B.S. a bit. Our first night in lean-to.

JUNE 29, 1944

Up at 6:00. Lt. Moore woke us. Slight slant to ground—slid down during night. Slept o.k. A pleasure to be able to stand up and dress. Chow at 6:30. Fell out at 7:30. Lectures all morning. Compass, map reading & individual weapons. Back at 11:10. Ate chow. "K" rations. Fell out at 12:30. Tactical deployment of the point demonstrated. Back to area at 1:30. Carried water for lister bag and G.I. cans. 55 gals. Afternoon off. Russian & I went down to old lumber mill. Boards for shelves. Ate at 5:30. Spread pine needles on floor. Built fire in fireplace. B.S.d around fire. Sang songs. Practiced for big pow-wow Sat. night.

JUNE 30, 1944

Up at 5:45. Weighed in 174. Up 3. Fell out at 7:20. Fired 12 rds. and on our way. M-1s and combat packs. Break every 50 min. Little toe developed a blister. Ate chow at 12:00. Started back at 12:30. Walked three miles and stopped 20 min. Tarryall River. Filled canteens. Water at school house where we ate dirty. Back at 5:00. Fired 12 rds. & back to chow 5:45. Washed mess kit & utensils. John shaved me-I him. Soaked feet after trip to medics-puncture blister. Leave guns for tomorrow. Sat around fire B.S.ing, singing, etc. before hitting hay.

JULY 1, 1944

Awake at 8:00. Laid in sack & dozed until 10:30. Got up for pay. Red-lined. Incomplete remarks. Will be 3 mos. in Aug. no pay. Over $200 coming. Put on swimming trunks to get tan. Hungry as hell-no breakfast. Now 11:30-chow soon. Ate bacon I missed at breakfast. "K" ration meat getting sickening. Laid around after chow waiting for shower trucks. Mail call. Rec'd Fargo Forum only. Recognized a few people. Left area for showers at 2:00. Showered & back at 3:15. Chaplain in lean-to. Had chow with us. Bummed smokes. Drew tomorrow's rations at 6:15.

Opened them—took a chocolate bar. Men at church now. (Some of them) Show after church. "Foreign Correspondent". Russian, Pulaski, Ed & I discussed *Jews*. Kill the dirty bastards. Show started at 8:00. Had seen it long ago. Saw it with someone much different than a G.I. (John & Ed). Some day I'll see more with her. Edna, to whoever is curious. The last few lines written by candle-light in lean-to.

JULY 2, 1944

Entire Co. overslept. Up at 6:30. Fell out at 7:30. Fired 12 rds & on our way. Head for mt. near Tarryall River. Reached water depot at 9:40. Filled canteens and rested. At 9:50 started up. Rocks rolling loose made climb dangerous. Leo just missed. Rock split just on reaching him. At 11:50 we called it enough. Ate chow. "K" rations. B.S.d until 12:40. Took off to go down. Followed Mt. a couple miles on descent. Reached Tarryall about 2:30. Picnicers there. Hot dogs, etc. Hard on eyes and guts. Started back at 3:00. One bad hill. Reached range at 4:20. Fired 12 rds. Last two hours in slight rain. Cold as hell. Chow at 5:00. Was going to wash & shave—still raining, skip it. Now 9:05. Coffee on outside. Blow out candles and get a cup. Eat some ham and eggs also. Hungry. The Chaplain's first words on hearing the type and extent of the men's profanity were "It's amazing".

JULY 3, 1944 Fire in front of lean-to. 9:30 P.M. While chicken is cooking

Up at 6:00. Ate chow at 6:30. Clean mess equip. Fell out at 7:30. M-1s & cartridge belts. Lecture on advanced guard & rear guard. At 10:00 we practiced both. I was flank guard both times—sweet stuff. Back to area at 11:20. Ate chow. John, Foggy & I "K" rations. Caught a baby rabbit. Let it go. Felt like eating it raw. Fell out at 12:30. Over to range. Practice throwing hand grenades. Started raining about 1:15. Hailed. We ran back to area for raincoats. Rained harder so stayed in lean-to until 3:15. Fell out again for continuation of h.g. throwing. Ate chow at 5:00. John, Foggy & I took off for woods. (The hell with the ration cans). Walked to a farm house we had passed on a hike. Talked a bit to one rancher driving tractor on road. He left & we went up to house. A wreck—old logs & wood all over the place. There until 7:30. He was an old bachelor—been there since 1918. Had 37 sheep. Old war veteran. 41st Div. Bought a chicken $2.50. Had him get us 3 loaves of white bread next Sun. Carved up chicken in woods. Left bayonet—get it tomorrow. Washed chicken on arriving back in lean-to. G.I. butter-"C" crackers. Fried it from 9:30-10:30. Not bad. A bit like rubber. We devoured every scrap. Cleaned cooking equip. & went to bed.

JULY 4, 1944 Today 4 years ago 1940 Edna 1944 mts.

Fell out for compass problem. Over to same area as fox holes. John, Russian, Foggy & I teamed up. Started at 10:00. 15 different azimuths. Finished at 12:30. Ate chow, "K" rations. The four of us laid down and went to sleep in lean-to. Woke at 3:00. Fell out—raincoats. Orientation of night problem 8-12. Out guard security. To fire blanks. Celebrate the 4th. Drew 5 blanks. Walked 2 miles to area. Into position at 8:30. 3rd platoon was the enemy. They started advance at 9:00. Everybody firing. Would have killed both friendly and enemy if we were using ball ammo. A total mixup. Lots of fun, however. Started back at 11:30. Raining cats & dogs. Wet as hell when I reached lean-to. Hung up clothes to dry. Washed black off face and hit the sack after about 10 "C" biscuits. Easy to eat when hungry.

JULY 5, 1944

Up at 8:00. 2 hrs. sleep gratis. Ate chow. Cleaned barrel. Blanks eat steel in a hurry. Fell out at 9:00. Down to lecture. Practised rushing & hitting ground. 10 question quiz. Back to area at 11:30. Ate chow & lay down in lean-to. B.S.d. Fell out at 12:45. Refresher lecture on advance party. Started to rain at 2:00. Over to rec. tent. At 3:30 we had practical training. Advance guard. Back to area 4:30. Ate chow 5:00. Carried excess to observer tent. Buried cans. Steel wool on mess equipment. Gen. McNair to inspect tomorrow. Cleaned rifle thoroughly. Put fatigues & towels to boil. Dirty as hell. John shaved me & I shaved him. He trimmed mustache. Getting just right. Dug two new latrines. After clothes had been rinsed and hung up we sat around fire & B.S.d. John played the bugle a bit. Sang songs from a hit book he had.

JULY 6, 1944 Sunny and warm all day. Too warm.

Called us at 6:00. We got up at 6:30 (the privileged four). Breakfast waiting when I got up. After chow I ran a couple of patches thru rifle. Got pack straightened and canteen full. At 7:30 we fell out. Over to range. Fired 24 rds. On our way at 7:50. Sharon has internal piles & Moore a fever. Reached chow area at 11:25. "K" rations. Started back at 12:45. Followed road until 1:35 & then took off across country. Back to area. Cleaned M-1 after chow. Read a sex book with John a while but quit. Too childlike. Only common sense. Went out by fire a while. About 10 guys. B.S.d until about 9:30. Subject was mostly women. Talked over and compared different happenings. Discussed marriage. Asked John & Russian some very personal questions. Checking up on their knowledge of life.

JULY 7, 1944 Writing on table we just built. Eating table.

Took off for hills. Another outpost problem. Lasted until 11:30. 1st platoon of 3rd sq. of 2nd platoon enemy. One hell of a lot of fun. Firing point blank at each other. Critique at 11:30 & then dismissed. Ate chow at 12:00. "K" rations. At 1:00 we took off for the old lumber mill. Got wood for table. John, Russian & I took off from mill for abandoned mine shafts. Get 2 x 4s. I climbed down and got some black sand. Full of fine mica. Panned it but gold dust too fine. Bumped into captain on way back. He was in another shaft. Picking gold from rock. Also fine. Back to area. Table built. Cleaned rifle & bayonet. Rifle inspection at 4:00 Ate chow at 5:00 with 3rd sq. at new table. Washed whites again after supper. Raked area. Moved stones to clear area around fire pit. Snuck off in dark to table. Polished up wash basin. A reflector for candle.

JULY 8, 1944 Dozed off & on until 11:30. J.,R., & F. came back from hills. Had 2 eggs & a chicken. Zeke's place. I heated some sausage & ate "C" biscuits and jam for breakfast. Pulaski & I took off for ranch. Try & get some bread, eggs, or potatoes. No luck! No one home. Cut across flats instead of mts. to place where chicken was hid. John, Russian & Dean were there. Had water boiling for feathers. We stayed a while & then took off for area. Fargo Forum waiting. One clipping interested me. M.M. getting married. Funny, I never figured it this way. Still single & intend to stay so, I hope. J., R. & Dean came back about 3:15. Chicken plucked & cut, ready to go. Will fry tonight during show. Ate chow at 4:45. Fed peanuts to chipmunks. Getting tame as hell. Shaved & washed feet. Put on some of John's after shave "stink" lotion. Can smell it 100 yds. Started frying chicken at 7:00. Just after co. meeting. Chaplain held services after meeting. As usual I didn't go. Show started at 8:00. Short on war material and enemy strength. G.I. movies. Main show was "Housekeeper's Daughter". New generator so went along swell. Show over at 10:40. Ate chicken & hit the sack. Had to rise early.

JULY 9, 1944

Up early 4:45. Dam tired. Hard to get up. An extra cold morning. Platoon urinated together at 5:00. Weighed in after that. 173. Mounted trucks at 5:30. Cold as hell riding to topside. 17 miles. Urinated again at 5:45. 1st half drank "C" vitamins. Ate at 6:00. At 7:30 they drew blood specimens. At 8:00 they gave us a physical checkup. Skin, reflexes, eyes, etc. Tests started at 8:45. Harvard tests started then. Finished at 11:15. Off until 1:00. "K" rations. Laid around in U.C. trunks absorbing sun. Start A.G.F. tests at 1:00. Finished 3:20. Took off for showers. Really felt good. Clean for the first time in a week. Mounted trucks at 4:30. Took off for camp area. Tired as hell. Out to table after chow. John and Pulaski played black jack. I joined in. Fritz, J., F., and I played hearts until 9:00. Big hike tomorrow. Hit the hay after a cup of coffee which DeLucca is making. Put 2 boxes of sugar in coffee. Can use energy.

JULY 10, 1944 A hike. Dead tired

Up at 6:00. Policed up. Fell out at 7:35. Combat packs & M-1s. Over to range. Fired and on our way. At end of break—10:20, we started across open field for Lake George. Looked close but oh! God! Distance deceiving. Walked until 12:35. 2 breaks. Finally called it quits and ate chow. "K" rations. Started back at 1:20. Hit some water but capt. said no. Not moving. Walked until 3:30. Found a well. Ice cold but strong sulfur taste. Rested there a bit. Took a small short cut. Couple of short breaks. Up hill all the way. Reached range at 5:50. Fired-then back to area. Supper waiting. So dam tired I didn't eat much. Washed my feet 7:15 and hit the sack. The four of us talked. Started feeling worse. Fever. Finally dropped off to sleep. Awake off and on all night, John coughing excessively.

JULY 11, 1944

Up at 7:00. So weak I could hardly stand. Ate very little breakfast. Fell out at 9:00. Tried to keep up but couldn't. Gave up about 9:30 & went back to lean-to. Medic took my temperature. 96°. Slept all day. Awake occasionally. Got up at 4:30. A little better. Still weak. Ate a little supper. Took some medicine DeLucca had. He also had been sick. His stomach. J., R. & P. left about 6:00 to get some rhubarb. Played with baby prairie dog John had caught. J., S. & P. came back about 9:00. Had been to Zeke's. Had 2 doz. eggs. Bread, potatoes & syrup. Had egg sandwiches & hit the hay 10:00.

JULY 12, 1944

Up at 6:00. A little weak yet. Ate a little chow 7:00. Fell out at 7:30. Fired and on our way. Hit the hills at 9:30. Lt. Patrick shot a coyote on entering hills. 2 shots-carbine. First in stomach-broke front left leg on leaving. Second in head. A young one. Hit Tarryall River. Crossed on rocks. Got one foot wet. Gomez picked up my helmet down stream. Ferguson got completely wet, rifle and all. Reached water area at 12:00. Ate a little of "K" ration. Hailed about 15 min. Ground white. Lightning struck a rock. Knocked Wes Moreland off. A close one. Left at 12:30. Reached range at 3:00. Fired 24 rds. Back to area at 3:30. Ate at 4:30. Potatoes, eggs and onions along with reg. rations. John, Hodge, De-Luke & I played poker until 9:00. Borrowed a buck to start with from John. Repaid it during game. Quit $1.65 to the good.

JULY 13, 1944

Up at 6:30. Overslept. All four of us. Conrad woke me up. Late for chow. Fell out at 8:00. M-1s, cartridge belts & bayonets. Lecture on target designation. Lt. Noonan. From 9-11:15 we had bayonet instruction & practiced training. Back to area at 11:30. Mail call. Letter from Edna. She's in Frisco now. Marriage pressing. Like the idea in ways. No job or dough ahead in future, however. Fell out at 1:00. Compass course. Paced ourselves cross country & road. 53½ strides to the 100 yds. average. Took off at 2:00. 2nd sq. didn't get back until 6:00. Last sq. in. Fairfax took off on his own. He wouldn't make a pimple on a PFC's ass in my opinion. Ate chow. Cleaned cooking utensils. My turn. J., R. & Pulaski catching chipmunks. Caught one but DeLucca let it get away. Caught another later. Tried our luck on smoking out prairie dogs. No good. All bedded down for the night. Took off for rabbits. I caught one right away. From then on until dusk—no luck. How those little b——!! can run. Quit at 8:45. Russian made coffee. I hit the sack about 9:00. Too sleepy for coffee. Plenty on my mind.

JULY 14, 1944

Up at 7:15. Weighed in. 170 lbs. All I care to lose. Haven't been in the 160's for years. Today we have off. No sleeping, however. Personal work. Put fatigues to boil. John shaved me & trimmed mustache. I the same for him. Russian was cleaning his rifle & catching chipmunks. 6 so far this morning. Ate with 3 sq. Dehydrated hash. Skip the "K" rations. Wrote letters after chow. Russian & Pulaski made a cage for chipmunks. Have 6 in cage. Major Bean was around to inspect our area. O.K. Fireplace excellent. Wrung out fatigues & hung up to dry. Traded Chief a pair of coveralls. His longer. Ate chow with 3rd sq. & 2nd. Off until 8:30. Sat around table B.S.ing most of the time. Let a couple chipmunks go. Chased them. Fell out at 8:30. Combat packs & M-1s. Wore field jacket-a bit chilly. Took new route after reaching crossroads. East. 2 breaks. Stopped at 11:30. Ate "K" rations. Capt. checked up area for cans with flashlight at 12:00. He was disgusted. 1st platoon bad. Started back 12:05.

JULY 15, 1944

After first break we took a short cut. Crosscountry. About ¾ mile east of route we took out. By Zeke's place. Reached area at 2:45. Early, thank God! Hit the sack at 3:00 after a cigarette. March was tactical so no smoking. Up at 10:30. Just laid & tossed from 8:00 on. Fell out at 12:45. Mounted trucks for topside. Showers. Reached there 1:20. Water warm. Best yet. Bought 2 boxes of stationery, lip chap & plug at chaplain's px. Back at 2:30. John, Russian, Pulaski & I took off for Zeke's at 3:30. (His name really—Frank Williams). Visited with Zeke until 5:00. Wormed the following items out of him one by one. Pail of spuds, can of tomatoes, lb. of lard, loaf of bread, bottle of pepper, onion, and 1 doz eggs. Gave him $3.50. High but worth it. Back to area at 5:45. Ate and hid supplies. Show call at 7:00. "House Across the Bay" Felt good to see Frisco again. Two G.I. movie reels. Community sing. Made coffee after show. Dean fried 5 eggs. We each had one on a slice of bread. The coffee also from Zeke's. Fixed pine needles under myself & hit the sack after a cigarette.

JULY 16, 1944

Up at 6:30. Slept like a log. Fell out at 7:30. Fired at 7:45 & on our way. Stopped at highway No. 24 11:05. There until 12:30. "K" rations. Can't stomach them any longer. Ate fruit bar & 4 crackers only. Water truck came at 12:30. We filled up & started back. Reached area at 3:15. Mail call. Edna on way to L.A. Don't get the angle. Even with her I'm mentally lost. Signed payroll 5:45. Looks O.K. this time. 3 months coming. Can surely use it. John, Russian, Kurt & I took off at 7:00 for hills. A lion killed two cows last night. Kurt knew his lair. Filed 8 06's down to lead. Dum-dum's. Took off. Saw something big in a hole but couldn't get him out. Chased rabbits on way back. No luck. Couldn't throw worth a dam with rifle on my back. Back to area at 8:30. Hungry. Put can of tomatoes, 4 slices of bread & 2 eggs. Heated them. Rest of guys didn't like it. Ate entire contents myself.

JULY 17, 1944

Fell out at 7:25. Lecture. Target designation. Lt. Noonan. Practical work from 9:00-10:00. B.S.d most of the time. From 10:00-11:00. Demonstration of patrol & 5 paragraph field order. Thru at 11:00. Ate chow. Made some oat meal—can't stand "K" ration meat. Fell out at 12:30. Lecture. Platoon in defense. Started raining at 2:00. John, Russian, Pulaski & I hid in lean-to. Rest of co. in recreation tent. Didn't miss us. Co. thru at 3:30. 2nd sq. cleaned out fire pit & changed water in G.I. cans. 1st & 3rd dug latrines. Tried new pudding. Melted chocolate bars. Not too good. DeLucca started a fire in the pit. About 15 guys came down. Just stood around and B.S.d. About 9:00 most of them left. At 9:30 put 15 spuds in to roast. John made coffee—enough for the four of us. Took spuds out at 10:00. Ate peelings and all. Delicious. Put scrap in the fire and hit the sack after a cigarette.

JULY 18, 1944

We have another all night session. Fox holes again. At lecture Lt. Sharon wanted 3 men from each platoon. We figured it was good—saw him, volunteered. Took off for designated area at 8:45. Out by cliff. Helped Kofax dig. I report at 12:00 to Lt. Sharon. Enemy patrol. John, Russian and I. Back to area at 11:00. We reported to Lt. Sharon for orders. Recon. patrol. J., R., and I. Took off. Drew a pair of field glasses. New. Night glasses. 7 power. Walked out to cliff. Observed 2nd platoon. Rained a bit at 3:00. Started back at 3:15. Back at 3:45. Started making chow. Made oatmeal. John made coffee, fried eggs, heated cheese. "C" biscuits in lard. All delicious. On alert for brass and observers. Retired to lean-to after chow. Built fire in pit. Baked potatoes. Meeting at 9:30. We took off at 10:00. Wore mt. jackets. Reached area proper at 11:30. Started in. Crossed ditch and road. Pete and Jackson passed 20 ft. from us with flashlights. Missed us. Crawled up to Pulaski's fox hole. Dumped a box of powder on him. Woke Dugan up to tell him he was dead. Put swastikas on rox around f.-holes. 12:00 then.

JULY 19, 1944

Got DeCola next. Finished killing all the 3rd sq. Took off for second. No one awake. Quit crawling and walked slowly. Had found all of 2nd by 1:15. Camouflage excellent in some cases. Started looking for Command Post. Noticed a shaft of light by cliff. Investigated. Found Lt.

Walsh, Osaski, Jackson, and Pete. A small fire gave them away. Sat by fire and gabbed a bit. Left for camp at 2:45. Signed in and hit the sack. Got up at 12:30. No chow left for me. De Shazer had taken all out to fox holes.

JULY 20, 1944

Fell out in rec. tent at 8:00. Lecture. Lt. Sharon. MLR's outposts & review. Lt. Patrick took over at 10:00. Problems of patrol. Dismissed at 11:30. Ate chow at 12:00. Fell out at 12:30. Lectures in rec. hall. Lt. Moore (Lt. Walsh & Noonan transferred today). Announcment by Capt. Gen. and 2 Cols. coming today. Review of 5 paragraph field order. Dismissed at 3:30. John & R. took off for ranch. Try & get supplies (food). Started raining at 4:30. Hardest yet up here. Came down in buckets. Washed thru DeL.'s & Jack's tent. Ate chow at 5:30. Rain let up then. Played football till 8:30. Kicking and passing. Got some beautiful punts & drop kicks off. Quit at 8:30. Stood around DeLucca's fire and B.S.d. Rode the dagos (wops). About 9:00 I went to the lean-to. Sleeping bag cover still damp from washing.

JULY 21, 1944

Chief had a fight with Herring. Hit in head. 3 stitches and bit in the ear. Chief went to top side. Wind got worse about 8:30. We threw rocks on tarp. Pin it down. Rest of guys tying tents down (They're worried). Wind died down about 9:00. Before I hit the sack I borrowed Beah's file and made 12 dum-dums. They open and have much greater shocking power on game. Tomorrow we're going into woods to see what we can get.

JULY 22, 1944 Our day off

Up about 8:45. Hoag had chow started. Rest of guys peeved. We were going to save breakfast for noon. We left about 9:40. I carried M-1 and 20 rds. John had his rifle. Dum-dum's in mine. Went straight for deserted farm house. Went in, looked around. Played piano. Over & looked at barn. Full of chipmunks. No rats home. Down to look at spring. Water ice cold but not too clean. Left on road for farm house. Went into old mine shaft. About 60 ft. The other guys then left for ranch. I had no shirt so headed for hills. 1st shot a rock to test rifle. Hit. Shattered rock. 125 yds. 2nd dove-missed. 3rd p. dog. Hit. 4th, 5th & 6 2 chipmonks & rabbit. Hits. The dum-dums left nothing. Disintegrated them. 7 & 8 p. dogs. Hits. Came in about 1:15. Wrote 3 letters. All 2 pages-both sides. Took time out for coffee, biscuits & jam, however. Fixed pack. Weigh it at 5:30. Has to weigh at least 19 lbs. Put a stove lid in pack. No mountain jacket. Exactly 20 lbs. Co. meeting at 6:00. New dope on rations. 10 men to box instead of 8 for 10 days. New biscuits Mon. Show started at 7:40. Rancher, wife & baby present. Just plugged projector in and it shorted. Transformer burnt out. We built a big fire.

B.S.d until 9:00. Hit the sack soon after. Hard day ahead.

JULY 23, 1944 Quite tired-Tough day

Up at 4:45. Urinated, drank a primer. Weighed in. 168 lbs. Mounted trucks at 5:15. Mt. jacket, M-1 & 20 lb. pack. Reached topside at 6:00. Urinated. Dr. drew 1 oz. of blood. Skin, reflexes and eyes tested. Harvard test started about 8:30. Thru at 11:00. Lunch "K" rations. Read a paper. Germany looks as if she's finished. A.G.F. tests started at 1:00. Raining a bit-sprinkle. Started on 4 mile hike at 2:40. Thru at 3:28. Showers. From showers to show. Same one we were supposed to see Sat. night. Ate chow at topside. Mounted trucks at 6:30. Back to area at 7:00. Straightened out pack & other equipment. Hit the sack at 8:30. No B.S.ing. Right to sleep.

JULY 24, 1944

Up at 6:55. Capt. pleased at results of yesterday's tests—let us sleep. Ate chow at 7:15. 10 men to rations now. For 10 days only—thank God. Fell out at 8:15. Fired. Started on hike. Capt. leading. Slow easy pace. Men a bit tired from the 23rd. Reached range at 3:15. Sat for a while before firing. Capt told us of set-up to come as follows: Two hikes a week. Go into camp Aug. 14 1 qt. of ice cream apiece the night of the 13th. Each "B" rations that night. Close to 100 miles the last 4 days. Ate at 5:15. Not enough chow. Played a little volley ball after chow. Cleaned rifle afterwards. Watson and Cariaga skinned 2 rabbits. Dean cooked them. I made oatmeal. Had saved a jam can full. Added sugar, salt, condensed milk and $H^2O$. Washed pot—bottom like glue. John, Russian, and Pulaski came back about 9:00. Just twilight. Kurt and I came down to meet them in woods. Carried can back. Get box when dark. Put coffee on about 9:30. Dean fried a dozen eggs. 2 eggs apiece and 3 slices of bread. Delicious. We smoked a cigarette and hit the sack at 10:20.

A list of the food they got for $7.50: 5 cans (large) condensed milk, 5 cans assorted soup, ½ bushel potatoes, 2 loaves of bread, 1 bottle pepper, 2 lbs. lard, 1 carton rolled oats, 1 sack of onions, 3 lbs. of coffee, 1 can tomatoes, 2 doz eggs, 5 lbs. white flour.

JULY 25, 1944

Up at 6:35. Ate chow at 7:00. Police call today. Officers supposed to visit area. Fell out at 7:30. ½ hour of exercise. Chin ups, sit ups, burpee's. Arm & leg exercises. Fell in at 8:15. M-1's & bayonets. Short review & then practical bayonet training. Lt. Sharon in charge. Used padded pole for parries—hoop on end for thrusts. Unarmed defense lecture from 9:30-10:20. Dismissed. Mail call. Two letters. Edna & folks. Future plans shot it seems. Can't see L.A. on furlough. Rested ½ hr. Fell out at 12:15. Demonstration of assembly areas & squad in the attack from 12:15-2:00. Lt. Moore in charge. Back to area at 2:15. Lectures until 4:00. Lt. Patrick. Platoon tactics. Dismissed at 4:00. Washed up. Chief had potatoes peeled. Dean sliced them. Wrote Edna after supper. Laid cards on the table. Face up. If she doesn't like my brand of playing—I'm sorry! Made some oatmeal. Traded Beak some for a cigar. Told him we got it topside. Hit the hay about 9:30. We talked about women & their unpredictabile habits for a while & then the sandman came (coffee kept me awake until about 10:30).

JULY 27, 1944

Fell out at 8:30 for physical exercise. Got c-belts and M-1's at 9:00. Problem! Drew blanks. 16 rds. Took off for cliff. Other platoons came thru about 10:00. Sudcliff surprised me with bayonet and I shot at him too close. Burned in chest. Lucky it wasn't higher. Problem over at 11:00. Back to area. "K" rations. Capt. called me over—wanted to know how it happened. Mail call. Letter from Edna. Different from any I've ever rec'd. The girl has guts. Afraid, however, our plans are shot. No trip to L.A. for me. Laid in lean-to and B.S.d until 12:30. Fell out then, M-1s and bayonets. Bayonet practice until 2:00. Practice pole used. Stripped to waist. Sun really beaming. At 2:00 we had to fill out a form on equip. Man from QM here. From 3:00-4:10 a lecture on organization of inf. regt. by Lt. Sharon. Dismissed at 4:00. Wrote Edna. 3 pages-both sides. Hope situation is clear now. Pulaski & Russian made sandwiches—1 egg & 1 jam. 1 boiled egg also. The hell with "K" rations on night hikes. Fell out at 8:00. Fast cadence. 45 min. Met "Y" Co. Watched night vision demonstration. Left at 9:30 for march.

JULY 28, 1944 Day off

Reached area at 2:10. Made coffee and hit the sack. Up at 10:30. Made 3 clips of dum-dums. Sackett & I left at 11:30 to hunt. Got 1 prairie dog apiece & 1 chipmonk. Couldn't seem to connect. Back to area at 1:45. Cleaned rifle. Russian catching chipmonks. Ties string on them & lets them run. John fixing watches (trying to). Wrote a letter to the folks. Read funny books until 6:00. Emptied and cleaned G.I. cans. At 7:45 John, Russian, Pulaski, Biggs & I took off with all supplies. We headed for deserted farm house. Took 2 gals of gas with us. Reached house at 8:20. Poured gas in Coleman & lit it. Put blankets over window. Lit two lanterns & candle. Pulaski & Russian cooked. Made graham flour cakes, soup & corn mixed. I boiled wild honey & water for syrup. Biggs on guard in front room. Thru at 11:00 with chow. Really full. Hit the beds. I slept alone. Warm—used mt. jackets for pillows. Woke about 4:30. Back to sleep until 9:00. Started breakfast. Folded blankets. Swept floor. Banks & son came up road on horse. We took off for hills. Came back, finished cooking. Took all food into hills. Hid in rocks & ate. Started back at 10:15. Reached area at 10:45.

JULY 29, 1944

Trucks came at 2:00 for showers. Mounted at 1:10. Reached topside at

1:45. Gave Canadian Capt. boot size. Try & get a new pair. Took shower. Bought hair oil & 8 cigars from Chaplain's PX. Started back at 2:30. Reached area 3:10. Fargo Forum in mail call. Put fatigues to boil after chow. Church call. Didn't go. Show started at 7:30. Rancher, wife & another woman. 2 small girls & a baby also present. Capt. invited again. "Topper Takes a Trip". G.I. movies a bit spicy—hardly fit for girls. Over at 11:00. Beautiful moon. Hated to hit sack—but did.

JULY 30, 1944 Tired. A hot, windy, dusty day. About worst hike yet.
Fell in at 7:15. M-1's, C-packs. Drew 12 rds. Fired & on our way. Cut across country about a mile after first 3 miles. Hit Highway. Quite a few Sunday drivers (good to look at young women). Fast cadence. About 124. Finally made destination, Platte Springs, at 11:45. There until 12:50. Water cold & clear. Found a dead gopher in well after drinking it. The hell with it. Took it easier going back. Many breaks. Every half hr. Finally reached range at 5:50. Fired and back to area—6:15. Washed up and helped with supper. Thru cleaning pots and pans at 7:00. Rested until 8:00. Co. meeting at 8:00. Latest dope. Tear down mansions. Sat. 22 miles a day. In camp by noon Aug. 14. Battalion dance Wed. Aug. 16. Beer party Fri. Aug. 18. All day. $2000 bucks to spend between "Y" & "H" Co. Get paid either tomorrow night or Tues morning. John, Pulaski & I sang songs from Hit Kit while oatmeal cooking. John and Russian hit the sack at 9:30. Pulaski & I sang till about 10:00. All hit the sack for good then.

JULY 31, 1944
Slept late. Up at 8:00. Police call at 8:20. Conrad and I filled lister bag. 30 gals. Physical exercise at 9:00. Fell out at 9:30. Lecture. Lt. Patrick. Map reading. Thru at 11:00. Ate a mess cup full of cold oatmeal. Still good. Filling. Stripped to waist. Sun beaming down. Cleaned out G.I. cans and fire pit. Fell out at 12:30. M-1's and bayonets. Straight bayonet practice until 1.15. At 3:00 we went on a problem. 4th platoon enemy. Problem over at 4:45. Critique until 5.10. Back to area for show. Thru at 6:00. Started cleaning rifle. Called to hdqrs. Had to go topside for new boots. Dusty as hell going. 15 guys in ¾ ton. No boots in. Mosquitoes thick. Started right back. Reached area at 7:30. Almost all guys paid. Received $225.05. Put in 2 $100 money orders. Helped John carry water to wash. Soaked feet and washed legs. Useless to try to keep clean up here. John wrote a letter by candle light to his wife. John blew out candle about 9:30 and we both kit the sack.

AUG. 1, 1944
Weighed in. 166 lbs. Cleaned trigger mechanism of M-1. Fell out at 7:30. Physical exercise from 7:30-8:00. Fell out for lecture. Lt. Moore. Hand grenades out of T.N.T. blocks. Made 2. Had 60 sec. fuse (1 ft. 60 sec. in burning). Used blasting caps. Quit at 9:00. Problem. 3 problems

in row. Squads. 1st we attacked an enemy artillery post. Best squad. Next a village. Used practice hand grenades. Then about 1500 yrds. around a large hill. Drew 8 rds. ball ammo. Attacked an ammo dump. Assault fire mainly. Back to area at 12:30. Ate supper rations—use "K" tonight. Laid & rested until 3:00. Fell out at 3:00. Marched 2 miles to fox hole area. Started digging. Small storm at 4:30. About 3 ft. down it got hard as hell. Chipped away. Ate "K" rations at 6:00. Finally gave it up as a bad deal at 9:00. About 11:30 we decided to try & sleep. Galata in fox hole. The 3 of us on top. Moon shining.

AUG. 2, 1944 Edna's birthday-forgot until now. Too late.

A miserable night. Dozed off & on but cold. Cummings & I up at 6:00. Built a fire—daylight. Ate & hit the prone again. At 12:00 we filled fox holes. Left for camp area at 12:20. Trucks for showers came at 2:15. Took off for showers. Boots not in yet—maybe tonight. Took shower at 3:45. Bought 2 bars soap & 6 cigars from Chaplain. Left for camp. Reached area at 4:30. Shaved & trimmed mustache. At 6:00 we headed for topside. Reached topside 6:30. Mosquitoes thick as hell. Dive bombers deluxe. Mail truck came at 8:00. No boots. Boots in at 10:00. Waited for Lt. Sharon until 8:30. In poker game. He drove back. On 2 wheels most of the time. No dust-thank God! Reached area at 9:00. Too tired to go to Zeke's for food as planned. We turned in about 9:30. Get boots tomorrow.

AUG. 3, 1944 11 more days to go.

Fell out at 8:00. Practical training for ½ hr. ½ hr. of disarming. Fell in at 9:30. Walked about ½ mile. Training—squad in attack. At 11:15 we fell in-back to area for chow. Fried cheese in bacon grease. Fargo Forum at mail call. Read paper, LIFE & LOOK until 1:00. Fell out. Over to range. Threw practice grenades. Threw about 8 grenades & quit. The hell with it. Lay around B.S.ing & smoking until 4:00. Back to camp. At 6:00 we hit trucks for topside. Really flew. Boots in. Drew a pair of 9 ½ D. No "C" size available. Really nice. Back to area at 9:00. A fast ride. Letter to Edna must wait. Dark.

AUG. 4, 1944
REMARKS

1. The slightest exertion at this altitude and you breathe deeply. A small hill makes one feel weak and exhausted. Lack of oxygen.

2. Fox holes weren't meant to live in comfortably.

3. Hard work in hot sun and dry wind up here makes one feel faint.

4. All the biscuits are lousy. K 5 the only decent tasting. Others metallic.

5. The chocolate issued if eaten fast has a laxative effect.

6. The ticks we were warned about so repeatedly we have yet to see on

ourselves. Sheep are covered with them, however.

7. Effective this date-we stop throwing rocks at chipmunks. They steal our biscuits—a blessing.

8. Like to try my luck at gold mining but too fine for rough panning.

9. M.M. getting married a complete surprise. Wonder what the future will bring for yours truly.

10. Prairie dogs are numerous. Gripes me to watch a set up with an empty rifle.

11. Sulfur water may be good for one in a beneficial way but certainly doesn't agree with me on a hot day. Esp. 2 canteens full.

12. Marriage seems the alternative to our situation. Encounter the other party on furlough and decide.

AUG. 6, 1944 First day of 4 day march 22 miles-a long 22

Up at 4:45. Weighed in. 169. Up two. Put barracks bag in platoon pile. At 6:10 we mounted trucks. Topside at 7:00. Fired 12 rds. On way at 7:30. Ate chow at 11:00. "K" rations. 13 miles behind us. Passed thru Jefferson about 3:00. What a dump. Grocery store looked tempting. On highway from 3:00-3:50. Reached area then. Pitched tents. Slight rain for a few minutes. Cleaned M-1 after chow. Ed and others B.S.d about marriage.

MORE REMARKS

13. "K" rations getting monotonous-can hardly stand canned meat. Look forward to evening chow—only enjoyable meal.

14. Chipmunks are getting to be a problem. Steal everything. Ate 5 chocolate bars today.

15. Judging from the no. of ants around here, I'd say it must be ant heaven. About 1000 per sq. ft. everywhere. Black and red headed mostly. Bit like hell.

16. Can't say I'm as satisfied with garrison life as I thought I'd be. Too hot, no privacy, too much cleaning & too much crap to take.

AUGUST 7, 1944 2nd day of 4 day march. 23 miles-a longer 23.

Up at 6:00. Cold as hell. Heavy dew. Struck tents. On the way at 7:30. 3 miles on black top. Cut off on country road. Flat plain. Sun beaming down. 3 breaks and then "K" rations at 11:30. 10 miles to go. Stripped to waist. Enjoy sun. At 12:30 we started again. Capt. had drove up with water so we had full canteens. Hot & dusty. Walked 1 hr. 10 min. before break. NO decent place to stop. At 4:00 we were slightly discouraged. Finally reached area. had started to fix shelter half over my sack. Quit. Conrad asked me to sleep with him. (Two shelter halfs) Put mine in front on left side. (Wind blowing that direction.) Rain coming. Thundering. Let it come. A soft pile of needles under us. Mail call in rain. Folks and Andy. Read both by flashlight. Conrad and I B.S.d an hour about cars, pre-war times and women. Mostly women. Had a cigarette about 9:00 and hit the land of dreams. Put raincoat over equip. in case of heavy rain.

AUG. 8, 1944 3rd day of 4 day march. A long, hot 26 miles.

Up at 6:00. Slept like a log only slid down a bit. Helped with chow. Packed equip, tore down tent after chow. Left area at 7:20. Hit highway then black top. It stretched like a ribbon ahead of us. Seemed as if we gained nil in distance. Pace slow. At 11:15 we halted for chow. "K"! Capt. had water truck there. Filled canteens. Started up Wilkenson pass. Reached top about 2:00. Elev. 9525. W. truck there. Hot as hell so really used the $H^2O$. 9 qts. in all today counting meals. Capt. told us at 2:15-6-7 miles to go. The longest 7 I ever saw. At 4:00 we were all pretty well shot. I had no blister and didn't chafe as of yesterday. Many men had bad feet. Moved in with Conrad again. Extremely warm evening. Didn't zip up bag.

AUGUST 9, 1944 4th day of hike. Easiest day & last one.

Up at 6:00. Struck the tent. Warm as hell. Didn't sleep too well. Kept sliding down and warm evening didn't help. Packed bag & ready to go. Kept towel & soap in c. pack. Showers at end of hike. Left area at 7:20. Easy cadence. 112. Reached Tarryall at 9:00. Lunch from 11:10-12:10. Capt. had water truck—filled canteen. Fast cadence in afternoon. 124-128. Lt. Sharon leading. Really covered ground. Reached last mile at 2:00. Mosquitoes thick as hell. Terrible. "Y" had just started 4 mile forced march. Closed up and took off. Fox Movietone taking pictures. I walked about 6 ft. from camera. Up to firing range. Drew 12 rds. Pictures of us firing. Down to showers. Really hit the spot. Hit trucks at 3:00. Back to area. Slept from 4-5. Unpacked barracks bag after chow. Good to be back 'home'. Burned pine needles (green) chase few mosquitoes away. Got disgusted & hit sack 9:15. Russian tells me that mice were running all over Pulaski & I.

AUGUST 10, 1944 Everybody washing and cleaning. Stripped to waist.

Up at 7:15. Weighed in. 165 lbs. Down 4 lbs. Got a haircut and had mustache cut off. Put fatigues to boil. Cleaned rifle. Linseed oil on stock. Gasoline on parts. Wrote a couple of letters after chow. Slept from 3:30-5:00. Flies thick! Results of hike—"H" first by long margin. Rifle inspection at 6:30. O.K. John & Russian went down to Zeke's. Into hills & cooked food 8:30-10:00. Corn fritters. Back to area & sack at 10:00.

AUG. 11, 1944 Another easy day before the final storm.

Fell out at 8:00. Manual of arms & close order drills. 8:00-9:00. Capt. talked on military courtesy from 9:00-10:15. Brush up for our return to camp & civilization. Bayonet from 10:30-11:00. Off until 12:15. Lt. Sharon—demonstration on demolition. Blasted tree with 14½ lb. blocks of T.N.T. Set off smoke pot. Dismissed at 2:00. Cleaned M-1 and bayonet. Inspection after chow. Storm brewing. Watson & boys ate a rabbit.

AUGUST 12, 1944 Last day in this area.

Pulled down tarp & poles after chow. Started packing bags. Put stuff I won't use in b. bags. Stuff I'll need in sleeping bag cover. Cleaned stove in gasoline. Policed up eating area for last time. Laid around until about 3:00. Fell in—police call. After p.c. carried barracks bags about 500 yds down road. Meet trucks in morning there. Came back to old area and had a co. police up. Last one, I hope. Mail call—Edna & paper. Read letter & hit sack 9:30.

AUG. 13, 1944 Last day in mts. A.G.F. and Harvard tests

Up at 4:30. Weighed in 164. Mounted trucks at 5:45. Cold as hell. Topside at 6:20. Urinated in unison. Drank primer. Ate breakfast. Blood drawn at 7:30. Started Harvard tests at 8:00. Finished at 10:30. Took it easy. Last tests. Ate chow "K" at 11:30. Started A.G.F. at 12:30. Finished 4 mile hike at 3:30. Test *over*! Showers. Supper at 5:30. "B" rations. Steaks, potatoes, etc. Ice cream 6:30. Ate 7 bars. Show at 7:30. "Trade Winds" Fredric March & Joan Bennett. Excellent. Ice cream after show. Mosquitoes terrible. Hit sack about 11:00. Lay & thought a long time. Asleep at 12:00.

AUG. 14, 1944 In to camp

Major gave us a short talk 8:00. Mounted trucks at 8:30. On our way. Trucks really high balled it. 65 at times. Helmet blew off. Last truck got it. Reached camp at 10:45. Started straightening up. Polished boots after chow. Mail call—folks and cake. Left barracks at 3:00. Post office-cashed money order. Over to 89th area. Paid off $35.00 I owed. Ate chow there. PX with Holt. Back to 201st at 8:30. Caught up on diary. Wrote a letter-Edna. Boys started coming in. Drunk as hell. Making more noise than ever before. Dropped off to sleep finally about 10:30.

AUG. 15, 1944

Reg't meeting at 1:30. Filled out questionnaire after the talk by a capt. & 1st Lt. Pertained to allotments, etc. while overseas. Vic & I went to service club. Ice cream, grapes, malts. Back at 4:00. Filled out public relations slip. Get names in home town paper. Top side experiences.

AUG. 16, 1944 Beer party

Laid around until 9:20. Hit trucks then to Palmer Park. 50 cases beer, 12 cases assorted pop. Eats, etc. Felt quite pleasant about 3:00. Back to camp at 4:30. Shaved and slapped on sun-tans. Russian & I going to town. Wore boots—bloused—against r. but what the hell. Look dam nice. Bought t shirts, couple souvenirs, belt & buckle-chevrons. Caught taxi at 10:00. In sack by 10:30.

AUGUST 19, 1944 Another easy day

Up at 6:30. Reveille. No duty day. Supposed to oil M-1's and return. A detail did it. Laid around in barracks until 12:00. Passes at 3:00. Stayed in barracks. Chow at 5:00. Guys dressing for dance. I bought popcorn & potatoes & read. B.S.d about coming furlough, women, mts. & women. Drunks started coming in about 9:00. Dance started at 8:00. Quite a few went. Fooled with exerciser for a while. Reed & I only 2 who could stretch across chest. Hit sack at 10:15

AUG. 20, 1944 Sun. Last day before furlough

 Woke up at 5:00. Ed & Ronson came in drunk. Got up about 8:00 & ate chow. First time in months I've been up on Sun. morning. Got bag & started packing. Sorted ration souvenirs. Had caught cold during night. Over to medics about 4:00. Throat sprayed & aspirin. Chow at 4:30. Everyone in after chow. No passes. B.S.d and then got dressed. Everyone nervous, restless & tense. Furloughs given out at 10:30. Caught bus to town. Ate in bus cafe. Bus left at 12:00 for Denver. All 201st G.I.s

# FRANK LOVELL

Frank Lovell, of West Roxbury, Mass., had kept a diary before the war and was never told he should not while in military service. He used his diary, kept in standard diary books, as reference when writing reports that he was required to supply in line of duty, in fact.

Throughout his service at Ft. Bragg, N.C., in French Morocco, Algeria, Tunisia, Sicily, England, France, Belgium, Germany, and Austria, he maintained the diary and indeed continued after the war. As Mr. Lovell says, his complete wartime diary would make a book all by itself. We have had to limit what we include to a few pages written during the campaign in North Africa.

Holding the rank of Warrant Officer at that time, Lovell served as Personnel Officer, required to follow a few miles behind the 105 howitzer guns. He was attached to the 9th Infantry Division of the 60th First Army Battalion.

After the war Frank Lovell returned to his job in the U.S. Government Post Office. A graduate of the Boston School of Accounting, he is married and the father of five children.

*******

TUESDAY, MARCH 16, 1943 Thelepe, North Africa
Bivouaced with Serv. Btry., Kasserine Pass, Tunisia

We had breakfast this morning and then struck the Pyramidal tent. We traveled at 20 miles an hour. We passed burnt and destroyed German and Italian trucks (about 6) We passed some of our airports. We traveled through 300 yds. of mined road into bivouac. It is in the open, no camouflage, about 14 miles from the other place. There are planes flying over all the time. We all dug fox holes. I dug a sleeping hole near the rock wall, probably the ruins of an old Roman city. We are to pull out of here about 9 this evening. We all put the tops of the trucks down and got in convoy position, moved about 600 yds. and then spent the rest of the night like this. It was quite chilly.

WEDNESDAY, MARCH 17, 1943
Biv, with Serv. Btry, near Bou Chebka, and Thelepe, Kasserine Pass, Tunisia

We moved back to our old spots just before dawn. I dug my foxhole a little deeper, mostly to warm myself up. We had C rations and hot coffee for breakfast. We heated the C rations on a little fire. I did a little work on the back of the truck. We ate C rations all day. Before we ate we got "march order". We moved out into convoy position. The other personnel truck would not start. We moved out of the area after dark. We ate supper, C ration, while in convoy position. The moon gave enough light thru the clouds to see pretty well in blackout driving. It began to rain and was quite cold. We traveled over American-made roads thru the mts. It was made by the Engineers. It was slippery and we finally pulled in to the bivouac area early in the morning. We went 54 miles in about 7 or 8 hours.

## THURSDAY, MARCH 18, 1943
Bivouac with Serv. Btry and with the Bn., near Sened, Tunisia

I slept sitting in the front of the truck. It was raining something terrific and the wind was very strong. We were told to put on our chains, that we will move. The mud, rain, and wind are terrible. The trucks are all bogged down. We are in an open field and the grassy spots are soft. Not knowing how to put chains on, we tried to put them on backwards. We got all wet and mud. We got the right front on and then quit. We got out when the rain let up a little and put one on the left front. We pulled out to the edge of the field. At noon we had coffee, given by the kitchen, and we put the chains on the rear wheels. We pulled down the field after supper and dug fox holes. We moved down because we were in front of some guns used for defense. I slept in my bed roll inside the truck on top of the boxes.

## FRIDAY, MARCH 19, 1943
Bivouaced with Serv. Btry and Bn. near Sened, Tunisia

I had a swell night's sleep and for breakfast had a little cereal with no milk also black coffee. It was good. I washed and shaved using only a C ration can of water. I stripped down and deepened my fox hole. In the afternoon there was an explosion and some smoke appeared (black) about 2 or 3 miles down the road. It turned out to be a Messerschmitt that crashed. The pilot jumped without a chute just as it was about to hit and did not get hurt. He had engine trouble. The Serv. Btry boys got a few souvenirs. Late in the night, after I had retired, the Bn. except Service Btry, pulled out. They are going to fire on some Germans and Italians over on the first ridge, about 10 miles away. They did not open up tonite, however.

## SATURDAY, MARCH 20, 1943
Bivouaced with Serv. Btry, near Sened, Tunisia

The Btrys opened up fire this morning. They are about ten miles away and we have a grandstand seat. We can see the guns and the smoke of the shells as they hit. I took a picture of it. We drove them back but there are many Germans on the next ridge over. This is on the edge of

Maknassey. We ate B rations today and it tasted good. Two enemy planes came over low, climbed, peeled and then dove a little at us but did not attack. Our cub plane attracted their attention. I believe they thought it was an airport.

SUNDAY, MARCH 21, 1943
Sened, Tunisia

We ate breakfast in shifts so too many people will not be at the kitchen at once. About 10 o'clock 6 German planes came over and dropped bombs on the forward echelon. There was anti-aircraft fire. There have been planes over all morning. 17 flying (German) fortresses and four fighters. One fortress fired about 8 rounds of machine gun fire. The smoke came from the bomber and then the shots could be heard about 2 minutes after. There were many planes all day. The 6 German planes came over again and then beat it. We had march order about 6 o'clock.

MONDAY, MARCH 22, 1943
1st day at front-2nd Bn. echelon
Bivouaced with Serv. Btry, near Sened, Tunisia

We bivouaced between some hills on this side of Sened (the town where there had been so much fighting about Feb. 4th and 5th. The French had control of it then, but the Nazis had broken through all the way to Kasserine Pass, taking it over). We had a rough convoy (20 miles) through the fields. It was not a road. I took pictures of a herd of camels and of some Arabs and their tents. We got stuck and had to be pulled out by the Brty motors. The ruts are so deep that the under part of the truck plows the dirt. This stretch was too much for the ½ ton. We ate after sleeping all night and continued on. We passed through heavily (Italian and German) mine fields. There were German and Italian clothes strewn along the road. We were attacked by 6 Stukas in the afternoon. They hit the scout car about 6 in front of us. I ran in a field and then had to pick cactus spurs out of my knees. They blasted the town (Maknassey) ahead also. We saw the aid men tending two patients. We had to detour the scout car as it was on fire and contained ammunition. We bivouaced in a field a little further down and dug fox holes. I shot my Thommy gun (full auto) at a German plane, just overhead. We were attacked constantly. 15 German bombers and 4 fighters tore the town up, ahead. Slept in fox hole.

TUESDAY, MARCH 23, 1943
2nd day at front
Bivouaced with Serv. Btry outside Maknassy, Tunisia

I had a fair night's sleep in the fox hole (outside of dirt falling in my face and ears). My head was kind of clogged though. George brought over some coffee and C rations before I got up. One of the boys in a ½ track shot himself last night. I heard planes going over early this morning. Shortly after daylight the Germans came over again. I was forced into my fox hole twice before 9 o'clock. They bombed the town ahead again this morning. I am writing this from my fox hole. The rumble of Arty. and occasional bombing and anti-air firing is going on intermittently. The Stukas attacked the town and road once or twice in the afternoon. I put my bed roll beside my fox hole and it was a swell night. Late in the night a Flying Fortress (German) came over and bombed the town. Some of the fellows fired, like saps, and the fortress strafed the area. She dropped a flare then circled until it neared the ground and then bombed again. I hit the fox hole once again as it sounded like she was diving but it passed over. I got some mail today brought from Div. Rear Ech.

**WEDNESDAY, MARCH 24, 1943**
3rd day at front
Bivouaced with Serv. Btry outside Maknassy, Tunisia

I was awake off and on during the morning. The German Flying Fortress was circling around all the time. There was plenty of Arty fire this morning by us, laying down smoke so our foot troops could advance. I went all the way back to Sened (25 miles) and through the Mt. pass looking for 1st Arm. Div. Hqs. I found Message Center Rear and mailed some official mail. I was back shortly after noon. The Stukas attacked Maknassy about 3 times this afternoon, about 8 of them. They started big fires in the gas dump. I did a little work today, between raids. Six or eight bombers bombed and strafed the road just after I had left for Sened. The whine of the diving Stuka sends a chill down your spine. I haven't seen any actually shot down although there are all kinds of rumors about it. I got the report of casualties. There were 6 hospitalized and 2 returned to duty. One boy lost his leg (Lynn boy names Symonds). It was hanging by a piece of skin, below the knee. Doc. Tingwald cut the rest.

**THURSDAY, MARCH 25, 1943**
4th day at front
Bivouaced outside Maknassy, Tunisia with Serv. Btry

The planes were early this morning and bombed Maknassy again. They are trying to wreck our supplies, I guess. Eight planes came over about 11 and started the fires again. We are still eating C rations. All the boys strip down and enjoy the sun. Again today we are in and out of our fox holes. There were quite a few raids on the town of Maknassy today. I readdressed Hosp. and mis-sent mail in the afternoon. I also read papers. Capt. Elliott came over to Serv. Btry in the evening. They are doing fairly well up there. The Germans are dug in and have metal shields in the rock, also telescopic sights on their machine guns behind these. They are doing a job on our infantry. We need air power, I believe.

We believe now we are just to hold them until our flanks move up. The nerves of the boys from the Col. down are beginning to feel the strain. Sgt. Woods of Serv. Btry. was taken to the hosp. (crying at night, etc.). Personnel isn't so well either, a bit jumpy.

FRIDAY, MARCH 26, 1943
5th day at the front
Bivouaced with Serv. Btry outside Maknassy

I got up at 6:45 as the chaplain was coming over to take the mail back to the Division Rear Echelon at Tebessa. I got a piece of bread and butter from the kitchen, also a cup of coffee. I drew our two (George Neuhardt and mine) three meal ration (C ration). I got the boys to work today and we accomplished quite a bit. We dug our truck in. There seems to be more of our planes flying over today. They look like they have been bombing for the British 8th Army. There were a couple of formations of 15 to 18 bombers with about 24 fighters. One group of fighters seems to be having a dog fight in the clouds way up as there were streams of smoke in the sky, like sky writing, and there was much noise. Capt. Elliott slept in my pup tent with me. He came back from Bn. to do some work tomorrow. The German bombers flew over all the early morning and bombed Maknassy as I heard about 5 explosions and anti-aircraft fire. The forever rumble of the Artillery can be heard plainly.

SATURDAY, MARCH 27, 1943
6th day at the front
Bivouaced with Serv. Btry outside Maknassy, Tunisia

There was the usual morning raid on Maknassy by the Germans. We did a lot of work today. There were many planes over all day, mostly Allied. There is evidence of more American planes. The booming of the Arty is going on all the time. At night the sky flashing. I did not sleep too well and neither does anyone else. The boys have guard to pull. Capt. Elliott didn't go back to Bn. and is going to spend the night here with me.

SUNDAY, MARCH 28, 1943
Bivouaced with Serv. Btry outside Maknassy, Tunisia

Capt. Elliott slept in my pup tent this morning. I am now in charge of all outgoing mail and Sp. Orders. I worked most of the day. We only hit the fox holes once today, that was when four Spitfires roared across the field just off the ground. One fellow was hurt when he jumped off a moving truck. We had B rations all day. They sent Sgt. Jones back today from the front—too nervous.

MONDAY, MARCH 29, 1943
8th day at the front
Biv. with Serv. Btry outside Maknassy

I heard planes early this morning but no action. We had a good breakfast but are going back to C rations. Some German large artillery is landing about 1 mile from here. They are evidently looking for the 155 rifle outfit who are further up. They have put in quite a few shells here. They do not reach us. I worked most of the day. I went to bed just after dark. The excitement started at about 3 A.M. I heard two bombs and excited voices so I looked out and it was like daylight out, flares having been dropped by German planes. I ran to my fox hole in my underwear and wool shirt, in bare feet. The ground was wet with dew and the air cold. I almost froze and my knees were knocking before the flares landed and went out. I could hear the planes waiting for the flares to near the ground so they could bomb. They bombed near the hills where they think there is a battery or two of 155's. I went back to my tent to sleep in my clothes. Soon they were over again. This happened about 5 times till daylight. They laid flares in a gigantic circle and bombed and strafed Maknassy. They bombed the hills near us with those leaping bombs (personnel bombs). It was quite a sight to see the tracers coming down and going up. None of our men fired. They flared and bombed up the road by Sened. It was quite a time and no one slept. I did not see one of the planes during all this. We could only hear them.

THURSDAY, MARCH 30, 1943
9th day at front
Biv. with Serv. Btry outside Maknassy, Tunisia

A German plane passed right by, low, at the kitchen this morning as I was having coffee. Everyone thought it was ours but some nearer to it saw the cross and then it was fired on by our anti-aircraft. The 2 planes that went down by the hills the other day were also German. I worked all day and censored mail. There were some photo planes away up today and many of our planes flew over. The news sounds good lately. The rumors have us going back to the States after the African campaign.

WEDNESDAY, MARCH 31, 1943
10th day at the front

I slept very well last night despite the fact that a little dirt fell on me and there were four or five German planes flying over while it was dark. They dropped flares and did a little bombing up the road but not near here although the flares were. I stayed in bed in the fox hole and did not bother to get up like the rest have to. A few German planes came over this morning about 9 or 10 o'clock and bombed the spot where they think the 155's are or they think there is something there. I read some papers and worked most of the day. I rounded out my fox hole for better sleeping.

MARCH-SPECIAL DATA.

We moved from Biv. (with Division) near Tebessa, to Serv. Btry near Thelepe. From here we went near Bou Chebka. We ended up outside

Maknassy. It is bombed three or four times a day. We are in an open field with many wild flowers growing and many birds. The sun is getting hotter. It actually burns. We are eating a B ration breakfast, a C ration dinner, and a B ration supper. We have the observation Cub bivouaced in the field with us. I am carrying a 41 caliber Italian Automatic. It belongs to Capt. (Doc) Tingwald. I am holding it for him. We had 2 more casualties from Hqs. Btry. the other day. They were hit by a German 88 MM.

THURSDAY, APRIL 1, 1943
11th day at the front

Well, it is my birthday once again today (26 years). This is the third one since I have been in the army. I received 5 letters today. The current rumor is that we will go back to the states when Africa falls (what a thought). "Freddy Flare" was over in the early morning and bombed a bit but I slept through it. In the afternoon 20 bombers and 3 or 4 fighters (German) came over and bombed and strafed near Maknassy. As they disappeared in the clouds I came to the truck to get my helmet as I figured they would be back. George Neuhardt was there also. A bullet came screaming through the air and I hit the dirt instantly, also George. It gave us a scare as did the many planes. I think the planes sort of sprayed the area with machine guns as they were leaving. The German planes have an unmistakable heavy chugging-drone, like the stalling of many motors. A German plane went over about 9 o'clock. It had dropped bombs around Sened Station.

FRIDAY, APRIL 2, 1943
12th day at the front

I had a good night's sleep after a poor start. The planes had been over during the night and flared and bombed. The new replacements for the doughboys bivouaced along side of the road were quite excited. I slept through all of this. I read quite a bit today. Capt. Elliott dropped by and the Chaplain opened up his canteen and I bought a few things, especially chocolate bars. The sun is very hot and I stripped down and am acquiring a good tan. I wrote two letters home. I was in the fox hole 3 times during the day. It usually turned out to be "Photo Freddie". We can tell by the sound of the motors now. A big group of bombers and fighters (American) went over in a Northerly direction this morning.

SATURDAY, APRIL 3, 1943
13th day at the front

It was windy and the sand filtered on everything last nite. The German planes were over all last night. "Freddie Flare" or "Lamp Lighting Freddie" was over and did a little bombing around, also dropped flares. I heard one or two of the planes, that was all. It was windy all day and sand filtered all day. I did some work, also read.

SUNDAY, APRIL 4, 1943
14th day at the front

I got up early, about 7 o'clock as usual. There were a few high-flying German planes. I read Mass and worked. I washed and took a sponge bath. I fixed the mail in the afternoon. It was a nice day although the guns boomed and the tanks could be heard all day. About 6:30 P.M. the German planes, 8 of them, bombed the field about a mile back. Two of them came up the road and cut across the field. One of them cut between George and my fox hole. He was so low I could have hit him with a brick. There was a lot of anti-aircraft fire and I could hear the bullets whistling overhead.

MONDAY, APRIL 5, 1943
15th day at the front

I got up early and packed my things away and ate breakfast, censored and stamped some letters and then went to the rear echelon of Division near Tebessa, 140 miles away. We went in an open command car. We went back to Sened and then to Gafsa, on dirt roads. Then from Gafsa we had a good road to Feriana and Tebessa. Gafsa is a pretty place with the mud fences, palm trees, native stone houses and narrow streets. It is an oasis. There were palm groves with water and little eroded places with grass and flowers. We reached the rear echelon and ate dinner. I talked with Frank Page, did some errands, and received some mail. I ate supper there, drew four blankets and then joined Frank Page. We talked by the fire. We went to the Medics' tent after dark and talked, had hot coffee and crackers and jam until 12 o'clock. I then slept in the 15th Eng. Personnel tent. It was chilly at night. I got paid for the month of March-$32.02.

TUESDAY, APRIL 6, 1943
With Div. at Tebessa, Algeria and Maknassy, Tunisia

I awoke and picked up my things. I slept fair as it was kind of chilly. We had a good breakfast. I did some more work and got some more mail. I took "Doc" and another fellow from the 9th Medics to Gafsa. We heard that they had bombed the air field at Thelepe just after we went through yesterday. We have a ½ ton, full of mail, belonging to the P.O. and our command car with some mail and supplies. We saw three two-star command cars in a row. We stopped for a rest outside Sened and the brake bands tightened and we had to pile in the ½ ton and come back. It was dusty. I have a lot of work to do. I did a few things and retired early. I had a good night's sleep. There was action on the flanks and a little up front. The planes bombed and dropped flares across the mountain on our left flank.

WEDNESDAY, APRIL 7, 1943
16th day at the front

Biv. with Serv. Btry. outside Maknassy, Tunisia

I got up early and had a good breakfast. We are only eating two meals a day. They are two good ones though. The Germans are on the run and the American bombers and fighters went over the other side of the mountain range and did a job on them. We could see the German anti-aircraft fire and the planes circling around and diving. It was a great sight. We accomplished a lot of work. There were flares and flashes in the sky and we could hear the guns on Jerry's tail on the right flank. The 8th Army (British) are also near here. There was some kind of a tank battle raging this morning.

THURSDAY, APRIL 8, 1943
17th day at the front

I got up at the regular time and worked steadily all day. The mail was quite a problem. I did not even get a chance to write, myself, between personnel work, censoring, stamping and re-addressing mail. My nerves were about to give out. We are still eating two good meals a day. It was windy and cool and the sand filtered through everything. I am getting filthy but there is not enough water to clean clothes. We usually just bury them. There were no planes all day and little action up front. The British 8th Army are up front having come from the South and taken over the town ahead. This is where the big gun was.

FRIDAY, APRIL 9, 1943
18th day at the front

I got up late this morning. The flap had fallen from the front of my tent and the breeze was cool. The wind is strong (Sirocco) and noticed by all. I had a good breakfast and gave the mail to Sgt. Jones and Sgt. Nix and he went back to the rear echelon. I read all morning and afternoon. There was a terrific explosion over at the mine about 8 miles from here, where the Italians had been holding out until recently. It was a quiet day and everyone is getting rested. I got a good night's sleep last nite even though there still were flares and bombs dropped in the distance. The 8th Army has passed by going North so things should be quiet from here on. I am dirty and the barbs on the grass stick to you.

TUESDAY, APRIL 13, 1943
Form Biv. outside Maknassy to enroute and Biv. near Bou Chebka

I got up at 4 o'clock in the morning and had breakfast. I had coffee and two crackers. There were C rations which I did not eat. We pulled out of the area about 6:15, on schedule, no less. The convoy moved right along. I took various pictures as we went (Sened, Zadgena), a camel led by a boy, and Gafsa. We arrived at the bivouac about 10 o'clock. It is near Bou Chebka. We had coffee and C rations. I could not eat it. We had a poor supper. I found some interesting bricks around here. Some look like flint and others like petrified wood. I found a fossil, the imprint of a shell in the rock. I put them in my foot locker. I pitched my tent and retired early.

**WEDNESDAY, APRIL 14, 1943**
Biv. with Serv. Btry. near Bou Chebka, Tunisia

We had a marvelous breakfast and it hit the spot. I washed some clothes and shaved. It is raining off and on. The boys finished their payrolls and took them to the Btrys. We are to leave this area tomorrow and head for the Mediterranean. The rumors are flying thick and fast. Some say it is a jumping off spot to Europe or Turkey. Some think we are going home. Some say we will train (Amphibious) and some say it is a rest. I don't know which one to believe. It sprinkled off and on. We all went to bed early. I washed almost all my clothes.

**THURSDAY, APRIL 15, 1943**
Biv. with Serv. Btry near Bou Chebka, Tunisia

We had a swell breakfast. Some of the boys worked this morning. I took the rest down to the shower. They are inside a special truck. There are two entrances, you take your clothes off in a tent (12 at a time), 12 are taking a shower and the other twelve are dressing. After dinner I headed back to drop some of the boys off at the shower as I was going on to Tebessa. We all went to Tebessa instead. I mailed some letters and then walked all around town. The city is enclosed inside a large stone wall. The streets are narrow and some have small inclines reminding me of pictures I had seen of Malta. I took a few pictures, one of a reclining female statue in the square. A couple of the boys got haircuts. There is nothing in town to buy. We got back a little late for chow. We are going to move out tomorrow so we cleaned the area.

**FRIDAY, APRIL 16, 1943**
From Biv. Bou Chebka to enroute north to Mediterranean (La Calle, Algeria)

We ate breakfast at 5 o'clock. It is chilly. We packed and left the area about 7:40. It is a slow trip and chilly. The windshield has to be down as well as the top. I took pictures of the ruins at Tebessa. It is the ruins of the ancient Roman city of Theveste. We ate dinner near Djerde, C rations. I have seen a few phosphate mines. It is dusty and chilly. We went through small towns and walled cities. We passed through La Kef and as it grew dark we entered the mountains. They are high and are supposed to go as high as 7000 feet. There were hairpin turns and twisting roads. We passed through Souk el Arba just after it had been bombed. We heard it just a short while before. We came thru some mountains and came face to face with the Mediterranean. We turned and went east thru La Calle and into bivouac about 10 miles further. We got stuck entering the area. We ate, pitched tents and retired.

## SATURDAY, APRIL 17, 1943
Biv. with Serv. Btry. near La Calle, Algeria, N. Africa

We had a good breakfast, did some cleaning up. We did some work. Joe Devine joined us once again. In the afternoon I took the boys swimming in the Mediterranean (took some pictures). We went to La Calle. The hills give away at this point and round into a curve. There is a beach at this point. The sand is fine and white. The beach was crowded with about 2000 soldiers. Some with underwear, some without. The water is clear and blue. It was about the same temperature as Nantasket. Just cool enough to make it invigorating. We drove thru La Calle and then came back to camp. We are going to stay over nite.

## SUNDAY, APRIL 18, 1943
Biv. with Serv. Btry. near La Calle, Algeria

We worked after breakfast this morning. In the afternoon I took the boys swimming in the Mediterranean (2nd time). The sun was not so hot but it was still nice. We stayed in swimming quite a while and then sat around the beach. There were some Arab shoe shine boys around and we had some fun with them. Some were in swimming. We came back, ate early, 4 o'clock, and pulled into convoy, ready to move out. The roads were too crowded so we stayed here.

## MONDAY, APRIL 19, 1943

I had a good night's sleep and awoke early. There were plenty of bugs around. There are the big black ones that fly around at night and sound like P-40's. There are many mosquitoes also. We had a good breakfast and laid around waiting to pull out. We had March Order about 2:00 and pulled out soon after. It was warm and we were compelled to travel with the top down and the windshield down and mudded. We traveled slow and thru beautiful country. Thru mts. and ravines. The mts. fall off into the blue Mediterranean. I took some pictures at different spots. We went through La Calle and Tabarka. The latter was heavily bombed in the past and the buildings and homes demolished. (There is an ancient island fortress here). We had to wait outside Tabarka until dark as it is too dangerous to travel this road in the daytime. The 84th FA lost men on this road the other day. We traveled slowly and thru many demolished towns. We arrived in bivouac about 12 o'clock. We dug holes and retired about 2:30. It was hot and the planes were over all night. We had traveled about 65 miles yesterday to get here. We passed many bomb craters, one large enough to park a truck. It was about 20 feet with water in the bottom and 30 ft. across.

## TUESDAY, APRIL 20, 1943
Near the front
Biv. near Sedjenane, Tunisia, North Africa

I did not sleep so well. The sand fleas and mosquitoes were thick and it was hot most of the night. The planes flew over all during the early part of the morning up till daylight. Just before daylight they bombed, not very near here. We had breakfast at 5:30 A.M. We hung around all day sleeping and resting. We ate our second meal at 3 o'clock. We will eat two meals a day from now until everything is under control. I put up my tent under a large tree in the clearing. We are all sleeping this way. It is in some Arab's bean crop. There are about 15,000 doughboys bivouaced around waiting for the zero hour. I had a good night's sleep.

SATURDAY, APRIL 24, 1943
Biv. with Serv. Btry. near Sedjenane, Tunisia

Worked until noon. I went back to the Div. Rear Echelon (7 miles) and turned in some papers. I went to a Pers. Adj. meeting and then got 22 F.A. replacements. I ate at the Pers. mess. I met Frank Page. It was black as pitch after dark. I had to wait until then to move out as no large trucks are allowed on the road during the day. It was slow and took a long while until we got to the appropriate spot to stop. I rode up and down the road for about 2 ½ hours looking for Serv. Btry. I did not see the sign so I had the boys (22) bivouac and I slept between two overcoats.

EASTER SUNDAY, APRIL 25, 1943
Biv. with Serv. Btry. near Sedjenane, Tunisia

I found Serv. Btry area up the same road. They had moved. I hung around all morning as we can not move up until night. I took 4 of the replacements and brought them to the 84th F.A. I stopped at the 34th F.A. and talked with them. We ate some of the new U ration, it was very good. After dark we came up to the new area. It was dark and the area was rough rocks and low bushed. I slept on my bedroll in the open and slept well.

TUESDAY, APRIL 27, 1943
2nd day at the front
Biv. with Serv. Btry near Sedjenane and Bizerte, Tunisia

It was misty this morning but warm. We had C rations for breakfast. There is the occasional rumble of guns this morning. We had 7 Messerschmitts over this afternoon. We thought that they were ours at the time. We had mass at 5 o'clock. It is the first time since about Ash Wednesday. One man was killed in B Btry this afternoon. The Germans have been shelling the Btrys. They brought through a German prisoner this evening. He was given to Serv. Btry. by the infantry. Serv. Btry. treated him like a long lost friend. They gave things to eat, candy, cigarettes. We can watch the shells landing on the ridge where the front is. It must be about 10 miles away.

THURSDAY, APRIL 29, 1943
4th day at front

Biv. with Serv. Btry. Between Sedjenane and Bizerte, Tunisia

We had eggs and bacon for breakfast. We worked most of the day. I took a bath and shaved in the morning. It was hot today. There is plenty of firing today and another boy in B Btry was killed (Jim Doherty, Charlestown, Mass.) while 4 were injured by mines. I sent 6 of the replacements up to B Btry with the ration run. We can sit on the side of the hill and watch the shells landing.

FRIDAY, APRIL 30, 1943
5th day at the front
Biv. with Serv. Btry between Sedjenane and Bizerte, Tunisia

It rained all during the morning up until about 5 A.M. It was clear and cloudy all through the day, however. There was a great deal of firing today. There were heavy concentrations. The 155 rifles on either side of us were firing. We were talking to an old Arab and he told us that the Germans were 25 kilometers (15 miles), that there is 15 kilometers from them to the plains and that we are 30 kilometers from Bizerte and 40 from Tunis. There is an old rifle up there where we were talking to him. (English, the Arab says). We had the men pack the things in the truck as the word is that the spitfires that have been flying around are captured planes flown by the Germans. That the Germans are fairly close and we are in range of their guns. The Btrys are only 1500 yards from "Jerry".

APRIL-SPECIAL DATA

This land has seen terrific fighting as the trees are shattered by shrapnel and there are huge bomb craters. The hills are large and the brush is heavy and the land rocky. There is difficulty evacuating the wounded. We have 5 mules to help out. It is getting hotter once again and we now take Atabrine tablets for the prevention of malaria. There are increasing numbers of insects.

SATURDAY, May 1, 1943
6th day at front
Biv. with Serv. Btry, between Sedjenane and Bizerte, Tunisia It rained during the early hours of the morning but stopped before daylight. It clouded up after breakfast. I was going to the rear echelon but figured it was going to rain so I gave some of the papers to Capt. Elliott to take back. It is extremely windy and too strong to work. The brush is low and the camouflage poor, so we have not put up a tent. Later in the day I had to take a record back to Division. We borrowed a jeep from Serv. Btry. We started about dark, Nix, Devine, and myself. Most of this is vague as on the way back the jeep hit the ditch and threw Devine and me out on the side of the road. The next thing I can remember is waking up in a hospital. It seems that we got to Division after missing the road once and then using our lights we arrived there, did a few things, such as deliver Burke's Service Record. It rained and lightning in the sky. We started

back, it was dark and we evidently went off the road a while later. I guess I had a slight concussion as I do not remember many things and the things I remember seem like a dream.

SUNDAY, MAY 2, 1943
7th day at the front

I awoke about 3 o'clock (guess) and in a sort of fog. I knew I was in a hospital. It was a field hospital. I could not figure what had happened to me. I thought I had been blown up by a land mine. I walked outside the tent, came back, putting my hands on men's faces, looking for my cot. In the morning Nix came up, we got Devine and saw the Dr. then left. We got Atabrine pills today. Most of the men were sick to their stomachs.

MONDAY, MAY 3, 1943
Biv. with Serv. Btry. between Sejenane and Bizerte, Tunisia

I awoke this morning at the heavy droning of airplane motors. It had been raining earlier but it stopped. The clouds were still low and ideal for aircraft. I heard these planes bombing so I knew that they were German. They must have been bombing around Sedjenane. I got up rapidly and half dressed and went to a fox hole on the side of the hill. I could see some of the planes returning and streaking through the clouds. The ones I saw were probably Stukas. I was leery of whether or not they would come across this area, strafing on their return. A shortwhile later American bombers and fighters passed in the same general direction. We had 'march order' about 10 o'clock. We shuttled to a new bivouac area where the Btrys had been, about 15 miles forward, toward Mateur. We are bivouaced in a grove of trees where Arabs did live.

# MAX B. SIEGEL

It has been a principal of the selection of diaries for this book to reject all those written or significantly expanded and polished after the war. This has resulted in the loss of some "diaries" which had much to offer in the way of interesting detail and hindsight but which could not, written so long after the events, give the sense of immediacy which is a true diary's greatest value. Such manuscripts, even if mimicking the diary form, fall more into the category of memoirs, a valid and fascinating category in itself, but one outside the scope of this book.

The account Max B. Siegel wrote of his early Army experiences was not written day by day but neither was it a post-war creation. Finding an abandoned blank notebook on a Sicilian hillside just taken by the Americans from retreating German forces, Siegel also found himself with time on his hands during a hiatus in the Italian campaign. Newly appointed a military policeman and awaiting shipment for duty in England, he set about recording his experiences up to that point with the intention of keeping a diary thereafter. Unfortunately he discovered that when his account reached the fighting he had just experienced in Sicily he could not remember all the places he had been and what had transpired there and so abandoned his short-lived effort.

Siegel, born in 1913, was, at the time covered by his fragment of diary, a private in Co. K, 18th Infantry Division of the Army. His duties were rifleman, then ammunition carrier in the machine gun section. He had worked as an elevator operator in a New York City hotel before the war. After the war he returned to hotel work for a while, owned a bar for 6 years, and in 1979 retired after 25 years as freight car operator in a New York City office building. He and his wife now live in Long Branch, N.J.

*******

I left Camp Kilmer on March 4 (1943). It was a cold day. There wasn't any happy faces. We all realized where we were going.

Still, we had hopes of going elsewhere than overseas. We left our barracks about noon time. The girls in the P.X. all waved us goodbye.

We marched down to the trains about ½ mile away. The camp was now getting deader and deader.

Only 2 days ago the camp was crowded as it could be. Many others had made the same march we were making.

On the march we met others including nurses leaving with us too. We were placed into our special train. Then we waited until all the others were ready.

Finally we pulled out. At once all were anxious to see which way we were headed. It was North. Our hopes were still there. We were moving fast now and our hopes were for a long ride.

We passed small towns in New Jersey and all the people stopped to wave to us. More than once we would pass a large factory and there would be banners waving "God bless you".

It seems everybody knew where our train was going to. At last Jersey City and our hope's gone. We were told we're getting off the train.

Our last train ride in America ended. We were at a Hudson River ferry line. We marched into the ferry. Our faces long. No band here, things were already changed. There on the other side lay New York City. It was my home and many others'. I almost cried. Would I ever see it again? How soon? I saw a few tears on some faces.

Off we went and I got next to the rail so I can get a view of old New York. We headed for the bay and there was the Statue of Liberty. What a picture it was.

Now we were passing some big warships. We sailed into a dock at Staten Island. The pier was full of soldiers. On both sides were two big transports. We lined up and waited for our names to be called. They called "Siegel", I answered with "Max B." and boarded the ship.

We climbed up the stairs carrying our loads. What a load. I had a full pack plus 2 barracks bags full. It sure was heavy.

We reached the prom deck which was going to be our home for a while. The ship was full of bunks everywhere and all close together.

The room I was in had 32 bunks so I had plenty of company. It also was next to the mess hall. I got talking to the other fellows. They said they have been on board a few days. Now the ship was almost full.

Now we were wondering where we were going to. It was said that the last two trips our ship had gone to Casablanca in Africa.

I was hoping for England. The first chance I had I looked over the boat. In peace time it was a luxury liner which made runs to South America. Its name was Santa Helena.

My friends from my platoon back in Camp Wheeler were all close by me. I was thankful for that.

At last it was time for bed, my first night on a ship. I awoke in the morning. The ship was rocking and I soon realized we were at sea.

I quickly ran out on deck and there we were right in the middle of a large convoy with many warships for protection. It was cold and windy on deck. I went back. It was also time for breakfast.

Each company ate in turn. We were lucky because we were the closest to the mess hall. We ate first and the food wasn't bad. Our officers then told us that we would be on K.P., the whole company, 2 days on, 2 days off.

After a while we liked our job. The food was good, we had ice cream and fruit, and we stocked up with everything. There was a P.X. on the ship. We bought candy by the boxes.

The sea was getting rough and we were getting seasick. All along the boat you was able to see sick soldiers. I felt it too so I lay in my bunk most of the day.

The next day I was much better and wasn't bothered by it any more. We soon realized we were going South. It looked like Africa. And when they handed us booklets about North Africa we knew then for sure.

About the fourth day the weather had gotten warmer so we really hugged the rail and watched the waves beat against our ship.

The Red Cross had presented us with a ditty bag with many articles in it. We received cigarettes too. Our officers got some games for us to play. One of them was a Bingo game and it was very popular with us. We played it every chance we had.

The most famous soldier on the ship was "Zeke" Bonura (*a major league baseball player*). He is one of the nicest of men a guy could meet.

He played bingo with us and he enjoyed our company. At night there was a movie in the mess hall. A picture played for 3 nights. That way it was possible for everyone to see it.

Another favorite game, of course, was craps. Everywhere there would be games. Some were real big and a guy could win a few thousand.

I only played a little rummy with my friends. My favorite game was Bingo. I even came out $5 ahead at the end of the voyage.

At the 8th day our convoy split up. The word was they had left for Casablanca. We were going to Oran.

The 12th or 13th day at noon we seen land. I stared at it for hours. It was Spanish Morocco. That night we passed cities in S.M. which were all lighted up.

Later we passed the famous Rock of Gibraltar. It was midnight but I stayed up to make sure I didn't miss it.

It was not easy to make out. It was a dark night. There it was alright and what a thrill. Now we were going through the Med. Sea.

We stayed close to the shore line and finally the 14th day land got closer all the time. The mountains got bigger and bigger. We were pulling in.

Supper time came and I went in to work for we were on K.P. When we finished our work I ran out again to see the sights.

There layed a modern city with beautiful buildings. I couldn't believe it. It was Oran. All the ships were being docked in the harbor. We all lined the rails and soldiers came over to talk to us.

The question we'd ask was how far was the front from Oran. They said 600 miles away. They also gave us the lowdown on Oran. That night we slept on board. The next morning we got off.

We all piled into the trucks we were assigned to. I was anxious to see what the Arabs really looked like. At last our truck convoy started to move.

We were moving through the center of Oran now. The people all waved at us, raised their two fingers for victory. Many French were in Oran. Many Arabs were dressed in civilian clothes except the head wear.

A lot of people were asking us for cigarettes so the boys were throwing them to the crowd and watched the fun. The people sure ran for an American smoke.

Now we were passing into the poorer section of Oran. Up until now their buildings were modern and main streets wide. People were milling around going about their business. The buildings were not like we had at home. They used bright colors and had fancy doors. The poor section had one story houses and narrow streets and was shabby and old, not like the modern 5 story buildings we had just seen.

We soon were on the road leading us to our camp. We arrived there, it was only 5 miles from Oran.

The truck stopped, we all piled out. Then we waited until we were assigned to our area. Meanwhile I ate for the first time C rations, which consist of two cans, one meat and one biscuits and coffee.

I pitched a double pup tent with 3 other friends from Wheeler.

It was here we tasted our first vino. Our mess hall was an open field. We sat on the ground to eat.

The second day they had us on a training schedule which kept me busy. The day ended at retreat. We paraded in O.D. about ½ mile every day for retreat.

Zeke Bonura was there too. One night we toured the town with him. He showed us all the famous spots. One was where the Prince of Wales met Wally Simpson. Our camp was really in one of the beautiful spots in the world.

The sea was 1000 ft. below us. We could see the harbor. There were warships in.

I went to Oran about the 8th day. We hitched in, there was quite a bunch doing the same thing. We were dropped off in Oran. The streets were jammed and had plenty of bars.

American boys were all over. Soldiers & sailors. Many French soldiers were seen too. I visited the American Red Cross. We ate a meal for 10 francs. Not bad, then we visited the Red Cross Club & seen a movie.

It was now time to get back to camp.

The next day it started to rain. It rained for 3 days. Everything I had was wet. We never had a chance to dry up.

At last the first shipping list. I was on it. I changed my clothes and put on my wet O.D., packed my barracks bag. One bag I left behind. I was given a rifle with ammunition.

For hours we waited in the rain. Just before we left a priest gave us his blessings. Most of my friends were left behind, including Larry.

Our truck convoy headed to town. We had no cover and it rained harder. We finally reached the railroad station in Oran. It was a pretty place.

Our trains were there. What a funny-looking train. Not like trains back home. We took our seats and loaded our compartments with cases of C-rations. It was easy to see we were going for a long ride. It looked like the front for us. I still didn't know what I was in or what outfit. I had hoped to get out of the infantry. My hopes were not high, however.

We soon pulled out. We went East toward Tunisia. There was eight of us and for 3 days we ate & slept there. There wasn't enough room. I couldn't eat the meat rations. The light can was all I'd eat. The cocoa I liked, the coffee and sugar even candy we gave to the Arabs every time we stopped in a town.

From all sides they came, even the French were there. We gave them all rations. More was given out than we ate.

It looked as if we had stopped at every town. We never really made good time. The country was not bad. Never did see many trees, plenty of hills.

It was about 3 in the morning when we reached our destination. We were near Constantine.

It took 8 hours before we left for our new camp. We rode about 2 hours and finally got there. It was the 5th replacement camp. They told us we will stay there between 1 & 5 days.

While there I could have gotten in the Rangers. Some of our boys did join them. The second day I left. We were replacements for the 1st Division.

I was glad because everybody was saying the 1st was going home after the African campaign. There were only 2 of us left now. Once more I piled on a truck and off we went.

It was hours that we rode. It was late night when we reach another camp near Tebessa. We stopped, the boys there were having a picture show. We see the picture and later marched to where our area was and layed down to sleep. It was the 1st Div. training camp.

The next morning we were formed in to a company and was given Sergeants. They explained our training schedule to us plus giving us the history of the 1st Div.

They said our training may last 4 weeks. Then we join our regular outfits in the division. Our teachers were men who had been in the front lines. We listened to all the stories they had to tell us.

We learned more there than we did at Wheeler in 13 weeks. The fellow I was bunking with was a handicapper in civilian life. We got along fine.

We worked hard and had no recreation there. We were far from any town. The sixth day the shipping orders came. Now we started to reduce our packs. I left my one barrack bag behind, knowing I may never see it again.

When they called us that noon they handed us slips that named our outfits. Mine said K Co. rifle man 18th. My partner went somewhere else. My buddy from Wheeler was also in the 18th but in another company.

The order came to get ready, which we did. Now it was the front, no more kidding around. The trucks were ready for us. I piled in again, still carrying a heavy load. I was sure they would still make me reduce it in K Co.

We pulled out about 3 p.m. and soon we hit the road. While on the highway I had my first experience. I was setting at the end when I heard a shot go off. We all laughed, believing some one had taken a shot at one of the Arabs. Another shot went off. Then another shot and it was the real thing, it was fired at us, probably me, being I was the front target for the direction the shot came from. It was a sniper and the joke was over.

Again we rode for hours and we passed Gafsa where the Germans started their retreat back.

We stopped at night. It was a rocky field. It was another area and we still didn't join our outfits.

By this time I was getting used to sleeping on the hard ground. The nights were cold. There three blankets and my overcoat were sure handy. That night we were warned about smoking because recently planes had bombed that area.

I went to bed looking at the sky. A million shining stars looking down at us. What was next?

It was way after noon when we packed and marched down to the road. We waited for hours until the trucks arrived. Then we traveled on a bad road. The dust was terrible and I was white as a ghost at night. We finally came to the area where our K company was.

An officer was there to meet us. We unloaded then got ready to move to K company. We climbed a hill and in the valley we stopped. They told us to take our packs off, we were there. Now we were given C rations, that was our supper. I was hungry. I then went to bed. It was a dark night.

Morning came at last. Then I saw all the other guys of K. Co. What a mess they were. All were dirty and needed haircuts, spots all over their clothes. One officer had a 10 inch hole in his pants. It was easy to see that they had had hard days. Now I was one of them.

The captain called all us new men and gave us the lowdown. Most of us were put in the 2nd platoon. The co. had not many men left.

They soon had us organized into squads. We were all set for action only there was no front left for the 1st Division to fight on. The Germans were retreating fast.

In two days we left the area for a rest area. Looks like we got here in time. 4 days were spent in El Guettar.

Then we travelled a day to a new area. Our rest continued and was told the British are going to finish the job themselves.

But in case of help we would be called. Our hopes were high of not seeing action.

Things changed and we were called so we finally are going up. We moved out and again rode all day. Stopped in time for the kitchen to make hot chow then slept. The next day we moved again. We rode all night, till about 11 p.m. We got off because we now were close to the front lines. We could see the flashes of artillery now.

The companies started to hike now. We carried our full pack and it was heavy. For 4 hours we marched over hills and in valleys. It was the hardest day I ever put in.

After the 3rd hour we dropped our heavy pack and made a light pack. That was the only way I was able to last it out.

The artillery was loud now, also some British soldiers passed by. We were going to relieve the British.

At last our hill was reached and finally I laid down to sleep. Only to get up soon and pull guard for a couple of hours. I had no blanket to sleep in. I used my raincoat. I was cold.

Morning came and hot breakfast. The boys started to dig in. I got myself a fox-hole which was already there.

The 3rd day our hill was heavily shelled by the Germans. For the first time us new guys are feeling what war was like. The shells kept on coming & coming louder & louder. I got as low as possible in my hole & hoped for the best.

Finally the shelling was lifted then we climbed down the hill to get our chow. As soon as received our food, right back we went to our holes.

About 6 boys were wounded. One killed. This was no joke. That night I went on my first patrol. Our mission was to cross the valley to a village on the other side, contact the 2nd Battalion then return. The whole thing should take 3 hours.

We left on time, 7 of us. None of us hardly spoke a word the whole march. We sweated out running into Germans who were nearby. Also machine gun fire opened up somewhere.

We arrived in the village. Not a soul was there and it was pitch black. Our feet sure made good time in getting out of it. Back we started and glad of it. On schedule we got back to our hill.

The night after we had 2 boys lost. I didn't have to go out. Meanwhile the shelling continued every day. Our boys were laying it in by now. Many of our planes were in the sky. I saw a few dogfights over head.

After about the 9th day we were to attack. It was a large-scale offensive at all fronts. At 1:30 we eat then moved out in columns of two. The day was here for all us new guys.

We moved slowly and our artillery was shelling the German positions. Each company had a hill to take.

In the midst of a terrific artillery barrage by both sides our squad scout lost contact with the squad in front of us.

By the time our sergeant realized, our scout was too scared to follow. We were lost. Lucky for us we were last so nobody else was lost. We turned left hoping we could find our company. It was dangerous to roam around because the Germans were around somewhere. Meanwhile the battle was on.

We climbed the hill near us and waited to scout it before we moved further.

After wasting some time our sergeant started to move us in the direction of our starting point. It was now getting daylight. We marched in a squad column in the valley when out of a clear sky we started to get shelled by mortar fire. Lucky for us the range was bad. We all ran. The shells were still dropping behind us.

Now it was machine gun fire. We all again ran like hell, even as tired as we were. Soon the range was too far for them.

We took safety in a river bed and waited a while before we moved again.

Our break was over and off again We were able to see our tanks hiding behind a hill, waiting until the time to move.

After ½ mile further of walking we took shelter on a hill. We waited there all day until dark. Then we would cross a valley to our hill.

The artillery shells were over us all that day going back and forth. More than once I'd jump. Night came and we crossed over to our hill.

We climbed the hill and no one was there to stop us if we were German.

Down the other side to the kitchen we went. The sergeant asked how the company made out. The cooks said the hill was taken at a cost. The company was coming in late. Another battalion was relieving our Bat.

We had a hot cup of coffee then climbed the hill again to our holes at the top. Then to sleep after doing some guard duty. The troops came back while I was asleep.

Morning came and there was many faces not there. 40 men were hit, 7 of them dead. The machine gun section of 10—7 were hit, all wounded. Our company was getting smaller now.

We rested all day and moved out at night. New positions had to be taken now. The Germans had been forced to pull back again.

9 miles we march that day. Another hill in the Mateur sector. Again I was tired for I was now in the machine gun section as an ammunition carrier. I carried a box of ammo. I was dead tired and not a drop of water I had. None of us had any water left.

We were told that hot chow & water will be in. Meanwhile the boys started to dig in. I waited for a tool. I had none. In the best-equipped army in the world half of us had no entrenching tool.

It was late and I was on guard duty about 3 a.m. when the food reached our hill. A detail of men carried it in. I filled up with water. The best drink I ever had. Later I had chow. Some of the boys didn't bother to eat, just slept on.

We moved around to the other side and set up our machine guns. More than once a counter attack was expected at any moment. One of our platoons while out on a outpost was almost wiped out. Not many came back.

Our artillery was very close to us. We were shelled often. Our company was small now. After a week we moved out. Mateur was taken. We took new positions, dug in, then were relieved by the 34th Div.

We marched along the road then turned off into the country when 3 miles more to our hill. Waited for supper then moved out to form a line 2 miles out. All night I dug. I used my helmet and bare hands until my fingers were sore.

Planes nearby dropped flares the whole place was lighted up. Soon they returned and bombed the hill we left. We all wondered if they see us but they didn't.

I finally got some sleep only to awake for a early breakfast. They fed us before it got light. They were afraid of being seen.

It turned out to be hot that day, no shade anywhere so there was nothing we could do about it.

The time came for us to attack again. It was another push. This time we all hoped the last one.

Night came, we moved out after receiving our rations. Our weapons were loaded on the jeep. That made it easy for our heavy weapon platoon.

Forward we marched along the road in columns of two. It was a slow march with plenty of breaks. Now we reached the point where we unloaded the jeep and started carrying our weapons.

I was loaded down with 2 boxes of ammo. All we had was 7 men in our section. Short by 3 men. In fact the company now was less than half strength.

Slowly we went along. Our hill was in sight now. The companies all were headed for their sector of the front.

Soon a machine gun opened up and all hit the ground. We waited then started again. Further in we went with pitched bayonets. Nobody cares for a bayonet. I don't either.

We reached the foot of our hill and soon formed our line. Now along the skyline were men running. They are Germans going to their positions. In further we went only to be pulled back a few hundred yards then started to dig in. Only to be called to move forward again. It seems they couldn't make their mind up. It was getting light now fast.

We had wasted good time, moving around. Now we were set only to have the Germans open up on us.

The two machine guns were set up in the center of the field, about 50 feet from each other. My gun was the No. 1 gun on the left. I was 20 feet back, nearer to the left to make sure no one could creep up on us from our left.

The battle started off with a bang. Men were now yelling. Already we had casualties. The German fire was terrific, their guns were at all angles.

Our gun was still not in action, the other had got in action fast. I looked around and there was our gunner working on our gun. The other guy had his head buried in the ground.

Bullets were zinging all around now. I found a target to shoot at. I fired 4 shots. Our boys were not doing so good. Many were hit and calling for the medics for first aid.

Now our troubles were just beginning. Three mortars are landing among us. It looked bad now. The German fire was worse.

The order came to withdraw. I got up on my knees, slung the rifle around my back, grabbed ahold of the two Amuno boxes then started back. I seen a few boys running back. I tried to keep low. The German fire continues. I ran about 20 yds. when I tripped and fell hard. I laid there about a minute, up again with the boxes and off I went fast and hard as I could go. I tripped again after about 20 more yards. I was sore in the knees now. The fellow running next to me was just hit, he was in terrible pain and hollering. I couldn't recognize him or help him. There was nothing for me to do but keep going. I couldn't lay there and I couldn't travel very well with the Amuno. I left one behind and off again I went. It didn't help. I fell flat again on my face. I laid there, I didn't move, I was too tired. I now was in the plowed field, the running was hard, not far ahead was smooth ground with bushes for cover. This time I left the last box behind and took off. I ran about 50 yds. and this time I hit the ground myself. I took cover and rested a minute. The fire continues all the time. Once more I ran. I ran like hell, my feet just carried me. I was too tired to hit the ground, I just didn't care. I took my chances of reaching the spot I was after for I made it and jumped down there a tired man. I found a spot and just laid there. There was 2 other guys there, we were all pretty well beat. 5 minutes I didn't move or say a word.

Now to find my company. Not many boys were there. I seen about 5 boys from my co. A few guys were coming in, some badly hit. A few men soon placed some guns in position in case. Some fellows soon continued the trip back. I was all set to do likewise when a officer came around the bend and told us to wait. The order came to continue back. I then dropped my pack and started off. I crawled out on the field and started to run out in the wheat field. I was about 50 yds. out when at my left I seen some soldiers following along the gulley. Their cover was perfect. They waved for me to come over. I did and was glad. It looked safe and the trail led us back. I had no worry now about small arms fire, only artillery.

All along the trail it was easy to see that the Germans had been around. Their papers and letters were all over. Also some of their equipment, which none of us took because of booby traps.

Our trail now led us in another draw and there was a creek running along it. We turn right & we seen soldiers all along the bank digging fox holes. I soon found out they were the 2nd Bat., our relief. Now to find K Co. I walked along slowly. I was sore & tired. Only a few of our boys I found. They all had the same story to tell. Our boys were captured. I couldn't believe it but it was true. Many were hit, our captain was killed with 6 others. The company on our right was also hit very hard. I found a few boys and laid down to rest and to get orders of what to do next.

I ate some K rations and that cleaned me out of my rations. I had no water. It was still early in the morning. I tried to get some sleep but the sun was too hot to sleep under. There wasn't any shade around. Hours went by—boys were coming in one at a time.

The medics were busy with thier first aid. Their job was to get those fellows who were in the forward draw and bring them to us. Then they would still have to carry them across another few miles to where the jeeps were.

I now heard that two boys of our other machine gun were killed, one wounded bad, the other captured. In my gun one fellow was wounded, only myself & another guy was around.

Meanwhile the hills were being shelled and also bombed by our planes. Later on some of our tanks went up the side of the hill and laid it to the Nazis.

Hours more went by and I was forced to drink the creek water. It was good & cool but sure looked dirty. A few boys of K. Co. took off and tried to head to town. I hung around. I was sore all over and some officers stopped me to ask me questions of the fight. I walked with a limp.

One of our boys couldn't see with one eye. I guess he's blind now for life. The story we hear is that we are leaving at dark. A officer finally came around to get K Co. list of boys there. All officers were captured, killed or wounded. I never seen this one.

I gave him my name. All he had was only 7 other names. He told us to wait in one spot and at dark we will start back, also hot chow was waiting for us.

We moved at night. K. Co., just about 20 of us. After a little hike we finally reached our area. After chow then got some blankets and went to bed.

Morning came, our both companies ate together. They piled our mess kits up high. Too much chow & nobody to eat it. We heard the good news about Bizerte & Tunis falling. That about ends the war here and glad we were.

The captured boys now had a chance to get set free, we all hoped. The day went along and boys were coming in one at a time. All talk was about going home, everybody had one idea. It was late the next day when we were all packed and ready to move back when some of captured boys returned. They told us the Germans couldn't get them on board ships, our planes were raising hell in the harbor. The British marched in to Tunis and that freed everybody. The Germans now were the prisoners.

# OTTO V. PETR

Of diaries dealing with naval warfare in the Pacific we have several examples in the At Sea section. All that turned up by members of the ground forces is this fragment by Otto V. Petr, of Cicero, Illinois. Even this, as it happens, finds him not for the moment in active combat but between engagements. It gives, however, a good account of what it is like to be on the ground at a target of air raids.

Now a World War II historian (Pacific Theatre), Petr was a Private First Class at the time of this diary, having garrison duty with Company I, 132nd Infantry, American Division. Born in 1915, Petr's work before the war had been hotel catering. After the war he held a variety of jobs—factory, farming, etc.—meanwhile amassing a great deal of published material about the various World War II campaigns in the Pacific. What began as a hobby eventually turned into a profession as he made a speciality of the history of that sector of the war.

*******

MARCH 13, 1943 Guadalcanal Island

My barracks bag No. 2 finally came. We have given up hopes of seeing these bags again. Our bags have been kept in storage in New Caledonia since we have boarded the President Adams in last November, for Guadalcanal. Today Tom Marren and myself worked all day building crates to crate up our company kitchen equipment for our expected trip to the Fiji Isles. Everybody has great hopes of going home from there. I made a necklace for Marianne. As like any other previous night, we had a lights out order for a few minutes but no alarm for an air raid. Father Gorman said Mass in our area. Yesterday the 10 wheelers hauled mail all day long from incoming ship . And today about 4 bags reached the Co. Got a letter from Helen Croft and also a letter from my old buddy Stanley Janusz.

MARCH 14, '43

Rained most of the day. Quite night. No air raid. We felt pretty good in our tent so we did a little singinq of some of our favorite old songs, to the playing of a couple of mouth organs.

MARCH 15

Weather cleared. Washed clothes. Kept building crates. The General called the officers together and after the conference we were told we would leave for the Fijis after the 1st of April. There we will train for three months and then back into combat. And that we are not going home as rumored. Went to see 132nd Band play and a movie. Quite night. No air raid.

MARCH 18th

Bob Kline, Tom Marren and I took the morning off to bum around on the main road. We tried to go aboard ships but the ships were too far beyond Lunga Point. Finally we came back after all that time spent getting nowhere. The movies were cut short because of an air raid warning. But no planes came in.

MARCH 20th

Nothing unusual. Quite night. Two formations of B-24 bombers took off for Munda Bay, Georgia Islands at 6:00 p.m. Planes returned about 10 p.m. It took a long while for all 33 planes to land.

MARCH 21st

No interference with the nightly movies because of air raid. Again, with a full moon, 40 Navy dive bombers, 5-24's and 4 B-17's took off at 6:00 pm. for another crack at Munda Bay, Georgia Isles. All planes returned both nights.

MARCH 23rd

Went to the movies. A very interesting picture was being shown. Just after the third reel started the generator broke down. A few minutes later, the lights out order came in. However we had plenty of time to get back to our area before the sirens sounded Condition Red 4, to get near our fox holes and bomb shelters. Then a plane or two came, and dropped a couple of eggs on or near a B-17 Fortress and set it afire. The fire grew bigger and bigger and .50 cal. ammunition started to go off. From our area it sounded as if a big battle was raging. We were pretty certain the Hell's Point Area (one of the largest ammo dumps) was on fire or was burning in one of the many gas and oil dumps. Maybe most of the planes at Henderson Field were on fire and exploding. The tall blazing flames died down, but a large cloud of smoke covered the sky. In came another two planes. I've been wishing for what happened next to see, before leaving this island. A plane was hit by the A.A. guns and burst. It was a direct hit and a flash from the burst lighted the area like lightning. The flash lasted only a few seconds and a rain of bits of metal was heard next. The other plane got in on a dive to start the fire and exploding of ammo in another part of Henderson Field. Once again the flames shot up and all Hell seemed to be loose in that direction. Three large bombs went off within ten minutes. The fire and all this lasted about an hour. After a general bull session and even an argument, I went to bed, still shaking and a bit upset, from all the excitement and the jolts of the exploding heavy bombs and the continuous racket caused by the exploding of ammo and the anti-aircraft barrage. This was my 1st chance to experience the jolt of concussion of a 500 lb. bomb. This was the Japs' first successful air raid, which has inflicted so much heavy damage since our arrival here. Several previous raids have caused a few deaths and casualties. Earlier in the day we got the good news that the Lunga River over-flooded and washed out the bridge over the main road.

MARCH 24th

Came a new day and made up my mind to see what happened. So I hitched a ride up to the bridge. Work to repair the washed-out bridge was well started by the C.B.s. It was already possible to cross the bridge by foot this morning. I watched the home-made pile driver (a weight, sliding down on a couple of rails, it was lifted up and dropped by a huge crane) dropping the weight, sunk the log another foot and a half, every blow. When I got to the bomber strip the damaged planes were only a pile of wreckage, scooped up with bulldozers. A bomb crater where a Fortress was hit was already filled up. Scraps of metal were scattered for about a block square. One of the Fortresses' motors was lying 110 ft. from the plane. All that seemed to happen to the planes near by was that they were covered with flying dirt and spared even slight damage. In all seven planes were lost in both raids. 3 B-17 (Flying Fortresses), 1 B-24, 2 Naval dive bombers and one of the New Zealand Air Force's Am-made Lockheed Hudsons. The 3 bombs (500 lbs.) that caused the big explosion and lit up the sky a bright red were lying near the Lockheed Hudson. Two bombs missed the airport completely and dropped into the swamp just twenty feet short. I was really surprised to know how little damage was done. Divine Providence surely was with us because no casualties occurred. I must praise the fellows who put out the fire and checked further damage. The 57th Eng., 101st Med. and 182nd Inf. units that have been boarding the ships since yesterday morning left at 3:00 p.m.

MARCH 25th

The day started with an air raid alarm at 4 a.m. The A.A. guns opened up in other parts of the island but the plane never did come in. The all-clear sounded about ½ hr. after the alarm.

MARCH 26th

Had another air raid alarm at 4 a.m. but no planes came in. Our boys who were picked for Cadery left today. Medics came around to give us a couple of shots for diptheria. Saw Don Amichi and Joan Bennett in "Girl Trouble". Everybody at the show got in a lot of good laughs and enjoyed it.

MARCH 27th

Another air raid at 4 a.m. Tojo time. Two planes were picked up in the lights in a moment after being turned on. A.A. fire was well placed around the planes but they were not hit. No bombs were dropped and the plane flew out of sight. About 15 min. after the A.A. firing ceased, a lone plane came in and the lights had a hard time trying to locate it in cotton-like clouds. The plane tried to outwit the A.A. light crews so it could fly in at low altitude and dive at a target. It almost succeeded but the lights picked it out at 12,000 ft. and just as it was coming in from the sea, towards us. And it just turned and fled at about 300 m.p.h. When the A.A. guns finally opened up, it was well out at sea. All clear and back to bed. Saw the picture WAKE ISLAND. We all took the picture in, in great admiration for the heroic stand made, by so few men, and against such unbelievable odds for so long a time without any aid in sight. And from our own experience pictured ourselfs fighting alongside of them and going through the same hardships.

MARCH 29th

Plenty of trouble for the P-38 planes. One came in with a dead motor, overshot the runway and didn't have enough power to rise again. Still traveling at high speed, taxied beyond the runway, a furrow of earth caused it to throw its tail into the air. It went about 25 yds. farther before it spun off the road. Plane was damaged beyond repairs, but the pilot was unscratched. A second P-38 came in with the tip of a wing knocked off while strafing a bombed destroyer and colliding into its smoke stack. Plane landed safely. Plane No. 3 made a perfect landing with only one motor in running condition. I have seen all this happen within ½ hr. or so. Quite night.

MARCH 30th

A quite day and night. Went to the show. As usual. Saw "Flying Tigers". About half way it started to rain. But the fellows wanted the show to go on. It rained for about 20 min. but the picture worth seeing in spite of the rain, and also taking a chance of not seeing it again. Getting back to our area, I found one of my barracks bags wet, and the foot of my bunk too. So I hung up the wet clothes and lucky for me that I had my shelter half beneath the blankets, the rain did not soak through. I managed to drain the water off. All this happened because I left the side of my tent wall up.

MARCH 31st

Dried all my wet clothes and started to pack my bags to move to the Reg. Area.

APRIL 1

We moved out of our Fighter Strip No. 2 area into the Battalion Area. We bivouaced in the Fight Strip area for almost two months. Our company was assigned to guard duty. In the afternoon we started to whip the area into shape. We picked up all the trash and all dead coconut palms and set it a-fire. We went to work improving the deep

ruts in the road and cut down the weeds in the area. This same area was the rear area and the kitchens during the drive on Mount Austin.
APRIL 3rd
A General inspection in the morning. We had a 20 min. "condition red" period about noon. No plane came in. They must of got the H—l beat out of them again by our fighters.
APRIL 5th
An air raid alarm spoiled the evening's movie. But no planes appeared. Our baggage was sent off.
APRIL 6th
Got up at 4:00 A.M. At 6:00 A.M. we started a three mile hike, with field equipment, to Kolie Beach. Arrived there about 7:00. The four transports and an oiler sailed in a few minutes later. The ships were the Penn, Climmer, Hunter Ligett and the U.S.S. Fuller. After a small lunch we boarded the Fuller about 2 P.M. We were fully loaded at about 4:00 P.M. At about 7:00 while our planes were returning for the night a lone Jap bomber followed and was not detected till a few miles away. The search lights picked it up almost at once. On shore all lights were on because of no warning. A naval blinker light was sending out messages to ship in the channel. When the alarm was given the crew aboard ship was rushing to Battle Stations and sailors seemed to be popping up from every direction. They had a hard time of it, for the deck was crowded. We were ordered below deck. Something very unusual for us as we always liked a ringside view from our foxholes of the battle the anti-aircraft artillery put up, to try to knock the planes out of the sky. We have also learned to judge whether we were in the path of the approaching plane or not. And it was second nature for us to hug the ground at the known sound of the falling bombs. On my way to the hatch below I seen the first anti-aircraft shells burst in the air. I also seen what appeared to be starshells going off, to warn our own planes a raid was in progress. Just before getting below, I hit the deck, for a "hit the deck" order was given. I managed to crawl to the door of the hatch and sped down below in order not to block anybody else from getting down too. Down below it was nasty. The air circulation system was stopped and most of the lights put out, to help the ship make use of all its power to get moving, to make a zig-zagging target. Before I got below I seen a few of our own planes navigation lights and thought they were our night fighters taking after the Jap. No doubt the plane got away or at least sent out messages of the convoy in the harbor. The plane seemed to head for the big tanker at anchor, pumping her fuel cargo of 1,000,000 gal. or so of 100 octane gas (On Guada an average of 40,000 gal. of gas was consumed every day. Some days, well over 52,000 gals.) The anti-aircraft barrage kept the plane away. It must of been well over half an hour

before we were again allowed on deck. In the meantime, there was a lot of misery below. Fellows smoked. Some birds stood in the doorways and blocked the air from entering. Fellows shouted "Get the hell out of there!". And those smart alecks swore back and stood. We were on the move all night, just going in circles to keep from making a target for any submarine that might of possibly got through the even extra heavy surface patrol by patrol craft of all kinds. If I am not mistaken I counted 13 destroyers around Kolie Point in the day time. Could not sleep on the deck because of a shower about nine o'clock or so. So I slept below. We were pretty lucky out our end because somebody aboard before us punctured several holes into the air shaft in our aisle and we got enough air to make it a lot more comfortable in a hatch of smelling sweating bodies.

APRIL 7th

We waited at Kolie Point for the other ships to finish loading. At 9:00 A.M. we took off for Lunga Point, about three miles up the channel. Here the Hunter Liggett was to pick up more troops. Four Liberty freighters were busy unloading their cargoes also at this point. About 11 A.M. an air raid alarm sounded. The planes were expected at 12:45 or so. At once all of the crew was again rushing to their battle stations. All ships raised their anchors and were in a few minutes at full speed steaming to get out of the channel. The Hunter Liggett took off without getting its remaining troops to go aboard ship. And even without its Higgins boats and its crew that manned these boats. A destroyer, alongside of her, took off at full speed. It picked up speed like a Ford V-8. Out of 98 attacking planes only 2 came after our four ships. All ships gave them a hot reception of A.A. fire. We thanked Almighty God, for we were spared. But four ships were sunk in the bay. A destroyer, a small tanker was loading at Tulagi, a corvette, a cargo ship. One of these, if I am not mistaken, was later reported only afire and was saved. 34 of the Jap planes were knocked out in the fight that went on. Our own forces lost six Grumman Wildcats and one Aircobra. One pilot was rescued. We kept right on sailing.

APRIL 8th

In the morning we got news of a prowling submarine that was sunk overnight. It was caught above the surface. 40 mm. guns of a destroyer opened up on it. It submerged. The destroyer knocked it out of the water with depth charges. The destroyer kept around where the sub was sunk. And about noon it joined our convoy with the big tanker that brought in fuel for Guada's planes. It too come out of the fight without being hit. It made an attempt to get out, in case of further raids. About 9:30 we sighted one of our aircraft carriers, three cruisers and eight destroyers that either came for added protection for our convoy or else heading to Tulagi for a future task-force raid. It rained again at night. In our convoy were the four transports, the tanker, four destroyers. Throughout the voyage various planes were sighted. Navy fighters, scout bombers and Catalinas, also several converted transports. Seen one flying towards Guada one night. Just the flames from the exhaust were visible and it flew up very high.

APRIL 9th

Our third day at sea. About 4:00 A.M. lights were visible in the New Hebrides somewhere. From ashore messages were sent out by a blinker light. A light was seen on one of the destroyers and a sailor remarked "It's only the Admiral in the toilet". We were now pretty well safe from air attacks and doubly so because we were in range of our own fighter planes, never far away. In the channels it was pretty rough sailing and some of the fellows became seasick. It was a little better out in the open sea. It was pretty cloudy and cool the rest of the trip, with now and then a tropical shower for at this time, in the semi-tropics, the rainy season was coming to an end.

APRIL 17th

Sunday morning the ship was made ready for a stop and our debarkation. The crew started long before daylight. An earlier breakfast was served. The final rolling of tenting was being finished, also the last showers, shaves and washing before going ashore.

ABOARD THE S.S. FULLER

We were well crowded in the troop berthing. The ship was the smallest and oldest we so far traveled on, launched 1923. Its winches and most of its operating equipment was propelled by steam from its oil-burning engine. This ship has earned a High Honorable Record. It took Marines to the Solomon Islands Aug. 7th. It survived bombing attacks by airplanes. It was laid up in New Zealand because it was rammed by one of our own destroyers. Its anti-aircraft guns knocked out several planes. In the early part of the war it made a trip to Iceland and Glasgow, Scotland. Its crew had a wild time ashore in Scotland.

# ANNE McCAUGHEY

The only woman represented in this collection, unfortunately, is Anne McCaughey, who served as an American Red Cross Aide, with the assimilated rank of Second Lieutenant. Her duties, not gone into in much detail in the diary, were to provide recreational and social service needs to patients of the U.S. Army's 50th General Hospital.

Born in 1915, Anne McCaughey graduated from Pennsylvania State University and went to work for Woman's Day Magazine. After the war she returned to her work as a journalist with the same publication and later was on the staff of the Germantown Courier in Philadelphia.

A diarist both before and after the war, Anne McCaughey brings a woman's sensibilities to the task of describing the impact of foreign landscape and of war on an idealistic young American. This diary makes all the more poignant my regret that I was unable to flush out any diaries by the women who served in the women's branches of the armed services, for it gives a glimpse of how different their viewpoint might have been. Women had, of course, served as nurses and Red Cross workers in previous wars but had never served in the armed forces (with the exception of such as Deborah Sampson, who masqueraded as a man and took part in the Revolutionary War). It might have been both interesting and useful to have had women's private reactions as pioneers of a sort. I have mentioned in the introduction my theories as to why women seem to have produced almost no diaries of their wartime service years, but I am grateful that we have at least this one example by a woman who was involved, even if in a more traditional nurturing way.

*******

DECEMBER 15, 1943 Camp Carson, Colo.

A day to be remembered because it was our readiness day. A day to be remembered because it was the day I discovered the mountains were real and not picture postcards. When I first saw them last Friday, they seemed too much like pictures out of the National Geographic to be true. It took almost a week for them to penetrate my consciousness as real, honest-to-God mountains, glorious to behold. Altogether a sight to love and cherish.

THURSDAY, 16 Dec. 1943

If I thought yesterday was a day to remember, it was only because I

didn't know about today. Until you have risen at 5:30 a.m., folded your tent like an Arab and taken it and the mattress and all the linen, quilts and blankets next door, stood in line for breakfast at 6:30 a.m., packed a suitcase, a duffel bag and a musette bag before 7 a.m., climbed aboard an open truck where you stood in the cold, wintry wind of a Colorado morning, holding on with both hands as you go around corners, and riding a few miles to board a troop train, with helmets falling off on the average of twice a mile so that the driver has to stop the truck with a terrific jolt that sends everybody flying to the forward part of the truck. Well, if you haven't done all those things, you haven't lived. All my life to date has been just preparation for today. There was a feeling that came to me as the truck started out that rutted road back of the Nurse's Residence buildings that I have never had before. Behind us, literally as well as figuratively, lay the great peaks of the Rocky Mountains, representing America, fine and big and clean, room and place for everyone. Ahead of us lay new experiences, untried talents for great challenges. It was good to be a part of it. It was good to climb off the truck as we reached the troop train and march along in our slacks and uniform coats with the heavy musette bag hitting the right hip and the light musette bag hitting the left hip. We Red Crossers were at the end of the line of nurses and as we passed the lines of enlisted men one of them said, "Look, something new has been added—the Red Cross."
(From Camp Carson we traveled by troop train to Camp Myles Standish near Boston, Mass. We sailed from Boston 28 Dec. 1943.)
28 DEC. 1943

Leaving the staging area on one shoulder I had a blanket roll and a musette bag, on the other shoulder another musette bag and a gas mask. Around my waist was a pistol belt with a first aid kit and a canteen. On my head I wore a wool cap, helmet liner and a steel helmet, weighing down on my brains. The whole thing was so heavy and cumbersome and so precariously balanced that I could hardly hold myself erect. When I saw the truck into which I was supposed to climb with all these impediments, I thought, "Shall I tell them now that I should never have joined the Army and that it's a terrible mistake. It's better to admit the error right now. Sorry and goodbye." Somehow when it was my turn to get into the truck I stepped forward and placed my left foot in the stirrup which was about halfway up the five foot ascent and fell forward into the truck. Surprisingly enough I was able to reassume an upright position in spite of all I was wearing. A WAC drove up in a car, jumped out and said, "So you're going across. You're a wonderful bunch. All the luck in the world to you." No one in our group had ever seen her before and we stood open-mouthed as she drove away. Ave atque Vale. 50th General Hospital sailed from Boston 28, Dec. 1943 aboard E. B. Alexander. Docked in Liverpool 8 Jan. 1944

14 JAN. 1944 Oulton Park, near Chester, England

Impressions of living in a Quonset hut with 10 Army nurses, one other Red Cross worker and one not very efficient coal burning stove. The latrine (labeled sanitary as separate and distinct from ablution center) is half a mile away and largely under water. The bed in a Quonset hut consists of three pillows of straw which divide themselves where your shoulders hit and where your hips hit. Sheets are not what the well-dressed Quonset hut is wearing this year. Rather the fashion calls for rough, heavy blankets which wear off hunks of your skin wherever they touch and of which you get pieces in your mouth. After several nights devoted to study of the problem, it has been determined that the best costume for sleeping in said bunks is heavy underwear (two piece and overlapping), one pair of heavy wool socks, one pair of pajamas and one fatigue suit. The advisability of wearing gloves and kerchief has been considered but not yet adopted.

The conversation of Army nurses is something unique in this world. They have a cynical attitude toward life and people, yet withal have managed to preserve a childlike innocence which makes it possible for them to believe the most astounding scuttlebut the Army can produce.

IMPRESSIONS FROM LONDON IN JAN. 1944

I've been looking in Selfridge's window just like the lady in Vincent Sheean's book. How much water has passed over the dam since then. When I walked past the BBC Building and down Oxford Street I had the feeling that the whole world to that moment had been made for me to be born in, to live for 28 years, to come to London in January 1944 so I could walk down Oxford Street.

6 MARCH 1944

This morning I discovered the University of Glasgow, rising up out of the fog. There was a dreamlike quality to my stroll, through Kelvingrove Park, coming upon the lake with the ducks and swans, climbing the steep hill and then the steps to find at the top the University, quiet as if deserted. A citadel in a war-torn world, arches and towers rising through the fog. I went into the library where the professors come in their caps and gowns, the students in their red flannel coats. I saw the collection donated to the library by an insurance agent, containing folios of Shakespeare and illuminated manuscripts. It's wonderful the way the British always apologize for what they have. They say quietly, "Of course, it's not so grand as your Library of Congress." Or, "Of course, it's not so large as the Empire State Building, or so handsome as the George Washington Bridge." And all the time they wouldn't exchange theirs for ours if we diamond-studded ours first. It's the epitome of all self-assurance. When you feel really sure, you don't have to brag. You can admire the other fellow's and at the same time know yours is the best of all possible.

Here they have a fog you can smell, taste, touch and see. In fact, you can do everything but hear it and in a negative sense maybe you can even do that, because it has a muffling, deadening effect on other sounds. It's like wrapping a trip-hammer in velvet. Fog has color here. It comes in yellows and blues and greens and purples—and sometimes the more ordinary greys and white. The taste of it is not pleasant. It is rather like chewing on a piece of coal with copper fillings in it.

10th MARCH 1944

A wonderful ride on my bicycle to Erskine Ferry, through country roads with the Scottish mountains across the Clyde River. I had the feeling that if I were to die the next minute, life would have been worth all the effort because of moments of peace and beauty like that, the cool, sweet air rushing past my ears as the bicycle whizzes downhill.

I met a small boy in Paisley who wanted to help me fix my bicycle. I asked him where the Cross was and he insisted on taking me on a personally conducted tour there. On our way we passed another small boy on a bicycle. They shouted a greeting and then he explained to me, "That's my wee chum."

16 MARCH 1944

My bicycle trip today was a fiasco. The weather is agin me. I get a flat tire. I have the tire pumped at that big bus terminal outside Renfrew. I get another flat tire. A dog comes along and bites me as I am flapping by on my bum tire. What next? I shudder to ponder. (The answer was that on the way home I ran over a small boy.)

Sunde, one of our patients, is a Norwegian boy, who is named after the farm in Norway where he was born. He fought against the Nazis in his own country and escaped in a fishing boat. He came to Brooklyn to live with his sister. He is going to be adopted by a couple in Cedar Rapids, Iowa, who will turn their business over to him because they have no children of their own. He is what the war is being fought for.

22nd MARCH 1944

There's a small hotel—maybe no wishing well (it has an E.W.S. on the front lawn instead)—but it's in Ayr and it's called the Dablair and through the window you can see the park and in the park the birds are singing and the grass is green and fresh. When you come from Glasgow to Ayr on the bus, you ride through the beautiful Scottish countryside, which looks as you had always imagined it would look and yet didn't really believe it could. Sometimes you catch your breath and say, "Oh, my God," because it's too perfect, the scene of peace and contentment. Hills stretch away to the far horizon, with sheep grazing on the hills and farmers cutting the fields into perfect symmetrical patterns. Through the windows of the cottages you pass you can see the tables laid for tea—shining white linen and gleaming silver and sparkling china in even the wee house. There are daffodils in many of the windows and the mirrors on the wall catch and reflect the sun from the west and the sun yellow of the daffodils. It's such a good feeling—and the war far away. "And what was all the strife about, for the myrtle or the rose?"

24th MARCH 1944

Naefach, who, when in a class on gas warfare, is asked what he would think if he got up one morning and saw that the white stars on the U.S. Army trucks had turned red, answers: "I'd figure that several divisions of the Russian Army had come to camp during the night."

2 APRIL 1944 A snowstorm in Scotland—and yesterday it was Spring

The other day when I was trundling my book cart around the corner of H and down the hills come the boys from Upper J just back from a hike (these are the rehabilitation kids). We reach the foot of the hill at the same moment and Private Zeppi brings the group to attention and says "Salute". The whole group snaps to attention and salutes while I stumble past them in an embarrassed fashion, saying "This is very nice," not having the vaguest idea what I should do.

NOTE ON ZEPPI, inserted Jan 6, 1946

He and Maxine were having a conversation one day about his super-size of 200-odd pounds. She asked him why he didn't do something about it and he told her in a humble, reverent way, "God knows best".

11 APRIL 1944

Visiting in Scottish homes is an experience. Mr. McLaren, who looks like a leprechaun, has eyes that twinkle and a face that wrinkles up when he is about to make some particularly elfish statement. For 24 years whenever he has left the table at the end of a meal in his home, he says "Thank you" to his wife. Mr. McLaren's greatest rival for his wife's affection is the Duke of Windsor, more commonly known among the McLarens as the late Prince of Wales. Mrs. McLaren loves him with the devotion of a mother to her only son. His suffering and anguish under the rule of his tyrannical mother still brings tears to her eyes when she thinks of them. No one can say a word against him without her taking it as a personal insult and rising magnificently to his defense.

Easter services in an army camp overseas are different from Easter services at Summit church, but somehow better. There are daffodils instead of deep-cupped lilies. There are bare rafters in a Nicean hut instead of oak beams in a high-vaulted arch. There is a piano out of tune with keys that stick, rather than a richvoiced organ. There are o.d. uniforms or blue bathrobes in place of new Easter finery. There are G.I. boots rather than Steigerwalt's latest and finest $22.50 model. But I think the spirit is there in more sincere form.

**14th APRIL 1944**

So you'd be interested in having an interview with someone who has just completed 50 miles of bicycling in one day and who is looking forward to five more before she calls it a day? Well, you see, it's like this. The effect is rather the same as that of three daiquiris in rapid succession. You are feeling no pain. There is a certain numbness which extends to all parts of your body down to toes and fingertips. The brain has long ceased to function. Everything that happens seems a little unreal. Trams have brushed past you, baby carriages may run over your feet, small children may fall across your path and you are above and beyond being affected by such trifles. Onward and upward—upidee-adee-adi—or there's always another hill beyond the next bend. The rain falls, the wind blows, the cars whiz by and knock us off the road, the road continues to wind up hills—yes, all the way. But does that stop us? Nay, Gourock, Greenock, Kilmalcolm, Bridge of Weir, Paisley—we knock them all off in our stride and cry for larger game.

**12 MAY 1944**

It's a rich and deep human experience to send a telegram over the telephone in the British Isles, especially when it contains such words as "best-manning" and "adMary" and "Londonwarding". It's a trifle disconcerting to a Scottish operator to understand such Timestyle.

Having lunch with a couple of other white collar girls at Terry's (more commonly known as the Grosvenor in Glasgow, I believe) is fun. It's interesting to compare notes and see wherein we differ and wherein we are alike, having been a white collar girl myself for a good many years.

**6 JUNE 1944**

And where were you on D-Day? I was in a peaceful hospital in that most peaceful of all peaceful countries, Scotland. I was in a room with four or five patients who were on their way back to the States, some of them having already done their part and some of them n.p. cases who didn't have what it takes to do the job and whose only concern was that the invasion might hold up their departure for home. Which were which I will never know, for I was not even looking at them, so concerned was I with my own problems—mainly the one of where was the nicest, cleanest, handsomest young brother in the world at that H hour of D Day and dear God, bless him and keep him safe and strong, keep him fine and brave and clean and happy and, dear God, above all, keep him in one piece.

It's a day when all sorts of emotions well up within you—mental pictures of those ships as they loaded up, what was going on in the minds of the men, the fear that must have been in them, and yet the dogged determination to get this messy business over with.

**12 JUNE 1944**

Today I was sitting under a tree with rain pouring down on my head, my neck, my face, my hands, completely soaking each page of the New Yorker before I had finished reading it—and reading a story by Irwin Shaw in which the leading character is longing for "the rugged and manly weather of his native Scotland". It seemed pretty ironic at the time and I laughed bitterly and muttered—"He can have the rugged and manly weather of his native Scotland—and he knows what he can do with it." But an hour or so later, when the rain had stopped and the sun was shining and I came to the top of that hill overlooking Paisley, I took it all back. How many times during the past several months have I said to myself, "Earth has not anything to show more fair". I've meant it, too. And today I said it and meant it again. The dark, brooding hills with the low-hanging clouds, the streaks of sunlight falling over the slopes down to the city. The rhododendron in bloom before the mansions. The blue water in the reservoir looking like a lake. The wind moving through the scented gorse and the tall grass, moving them like waves on the sea. So I'm sorry I said mean things about the Scottish weather. Okay, so the weather is lousy, The country is more beautiful than it has any right to be—and I don't want to leave it.

25th JUNE 1944

A Sunday in Surrey, bicycling along the Thames, one of those things I've dreamed about since I was 12 and once I wrote a story about John and Anne, dressed all in gray, going to visit John in his country home in Surrey, complete with swimming pool. I was a crazy sort of kid with all sorts of illusions and wild ideas which I have surrendered slowly and reluctantly. So now I have come to Surrey in a gray suit, but it is a darker grey than I had planned and somehow it happens to be a Red Cross uniform which was not in the earlier picture. And there is no John, tight-lipped and with a secret sorrow, to show me Surrey. Instead there is 38 year old Nelsey Redman and her ten year old son, Creighton. The glamour and the romance are gone, but there is something more substantial, more realistic, less gingerbreadish left.

NOTE inserted 17 Dec. 1946: When Bea and Maxine and Tesse and I went to London in June of 1944 to get our battle dress preparatory to moving on to France, none of us was enthusiastic about the idea of going to London, which doesn't make very good sense to me now. We had a rugged trip down on the train, sleeping in our clothes in a third class compartment. But after we arrived we were assigned to the Mayfair Hotel. After engineering the deal so Bea and Tesse were rooming together, Maxine and I found ourselves in a suite. There was a bedroom and a bathroom with a tub the size of a small swimming pool. We kept opening doors until we found a sitting room opening off the bedroom with lovely, delicate pale grey-green furniture of Louis Quatorze or

Louis Quinze style—I wouldn't be knowing. The first day we were there I took two baths because it was the first opportunity I had had to take anything but a shower since we had been in London last time, in January of that year.

I can't remember all the things we did. I know we spent a lot of time at Debenham and Peabody's, getting fitted for our uniforms. I remember the first night when we were sleeping in those beautiful, wonderful, comfortable beds at the Mayfair, on those mattresses in which you sank up to there. Oh, it felt so good and I was so happy when I climbed in between those clean sheets and pulled the soft comforter up around me. About three o'clock in the morning Maxine wakened me. She was standing at the window looking out and she informed me that we were having a buzz bomb attack. "Do you think we ought to go to the air raid shelter?" she asked. "I can't think of a better place to die," I told her, "I couldn't be happier." And with that I turned over and went back to sleep.

18th JULY 1944

This is written in the midst of a rich and deep human experience—at Seaton Barracks, a marshalling area before shipment to France. I'm in a room with twenty nurses. They have just brought our bedding rolls to us because they are too fat and bulky and we must lighten them. It seems that the nurses' combat suits are not ready and that we can't leave until they are, so with this as a starter the rumors begin and grow in size and intensity until it is bruited about that the 50th General Hospital is about to be split up, never to see each other again, and it is all the fault of the Chief Nurse and the Quartermaster. Something within me makes it possible for me to feel completely removed from everything that is going on, because I know I'm not going to have to make any decision about anything—that somebody is going to tell me what to do and then I will do it. And that is all there is to it.

But to go back—last night I was standing on a corner in the small town just outside of Plymouth and the whole scene was something out of Saroyan. There were six G.I.s sitting on the wall, the sergeant with a harmonica had an appropriate tune for all passersby—Anchors Aweigh for the Navy, While the Caissons Go Rolling Along for the Field Artillery, Paper Doll for some lovesick G.I. and one long blast for any goodlooking babe who happened to pass by. As an indication of good Anglo-American relations some American soldiers and British sailors went by with their arms interlocked. The detail of six British shore patrollers paced by at funeral march pace, with sad faces and lowered heads. I was with Clara, who was waiting outside a public telephone booth, or kiosk, to get a telephone call from her husband. She waited an hour and a half, but when it finally came she was the happiest girl in all of England that night, I'm sure. Yesterday we viewed the Hoe in Plymouth, where Sir Francis Drake sank the Spanish Armada. The small island, the blue-gray water, the hills that looked like camouflage, the kids in swimming off the water front, the people sitting in deck chairs on the greensward sloping down to the water.

18 JULY 1944

You wouldn't believe all the things that have happened in the last five days. One thing I'll say for the Army is that when it moves, it moves fast. How many places have we lived—700 people, not just half a dozen or so (and with all our worldly goods) in the past 10 days. We have lived in our hospital—our old, common, ordinary workaday hospital where we were happy in a humdrum sort of way, we have lived at Crookston from Friday afternoon to the following Monday evening; we have lived on a troop train from Tuesday at 1 a.m. to that same Tuesday at about 9:30 p.m. (not forgetting sleeping in the same compartment with Captain Berkowsky that night with blanket rolls falling with monotonous regularity and window shades flying up with a great clatter at odd intervals—and tea being spilled on the floor. Not just one canteen cupful or even two canteen cupfuls but three canteen cupfuls until our cozy little compartment resembled a swimming pool). Then, to continue with this story, from Monday night until Saturday morning we lived in Plymouth, England. From Saturday morning to Sunday afternoon we were aboard a Liberty troop ship crossing an English Channel which was as smooth as Lake Ontario ever was, making all my fears groundless. For a few hours Sunday evening we were in a cow pasture somewhere in Normandy near Utah Beach, where I had my first experience at pitching a pup tent and we sat on blankets outside our new little home and supped on K rations. I can remember the first time I ever tasted K rations I thought they were delicious, but now that I have lived on nothing else but for two days, I might say in an understative sort of way that my palate craves something different. Well, to get back to the sequence of events as they happened and which I will never be able to recall in later years because they happened so quickly, unless I get them listed right now. A ride through Normandy in the dusk, viewing the world as seen from the back of an ambulance from which one does not see much. Then arrived at the French Naval Hospital recently evacuated by the Nazis and were told to be sure to sprinkle lice powder on the mattresses before we climbed into them. The girls started composing aloud letters which began "Dear Mom" and for the first time I was sorry I'd come. But I fell asleep as soon as my head hit the pillow and the next morning when I woke up the sun was shining brightly and everything looked much brighter and better, somehow.

Now to go back and try to pick up a few pieces—the negro ambulance driver who said, "The Americans are having inspections, the English are serving tea, and the Russians are winning the war."

Today when I was scrubbing years of dirt and dust accumulated in the springs of my bed, for the first time I felt I was really making a contribution to the war effort, that I was really sacrificing something (NOTE inserted 7 Jan. 1947—I can remember very vividly doing that scrubbing up act after the Germans. There was dried German blood on the night stands between the beds. I was using my helmet as a scrub bucket and I really felt like a martyr. Something else which the journal neglects to recount is the stench of the morgue, where the Germans had left their dead and dying when they departed in a hurry.)

I think I forgot to mention that I have had a ride on an L.C.A. In fact, I have had two rides—one to the ship at Plymouth and one from the ship to Utah Beach.

We were in a completely exhausted state when we threw ourselves on the sands of Utah Beach after carrying our gear down the long ramps from the landing place to the beach. For the first time we knew what war meant. On top of sweaters and combat suits we were wearing impregnated clothing, steel helmets, and as a final ridiculous touch, four-buckled galoshes. In years to come, I want to remember what we were carrying: a-gas mask; b-pistol belt with full canteen; c-musette bag, from which dangled secondary white bag containing those items which I could not cram into my musette bag; d-blanket roll, containing two blankets, one shelter half, tent poles, rope, pins, cigarettes, pajamas, fatigues and sundry other items. (NOTE inserted 7 JAN 1947—Once again this forgetful journal neglects to mention an important item. 16 July 1944 was one of the hottest days that ever came to the Normandy peninsula. And we had been instructed to wear our heavy underwear underneath everything else. It was only my good common sense that prevented me from being in a worse state of broiling than I was.)

The things that we have seen in France so far remind me much more of a movie set or something I saw years ago in the movies than anything real and actual. It all seems a part of "Wings" or "Lilac Time" or "What Price Glory?" and not anything that is actually happening to me in 1944.
21 JULY 1944

The whole thing is pure Hemingway—a mixture of "For Whom The Bell Tolls" and "Farewell to Arms". The hospital setting with nurses flitting about and French being spoken at the Cherbourg Naval Hospital—the bright sunlight, the white buildings, the white chapel reminded me very much of "Farewell to Arms". Now in our tent hospital, with the bridge half a mile away that the Germans are trying to blow up, I feel just like Maria only without the short haircut—and I haven't taken my sleeping bag out of my bedding roll. It's all too much like the movies to be true. Four or five miles from the front lines, air field on both sides, military objectives all over the place, airplanes zooming overhead going to and from bombing missions. The night we reached this spot—or rather the early morning at 4:30 A.M., after riding miles and hours through the French night, at times brightly lit with stars, alternately murky and sodden with fog. The strange French trees rising against the horizon, tall and slender as telephone poles until the very top where there is a strange furry growth. Mixed thoughts rise within you as you ride in an open army truck with a dozen army nurses from 11 at night till 4:30 the next morning. The start of the trip through Cherbourg, the winding cobblestone streets, along the waterfront where three explosions in rapid succession and glass clattering into the streets gave me the first taste of fear in my mouth. Then out into the countryside and through towns full of vacant, staring buildings.

No, I take it back when I said I had the first taste of fear in my mouth when the blasts went off on the waterfront at Cherbourg. I felt it first when we were riding through the narrow blacked out streets of Cherbourg and when I thought of the lady snipers whom the Germans were supposed to have left behind and I thought how easy it would have been for a sniper to be seated at one of those blacked-out windows and take a pot-shot at a passing truckload of army nurses. And for the first time in my army career I was glad I was wearing a steel helmet. I was frightened then and I don't like to be frightened. When we arrived here at 4:30 the next morning, we went first to the wrong hospital and tried to find familiar voices rising to us out of the dark and there were no familiar voices. When we rode on a little farther through the darkness to the guard who said, "Hubba, Hubba" and we knew that we were home. Colonel Buckner met us at the end of the road and told us that we were five or six miles from the front lines and that there were dog-fights overhead at all times and falling flak and shrapnel, but that we had nothing to fear except the mosquitoes. Then we stumbled through the cow pasture, not able to see six inches ahead of where we were walking and going on for what seemed like miles to the very last tent in the line. If we thought it was dark before, that was before we stepped into the tent. No matches, no flashlights under any conditions, so find your own suitcase and bedding roll and make your bed. Pretty funny. I spread out my blanket roll on the ground and slept on top of it, with different parts of me resting on the bumps on my bedding roll. The mosquitoes came, as Colonel the Buck had warned. They made more noise than the airplanes. And tired as I was, it was difficult for me to sleep until I pulled the blanket up over my head, leaving them no entrance way. The next morning, when I awoke, the sun was shining and everyone was busying around getting breakfast ready. First I crossed the cow pasture to use a slit trench for the first time. Then I too scurried around finding twigs and bits of wood to use in building the fire over which we cooked that wonderful bacon that came in the ten-in-one rations. Never did breakfast taste so good as that one.

29 JULY 1944

I don't so much mind having them run around like distracted chickens at night, clucking in and out of fox holes, but I do object to their reliving the whole episode the next morning—what who said during the third alarm, how who had to bend her knees so who else could fit into the fox hole, how who lost her socks and why. I think they're a bunch of scared rabbits. And of course the laugh is on me if anything happens to me while I'm lying dry and warm in my cot and they're muddy and dirty in their fox holes. Well, as I learned at my father's knee at an early age, "Sufficient unto the day is the evil thereof."

And what does one think about as one lies in one's small army cot in one's cozy sleeping bag during bombing and strafing and anti-aircraft fire? One says, "Dear God, let this one pass over" and one falls asleep again very quickly, thank the dear Lord. When once long ago I read Mrs. Roosevelt's statement that everyone in the world does something better than anyone else in the world, wracked and searched my brain to think what my special gift might be and the only thing I could think of was that I could go to sleep faster and sleep sounder and harder than anyone else. And now I thank God for that gift above all others.

Every day we move just to keep in practice. It's something to be able to move all your earthly possessions on this side of the Atlantic in a space of about five minutes flat. Every day they lower the time we do it in. I guess their idea is to have it become so automatic that we could do it in our sleep, or when we are so dead tired that we can't think any more. The delight in a warm shower and a fresh, clean, white towel—things which would be so much taken for granted before that you wouldn't even bother mentioning them. And yesterday it was the high spot of the week to ride three miles along the dusty roads of France to a place where we, eight of us at a time, took a warm shower in a tent with a tarpaulin on the floor. When they gave us white towels, something which even a third-rate swimming pool at home would provide, it was as if we had been given two seats sixth row center at a Broadway opening. The condition on which the Air Corps group invited us to come use their showers was that we bring plenty of bath powder and smell-good stuff along with us so that we would give that delicate, feminine scent to their shower room.

When yesterday's mail brought forth ten letters, it was the best morale-raiser that anyone could have devised. And when one of those letters was from the best little brother in the world saying that he had been made skipper of his ship—well, I could have bust with pride.

If anything should happen to me now in these air raids, which I don't take seriously enough, I want all and sundry to know that the game was worth the candle, that I'd be sorry to go because I'm not ready to die (not for about fifty years) but that I had a lot of fun, that I'd recommend life to anyone who was considering its purchase and hesitating because they weren't sure it was worth all the effort it cost. Even in the midst of this terrible war and the suffering I have seen and heard described, I would say that life is wonderful, the world is a miraculous sort of place and filled with never-ending surprises and new sensations. Like the morning you wake up after a rough night and it's raining and miserable and the first news that breaks upon your ears is that you have to move and everybody in the tent is being very bitchy and annoying, so you get up and make the preparations to move in a generally disgusted state. Then, after a hit-or-miss breakfast of leftover K rations, you stroll outside the tent and the sun bursts forth in all its glory, warm and bright and soul-filling and blue sky comes through all around and suddenly the world is a beautiful place and the people in it are gay and charming.

3 AUGUST 1944

And yesterday was my first birthday overseas. And I'm pretty sure it will be my last overseas, too. It was fun.

My self-appointed job in sunny France is to go around painting out the signs on the army trucks and jeeps and ambulances which say "Left-hand drive-No signals". Then one of our doctors pointed out to me that the French couldn't read the signs anyway, so in order to make my work effective, I should first translate the signs into French and then cross them out.

To record a little something of the birthday celebration—the 26th Bomb Disposal Group invited the Red Cross—Tesse, Bea, Maxine and me—and two nurses, Jane Brown and Ruth Bayles, to a steak dinner. True, we ate it from tin plates, but it was steak nevertheless. Dinner was served half indoors and half out. They were living in an orchard and their dining room was a porch arrangement in the midst of the apple trees. At the party there was Bill Benton and Bassalotta and Major Hallowell, who was my dream man. It turns out that he knew Caroline Tyson back home in Greensburg and he was the nuttiest guy it was my pleasure to meet in the Army.

7 AUGUST 1944

What am I going to do with the rest of my life? It's a pretty serious question and I'd like to find a pretty serious answer to it. From what I've observed of race relations during the war, of what the Southern white boys say they are going to do to the colored boys after the war, I think maybe the best place for me would be working for Negro rights in the U.S.A. Yesterday, listening to Chaplain England's sermon, standing leaning against the plank that serves as a table in the mess hall, when he was talking of the necessity of having convictions, I thought of my own convictions and those of the other people who were standing in the tent, and I thought I probably ought to use my convictions to combat their convictions, or lack of them. This sounds terribly smug and I don't feel a bit smug. I just would hate to go home and have to fight another civil war through our own ignorance and feeling of insecurity and inadequacy when I feel the whole thing could be avoided with a lot of education and a lot of tolerance and a lot of people working together toward that end. And why shouldn't I be one of them? I'm not at all sure how to go about what I want to do and I guess it will have to wait till I get back.

12th AUGUST 1944

Seeing GOING MY WAY last night was one of the pleasantest things that have happened since being in the army. Sitting on the rough ground, five feet removed from the sheet which rippled and swayed and gave everyone's face and figure a crazy mirror effect, the sound track alternately being completely absent or booming forth in deafening tones—these were inconveniences, I'll admit, but still and all I loved it. Today Frank Sullivan's column said that as long as there was a Bea Lillie in the world everything was worth while; that's the way I feel about Bing Crosby. He fills me with a feeling of happiness and contentment and being at home and at ease and having a helluva good time.

15th AUGUST 1944

I'd like to tell you something about the Beach at Grandville, if I knew the right words. As you lie on top of the cliff looking down over miles of white sand and water almost as blue as Bermuda and the sun warm and clear. To go swimming in that water and to lie in that sand were experiences long to be meminisced. You forget, at a time like that, that the water is probably mined in places, that there are still Germans on that pretty little island that lies about six miles off shore, that along the road where you walked down to the beach a man was blown to death a few short days ago.

Then there is another sensation which comes later as you prowl through a deserted German dugout where the Nazis sat and waited for D-Day to come. That is the sensation of fear. The piles of ammunition which have been collected—all of it deadly stuff that I want no part of. And I say prayers when Hallowell and Antonelli throw hand grenades that they all may be duds. The good Lord heard my prayers and they were duds. The German trenches which they had fortified against the invasion. The coops in which they kept their police dogs to be used in coastal defense, like those I saw on peaceful Nantucket this time last year. The rounds and rounds of shell fire stored away, but also with that not-yet-de-booby-trapped look and I didn't want to linger one little bit. And I shall try to tell you what I thought about as we rode along the dusty roads of France that sunny Sunday morning. The French people in their well-worn clothes on their way to church. The church in one town we went through which had been just about cut in half and still the steeple stood. The cathedral at Coutances—or is it a cathedral? And why don't I know more about the places I am seeing? And you realized the eternal wrongness of war. God made the countryside green and beautiful and even when men insist on tearing it up with shells and bombs and flak, God goes right to work on healing the wounds; and the grass and the flowers grow there and the trees spread their boughs to cover the open places. Later, same day: Today at lunch I was listening to the gals tell of their experiences in the field hospitals where they have been working on detached service. To have the boys look up at them and say "Women—and this far front. How can we be scared if women can be here?" Joan Greenwood, the best looking girl in the outfit, whose reaction is that she's sorry she couldn't have prettied up for them a little. I can imagine how good she must look to a poor sick kid who's just come back from a little over the border which separates us from the great beyond—saved by the skill of modern medicine. They were saying how hard it is to tell these kids that they've lost a couple of legs or an arm. Joan was telling about the day they were running short of blood in their hospital and they had to save it for the surgery cases, using plasma for the others. Then to have a wounded Jerry come in and to have to use the precious rationed blood on him when there wasn't enough to go around for our own boys. This war's a crazy business.

16th AUGUST 1944

Just a brief note to record my favorite vehicle name to date—on a mile-long ammunition truck—Woman's Home Companion.

30 AUGUST 1944

General Patton, a few short days after the face-slapping incident in the hospital, visited another hospital and started to give hell to one patient who did not snap to attention on his entrance. The man listened patiently for a time and then said, "Run along, bub, I'm in the Merchant Marine."

Some of our nurses went bathing at Barneville the other day and were mistaken for French gals. They blocked all advances with "Je ne comprends pas". Then when the G.I.s took off hesitantly to go in the water they yelled after them, "Go on in, you big sissies."

31 AUGUST 1944

The whole system of code words used to apply to the 50th General Hospital is depressing. First, our cable address is AMFUMU Downcast. Then our shipping code is Tuneless. Aren't they descriptive?

The patients in one ward told the French boy, from General LeClerc's army, that the name of the guy in the next bed is Snafu. He very seriously addresses him as M. Snafu. I laughed merrily when they told me the story but when he told me his name was really McGonegal I laughed some more and said I wasn't as easily taken in as the French boy. I wouldn't credit the McGonegal business until he showed me his dog tags.

There was a Chinese checkers game in our recreation hall last night with Tony, of Italian emigrant stock, another detachment man whose ancestry is German and one of our German patients who knew no English. And yet they all played happily together. Games are international, like love, and can get along without words.

6 OCT. 1944

Yesterday was the day Joy Mansfield died and you could feel the grief among our group. It hung over everyone like a pall. We went to the cemetery at Ste. Mere Eglise in ambulances. The white crosses, marked simply with name and serial number, extend as far as you can see. Some of them are marked X with a number and then "Unknown". Joy's slight body, covered with a flag, was carried out of the ambulance and lowered into the grave while the bugler played.

18 NOVEMBER 1944

How different is travel on this troop train from what it was almost a year ago at this time when we went from Carson to Standish. We gathered at the officers' recreation tent soon after the cold grey dawn, with the rain beating down on the roof. We pulled in to the station at Carentan where we were privileged to wait for two hours in the driving rain until someone had the brilliant idea that we might as well wait in the station. Even after the hospital train pulled into the station, we had to do more standing on one foot and then on the other until we and our baggage were finally on the train. But then the luxury of it all—compartments with real sleeping accommodations. We have been enjoying a slow, leisurely journey so far. St. Lo by that night at a snail's pace we could have walked (but think how heavy the luggage would have become). This morning we made it to Laval—then two hours in Le Mans.

24th NOVEMBER 1944

The new style hairdo which we in the ETO are wearing this year is termed Rumpled By Helmet. Speaking of helmets, it's quite disconcerting to be kissed in a helmet. To begin with, there's a fine juggling act involved in keeping the thing on the back of your head. Then it starts to go and you know it's going to go and there's nothing you can do to stop it, so you just hold tight and wait for the crash. There's a fine art, also, to being kissed in the back seat of a jeep riding over the bumpy roads of France. You're just as likely to come out with a bruised nose and bit lips and swollen cheekbones as anything resembling a kiss.

I'd like to tell you about Thanksgiving 1944 in France because it was such a nice day. We went to the APO shortly before four and I set to work immediately helping Louise. I learned how to make les oeufs mimosa—and very tasty and decorative they were, too, matching my yellow sweater.

27 NOVEMBER 1944

I didn't get far with telling about Thanksgiving so I'll take it up again. The table, laid with my bed sheets, was set in the mail-dispatching room. The silver was odds and ends from the kitchen, filled out with spoons and knives from various people's mess gear. The table was set for dix-sept, which is just about what 6902 would be seating on a similar day avant la guerre. The boulangier, his wife and his daughter brought in les dindons, two beautiful birds filled with delicious stuffing, as prepared by Rudy. The Bordeaux wine was the proper festive note. Randy (or Larry) said grace and I remembered other Thanksgiving dinners when Uncle Jim had said grace. Bing Crosby was singing "You Made Me Love You", when the electric current went off and we had to light the kerosene lamp. All in all, it was a piece of America that we had transplanted 3,000-4,000-5,000 miles across the ocean and set up in the little town of Commercy in France. I found out that Thanksgiving was a holiday which the French people didn't know about. Louise, the French housekeeper for the APO, had me write on a slip of paper "Happy Thanksgiving" so that she could get the spelling right to give to the patissier, or whoever it was who made up the beautiful cake which we had for dessert.

1 DECEMBER 1944

Shall I tell you about Paris? It's the wonder city, the magic city of the world. It's everything that anyone ever said about it. It's glamorous, exciting, breathtaking, well, like I said, magic. The first night we saw the Arc de Triomphe, le Tour Eiffel, Cleopatra's needle, the Bois de Boulogne—all by moonlight. We drank champagne and went to a night club with a dance floor the size of two middle-sized desks shoved together, with 70 people dancing there. I felt like Garbo in NINOTCHKA, toujours gai.

The next morning I rode on the Metro to find Navy headquarters. When I asked two distinguished-looking gentlemen at the Arc de Triomphe "Ou est La rue de Strasbourg?" they answered me in perfect English, which was a terrible blow to my pride. And then, of course, it turned out that what I was looking for was the Rue de Presbourg. I've had a marvelous time in Paris walking along the streets, looking at all the beautiful clothes and jewelry and pictures in the windows, all with too fabulous prices. Les tres chics femmes with the wild chapeaux and the soignée hairdos ride their bicycles as if they were in seven passenger limousines.

Yesterday we rode along the Seine in Bill Benton's car, along L'Avenue Longchamps. We saw the original of the Statue of Liberty, the Tuileries Gardens, Notre Dame, Madeleine, Hotel de Ville, Rue de Rivoli—so many things to see, so little time to see them. The afternoon we arrived I was wearing my four-buckle arctics, mud-spattered battle pants and was fat like a teddy bear with my red lining under my gray horseblanket coat. And for a chic Paris bonnet, I was wearing my helmet liner and steel helmet. Ah, c'est la guerre.

13 Dec. 1944

This is looking at Paris with a sort of hind-sight because I don't want to forget a lot of things that happened there. Friday afternoon when we took the Red Cross tour and met the two flight officers, we found that you get a beautiful view of Paris when you stand at the Trocadero and look down at the city spread out in all its splendor. While we were standing solemnly and silently in Notre Dame, one of the GI's in our party knocked down a chair and 20 chairs in front of it fell down like lined-up dominoes. Cocktail hour in the Cafe de la Paix where les tres belles femmes, smelling to heaven of high-priced perfumes, sat happily drinking raisin juice—or that's what it said on the bottle. Saturday morning Maxine sprained her ankle and cried great tears. We went to the dispensary and I packed her bag to go to the hospital but it wasn't necessary. She had to sit all day in Rainbow Corner while I went wild on a shopping tour. It was like being on a binge, after staying strictly away from the stuff for four months. I couldn't pass a shop without going in to buy something. While I was shopping along the Rue de Rivoli I met two GIs who had been in Iceland, England, France, Holland and Germany together for more than three years. Coming down the Champs Elysees that evening in the dusk, for the first time I had the feeling that I really knew Paris and belonged to it, as I watched the people hurrying home from work on foot and on their bicycles. I came back to the hotel that evening in a high state of exhilaration to find my surly friend, Sgt. Lowe, who wanted me to drink beer with him and that was the last thing I wanted to do. So finally we all had dinner and at nine o'clock on Saturday night in Paris we were back in the hotel. A hot bath felt so good, I took two of them for good measure. Sunday morning I went to church at St. Somebody Auxerois and the priest was saying that what was the matter with the world today is that people are too bent on pleasure and not enough interested in the serious things of life. At least I thought that was what he said. I walked through the driving rain along the Seine toward the Cathedrale de Notre Dame where last mass was just letting out. So back to the hotel to watch Maxine devour her delicious steak dinner and then I went to the Red Cross restaurant to find we were eating hot dogs and sauerkraut.

Sunday afternoon in the Louvre I looked in vain for two hours for the famous paintings and kept coming out at the same place. Finally I figured out how to ask somebody where the paintings were and I found that they were all stored away. Even the statue of Venus de Milo was only a moulage. Quel dommage. Sunday evening with Captains Benton and Bassalato, we went to see "Dough Girls". Bassalato told us the story of when Crosby and Dinah Shore came to visit the hospital in England where he was and he didn't recognize them. When Dinah asked him if she could do anything for him, he said, "Yes, fix the pillows." She did and she was so upset at the bad shape he was in that she had to leave the room in tears. Crosby told the patients that they gave him far more than he could give to them. I know just what he means—and it's true, too.

After the show we went back to their apartment in that swank hotel to watch newlymade Major Feldman packing his bags to take a plane home the next morning. What a happy chore for him.

Monday morning I went shopping along the Rue de la Paix with two disreputable-looking GIs, Lowe and Jackson, both badly in need of a shave. We went into the fanciest shops—Guerlain, Pacquin, Schiaparelli—and the sky was blue above and I had joie de vivre even if we did have to leave that afternoon.

Saturday morning when I was shopping in Aux Trois Quartiers, I looked at the Christmas decorations on the table spread as if for a party and my eyes filled with sudden tears as I thought of Christmas 3000 miles away at 6902 McCallum Street and 471 W. Ellet Street and how everything would be going on without Jim and me. It was a sad, lonely sort of feeling—a stranger in a strange land where they call it Noël instead of Christmas and where there are no Neddy, Bobby, Janice and young Jimmy for me to see their eyes ashine with the joys of Christmas and for me to share their rapture at "The Night Before Christmas".

20 DEC. 1944

Last night when the Negro choir sang "Silent Night, Holy Night" I could have bawled like a baby. I thought of those guys lying in cold, wet fox holes in six inches of water and how it would be anything but a silent night, holy night for them. I thought of a soldier lying there thinking what a hollow mockery it was even to have a Christmas. The shells are screaming, the machine gun bullets spray near his fox hole, he tries to make a Christmas Eve dinner out of cold K rations, he's lying there in the mud, looking up at a starless black sky, lit only with the bursting of shell fire—then he hears a voice singing "Silent Night, Holy Night". It's a woman's voice. It's his own mother's voice. And suddely there is warmth and bright lights. There is a Christmas tree in the corner of the living room. His young sister and brother are sitting by the fireplace watching the stocking which they have just hung up, his father is working on the wirinq of the tree, his mother is sitting at the piano playing "Silent Night, Holy Night". He is home for Christmas—with a bullet through his brain. When Kellum drove us to Nancy last week, he had to listen to the hollow chatter of four females all the way there, each of us giving him different directions. Then he sat at lunch with five of us, "Jabber, jabber, jabber" all the time. When he went to the Red Cross Club, a G.I. just back from the front says to him "Doesn't it sound good to hear an American girl's voice again?" And Kellum, gallant gentleman that he is, says, "It sure does." Cole says that the Red Cross are civilians once removed.

1 JAN 1945

Let me tell you about S/Sgt. Esmond, who is one of my favorite GIs to date. He came to France on H hour of D Day, has been fighting ever since and is one of only three men of his company of 500, counting replacements, who have come through uninjured. He told me about Gen. Roosevelt and how he would say, "Where are you from, boy?" Whatever their answer, he knew something about the place. He asked Esmond, who was in the Fourth Division, the question when they were crossing the English Channel, riding along in an LCA with the icy water washing in all around the general. He sat there with his cane braced squarely on the floor and asked, "Where are you from, Sergeant?" When Esmond answered, "Philadelphia," the general said, "Oh, the City of Brotherly Love—but I guess my cousin Franklin would know more about that."

Esmond endeared himself to me forever when he said, "Americans brag too much. They talk too loud and too boastfully." That's exactly what I think but I never heard a GI say it. Another reason he's wonderful is because he says he won't wear any of his ribbons because he says the guys would look at him and ask, "What do you think you are? A damned general?"

I saw the New Year in with the Champions, a real French family. The night was beautiful when we stepped outside their cottage to watch the ack-ack fire on the German planes. The white of the buildings was slightly less white than the snow washed with cold, clear moonlight. The stars were bright and far away in the velvet blue of the heavens. When we rode home in the jeep we saw the church steeple silhouetted against the moonlit sky. The whole night was so cold and still you could feel it in your lungs, your cheeks, your ears. There was a simple beauty about the whole Champion family and their New Year's toast to "Victoire bientot. Vive la France. Vive L'Amerique."

Tonight Ellen Vigneron went with us to see the trench foot GIs and she sang her little song about "Les Petits Champignons". It was good for those GIs back from fox holes and raiding German fortresses to see and listen to a little girl who reminded them of their own little girls back home and what the war is all about.

11 JAN 1945

This was Lt. Lyell's birthday and his last day in our hospital and my last day to visit him. I shall miss him very much. He had a great deal of vitality and he was good for me. Tonight was a strange affair while I sat sewing Captain Dahl's sleeve for him and the mood changed from joking about how Lt. Johnny Saldano had arranged it with his sergeant so that he (the sergeant) could get a Silver Star and Johnny a Purple Heart, to the true story, which is something more dramatic than anything Hemingway ever wrote—how they were ambushed by the Germans and everyone was wounded and the Germans came and killed all the wounded except Johnny, who pretended he was dead. He lay there for hours until it was almost dark and then he started walking painfully, with the aid of a heavy stick. He came to a figure lying to the right and, thinking it was a GI, he nudged him and asked him if maybe they could find an aid station together. The GI woke up and turned out to be a Heine. All Johnny could do was bash him over the head a couple of times with his stick and then, because he was afraid rifle fire would attract attention, he used the German's bayonet and jammed it down his throat. The German's tongue came out. He continued his lonely trudging for another five hours until he came to the road, where he was picked up by an American jeep. Captain Dahl and Lt. Murtaugh were flying rations to the beseiged soldiers at Bastogne when their plane was shot down and they parachuted down into the No Man's Land between the German and American lines—Dahl with a piece of flak in his elbow.

After all the grimness of those episodes, let us take off to the ridiculous. What does one do when one receives a package from one's dear mother containing two bedroom slippers—perfectly lovely, but both for the left foot. She must think I have changed a great deal.

26 JAN 1945

The trip to Nancy on Wednesday was good for me. I went riding through the snowy meadows of Lorraine in an open jeep with Dave, pretending we were in a sleigh. When we were at the Hotel Thier at cocktail time all of Nancy was there. The orchestra started out playing German waltzes and semi-classical stuff and Dark Eyes, and then they went into Franklin D. Roosevelt Jones. After a few glasses of white wine, I thought how wonderfully ridiculous it was that I, Anne McCaughey, should be sitting in a cafe in Nancy, half-filled with French floozies, and there was a seven-piece band playing Franklin D. Roosevelt Jones. It was all very good and funny and beautiful. Then the cold, cold ride back and just when you're so cold you think you're going to die, you get there. To the Hotel de Paris, where M. Marcel married Mme. Marcel, after they had lived together for only 16 or 17 years and so he decided to make an honest woman of her. And the story goes that he originally took her out of a house.

2 FEB 1945

Happy Ground Hog Day. It's the day the war is supposed to be over and it looks and feels like Springtime. Yesterday was the day I received news that Jimmie was home. Oh, glad day for the McCaugheys. What I wouldn't give to be there now. Jimmie, home after almost two years in the Mediterranean, looking bronzed and wonderful and telling all the things he couldn't say in his letters, and me 3,000 and some hundreds of miles away.

23 FEB 1945

It's a funny thing as Spring comes in this year that I find myself homesick for Scotland instead of Germantown or New York or State College or any place where I have seen Spring come in. I'm hungry for the green hills and the clean smell, the cool, moist air and the freshness and greenness of it all. I'm homesick for Zelda when the two of us could ride away to beyond the blue horizon and all the cares in the world vanished as we whizzed down hill with the wind cool and fresh against my face.

It was good shopping today in Nancy, with the people moving slowly in the afternoon sunlight. Later I walked through the corridors of the 2nd General Hospital, knowing their patients weren't as nice as ours, because ours are the nicest patients in the world. As I watched them play baseball in the open area between A and B buildings, I loved them more than ever. I wished so hard that they could be playing in real baseball suits or beat-up old trousers and sweatshirts and not in O.D.'s.

26 FEB. 1945

It's a ceaseless source of wonder to me how hard I have become. Emotions which formerly would have wracked my soul leave me almost untouched. It's a hardness of survival, I know, and it's a blessed hardness because I couldn't go on with the job without it. When those dough-feet come back from the front with their stories of how it feels when you see your first dead German and how it feels when you kill your first German and how it feels when you step on your first dead American and how bad they all smell, whether German or American—I can listen almost unmoved and my mind goes on thinking about if they would enjoy a Bingo game in this ward tonight. I think of the guy who said to me that in this war you can't make buddies because then when your buddies get killed, as ultimately they all do, you die with them. For their own survival they cannot become too intimate with anyone.

**28 FEB 1945**

I want to tell you about Private McCaffrey, who was a farm boy in Indiana with a lovely wife and two beautiful babies and who had to come way over here to fight a war. His elder boy is five years old and when he used to take him to the movies downtown, they'd look to see what was playing at all the theatres and then they'd go to a western. When the horses came rushing across the screen, Bobby would hide under the seat and then when the danger was past, he'd stick his head up and grin and say, "That sure was funny, Daddy, wasn't it?" Why does the war have to take a boy like McCaffrey who was happy in his life as he made it? Why does there have to be a war at all?

**7 MARCH 1945**

Last night Nick Livitro, the accordionist, went with me to play on the C Wards. My always dear "Patton's boys" were busy finding their pictures in Life Magazine. There was the Frenchman with the flashing black eyes talking Spanish with the Polack who followed in our train. Then the Polack talked Russian to the Russians in the little room. Nick was like the Pied Piper with his train following behind him.

**19 MARCH 1945**

Last night the French people held their first dance in Commercy since before the Germans occupied the town. It was something to be meminisced. The floor was jammed with beaucoup de people, the RAF, the GIs, white and colored. The music was supplied by a tinny French orchestra. All in all, it was quite a spectacle and I had a wonderful time. It's something wonderful when Joe Soeffel takes you to an affair. He delivers you there and then you're on your own, free to play the field of GIs while he does the same with the French babes. Then you dance the last dance together and he takes you home. And for once I was the belle of the ball, if for no other reason than that I was the only American girl there.

**22 MARCH 1945**

Luxembourg is a belle ville indeed. I was impressed by the sign on the town which I saw on the way here from Commercy. "This is the city of Lorraine—welcome to our American liberators." The payoff is that there is not a whole house left standing in the town.

**24 MARCH 1945**

The change from France to Luxembourg. From poverty to prosperity. From dirt to spotless cleanliness. From straggly farms to well-cared-for land which looks like Lancaster County, Pa. The people look like the well-fed, contented bourgomeisters in an old musical comedy. And all in the space of a few miles—it's pretty remarkable.

I had to laugh when Bill, the innocent, asked me if I had many promotions from Frenchmen—mean propositions. When Dave and I were in the Clou Barcafe we were talking to another GI who didn't notice my uniform in the dull lights and after listening to me jabber away for five minutes, said, "My, you speak English well."

The park around Radio Luxembourg by moonlight is something pretty special.

27 MARCH 1945

Would you like to know what real honest-to-God orange juice tastes like after fifteen months without it? Well, did anyone ever attempt to describe nectar? It's hard to remember how something tastes—and yet at that first, sweet delectable swallow, all the remembrance of it and how good it is comes flooding back to you and you gulp down the whole glass without trying even to savor the rareness of the treat.

1 APRIL 1945

Happy Easter in the ETO. This morning we had a sunrise service on a hilltop with a view of three small French towns, each complete with church steeple. Bells were tolling in the distance. All about us were ploughed fields where mines might have lain. When we went back to the mess hall after the service, feeling as if we hadn't eaten since we were small children, we were served real fried eggs, as a special treat because it was Easter morning. I told Sgt. Hyche (enlisted man at 50th GH) how hungry I was and, when he handed me the done-to-a-beautiful-turn eggs, he smiled and said, "Write and tell your mother that a boy from Alabama fried two eggs for you this Easter morning." And so I did.

I want to tell you about Adams (a patient at the 50th GH) who is going to go home as a neuropsychiatric case and whose Christianity has been tried by the war. He feels strange to be going home without an arm or leg gone, without a limp. He thinks people will not understand what can happen to a guy's mind as well as a guy's body. He told me a story of lying in a foxhole with another soldier. The shells were bursting all around them while he told his companion about God and faith and prayer. Adams asked him if he were saved. At Adams' insistence, the soldier tried prayer and they were untouched by the shells or bullets. The next day the soldier told Adams that he felt so much lighter. Now Adams thinks that maybe that experience was worth all the bad things that have happened to him in the Army. He thinks back a lot to things that have happened to him—like the time their platoon had orders to cross a river and the officers and sergeants turned tail and ran. Adams talked nine other soldiers into crossing the river with him. They crossed the river and then the engineers took the boat away, leaving them on the other side. Four of the men were killed and four were wounded. Now

Adams feels personally responsible for their deaths. It weighs heavily on his mind. In fact, his mind is always on the war. When he walks around the hospital grounds and looks at the hills of the countryside round about, he thinks how it would be if the Germans were on the other side of that hill and he and the men in his platoon had to take it. The weather, good or bad, is always gauged by what effect it has on the men at the front. The other day when he was in the ENT Clinic it made Adams homesick when somebody dropped a mess of pills into a metal tray, because it made him remember when his wife would pour beans into the pan preparatory to baking them.

15 JUNE 1945

Last night we were the guests of honor at the College pour Jeunes Filles at Commercy. It was a regular fete with ice cream and strawberries and garlands of flowers for the table. When they sang "Silent Night" in the middle of June with their French accents it was incongruous, but charming and delightful. When they sang "The Star-Spangled Banner" it was all I could do to restrain my tears. They pronounced it twee-light's last gleaming. They made crowns of flowers for our hair. They were so young and fresh and eager and, when they told us of the atrocities which the Germans had committed, I wanted to say, "N'oubliez jamais."

# DESIDERIO J. SAIS

Brief as are the entries in the wartime diary kept by "Desi" J. Sais, they build up a picture of a time, a place, and a man. One even meets Butch, a dog who took part in invasions alongside his master.

Sais, born in Albuquerque, New Mexico, and still living there, was a rancher before the war and afterwards spent 25 years as a law enforcement officer, work from which he is now retired.

At the time of the diary, Sais held the rank of Technician, 5th Grade, attached to a bewildering number of companies in the Quartermaster Battalions which were in charge of trucks and the amphibious vehicles popularly known as "Ducks".

Sais and his wife have one child and are grandparents.

*******

ITALY
Feb. 2, 1944

Went in to some of the houses here, and they sure are badly damaged. Many still have fine furniture.
FEB. 3 Wittenmaier brought me a spring bed. But I still can't sleep good at night. Could it be the noise?
FEB. 4 Was in Motor Pool when air raid occured. Jumped in small fox hole. Olson & Stewart beat me there, but I landed on top of both. All clear, not much damage done.
FEB. 5 Received first Stars & Stripes. So now we can get an account of the war. We are still pushing forward, as also are the British.
FEB. 6 It was very quiet last night. Whistling Willie (German gun) is still continuing to come over. One landed on the road. Did some damage.
FEB. 7 Big air-raid. We knock down four planes. Saw one jump from plane.
FEB. 8 Area hit by bomb lost kitchen tent & truck. C.O. wounded. Many other things happened on that same day (*me hit also!!!*)
FEB. 9 Received nice box of candy from Ursula and was enjoyed by all. It was kind of quiet today.
FEB. 10 Got up and found most of our trucks damaged by a nite raid. Shields went to the hospital.

FEB. 11 Today I received lots of mail. Glad to know that everyone at home are fine.

FEB. 12 Received Readers Digest so am trying to occupy my mind by reading.

FEB. 13 After so long a time I finally got a haircut by a G.I. I expect to take a bath soon, I hope.

FEB. 14 Went to QM. I found a pair of water boots. I jumped in another fox-hole. 18 of us in all, both black & white (G.I.)

FEB. 15 Went to the Day Room to do some reading and catching up with my writing. Hq. moved in with us, so had to move to other *cave*.

FEB. 17 Four air-raids last night. German mission was not accomplished. They lost four more planes.

FEB. 18 A P-38 landed on area. The pilot was not injured as he bailed out in time.

FEB. 19 Today was a big day for me cause I finally took a shower. The weather, I mean the water (the Whistling Willie is getting on me nerves) was nice & warm.

FEB. 20 Keeping busy in area, I also did my own laundry. It took me long to finish as I was always on the run. Yes, for a fox-hole.

FEB. 21 William & Freiburg went to hospital. Condition not serious. An air-raid is going on and I am here on my bed. My fingers crossed. Everything under control.

FEB. 22 Received letter from Ray saying he sold calves at KC and also that he is moving.

FEB. 23 Air-raid last night destroyed Ducks.

FEB. 24 Don't feel too good, had only one meal. Whistling Willie is around again.

FEB. 25 Today I feel better. No air-raids today. I washed, shaved, and did some more reading. A few more trucks were damaged.

FEB. 26 Took trucks to front. Four got stuck. Pull them out before daylite.

FEB. 27 Sgt. of guard again. Everything under control. Very little noise.

FEB. 28 Took laundry, mine & Sgt. Elliott to an Italian lady. Gave her some C-rations.

MARCH 1, 1944 Trucks came in from Naples. Another convoy left this morning. Quiet today.

MARCH 3 Bo-coo of bombers went by on a mission. I bet the Jerries are plenty busy making their fox-holes deeper.

MARCH 4 Small air-raid. Whistling Willie still active. One hit over the cave & another by the ducks. Doing a little damage.

MARCH 5 Raining. Old boys are getting paid. We won't yet. I heard that 2 platoons of the 80th were captured yesterday (my old outfit).

MARCH 6 Met a boy who came from front, name is J. Garcia & lives in

Albuquerque, N.M.

MARCH 7 Saw a show last nite, "Adventures of a Rookie", it was pretty good. Still eating "C" rations. Today I took a shower by the Palace.

MARCH 12 Plenty of Liberty ships in sight. Ducks still hauling. All the trucks are out.

MARCH 13 Ofc. brought five gal. can of vino. It was pretty good. Also gave me some fresh bread. Quiet outside.

MARCH 14 Raining outside. Most everyone is in the cave. Reading or playing cards.

MARCH 15 Today is 1 yr. this outfit has been organized. Lt. Loomis gave a speech. Two air-raids. Played poker. I won & then I lost so I'm now even.

MARCH 16 Shelling yet but doing no damage. Civilians are being moved to Naples—a few still scattered around Nettuno & Anzio. Rumors that we took over Cassino this morning. Three air-raids today. A bomb landed in the area, making just a big hole & landing by a duck.

MARCH 17 One air-raid. Ducks still hauling from the Liberty ships.

MARCH 18 Wittenmaier & Olson on Detached Service on paratroops duty. Played a little poker. Didn't do so hot.

MARCH 19 I was on guard. No air-raid. W.W. still comes around. Went after my laundry in jeep.

MARCH 20 All quiet on Anzio Beach. Big fight going on in cave by *cave men*. Battling "Willie" lands in Guard House.

MARCH 21 Big air-raid this morn. A German spy dressed in British uniform had chow with us. 1st Lt. Bockman was the one that captured him and held him prisoner.

MARCH 22 Went to the Assembly Area with Sgt. Elliott & truck commander. Had an air-raid. Went after my laundry. Listened to Radio Sally.

MARCH 23 Went with Ofc. to deliver bread to civilian. Took 8 trucks to Red Beach. It was a 'dry run'. Played poker using .50 cal. bullets for chips, value fifty cents, and match stick two-bits. As usual didn't win, but came out even.

MARCH 25 Was a dispatcher at the docks with Cromer. Weather a little cold. Went on a jeep. Starting a dug-out, expecting to move soon from the cave to a new area in same location. Six men to a hole. Drandorff, Dierskie, Wittenmaier, Cromer, Olson and Sais.

MARCH 26 Took some pictures. At night I listen to Radio Sally from Germany. The music was good.

MARCH 28 Went back to docks as a checker, working 12 hrs. shift, 12 midnight to 12 noon. Moved in to the dugout. It's big enough to hold six men. It's better here than in the cave. Shelling plenty last night. I was checker at the docks. Met a boy who was going home on rotation.

MARCH 29 Found a desk and some chairs to put in my dispatching tent. We now have a new Capt. and Lt. in charge of the trucks.//
APRIL 9 Easter Sunday, attended service at Municipal Palace. Large crowd. Received a victorial. Pretty good music. Whistling Willie. Navy doing some firing. Raining.
APRIL 10 Still living in Dug Out, got it fixed nice. Six of us live in it.
MAY 16 Left the 53 QM Trk Bn and landed in Naples. We are now attached to the 6723 Trk Group (Prov.) Co. We landed here the following day by an LST.
MAY 17 Fixing up our new area. We are living in squad tents with eight men in it.
MAY 18 I haven't been to Naples yet. Expecting on going tomorrow. Rumors that limited service men will get to go to the States on points. Received my Purple Heart. The serial no. is 19711. Planning on sending it home. It rained today. It's a good thing because it sure has been dusty.
MAY 19 Went to Naples and then to Caivano. Had a nice time. Stayed most of the time at the Red Cross.
MAY 25, 1944 Moved again, this time we are attached to 6748 Co. C. Just 17 men were transferred.
MAY 26 Went to see Nina and took her my laundry. She had films for my camera. We took pictures.
MAY 27 Went to Naples. MPs are on the ball. Many of our boys spend the nite in the Guard House. One boy didn't salute an officer (90 day wonder), others didn't have dogtags, etc.
MAY 28 Took my laundry to Nina. She does a good job and doesn't charge me anything. I take her gum and cigarettes.
MAY 29 Rode LST to Anzio with load of French Ammo. Reported to assembly area of 6723 Co. C. trk.
JUNE 2 Did some hauling. Also had a big night air-raid.
JUNE 5 Haul German prisoners to the cemetery to dig graves. Took a shower at 5 Army Hq. Received new issue of clothing.
JUNE 6 Took ammo to Rome. On the way saw many Germans (dead), "tanks", etc. People walking back to their homes that they left six months ago. Plenty of people in Rome to welcome us. Pretty buildings and beautiful girls. Yesterday was the first day for the GI's to enter Rome.
JUNE 7 Haul rations to Rome. Stayed over night but didn't get a chance to see St. Peter's Cathedral.
JUNE 8 Am assigned to Co. B 3338 QM Trk Co., stationed at Anzio. Cooper is also here.
JUNE 9 Nice outfit. Haven't done much yet so am getting a good rest. Am expecting to go to Rome on a pass.
JUNE 10 Didn't get a pass today. I drove a Duck today. Went after a load of rations from boat (Liberty). P.B.S. trying to get control of Rome. 5th

Army (Gen. Clark) still going strong. They are now 80 mi. beyond Rome. Received lots of mail today. Went to 6723 area and got Dave Malanut's dog (Butch). Rest of boys went to Replacement Center. Cooper, Elliott, Thompson & myself are assigned to the 53 (Duck Bn) Co. B in Anzio.

JUNE 11 Went to Rome on pass with Cooper. Saw St. Peter's Cathedral. Walked around town. Lots of people and G.I.s. Eat downtown. Meal wasn't so good.

JUNE 12 Drive the Duck again, from ship (water) to the ration dump.

JUNE 13 Went to our old area to take a shower but crew left for Rome. So we went in the beach. The water was nice but salty. Lots of GI's are swimming. Civilians are still coming thru, some going home, others to Rome and Naples.

JUNE 14 Went to the Ration Dump to get the rations. Also went to "C" Co. area. Boys in dug-out found a house mate. People still traveling on the hi-way going home.

JUNE 15 Went to Rome again. Saw the beautiful cathedral of St. Peter. Did a lot of sight-seeing. Met a girl, Agnes De Sintos. Invited us over to her house for lunch. Didn't have much but enjoyed it. She gave me her picture.

JUNE 16 Saw Ed Chavez & Augustin Eichwald on their way to Rome. Here in Anzio getting rations for the 88th Div. 5th Army. Are now about 100 mi. No. of Rome. We are expecting to move soon. Now we are hauling from the docks with Ducks.

JUNE 18 Rumors that we will finally get paid (last paid Oct.-9 mo.) My little dog (Butch) is OK and sure growing. Took him riding today.

JUNE 19 Forgot to mention that we are now living in buildings. The house we're staying in is pretty nice. I went to Littorio this afternoon—just looking around. The town is badly damaged. Met Brunano & family, had dinner with them. Helped the old man fix the door.

JUNE 20 Am going to do my laundry today. Might go to Littorio this afternoon.

JUNE 21 Went out on a Duck again this afternoon—all alone. Haul rations.

JUNE 22 Went to Rome on pass. Ate with family.

JUNE 23 Rumors that we will be moving soon to Salerno.

JUNE 24 Went out on the Duck to haul rations. Manage to get some cigarettes & rations.

JUNE 25 Played poker, won a few dollars. Butch is still with me. Took him for a walk.

JUNE 26 Went to Nettuno with Mike for a visit. Civilians moving in Anzio & Nettuno.

JUNE 27 Went to Rome. Saw Flora & family, had supper with them. I took them some candy & vino. Give her my address. She said she was going to pay me a visit after the war.

JUNE 28 Went to the *Dentist* to have a tooth filled. At the 59th Station Hospital. I met Tony Lucero's brother. In the afternoon he came over to visit me.

JUNE 29 Went to Rome again. Had my picture taken. Had dinner in town. Cooper went with me.

JUNE 30 Waiting to get paid. In the afternoon they paid us. I received two hundred & fifty.

JULY 1 On the alert. Rumors we will be moving soon. All passes cancelled. Went bathing in the beach. Captain took his girl to Naples.

JULY 2 Getting ready to move. No one to leave the area.

JULY 3 Left Anzio on LST and arrived in Salerno next day. Camp close to beach. We had C rations on the boat. My dog didn't get sick. I did!

JULY 4 Getting all our equipment together. Living in squad tent. Covering up all the fox-holes to make area for the Ducks.

JULY 5 We are about 30 miles from Salerno stationed by the beach. We bought some eggs for 20 cents apiece, also potatoes at 25 cents a kilo. We had a mid-night snack. There are six of us in the tent-Kitchen, Labo, Stewart & Ruzicki & me & Cooper.

JULY 6 We are stationed about 60 miles from Salerno in a town named Paestum.

JULY 7 We went to Naples to get some new Ducks. Not ready so didn't bring any.

JULY 8 We are now in the 7th Army (36 Division). Sure hot today. Am going to the beach this afternoon.

JULY 9 Went to church in Paestum (civilian). A few GI's.

JULY 10 Received PX and beer. Went to the show to see "Follow the Boys" Wrote to Ray Abeyta and today received the letter with the word "missing" on it. Also got a letter from Cromer. He is now in the Replacement.

JULY 11 Went in the beach again. At nite we fried more eggs & potatoes.

JULY 12 Left Paestum, now stationed about 40 miles from Salerno.

JULY 13 Hubbard, Cpl., was shot in the head. He died 2 in the morning.

JULY 14 Went to Paestum to get laundry. Had dinner with Vincent Vogi.

JULY 15 Funeral for Hubbard. Went to 48 Eng. with Ducks, Suppose to go on a problem but it was a dry run.

JULY 16 Went to Paestum and took pictures of the Cerere temple. Had dinner with Voza & family, Eva, etc. Vino pretty good. Took coffee & candy.

JULY 16 Took Duck out to practice Invasion Landing. Plenty hot.

## Desiderio J. Sais

Arrived back in area in the afternoon.

JULY 17 Had dinner with some people who live by area. Mike Ruzeki & I took some D-rations to the lady.

JULY 18 Went on detach service with the 540 Engineers. Practice Invasion. Cooper & I were on one duck. Stayed for 3 days. Unload from an LST. Navy didn't feed us very good. Butch also made the "Invasion".

JULY 21 Finish with training, we reported back to "A" Co. since "B" Co had already left to another new area.

JULY 22 Cooper & I walking around manage to get acquainted with some people. We had dinner—eggs & potatoes. The lady had two daughters. Marie (Vino Blanco) & Annie.

JULY 23 Being Sunday I went to Church at the 59th Station Hospital. Large crowd.

JULY 24 Meals here are terrible. Kitchen & I went to eat again with the Italian family.

JULY 25 Left area and arrived by Oversea about 20 miles from Naples.

JULY 26 Went to the Ord. to get new "ducks". Received a package and lots of mail from home.

JULY 27 Butch has a sore leg. But improving. I am now assigned to a Duck. No family near by so have to do my own washing.

JULY 28 Many vehicles being water-proof so expecting something to pop out pronto. Plenty warm today.

JULY 29 Went to Ammo Dump for ammo. Getting Ducks ready for another movement.

JULY 30 Got paid (35.80) Played poker, won a little. We are leaving this area soon. Had plenty of ice cream for dinner. Gave Butch a bath. I also took a shower. Going to write some letters.

JULY 31 1st Sgt. sold Gin. I bought a bottle. It was pretty good. Got a duck today.

AUG 1 Getting ready. Duck load-up. Gun & A-frame ducks out on 3 day problem.

AUG. 2 Dusty & plenty hot. Received letter from home, everyone OK. They also said they received the Purple Heart.

AUG 3 Got 5 months rations also received four cans of Good American Beer. PX amounted to five dollars.

AUG 4 Fried potatoes and with the chile sauce Claude send me it was a delicious meal. Edith Hixenbaugh send me her picture.

AUG 5 Went to Aversa with Michael Ruziski. Had dinner at Red Cross, also had Ice Cream. Bought a frying pan & coffee pot.

AUG 6 Went to the village, being Sunday we attended Church. Stayed in town all day.

AUG 7 We are on the alert & can't leave the area. All the Ducks are loaded and ready to go.

AUG 8 Still here. After chow I am going to take a shower. Snow & Stewart left this morning to the new area.

AUG 9 Took tent down. Tonite we will sleep outdoors. Fried eggs & potatoes.

AUG 10 Arrived in our new area. We are just 10 miles from Naples. Heck of a area. Butch is now sleeping on my bunk. Mike & Cooper are reading the Stars & Stripes. Went to the show to see "Riding High" with Dorothy Lamour & Dick Powell at the open air theatre (36 Div) area.

AUG 11 Part of the 53 Duck Bn. left for the Invasion. We are now Rear Echelon. Took a shower today. Put up a tarp as it looks like it is going to rain.

AUG 12 Went to the movie to see "Lost Angel" with Dick Powell and Dorothy Lamour. It was about the best show I ever seen. We are on the alert again. The Ducks are parked & ready to go.

AUG 13 Plenty warm. Took my laundry to be washed. A order came out today saying not to associate with civilians especially in the area. Girls are sent here by Germans that has VD to do harm to the GI's. Chow wasn't so good so we fried some eggs.

AUG 14 Still getting ready to move. Went to the show to see Joe E. Brown.

AUG 15 Invasion took place in S. France. A big success. We are getting along OK.

AUG 16 Arrive Staging Area. French & English troops also here. Went to Naples & Bagnolia.

AUG 17 Went to Naples again. Many troops pulling out. The harbor is full of LST's.

AUG 18 Went to Bagnolia to see Nina & also to get the films I left there before I went to Anzio.

AUG 19 Still eating "C" rations. We are getting ready to leave. I think tomorrow we will be going to France.

AUG 20 Loading up on LST. Ruziski & I are on the same Duck & Butch is still with us.

AUG 21 We are on our way. Smooth riding. Butch is getting plenty to eat from the sailors. We are eating "C" rations.

AUG 22 Saw some big fish. The water is getting rough.

AUG 23 Expecting to land today. We now can see land. We unloaded. Had trouble with the Duck but finally had it fixed. Was on land for about 8 hrs. Moved to our new area. Can't find Butch & "Anzio", so I reported them missing in action.

AUG 24 Reached our new area. We are now living in houses again. The nearest town is San Raphael. The buildings are not badly damaged. The French people here are kind & friendly. I am expecting to go to town after I finish packing.

AUG 25 Took a Duck to the docks to work, hauled rations & ammo. Took my laundry to Mr. Martinez. He's from Spain. Told me all about the Germans. Girls that went with them had their head shaved.
AUG 26 Went to town, San Raphael, to get a haircut. Vino cost 10 francs a glass (20 cents). Haul rations from Liberty ship. Polish prisoners working in Ration Dump. Before going to bed Snow, Brown & "Buck" & I cooked some bacon.
AUG 27 Raining plenty & I have to take my Duck out. The rest of the boys that were left in Naples arrived today. Hogan found himself a room mate. Wow!
AUG 28 Haven't found Butch yet but still looking for him. After work went to Antonio Martinez's house & had dinner (San Raphael).
AUG 29 Haul rations & gas. After work Malcolm and I went to town, met some people & had wine, then took pictures.

*******

NOV 27 Leaving Marseille this morning and will arrive in Vienne sometime tonight.
NOV. 28 On our way again to our destination. I believe we are going to Lyon. We were issued new Ducks. We arrived a few miles from Lyon. We are now going to school, "learn river crossing". We will be here for about a wk. We are staying in building (German Barracks)
NOV 29 First day of school. Took the Ducks to the Rhone river and had river practice. Plenty cold today. No accidents.
NOV 30 Practice river crossing with cable. Rain all morning. Getting a good rest now.
DEC 1 River crossing and detail work. Tonight we cross river with cable. Received a few Xmas packages.
DEC 2 Back from school. Went to town and had a Rabbit dinner. La Valbourne is the name of the town near to camp. Will be here for just two more days so won't bother going to town often.
DEC 3 Getting passes to go to Lyon (15 mi) but instead I stayed in camp and worked on my duck.
DEC 4-5 Training, plenty of rain. We manage to get some coal for the stove so we are now pretty cozy. Rumors that we are soon leaving for Marseille again.
DEC 6-7 Still training and plenty of rain. Today is the last day of school. We also got paid today. I received $35.50. Received more Xmas packages.
DEC 8 Went to Lyon on a day pass. Had a swell time. Very few GI's in town. The city is bigger than Marseille. Manage to get good eats & cognac. It's about 20 mi from camp.
DEC 9 Worked on my new Duck, getting ready to leave. We are expect-

ing on going down North. Went to Lyon again & had a nice time. I think we are leaving tomorrow.

DEC 10-44 Left Camp La Bonne (school) with the Ducks. Slept in Beaune and arrived in our new area, Langres on 12-13-44. We are staying in a school house. Hq. is eating with us. We unloaded our Ducks cause tomorrow we are suppose to turn them in. Langres is a small town.

DEC 14 We took our Ducks to Beaune. We are suppose to work in an ammo dump here in town. Arriving back to camp I heard the sad news that our Capt. Kelly was in an accident (Jeep turned over and froze to death). Tomorrow I am going to town and look for a shower.

DEC 23-44 Went to confession at the Cathedral. No Army Chaplain but the Parish priest understands good English. Might go to Dijon for Xmas service.

DEC 24 Went to mass at the Cathedral. It was plenty cold. In fact the altar boys wore gloves. Many GI's attended. Tomorrow is Xmas & expecting a big dinner. Today I didn't work since my feet are giving me trouble.

DEC 25 Xmas day. Went to Mass & Holy Communion at the Cathedral here in Langres. Snowing & plenty cold. Played poker & knock rummy. Will work tonite.

DEC 26 We are now off days & work at nights at Ammo.

DEC 27 Having trouble with my feet. Made sick call. Don't work today. Tonite we will.

DEC 28 Just about finish moving ammo. Went to town & got hair-cut. Received a letter from Simone from Marseille & also photo. Wow!

DEC 29 Finish ammo. Tomorrow we will go to Marseille and bring new trucks to Langres.

DEC 30-31 On our way to Marseille. We slept in Valence ate "C" rations and started next morning & arriving in the evening. Got a pass & went to see Feli. Family were surprise to see me. Had supper there. We slept in area "C". Kitchen went AWOL.

Jan 1-45 Went after our new big trucks. Had dinner with a Port Bn. Tonite they will serve chicken. Got ready & went over to see Feli. Had supper with her and then went to the dance at Connet. Saw Stewart & Cooper & girl friends.

JAN 2 Took trucks to Ord. to be loaded didn't finish until about 10 at night. Suppose to go over to see Feli but didn't since it was late.

JAN 4 Finally arrived here in camp. With our trucks empty (unloaded at Dijon). Kitchen finally came back (AWOL) Haven't eaten or slept much so tonite will retire early.

JAN 5 We are now on the alert & can't leave area. I was planning on taking a bath. Getting ready to leave again & this time we are going the other direction. Gilbert is my assistant.

JAN 6 We are leaving again. Last night we slept at Epinal. It is snowing and the ground is plenty slippery. We arrived at our destination OK. The name of the town we're in is Strasbourg. We are ordered to leave the town as the Germans are expecting to take over. So we are now in Molsheim. Just a few miles from the front. Most of the trucks went out. Gilbert & I have to haul (Infantry to the front). The boys were green, just came from the states (Rainbow Division). When unloading truck they marched to the front without the tools & a few without their ammo. We stayed at the CP & had coffee & bread. 4 o'clock in the morning Sgt. Lewis came by & we all went back but got lost & didn't reach camp (Molsheim) until the next day.

JAN 7 We are now hauling German captured ammo to the rear. The people of Strasbourg all speak German. The beer is good here & a nice town but can't trust the people.

JAN 8 Hauling French ammo to railhead. Sanchez found a dead soldier (G.I.), loaded him in truck & took him to the nearest camp.

JAN 9 Doing the same thing. The town is very big & the people are undecided to be for Germans or Americans. In most houses you will see American & French flags one day & then the next day they will be down.

JAN 10 We are now on our way back to Langres. It will take us two days to reach our destination.

JAN 11 We slept at Epinal. Still snowing but no accidents. We finally reached camp & glad to get here.

JAN 12 We are now working at the Railhead. It sure is cold here. But the building we are living is not bad compare to sleeping out-doors (pup tents!).

JAN 13 Rumors that we will be leaving again & this time to work at Epinal. This morning I made sick call (*my feet*) so didn't have to work.

JAN 14 Still mark quarters-sick. We played Knock Rummy & didn't do so good. I lost about $30.00 Want to get in a Poker game so I can win.

JAN 15 My assistant is taking treatments (VD) so I guess I will have to drive today alone.

JAN 16 Working at the Ammo Dump hauling. Took one load to Laverne (five mi. N. of Strasbourg) came back to Langres next day. Drive all night. Plenty of snow.

JAN 17 Left Langres in the morning with a load of ammo. Took it to the front.

JAN 18 Arrive at our new area in Epinal. We are now living in a French Barrack. Gilbert, Malloy & I are staying in one room. Still snowing. We are about 80 miles from Langres & 80 miles from Strasbourg.

JAN 19 Drove to Langres on convoy for load of ammo. Arrive back in camp next morning. Gilbert delivered it to the dump. 1000 franc notes & 500 are now valid and must be turned in for exchange. Due to counterfeit.

JAN 20 Took a shower & am getting ready now to go out on convoy. Had a show-down this morning & had to turn in all overage.

JAN 21-45 Moved again but still in Epinal, one platoon to a room. Still hauling from Dijon to Epinal and Luneville. Yesterday we hauled beer. We drank a few bottles and it sure tasted good. Still snowing and the roads are dangerous. Pvt. Pacquette was in an accident and died on the way to the hospital. Haven't been getting much sleep nor eats. Was out for two nights straight.

FEB 19-45 We are leaving Epinal and our destination is Langres again. Gilbert & I stayed behind and helped move Hq. & Med. Arrived OK. We are now staying in tents. I guess we will be hauling ammo.

FEB. 20 Kitchen, Pauline & 3 more left this outfit & are now in an infantry unit.

FEB. 22 Hauling ammo. We are staying in tents located behind the bath house in Langres

FEB. 26 Received a few letters. Everyone is OK. The weather has been good for a change. Planning on taking more pictures.

FEB. 27 Still operating COE (Cab Over Engine) and hauling ammo. Rumors we will be crossing the river soon.

FEB 28 Pay Day. Received $35.00 Played poker, didn't do so good. Tonight I am on duty.

MARCH 1 Raining but it hasn't been very cold. We just finish playing Knock Rummy & planning to get some rest. Five in the tent.

MARCH 2 Still working at the Rail-head. German prisoners are the labor.

MARCH 5 Rumors we will be getting Ducks again. Saw a few pass by going to Ord.

MARCH 6 Turn in trucks at Chaumont & received Ducks. 1st Plat. already left. We will probably leave tomorrow. 2nd Plat. will leave tonite. It is still raining. Most of the tents are down.

MARCH 7 Arrived at Valbourne with Ducks. At same living in buildings.

MARCH 8 Went to Lyon. Had a nice time. Met some English-speaking girls. Had a fairly good supper. Populaski went with me.

MARCH 9 Working on Ducks. Gilbert is my assistant. We are now instructing a Tank outfit on river crossing.

MARCH 10 After work we went to Lyon again. It's a big town. Met some boys that were with me at Anzio. Wilson & Sigler.

MARCH 11 Rumors that we will leave in the next few days. We are still giving training at the river.

**MARCH 13** We are leaving tomorrow but don't know where to. Tank outfit left this morning. It's a nice day today. Took some pictures but will get them developed on our next stop. We are now living 12 to a house. Deestra, Bell, Malcolm, Populaski, Humes, Gilbert & myself. The rest are new replacements.

**MARCH 15** Been traveling for the past two days. We are now in an area just a few miles from Nancy. We are living in tents. I believe we will train here and get ready for "the river crossing". Warm today, just like summer. Had no trouble on the road. We are 282 mi. from Lyon. There is a small village near by. Guess I will go in and get my laundry done. We are now with the 7th Army again.

**MARCH 18** Had a Duck inspection. We are getting ready to move. I think we will move close to Luneville or thereabouts. Dunlop & McGuire came back (AWOL) to area. Today it is cold.

**MARCH 19** Went to Nancy on a pass. Had a nice time. Took a shower & pictures to be developed.

**MARCH 22** Getting ready to move. I think we will go to Germany.

**MARCH 23** Got everything packed & on our way. We slept in a field and expecting to continue on our journey.

**MARCH 25** We are now in German soil. Many houses destroyed & people moving out. We are not allowed to speak to them. I guess from now on I will have to do my own laundry. Gilbert, Populaski & I rode on one Duck. It rained most of the way.

**MARCH 26** Put up a tent near a small town. It is Off Limited so can't go in. So I now find time to do some letter writing.

**MARCH 27** The 7th Army crossed the Rhine River. Don't know what we will do. Hauling ammo across the Rhine River at night. I got lost the first night but made it back to camp OK. Made two loads. Pupulaski is working with A-frame across the river.

**MARCH 28** I'm working nights. I cross the Rhine again. I have a good Duck. We can *not* talk to the people here. So when I get back I usually go to sleep. Many homes are destroyed. GI's are riding around in civilian cars & motor-cycles.

**MARCH 29** Still moving ammo. 7th Army are 75 mi. in now & connected with the 3rd Army. Ammo here about finished. The German soldiers left most of their equipment behind as they were in a hurry to leave.

**MARCH 30** Windy & still working nights hauling ammo to the front. For dinner today we all received one big bottle of German wine & champaign. It tasted pretty good. I went in a vacant house and manage to get a mattress, so now perhaps I will keep warm & sleep better. Many French civilians are on their way back to France (Labor).

**APRIL 1** I crossed the Rhine with lights on, but had a hard time getting to the other side. There was no one there to guide us in. I finally manage to find the entrance. We are expecting to move soon. A C D Cos. have already left.

APRIL 2 We are now in Limberhof, arriving today. Hauling rations from Dump to Depot across the Rhine. Expecting to finish within the next few days. Many houses destroyed & people traveling along the road. We are not allowed to talk or associate with them yet.

APRIL 3 We were paid in French money ($35.00).

APRIL 4 Still working days. Today I washed my Duck. Hauling rations & gas. Have to do my own laundry today.

APRIL 5 Haven't been feeling very well. I am driving nites.

APRIL 6 Made sick-call. Have a fever of 102. Have malaria. Slept all day & taking treatment. May have to go to hospital if fever don't go down.

APRIL 7 Feeling some better. Stayed in bed. Using Duck to haul ammo.

APRIL 8 Feeling better, made sick call, still taking pills. Nice day. Boy from "C" Co. hit last night during air-raid. He died on way in.

APRIL 9 Am up and feel better. Walked to the village with Pop & took some pictures. Ducks going out today.

APRIL 10 Went out & haul some rations & gas across the river. White flags are still out. Nice night. One of the boys had trouble with Duck in water. Helped him get out.

APRIL 11 Went out again. Had an air raid. Six boys got transfer today including Gilbert.

APRIL 12 Feel good today. Received a package with carne seco & slippers from Mother.

APRIL 13 Rumors that President Roosevelt died last night. Yes, it is true. He dies at Wash.

APRIL 18 Moved from Limberhof to another area. Haul 44 Division to the front, got scraped but no one was hurt. Arrived at night, chased civilians out & slept in house. Captured many prisoners. Found a radio, not much good.

APRIL 14 Went back to camp. Read my mail. Most of the other drivers are out.

APRIL 21 Took the 103 Div. to the front. Had no chow, traveled all day & night. Came back for another load.

APRIL 25 Took the 101 Airborne to new area. Haven't been feeling very well, driving both days & nights. My assistant can't drive nights.

APRIL 26 Went back to the camp, and made sick call. Had a fever of 104. Went to the hospital. (112) Have malaria. Logan also went.

APRIL 27 Spend one week in hospital and then went to the 2nd Con. for sev. days. Landed in the 71st Replacement Depot near Munich. Chow was *terrible*. Stayed here for three weeks, near the town where the S.S. troops starved the French & Russian slave workers. Many were found in box cars. Found a new bicycle. Did a lot of riding. Dachau. Weniger & I went out & found two rifles. Send them home. Manage to get plenty of eggs & beer. Refugees are doing a lot of looting, cars, etc. Nice weather just like summer.

MAY 1945 Played poker, lost a little. We have Russians working in the kitchen. Our meals are getting better. Trying to get out but no luck. Even wrote to the C.O.

MAY 8 *The war here is officially finished!* Went bicycle riding & also visited the concentration camp where the refugees are staying (French, Russians & Polish). We are staying in tents. The weather is nice & so are the girls but we can't fraternize. About everyone here in Germany have a bicycle. Had PX & finally got some cig. Haven't seen a stage show since I been over here. Went to the show.

MAY 13 Moved to another R.D. (2nd) which is in Worms. Major Frye is in charge of the Depot. Many soldiers are getting court martials. I figured my points. I have 117 points so have a good chance to go to the States. Played poker and lost what little I had. Sold my pistol for $25.00. The weather is warm. Took a bath & also got a hair-cut. Loan my bicycle to a Lt., will get it when I return to my unit. Gen "Ike" Eisenhower, charge of (ETO) forces says—Do not fraternize. Went to the show with Cpl. Weniger to see "Lost in Harlem" with Abbott & Costello. Weniger left 2nd R.D. I will leave tomorrow. I am on my way to outfit but landed in the 3rd R.D. in Kaufbeuren, Germany. It's a nice town, Go bicycle riding about every day. Two days later I loaded on truck to look for outfit. Landed in Austria. On our way back we landed in Schongau where 53 QM Bn. is staying. Left next day with Lt. Bringman to Co. in Ulm. We are staying in a big house. Today it is raining. The town is badly damaged. Officers do not censor mail. Met a girl (German) speaks good English. She told me the German soldiers were poorly equipped & had little to eat. Left my bicycle with Ruzeki at Bn. Hq.

JUNE 2 Haven't been doing anything lately. This morning I went to Bn. Hq. to check on my points. I now have 108. We are living in a nice big modern home by the Danube River. Most of the buildings here are destroyed. Some of the boys came in today that were in Paris on Pass.

Left Antwerp Belgium Aug 26-45 Arrived Camp Kilmer, N.J. Sept. 8-45 Discharged Fort Bliss, Tex Sept. 1945 Civilian again! Wow!

# EDWARD ROBB ELLIS

Very few of the diarists in this book continued their diaries once the war was over. Edward Robb Ellis, a newspaperman before, during, and after the war is a major exception. He had, in fact, begun his diary in the 1920's, continues it to this day, and is listed in the Guinness Book of Records as the author of the world's longest diary. He well may be, for the diary, now in the possession of the University of Wyoming Library, contains over 15,000,000 words and is more than 31,000 pages long. Begun when Ellis was a schoolboy in Kewanee, Illinois, it so far covers a span of 56 years.

Ellis was virtually the only diarist in this book who was distinctly told by the military powers-that-be that diaries were forbidden because they imagined them to be of potential use to the enemy if captured. Some of the other diarists herein heard vague rumors to that effect but never got official word. Determined that there would be no break in the diary he had already kept for so many years, Ellis put his entries into the form of letters to his wife for the duration. This, plus his background in journalism, makes for a somewhat unusual style. The diary has a far more self-conscious tone in the writing than most and tends to sound more like reporting than like either letters to a wife or the normal private diary. Because of his trained, observant eye, however, it is rich in telling detail.

Born in 1911, Ellis held the Navy rank of Corpsman, First Class, in the Lion 8 unit at the time of these diary excerpts and he was serving as editor of the Navy paper on Okinawa. I have arbitrarily decided to put the Ellis diary in the land section of this book rather than the sea division since he is on land at this point, not at sea.

Retired from journalism after years as a reporter in a variety of cities including New York, where he now lives, Ellis is the author of ECHOES OF DISTANT THUNDER: LIFE IN THE UNITED STATES 1914-1918 as well as A NATION IN TORMENT: THE GREAT AMERICAN DEPRESSION 1929-1939 and THE EPIC OF NEW YORK CITY. He is co-author with George N. Allen of a book on suicide. He is now working on a book with the ambitious title THE ENCYCLOPEDIA OF NEW YORK CITY.

Three times married, he is now a widower with a daughter and two granddaughters.

\*\*\*\*\*\*\*

SUNDAY, AUGUST 5, 1945 Okinawa

I could *smell* land. Prairie-born one that I am, I'd never before believed that land can be smelled. So this was the broadening part of "travel broadens one". What I was smelling was Okinawa. At 5 p.m., junked up with carbine, gas mask, pack, canteen, etc. I floundered over a rail and swayed down a cargo net into a landing craft. A smoke screen was whooshed around us, a thing that surprised me, since the island was supposedly secured. With salt spray blurring my expectant eyes, I strained toward this bloodiest battleground of the Pacific. It looked like a country club. From a distance its hills, sloping up almost from the surf itself, were green neatness. There was a look of cultivated precision about the island. It was so different from Mog-Mog Island, where we'd stopped en route here. The shores of that diminutive isle were a Hawaiian skirt of palms. So exactly did it look like a Hollywood version of a tropical island I was confused for a time as to whether Hollywood was copying nature or nature was copying Hollywood. But this was Okinawa, and despite the innocent greenery the boots of war had ground men to a coral death. As I hauled my White Knight paraphernalia onto that coral, I muttered, to mark the occasion, the single word, "Okinawa". Many men, I since have learned, did the same thing. It is a gesture to shatter the wide-eyed surprise that a little guy from a Kewanee, a Keokuk, a Walla Walla actually has reached such a distant, such a fabulous place-name as Okinawa. But here is a curious thing—more of that "broadening" process, I suppose. There is a daily-ness about distant places once reached, an ordinariness of routine, clutter of trivialities such as one is used to in the U.S. . The "Wow!" of landing tempered by a commonplace weariness and the tiresome familiarity of such things as uniforms. No, it is not all strange. And even when I later got into the more remote parts of the island where there was more strangeness, there was also a foundation of the ordinary. Okinawa is bedded in beet fields. Well, beet fields are beet fields, whether they be in Illinois or on a Ryuku island. That's what I'm trying to say. Five minutes after arriving I did see something that made me stare though. A Navy truck passed loaded with peasant women, and some of them wore the conical-shape hats I had seen in Japanese prints. These, and their smallness, did attract me. I'd always known, of course, that Japs and people of Jap blood were short, but actually they are much shorter than I'd expected. Men and women alike, they reach only to our shoulders and it's somewhat difficult to adjust one's mind to an acceptance that the race can be so under-sized. Anyway, since I was a one-man draft (Navy lingo meaning that I had travelled across ahead of my own echelon), I had to forage for myself. Some Southern hill-billy sailor drawled that he thought he knew of an empty bunk, so I trudged after him up the slopes on which this activity is based. He gushed conversation but I was too concerned with balancing my gear on my shoulders to make the attempt to understand his gibberish. So I found a bunk. And one with a mosquito netting at that. Then, wearily, I sat me down. The view was a big something. Far below me, as in a Greek theater, stretched the panorama of Buckner Bay, freckled with ships. From them diamond-flashes of signal-lights defied the engulfing darkness. My reverie was interrupted by the entrance of men occupying the tent. After the usual off-handish civilities were exchanged, they told me what to expect that night. To my awakening amazement, they informed me that while Okinawa was secured in the sense that organized Jap resistance had ended there, there were still an estimated 10,000 enemy soldiers infesting the place. "Whatever you do," they said, "don't leave this tent at night. There's a string of fox holes along the rim of this hill, just 30 feet away. There're security guards in them, and they shoot at anything that moves. You'll hear them begin to shoot as soon as it really gets dark." I unpacked some of my gear. It really got dark. Splaat! Whiiinnng! "Well," my new friends commented, "there goes the first one." Splaaat! Splaaat! Splaaat! On the hill above us, all right. I sprawled beneath my netting and for the first time in my life listened to the sound of war. Then the carbines began splatting to our right. Then our left. Then behind. "Damn Japs sneak down to the pier," I was informed, "Got 'em all around." Shuffling an arm through a fold of my netting I reassured myself that my carbine was near at hand. And my sheath knife. Then I stretched out again for a little session of analysis. For years I had wondered what fear is like. I'd third-degreed fliers when I was a reporter, I'd hounded helpless casualties as I dressed their wounds in San Diego. Mostly, they didn't know. The best answer I could get was that fear was the regret of feeling that a guy might never again see those persons and things he loves. Well, here I was on Okinawa with—and just then the siren snarled. "Alert!" the men shouted. "Geez, are we going to have to put up with them damn planes again tonight?" Being more newpaperman than sailor, I floundered out of my cot, sandalled outside. The lights were going out across the hills. BUT AS MATTER OF RECORD, NOT ONE DAMNED EXCITING THING HAPPENED AFTER THAT.

SEPT. 16, 1945

"Hey, it's Condition No. 2!" Charlie greeted me as I entered the office. Charlie Campbell is an enlisted Navy correspondent, a Negro and a good friend of mine. I'd gotten down to work early that morning and I'd noticed that the wind was blowing unusually hard. Condition No. 2 meant TYPHOON Condition No. 2. En route here our convoy had traveled in a vast circle one full day to escape a typhoon, but now, it appeared, I wasn't going to be cheated out of a little fun. Hauling on my rain trousers and parka, I hit out for the beach, about 200 feet from our office-tent. Crawling over a pipe labelled: "Danger! Aviation gas!" I teetered atop some empty—I hoped—gas drums at the edge of a rice paddy. The wind seemed to be funnelling in from Buckner Bay directly before me. It ruffled the sea into the semblance of a cat's back, the frizzy uprightness of a frighted gray cat. The surf was the tattered apron of a giant. As I licked salt spray from my lips an expecially strong gust caught and filled the hood of my parka, wallowing me back a staggered pace. Thinking of the fabled winds of Iceland, I leaned into it, and was disappointed because I couldn't lean my full weight against it. The clouds were a two-layered cake slipping off a blue table. Curving reeds were a rampart of parentheses marking the extremity of the land. Oblique blasts sent cobra-hoods slithering across rice paddies. The entire scene—the dimming peninsula across the bay, the warm menace of the wind, the devil's dance of ships at anchorage, the coronets of spray being broken against the sea wall—had the savage melancholia of a drunken Poe. It was stimulating. Man, for all his atomic bombs, has yet to tame brawling weather. It was inspiring, for power always inspires human beings. I bellowed in sensual enjoyment, and sucked the salt water that flicked into my mouth. But there was a paper to get out, typhoon or no typhoon. Throughout our entire work day, with the wind inflating our office-tent twice its size, our motto became: "The show must go on—but why?" At times the rain was as slantingly solid as a corrugated shed roof. It whipped through the netted front door, puddled our one typewriter. Raising our voices against the hoarse whoofing of the wind, we shouted to one another and made changes with the speed of theatrical property men. Charlie blew in—ah, for once this expression may be taken literally—to announce excitedly: "Condition I now!" Condition I, huh? Riffling through some papers, I found and read what that meant. Among other things it meant to be ready to flee from tidal waves. Verrry interesting! About 4:30 p.m. I slushed through the mud to chow. In that brief trip I became soaked through, parka and all. Coffee, I yearned. Hot, hot coffee! How I love you! So, of course, we orphans of the storm were served ice cream. Only the Navy could dream up something like that. Then I went to my tent. Let's see: That is a short sentence of seven words. The reality behind these words was clutching at tufts of grass to pull myself up grease-slick mud slopes, shouldering back the waxing wind, inching across a narrow board spanning a freshet, working the calves of my legs against the pneumatic pull of the yellow gumbo. But I made it. Sunday happened to be Monte's and Bill's day off, and they had spent the day double-staking our tent. It bristled with the lines attached to pegs driven nearly out of sight beneath the morass. I had eaten, but Monte was cooking dinner. This is to say that he

had a single open flame burning inside a discarded oil tin lying on its side in the tent. As the light grayed into black, we made repeated inspection trips around our bloated tent. Hooded figures of men ringed their tents. Dull thuds bespoke the frantic efforts of others to keep canvas over their heads. The wind became a pressure that made one heady. It was whipping rain before it at 90 miles an hour, rain that was a machine-gun burst. To face that force was a tortured impossibility. I wanted to see the bay but this gray madness impaled my eyelashes against my eyelids. The recreation hall, 25 feet away, collapsed. Tents were straining at their lines like Superfortresses on the line. Inside our uncertain haven, the single centerpole bent and relaxed and threatened at any moment to snap in two. Fearful of this, some of us donned helmets lest we be speared from above. So it was for this that we lugged steel helmets across the Pacific, we grinned. I unlimbered my sodden frame onto my cot, still wearing my parka. For the time being, at least, sleep was an impossibility. Fitz broke out his harmonica. Shoutingly, we argued about the European war. While all the time I was thinking: Well, I'll be damned! So this is supposed to be one of the tough moments of life, huh? Curiously enough, this isn't bad at all. I could take lots more. Thinking this, I heard Fitz waft into another piece. It was "Ave Maria".
SEPTEMBER 20, 1945

"Here comes Mr. Okuda now," said the commander. "He used to have a wholesale grocery and export business up in Korea some place. I think they ran him out. He's a candidate in today's election for city council." Through the break in the stone wall we could see Mr. Okuda advancing across his grass-matted floor toward our side of his sliding-wall home. A sturdy, brown little figure, he drew himself up into statue-like rigidity, thrust out his arm into something resembling the Nazi salute. As though making a speech, he barked: "Good-a morning. Thank you!" The commander, a former Los Angeles criminologist, relaxedly beckoned Mr. Okuda out of his house. The little man stepped down, ran toward us in quick, short steps, again imitated a statue making a speech: "A-meddica very good country, thank you! Yisss! Yisss!" The commander tucked a smile into the folds of his wrinkled face. "Mr. Okuda," he pronounced slowly, "this is an American newspaperman. Newspaperman." The Okinawan politician bounced toward me on naked feet, his white loin cloth flapping. "A-meddica newspaperman, vary goood! Thank you! Yisss!" And with that he grabbed my hand and kissed it. An emperor's grandson lighted my cigarette once, but, really, this was going too far. However, this was the island of Heianza, three miles off-shore from Okinawa. When in Rome—damned if I would! Before the day was out, a native woman at whose home I was visiting fell onto her knees, went all the way down to the floor onto her elbows, and touched her head against the grass mat in welcome. While a passing fisherman, having no hat to doff, whisked off a white cloth he wore about his head as a sweat-band. If I was supposed to feel like a conquering hero, I felt more like a constipated heel. The attitude of the Okinawans on Heianza toward us Americans varies: The old people are embarrassingly subservient and polite; young girls (there are no young men left here) are alternately timid and coy; while the kids are so effusively friendly they swarm beneath one's feet. This island of five square miles of rice paddies and sweet potato fields harbors 6,459 natives under the control of the military government. Some were born there; the majority were brought to the island from six smaller islands nearby. Entirely unfortified, Heianza suffered but little from the bombing that left Okinawa itself a broken skyline. When the duck which brought me to the island crawled up a stone ramp, I first was struck by the relaxing sight of intact buildings. Battle-rubble, I have sufferingly learned, wearies the eye with its multitudinous detail. Here, however, were clean-cut stone fences protecting red-tiled homes against typhoons, unscarred scrub pine and dainty plane trees providing beauty in depth against the towering central plateau on whose slopes rice fields showed as green rectangles. The village of Heianza, the only village on the island, is compounded of stone and smells. Strolling between the omnipresent white walls, I appreciated to the full the Crane Mfg. Co. and realized the truth of Christopher Morley's observation: "Man is an ingenious bit of portable plumbing". There is no soap on Heianza, for another thing. It would almost seem that the flatness of Okinawan noses is due to the century-old presence of heavy odors. But then, maybe American noses are sharp from centuries of poking them into other people's business. Benny's nose is sharp and he does all right. Benny is a 25-year-old M.P. stationed on Heianza, and his hair is golden and his mind is leaden. Leaden from 44 months of overseas duty. Benny isn't sure he wants to go back. He isn't sure he *can* go back. Literally, he's forgotten what his own sister looks like. And, months ago, when he tried to eat in a Honolulu restaurant, civilization turned all his fingers to thumbs, the sight of so many poised persons at once threw Benny for a loss. "Had to get up and leave," he says, "Couldn't stand it." No, Benny is strictly from the boondocks these years. And that's where he's likely to stay. Down irregular lanes he strides his booted strides among a scattering of bare feet. And from his booted toes to his golden crown, Benny is the half-feared, half-adored demigod of Heianza. Perhaps he is more than that to Hide Okuna. She is a 20-year-old Okinawan school teacher and, seeing her, I knew what servicemen mean about native girls beginning to look white. And I've only been here two—not 44!—months. Benny is a boondocker from all the boondocks of the Pacific.

(Translation: "Boondock" is "backwoods country") So when Benny led me to Hide's little house, she smiled at his coming and hastened to spread forth a grass mat and said, "You sit down awhile, yisss?" Benny would. And did. He sat with his booted feet outside the house, for no Okinawan enters his home without removing his shoes or sandals. Hide bustled about, boiling tea for us, laughing girlish laughs at Benny's drawling "Take it easy". Then the tea was ready, served us on orange enamelled saucers. And Benny, the tough military policeman, poured.

MONDAY, SEPTEMBER 24, 1945

The tip of a tennis shoe was growing out of the ground. Idly, Charlie kicked it. Rotten canvas was shredded by the blow, exposing a human toe. Out scurried maggots. We stood silent in the sun. At our feet, at a 45 degree angle in the coral-soil of Okinawa, a someone who once gurgled at his mother's breast was now but a something. Jap? American? What difference. Charlie Campbell, the Negro correspondent and I, had a Negro jeep driver with us. With that one ghoulish kick, the driver muttered beneath his breath, and the next thing we knew he was half way back to the jeep. Charlie and I laughed and were glad for the excuse to laugh, and turned to look about us. We stood askew on a yellow hill, the scene of a horrible tank battle. Ten feet from us, cocked at the angle of a drunk's hat, was a blackened tank. An American tank. Twenty-five feet behind it was another. And an even 25 feet behind that, yet another. Brobdingnagian beetles, they had crawled to useful death, specimens in the laboratory of war. Charlie and I closely inspected one. A curvaceous "Miss Atlantic City" smiled a wan smile at us from its side. And lettered beneath her proud thighs were the names of her erstwhile conquests: "Guam. . .Leyte". The turret was blown off. Chains of live machine gun ammunition festooned the charred hulk. While, inside, a spider threaded another trap of death. And then we saw the jackstraw pile that was the town of Shuri. Until a fateful April, it had been a slumbering municipality of red-tiled homes, a place the size of my home town, Kewanee, Ill; population 17,000. Now, in the very center of the city, one had to be told: "This was Shuri". On a cobbled street winding up to a jagged skyline we saw the bleaching bones of houses and in those skeletons we found a child's crayon book, partly filled in. Charlie stumbled dangerously near a hand grenade and, stooping, I picked up a fragile vase. On a bullet-pocked wall hung a dainty Japanese picture of flowers, while in our nostrils was the must of decadence. Out on the cobblestones adventuresome ants scaled the ribs of a horse. Only its hoofs remained intact, and they were 10 feet distant, crossed in the manner of a trick horse taking a bow. "LIFE," said Charlie, "should see that." He meant the magazine. On the outskirts of Shuri we came upon the remains of a mansion. Behind its now half-noble masonry a Japanese garden still patterned its beauty upon the earth, complete with pool and tiny island. "In Xanadu did Kublai Khan a stately pleasure dome decree". Slowly we strolled its grassy borders and we looked not for buttercups but for treacherous wires, for we had been warned against land mines. The mansion must have been owned by some bigshot, for two or three thick strongholds bulked across the slopes. The first we entered had the appearance of a battered shoe box. On the brick-littered floor lay a rigid black figure. When I was a little boy I had a doll. I would run to the top of the stairs and drop that doll downstairs. Then I would peer down between the rungs at the doll. This looked the same. Except for an added touch. Eight feet away a severed hand struck a silent chord on black and white pebbles. From there we jeeped to Naha. Naha, the capital, was old when gunpowder was young. In 1372 Chinese commercial agents were granted concessions there. And one of the first things I saw there was an empty bottle of Coca-Cola. That's one concession the wily Chinese missed. Until the Americans came, Naha had a population of 65,000—of whom 60,000 were not prostitutes. It also had two movie houses. Naha is easier on the eye than Shuri, cleaner-cut, for bulldozers have already scraped the city blocks bare. In a lone Christian church where converted Okinawans forgot their Shintoized ancestors, a chaplain's helpers were setting up rough benches in the light shining through naked Gothic windows. A few other buildings that escaped complete destruction had the single word "SAVE" painted on them, and this was not a religious exhortation but a military command. Lying outside what must have been a bank were a cash register and a Japanese typewriter. Musing over the thicket of keys on that typewriter, I understood anew why the Japanese language is so difficult. Then I picked my way into the ruins of the Jap military academy and sat in a window as empty as the eye socket of a skull to drink grapefruit juice in sight of the China Sea. A trio of huge Shinto symbols—the two upright and two horizontal bars—lured me out and on. Presently my companion and I found ourselves at the foot of a long outdoor staircase of shallow steps. They led past stone lanterns up to the site of what had been the largest Shinto shrine on Okinawa. Of all that I had seen, this presented the most typical picture of the Far East. But before ascending those steps to the ultimate, we saw something else at the base of the promontory. It was a tile chute-the-chute. At the same time, our eyes met in laughter.

# AT SEA

# FRANCIS H. BRUMMER

Francis H. Brummer, now a freelance cartoonist living in Council Bluffs, Iowa, was an 18-year-old youth from Woodbine, Iowa, when he was sworn into the Navy in 1940. He started a diary at once but for the first year or two it consists of little more than a record of his ship's movements in the Pacific, the Caribbean, and along the Atlantic Coast. In May, 1942, however, he began an adventure which he dealt with in somewhat more detail, an experience that still occasionally haunts him after all these years, and little wonder.

Though still very succinct, drawing being a more natural medium of expression for Brummer than words, the diary of this brief period is a stark reminder of an area of the world conflict that is now somewhat underplayed as former allies come to be viewed as enemies while former enemies gain the status of friends.

As Signalman, Third Class, later Second Class, and 50 caliber machine gunner in the Armed Guard, Francis H. Brummer was assigned to the U.S.S. Ironclad, making a run to Murmansk, Russia, with supplies. While keeping the brief written diary, he also kept a cartoon record of some of his Navy experiences but the nature of cartoons keeps them from conveying much of the gravity of events with the force of the few short artless entries of Brummer's diary.

Brummer served in the Merchant Marine for three years after the war then worked for the Chicago and North Western Railroad until 1954, since which time cartooning has been his profession, using RUM as signature. He has a daughter from his first, wartime, marriage and two daughters and a son by his second wife, Mabel Lea, to whom he has been married for 32 years. He also has three grand-daughters.

Mr. Brummer's diary was kept in an ordinary notebook until May 1943, when his sister presented him with one of the ubiquitous MY LIFE IN SERVICE diaries and he transferred all past entries to that.

*******

1942
JAN 21 Under way for we don't know where.
JAN 22 Joined convoy
JAN 26 Message from Washington, Proceed to Londonderry, Ireland
FEB 1 Moored alongside dock at Lessiholly, Ireland, at the American base. It is rainy here. It is a pretty place though.

APRIL 19 Underway in route to Iceland, hated to leave.
APRIL 22 Arrived in Iceland, very bleak place
MAY 27 Was transferred to the armed guard aboard the SS Ironclad.
JUNE 27 Sailed from Iceland in route to Archangel. 38 ships in convoy—3 destroyers, 2 AA ships, 4 minesweeps, 3 corvettes, 2 trawlers were the escort. Fog is thick here outside of Iceland.
JUNE 29 At 2 AM we hit heavy fog, some ice. Some ships are missing. 2100 2 ships returned.
JUNE 30 Got SOS from Richard Bland that she had hit the rocks off Iceland. The 2 AA ships joined convoy and three rescue ships.
JULY 1 At 1300 a plane flew over the convoy about 200 ft. high over the Ironclad. I was watching through a pair of glasses, identified Blohm Voss 138. Some ships opened fire on the other side of the convoy.
JULY 2 The patrol plane 138 is still with us. The destroyers have been dropping depth charges since last night. At 1400 4 Henkel 115's come out trying to come in on our side but fire was too heavy and then the USS Wainwright came over the horizon and knocked down 1 plane. Another landed beside it to pick up the pilots but I didn't see any climb on. The Wainwright is staying with us.
JULY 3 More planes flying over in the fog. No damage done to convoy. 1 bomb missed a corvette by 20 or 30 ft. and 2 straddled the SS Washington, still dropping depth charges.
JULY 4 At 0500 the Chis Newport was torpedoed by aircraft on the other side of convoy. Lost 4 men, found out later. At 1715 7 planes came out on our side. The patrol plane has been here all day. 1 of these planes is a Junker 88 land plane which is a fast plane with a torpedo slung under it and also 6 Henkel 115's. The Wainwright has been really putting out the shells. Very pretty barrage. First the Ju. 88 started between 04 column and 05 column with the other six following. She really came fast, everyone shooting at her over there. First she hit a English cargo vessel with a bomb flying between her masts and then going about 10 ft. off the water she put the torpedo into the English fleet tanker which I saw out of the corner of my eye go up in smoke. Nothing left when smoke cleared away. When Ju 88 started climbing she was hit and crashed. I never saw that part. 3 of the H 115's turned back and the other three came in on our side. I hit a tanker but didn't hurt her much. I was firing for all I was worth at one astern of us about 300 yds. She hit the William Hooper with a torpedo and we turned the other 2 back about 500 yds with stiff fire from all ships. We got hit by a 37 mm from the SS Troubador who was firing their tank guns. I heard a few go past my head and at 2000 they run up the scatter fanwise signal because surface craft were coming. Total loss for July 4th, four ships. My heart

sort of sunk when I read the signal. Now we are alone, headed for Spitsbergen.

JULY 5 We met 2 merchant ships and one English trawler, the SS Silver Sword, SS Troubador, HMS Ayreshire. We could see a ship where we was at 4 hours ago getting blowed up. Ice is all around. Icebergs as big as a city block.

JULY 6 Are lying to and painting ships. White ice all around. You cannot see ships very easy in ice painted white. They figured we should head for Nova Zembia, Russia. It is daylight all the time. We are 2 degrees from the North Pole. The trawler has heard 10 SOS so far.

JULY 7 Under way for Nova Zembia. We heard another explosion today and also just as we hit the fog a plane flew over astern of us. Pretty lucky.

JULY 8 The Silver Sword rammed us. We are taking in water forward. Pretty good jolt but for a few dents we are ok. Same for Silver Sword.

JULY 9 At 0200 we sighted land and we went in to cove at Admiralty's Pen Point. HMS Ayreshire came along side, says there were 30 planes in attack on July 4th. This place has snow and glaciers all over it.

JULY 10 0300 underway for the straits in Nova Zembia. 1420 run aground and abandoned ship, all but captain and six men. Took stores off the ship and put them on H.M.S. Ayreshire. At 1700 they had the Ironclad off after dumping off her 10,000 gals. of water and 20,000 gals. of oil. We are back on. The meantime we all sent a landing party on the land. Not much here. Very few people. Trawler went after some survivors who shot up red flares. There are thirty-five off the Fairfield City and also the Benjamin Harrison is here. She has survivors from the Paulis Potter. Their feet are in very bad shape from freezing. We got the news that 18 ships have been sunk, making it 22 so far. One was bombed ten miles from where we are now. It looks very bad for us. The Ironclad is taking in more water.

JULY 11 Tonite we got 8 survivors from the Fairfield City. They were bombed July 5th. 5 days in life boat. We are still in Tomosrakaya Bay.

JULY 13 Russian patrol plane came out. Still in straits.

JULY 17 A bomber flew over. We opened fire. Said to be friendly, but we don't know. Still in straits.

JULY 18 Today some survivors from the Potter came aboard.

JULY 20 Underway for Archangel, Russia, with three corvettes, one trawler, 5 merchant ships, no trouble.

JULY 21 Sighted plane. Went to battle stations.

JULY 22 Sight plane then fog set in.

JULY 23 We met 2 Russian destroyers, 2 English mine sweepers and 1 AA ship. Continued fog.

JULY 24 Today planes. Went to battle stations. Identified as Russians.

Land on both sides. In the White Sea now.
JULY 25 0100 anchored at mouth of river. First time I saw darkness in 27 days. Sure is nice seeing it again. Also the land. 0090 going up the river. 1400 moored alongside dock in Bokerettes 5 miles up from Archangel. I went ashore with John Stradsamire. Cigarettes are worth 10 or 15 dollars a pack in American exchange. Whiskey they call vodka is terrible.
JULY 31 We are unloaded of cargo. Only 8 ships got in. One was captured, the SS Carlton went into Norway, 28 went down, 1 turned back to Iceland.
AUG 3 We have no sugar or milk. We are eating beans, rice, and horse meat, black Russian bread, no white. The black is heavy and soggy.
AUG 12 Went to Archangel for first time. You have to ride a ferry. I bought some souvenirs.
AUG 16 We got some sugar, milk, flour and powdered eggs. In the morning we eat eggs and hot cakes.
AUGUST 18 Had an air raid alarm. Firing at different places.
AUGUST 19 Air raid alarm at night. Search lights were on. Practice, both.
AUG 24 Tonight at 2030 the alarm was sounded. At nine they came over. They dropped incendiaries first then H.E.'s. Big fires were started in Archangel. Heavy barrage. I opened fire with my 50 cal on a plane in the search light not far from us. You can see the incendiaries come down. 7 planes is supposed to been shot down. They say about 25 in the attack. Ending at 0200. Casualties is unknown. Quite a few I suppose.
AUG 29 Missed inspection and drill. Didn't get back from Archangel in time. No jerrys.
AUG 31 At 1530 the alarm. One reconnaissance plane. Heavy firing. 2300 alarm, 7 fires were started. H.E.'s and incendiaries were dropped. Secured at 0230. Beans and machroni for dinner and supper. Pears for supper. My eyesight is getting pretty weak. Bad health. No food. Damn this place.
SEPT. 3 Went to Archangel. Saw lots of burned out buildings.
SEPT 11 They took our passes today so we are about to leave.
SEPT 13 Underway standing, standing out but we damn near hit another ship then our steering gear broke down. We held the convoy up 8 hours then at 7 pm they pulled out. My heart sank to see them go. We are still broke down.
SEPT 14 We are fixed but too late. Are now going back to Archangel for we don't know how long. We tied up at Acanomic below Archangel. No passes so far.
SEPT 16 Moved to Solombia. Passes were issued.
SEPT 20 Went over to Bokerettes to see Zena. Had two air raids,

couldn't get back to ship until morning.
SEPT 21 Am on 4 days restriction. At 1500 air alarm, at 2250 heavy firing. No bombs.
SEPT 28 Today at 0830 A.R.A. 1230 A.R.A. At 1730 A.R.A. At 1954 A.R.A. The one at 0830 4 bombs were dropped by some ships that just come in. A convoy of 27 ships got in, 13 sunk. At 1945 plenty of action, about 10 blocks was leveled, plenty of fires. H.E.'s were dropped causing plenty of damage on train tracks and store houses. I was in Bokerettes and bombs were dropped in the water 300 yards away trying to hit some ships at the dock. It really shook the house. They say 9 planes were shot down and a heck of a lot over. Flares were also dropped. I got back next morning at 0900. Saw a awful pityful sight, people looking where their houses used to be. No restriction this time.
SEPT. 29 Tonight at 2010 A.R.A., plenty of bombs. Flares were dropped. They say plenty of casualties for the hospital was blown to pieces. They had a plane in search light but didn't get him.
OCT 16 First time I got lost in my life. Wandered around for 3 hours. Went back to ship. I was visiting SS Nathanael Greene.
OCT 18 No food this morning or noon. I mean none. So we borrowed horse and sled and went to ships looking for a handout. Virginia Dare gave us some.
NOV. 2 Tonight temperature 12 above.
NOV 7 River froze over.
NOV 14 Captain went to conference. Russians took up our passes.
NOV 15 We are ready to get underway but captain hasn't come back yet.
NOV 16 Are still waiting for fuel oil.
NOV 17 The tanker came at 1000. Pilot told Capt. we had to leave by 1400 to catch convoy. Capt. said no. At 2300 we got underway. At 0200 convoy had left so we are going back into Archangel for a while.
NOV. 19 Today we came back in. British Naval officers came aboard, said they were going to send us with a HMS Danman to Murmansk.
N0V 20 Underway for Murmansk but when we got to the sand bar we are loaded too heavy so they are going to have tugs tow us across.
NOV 21 Still on sand bar.
NOV 22 Still on sand bar.
NOV 23 At 1645 we started moving off. At 1800 we anchored.
NOV 24 0200 underway for Murmansk. At 2300 run on rocks on Russian Lapland in the White Sea. She has many holes in her now. The stern has settled so you can touch water by leaning over the rail.
NOV 25 Still on rocks. HMS Danman came over after we had lost her when we reversed course.
NOV 26 Russian trawler came out to pump water out of the Ironclad, which is very badly damaged.

NOV 27 Today half of the crew was taken off and put on the HMS Danman to take us some where. I am one of them.
NOV 28 Am on HMS Danman headed for Iokanka, Russia, a little ways from Murmansk.
NOV 29 Arrived Iokanka this day at 1300. A very lonely place. Lots of Russian ships. Vapor is deck high and hard to see anything.
NOV 30 10 below zero.
DEC 1 Received word to transfer to Russian trawler this morning at 0300 to go back to Archangel. 0230 on trawler. Plenty of bed bugs. Breakfast tea, bread. Dinner soup, hash. Very hungry ship.
DEC 3 Arrived Archangel. River froze over with ice.
DEC 4 Still on trawler.
DEC 5 Moved off trawler carrying our gear a mile across broken ice and pushing it on a stolen sled. We arrived at the Intourist Hotel at 1930. Am worn out and hungry but get drink to throw my cares away on conyac. Am staying in hotel now.
DEC 6 Still in hotel having the best time since I have been to Russia.
DEC 8 The Ironclad is at Malatov's and has the stern under water.
DEC 9 Sawed wood for American attaché.
DEC 11 About 20 below zero.
DEC 12 Plenty of snow
DEC 13 Went skiing first time in my life. Didn't do bad.
DEC 14 8 fellows went to Malatov's.
DEC 15 More went to Malatov's, leaving 8 Navy boys.
DEC 20 Went skiing.
DEC 25 Had a swell time. The American attaché put on a little party in the afternoon. Plenty of whiskey. And the English put on a party starting at 1900 ending 0400. I passed out. All the English beer and gin you could drink. I did. Dance. Lunch.

1943

JAN 1, 1943 Archangel, Russia. Am staying in the Hotel Intourist.
JAN 11 Was transferred to the SS Oromor to be sent to the states. Doesn't feed so good.
JAN 22 Sailing for Murmansk. The White Sea is all ice. Having a hard time getting out.
FEB 4 Arrived in Murmansk at about 2200.
FEB 5 At 1300 German dive bombers came over. We opened fire. One bomb just missed an oil tanker a mile from us. She had been hit once before by a bomb in the mess hall, killing five guys and blinding two. At 1530 they came over again. Heavy firing. 1800 come again, dropped

bombs on Murmansk, what there is left of it. Kept up till 2330. Very heavy barrage.
FEB 19 Another air raid starting at 1900 ending at 0230. Bombs were dropped. Heavy barrage.
FEB 20 Air raid 1830 lasting to 0300. Bombs on Murmansk. Heavy barrage.
FEB 22 1130 3 dive bombers dropped bombs straddling the S.S. Chester Valley. We opened fire all day 1330 4 dive bombers dropped bombs by C. Valley 1430 one plane no bombs. 1500 Russian fighter dove into German, both planes come down. 1545 4 dive bombers no bombs 1845 4 dive bombers dropped bombs by C. Valley a mile from us. That is the 2nd Russian plane I saw crash. For supper we had soup, biscuits and coffee 1900 planes again. Bombs were dropped up until 2400.
FEB 23 Breakfast oat meal hot cakes Dinner Fritters, Farina pudding Supper pea soup farina pudding.
FEB 25 4 English cruisers came in 1 German plane over.
FEB 26 Bombs were dropped twice by M 109 by ships mile and a half. Convoy came in, plenty of destroyers and corvettes.
FEB 28 Dive bombers twice again dropped bombs by tanker which was hit once before. At night heavy bombs were dropped in Murmansk. Russian shore batteries shot down one plane. The Captain went to conference. He also sent American stores out. The. S.S. Lorentia was hit at the dock with a bomb, killing two navy men and one merchant man. Also a English ship got 2 bombs in 2 hatches while at the dock. Is still burning when they towed her past us.
MARCH 1 1030 underway headed for home.
MARCH 2 Very nasty weather out. Cold and snowy. They dropped a few depth charges.
MARCH 3 Snow very cold. Dropped quite a few depth charges.
MARCH 4 Cold but is clearing off. Hit ice 2000. Destroyers sent up about 25 flares. Dropped a hell of a lot of "D" charges.
MARCH 5 At 0930 sighted two German patrol planes and one mine layer. 1000 a submarine came up in the middle of the convoy and sank the SS Executive and also putting a torpedo in the Richard Bland. She has 4 of our Navy men on her and one merchant officer. But the Bland is still coming along. 1400 from 12 to 15 big bombers came over on our side of the convoy. I could see them drop their bombs. Four straddled a Liberty ship, 4 fell right in front of the Waskatomska about 20 ft 11 between us and a oil tanker 4 off our starboard quarters and a lot more other places. No ships were hit. Also lots of mines were layed. We passed four in about one hundred yards.
MARCH 6 A terrific storm. Got a S.O.S. that the Bland was breaking up.

Also the SS Querry sent out an SOS she was breaking up. Storm is very bad, ships strung all over.

MARCH 7 Found the rest of the ships. All but eight. So we go on.

MARCH 8 Got a SOS from a straggler. They said they launched two life boats but they swamped. The sea is very rough. Snowing.

MARCH 10 Another ship sent out an SOS. Torpedoed. The sea is so damned rough.

MARCH 11 Sighted Iceland today but we are lost. The convoy tried to go into a inlet but it was blind. It is snowing terrible. At 1300 we lost the convoy and started around in circles. At 1500 a destroyer came up and said the convoy was 50 miles ahead so we are following the destroyer about 2030. She dropped some depth charges.

MARCH 12 Found convoy 0100.

MARCH 14 Arrive in Lochewe, Scotland. We are getting some chow.

MARCH 16 Was transferred to the S.S. Langdon for FFT at Gurock, Scotland. Left at 0930 for Gurock. This ship feeds swell. First orange and apple I saw since June.

MARCH 18 Was transferred to hospital for examination. Am OK. Met a fellow off the R. Bland. She got another torpedo the 5th of March. He said they had lowered two boats and they broke loose before anyone else could get in. Just 4 men in each boat. One froze to death in the boat. He don't know what happened to the rest.

MARCH 24 Was in Glasgow when an air raid took place. They dropped H.E. and incendiaries. Some damage. Haven't been paid yet.

MARCH 31 Was transferred to US Army transport Mariposa to go to the states on April 1.

APRIL 9 Arrived New York after 15 months out of the states.

APRIL 10 1750 was transferred to Arm Guard Center, Brooklyn. Very disappointing. I had no mail. It all was sent to London. Haven't had a letter in 10 months.

APRIL 12 Got 23 days leave. Am going home. Found out Mr. Carter, SM 3 H. K. Peterson, and John L. Stadamires S 1/C got off the SS Bland and are on leave. Robert Baker, Cox, is missing, a very nice fellow from Texas.

APRIL 14 2130 Arrived home, very glad to get home.

MAY 6 Checked in Arm Guard Station. Mr. Carter was transferred to the fleet. Mr. Carter, Pete, and John were in the life boat for 18 hours. John froze his feet but is coming along ok.

*At this point the diary reverts to being mostly a record of transfers and ship's movements. We quote only a few passages which go beyond that and show the wide geographic range of Brummer's wartime travels.*

MAY 31 Arrived in Oran, Africa. Quite a few merchant ships and Navy ships in. Also my brother Vince's ship, the USS Ordronaux is in. Right

alongside is the USS Betelgeuze which shot down 7 Jap planes in the landing of the Solomon Islands. A.P. Ayres, an old shipmate, is on her. He brought me over a gallon of ice cream.
JUNE 6 Went over to see Vince. He is first class S M now. Got some mail from him which was a year old.
JUNE 19 Went alongside of dock and took on German and Austrian prisoners.
JUNE 20 Underway, heading for home, I hope.
JULY 5 Depth charges were dropped between us and next column.
JULY 6 Admiral Cooke is sick. We took over convoy.
JULY 10 We arrived New York but too foggy to go in.
NOV 12 Arrived Swansea, Wales. Went ashore. Isn't nothing to brag about.
NOV 15 0700 Underway for Milford Haven at the end of the channel. 1400 arrived and went ashore with Captain Wolford.
DEC 9 On ten days leave NYC

1944

FEB 12 Underway for England. Brother Vince on one of the destroyers.
FEB 27 Arrived in Belfast. Went to Londonderry to see Cissie.
FEB 29 Sailed for the States. Vince coming back with us on his tincan.
APRIL 13 Underway for NY. A ship rammed us on our port quarters. Did some damage. No one hurt. 1850 depth charges were dropped about 3 quarters of a mile off our starboard bow. (The S.S. Sharpsburg, the one we were on before, was rammed in Mersey Bay and lost 7 men, the two signalmen Gowan and Seely, who is from Magnolia, 12 miles from home).
MAY 12 Went aboard the ATS Uruguay. A big transport taking about five thousand troops across. Escorts dropped some charges around 24. One enemy plane flew over when we were in sight of Ireland. I was in sick bay 3 days.
MAY 28 Sailed. On board we are bringing airforce men back for a rest after flying over Germany. Many are wounded. Also we have some insane soldiers.
MAY 29 Escorts dropped charges, plenty of them. (On way back we totaled 28 submarine contacts but we got through ok. Depth charges around 90).
JULY 10 Started working at the Armed Guard Center.
SEPT 2 Was put on standing to go to sea for sleeping on the job.
SEPT 4 Assigned to the SS A.V. Fraser with a SM that sailed with on a ship before. Went to Baltimore to catch the ship.
SEPT 10 The Capt., Sparks, Gunnery Officer and myself went down to

Norfolk on the ferry to a conference.
OCT 9 Arrived at the Suez Canal and went through ⅔ of it and anchored at Grand Bitter Lake.
OCT 16 Arrived Aden. Underway for Madras, India, running independently.
OCT 27 Arrived Madras. Went ashore, rode in a rickshaw. The people are small, they don't wear much clothes. The place looks very old. We unloaded half the cargo. Played ball. We won.
NOV 4 Arrived Calcutta, went ashore. Lots of soldiers (American).
NOV 8 Had shore patrol. One of the merchant sailors got hit by a taxi. He was banged up pretty bad. Played ball. We won.
NOV 16 Arrived Colombo, Ceylon. Went ashore to a dance.
DEC 4 Arrived Capetown, South Africa. Went ashore. Got plastered to the gills. A Navy man named Long, Merchant Seaman named Moe and myself broke up a house. Long and I will be tried in New York.
DEC 6 Underway for someplace.
DEC 17 Lagos, Nigeria. Played a game of soft ball with the Army. They beat us, 4 to 2. Our first defeat.
DEC 21 Arrived Takoradi, Gold Coast. We had trouble in Lagos. Long, S 1/C broke in the Navy cigarettes and jumped over the side. They put him in handcuffs and tied him. When Ronacher came back he took a butcher knife and cut Long loose, threatened to cut anyone to pieces if they came near him. They put both in the brig.

1945

MAR 2 Was assigned to new construction destroyer U.S.S. Gyatt DD 712 and am going to school for next 8 weeks.
MARCH 24 Patsy came down to Norfolk on Wednesday and we were married on Saturday at the N.O.B. Chapel. Best man and Bridesmaid were Floyd Balus, CY, and wife Laura. We are living with Floyd and Laura.
MARCH 26 Captain Wolford, my last Commodore, shot himself in NYC over his wife from Bristol, England.
APRIL 12 President Roosevelt died. Vice President Truman took over. I have been going to the Destroyers School and Cunningham for underway instructions.
JULY 2 Put the destroyer Gyatt DD 712 in commission.
JULY 15 Left New York for shakedown cruise in Guantanamo Bay, Cuba.
OCT 26 Left for Weymouth, Mass, to see Patsy, where our daughter was born dead.
NOV 2 Arrived Norfolk. Ship already left for Pensacola, Fla. Went to

the receiving station. Next night, Nov. 7, left for Pensacola by train. NOV 11 Rejoined the ship.

*Discharged from the Navy on Feb. 12, 1946, Francis H. Brummer joined the Naval Reserve in August, 1946 and was soon off for Curacao, Uruguay, Sweden. In the end he had served on 30 different ships.*

# JOSEPH McNAMARA

Of the eight children of Michael and Mary McNamara, five sons served in World War II. Joseph, born in 1911, was the eldest and served as Machinist's Mate, 2nd Class, in the destroyer division of the U.S. Navy. He had all engine room duties but mostly throttle duty in the forward engine room.

Before the war, Joseph McNamara was a skilled machine operator and afterward worked machining parts for guns. Now retired after 25 years with the U.S. Dept. of Justice, Mr. McNamara published his wartime diary in 1980 under the title TIN CAN DUTY IN THE PACIFIC 1943-1945. He dedicated the book to the one McNamara brother who did not return from service, "Lt. Robert J. NcNamara, 27th Troop Carrier Command, U.S. Air Force, who with his crew met death on a mountainside in China, 27 September, 1945. 19 years old."

Those who are interested in reading the full book from which the following excerpts are taken may contact Mr. McNamara at 60 Pleasant St., Danbury, Ct. 06810.

*******

I volunteered August 12, 1942, was sent to Newport August 13, 1942. We trained there for one month.

I was given 15 days furlough and was assigned to the Somerset Hotel on Commonwealth Avenue, Boston, to attend school at the Wentworth Institute—we leave for school at 2:15-arrive at 2:30. First class 2:40, power plant and Mr. Westover until 8 p.m. Electricity 8 till 10. The above for the first three days of the week.

Schedule for Wednesday, Thursday and Friday is Math from 2:40 to 4:00, machine shop from 4 to 8, mechanical drawing from 8 to 10:00 P.M. Hotel Somerset holds a thousand men who attend Wentworth Institute in two shifts. Boston is a good town.

On Sunday, October 24th, attended PRIORITIES OF 1942 with Willie Howard, Bert Wheeler, Lou Holtz, Bert Sheldon and Argentina—laughed for two hours. Boston Common reminds me of the old Lake Kenosha.

WEDNESDAY, OCTOBER 28

Had dinner of sauerbraten at Jake Wirts. A special draft beer that

Jake Wirts has is famous all over Massachusetts. I went with men who live in my room in the hotel. We're housed in rooms 6 to a room, three bunks high and two beds and you're housed by the letter of your last name.

NOVEMBER 22-SUNDAY Polyna Stoska sang at Symphony Hall—beautiful woman, beautiful songs. Went to see THIS IS THE ARMY at Boston Opera House. Irving Berlin in person and the original members of his group who sang in 1918. He sang "Some Day I'm Going to Murder the Bugler". Good show! First half marks at the institution: Electricity A; Power Plant A-B; Mathematics B-B; Shop C-A; Drawing C-C; Auxiliary B. Final average 84.5

SUNDAY, DECEMBER 6 Symphony Hall—Richard Crooks, middle row seat and best seat ever. Richard Crooks wonderful. In the evening went downtown. Noticed the spirit of abandon in the young couples, probably induced by the blackout. So dark you can't tell if the stores are open unless you peep in.

We're leaving the Somerset Hotel January 16, 1943 and my rate is now Machinist's Mate 2nd Class

JANUARY 16 to FEB 20, 1943

Arrived at Pier 92, West 52nd St.—a hell hole. Assigned as guard on the Camden. Camden is a prison ship—four hours on and four hours off. Three days later we were transferred to the Brooklyn Receiving Station. A hotel with 5 cent beer, etc. We slept in hammocks. Men going to school at Consolidated Edison for one month. A great experience! Get over to Manhattan two or three times a week.

Plays: I seen ARSENIC AND OLD LACE, UNCLE HARRY, ASK MY FRIEND SANDY, FARMER HAD TWO SONS, to the Radio City Music Hall to see RANDOM HARVEST, Colman and Garson. Radio City, one of the truly great experiences of modern man! Woke up at 6 p.m. February 20 and told I was to be transferred back to Boston to the U.S.S. Anthony DD 515 to outfit and be aboard.

MARCH 1st to MARCH 20 Were moved from pier to pier for outfitting. Had dock trials and trial runs out of the harbor.

MARCH 21 SUNDAY Ship under way for Casco Bay, Maine. 8 hour run. Seasick for two weeks.

MARCH 23 Left Casco Bay, Maine at 2:30 P.M.. Arrived in San Juan Harbor, Puerto Rico, on Friday March 26 at 11:00—steaming 70 hours—made 1500 miles nonstop. Ill the first night out—quickly recovered—avoided the mess hall.

Leaving Portland the sea was black—half way it was blue, light blue. In San Juan Harbor the sea is green. Looking over the harbor your eyes near the shore, the sea is even more green. The hills near shore are rolling with sharp peaks, further back the mist hides the hills. They are the greenest green I've ever seen. Villages sprawl all along the harbor's edge.

Planes take off from the harbor regularly. As I write this, sitting on the fantail on a pile of depth charges, evening approaches. The wind is cool yet warm. Some of the boys have liberty in town. The boys have a telescope and we looked the town over. As it grows late, it rains. As it does every night.

Left San Juan, Puerto Rico, March 27, Friday—steamed 600 miles run to Guantanamo Bay, Cuba. Made the run by Saturday at noon. Leaving San Juan Harbor was the most beautiful experience I've yet witnessed in the Navy. Guantanamo Bay is a military installation strictly. The marines have a huge layout here. I got my first liberty last night since leaving Boston. They have a good Navy canteen. The Marine canteen on the hill is the best, but the Navy is close second. The stay here has had all the earmarks of a cruise in the tropical waters except for a few bad days—14 hours duty—it has been enjoyable and interesting. Saw my first banana tree, papayas, cacti, and many beautiful native flowers. There are absolutely no women in all of this area except a few Navy nurses.

APRIL 12, 1943 Our depth charges sank a German sub. 3 DC's hunted it for two days. But the sub sank an American ship—all hands saved and we took some of them ashore and also the Bennett saved some of them. And the destroyer Stevens saved others. As we passed through the mine fields of the bay on Thursday April 20 I hear the welcoming words "Secure from Condition 2. We're going to dock." Have had a few experiences here, getting caught on the weather deck when the 5 inch rifles were firing over my head. Watching the barricuda and the swarm of beautiful tropical fish. Movies at 1900 on the fantail. The evening air is as good as sleep. Watching the activities of the great flying ships as they come and go. Most of all the magnificent sky, stars, moon, blue water. 80° all day, cool evenings in paradise. Nearby is the wicked city of sin, Camenera. The women all come up from Havana, they go for the marines. Seen my first troop ship alive with boys in khaki on their way to glory. I hear that it is freezing back home.

APRIL 27, 1943 Arrive in Boston. Clean, repair, replace parts in the engines. Left Boston, where I had two hours at home.

MAY 7, FRIDAY steamed through the Cape Cod Canal, Boston to New York. Very narrow, lined with homes and summer cottages. It's quite an experience to go through the Cape Cod Canal on a destroyer. You almost have the feeling that you're sailing through the back yards of the people who live along the canal and which is very true because it is their backyards. We arrived in Norfolk, Virginia through Chesapeake Bay on

Saturday May 8th. This is the greatest Naval Base I've ever seen. There are two new aircraft carriers. Planes aboard—ready to go. The bay is full of destroyers, troops ships, and freighters. The general feeling is that we are bound for Africa via the Mediterranean Sea. We get no liberty in Norfolk. While in Boston attended the Boston Pops on Wednesday and Thursday May 5 & 6.

Steaming for six days now and on the fourth day set clocks ahead 60 mins. On the fifth day set clocks back 60 minutes. We are still escorting the aircraft carrier Essex in company with the U.S.S. Rowe, a one-stacker and the Bennett (destroyer). A sister ship. Under way since May 8th. The opinion now is that it's first Panama and then the Pacific Coast. Then Hawaii.

MAY 16th 1943 SUNDAY Went through the Panama Canal then to Balboa at 9 p.m. Took all day. Had liberty from 8 to 11 o'clock in Balboa and Panama City. Both places stink. Holes of iniquity. Had two banana splits and one fruit parfait at the Astor Restaurant on Central Avenue in Panama City—50 cents each. Ice cream is pure white, very, very, good! Some native women of a Spanish type that looked good. Canal itself is a wonderful achievement. Guantam Lake at the highest point is a big body of water. Entire length of the canal—40½ miles, is lined with soldiers, great encampments of them.

Also, barrage balloons in great numbers line the canal. So do the 16 inch guns. The rise from sea level is 90 feet and two sets of locks coming up and three sets going down to the Pacific. In Culebra Cut the canal is only wide enough for one ship at a time.

MAY 19th We left for Pearl Harbor, in company with the Essex and the Bennett. Drills with the Essex in which some 45 planes left the ship. We stood by for crashes. On Thursday one plane crashed into the sea. I saw the complete event. The fuel line broke, he came alongside flying as slowly as possible, then he hit, nose first. The plane submerged, all but the tail. Almost immediately he got free and his life jacket buoyed him up. Our boat put out and he was aboard in 20 minutes after he crashed. His plane stayed afloat about five minutes. He looked about 35, did not seem very nervous, laughed and shook hands with the officers. On Friday one of the planes caught fire and although he was expected to crash he made the carrier in a cloud of smoke. Planes came off the Essex like bees from a hive. Torpedo planes, dive bombers, scout, fighters, 96 planes in all.

MAY 22 SATURDAY—A beautiful day in the Pacific. This ocean is not as blue as the Atlantic and the sunsets are not as colorful, yet they say around the islands there's plenty of beauty. On our 5th day out, May 23rd, we refuel off the carrier Essex.

To refuel we travelled at 12 knots, quite a job of skill, ably handled by both groups. She sent over ice cream and cake for the crew.

MAY 30, 1943—We arrived in Pearl Harbor—22 days underway. Islands are beautiful! Softly rolling hills, emerald green, they go right up from the sea to fade into the clouds that shadow the hills. The sunset and sunrises are unbelievably beautiful!

JUNE 6 First liberty in the city of Honolulu. Spent most of the day at the Royal Hawaiian Hotel. A pink and green monstrous hotel, beautifully landscaped lawns with big palms, great old trees, mosaic tile floors, cool wide corridors. Waikiki Beach in the rear of the hotel is very pleasant. And the sand beach is very narrow and the water is shallow for some distance out.

Bought souvenirs—they are very expensive. Mailed them home. Had photos taken with a Hula girl.

JUNE 16th Great liberty. I was fined $60.00 for mailing a postcard home while I was ashore. I made the terrible mistake of thinking a box that said Servicemen's Mailbox meant that was for the Navy. I just found out that we're not in the service, we're separate. So, it only cost me $60.00. A picture of a golden flower tree for my mother.

JULY 12, 1943—Have been operating with the Essex and the Enterprise. Many plane crashes on the carriers—two in one day. Many pilots are lost. Most dangerous kind of work, especially the night landings.

AUGUST 7—Operations underway to make us shellbacks, when we cross the equator. We're polywogs before we go and then we get through the garbage and swill that they make us crawl through and paddle our cans with a board and then we will become shellbacks.

AUGUST 10—11:10 crossing the equator. Initiated into the Royal Order of the Deep. A brutal initiation in which officers and all aboard but two men took part—they were sick.

AUGUST 14, 1943 First anniversary in the Navy! What a celebration!! Arrived in Pago Pago Harbor at 8 o'clock. Harbor very beautiful. A dog leg surrounded by sharp high green mountains so steep they seem unclimbable and inhabited along the shore only. Not a large base. First thing one sees on entering is the white New England-style church on the shore. Very reminiscent of the Congregationalist Church we have in Danbury. Native men in Samoa wear long skirts. Native boys dive from the docks into the clear blue water for coins. The mountains are sharp and a solid stone cloaked in green. Half way up the mountains—a white house. Could this white house have been Sadie Thompson's Inn? Underway Sunday at 7 o'clock for some unknown destination.

AUGUST 17 The air is chilly and the first night in months I have put on a blanket. Sleeping is now looked forward to. Captain told us we had 7,000 soldiers in convoy. Kept my life jacket within five feet. We have bypassed the Fiji Islands. Crossed the International Date Line on Tuesday, August 17, next day being Thursday. Every unidentified ship we pass brings general quarters. We are always constantly on the alert.

AUGUST 24, 1943 We anchor. Noumea protected by a coral reef several miles outside known as the Great South Reef. Small island with a lighthouse at the entrance. After getting in, the great chrome mines that are open pit on the mountainsides are visible from the ship and the activity goes on in those mines day and night. And their great glow of fires at night certainly is a beacon for any enemy that might think to do anything about destroying them. We laid along a tanker containing 9½ million gallons of fuel. These tankers lay in those harbors months and months until their fuel is exhausted. I talked to some of the men that have duty on them and it's a wonder they didn't go crazy just sitting out there in the harbor aboard a tremendous quantity of fuel and doing nothing but pumping it on other ships, but that's all they had to do.

I have been out here a year and have had six liberties which gives you some small idea of how much time we have spent underway and how little time we've had either at anchor or tied to a buoy in a harbor where we could make it.

AUGUST 26 Underway with the "Bennett" to Efate Island, southern end of the Hebrides group. Tied to Buoy No. 20 in Efate Harbor at 1400 August 27th. Efate is a table-like island with no signs of native village. Green foliage and that's about all you can see.

AUGUST 29th Took liberty ashore—given two bottles of beer. There were two or three softball fields hacked out of the jungle. I looked over a fighter strip running alongside the beach. They had Grumman torpedo bombers and Grumman fighters there. The lowest price for two-beer chit is $2.00, rising up to $5.00. This racket is run by the officers. They pick up their chits from the kids that pick them up from me and then they sell them back to me later on. But for five bucks it isn't bad. We can still go for a couple of dollars there.

SUNDAY AUGUST 29th Mass on the Battleship North Carolina under the No. 2 Turret Gun.

AUGUST 30th Underway from Havana Harbor, Efate Island, to make a sweep around Guadalcanal.

TUESDAY, SEPTEMBER 7th—Our task forces are to my mind the greatest I've ever seen assembled. Total of 25 ships of war. This feint took us north of the Solomon Islands, took 7 days. Our force from Hawaii went by way of Midway Island at the same time we went out. They hit the Marcus Islands—the Japs refused to come out to give this task force battle. Put anchor in Havana Harbor, Efate Island 1700. We had 700 gallons of fuel oil left. We were almost empty from this sweep.

WEDNESDAY, SEPTEMBER 8th ITALY SURRENDERS—UNCONDITIONALLY says Eisenhower. The official date is September 3, 1943.

Walter sent me a card telling of his injuries at having sustained bullet injuries on Mundia about August 13. He was hospitalized and then the good news that the North Carolina was going to go back to the States on August 20. The lucky guys out there—15 months and they are going back for rest and rehabilitation.

SUNDAY, SEPTEMBER 12th—Attended the smoke aboard the Massachusetts. Boxers from the Massachusetts and the Washington. Eight bouts and very good. Free cigarettes!!! Lasted from 1430 to 1630 hours.

SUNDAY, SEPTEMBER 26—Mass on the "Fullum"—Father O'Brien. The sermon was on profane language.

SATURDAY, SEPTEMBER 27th Underway with the Battleship "Alabama", "South Dakota" and three other cans, the "Houston", the "Guest" and the "Fullum". Firing all guns—full week of practice. Fire at sleeves pulled through the sky by an airplane. Shore bombardments, star shells at night. A very intensive training with ships at high speed.

SEPTEMBER 29th Weber from the engine room throwing trash over the fantail fell over into the Pacific. The Bosun's mate signalled the ship directly back of us, which was the "Guest", to veer away. They did. They just barely missed Weber. He stayed afloat. We slowed down, stopped, sent our boat back and picked him up, and he was aboard in half an hour—a little bit wet but his life had been saved. He's a lucky kid.

OCTOBER 20th—Went ashore in Meli Bay, Beach 19, where the Marines practice invasion tactics. Had a swimming party. Talked with the Marines, members of the 3rd Division. Told about the battle plans, how the 9th Division will land alongside of them in a swamp on some Jap island, Raboul or Bougainville. They can unload a ship in 4 hours. Communications and water come ashore first. We were told why officers now dress like privates. The Japs made special effort to kill those with shoulder bars. They have two meals a day while on a problem, which is an invasion. Played cards in the jungle with the bear, A. R. Mitchell and Max Pence. Picked up good coconuts.

OCTOBER 21st Back to Havana Harbor to take on AA ammunition.

OCTOBER 30, SATURDAY Convoy arrived at Kali Point, Guadalcanal, to anchor. We serve as a screen in company with the "Renshaw" and the "Sigurney".

Battle plan—general quarters expected late Sunday. This is for the Bougainville operation. This will last 24 hours on battle stations. Early Monday morning the marines will land on Bougainville. We will be 5 miles out to sea, firing 200 shells in 10 minutes at Target No. One. Then for 15 minutes we will shell target number two. Salvo fire. 50 rounds. Target number three is 3,000 yards further inland. Also may be asked for call fire on targets 11, 12 & 13. The transports with the marine division number 3 will be inside of us, so will the "Terry" and the

"Wadsworth". They will lead the mine sweepers in. Harbor bottom is unknown.

MONDAY, NOVEMBER 1, 1943 General quarters sounded at 0518 while I was on the throttle watch. Firing commenced at 0550. Fired 457 shells. Firing stopped at 0735. Secure from general quarters at 1930. First Jap plane shot down at 0805. Third Jap plane shot down at 0850. Two men killed and four wounded and a near miss of Dive Bomber on the Wadsworth, which was just alongside of us. General quarters lasted 14 hours and 15 mins. Had K rations for dinner and supper. Pretty darn good. Also cans of fruits and vegetable juices. Marines had little opposition upon landing. The tactic then we found out later was to let them land and get them started inland and then to hit them.

Left Bougainville at 730 with 8 other destroyers and 8 troop ships empty for a safe port. We had landed all our troops.

Some 17,000 to 20,000 marines landed—opposed, they say, by 40,000 Japs. Task Force No. 39 encountered Jap task force and sank a cruiser, one can and left two burning. The pursuit was taken over by bombers. We had a cruiser hit, a hole through the bow. Not serious. It was the "Denver". Also the "Foote" was torpedoed in the fantail and killed 19 men. Ship almost a total wreck. Good only for salvage. The "Spencer" and the "Thatcher" rammed each other while making a torpedo run.

NOVEMBER 1st—Anchored in Purvis Bay, Talagi Island, just around the corner from Taluga Harbor. All the damaged ships came in here. This completes our part of the Bougainville marine landing.

NOVEMBER 5th—Liberty beer party on shore, Purvis Bay. On the jungle's edge—if you took a step in the wrong direction and didn't watch your foot, you'd step in 6 feet of water. A hand-woven shack and some grass to sit on plus 3 bottles of beer. Quite a treat.

NOVEMBER 6, 1943 SATURDAY On the way for Bougainville with troop and supply ships. Now we're gonna back up the guys we put ashore.

Halted in Guadalcanal for orders. Troops ships close by. Surprise of the year. A message from Walter who is on the "President Hayes" a few thousand yards away. His message reads "Keep Your Chin Up. Reply. Good Luck. Red" These signals were sent by flags and we had the Captain's permission to both send and receive these messages. We are taking Red to Bougainville with a destroyer escort of ten ships. We are followed by the "Saratoga" and just 200 miles off the Task Force No. 39 just out of sight and on the loose.

NOVEMBER 7 SUNDAY Steaming at 15 knots. Planes appear—sub sounded and lost. Should arrive at Bougainville tomorrow morning. Engine room temperature 118 degrees.

NOVEMBER 8, 1943 Had 8 to 12 throttle watch. Urgent call for destroyers immediately in Empress Augusta Bay, Bougainville, to break up a Jap landing of troops behind our marines. Full flank speed called for not only for as fast as the ship will run but it also calls for superheated steam at 850 degrees. That temperature makes the steam pipes turn red. You would think they were going to melt. They glow. Of course, the tremendous heat of 850 degrees and 346 RPMs is almost the extreme limit of our engines and that's around 42 knots which is so far as the ship is concerned almost flying.

Arrived with the "Hudson" Destroyer at Bougainville 2400. At 0030 first fired salvo at a PT boat behind us trying to make a run on us. Just a moment before we fired we got word that they were our friends. They were Americans and they were making a run on us and of course we had them lined up, and if they'd waited another minute we'd have blown them up and killed them off. They were U.S. boats and did not know of our being in the vicinity. Of course we'd come up so fast from the south that they probably hadn't got word that we had actually arrived.

At 0100 fired on Jap barges making a hit. At 0200 Jap dive bombers missed us by 150 feet. Yet his bombs blew out plugs in our ejector lines which causes no end of embarrassment. We had about a foot of water in the forward engine room. Plugs which are used as safety measures in the line were simply blown out, threads and all, so we had to go to work and repair them. This bomb fell just opposite of the forward engine room which is the reason for the plugs being blown out. Fired at intervals all night at Japs on the beach. Now waiting for our convoy to catch up with us.

At 0300 we left the PAs and all these troop ships far, far behind when we went to flying speed. At 0530 attacked by 25 Jap planes. Ship fired all guns from 5 inch to 40 millimeters and 20 millimeters. And so did the fleet of destroyers. Troops began to land at 730, Walter, my brother, included, and cargo being unloaded. We're being under constant aerial attack. Have been hit by 50 caliber machine guns from Japanese torpedo planes. They released a bomb and we saved ourselves by an emergency astern at 0100. Ship has now shot down 11 (official count) planes—some great work and hair-breadth escapes by us.

One way we found out to beat the torpedo bombers was when the torpedo bomber made a direct run at you, you would present your bow to the Jap torpedo bomber and all that gave him was a knife-like edge of the bow and then if you kept going at them straight ahead eventually he'd either crash into you or you'd cut him in half, so 99 times out of a hundred they'll give up this plan and veer away. When they would veer away, then we would bring our guns broadside to bear on him and that would eliminate him. Otherwise he's got us at a disadvantage because firing straight ahead we could only fire the number one gun which was the only gun that could bear down on them. And if he gets in low enough and close enough then the number one gun can't bear down on him. We got to go back to our 40s and 20s and God help us when we go back with our 20s because we know that ain't gonna do us any good.

News of our sister ship, the "Hudson", being hit by a bomb. Two men killed. By noon the battle was over. Back to Tulagi, Purvis Bay.

NOVEMBER 11 Underway to Guadalcanal with six other destroyers to pick up convoy. Arrived at Guadalcanal 1800, four troop ships and two cargo ships. At 2000 hours—underway for Bougainville. This is our third trip in less than three weeks with convoy.

NOVEMBER 13th 2:30 general quarters, ships fired on torpedo planes. Secured at 3:30. General quarters—fired on Jap planes. Breakfast has been down but no one can eat. At 5:30 commenced firing at Jap torpedo planes which have just put two torpedoes into the cruiser Denver.

At 0545 torpedo wake, port side. It missed us. One of the torpedo bombers laid a torpedo down and sky watch caught it in time and we avoided it. Of course we can turn quickly.

Daylight finds us off Empress Augusta Bay with convoy intact. Good news! We are covered with 8 divisions of planes—88 in all. At 900 went topside for the first look at actual unloading operations. Transports line up along the beach—our P38s overhead.

NOVEMBER 23 0600 hrs. Underway with empty transports and 6 destroyers for Noumea Harbor, New Caledonia. Passed the Denver again underway with one screw and one tug pushing her to make repairs at some destination.

NOVEMBER 24—Anchored in Noumea Harbor. A high harbor, the largest outside of Pearl Harbor with a vast amount of shipping in it. I counted 50 transports.

NOVEMBER 25—Liberty in Noumea—2 to 5 o'clock. A poor little town. French in origin with nothing to sell but souvenirs at outrageous prices and skull-popping rum at $20 a quart. It is the most cosmopolitan town I've seen with Australian and New Zealand troops, Aussie wacs, British tommies, French saudats, Black French saudats, and of course our soldiers and sailors.

My first look at Japanese women—who were tiny, the most frail people I've seen. They carry their baby in a sling to one side. The redhaired bushy barefooted black natives are really gruesome. It's spring here and after being five degrees below the equator for some time, it's actually very cool and so much to be thankful for.

The buildings in Noumea are old and cheap but with elegant names such as The Grand Theatre, the Grand Hotel, the Hotel de France and

the Marshal Foch Hotel. Also the Roue de Margin. Parks run through the town with benches to sit on. All the trees are golden shower-type trees. But the park is dug with trenches. Ice cream is 10 cents for a 5 cent scoop. They sell lemonade and that's all. French babes are pretty and exciting to one away from them so long. This is a vast military establishment—one of the greatest army posts I've ever seen. Chrome mines still smoke—the harbor is like Broadway at night.
NOVEMBER 31—A Marine group came aboard with good entertainment. Somewhat risqué. Also the officer had four Army nurses aboard. They will never again claim the attention they received last night. The first woman I've seen aboard since I came on board the ship. I was given a piece of paper money printed by the people of Noumea because their money has become unusable. The hills here remind me of the mountains of the moon.
DECEMBER 15 General quarters sounded 0034. We started firing at 0045 on Jap torpedo planes. Secured at 0125, breakfast at 0400. General quarters at 0530. Ship firing on beach, bombs could be seen to drop, being able to see great red flashes. 0900 went topside to watch the show, all LSTs busy unloading. We are covered with a heavy air arm. Secured from General Quarters at 1800. Marines are going one way on the beach, Army goes the opposite.
DECEMBER 17, FRIDAY 1200 Arrived at Purvis Bay, Talagi. Laid to from 17th to 22nd. No liberty for crew because of two stolen cases of beer. Never did find out who stoled the beer.

1944

JANUARY 1 1700 Underway to Russell Island to refuel and to pick up ten LSTs and one cargo ship for Bogy (Bougainville). Eighth trip to Bogy.
JANUARY 22—0125 Started firing on Jap barges in Bougainville Strait. Fired all night, all guns, got seven barges, one hundred men each, and "Pringle" got several also. We received several 50 calibre hits which did no damage. At 30 knots left the straits. At 0600 steamed back to Deamond Straits. Arrived and refueled and took on ammunition with four hours sleep. And engine rooms at 124 degrees. We are going back tonight, the 22nd. Patroled all night, not a shot fired.
JANUARY 23 Arrived in Naumia for ten day overhaul of destroyer tender. We received the congratulations of Ahnsworth, Commander of Task Force No. 23 on our barge destroying operations. Lay to alongside repair ship "Prometheus". World War I ship-repair ship. The "America", new luxury liner, was in Naumia when we arrived, left shortly. Beautiful ship, now called "West Point". Had liberties in Naumia—just a

small unsanitary village. Looked at paintings and drawings at the Red Cross, they were excellent. All done by soldiers and Marines, thoughts of war on paper.

FEBRUARY 10 Underway at 1600 for Russell Island. Had liberty on new recreation center put up by Seabees, group No. 1008. Four bottles of beer and won $45 at stud poker.

MARCH 11 Began to paint ship with new camouflage—liberty with two bottles of Pepsi and three hours of torrential rain.

MARCH 14 Out to sea to try radar.

MARCH 17 St. Patrick's Day—underway to Guadalcanal. We arrived, took aboard a 4 star General. 80 ships in this operation. The Captain told us today we will land Marines on Emirau Island in St. Matthews group 2 degrees below the equator. We will be very close to a Jap fleet plane base used as a submarine base. We have 1600 Marines.

MARCH 21 Landing made at 0800 on Emirau Island. Fourth Marines 6000 troops in all. No opposition to speak of. Snipers on small island blasted by all our 40 mms. We being just off the beach. Now called the Hollywood Squadron because of black and white stripes. Our new paint design. Carrier based planes and land based gave heavy cover. Jap snipers could easily have picked off men lining the life lines. 16 hours General Quarters.

MARCH 23 Arrived Purvis Bay—trip of 2000 miles. A most uneventful trip and the invasion a success with no casualties to us.

MARCH 28—On report for improper performance of duty in forward engine room. Deck court. Reduced to next lowest rate as of April 1. There can be no mistakes.

APRIL 2 SUNDAY—Proceeding as usual when looking up at the evening sky I beheld first a few parachutes then they blossomed out in a long line across the sky. 9 in all with a great 4 engine Liberator as the source. The ship held a level flight going on its way. On looking back to the men as they neared the sea, the entire convoy stopped. The plane crash party was sent away. We picked up 4 new men. They were really boys and scared to death. A pitiful sight. A man in the sea. Darkness was only a half hour away so all ships sent out small boats. 10 men. The entire crew was rescued. The plane circled part way back and crashed into the sea. Out of fuel while returning from raid on Truck Island. Quite a thrill. They say they were on two motors and losing oil pressure on the others. Went into Munda with them at 29 knots.

APRIL 10th Arrived in Empress Augusta Bay just off the airport. In close look this is a rugged hell hole. Captain gave me permission to send message to Red, my brother, "Hope you get off that rock soon," my message. His message, "Keep your chin up."

APRIL 23 Arrive Havana Harbor to find the weather cool and delightful. Took on provisions, ammunition, and fuel. The cool weather is a gift from God.

APRIL 29, SATURDAY Arrive Sydney. The realization of a cherished dream. On April 27th, joined by DD 630 "The Braine", with recent mail. Two St. Patrick's Day cards from Mazie and Rita. We are in company with Braine, the Bosch, and the Wearington. All hands have blues washed and pressed.

APRIL 30 In Sydney liberty begins at 1300, expires at 1030 next day. We have three out of four liberties. We had 2 ship parties with no officers present. All you can drink. Captain wants all hands to have a good time. A good many extra girls arrive, all pretty and very much alive. Took Dulcie Robinson. Dates on all liberties. Boys rented room at Mrs. Smith's Chester Hotel, corner of Hunter and Elizabeth St. A fine small hotel. Fine people as are all Australians. Of course we are treated as heroes.

We have tickets for enlisted men's liquor club on Maelay Street. Under Navy supervision you draw liquor at correct prices. Rye about $3.00 a fifth. While across the street the bootlegger hangs out doing a tremendous business at $4.00 a fifth—a fair grade of whiskey.

Attended the Minerva Theatre to see "Boy Meets Girl". Only a fair show with Dulcie, getting back to the ship about 4 A.M. Liberty three days with only a few hours sleep.

These are the finest people we have ever met. They are so very grateful for American help. Sydney is a beautiful harbor, very deep with many bays. King's Cross section is ten minute's walk from ship. The Red Cross is the big American gathering spot. They have a fine one.

They have five parks full of pretty girls looking for "Yanks". No central heating, homes cold. And so with regret we leave Sydney, the best liberty port I've ever seen.

JUNE 1st Inspection. We now have ship in first class condition. Edmund Taylor, Commodore of our division, leaves today to assume command of our entire squadron. Today while awaiting captain, a corsair fighter crashed into the sea a few hundred feet way. He was going at a terrific speed with wheels down which caused him to nose over. He came up a few minutes later and was taken aboard a battleship crash boat. Badly injured.

JUNE 2nd Underway from Efate with the Terry, Braine, Wadsworth, Idaho, New Mexico and Pennsylvania. Very rough sea. We leave the beautiful coolness of Efate. Underway 3rd and 4th joined by 6 destroyers, 2 light cruisers, Honolulu and St. Louis, 2 baby carriers. Now quite a force. Dope is that we are on the way to Kwajalein in Marshalls. Expect to strike Saipan, Tinian, and Guam.

JUNE 6 At 1900 heard over Los Angeles radio armed forces radio that the allies had invaded France on a 100 mile front in Normandy.

JUNE 10 1000 Underway for big adventure. The force has now been split in two. Bombardment group No. 1 and No. 2. We are in No. 2 and our entire destroyer squadron No. 45 is with us, also the Kidd, Black DD and one other. Also heavy cruisers, 8" guns, Wichita, San Francisco, Minneapolis, and New Orleans. Battleships New Mexico, Idaho, and Penn.

Also 4, now 3 BB's—one collided with the Penn and had to go back. An APD with 50 tons of dynamite to blast a passage through the reefs. Preceding us by one day is the Class No. 1 Task Force composed of the "Essex" and "Princeton" type carriers, New Jersey and Iowa, also BSs of Washington, Massachusetts class—a tremendous force. They will strike the island 24 hours ahead of us on June 14. We will bombard from one side of these islands while No. 1 does so from the other.

Address by Captain. Our objectives Saipan Island, Tinian Island, and Guam Island. We will shell Saipan for 26 hours then go to Guam for 72 hours then cover Marine landings, keeping sea and sky control. We have been told that a Jap force is moving north from the Philippines. I hope they come our way.

JUNE 13 Refueled off the New Mexico, took on ice cream. Reports begin to come in of our strike at the islands. Tokyo Rose tells us of our defeat. She has a pleasant English voice. We can also pick up TBS (talk between ships) telling one another of new bombing objectives.

JUNE 14 Reveille at 0200 breakfast 0300. General Quarters 0400, the big guns have opened up on Saipan—went topside at 0630 to view the bombardment—a colossal sight, the island as fires break out begins to burn from end to end. Watched dive bombers peel off to bomb AA batteries. Saipan under extensive cultivation—a very pretty island with rolling hills and soft green vales. Cliffs are on one side. Tinian is also under cultivation and pretty.

At 1100 in to bombard at 1145 open fire—secured from firing 1230. The BB battleships have been firing all day at gun emplacements on the cliffs' edge.

Secured from General Quarters at 1800 for supper. General Quarters again at 1920. Topside to see cruiser and battery on cliff exchange fire. At G.Q. 2000 opened fire—ceased fire 2230. Secured from General Quarters 2300, going topside. At midnite I see the sky glow with star shells while others pound the shore.

JUNE 16 On way to bombard Guam Island at 0400. The BBs and cruisers are firing three gun salvos at Guam. A huge island. Very rocky and hilly, 35 miles long. A continuous thunder of guns. Truly the sound makes one deaf. Secured from General Quarters at 1100. Informed that Jap Task Force is on way to relieve her troops on the island. We cease firing and form into battle line, proceeding toward Saipan with all of force. At 1800 told to refuel and join the A 1 Task Force Marines. Will do battle with the Japs.

JUNE 19 At 0230 the carriers sent off their planes. One man fell overboard off the Belleau Wood. The Lexington gives us our orders now. We hear that the tanker we fueled off on the night of the 16th has been torpedoed. General Quarters at 1030. Attacked by Jap planes. They have penetrated the screen of carrier fighters. All shot down. Dog fights take place all over the sky. Very high. Fired a few rounds with no results. We are in between 7 great carriers—their last protection. Passed dead Jap pilot in sea. There are 13 carriers in this force.

At 1830 took two pilots off S.O.C. (type of plane) which was unable to rise from the water. Fired and sank plane. Secured General Quarters 2130—10 hours. Shot down by force—200 Jap planes.

JUNE 20 Force still steaming off Guam. No news of carrier attack on Jap fleet. Our planes have gone to attack. Due to inability of planes to get in touch with carrier about 50 of them fell into the sea. At 2100 we picked up two pilots off yellow life rafts. We now have four aboard.

JUNE 21 No news of plane attack on Jap fleet. Have picked up several life rafts. Things on Saipan are going okay.

JUNE 22 Fueled at sea. Tanker No. 43. Two ships at a time. DD 547 on the tanker's port side. 5 tankers in all. We return to the 5th fleet.

JUNE 23 We take on fleet mail from a carrier escort. We have over 100 sacks for 15 ships but none for ourselves. We get ice cream from the Lexington and San Jacinto. News is released of our damage to the Jap fleet which has caused them to fall back to the Philipines.

JUNE 25 Compliments of Admiral Michener on picking up pilots who crashed at night—4 in all. Fueled from the Minneapolis No. 38. Ice cream. At 1800 torpedo plane went into spin at low altitude and pilot baled out only a few feet from the water. He was torn into strips. I hope I don't wake up screaming. We will bury him at sea. Pilot name unknown. His plane engine failed. He baled out and his parachute failed to open. He struck the sea like a sheet of steel. Send body ashore. Sewed him up into a semblance of the image and likeness of God. If all people could only have seen him. We passed Jap pilot's body in sea.

JUNE 27 Take Commander Tedder aboard from Santee. 21 consecutive days at sea. Food low.

JULY 2 Captain Van Mateer swings over to the Shawnee (carrier). He swung over on Bo-sun Chair, leaving his ship some hundreds of miles off of Saipan.

JULY 4 Still underway. Chow very low.

JULY 7 Came back into Saipan Harbor. Anchored under the mountain. Watched the line of No. 105s fire on Japs trapped in the corner. Watched planes dive bomb and strafe on Tinian. Talked with amphibian jeep driver. Told that the 27th Division from Brooklyn and the 2nd and 4th Marines were on Saipan. Jap women unbelievably dirty. The Geishas are held separately. The Koreans are in charge of the Jap prisoners.

JULY 9 1000 all night harassing bombardment of Guam. Cruisers fire all day. Again as at Saipan the sugar refinery has been destroyed but the stack stands. The town of Pate is quite large, running all along the shore. Guam looks rugged and will be difficult to take,

JULY 13 Underway for Eniwetok Atoll for a 48 hour layover. We will have to work all day and night to provision the ship. We will have been underway 37 days. Chow now amounts to a sandwich. War is a terrible bore.

JULY 24 We pick up at sea 5 men who claim to be off American ship sunk by Japs in 1941. Delirious with joy to be back on ship. Sent to flagship Clymed PA#27. The BB and cruisers fire day and night on island—this is the 23rd day.

JULY 27 Still on patrol. With many shows put on by dive bombers who lay 1000 pound bombs, strafe and scout the Japs. The concussion is now part of the routine. Received absentee ballot for presidential election. Received mail for May, June, and July.

JULY 31 Still on patrol off Guam—all organized resistance on Tinian ceased. Watched seven water spouts at the same time take up water from the sea.

AUGUST 7 On patrol off Guam. All day and night the cruisers and battleships fire on Japs. At night we watch the line of infantry artillery flash as it fires on the beaten enemy, while at sea the ships pour in a deadly hail of shells. The different color tracers make it look as though great numbers of Roman candles were being fired at the beach.

AUGUST 13 SUNDAY 1400 arrive at Eniwetok. No man has been off the ship for the past 74 days.

AUGUST 20 Arrive Pearl Harbor. At anchor on Marine Railway No. 2. Ship sandblasted for new paint. Liberty from 0900 to 1830—Sunday, Monday, Tuesday, and Thursday. Over to sub base on duty days for beer. Then also to "Sierra" supply ship to repair my denture. More sailors here than I've ever seen. Buy new grip baggage at Rec. Station. No ditty bags at Royal Hawaiian. The beer garden has been remodeled. Very nice with band. Barb wire has been removed. Still the same beautiful island and soft skies. The trade winds are very cool and pleasant. Have eaten great quantities of ice cream, sirloin steaks at the "Tropic" across from Royal Hawaiian. Beer. No good whiskey. Have great hopes of the States by Christmas.

SEPTEMBER 1 Underway to sea where we did sub patrol while LST and troop ship made practice landings on other islands. Have had cold.

Often catch cold when coming back to land base.

**SEPTEMBER 10 SUNDAY** Mass at Block Rec. Center. Letter from home tells me they receive orchids at home. "Breakers" Hotel have swanky beer garden on seas with dance band. Good chow.

**SEPTEMBER 15** Underway at 1600 with convoy of 22 troop and cargo ships, two aircraft carriers and 8 destroyers. Also on horizon can be seen another large convoy. In all there are 3 convoys with 180,000 troops.

**SEPTEMBER 25** Arrive at Eniwetok, Marshall Islands. Go alongside tender "Markab" to overhaul feed pump which was supposed to have been repaired at Pearl Harbor. Found evidence of sabotage in Pearl Harbor repair yards.

**SEPTEMBER 29** Liberty on Eniwetok Island. 4 cans of Acme beer—cold—plus a few extra. All sand. A beautiful beach with sunken Jap cargo ship containing live ammunition just offshore. Picked up some coral. Replace our new torpedoes with old ones. There was also torpedo sabotage. Have been given 5 day extension. The invasion force has left. What is our destination?

**OCTOBER 9** Stateside is now certain. The executive officer will fly ahead from Pearl Harbor to try and make train reservations for three ships' crews. There are 164 men aboard of the original crew. Plank owners who each will receive a piece of the going-home pennant which we will break out at Pearl Harbor from the main mast.

**OCTOBER 14** Saturday and so is the next day. Cross International Date Line. Same date. We hear a broadcast of the Ohio State-Wisconsin game—very clear and good to hear. We are midway between the Marshalls and Hawaii.

**OCTOBER 17** Payday—our last until after the furlough. Draw $129.00.

**OCTOBER 19** Underway for U.S.A. We will dock at Hunter's Point in Frisco Bay. We will get 20 days for 20 months at sea. The Captain and Commander have quarreled about giving those of us who have been at sea 18 months 20 days. This is a typical Navy disappointment. I have the second leave party, which starts November 15 at 0800, ending December 5, 1200.

**OCTOBER 24** Steamed into Frisco Bay at about 0500. Being on deck I could see ahead there the light fog and the first gleam of dawn, the beautiful sight of the Golden Gate Bridge. All lights and with a constant row of cars, with headlights, moving over it. On one side the blazing city of Frisco and on the other Oakland. The finest view I've ever had of the greatest country on earth.

**OCTOBER 25** Dock No. 16 at Mare Island. We are moved with all our personal gear over to Barracks No. 6 South. Especially for men whose ship is to be torn apart for overhaul. This place is a madhouse. Just across the street is a beer tavern-open at 1130 to 1230 and 1600 to 2045.

No limit. First leave party shoved off.

OCTOBER 26 First liberty. Went over to Frisco on bus. $1 for round trip—takes one hour ten minutes. Bus is Greyhound, women drivers. Went to Curran Theatre on Geary Street to see THREE IS A FAMILY with Una Merkel. Had a filet mignon in the Somerton Hotel—$2.50—very good. Drinks in the show room. Frisco is a boom town—a blaze of lights and pretty women.

OCTOBER 28 Again Frisco—same rountine except that show at the Geary Theatre and it is A DOLL'S HOUSE with Francis Lederer. They have some fine hotels and swank bars. Shot $.50 Beer $.25.

NOVEMBER 1 Liberty in Frisco. Took in light opera, H.M.S. PINAFORE at Savoy Opera Company. Excellent.

NOVEMBER 3 In Frisco. Over to Fisherman's Wharf for supper. Everything one could desire. All fish fresh from the sea—cracked crab speciality. After eating took cab to Grant St. and went through Chinatown.

NOVEMBER 7-13 Liberty every other day in Frisco.

NOVEMBER 14 1600 started our leave by truck to Oakland on the Western Pacific Railroad "The Exposition Flyer". Aboard at 1645. Seats in a cattle car. Emergency measure. The poorest sort of car, dirty and cold. The worst stretch of railroad in the country. Lakeland to Salt City. A wreck ahead on the Sierra Nevada Mountains delays us 11 hours, a heartbreaker. At Salt Lake switched to Denver Rio Grande Western—much better known as the Scenic Limited. The most beautiful railroad route in the world, through the Rocky Mountains. Very cold. Snow on all sides. Through the Maffatt Tunnel at 9,000 feet above sea level and underground 4,000 feet. The car during the 6.2 miles in the tunnel became black with smoke and fumes. At Denver switched to Burlington Route with diesel power. We fairly fly about 70 miles an hour. Arrive at Chicago at 79 hours on day coach. A 10 minute break and I board the crack Penn "Golden Triangle" with air conditioned soot-tight windows—a luxury train. But there is a wreck ahead. We lost 6 hours. Only a few stops—Pittsburgh, Philadelphia, Trenton to Pennsylvania Station New York. Stop at railroad YMCA on 47th. Swell night's sleep. Catch the 8:15 on N.Y., N.H. Railroad to Danbury. Arrive home Sunday 1100—a total of 117 hours from Oakland. So with 20 days leave I will spend one-half of it on board the train. 5 days coming and 5 days going. The trip is a wonderful education for anyone. But should be broken at main points.

So ends my cruise—20 months at sea. 6 engagements, 4 major ones.
MAJOR ENGAGEMENTS
   Treasury-Bougainville—November 1943
   Green Island 1944

Marianas-August 1944
Battle of Philippine Sea-July 1944
   A word about General Quarters. When you get to General Quarters or G.Q. a gong rings in all compartments. It would wake you from the dead. Then the Captain's voice is heard, "All Hands, Man Your Battle Stations". If you sleep aft of your station and must go forward, you run up the starboard and fall down to the forward engine room, which was my station. And if you sleep forward of your station, you run down the port side. Every man on a ship of war has two jobs—one job to maintain the ship, sweep, clean, cook, radar and a second job—his battle station.
DECEMBER 29 Arrive Pearl Harbor. Both holidays at sea. A terrific storm on way. Our ship rolled 42 degrees. It lasted three days.

1945

JANUARY 20, 1945 Underway to sea. Practice fire. Today to fire over heads of Marines who are to dash in to the beach and pick up survivors. The coming invasion will be great force with the 1st Marine Division. We now rate the No. 1 air firing spot in the destroyer class. Received news of loss of "Spence" in typhoon off Philippines.
FEBRUARY 11 Arrive at Saipan Island in Marianas. I see great changes—near coast is B29 airfield with some ships standing out. Army tents all over this green island. The amount of shipping in Saipan is tremendous. We will fuel here and go on to Guam. Our generator in aft engine room is secured awaiting inspection to check for damage. Sabotage at Pearl Harbor. Also No. 3 feed pump has burned up due to a unit being left inside, causing the shaft to become so hot as to crystalize.
FEBRUARY 16 Liberty this noon at GAB Beach, Guam Island. This is a great coral rock, sharp as a knife. Our liberty beach is just a clearing hacked out of the junge. Ration 3 cans of beer. Inspect Jap pill boxes made of coral. Three feet thick. Talked with CBees, who told us stories about Japs still on island, how they kill off small groups of Americans.
FEBRUARY 19 MONDAY We are now less than 100 miles off Iwo Jima Beach. The plan now becomes clear. This force of ours, 20,000 Marines, is to be reinforcements. We are in direct radio contact with the Marines who at 0815 landed the first wave. All one can do is say a prayer for those of them who meet destiny on the strange beach so far from home. The air is cool now. No word from the carrier planes who hit Tokyo three days ago. We heard the invasion of Iwo Jima is going very well.
FEBRUARY 21 As dusk fell we had to transfer one of the men, Connall, to PA No. 11 by sling, with acute appendicitis. The thousands of Marines aboard stood out in the cold driving rain to witness this neat bit of seamanship. The weather for the past three days has been cold with

almost constant rain on Iwo Jima. The visibility is zero and the operation is 24 hours late. Our part is as yet unknown.

FEBRUARY 22 During the night 8 of the transports left and went in to reinforce the Marines on Iwo Jima. This invasion, according to Howland Smith, Marine Chief, is the supreme test of the Marines, hell on earth. The fog, rain, and a heavy sea has kept planes grounded and even supplies are not being unloaded. The death toll will be severe.

FEBRUARY 23 Severe weather—20 degree roll—unable to refuel ship—4185 casualties in first three days on Iwo Jima. 3rd, 4th, 5th Marine Division on island.

FEBRUARY 24 Weather terrible. General quarters when planes go overhead. Japs jammed our radar with tin foil.

FEBRUARY 26 TWO YEARS ABOARD. Today our anniversary. Special ship's paper. Big birthday cake—still steaming off Iwo Jima with six liberty ships.

FEBRUARY 27 Into Iwo Jima with our reinforcements-no enemy action directed against us. But the cruisers and old line battleships shell the island. The huge rocks are extinct volcano—like a great loaf of bread. The island itself is not long with a rather even terrain. The planes this noon are dive bombing the Southern half of the island. A great fleet of supply and transports lie in here at anchor. Sky always overcast. The B29s fly over on their way to Tokyo. There is a constant rumble of gun fire and the blooming of smoke clouds on the island.

FEBRUARY 29 We move into Iwo to take up our position for precision firing—500 yards from the beach on the southern end into which the Japs have been driven. This is a devil's dream, a bad land like a nightmare. Rock piled upon rock and the base itself is rock. There are thousands of caves, every stone is split, being volcanic they are heat riven. We have a plane overhead which spots likely looking caves and ledges into which we fire. Going topside several times today I witnessed the greatest show on earth. Just in back of us the Salt Lake City firing salvos. To the left are other destroyers, cruisers and even PCs. The planes come in waves to strafe and fire their rockets. They make a swoosh sound and leave a trail of fire, making a great explosion on contact. The TBFs (torpedo bomber fighters) unload cargoes of bombs, two 500 pound bombs make the isle tremble. One TBF follows another. The concussions are waves of sound which shake the ship. How life can go on is a mystery to me. Yet as twilight falls, they fire rockets out at the shipping.

MARCH 1 0230 General quarters-Jap planes overhead. They hit the Marine ammunition dump. It blows up for 5½ hours. A description is impossible with a full moon shining down from a peaceful sky. At 0730 General quarters again—planes overhead. At 0800 Terry (513) hit in forward fireroom. 27 men injured, 9 dead.

At 0830 DD Calhoun hit-6 injured. Shell on fantail-one man killed-7 injured. Both ships occupied the same position we held only yesterday. We had been relieved to let the Commander off the ship.

1120 General quarters sounded—opened fire again on island. Our planes leaving spotted a target, at about noon, they shot down one of our planes. We fire star shells all night.

MARCH 2, 1945 0800 My birthday-34 years old-my third trip aboard the Anthony. The Marines have half the isle, including the big airstrip. We fire on the island all day. The fall of shells is like red rain on the Japs. All night firing star shells. We have five General Quarters during the day.

MARCH 3 Our ammunition is very low. We fire at request of our spotting plane who calls our accuracy excellent. Fuel at sea. Screen retiring vessels at night.

MARCH 4 SUNDAY The boys have ¾ of isle. Firing by all ships and planes continues. Our ammunition is exhausted. So today we patrol ten miles off Iwo Jima. They expect to secure today. See the first C47 land on airstrip. Just off to one side of strip is a huge pile of Jap wrecked planes. Firing on fog bound island very heavy. Yesterday watched Marines use flame throwers on pill boxes.

MARCH 6 Routine patrol off Iwo Jima. Today a B29 with two motors shot out while over Tokyo came over the ship and told us they might bail out. But the crew decided to land on Iwo's airstrip, which they did successfully. The Japs are putting up the most savage resistance in all the records of Marine warfare. They must be clubbed to death one at a time. Underway this evening for Saipan, due to arrive on the 8th, with six transports and three DD's.

MARCH 13 Move to Dixie (14) repair ship for necessary work, especially generator. Off to starboard is Samar Island. Rain several times a day. Turn to on engines which were left in terrible shape at Pearl Harbor. More sabotage.

MARCH 17 Went to Communion. A peaceful setting as sun rose in the early sky. Over jungle green hills wreathed in clouds half way up. Take ammunition from Dixie and stores also. St. Patrick's Day.

MARCH 18 SUNDAY Getting underway from Dixie to go out in stream. Generator fixed by taking two blades on opposite side of 5th stage wheel. Natives come alongside every day to sell Philippine pesos for twice their value—50 cents 1 peso. Also Japanese invasion money, for mattress covers or food. A needle has big value. Some of the lads being propositioned on beach at Tacalban with clothing being the measure of value. Also Saki (wine) for $1 a beer bottle full.

MARCH 19-20-21 Underway each day for practice with troop ships for invasion to come. Back in Leyte Gulf each evening for movie. Go every day. The new Commander Young is in command of about 50 other ships. The entire screening detail for invasion. Water taxi or native outriggers come out and pick up lads who want Pom-Pom at 20 pesos apiece-$10.00—risky business.

MARCH 22-23-24-25 Lay to in San Pedro Bay-alone. Weather moderate-nights cool. Work 8 hours a day on ship getting ready. Invasion due on march 29 with 300,000 men.

Total dead on Iwo Jima-5,000 Marines, 15,000 injured. Worst battle of Pacific war to date. 20,000 Japs dead.

MARCH 27 Underway for invasion of Okinawa! We steam to battle line. We are the squadron leader of Squadron No. 24 out to sea, leaving the very pleasant climate of Leyte Gulf, in which I have never seen more romantic nights, cool with a silver moon. It is full and will be so for this great invasion.

Our squad of 8 destroyers, one a 2200 class Van Valkenburgh, gleam with a new paint job. Everything is in ship shape. We are in number one position steaming in a straight line in front of 27 troop and supply ships. They come out of the harbor appearing on the horizon like the great galleons of old. They fill the horizon. Off to the port side low in the sky is another fleet of destroyers and ships. Again forward off the starboard bow are two aircraft carriers and their escort of DDs.

Our ship with Commander Young aboard is in command of 32 ships. We will be in charge of the screen which will send the first two waves of army ashore. Our position will be about 500 yards from here. They tell about a sea wall which will have to be blown either by a demolition ship or with torpedoes. We will open the shore bombardment the night before the invasion.

MARCH 28 Underway—the sea is very heavy. The 100,000 troops just back of us must be seasick. Half our crew is ill. The Captain just spoke to us on the three phases of this invasion. We are to be in the most important spot—the "Southern group" that will land on Okinawa proper. The Jap has 55,000 men there and the island has half a million civilians who will no doubt take up arms.

We are worried about strong swimmers who'll come out with explosives and suicide motor boats loaded with TNT who will drive on into us. Mines are to be watched for as well as sustained air attack from the enemy. Eleven air strips in the vicinity. Also from Formosa, which is 300 miles away.

We, the "Wadsworth", the "Beal" and one other DD ("Dailey") will be called upon for fire in close up screening of the landing. The sea is now a great sea. It may change all the plans.

The seventy Jap submarines are also expected to be on hand. Our most dangerous operation—about time the coastal guns dropped out on us. Only God knows.

MARCH 28-29-30-31 Sea is heavy—15 to 20° roll. The harbor is full of mines. Two ships have already been sunk with heavy loss of life. Six other ships have been hit. The British fleet "George the 5th" and "Illustrious" are pinning down Formosa. The Japs are waiting for us. There is a very pessimistic feeling among the crew—unusual number of suicide planes are active.

Easter Sunday will be D Day for many soldiers and sailors.

EASTER SUNDAY, APRIL 1, 1945 Off Okinawa Island. Full moon-calm sea-cloudy. It promises to be a beautiful day for the invasion. All hands wear Easter garb of blue dungarees, blue shirts and Kopack life jackets.

General quarters at 0150—Jap planes over island. Bennett shot one down. General quarters at 0400. We are now approaching inner harbor, sounding for subs. Secured General quarters 0530. Chow-beans before—officers have ham and eggs. Of course this is their outfit but they tolerate us (envy and dissatisfaction). While in chowline we see horizons aflame with a curtain of AA fire and then a Jap plane is hit, it flames, grows into a mass of flame and falls slowly into the sea. The AA follows him down into the ocean. General quarters 0600-no breakfast. The fleet opens fire on Okinawa beach. Going topside at 0800 as the invasion starts. It seems as if all the guns in the world are firing. The LCI's in front fire into the water, searching for mines, immediately behind come the troop-laden alligators and some barges, they are moving in—100,000 of them—a vast wave which is unstoppable. Over their heads all ships fire—16 inch shells—toss trees into the air, dust rises in a great cloud. The planes by hundreds fire showers of rockets and strafe the beach. We commence firing at 0755, fire 545 shells in 45 minutes, the barrel's hot, the paint blisters. The beach can no longer be seen, obscured by clouds of dust and smoke. The express trains roar overhead-16" shells.

Report 1100 from beach driving inland with no opposition. Fires burn along the beach. The tall smoke stacks of a factory stand tall and alone. Big radio towers stand out all through the city of Beraba.

Watching all this topside, after half an hour the constant concussion makes one almost physically sick.

At 1830 fleet lays down a smoke screen and we lay stopped beneath it. Jap planes coming in at sunset look in vain. Engine room fills with smoke. A great cloud of dust and smoke lays over beautiful Okinawa as the day ends. Night drags on with firing all around at 7 o'clock—very sleepy. One empty transport hit by a bomb.

APRIL 2 Off Okinawa, weather beautiful. General quarters all night, slept from 1 to 6:30 on deck, lower level with Hannus on watch with me. Two smoke screens layed down during the night to conceal battleships, cruisers and destroyers from night fires. Secured from General quarters for breakfast but before eating General quarters sounded again. Firing inland.

APRIL 5 General quarters 0945. Fire on Niki Jima, small isle off Okinawa. Secured 1130. While in chow line watched first Piper Cub plane taken on LST at sea. He flies at slow speed into cable which catches a hook above his wings. He is then swung inboard, a very tricky business. If he misses, he crashes into the LST. Told to expect air attack in 36 hours. Late evening leave Nevada to fuel in Kakagusukee Bay. While there the Nevada is hit by shore battery. Sea is heavy. We go outside to screen the cruisers tonight. Quiet until after midnight.

APRIL 6 At noon lay to to take on ammunition. General quarters at 1230-planes-smoke screen-other ships fire-secured 1300.

General quarters 1515-planes overhead, proceed with ammunition and stores-25 planes overhead, situation is serious. We are inside with hundreds supply and troop ships. Planes begin to fall out of the cloudy sky—3 fall within one mile radius. News of suicide planes making hits—1 on DD while it is burning badly-1 on DE which blows bow off—they hit four ships-9 are shot down.

The Japs will make stand near Naha, capital of Okinawa. We have air fields but they are under Jap artillery fire and so useless. No Army planes as yet. They would be a God-send. Still at General quarters as we go into Saturday.

APRIL 7 We fire all night—will sleep lower level in engine room on rag mattress on deck plates, splitting watch with Hannus. News of Jap planes in large numbers—our luck still holds having left our screening spot just before Jap suicide plane dived on DD off to starboard. Tonight the Japs are making heavy counter attacks on the island-fire all along the ridge while an LST burns brightly in the bay. Very tired at this time—7 days of constant battle. We stood G.Q. two days and two nights and on the third night secured.

Secured from General quarters at 0700-then General quarters at 0800-secured 0830-with coming of day air attack stopped—1300 we take on ammunition—1700 the Executive Officer tells us there were 125 Jap planes overhead, we shot down (combined forces) 103 of them-they hit 18 ships, 3 destroyers sunk-Bush, Calhoun, and Emmons-with the Bennett, "Mulaney" and "Amen" badly hit but also 11 others. We shot down two of our own boys—also at 0700 this morning Task Force No. 58 sent 238 planes off to attack the Jap fleet heading in our direction.

So at 1800 all war ships of this area form up into battle lines and proceed into the East China sea to meet any of the enemy who escaped

No. 58. There are 6 battleships, 8 cruisers and 17 destroyers—a great armada. We will steam in the sea off Rykyu Islands all night. Twenty-one ships in line. With coming of dawn we steamed back to Okinawa, no action. Task Force No. 58 has sunk the "Yamato", forty-thousand ton battleship, 2 light cruisers, 3 destroyers, left two DD's burning and 3 DD's escaped. All this in one strike. They lost only 7 planes.

At dusk watch Jap suicide plane hit the Maryland BB—kill 16 men—he was heading our way but veered off at last minute to hit BB.

APRIL 8 All night General quarters again-General quarters 1000 to fire on island and remained at General quarters all day. During the day two more destroyers were hit by planes and bombs, 4 of our squadron have been hit, two sunk.

APRIL 9 Five hours sleep then General Quarters. 0500 news of new Jap cabinet, Premier Suzuki in power. One of the men went loco last night. Looks okay this morning.

APRIL 12 General quarters at 1300-planes. By midnight will have had 42 straight hours of General quarters—no sleep. Suicide planes get 2 more destroyers today, making 13 hit, 3 sunk.

APRIL 13 FRIDAY FRANKLIN D. ROOSEVELT DIES. Stupendous, unbelievable news. We now have a political hack, Harry Truman, as president. Mail goes off. Generator No. 2 breaks down again. Great news RUSSIA DECLARES WAR ON JAPAN—GERMANY SURRENDERS-two hours later it is found to be false news.

APRIL 15 Star shells all night. Army makes no progress on Okinawa. Forward engine room electric board burns up-Diesel generator blows gasket, electric service in very bad condition—we go on four on, four off General quarters.

APRIL 19 After firing all night, we get underway for Ulithi, Caroline Islands. 1300 miles, should arrive April 23.

APRIL 23 Arrive Ulithi to go alongside AD 20 "Hamul" for repairs, mostly to generator No. 2. We finally take turbine rotor from generator of U.S.S. 661, "Kidd". We are two ships outboard of Hamul with Kidd between us. She with Task No. 58 was hit by suicide plane which struck on starboard, crashed through her deck by fake chance-smashed across the fire room and exploded on the port side going upward-it kills 40 men who ran across the ship in vain effort to escape the crazy pilot. The hole on both sides is 20 ft. by 20 ft. The boiler blowing up—no person in the fire room escaped.

APRIL 25 Liberty on small island called Waterfall Beach—four cans of beer. Cool, somewhat, under coconut palms. Water like liquid glass. A surf rolls far out on coral reef.

Get three months newspapers—read of Billy Stolzenberg dead on Iwo Jima—a blow. A good friend who loved life.

APRIL 29 Liberty on beach—the island a mile long. Very narrow, a few feet above sea level and crowded with palms and coconut trees. We have movies-TO HAVE AND TO HOLD with Lauren Bacall-excellent-nights it cools down enough so that sleeping on deck with only shorts is cold.

I wonder if Kenny Williams was on No. 777 DD. We passed in Okinawa cove with bomb hit which tore out entire side of ship.

MAY 1 Liberty today-1130-1430 with six beers each—biggest handout since I been going on shore parties.

We hear of 28 groups of planes coming down to Okinawa. The hospital ship, Comfort, is hit. The "Wadsworth" and the "Von Falkenburgh" are hit, leaving only the "Basch" and "Anthony" still unhit out of the squadron of nine ships which arrived off of Okinawa on April 1st.

MAY 2 News that Hitler was killed in the center of Berlin and (false news) that Donitz takes over. The end is near. We have worked all day and late at night on engines for the past week. Number 2 generator is again operating, by having taken the rotor from the Kidd, who left for the states with 30 days leave.

MAY 6, SUNDAY Underway to Okinawa to take No. 1 picket on lines, sixty miles north of Point Balo. If we survive this operation we will see the war through.

Sea calm. I am worried as hell.

They have sunk 24 DDs and damaged 35 others. Some day this operation, particularly the radar picket line, will be rated in history. We go up with the feeling that only God can save us.

We watch the "Hazelwood", our type DD, come in with all the bridge blown off. Eleven officers killed, the forward stack leans over the rail. Many ships are unable to move from the anchorages at Okinawa.

With Berlin in the hands of the Russians, the war in Europe is over. Two million Army men will be discharged while 7 million come out here to fight.

MAY 10 0800 arrive Okinawa to find the same conditions we had left. Battleships, cruisers and destroyers fire constantly on the island while planes are doing their stuff. The area is enclosed in a heavy blanket of dust which like a curtain is noticeable when you come in from the sea. The harbor is crowded with hundreds of ships.

MAY 11 All night planes overhead, some firing. General quarters 0930-1030—planes attack picket line off Balo Point. They sink 1 DD hit 1 DE. Ships go out to pick up survivors. How long can this radar picket line destruction keep up? Either we will run out of DDs or they will run out of suicide planes. We take up patrol off main anchorage to prevent planes getting in to the troop and cargo ships at anchor. The land battle goes slowly forward. Heavy firing all night.

MAY 12 General quarters 0500. On patrol off Naha, where the main enemy line is being hammered unceasingly. How can men still live in such a hell on earth? The thunder is constant.

General quarters 1915—Jap planes over the beach and seconds later were diving on the BB New Mexico, which was passing just off the port bow. This attack was a complete surprise. I fell into the forward engine room just as the BB opened fire on a line at 45° over our ship. One plane came down our starboard side and was the center of fire. We, too, opened up on it. This plane finally crashed just past our starboard bow, short of the BB New Mexico, while his partner had sneaked down our port side and opened up, strafing the ship with no opposition. A minute later he crashed just at the stack and bridge to envelope the ship in flames, killing 52 men and injuring 70 others on the New Mexico.

This attack was a daring move because they followed the regular fighter patrol in over the island and then detached themselves when the target was in view. They say Admiral Spruance was aboard. A horrible business. They could have hit just as easy as not. Lucky for us again that the BB was passing at that time.

Shrapnel fell heavily on the ship. My heart was hammering hard, frightened!

MAY 19 Go to Kerma Rhetta for ammunition and supplies, which crew promptly steals. We have two cases of fruit cocktail in bilges while forward engine room has two cases of milk and one case catsup. Also case of pineapple juice.

MAY 23 Underway for picket duty-35 miles north of Point Balo or 80 miles closer to Japan than the boys on Okinawa here. We may meet death. We may find out if we can take it. The water is 76°-too cold to live in long but beautiful sleeping weather. Of course it's only possible to sleep in the daytime.

MAY 25 General quarters 0100—planes coming in low—300 ft. away—very close. We open fire with every gun on ship. Of the five, four are shot down, 2 on their first run at us and two about 0230. They were close. When shot down they burned brightly, one a two engine bomber.

General quarters 0900—plane overhead above the clouds, which are hanging low. We opened fire and he comes plunging on fire through the clouds, releasing his bombs before he hit the sea. He never knew what hit him and radar catching when he could not even see the water—still he came down in flames.

The "Braine" No. 630 is with us. She gets credit for two. We get credit for four.

MAY 26 Heavy downpour with no visibility makes us secure against raids but it must be hell on the boys on the beach.

SUNDAY, MAY 27 A day of horror-unbelievable. The "Braine" just off to starboard is hit by two suicide planes. One on No. 2 gun, the other on the afterstack. One, flaming, comes at us only to miss by inches, going over the No. 5 gun.

We shot down two. We take the "Braine" under tow at 0930, death toll unknown.

Our ship has all compartments full of badly wounded men. Some have already died, others will soon go, under morphine shots—they look yellow and half dead already.

The injuries are beyond belief—eyes burned—both legs, both arms broken—burned all clothes off others beyond belief. The ship itself is almost a total wreck.

One Jap hit the water so close to us his body was thrown up on the forward torpedo tubes. The men found him, covered with rag dolls, charms, etc. He was immediately pitched into the water—sharks in schools tore him to pieces. They hang around us.

I feel sick and my mind is dazed. These Japanese men in planes *cannot be stopped by destroyer fire*. All flaming—one jet went on to hit the "Braine". We will take the men to the hospital ship.

By 1800 three men have died aboard, many others in a bad way. We proceed at 30 knots to the hospital ship in the southern anchorage. On arrival they will be transferred to landing barge then to the hospital.

At anchorage. Men going off. General quarters sounds—secured one hour later. They cut off one man's leg at the knee and one man lost both arms at the elbow. Used 28 units of blood plasma. The Doc Elder, Evans George, aid surgeon aided by deck hands and many others do great work. Several of the men boarded the "Braine" and moved the hoses to extinguish the fires.

MAY 28 General quarters several times-seven during the night. Planes.

At 0530 again as I go down portside, Jap plane burst into flames just off portside.

0930-firing just a few hundred yards away with our fighters close to the water because of rain and fog. The ship shot down 2 Japs almost at our bow.

MAY 29 We go up to Kerma Rhetta for repairs to radar damaged by Jap plane exploding as it passed by on plunge, also repairs to up-risers in aft boiler space. We will spend five days alongside the Hamul.

The No. 638 under tow by two tugs goes by. She is almost blown in two at gun No. 4. "Braine" killed 90 men. Many others injured for life.

The bay is full of ships with holes in sides, guns blown off, burned and broken. The Jap suicide plane is the greatest weapon ever devised by the enemy against our Navy.

The other side of this repair ship is No. 458 with only 75 men survivors, blown apart from fantail to bridge. All engineering spaces blown up, all hands killed. 29 damaged ships now in harbor.

MAY 30-31 General quarters—average every 6 hours.

We are to paint up six new Jap kills, making 17 in all. The Okinawa isle had 35 raids in 24 hours.

On "San Mateo" ship, hit by two suicide planes, 4 men were trapped two days in the number 4 magazine, the aft component being under water. Rescued when compartment was pumped out—okay.

Here is the PBY and PBM base—three floating drydocks with 3 DDs in them.

The time-ravaged rocks that surround us towering hundreds of feet in the sky are very beautiful. Clouds surmount their tops, the sides even terraced completely, the gardens being bright green with the natural surrounding browns.

We hear that we are to join the third fleet.

JUNE 4 Move from Kerma Rhetta—repairs completed to transport—anchorage on southern Okinawa.

We have had no General quarters for 48 hours. This evening a typhoon is reported heading this way. Resistance on Okinawa is about to break. Still the battleships and cruisers and DD's fire on island going into the third month.

JUNE 6 1620 General quarters—when Jap plane with 4 corsairs on his tail breaks through the clouds off our stern. He is already hit but seems to be trying to run away. We open fire and score hits, but credit goes to fighters who follow him into our A.A. fire. He splashes off to port but tries vainly to bail out just before plane hits.

New Chief Engineer officers come aboard (Lt. j.g. Lawrence Boyd goes ashore). The raids have me very nervous, more so as time goes by.

JUNE 8 General quarters 1830—without the fighters being aware of them, two Vals come in low on the water. We were almost caught asleep. Seen by the repair party, we opened fire, the planes parted one to stern, one to the bow. The bow plane is hit bad and veers off and is finished off by C.A.P. while the stern comes in, going just past the fantail. As we maneuvered the ship at high speeds—33 knots, he swings and arches back into the port side under intense fire and flaming he comes back! Men on deck jump overboard (5 of them) including the Ship's Dr. Elder off the bow. The plane tilts over on its side as it nears the bow, past the bridge, and just as it hit the ship it explodes.

A great sheet of flaming gas envelopes gun No. 1, but the Captain putting the ship hard to port drives our bow under to extinguish this blaze. Part of the engine is driven thru the hull into the chief's quarters where the force of it against the bulkhead causes the radio to fall, hitting a chief on the head. There were 3 of them hiding in the chief's quarters—all regular Navy. Another one jumped overboard.

Ship's damage light. The pilot's boot was found on deck. This makes two boots that now have fallen on the ship from Jap pilots, also his hand and glove. One man jumped from gun No. 1. Another was swept overboard on the fantail when he was knocked down by the five inch gun blast and our terrific turn put the fantail under water. We are credited with both planes down, a total of 19.

At 2100 we are again under attack from high altitude. We open fire. They return. We are at battle stations all night.

JUNE 9 Underway to Kerma Rhetta to fuel and arm at 1300, go to transport anchorage to anchor. To repair same. Especially boilers—they put them boilers on the line.

Two yellow jerks claiming battle fatigue get off ship. All hands are in a highly nervous state.

JUNE 15-1900-1930 A low flying torpedo plane was observed coming in—due to confusion brought about by fighter control officer on one of the other two 2200s, he said it was one of our torpedo bombers, but we opened with all our guns. He swerved away with some 200 yards off. And a minute later, a terrific explosion occurred between our three ships. He had dropped a torpedo, set to a time-limited run. The officer's stupidity could easily have cost hundreds of lives. The Jap was smoking as he disappeared.

They are well aware that our fighter cover goes in at 1900 o'clock. We reached 380 RPM in three minutes.

JUNE 19 Underway for Leyte after two days rest.

Several men aboard are being recommended for citations because of work done to men taken off the "Braine".

JUNE 20 Orders changed. Hi-jinks on sea plane tender No. 18, which puts us back on the picket line.

0300 I start the engines and we proceed with one other DD to relieve two ships at Rodger Peter Station No. 15.

Will death come to the ship? Many of the men feel we may not survive. My nerves are in the poorest shape to date in my lifetime. Morale is very low.

JUNE 22 Organized resistance ceased today on Okinawa—80 thousand Japs dead. Two Generals killed in last days including Simon Bolivar Buckner, General of the 10th Army. His place is taken by General Joe Stilwell.

JUNE 24 Arrive Hagushi Beach—Lay to until 1500 when with convoy at 15 knots we get underway for San Pablo Bay, Leyte Gulf, Leyte, Philippine Islands.

Seven thousand prisoners were taken on Okinawa—a record.

Thus ends the Okinawa operations. The most horrifying, deadly business the Navy has been in since the Guadalcanal period.

JUNE 29 Liberty on Samar Island at Asema Rereato area. Thousands of sailors and a two beer ration. Bought beads from natives. We have an area along the shore for miles, all in the process of building. Went to the show twice. Wet to the skin twice.

Typhoid booster shot for arm—in bad shape.

JULY 4 Still at Leyte Island. Passed up liberty today, the two beer ration spoils the idea. Ship being repainted, all machinery in top shape. Letter from home tells me Ray has his first job on a farm in Litchfield for the summer. Okinawa picket line claimed one in every three ships sunk or hit. Greatest ship-plane fight in history.

JULY 6 We take on six 50 caliber machine guns, two on the bridge, four forward of the quarter deck, the men on their own effort get guns and ammunition and mount same.

Liberty every other day—can buy all the beer you can drink for $1 a can. On the 7th we go out to fire all day on sleeves.

JULY 11 Still in San Pedro Bay alongside the Wadsworth. Walter, my brother, expects to go home in August. 1000 carrier planes hit Tokyo and 550 B29s hit Kyushu cities. Nerves back to normal state of jitters.

JULY 16 Arrive Buckner Bay, Okinawa, fuel from "Guam". Heat is terrific. 122 degrees in the engine room with super heaters lit off all the time. This condition allows us to go to flank speed. A few hours in and we get underway at 1800. Captain, for whom the crew are buying a $750.00 wrist watch will give us the details this evening.

Captain tells us we are to sweep down to Formosa, then to China coast about Foochow, then north to Shanghai in shallow mine-infested waters. This evening we are told a typhoon is coming down the China coast, so we will delay 49 hours.

JULY 19 Driven south of Okinawa by typhoon, being on the outer edge. Seas are colossal, waves 100 foot—40 degrees roll. Slightly ill. Close calls on going overboard by a few men.

JULY 22 SUNDAY Clear, hot day. At dawn we can dimly make out the outlying islands off the China coast. On the horizon could be seen the sail of a fairly large two-masted schooner fishing boat. It turned out to be with 14 men aboard. Our commander sent the Dailey 519 to investigate. She reported fishing craft.

The Vice Admiral Lowe on the "Guam" ordered all destroyers to open fire. As we steamed in closer, a fleet of these small craft were to be seen. Some moved by, only two or four Chinese fishermen. So the wanton murder began. I stood on deck in bewilderment when the 5 inch shells scored direct hits, blowing men and boats into the sky. We closed to 40 mms. range and the slaughter continued. Only a few boats escaped.

The Navy claims that these simple people gave the Japs information which lead to the heavy sinking of our submarines. Especially along the coast.

This string of washed-out islands runs along the coast, being from 10 to 50 miles off shore.

In the afternoon we steamed north toward Shanghai. The admiral had a change of heart and we did not destroy any more boats. We went alongside one. I looked down on the four fishermen, burned almost black by the sun. The boat was as old as Noah's Ark, built on lines as ancient as time, curved sharply both fore and aft with a brown rattan sail. Also in the stern, a sweep used manually to turn the craft. As we drew near they waved friendly greetings, holding up large silver fish.

We have a Chinese interpreter aboard who asked them if they had seen any Jap warships in the vicinity. Answered no.

One of the men continued to bait a long line with many hooks on it and kept throwing it overboard. Little did they realize that death hung like a cloud over them had they made the slightest unfriendly gesture—they would have been instantly riddled with fire. The crew as a whole felt badly about this business. Not all American. Other than fishing craft and a few mines, we sighted nothing.

Our squadron of DD's blew up four mines. One just missed our ship. So, finally, we get half way around the world and kill fishermen.

JULY 27 Steaming at high speed—20 knots, during the day. We, as leading ship of the force, narrowly miss a mine after passing it—we go back and sink it with the 40's.

At 0100 we have surface target, open fire as do other 3 DD's. Our commander sends the Dailey over to investigate the sinking target. It turns out to be a 50 foot motor launch filled with Korean men, women and children. Two are dead, others badly wounded. The "Dailey" captain picked up survivors—12 in all, against our commander's orders. They come back to Okinawa with us. They were killed without cause. We conclude sweep about 0400 and start back.

AUGUST 8 Arrive Buckner Bay. ATOMIC BOMB DROPPED ON JAPAN-two billion dollars-greatest discovery in recent times. 300,000 dead at Hiroshima.

AUGUST 10 Silence from Japan. Russians advance into Manchuria. Our new Captain Raymer is a martinet, turning the ship into a peace-time Navy routine. Utter nonsense.

At 2200 while in the machine shop with 5 other lads we heard that PEACE has come. Going topside we see all ships in the harbor firing their guns, using green and red tracers. Flares of all colors go off. All hands to topside and cheer. Many had a prayer of thanks to a Merciful God.

AUGUST 11 Three years in service today. Peace turns out only to be a

Jap note with provisions to keep Emperor. We reply that he can stay, but an allied commander is to be over him.

AUGUST 12 Sunday—Mass on the Hamul AD 20. The allies have agreed to Jap surrender and have sent note to them with promises about overall commander. They should reply by tomorrow.

AUGUST 13 Still on pins and needles—underway to sea to prevent a last minute attack. The Pennsylvania was torpedoed in the transport area last night. 25 dead. We went to General quarters.

AUGUST 15 PEACE-the long wait is over at about 0830 while securing the main engine in the forward engine room the Exec announced that President H.S. Truman had told the world that peace was here. General MacArthur is supreme allied commander over the Jap empire. All arms are to be laid down. Mass today at 1230 on the Hamul. On Feast Day of the Assumption of the Blessed Virgin Mary. We lite off at 0400 to get underway for sea.

AUGUST 16 Back into port to secure and turn to on polishing brass and steam hosing the machinery. The radio reports that a great celebration is in progress. We turn to and sweat it out over the engine room. Only fit for a dog.

POINT PROGRAM-½ point for each year of life, ½ point for each month in the service. I will have a year and a half to go. The reward for three years of combat. Pretty low in mind.

The Chief of Tokyo radio said, "We have lost at this time, but only temporarily." As long as I live I shall look with suspicion and distrust on the Japanese. Another commentator said, "The nation must build the mechanical equipment now in use by other powers." Hirohito told his nation only yesterday.

AUGUST 17 At sea this morning at 1207 we were missed being sunk by the larger cruiser "Guam" by 30 sec. The "Guam" when we changed course at midnight we found ourselves off course and at above mentioned time the staff found itself running parallel with the Guam as she approached our fantail. (I sitting on the 20 mm ammunition box aft of gun No. 5). She came in on us. I sat there as she flashed her red and green collision lights on. My mind became dupped. My feet would barely move. I staggered to gun No. 5, leaned on same and waited for death. Physically sick. She missed us by 30 seconds in time, or by a few feet. 40,000 tons at 20 knots.

The admiral sent a note to our inefficent captain—stating that such a performance again and he would be relieved of duty. The plane catapult actually swung over my head. Death missed us in peace as it had done in war. God is merciful.

AUGUST 20 On three hour liberty on Ise Cira Shema. Four beers. Hot as hell. Lads pick up live shells, hand grenades, dynamite. One boob

threw a 5 inch shell down a well and when it exploded he was looking down. A Marine band on the Anthony played some entertaining jazz.
SEPT. 2 V-J Day-the peace terms were signed aboard the Missouri in Tokyo Bay about 1030 this morning. We heard over the Okinawa radio WXLH speeches by Truman, MacArthur and Nimitz.

A great day for the unbeatable forces of free men. It is our last chance to sign the peace terms. Next time no one will have to sign them. Our spiritual development is 2,000 years behind our material advancement.

A heavy sea in the bay today causes all small boats to be cancelled so no one gets off to go to Mass. The harbor is full of warships. The New Jersey with Admiral Spruance aboard lies just inside the nets. We are at anchor between four aircraft carriers.

We have movies now on the fantail.

When will we go home?
SEPTEMBER 3 The lights came on again. This evening we did not have to darken the ship for the first time since March 28, 1942. A great sight for us in Buckner Bay. The 5 hospital ships are a blaze of lights like the river boats. All the warships have anchor lights fore and aft. The nearby carriers look like tenement houses. Light is a part of man's being. He is brighter, more cheerful in the presence of light. Peace is wonderful!
SEPTEMBER 4 Out to sea with 5 other DD's and 4 cruisers for A.A. practice and tactical maneuvers. What a sad joke this Navy is—no doubt this routine will go on for some time. Back in at 6 o'clock. Sea is moderating.
SEPTEMBER 8 At sea, the Captain tells us we are to cover a mine sweeping operation in the Nagasaki, Sasabo area of Kyushu.

We will pick up plane crash pilots from carriers, if any. Look for mines and cover the mine sweeps.

We are attached to Admiral Spruance's fleet, the fifth. He will bring up the fleet when we have cleared the path.

Today the "Birmingham" and the "Wadsworth" left to pick up allied prisoners held on the main island.

Every day, new stories of Jap savagery comes into the news. Several thousand Japs are now on the list as war criminals. Members of the "Houston" which disappeared, were found. All had been given up for dead.
SEPTEMBER 10 Still steaming—new point system gives me 43 ¾ points as of September 15. On October 15 I will have more than enough to go out.
SEPTEMBER 14 ENTER NAGASAKI HARBOR. Moor alongside the Dailey and Wadsworth. This harbor closed closely on both sides by high, steep emerald green mountains, is about 15 miles deep. We pass ruined plants of all descriptions. Finally arriving at the foot of the

demolished city. The harbor water is contaminated, so we cannot use it for any purpose. There are several other warships in here with us. We passed many sunken ships on the way in. The shipyard with three ways is completely burned out.

SEPTEMBER 19 The Wadsworth leaves here for Okinawa with 120 Japanese and Dutch POWs from Sumatra and Java. There are some cases who received brutal treatment. One man stood in a beheading line only to have them secure the line at 60 men. The carriers and cruisers continue to go out loaded with POWs.

SEPTEMBER 20 At 1230 took landing craft to landing at Nagasaki. We were given two cans of beer. All buildings in the vicinity completely bombed out. Picked up many Japanese writings and red pillow roll. Then the Marines came along in trucks and we climbed aboard several of them for a ride through such total destruction as has never been seen by man. The atomic bomb fell in an area devoted to industry.

All buildings not of steel construction were blown to bits. All buildings leveled to the gound and all construction is in pieces, stove coal size. The great steel-built factories are knocked into a mass of twisted steel. Everything melted into a mass. The lathes and milling machines stand in rows on the ground floor.

On one mountainside all of the trees are torn up by the roots and burned into charred logs. Everything on the side is dead. Some of the ruins have skeletons rotting away in them. Everywhere is the stench of death. All the wires are down so we often had to duck as we rode along.

The Jap police are still in charge and most cooperative. They wear black suits and rubber jungle shoes. The people seem dazed but are working. They possess a great deal of the spark of life. They are so tiny. They don't know what to make of the sailors or marines and will do anything to please.

I shall never forget the desolation in Nagasaki. The sad look of a woman pushing all her wordly possessions in a two-wheel cart. The three Japs neatly dressed walking single file with three boxes wrapped in white cloth containing all the remains of three dead.

OCTOBER 1 Go alongside Yosemite for five day overhaul. 14 men go off ship each day for a tour of Sasebo. This is another harbor full of ships with nothing to do. Watched a trainer plane take off from shore and zoom up at about a 90 degree angle and stall—fell into sea and sank. Both dizzy would-be pilots rescued.

OCTOBER 13 All plans cancelled but have sea bag fully packed. The typhoon killed 89 men on Okinawa, sank several mine sweepers, tore all tents down. That would be a hellhole for a naval base. The U.S.A. produced 277,000 planes from July, 1940-July 1945 or 186 billions of war equipment.

OCTOBER 15 Leave Anthony to go aboard DD 438 "Corbieser". We get underway with homebound pennant flying. My discharge station is Lido Beach, Long Island. Will stand watch in after engine room 412.
OCTOBER 24 The second Wednesday, we eat only sandwiches at three meals. Seas are typhoon high. This condition for the past 24 hours makes one very tired. No sleep. No chow.
OCTOBER 27 Arrive Pearl Harbor tomorrow-Sunday. It's been a rotten trip-poor chow and heavy seas.
NOVEMBER 5 MONDAY Arrive San Diego at 0500—while on watch go topside and see the horizon—a string of twinkling lights. It's a great feeling. My last day at sea-Two years, 10 months, 10 days.

At 0900 we leave ship at pier to board the busses. Red Cross gals give us bottle of milk and doughnuts—good. Then on to Camp Elliott—a huge receiving station. Fill out six forms and finally get our bags shipped by express at government expense. Then hand in orders at Building 96—fill out form and go to Building 36 for bunk. Stand in line for hours for chow—a hectic morning. The weather cool. The gals beautiful. We may leave Wednesday.
NOVEMBER 15 Discharged from United States Navy. On arrival home told of brother Robert's death. Age 19.
AFTERWORD BY JOSEPH MICHAEL McNAMARA taken from TIN CAN DUTY IN THE PACIFIC 1943-1945

I must take the time to say that my remarks about Harry Truman were to prove not true. Mr. Truman became one of our greatest presidents and again my harsh remarks about the six or so men who had mental breakdowns and had to be taken off the ship. We are not all cut from the same piece of cloth and I now realize that it was to be expected that constant fear must be harmful. Looking back, I now realize that I had begun to feel the tension, for the last six months I had slept on my blankets on the top deck. I no longer went below to my bunk. I propped the canvas movie screen against the bulkhead to ward off the nightly rains and no one bothered me. When I returned home, the blowing of an automobile horn startled me. So I rented a cabin on Round Lake, Maine, and spent a month walking through the deep Maine woods and sitting on the lakeshore listening to the call of the loon. To the thousands who did not come back I ask WHY????? For what????? Truly, where have all the flowers gone?????

# CASIMIR BIELIK

Casimir ("Casey") Bielik, of Wyandotte, Michigan, was 21 when inducted into the Navy. He had been working as a salesman at Sears, Roebuck Co. and after the war returned to that work, in the hardware department. His diary illustrates that even in the line or two of space allotted in a tiny pocket diary a diarist with powers of observation may keep a record which captures a personality and the pattern of days. The staccato style does not make easy reading but no other would have been possible if so much detail was to be fitted into the miniscule space allotted to each day. Bielik clearly had the true diarist's urge to record what he experienced during an extraordinary period in his life which took him so far from home. When his first little diary was filled up and a new year was beginning, Casey Bielik obtained another small diary book in Brazil, months and days all given in Portuguese, of course. He did not, however, continue his diary after the war. A fun-loving young man who kept his eyes open, Bielik's rank during the period of the diary went from Seaman, 1st Class, Coxswain to Boatswain 2nd Class in the U.S. Naval Armed Guard. Bielik is now the father of four and grandfather of three.

*******

AUGUST 25, 1942 U.S. Navy Armed Guard Center from gunnery training at Amphibian Base, Little Creek, Va. Assigned work detail in Bakery shop 0400 making hot buns.
AUG. 29, 1942 Waiting to be assigned to my first ship for the high seas.
AUG. 31 Brooklyn. In Armed Guard Receiving Station. Got detailed on SS Florida. Had short arm inspection. Packed our gear & got ready for morning to board ship.
SEPT. 1 Got on board the S.S. Florida, stayed in dry dock. Few days at Bayonne, Jersey, and till the 11th in South Brooklyn on 27th St. dock.
SEPT. 3 Docked in Bayonne, N.J., unloading gasoline. Had Liberty. Went out with girls. Took Alabama's girl away. Had fun. Alabama was sore and argued.
SEPT. 7 Liberty. Went to night club. Felt good. Met girls. Me and Butler took girls home early in morning. Came back to ship 0730 morning in time for breakfast. Had fun with girls and soldiers.
SEPT. 8 Had date with girl I met last night. So did Butler with his. She

waited for me at Journal Square. Came back late again, Butler and I.
SEPT. 11 Dry Dock-repairs. Liberty-Went to Jersey City Carnival-Butler, Alabama and me got popular. All knew us. Went to a Polish gin mill. Met some girls.
SEPT. 13 Anchored in harbor, New York. New Gun Crew came aboard. Just what we needed, more men. 18 men now and one stiff Ensign, Mr. Huffer.
SEPT. 14 Anchored in harbor, waiting for convoy.
SEPT. 15 Sailed in harbor for compass correction. Gun drill.
SEPT. 17 Sailed from New York harbor at 9099 with convoy. Day was nice. At 0830 had gun drill. Seen British come in Hudson Bay. Queen Elizabeth ship.
SEPT. 18 I got sea sick every time Steve did. We stood all night watch. Looking to see action stood by gun. Corvettes dropped depth charges. I got little sleep.
SEPT. 19 Feel better. Watch 2 on 4 off. Day clear. In evening submarine at stern reported. Double watch.
SEPT. 20 Doubled watch, two hours sleep. Stood watch in big squall & rain 3 on 3 off Sunday morning.
SEPT. 24 Passing along coast of Cuba, ½ mile off coast. Left few troop ships and tankers, went on our way. In evening sea got rough—seasick myself again. Bandaged Butler's sore knee.
SEPTEMBER 25 Early morning storm, rough sea. Few men caught sleeping on watch. Hell raised—by Ensign Huffer.
SEPT. 27, 1942 Feel fine-sea calm. At 1600 Land Ho. Aruba Island, place where we dock. In port to take load of aviation Ethyl, just as bad as nitro. Whew!!
SEPTEMBER 29 Had Liberty. Me & Alabama had fun, visited gin mills, got drunk, spent about 8 dollars. Very expensive. Went with Steve later part of evening. Blackout-couldn't find my bearings.
OCTOBER 1 Went to Army Base, got medical supplies. Eat supper & had beer there, 10 cents a can. Seen bloody fight—went to few gin mills and came back to ship.
OCTOBER 2 No Liberty—cleaned quarters. Slepped during day and read book. Got watch 2000 to 2400. Very hot day.
OCTOBER 3 Had Liberty-8 of us went swimming at American Colony. Water very salty but good swimming. Me and Steve buddies for swimming. Later Steve and I went to some gin mills. I got a little tight. Came back on watch. Day very hot.
OCTOBER 4 Liberty again, went swimming-same place. Came back to ship & had supper. Andrews & I went out again, walked around & went to Stars and Stripes Club. Seen Butler drunker than hell. Came back. Have watch 2000 to 2400.

OCTOBER 5 Still in Aruba. No Liberty. Read book & rested all day. Had watch 1600 to 2000.

OCTOBER 6 Left Port today-left Aruba at 0100 Arrived at Curacao at 1900. Beautiful site, especially at evening. Docked and waiting for convoy. Admire this place very much.

OCTOBER 7 Left Curacao 0630 morning (3 ships), nice day but hot. Met convoy about noon. 17 ships. Sea little rough. We argue about religion & we won. Had fight about 4 days ago. Butler stopped it.

OCTOBER 8 Sea little rough. Sun very hot. Me and Alabama sat at the bow and sang in the cool breeze with our bathing trunks on. At 1800 had gun drill for ½ hour. Got watch from 2000 to 2400. Really hate this watch business, rather sleep.

OCTOBER 9 This morning "Land Ho" Trinidad. Anchored about 1730 in Port of Spain. Beautiful scenery, especially the mountains as we passed thru the Dragon's Mouth. No watch tonight. Me & Butler fooled around with Alabama.

OCTOBER 10 Eating rationbars. Still anchored in Spain. We had exercise then a class for knots. We had boat drill & abandoned ship. I stood watch & then after supper we had a pillow fight—pretty easy day, no gun drill or cleaning. I washed & now I'm playing my mouth organ.

OCTOBER 11 Beautiful hot day. Sunday, read my Sunday Missal. Swimming alongside ship. Still anchored in Port of Spain. Had watch, no relief for supper, raised hell at Bablinkas. Very good fishing—Steve pulling up a fish pretty often, then he would throw them back in just for fun. Today I washed my undress whites, expecting Liberty.

OCTOBER 12 No Liberty. Busy Day. Still in Trinidad. Port of Spain. Learning semaphore signals. Took 20 mm. apart & put together. Read magazine. Had wrestling match with Alabama. Had jam session, me and Rasnake. Boys went swimming off ship. Water full of sharks.

OCTOBER 13 Still in Port of Spain. No Liberties yet, damn it!! Played checkers with Steward—lost. Had music at Focsle head. Watched Steve dance with Alabam (Polish).

OCTOBER 14 Still Port of Spain. Learned all parts of 20 mm. from stem to stern. Learning semaphore, I would get to J then get all screwed up. After supper bunch of us went swimming, water really salty and a very strong current. Few fellows would ride up & down in a small motor boat to scare off the sharks while we swam.

OCTOBER 15 Same old routine. Had a little fun. Butler, I & a few more guys told the coxswain off & I have an invitation to kick the ___ out of him when we get ashore and will be a pleasure.

OCTOBER 26 Exercise & semaphore. Field day. Blackwell did most of work, I didn't do any, pretty soft. Seen Spanish refugee ship come in, seen pretty girls aboard thru sight on 5" gun. Green bananas on the table for breakfast. Loaded more oil in forward hold.

OCTOBER 17 Same old routine. Had boat & fire drill, abandoned ship, rode in life boat. Me and Butler whittled a small sail boat. Few boys catching ringworm.

OCTOBER 18 In the morning went for a boat ride to another ship & found a buddy from "Boot" camp, Watson, his ship torpedoed 75 miles from Dragon's Mouth, seen another blown to bits. His ship has a big hole in her side, stbd. Afternoon went for a ride around the Spanish ship, music & waved to girls. Today my slight case of ringworm.

OCTOBER 19 Put medicine on my ringworm. Read a few stories. Butler gave me the hot foot while sleeping. Alabam & I had a wrestling match. Crew raised hell about the food.

OCTOBER 20 This morning brought Vice Admiral's car aboard-42 Ford. Loaded with fresh water. A big load of Navy mail, worked our____ off putting it away. To be taken to Brazil for the Navy. Gun Crew argued about States, Rebel & Yankees. We won, ha, ha. No ringworm today. We have big arguments very often about the Yanks & Rebels.

OCTOBER 21, 1942 Visited Winonia, Watson's ship. Seen Watson & the gang from Little Creek. Had a good shot of rum (Trinidad), some stuff. Had good workout rowing boat. In evening had watch. Locked Alabam in magazine hatch. What fun. Listened to music from Spic ship. Another man from gun crew got rid of his ringworm & Alabam caught it today. Kid Arujo caught 4½ foot barracuda.

OCTOBER 22 Raining all day (squall). I'm reading a book "Myths After Lincoln". Have watch tonight in rain. Playing Carver's guitar. Calling me "one piece Casey". Alabam locked me in a hatch.

OCTOBER 24 Watch from 0400 to 0800. What a relief, beginning to get Liberty. 3 other boys had Liberty today. Picked names from hat, only ones who rated!! Played catch with Barron. Washed clothes. Played pinochle. Very interesting game. Expecting to get Liberty tomorrow.

OCTOBER 25 Made fishing net and done fishing. No Liberty today. Played pinochle.

OCTOBER 26 No Liberty. Had watch this morning. Played pinochle. Rode to shore with our motor boat with the Chief Mate & Engineer. Nice ride, got wet from rough water. Came back to supper then played some cards. Seen a ship torpedoed anchored here in port. Engine shot off.

OCTOBER 27 Up at 0630. Exercise and cleaned up barracks, me & Alabam. No Liberty today. Brockschmidt & I painted ships bearings on gun turrets forward 20 mm., other boys scraped paint off 3". Busy all day. After supper played pinochle and wrote a few letters.

OCTOBER 28 Up at 0630. Exercise, breakfast. Painted stenciling on after 20 mm. gun turrets, me & Brocky. Barron sleeping on watch, bunch of us splashed a pail of water on him. Ensign caught him too.

OCTOBER 29 Up at 0630. No exercise. Raining this morning. Brockie and me stencil painting gun turrets 5" & 3". Seen survivors on PT Boat come in, must have been torpedoed because big convoy went out this morning.

OCTOBER 31 Port of Spain. Exercising this morning. Brocky & I painted beddings. Fire boat drill in squall. Had stiff talk by Mr. Huffer (Ensign) on Sub attack & bawled out some men in gun crew. Should pull out in the morning & headed for "Torpedo Junction". Will get some sleep tonight, get set for sea watch. Trip should be about 10 or 12 days.

NOVEMBER 1 "Anchors Away" at 0600. 12 ship convoy. Hot convoy. 2 cruisers fore & aft, 5 destroyers. Sea Calm. Had 4 hr. watch in morning and put gun ready for action.

NOVEMBER 2 At Sea (Atlantic) All Souls Day. Watch 0400 to 0800. 1200-1600 Submarine reported 50 miles off. Sent sea-plane off cruiser for it. Firing Key broke on 3", using a laniard now. Time for me to get some sleep, have dog watch tonight.

NOVEMBER 3 At Sea-regular watch. Couldn't sleep on account I drank so much coffee. Feel tired. Small squall, sleeped and watched in rain. Me and Archibault talked all night on watch. Quartermaster Jim raised hell about it.

NOVEMBER 4 At Sea-sea little rough-not sea sick anymore. I guess I'm getting over it. Cruisers practising today with guns. We had gun drill. Sun hot today. Archibault urinated in gun turret, he will scrub it tomorrow with brush. My eyes bloodshot from standing watch. Have another dog watch tonight. Bunch of us wrestled on foc'sle head—me, Alabam, Butler and Jersey.

NOVEMBER 5 At Sea-overslepped. Exercise. Sea calm, day nice & hot. Destroyers refueling alongside a tanker. Seen 3 lifeboats in sea with bunch men. Seen the Marblehead coming past us, seen boys fixing motor on plane. Had general quarters & cleaned gun.

NOVEMBER 6 At Sea. Fine day, feel fine. Cruisers & 1 destroyer left us this morning, passed "Torpedo Junction". Cavanaugh laid hand on Archibault, bunch of us sympathized with him. We don't blame Cavanaugh because he lost his temper, he's still O.K. General Quarters 3" Watch 2000-2400. Made coffee and drank on watch. Played harmonica on watch.

NOVEMBER 7 At Sea-Fine day & very hot. 2 ships left convoy. After watch took exercise & cleaned up quarters. Had fire and boat alarm. Cavanaugh really rushed out of quarters, thought was the real McCoy. Me & Archie played harmonica on Standby over the phones. Station RUM broadcasting from 3" gun turret. Should be crossing the equator sometime this fine cool morning. Now I'll go get some good old sleep.

NOVEMBER 8 At Sea. Wind Blowing. Ship taking sea over bow. Had anniciation today-first time crossing the equator. Jim (quartermaster) dressed as King Neptune. Soaped up and bathed, went thru pipe-line and patted on buttox and dipped into salt water in life boat. Some got all greased with black oil. All stripped naked and taking the works.
NOVEMBER 9 At sea. Fine day. Had good sleep this morning in 5" gun turret alongside Carver. Sea little rough, water coming on decks. Sun hot. Subs in vicinity. Had General Quarters.
NOVEMBER 10 At Sea. Fine day. Gave boys exercise this morning. Up this morning 0515 for general quarters. Ship on Port side had funeral for a man, threw man in the sea wrapped in canvas. Played harmonica today for the boys. Same watch. Sea little rough, sea coming over the side. Got wet standing watch at forecastle on Port side.
NOVEMBER 11 At Sea. Armistice Day. Eat seagull for dinner & supper. No exercise this morning. Feel fine. Regular watch. Destroyer came alongside, inquired about our cargo. Ironed my trousers. Didn't do very much today.
NOVEMBER 12 At Sea. Exciting day. Fired all guns 5",3", 20 mm. & automatic machine guns. Regular watch. Cleaned guns. Fixed Carver's hat up like Commandos. I originated the idea.
NOVEMBER 13 At Sea-Friday the 13th, the unlucky no. This morning general quarters 0900. Sub on our starboard side. Guns ready for action. Destroyer dropped depth charges about 1000 yds off our side, change course, all is well. Secured. Ration our water, supply is low. Going to Bahia, Sao Salvador. Ships there need our fuel. Before bed drank cocoa and played harmonica.
NOVEMBER 14 At Sea. Early this morning seen lights on horizon of Pernambuco, Recife, S.A. General quarters. Dangerous waters. 5 ships left in convoy, 2 cruisers, 2 destroyers, 2 subchasers. Good escort. Slepped this afternoon then went on watch.
NOVEMBER 15 At Sea. Sun hot today. Regular watch. Alabama won cigarettes in card game. At 1915 left convoy with another ship. Reached port at 2300 & dropped anchor. See the lights on shore of Bahia, Sao Salvador, South America. Standing sea watch, hell.
NOVEMBER 16 Port of Bahia. No Liberty. Cleaned up quarters & then stood watch 4 hrs. Read Bluejackets manual. Admiring the beautiful shore of Sao Salvador. Glad to be in Port. Will get Liberty soon.
NOVEMBER 17 No Liberty. Alongside another ship taking water in morning. I am *restricted* from Liberty for not being on General Quarters at sea one morning. Bablinkas, Arujo & Archie went to shore. Arujo got pet monkey for ½ pack of cigarettes. Liberty here is good. Women galore. Especially for American sailors.
NOVEMBER 18 Bahia. Other boys got Liberty, some of us didn't. No

Liberty for me. Alongside the Empress of London fueling here. Many British soldiers on it, threw packs of cigarettes at them. Traded natives fruits for cigarettes. Had lot of fun doing it. They're crazy about our cigarettes.

NOVEMBER 19 Bahia. No Liberty for me (restricted). Boys had Liberty & said it was fine. Stood gangway watch & talked with natives, tried to sell me pistol, 32 cal. & German lugger. 600 milroys, jewed him down to 400. Came to dock & scenery is fine.

NOVEMBER 20, 1942 Bahia. No Liberty. Stood watch at gangway and was learning Portuguese from a cop. Seen an octopus. A native killed it. Good food. In evening had drinking party with Sparks and Shorty. Got drunk. Alabam brought me some beer from liberty.

NOVEMBER 21 At Sea. Left port early this morning, headed for Pernambuco. Feel lousy today from the aftermath of last night. Stood sea watch, condition two. Vomited while sleeping on Forecastle. Never again, I hope.

NOVEMBER 22 At Sea. Sea little rough, wind blowing hard. Regular sea watch and general quarters. Played my harmonica during the day. Cleaned quarters, Alabam, Butler & me. Beautiful moon out tonight. Reached our destination but kept circling out at sea till daylight to anchor in port.

NOVEMBER 23 Port of Pernambuco, Brazil Part of day at sea, at 1500 came to docks. Day hot. Condition 3 Port watch. Have watch tonight 2000 to 2400. Cleaned 3" gun. Washed & ironed my clothes expecting liberty tomorrow.

NOVEMBER 24 Recife, Brazil. Small stores off U.S.S. Patoka. Liberty today. Had swell time. Women are fine. The beer is good. Went to interesting places. Got my haircut and a massage for 10 milroys. Back at 2400.

NOVEMBER 25 Recife, Brazil. No Liberty today. Shoved off today in late afternoon, headed for Belem. Left aviation gasoline in Recife. Have 10,000 barrels left to Para.

NOVEMBER 26 At Sea. Thanksgiving Day. Never expected to have thanksgiving out at sea. Had turkey dinner. Stood regular sea watch and general quarters. Seen lot of phosphorus at night on the bow.

NOVEMBER 28 At Sea. Exercise this morning & cleaned quarters. Regular sea watch & general quarters. Dropped anchor at 1900 at sea, must be at the mouth of the Amazon. Destroyer circling. Standing sea watch just the same.

NOVEMBER 29 Pulled anchor this morning and got a Pilot aboard, going up the Para River, branch of the Amazon. Cleaned out gear locker & washed my blues. Large River. Dropped anchor 2000 in

middle of river channel. Destination 90 miles up the river. Tomorrow port.
NOVEMBER 30 Belem. In port-docked. No Liberty today. Ensign went ashore and we raised hell by drinking rum and me & Rosnake playing guitar & harmonica. Had swell time. Aruajo jitterbugged.
DECEMBER 1 Belem, Para. In dock. Nice warm day. Liberty from 0800 to 2300. Went ashore with Dean, Laurence, Brock. Eat in Grand Hotel. Drank good beer. (Women) Ah! Went to many interesting places. Really had a good time of my life in Brazil.
DECEMBER 2, 1942 after the boys came from liberty, Belem, Para Trouble started with merchant crew over Brockschmidt bringing over a pair of shoes for one of the crew. "Red" the fireman cussed him (Ensign) for looking in *his* suitcase. Wanted to fight with him. Later the Ensign took Brockschmidt with him for shore. "Red" tried to stop him but the Ensign had his .45 on him and fired one shot. The ensign went to shore with Brockschmidt, will find out results tomorrow. *Very exciting night.*
DECEMBER 3 Pulled anchors, going to sea. Put "Reds" in irons & brig with force. Ensign gave me, Rosnake & Bohic orders to shoot any man that starts trouble. Put ship under martial law. Getting tough with them now. Big squall tonight. Exciting day. Bay inspection.
DECEMBER 4 At Sea. Nice day. Standing sea watch. Had seaman class. Joined convoy tonight, 14 ship convoy. "Red" still in the brig. General Quarters. New watch list made out. Started to bitch again. Even "Dean" has to stand watch.
DECEMBER 5 At Sea. Cleaned quarters & gear locker "Reds" still in brig. Headed for Trinidad. Bailey has venereal disease, will be left off at Trinidad for treatments. Had classes today. But I was catching butterflies.
DECEMBER 7 At Sea. Pearl Harbor day. Ship rocking like hell, making Brockschmidt sick. Took 45 all apart & had classes. "Red" still in brig.
DECEMBER 8 At Sea. Sea little rough. Ship rocking like hell. Didn't feel so good. Brockschmidt got sick. Year ago today we declared war on Axis. Cleaned 20 mm. with Steve then went on watch.
DECEMBER 9 At Sea. Sea rough, day cloudy. Learning the flag signals (international). Worried about having chancroid. "Land Ho" Trinidad. At 1930 passing thru the Dragon's Mouth. Sub sighted off starboard beam, 2 destroyers blasting with ash cans.
DECEMBER 10 Port of Spain-going to Venezuela. Anchored, till morning. Hauled anchor then up the River Caribina. Lng river but narrow surrounded with thick jungles. Seen native huts built from trees & straw or leaves. 1830 docked. Done some typing on Sparks' typewriter.
DECEMBER 11 River Carapito, Venezuela. In port. Up at 0630. Exer-

cise. 20 mm. classes. Wrote few letters on typewriter. Type two for Aruajo, one to his girl. Had watch today. No Liberty in this port. Loading on naphtha.

DECEMBER 12 Venezuela. All loaded. Leaving port this morning. Looked at scenery from bow with Aruajo while going up river to Trinidad. Watch 2000-2400.

DEEMBER 13 Port of Spain, Trinidad. Exercise. Had exam in 20 mm. (passed). Came to Trinidad sometime during the night and anchored. Me & Steve learning the international flag signal.

DECEMBER 14 Port of Spain, Trinidad. Quartermaster learned me how to make lace. Liberty. Drew 40 bucks, went to N.A.S., talked to sailors & soldiers. Went out drinking with Aruajo, Alabam & Andrews. Left Bailey ashore in hospital.

DECEMBER 15 Port of Spain, Trinidad. Took "Red" from Brig & took him ashore. Finished my square knot lace. Aruajo & Alabam went ashore for small stores. I got a rain coat. Had brig watch this morning 0800-1200.

DECEMBER 16 Port of Spain, Trinidad. No exercise. Cleaned quarters. Officers came aboard. Carver & Andrews had fight. Hoisting anchor, going out to sea to Aruba at 1400. General quarters. 21 ship convoy.

DECEMBER 17 At sea-fine day, sea calm. Washed my whites for Liberty at Aruba. Mr. Huffer informed Alabam that he's getting more like a sea lawyer. Clothes inspection. Knot class but fooled around. Butler blowing about his best girl friend.

DECEMBER 18 At Sea. Very hot today, took sun bath. Sea rough—coming over our decks. I got all wet by one splash. Cleaned guns today. Fooled around on general quarters-got hell. Left convoy at 1500, all alone—docked in Aruba, Curacao at 2000. Port watch.

DECEMBER 19 Aruba, Curacao—LIBERTY-what a day! Me, Butler & Andrews with 3 soldiers got drunk, raised hell & got into a fight. My arm bruised & so is Andrews'. Really had a swell time. Even played the piano (Elmer's Tune).

DECEMBER 20 Aruba. Sunday morning, up at 0745. My head really hurts after last night's PX. Rested all day today. Feel good in evening. Liberty tomorrow. Alabam went on shore patrol duty.

DECEMBER 21 Aruba. Exercise. Stood 8 hours watch. Done some typing for Mr. Huffer. Navy forms. Then LIBERTY. PX Me, Steve & Andrews. Had swell time. Even went to the *beach*.

DECEMBER 22 Aruba. No Liberty today. Had gangway watch. Fixed up my lockers, which was a mess. Clothes inspection. Bunch of us practised making knots. Next Liberty on Xmas day.

DECEMBER 23 Aruba. Up at 0630. Exercise. Stood watch & showed

Brock, Ash & Rosnake how 20 mm. works to cock it. Took exam on Seaman test. Power boats & pulling boats. Spliced a rope for some men on the dock.

DECEMBER 24 Aruba. Xmas Eve. Exercise. No Liberty. Learning knots & splices. Had watch. At 2300 left the docks, out to sea. General Quarters. "Some Xmas Eve!!" Sang Xmas carols at the bow before we left, some felt homesick at this moment.

DECEMBER 25 At Sea. *Christmas Day*. Warm day, sea rough. Had Xmas dinner & supper with nuts & candies. Regular routine. General Quarters. "Hell of a Christmas for us". Six ship convoy.

DECEMBER 26 At Sea. General Quarters this morning stood till 0810 on account Bab didn't tell us we were secured. The Ensign restricted Bab & Archie for gabbing over the phones & talking on watch, really raised hell. Cool day, sea coming over the bow.

DECEMBER 27 Land sighted at starboard bow. Trinidad. British destroyers outside Dragon's Mouth, 4 of them. Place where we sank 3 subs last trip. Dropped anchor at 1500 in Port of Spain, Trinidad.

DECEMBER 28 Port of Spain. I was barber to Butler & Cavanaugh. I cut their hair—not a bad job either. I read a good book most of the day, "The American Tragedy". Washed my clothes. Aired out our bedding.

DECEMBER 29 Trinidad. Hot day, no liberty. Admiral's barge came alongside-a beauty. We will take it to Pernambuco. Officers aboard & some Navy personnel. Took Navy cargo to be taken for U.S.S. Milwaukee & U.S.S. Cincinnati. Had dog watch & watched army aerial gunnery.

DECEMBER 30 Port of Spain. Hot day. No Liberty. Had good night's sleep, no watch till morning at 0800. Aruajo caught sleeping on watch by Mr. Huffer. Put in brig this morning on bread & water for 3 days. I have Brig watch from 0000 to 1600, dog watch.

DECEMBER 31 Port of Spain. Exercise. Cleaned 3" gun. Grounded some meat for steward. Steve caught 32 lb. barracuda. He sure got a kick out of it, catching his first big fish.

## 1943

JANUARY 1, 1943 Port of Spain. Mr. French came aboard, our old gun crew officer, was glad to see him. Liberty-Alabam, Carver, Dean & me. I had a picture taken. Went to show. Met 3 Greek sailors, torpedoed 3 times.

JANUARY 2 Port of Spain. Up at 0630. Exercise. Had S 1/C class. Stood watch. Took on Navy supplies & airplane flap to be taken to Brazil. No watch tonight. Aruajo got out of the brig 0800.

JANUARY 4 Port of Spain. After breakfast went to shore to draw small stores but at 1130 found out ships sail soon. Got Navy launch & rode back to ship in squall. Got wet from rain & sea. Weighed anchor at 1500. 9 ship convoy.

JANUARY 5 At Sea. Rain-regular sea watch. Ship taking sea in turret. Brocky is sick. I cleaned 3 .45 pistols which got wet in turret. I wore all three pistols, looked like a commando.

JANUARY 6 At Sea. Day cool. Regular sea watch. Most of day I rested. Brocky is awful sick. Had gun drill at G.Q. Sea rough. Fooled around with my buddies. Have dog watch tonight.

JANUARY 7 At Sea. Day warm. Rain. Cleaned quarters. Stood watch in rain. G.Q. talked all the time & telling stories. 3 ships left our convoy to B. Guiana. Later they were torpedoed (all).

JANUARY 9 At Sea. Rain-sea rough. Subs ahead. Condition 2 at 2000. The fighting 463. What a gun crew, always quarreling. Have dog watch tonight, Cond. 2.

JAN 11 At Sea-No rain. What a relief. Cleaned quarters. Sea rough. Should cross equator in morning. Alabam & Butler wrestled. Cleaned our tools. General Quarters 1800.

JAN 12 At Sea. No rain. Sea calm. Subs ahead. Cond. 2 at 2000. Brocky & Lawrence had quarrel, will have fight ashore. Have dog watch tonight, me & Alabam.

JANUARY 13 At Sea-sea calm. Sub packs in vicinity. Cond 2 & slept in gun turret ready for any attack. Tested everything for emergency. Waters are hot around here. 3 ships sunk at Guiana & one straggler from Trinidad.

JANUARY 14 At Sea. Sea calm. Cond 2 & whole bunch in gun turret. Me & Alabam & Butler wrestled in turret on G.Q. Got hell for it, might get restricted in next port.

JANUARY 15 At Sea & calm. Butler and Alabam had fight in gun turret. Alabam was looking for pliers to hit him with.

JANUARY 16 SUNDAY Recife, Brazil. In port in morning. Liberty afternoon after cleanup of ship. Me, Alabam, Butler, Brocky & Barron fooled around ashore. Butler & I got feeling good. Visited many places (Girls).

MONDAY, JANUARY 17 Recife, Brazil. In port. Day hot. Washed clothes. No Liberty today. Stood watch. Unloaded supplies for Navy ships. U.S.S. Patoka. Some of us played baseball.

THURSDAY, JANUARY 18 Recife, Brazil. In port. Day hot. Liberty again. Me, Steve, & Alabam went together, had our pictures taken. Went to a dance ballroom, met Sparks there with his girl Betty. Had fun. Later met rest of gang, more fun with girls.

WEDNESDAY, JANUARY 19 Recife, Brazil. In port. Up at 0630. Exercise. Stood watch. Walked around the docks & talked to other sailors of different ships. No Liberty today. Went to a movie aboard No. 396

destroyer. HONKY TONK-Clark Gable & Lana Turner. Swell picture—
THURSDAY, JANUARY 20 Recife, Brazil. In port. Up at 0630. No exercise, only a little semaphore. Yesterday I went to shore in morning to get haircut, came back at 1200. Had a ball game, lot of fun. Played my new harmonica.
FRIDAY, JANUARY 21 Recif. Day hot. Pulling in mooring lines getting ready to shove off. Pulling anchor at 1600 and got fowled with another anchor which was on the bottom. At 1830 on our way to Rio de Janeiro. General Quarters & Condition 2. Going all alone & zigzagging.
JANUARY 22 At Sea. Sea very calm. Took sun bath in gun turret. Didn't do much today only cleaned quarters & rested when off watch. Cond 2 4 on 4 off. Played my new harmonica on watch.
JANUARY 24 At Sea. Sea calm, day hot. At 0900 had G.Q. for Spanish ship on our starboard bow. Zigzagging our course at night. Played harmonica on watch. Had fun today giving Alabam a bath with all kinds of solutions. He spilled ink all over me while taking bath. Land sighted on the stbd side 1200.
JANUARY 25 Rio de Janeiro. Came in about noon. Beautiful sites. Three Brazilian destroyers greeted us. Had Liberty at 1600. Had fun at Cabaret, dancing with beautiful girls. Stayed ashore all night, met Ensign Huffer. Back 0700.
JANUARY 26 Rio de Janeiro. Other boys went on Liberty. I sleeped all day and went on watch at 1600 to 2000. Will go ashore tomorrow. Yesterday met another sailor from River Rouge, Mich.
JANUARY 27 Rio de Janeiro. Liberty from 0800 to 1600 but me, Steve, Aruajo & Andrews stayed over leave. I stayed till 2330 came back, the rest stayed. Had fun dancing, sightseeing. Bought souvenirs. Boys didn't come back yet. I have watch 0400-0800.
JANUARY 28 Rio de Janeiro. Boys came back from Liberty (over leave). Ensign said they will get court-martial. Held up ship. Weighed anchor at 1230 on our way to sea again. I got restricted from 2 ports for coming late from Liberty. Cond. 3 sea watch. 4 on 8 off.
JANUARY 29 At Sea. Exercise this morning. Ensign read everyone's record, individually. I have 2 offenses, which he will forget about if I behave. Some have it bad, especially three. Done lot of washing today. Our destination north.
JANUARY 30 At Sea. Sea calm. Stood watch. Pressed my clothes. Had signal classes. General Quarters—passing sail boats. Condition 2 at 2000 slepped in rain in gun turret.
JANUARY 31 Bahia, Brazil. Reached port this morning, dropped anchor at 0845. I was awful sleepy this morning on watch, didn't have much sleep. I slepped in aft quarters for a few hours. Practiced semaphore with Carver & sent messages. Took shower and went to bed. The

month of January was an exciting one. Early part of January we lost some ships coming from Trinidad to Brazil. We were pretty lucky not to get torpedoed. While anchored in Bahia today we are the only tanker here. The rest are freighters. Waiting for convoy here in Bahia.

FEBRUARY 1 Bahia, Brazil. Up at 0630. Exercise. Cleaned 3" gun with Alabam. Took a nap in hospital but was woken by fire & boat drill. Practiced semaphore with Deane & Carver.

FEBRUARY 2 Bahia Weighing anchor at 0700. Pulling out with convoy. 20 ships. We are the only tanker in the convoy. Have sea watch Cond. 3. Fine day and sea calm. Have 0400 to 0800 watch, the best watch at sea or in port.

FEBRUARY 3 At Sea. Sun hot in afternoon. Practiced semaphore & flags. Had S 1/c classes. Condition 3. Had exercise this morning at 0700. Going along swell. Had plenty of rest.

FEBRUARY 4 At Sea. Sea calm. Exercise. Day hot, 125°. At 1600 4 ships joined our convoy coming from Recife, Brazil. Practiced semaphore with Butler & Dean on flying bridges. General Quarters.

FEBRUARY 5 At Sea. Day hot. Exercise 0700. Painted the gun with red lead. Passed my flag test & practiced semaphore with Butler. In evening listened to Rasnake play guitar & bunch of us threw the bull.

FEBRUARY 6 At Sea—Sea calm day hot. Painted forward gun turret all day. Coffeetime at 1000 & 1400. We have them every day.

FEBRUARY 7 At Sea. While on standby this morning I painted the forward gun. Had personal inspection today. Slepped in the afternoon. Have dog watch tonight.

FEBRUARY 8 At Sea. Shine the brass on the gun. Shicklegroober around today, depth charges thrown all around at 1200 & in evening at 2000 on port bow. Torpedo Junction. Cross Equator.

FEBRUARY 9 At Sea. Stenciled clothing this morning. Brocky read a good story to us before G.Q. Visibility zero tonight, very cloudy. All is well.

FEBRUARY 10 At Sea. Sea rough. Rain-storm. Visibility poor. Refused to take classes, me & Alabam, had to clean quarters for punishment. Have bad cold, feel lousy. Bablinkas got sick, vomited, too. Rain all day.

FEBRUARY 12 At Sea. Sea calm, day hot. Took nice sun bath. Seaman classes this morning. Aft crew got hell for making noise during G.Q., they blamed Alabam for it. Dogged the watches tonight. Condition 3. Part of convoy separated today.

FEBRUARY 13 At Sea. Sea calm. Took test in Seaman 1/c. Coming near Trinidad. All is well. Signal lights flashing all night.

FEBRUARY 14 Trinidad, B.W.I., Port of Spain. Came thru Dragon's Mouth at 1215. At 0130 dropped anchor. Me & Cavanaugh reading slide rule. Day hot. Archambault has the itch. Will disinfect our quarters tomorrow.

FEBRUARY 15 Port of Spain. Day nice. Happiest day of my life. We received our Xmas gifts today but I didn't get no mail, but enjoyed the Xmas gift from home. We missed 3 bags of our mail. We painted quarters & general cleanup. Aired out mattresses. Busy all day.

FEBRUARY 16 Port of Spain, BWI. Up at 0700. Exercise—only had 2 hours sleep. Painted in forward turret. Cleaned & disinfected our quarters. Me & Archie & Aruajo played harmonica, the trio. Had nap in afternoon.

FEBRUARY 17 Port of Spain. Exercise. Boys went ashore on Liberty. I am restricted in this port for being over leave in Rio with Steve, Joe & Andrews.

FEBRUARY 18 Port of Spain. Up at 0700. Exercise. Painted relative bearing in forward turret. Painted top side in quarters. Brockschmidt hoisted ensign upside down. But was right because ship in distress call for shore. Wanted slop chest opened up.

FEBRUARY 19 Port of Spain. Few boys got Liberty. Stood watch today 1200 to 1600. Played harmonica for the crew on the fantail.

FEBRUARY 20 Port of Spain. Learned parts of large guns. Took seaman's test today.

FEBRUARY 21 Up at 0700. No exercise. Took boat & rowed over to Ticonderoga ship, visited some boys. Aruajo met one of his pals. They were at Gibraltar and South Africa. Played poker in evening, me & Lawrence won 7 bucks. Had watch 2000-2400.

FEBRUARY 22 Still in Port of Spain, Trinidad. Learned parts of 3" guns. Played poker, lost about a buck. Went to bed about 2100 & up for dog watch.

FEBRUARY 23 "Anchors Away" at 0600. Cond. 2 at 0800. Passing Dragon's Mouth. 18 ship convoy. Stood sea watch and bridge watch. On Cond. 3.

FEBRUARY 24 At Sea. Sun hot. Mr. Huffer gave S 1/c class today. Will be finished by Monday. Passing an island on the starboard side in the afternoon. Dean sent semaphore to other ship. Signalman from Detroit. Regular sea watch Cond. 3 & General Q.

FEBRUARY 26 Aruba, Curacao. Up at 0630. Exercise at 0700. Cleaned and swabbed quarters. Layed bag out for bag inspection. OK. Had classes & took tests. Some boys had Liberty, not me, restricted. Had port watch 1600 to 2000.

FEBRUARY 27 In Port of Aruba D.W.I. Up at 0330 for watch. Had classes this morning & afternoon. One more assign. to go. Took tests. Washed my sea bag & put my clothes away. Putting winter clothing on top for the States.

FEBRUARY 28 Aruba. Had watch from 0400 to 0800. Cleaned up the quarters this morning. Had classes and took tests. In the afternoon some of us went to sea shore and played ball then went in for a swim. Very rocky shore. Me and Steve walked along the shore picking up shells. Had another watch at 1600. Pressed my blues & getting ready to go back to the good ole U.S.A. The month of February was a month of restriction for me and three of my pals. Restricted at Rio de Janeiro. Today 2 Spanish ships came in and one Portuguese tanker (many tankers).

MARCH 1 Aruba. Up at 0630. Exercise. Review of Seaman's tests & took final test and passed. Whole bunch went ashore & played ball on seashore. I'm off restricted list today.

MARCH 2 Up at 0630. Exercise. Left Aruba at 1100-4 ships. General Q. & Condition 2 till we reached convoy at 1600. Cond. 3 Convoy of about 35 ships headed North. Home, I hope.

MARCH 6 In the Caribbean Sea. Sea little rough. Changed watches today. Me & Butler cleaned 20 mm. today. Stuck salt water hose on Alabam thru port hole while taking shower. Me & Butler. Cleaned 30 cal. machine gun. Played around with it. Have dog watch.

MARCH 7 At Sea. Sea calm, day hot. Had interview with Mr. Huffer today concerning our voyage. Took sun bath in 3" turret.

MARCH 8 At Sea. Sea little rough. Rain & wind, cold today. Nearly froze on watch in the rain.

MARCH 9 At Sea. Sea rough, winter gale. No watch in fwd turret. Stand 2 hrs. watch on flying bridge. Some guys sea sick. Sea came thru porthole & got my bunk all wet. Really getting rough & taking sea. No general quarters.

MARCH 10 At Sea. Sea rough, winter wind blowing. No. G.Q. in morning, stood my watch. Had general quarters at evening, got cold spray when ship took sea at bow. Brocky got sick. Have watch tonight.

March 11 At Sea-Wind cold, sea getting more calm. Cleaned 3" gun from salt water & 8 shells were corroded from salt water. Stood 4 hr. watch. Nearly froze on watch. Had General Quarters. Training gear was frozen.

MARCH 12 At Sea-Sea calm. Day cold. After coming from South A. it feels like North Pole here, so cold. Regular watch. Seen 4 whales and a school of porpoises playing at the bow. Will be in Port tomorrow. Good ole N.Y.

MARCH 13 At Sea in morning. In afternoon coming thru New York channel. Good ole New York after 6½ months. Snow today. Stood watch in rain & snow. At evening dropped anchor. Waiting for our leave now.

MARCH 15 Received our leave to go home—Happy Happy-Back to the trains.
APRIL 26 Got aboard a new ship, SS San Antonio, 28 men in our crew. Mr. Wellman, our Lieut. (j.g.) in charge. Got aboard at Chester, Pennsylvania.

*Hereafter the diary becomes very sporadic*

1944 Left Lagos, Nigeria on the 4th of March 1944 and headed West with a convoy of 11 ships and 8 escorts (British). 5 gunners are down with malaria which they caught in Nigeria.

On October 14, 1944 about 1830 had a collision in our convoy, a freighter and a tanker. Tanker was carrying 100 octane gasoline which blew sky high. About 70 lives were lost and only about 8 were saved. The freighter also caught fire but was put out because only deck cargo was afire from the squirting flames from the tanker. 3 destroyers went to the aid of the tanker to pick up the survivors. An hour later the ship was still visible, red as a red hot rivet on the horizon. This happened about 4 days from Gibraltar.

NAPLES, ITALY I had liberty for 2 hours, going for mail and done a little hunting for souvenirs. We left the dock Sunday noon and anchored out in the harbor for further orders. November 3, 1944 Friday, got orders to go 10 miles up the coast and anchor. We anchored and waiting again with 17 other ships. Tuesday, November 7, 1944 in the morning we left for Leghorn, Italy. We loaded with tanks and tents for the Army, 30 miles from the front at Leghorn. Arrived at Livorno (Leghorn) Thursday, November 9, 1944 and to discharge our cargo. Livorno is all bombed and shelled, whole city is ruined. Wednesday we'll go and see the city of Pisa, the leaning tower. We borrowed a truck from Navy port office and I drove ½ the crew down to Pisa, Italy. On November 22, 1944 we left Livorno, Italy, and our way back to Naples. Loaded with 1000 American troops and left Naples Saturday 25 November. Convoy of 6 ships loaded with troops. Arrived at Leghorn, Italy, Monday, Nov. 27, 1944 and leaving of troops. Met soldier from Dearborn by name of Frank Troddel. Left Leghorn next morning the 28th. Arrived Naples, Italy on the 30th of November, got orders to go on to Oran, North Africa, the same day. Arrived at Oran on the 3rd of December. Got orders to join convoy headed for the states so at 1030 we weighed anchor and joined convoy of 129 ships. Arrived at Norfok, Va. on the 21st of December at 0800.

*With which entry the diary comes to a permanent halt.*

# JAMES J. FAHEY

The first diary of an ordinary World War II service man to find its way into print was probably that of James J. Fahey, then working as a sanitation man in Waltham, Mass. Under the title PACIFIC WAR DIARY it was brought out in 1963 by Houghton Mifflin Co. and was later issued as a paperback by Avon. Its wealth of detail about what it was like to serve as Seaman, First Class, on a ship such as the U.S.S. Montpelier during sea warfare instantly won acclaim for the book.

There had been some attempts on the part of the Pentagon to suppress publication of the diary because the writing of it represented a flouting of the rules against diary-keeping in service, though these rules were often unknown to service men. Cooler and/or more highly placed heads eventually prevailed and the book was issued with the blessing of admirals with a feeling for history. The war, after all, was already 18 years in the past, many top officers had by then published memoirs, of far greater potential usefulness to the enemy than the diary of a sailor not privy to strategy, and the merits of the book as a historical record of the look, sound, temperature, and feel of naval warfare were undeniable.

Despite the wide circulation the book has already had, I felt it would be unfair to such a prime example of the documentation of the ordinary fighting man's lot not to include at least a few excerpts in this collection.

Gratitude must be expressed to Mr. Fahey and to his publisher, Houghton Mifflin, for permission to include here these few pages from a remarkable book.

*******

JANUARY 29, 1943

It rained last night. I slept topside, it was too hot below I used my hat for a pillow, put it on top of my shoes, we kept the rest of our clothes on. The steel deck is very hard. My sleep was interrupted by rain at 3 a.m. I changed my wet clothing and then it was almost time to go on watch. It is too hot to sleep below in the compartments so the men sleep topside under the stars. The ship is covered with sailors all sprawled out. In the darkness you will trip over someone who is sound asleep if you do not watch your step. When the rain comes there is a big scramble to get under cover. The rain will not last long so they can go back to their spot again and continue their sleep. Some nights your sleep is interrupted several times and you hope that the next night you can get a night's rest but something always comes up to prevent you from getting that sleep. We had field day today, everything was cleaned up and put in order. We will be ready for action in case we should run into the Japs. We are only twenty-five minutes from Jap air bases and we are getting closer to them every mile we travel. Today is Friday, Fish Day.

SUNDAY, FEBRUARY 21, 1943

Not much to say for Fr. and Sat. We came across some of our pilots who crashed into the water. We don't know how long they had been drifting on the raft. It was a good thing we came across them because they could have been picked up by Jap subs or maybe land on one of the Jap-held islands in the Solomons. If that happened it meant certain death and the Japs like to cut your head off with a sword. The waters are also full of sharks.

Saturday night while I was on the eight to midnight watch we sighted the Solomons. We were going to stop at Tulagi, it is across from Guadalcanal. As we approached the island we were told to be on the lookout for a blinking light. It should be easy to spot because it is a very dark night. This would be our signal telling us that it was safe to enter one of the harbors. The hours passed and about 4:15 the next morning, while all hands were at battle stations, the blinking light was spotted, our mount was the first one to see it, it was reported to the bridge at once. Now all hands could relax, some Jap subs are in these waters and you never know when you will come across one.

The weather is like a hot summer's night at home, it was very still and quiet. The air had a nice odor, it must have been the flowers in the jungle. We are not too far from where the five Sullivan brothers lost their lives when their warship was sunk by Jap warships. There are still plenty of Japs hiding in the jungles here. About 4:30 the earphones on our mount broke down, so I had to take them down to the repair shop. When I entered the shop the men were asleep, I felt foolish asking someone to repair a set of phones at 4:30 in the morning but it had to be done because we never knew when the Japs might attack us, we are also in the Japs' back yard. I returned in fifteen minutes to pick up the phones.

When the sun came up we got a good look at Tulagi because we were very close to land. You could see where the Marines and Japs had fought some bloody battles.

The trees were blown to bits and huge holes from bombs and shells were all about. The hills had a lot of caves, some were sealed with dead Japs inside who would not come out to surrender. The jungle here is very thick and you can hear the monkeys squeaking and the crocodiles are not very far away. We will be in for a hot day in the Solomons because it is very warm early in the morning. This is a pretty good size harbor. We are ready to get under way in ten minutes because you never know when the Jap planes from their base just up the line will attack. We would be sitting ducks for their planes in here. In time this will be our regular base. This will be the pushing-off place for the coming invasion against the Japs in the Solomons.

Capt. Wood was in for a big surprise while we were here at Tulagi. A PT boat came alongside and who should come aboard but Capt. Wood's son. He is in command of his PT. They had a great reunion, it was a very happy day for both of them. Some other PT boats also came alongside during the day and we gave them candy, cigarettes, ice cream, etc.

The PT boats had Jap flags painted on them. The PT boats carry 4 torpedoes and some machine guns. There is no privacy, when it comes to the toilet it is just a toilet seat at the rear of the boat. It reaches out over the water. One of the crew from the PT boat told us that they picked up 5 nurses at Guadalcanal who had escaped from the Japs. Some of them were almost insane after what they had been through while being held by the Japs. He said the Japs also raped the nuns and then killed them, some had their heads cut off.

Some of the Jap prisoners are fellows who went to our colleges in California before going back to Japan. This is the hottest place we have hit so far, you could fry eggs on the steel deck, there is no air in here, the Dr. and some of the crew threw a line over the side of the ship and got themselves some fish. You can catch them on an empty hook.

WEDNESDAY, JUNE 30, 1943

We are still at sea. I got up at 3:15 A.M. this morning for the 4 to 8 watch. About 5:15 this morning we could see land, it was the Solomons. The rest of the ships had left us. We made our way to Tulagi with the rest of Task Force 39. It is a very hot day.

While we were in Tulagi, a working party brought up a lot of food in cans from the hangar deck. We will eat this food at battle stations, the mess hall will not be used. It is up to the cooks to get this food ready. We will eat sandwiches during our many hours at battle stations. The fellows usually take clean clothing and soap with them also. Our gun mounts will be our home for some time. I got a few apples from Floyd when he was taking them up from the icebox. I took a shower this A.M. Smith and Floyd borrowed $1.00 each from me and Blankship borrowed .50 this left me with the big sum of $2.25. Money is no good out here because there is no place to go or anything to spend it on. The only thing you see out here is jungle, and water. I saw our latest fighter plane, it is put out by Grumman. Late this afternoon everything was in readiness and at 6:30 P.M. Tulagi was behind us as we made our way up the

Solomons. We are all by ourselves now, good old Task Force 39, Cruiser Division 12. They should call us Merrill's Lone Wolves because we operate as a small task force, without carriers, battleships or even heavy cruisers. We are always snooping in the Japs' back yard. We could not afford to send carriers or battleships up the Solomons because they would be easy targets for the land-based planes, and also subs that would be hiding near the jungle. We don't mind losing light cruisers and destroyers but the larger ships would not be worth the gamble, when we can do the job anyway. The Solomons are over five hundred-miles long and most of the islands are Jap-held fortresses. We call this going up the slot. It is like going up an alley at night in the tough sections of any big city. You have to be on your guard at all times. You never know when a Jap sub will be up ahead of you dead in the water, just waiting to spring the trap. It is also a good hiding place for PT boats and warships. The Japs also have many airfields on these islands.

We did not eat supper in the mess hall tonight because we could not take the chance. We had 1 ham sandwich, 1 cookie, and 1 apple for supper at our battle stations. One of our pilots went to his battle station with a machine gun, he was very close to our mount, which is one of the highest places on the ship. If Jap planes attacked us, he wanted to get a shot at them. Capt-Tobin spoke to the crew at 7 p.m. said we would bombard the Shortlands at 1:58 tomorrow morning.

The Japs have barracks there, a radar station, big fuel dumps, and plenty of troops plus ammunition dumps. We expect to run into big 6 inch shore guns.

Our bombardment will take place in darkness as usual right in the Japs' backyard.

It will be a bad place to get hit because if you land in the water the sharks will get you, and if you land on one of the islands the Japs will get you, and of course that means torture and death.

JULY 1, 1943

The hours passed and we finally reached our destination. About 30 minutes before zero hour it began to rain but it did not bother us because we were going to have a ringside view of the whole show. They were not going to fire the machine guns so that would enable us to see what happened. We would have the night off, if we were needed we would begin to fire at once. The 5 and 6 inch guns will do the firing. When the word was passed for our ships to start firing on the Jap-held island we were soaking wet, and during most of the time we were here it rained. The Japs did not know what hit them as our ships sneaked in on them while they were sound asleep and ripped the place with 5 and 6 inch shells. Many a Jap died in his bunk. You could see big explosions as the ammunition dump went up. The visibility was very bad because of the rain and darkness. Our task force really poured it on the Japs as they knocked out the Jap targets and slaughtered the troops. Our battle station is only a few feet from the big guns and when they fired, the big flashes were blinding. We were so close to the guns that we could almost look down the barrels. The concussion was awful, it felt like our eardrums would be blown to bits, and the pain in our throat and chest was almost unbearable. The cotton and rubber plugs in our ears did not help, because we were too close to the guns. When these guns fire like this, they even snap the steel plates and ladders that go up to the mount. Jap shore guns opened up on us but no damage was done to our ships. While all this was going on, our ship was hit by a torpedo but lucky for us it must have been a dud. We did not know if it came from a sub or PT boat. This would have been a great place to get stranded. When we completed the bombardment Admiral Merrill ordered the task force back to its base, many hundreds of miles south of here. It rained until the sun came up on this cloudy Thursday morning of July 1, 1943. We had some peanut brittle candy for breakfast and for dinner we had two hard-boiled eggs, 1 orange, and 2 donuts. It was a cloudy day as we raced south. We were in the midst of Jap-held airfields and we never knew when they would attack us. We had three air raid warnings but the Jap planes did not attack us. The cloudy weather must be interfering with their search for us. Everyone could stand some sleep but we will not get that, for some time. They say we might be back in a day or so for more bombardments against the Japs.

It is late in the afternoon as we pass good old Guadalcanal. The sun is out now and we were lucky it did not come out this morning, we would have made good targets for the Jap planes, My glasses broke again, but I patched them up. It is the glass that is broken.

The sun and glare from the water does a job on your eyes, it is almost blinding and lack of sleep does not help.

JULY 11, 1943

We are now at Purvis Bay in the Solomons, it is not too far from Tulagi. We will bombard the Japs at 3 A.M. tomorrow morning. After our bombardment our troops are to advance from 3 sides and destroy the Jap troops not killed with our bombardment and in 24 hours Munda and its important airfield will be ours.

This bombardment will also take place in the dark. Every time we go up the Slot to take on the Japs it is dark, it is near midnight or early in the morning. We get very little sleep with this schedule but it is the only way we can do it. We are not strong enough yet to do this in the daytime. We would run out of warships and our air power is not strong enough either, there are too many Jap airfields in the Solomons. We only get about 10 per cent of the war supplies down here while the European theatre of war gets about 90 per cent. We are hanging on with a big prayer.

I think the rugged routine that we have had for the past 7 months has something to do with the way the men have been acting lately. The men have noticed it themselves doing it. Your mind goes blank and you find yourself walking around some part of the ship, some distance from where you want to go, and then it dawns on you that you are not supposed to be there. You forget what day it is, what you had for breakfast, what you did in the morning. You find yourself in the washroom with no soap or towel. When you turn the water on, then it dawns on you. You forget to take your toothbrush and paste with you, until you begin to brush your teeth. You go in to take a shower without towel or soap. Some of the fellows have a lighted cigarette in their mouths and ask for a match to light theirs. When you wake up, you think it is time to go on watch, etc.

These things sneak up on you before you know it. You will find yourself somewhere and ask yourself, "What am I doing here?" Our routine for almost 7 months has not helped the situation. We spend most of our time on the ship, which is 607 ft. long and about 50 ft. at its widest point. Our recreation consists of a few hours a month in the jungle. Some of the men have not left the ship in months because there is nothing to amount to on the recreation parties. We seldom get a night's sleep. The only thing we see is, glaring ocean, thick green jungle and tropical rain storms. The heat and the tropical storms and humidity are wicked and of course the Japs always keep the pressure on us, you never know what the outcome will be when you take on the Japs.

As our task force made its way up the Solomons tonight, I got a good look at the photographer we have aboard with us. He will cover our bombardment of Munda tomorrow. He is a photographer for the Life Magazine and will stay at battle stations from now until this operation is completed, that means another night of no sleep.

MONDAY, JULY 12, 1943

After many hours at our battle stations our task force finally reached Munda and at 3 A.M. this morning we started our bombardment on the Japs. They must have been sound asleep this early hour of the morning but it didn't take long to wake them up, the others died in their sleep. It did not take long after we opened up on the Japs, we could see great explosions. They looked like fuel and ammunition dumps, they went sky high. It was a pretty clear morning, not as dark as some of our other attacks.

The reporter for Life Magazine was up on the highest spot of the ship taking pictures of the action, he was very close to the searchlights and was in a perfect spot to take in everything. We gave the Japs an awful plastering. I would not want to be in their shoes. During the bombardment the sprinkler system on our 40 mm machine gun broke due to the heavy bombardent and the water began to pour down on the ammunition. Not long after that happened Red Longfellow, our Mount Captain, received word for all hands on our mount to leave, because the twin five inch mount not too far away from us had a 5 inch shell stuck in the barrel and it could go off at any time, they call this a hang fire. If it went off it might cripple the ship.

After about a half hour of very ticklish work the shell was taken out and dropped over the side. A big redhead was the big factor in freeing it and he was later commended for his bravery. When the shell was first fired instead of going through the barrel and into the Japs it got stuck. While we were waiting for the shell to be freed it felt like we were sitting on a time bomb.

Jap planes also appeared on the scene but they were driven off. This was also navigation at its best on our part because we had to go through the very narrow passage of Blanche Channel which separates the islands of New Georgia and Rendova.

When our bombardment was completed Admiral Merrill and his task force headed for our base at Espiritu Santo, we would reach it in 2 days. When the sun came up we had to be on the alert for Jap planes. Nothing happened during the day, but still we could not take any chances.

At night we could see the Southern Cross in the sky, it was a very clear night and the sky was full of stars.

I guess this is the only place you can see it. It looks like a group of stars in the shape of a cross, it is something to see. It looks like another night with no sleep. Another task force will take our place up the Solomons while we return to our base for ammunition and fuel.

Each task force takes turns relieving the other.

JULY 15, 1943

We returned from our prowl up the Slot in search of Jap ships and nothing happened. I guess the Japs are licking their wounds. We are now in Purvis Bay and tonight we will not go up the Slot. This will be the first time in quite some time. Two of our cruisers left today, we don't know where they are bound. A big LST pulled alongside today, they can carry 200 trucks, hundreds of troops, tanks, etc. The proper name is Landing Ships Tanks about 300 ft. long. It was about 6 P.M. when it got here. I spent some time talking to the crew and this is what they had to say. They brought close to 300 wounded troops from Munda to Guadalcanal and then came alongside our ship. A lot of the wounded were cut very badly by Jap knives. Many had to be strapped down because they were insane, they were given something to put them to sleep.

They said our troops go for days with very little sleep. They live in foxholes and when they get wounded or hurt, cut their clothes off to bind their wounds. The wounded troops whom they brought back had hardly any clothes on so the sailors gave them theirs. Fighting the Japs is like fighting a wild animal. The troops said that the Japs are as tough and fierce as they come; the Jap is not afraid to die, it is an honor to die for the Emperor, he is their God.

A lot of the fighting is done at night and you can smell the Japs 25 yards away. The jungle is very hot and humid and drains the strength quickly. The jungle is also very thick; you could be right next to a Jap and yet you could not see him. The Japs also have Jap women with them. The Japs watch from coconut trees in the daytime and then when it becomes dark they sneak into your foxhole and cut your throat or throw in a hand grenade. A 200 lb. soldier was pulled from his foxhole and killed in short time. You also hear all sorts of noises made by the animals and you think it is the Japs. This is too much for some men and they crack up.

They say the Japs also have some Imperial Marines who are 6 ft. 4" tall. The Japs are experts at jungle fighting and they know all the tricks.

We also have some Fiji Islanders fighting here. The Japs are afraid of them. They love to cut the Japs up. One Fiji had 40 Jap dog tags which he had taken from the Japs he killed. They said the Japs bury their dead at night so you will not know how many Japs had been killed. When the Japs hear our wounded moaning, they fire in the direction of the sound. When the Fiji Islanders see a coconut tree with mud on it, they know a Jap is up in the top hiding. Jap bombers fly very close together and this formation makes it easy for the guns on the ground to get them.

When I finished talking with the crew on the LST they showed me Jap guns, swords, etc., that they picked up at Munda. They said that they landed troops, supplies, etc.

WEDNESDAY, AUGUST 11, 1943

We left Purvis Bay in the Solomons yesterday and expect to pull in to Espiritu Santo, New Hebrides, tomorrow. We had a bad accident today. One of the men from the 7th division was crushed to death this morning. He was standing near the 6 inch director as it turned around. It crushed him against the steel bulkhead. The men are having a lot of trouble with skin rash from the heat. This has been going on for some time. Out here you sweat 24 hours a day, and that makes it impossible to cure the rash. Some of the fellows are in bad shape but the Dr. cannot help them. Some of the men's rash have turned into big sores. Many of the men also have trouble with their eyes, they are full of pus. My eyelashes fall out and when I wake up in the morning I have to put some saliva on my eyes to loosen them because they are stuck together. Some days I have a rugged time with my eyes owing to the pain. The climate and our diet plus very little sleep are to blame for our ailments. Some of the men have their whole body covered with a rash and sores. The rash gives you no rest, it itches and it is impossible to sleep because of the heat. It is hard to breathe and you would wake up in a pool of sweat. Some of the men sweat so much in their bunks that they could not stand up, they were sick and dizzy from the heat and sweating. We had to take them to sick bay. The steel bulkhead is so hot during the day you cannot touch it in the compartments. When you go to the toilet the sweat just rolls off your body. It is just like standing under a shower. Sleep is also a hard thing to get because you never know when a shower will come up and you have to run for cover. You stand there until it stops. It is too hot to sleep below in the compartments. We have been eating bread that is full of little hard bugs for quite some time and this will not change because of the heat. When you put a slice of bread up in front of you there seems to be as many bugs in it as there is bread. The flour is full of these small bugs. It would be impossible to separate the bugs from the flour. The bugs breed very fast in the heat down here. The bugs in our bread do not bother us, we are used to them. When you carry a bag of flour on your shoulder you get covered with these bugs. On Sunday, August 1, I started my 3 months of mess cooking.

SEPTEMBER 18, 1943

Today was a very outstanding day for the men who went over to the beach in the afternoon. We saw our first woman in almost 10 months and it happened to be the First Lady of the United States. It was President Roosevelt's wife, Mrs. Franklin D. Roosevelt. She spoke to hundreds of sailors and marines who are stationed on the ships here. Her talk lasted about 10 minutes, then she walked around to see what the place looked like, she was with some officers and a woman from the Red Cross. The outfit she wore was very nice, she is much better looking in person. While she was here she also paid a visit on the other side of the island to see the wounded troops in the hospitals. Before coming here she visited New Zealand and Australia.

TUESDAY, OCTOBER 19, 1943

About 6 A.M. we sighted Australia. We dropped anchor at 12:01 P.M. I should know the time because I won $250 in the anchor pool. The ship moved very slowly as it came alongside the pier but just slowly enough for me to win. You do not have to walk very far from the ship to the street outside the pier. The houses and buildings are not too far away. Everyone was in dress blues and at quarters as we pulled into Sidney. It looked like any large city in the States and appeared very clean. The bridge reminded one of the Golden Gate Bridge in California. The weather was beautiful, like a warm spring day at home. A ferryboat passed close by as we were pulling in. It carried many people. They began to wave to us and we waved back. It was quite a sight and also quite a feeling to be back to civilization for the first time in almost a year. It was just as if we were coming home. A feeling came over us that we could not explain. It seemed like paradise. Summer begins December 21 in Australia so it must be spring here now. Australia is larger than the United States but its population is only about six million. It is also the oldest continent in the world.

LATER: Liberty started at 1 p.m. and we did not have to be back to the ship until the next morning at 11 A.M. There are three sections of us so that means we stay on the ship one day and have two days off. I am in the second section so we left the ship at one in the afternoon. The first thing I did was to go to the eye doctor and make an appointment. The secretary asked me if I was sure of keeping the appointment and I said I would, not knowing that I would be refused permission to go because it was one of the days I did not rate liberty. The doctor was the best in the region. He took care of the Australian Air Force. It did not take us long to find out that the Austrialian girls really went wild over the American sailors. The Australian people are very friendly and love the Americans. Some of the girls knew every state in the Union and its capital.

This was the first time in over 10 months for some of the men to leave the ship and put their feet on land. Donovan went 9 months.

LATER: I will now try to cover some of the things we did while in Sydney. We had a big dance for the crew at the Grace Auditorium. The auditorium was full of girls. They also had a good floor show. You could have all the food, beer and Coca-Cola you wanted. The mess cooks had to serve. I waited on Admiral Merrill and Captain Tobin. Everyone had a great time.

When you leave the ship you go through a big beautiful park to get to the business section of Sydney. The name of the place is Hyde Park. The first thing that catches your eyes are all the beautiful girls. The place is full of them. There are supposed to be five (5) girls to every man but I think there are even more than that. Everyone is so friendly down here. I never saw such friendly people. The girls in the States could really learn something from the girls here. They treat you as if you were related and invite you to their homes to meet the family. The little towns on the outskirts of Sydney were very pretty, most of the houses had a lot of flowers and a fence around it. You could smell lilacs as they were everywhere. Because of the war the taxis were run on coal and wood. Things are very cheap here and it does not cost much for a good time. We got fresh food for a change and our fortunes turned to the better as milk was acquired. It was our first milk in almost a year. All the beer parlors closed at 6 p.m. in this city of about two million. Nightclubs were open very late. The dance halls are always full. They are very nice and the orchestras are very good. Only two movies are open on Sunday and they are for servicemen and their girl friends.

SUNDAY, OCTOBER 24, 1943

We were told to be back to the ship at midnight instead of 11 A.M. Monday morning. That means we stay here only five days and get only three days of liberty. We were supposed to stay here ten days but will have to cut our stay short because we are going to invade Bougainville, the largest island in the Solomons, and also the last island in that group. If we take that, the Solomons will be ours. They say we might come back to Australia again sometime.

On my last day of liberty I bought a carton of cigarettes on ship for an Australian friend of mine as a gift. I left the ship with the cigarettes tied under my pant leg and would have looked foolish if they had fallen down as I walked the gangway after saluting the flag and an officer of the deck. American cigarettes are like gold here. The last night we spent in Australia, everyone had to be back on the ship at midnight. Everyone had a great time and met many nice people. We did not like to leave. When you know it's your last night in civilization, you would walk on the soil all night, and just breathe the fresh air. It feels so good. You know it will be some time before you put your feet on anything like this again. It reminds you of when you go swimming and the water feels so good you hate to get out. As you walk back to the ship it is very dark and quiet, everyone is asleep. The streets are deserted. Everything is so peaceful and quiet, you would not know there is a war on. Then you think of the nice time you had and the friendly people you have met. They make you feel as if you had known them all your life. For many a day to come your mind will be miles away, thinking of the people you have met and the places you have visited. It is an experience you will never forget. You will put Australia down as the best liberty port in the world. You will also put the Australians in the same class as the Americans. The Australians think there is no one like the Americans and the Americans think there is no one like the Australians. When you go to Australia it is like coming home. It is too bad our country is so far away. Our best friends are Australians and we should never let them down, we should help them every chance we get.

SUNDAY, OCTOBER 31, 1943

It is the last day of the month and also the last day for mess cooking. These three months sure went fast. Now I shall go hungry again. The only good meal we get is at noon. I shall start standard gun watches again. On the regular watch on our 40 mm. machine gun mount we have about six men on watch. When you step in to the mount, it is like going into a hot oven. You say to yourself, "How can anyone stand that terrific heat for four hours with the hot sun beating down on you and the heat from the blowers pouring it on, not to mention the hot steel of the mount that almost surrounds you." You could not stand on the steel deck without shoes on. The temperature is way over 100 degrees. The sweat just rolls off you and into your shoes and onto the steel deck. We have to keep wetting the canvas that covers the ammunition. The humidity just saps the strength from you and you do not get any breeze. You and another man stand one hour on the lookout and then you sit in the hot pointer's or trainer's seat for another hour, this is the toughest because you cannot move around. You just sit there in the hot steel seat and sweat. The glare from the sun and the water is very tough on the eyes. The 12 noon to 4 p.m. watch is always the hottest. It is also hard to stay awake when you are in the Japs' backyard at two or three in the morning when you are standing lookout in front of the gun mount. You have had very little sleep to start with and while you are on the lookout for Jap subs or torpedoes your feet just buckle under you. You are dead tired and actually fall asleep standing up. You force yourself to stay awake but it is a losing proposition. You continue to doze off for a split second, your head droops, feet buckle under you and then you are awake again to do the same thing all over again. While this is going on the Mount Captain is walking back and forth pushing the fellows and barking at them to stay awake. It is really the Agony in the Garden. This is what you call torture. If the guns are firing we have no trouble staying awake. When we stand watch in port at night and one of the fellows should doze off in the pointer's or trainer's seat, he gets two buckets of water in the face. Everyone goes up to the fellow asleep and someone puts his hands in front of his eyes; if he does not move, we know he is asleep. The bucket brigade then goes into action. When he gets hit with the first bucket of water, it almost knocks him out of his seat, and when he opens his eyes he gets the second bucket. It is better than a circus. The rest of the crew break their sides laughing. The payoff comes when he says that he was not sleeping, he was resting his eyes. It does not take very long to dry your clothes because the water is warm and the weather is very hot. This ceremony usually takes place on the midnight to four in the morning watch.

    After all this talk about what we do while on watch, it looks like we are going to spend many day there, starting today. At 2:30 A.M. we left Tulagi in the Solomons. It's very dark as usual. Every time we hit the Japs it is pitch black. There is no moon. This way the Japs will not see us. We are going to travel about 500 or 600 miles up the Solomons to bombard the Japs on Buka and Bonis. This will take place after midnight. When we finish we will turn around and pull off our first daylight bombardment of the war, on the Shortlands. It is also heavily defended.

Bonis is a strong base on the furthest tip of Bougainville. The Japs will have plenty of planes on the airfield there. Above Bonis is the Jap-held island of Buka. Buka is between Bougainville and the Jap fortress of New Britain and New Ireland. It looks like we will have our work cut out for us. All hands were told to get as much rest in the afternoon as we could. The sun is shining and it is hot as usual. The sea is calm. As I look out on the starboard side I can see many transports, supply ships, invasion barges, etc. Large barrage balloons fly above many of the ships. They will come in handy against Jap planes. This is the first time I have seen these in a convoy. We must have about 70 or 80 ships with us.

Bougainville is about 200 miles long. It is also the largest island in the Solomons. The jungle there is about the thickest in the Solomons. It also has high mountains. Most of the waters around Bougainville are uncharted and we have to go by photos taken from the air or old charts that are not complete. You never know when the ship will get stuck on a reef and stay there. The Japs would love to see that happen right in their own backyard. Our five and six inch guns will fire thousands of shells during these bombardments.

TUESDAY, NOVEMBER 2, 1943

We got two hours' sleep as we continued south but at 12:45 A.M. this morning General Quarters sounded. Everyone was very tired as he ran to his battle station in the early morning darkness, not knowing what we were in for. We did know that when we left our base at Tulagi, Sunday at 2:30 A.M. that most of the time would be spent at battle stations without sleep. Our food during that time was mostly sandwiches. The reason for battle stations was that a task force of Jap warships were on their way down from Rabaul to sink our transports and supply ships that were unloading at Empress Augusta Bay, Bougainville. Their objective also included bombarding our Marines and Army troops on the shore. The Japs' force packed a bigger wallop than ours. They had two heavy cruisers with them. Our biggest ships were our four light cruisers. The Japs had eight inch guns, our biggest were six inch guns.

About 2:45 A.M. all hell breaks loose. The battle is on. Our guns are pouring it on as they maneuver. It is very dark and heat lightning can be seen during the battle along with a drizzle. Our ship did not waste any time in that it hit a Jap heavy cruiser. Flames and explosions were everywhere. When it was all over, the ship was dead in the water. It finally sunk. Jap shells were falling all around us and some of our ships were also getting hit. Both sides were firing away at each other. The water was full of American and Japanese torpedoes as destroyers from both sides attacked. The big eight inch salvos, throwing up great geysers of water, were hitting very close to us. The water sprayed the ship just in front of our mount. There are great explosions as some ships sink very fast. We received reports from the other ships that they had been hit. The cruiser Denver was hit and had another close call as a shell went through the smokestack. It would have been all over if it went down the stack. During all this action our ship was hit by two Jap torpedoes but they did not explode. There was also a near miss for one of our own destroyers as it came out of the darkness and came close to ramming our starboard side. It was going in the same direction in chase of a Jap warship. For a while we thought it would crash into our ship. Our force fired star shells in front of the Jap warships so that our destroyers could attack with torpedoes. It was like putting a bright light in front of your eyes in the dark. It is impossible to see. The noise from our guns was deafening. The guns on the port and starboard had plenty of firing as we kept cutting back and forth. They say the maneuvers Admiral Merrill pulled off in this sea battle would put German Admiral Sheer of World War I fame to shame. Sheer pulled his tactics in the daylight off Jutland but Merrill had darkness to cope with and twice the speed. These maneuvers are very dangerous as collisions are the rule. It's a wonder the ships could work as a team in the darkness, each picking out his own target. The Jap Admiral was the best the Japs had and he tried every trick in the book. Admiral Merrill was better. When things looked bad and the sea was lit up by the Jap star shells, Admiral Merrill ordered a smoke screen. Thick black smoke engulfed the area. The Japs found it next to impossible to strike at us. We also were on the alert for Jap subs, and torpedo boats and to make sure none of the enemies warships would sneak into the bay and fire on our transports and troops there. The battle raged hour after hour. No quarter was given by the Japs or us. During the battle one could see that the Jap star shells were brighter than ours. They really lit the place up. It's a funny sensation expecting to be hit by Jap or for that matter any shell or torpedo. I'll feel much better when it gets dark again. Sometimes we fired at Jap star shells and put them out. The sky was full of shells.

As the sea battle was coming to an end we passed a Jap ship under attack at close range. We did not fire on the Jap ship because we were very low on ammunition and our help was not needed. This action took place on our starboard side not too far away. It seemed like it was getting a little brighter as I watched the action. The Jap ship was dead in the water I did not notice any other ships around but the three of us. The Jap ship was a mass of flames and red hot steel as the big guns covered it wth exploding shells. It gave off a red glow that lit up the area around it. It must have been a nightmare in hell for the Japs as they were roasted and blown to bits. I don't see how anyone could escape. It was a horrible way to die, it was a slaughter. This type of warfare tops them all for horror. There is no safe place to hide and if you land in the water the huge sharks that are longer than a good-sized room are always close by. Our ships are now running low on ammunition and some of the destroyers have only star shells left, because of our earlier bombardments against the Japs. Our ship is also getting low on fuel. If this keeps up, we will have only machine guns and potatoes to fire at the Jap warships. After three hours of fighting, the Japs have had enough and head for their base at Rabaul. It's approximately 5:45 A.M. We started the engagement at 2:45 A.M. Losses for the Japs—at least one heavy cruiser and four destroyers sunk and two cruisers and two destroyers severely damaged. Our ship accounted for one destroyer and one cruiser, the rest of the task force took care of the rest. Every ship in the force was in on the kill. At daylight nothing could be seen on deck except empty shell cases. The men on the five and six inch mounts and turrets looked like a bunch of ghosts. They were all worn out from lack of sleep, heat, very little food and the bombardments. Oh, yes, I forgot to mention the sea battle. The men had spent the past three hours in a hot steaming steel mount or turret passing shells or powder cases. The six inch armor piercing shells weigh 135 pounds and the heavy brass powder cases are approximately four feet long. They get very little air and the heat is unbearable. I imagine they believed that the firing would never stop. The steel decks were rivers of water from their perspiration. The weather from beginning to end was simiar to a heat wave back home in August. Why they did not pass out from exhaustion is a miracle. They were all out on their feet. I would not want to be in their shoes for a million. When we go into action, the air blowers are shut off and the ones who are shut in really suffer. They actually gasp for fresh air. The ships keep twisting and turning and they don't know what to expect from the enemy. The men who are many decks below in the handling rooms had a tough job sending the ammunition up. They are surrounded by tons of ammunition. If a torpedo happens to explode close by, they drown like a bunch of rats. It's a long way to topside.

It's still Tuesday morning, November 2, the same day of the sea battle. It is a beautiful warm sunny day as we make our way south to our base at Tulagi. We have still to be on the alert for Jap planes as they will be looking for us.

LATER: Approximately 8:30 A.M. we were attacked by 70 Jap planes Our four cruisers and seven destroyers had plenty of target practice. The destroyer Foote, our eighth destroyer, is dead in the water as previously mentioned. All ships break loose as Jap planes come in on us from all directions. We fire every gun on the ship at the Japs, even our big six inch guns. The first plane we hit was blown to bits by a 6 inch shell. Jap planes can be seen falling all around us. The Japs are also doing some damage and one can see many bombs explode very close to our ships. At first you think they have scored a hit as the water shoots high into the air. Their machine guns are also cutting up the water. Our ship is also bit by a bomb that destroys one of our catapults that we use or shooting planes off. It's a good size steel ramp. When the bomb exploded the stern of the ship was covered with smoke. It looked very serious at first. If one of our planes had been on the ramp it would have been blown to bits. One of the machine gun mounts was also knocked out by the bomb. No one was killed. About fifteen men were wounded. We also received a hit up forward and more casualties, all wounded. One of the fellows almost had his head taken off.

A few Japs parachuted when they were hit but a few sailors and Marines on the 20 mm. opened up on the ones in the chutes and when they hit the water they were nothing but a piece of meat cut to ribbons. The men were blasted out for doing this. They were told not to waste ammunition in such a way. They were also told that it was good shooting. The Japs were the first to do things like this. They asked for it and we returned the favor.

During the air battle, our air cover did a mop-up job on what was left of the Jap force. They were a little late getting here but we were very happy to see them. We secured from General Quarters at noon and received some food for a change. We stayed in the waters near Bougainville all day. We are making sure nothing happens to our empty transports as they head for their base at Tulagi. If the Japs send down any more warships, we will have to use potatoes against them. We must have fired at least 5000 rounds of five and six inch ammunition during our sea battle. The concussion from the twin five inch mount knocked out Fuller and ripped Babe's sweater off. It also knocked him to the steel deck twice during the air attack. Babe is a rugged Jewish boy from New York who weighs around 200 pounds. Sometimes when these twin five inch mounts turn around, the men on the machine guns can look right into the barrels and almost touch them. The concussion from these, with all the steel around, is wicked on the eardrums. Many a man has had his eardrum broken with the guns. Our ship has close to a hundred guns on it: 20 mm., 40 mm. machine guns and five inch mounts, two guns each. Admiral Merrill used the wisdom of Solomon when he let the men in his task force get some rest before going into action. At first we got very little sleep but after a while one can get along with what he can get. The little sleep we received went a long way. Old Bull Halsey knew what he was doing when he put Admiral Merrill in command of this task force. Old Bull knows how to pick them.

The new men we picked up before going to Australia were shaking like a leaf during the air battle and we did not waste any time kidding them about it.

## THURSDAY, NOVEMBER 4, 1943

I did not get any sleep until 2 A.M. this morning. We were receiving fuel from one of the tankers. They told us to get some sleep while the ship was fueling. We fell asleep on the steel deck. They woke us up in one hour at 3 A.M. when we were refueled. I did not get to bed again until 4:15 A.M. We usually crawl under a near mount or turret and fall asleep. Reveille was 6 A.M. There was no resting for the weary today. All hands worked all day under a hot blazing sun, carrying tons of ammunition. The sun gave us qute a burn because we wore no shirts to beat the head-sapping sun. We continued into the night. Even some of the officers helped. It makes you forget the heavy work that you are doing when you see the officers pitch in and help. They did not have to do this. They could be catching up with the many hours of sleep they lost. It's no joke carrying a 135 pound armor-piercing shell almost the length of a ship that is 607 ft. long. Two men are used to pick the shell up and put it on another's man's shoulder which is bare. It's then carried or staggered on its way, always with the hope that it doesn't drop. Thousands of shells were carried plus the powder cases. Some of the smaller fellows could not carry the armor-piercing shells because of the extreme weight. Usually a piece of cloth on the shoulder was used in vain for the heavy shell still cuts into the bone.

A very special guest came aboard this morning. It was the brass himself, the number 1 man, Admiral "Bull" Halsey. The men would do anything for him. He rates with the greatest of all time. A PT boat pulled alongside and he came aboard. He had a long handshake with Admiral Merrill on the starboard quarterdeck. Everyone wanted to get a look at the "Bull". Halsey is a tough-looking man and looks as if he could take care of one of his namesakes. He had on a pair of shorts, tan in color and a short sleeve shirt of the same color, the shirt open at the collar. You would never believe that he was the number 1 man in the Souh Pacific. He wants his men to be comfortable. He doesn't go in for this regulation stuff. As they were putting a six inch 135 pound armor-piercing shell on my shoulder, who was standing in front of me but "Bull" Halsey and Admiral Merrill. As he stood there watching us carry ammunition, I tried to look right through him. I tried to study him and see what he was made of. I left him standing there, with the shell on my shoulder and the knowledge that he came from good stock. It did not take long to draw that conclusion because he had it written all over him. We got the best man in command down here in the "Bull". Admiral Merrill showed him the damage we received from the Jap bombs. Before he left the ship, he congratulated everyone for the great job they did.

Francis McCarthey, the news reporter for United Press, was also aboard our ship during all this action. He was the only correspondent with the task force. When we reached Purvis Bay, he had to share his scoop with the other reporters. Mr. McCarthey should get some kind of award. It's tough when you get a scoop like this and then have to share it with several other syndicated reporters. Everyone thinks the world of Mr. McCarthey.

## WEDNESDAY, NOVEMBER 10, 1943

All hands arose at 5 A.M. It's another very hot day. We had our first good meal in quite some time., the apple pie really hit the spot. This afternoon, while we were south of Bougainville and just off Treasury Island, we came across a raft with four live Japs in it. Admiral Merrill sent word to one of our destroyers to pick them up. As the destroyer SPENCE came close to the raft, the Japs opened up with a machine gun at the destroyer. The Jap officer then put the gun in each man's mouth and fired, blowing out the back of each man's skull. One of the Japs did not want to die for the Emperor and put up a struggle. The others held him down. The officer was the last to die. He also blew his brains out. The SPENCE went in to investigate. All the bodies had disappeared into the water. There was nothing left but blood and an empty raft. Swarms of sharks were everywhere. The sharks ate well today. The Japs must have taken the 7.7 machine gun from one of their planes before leaving the islands to escape advancing troops. We went to battle stations at 6:30 P.M. At 10 P.M. we were attacked by enemy planes. We emerged without damage. The night was as bright as day and rendered us clear targets for the Jap bombs and torpedoes. Later, darkness descended and the rains came.

## THURSDAY, NOVEMBER 25, 1943

Back home in Massachusetts, it was Thanksgiving, one of the real big holidays. Everyone, or it seems just about everyone, goes to the high school football game in the morning. Then it's home for a big turkey dinner.

On board ship we celebrated Thanksgiving with a big turkey dinner and all of the trimmings. It really hit the spot.

Nickelson had a heat stroke from sleeping in the compartment last night. We carried him to sick bay as he was too weak and dizzy to go it alone. The flashproof cover where he lay was covered with his sweat. He was kept in sick bay for a day. I can't understand how some of the fellows sleep in the compartment, especially ours, as it's above the waterline. The sun beats against the steel sides and the deck all day. The side of the ship is so hot that you cannot touch it. On top of that, there is very little air to breathe. Sleeping there is out of the question.

We had Captain's inspection in whites this morning. What a joke. How stupid can intelligence get. We were told that these orders had come from the states. .that figures.

I was talking to one of the crewmen today. It seems that the duty here is getting the best of him. He told me that he was going crazy. He appeared very nervous. We've been in continuous action for almost a year now. Some of the younger men in the 17-year-old group wish that they were back in the States and out of the Navy. One of them is here on watch with me now. He really does look homesick. He's sorry now that he was in such a hurry to enter the service. He's only 17 years old. I told him that after a few months he would recover and the Navy would seem like a second home to him and he'd never care if he saw home again. I also told him to forget about being homesick and think of something else. I never felt lonesome in all the time we have been here, in fact I never give it a thought.

Some of the new men cannot wait to get into action. They say "I came down here to fight a war and that's what I want." It takes all kinds. After being in so many campaigns, you're disappointed if one passes you by. There's always the next one. When you find yourself in it, there's always the realization of how crazy you were in thinking that way. When this one's completed, never again. When it's finally terminated, you're always ready for the next one. It gets to be a disease after a time.

Following chow, the fellows like to sit around and listen to the recordings piped over the loudspeaker. The songs are old but we enjoy them very much. It lasts for half an hour.

## SATURDAY, DECEMBER 4, 1943

I received shocking news today. The Press News reported my brother John's aircraft carrier was sunk in the battle of Tarawa in the Gilberts. The communique stated that at approximately 25 November, 1943, the carrier went down. It was a converted job and the first of its kind to be sunk in the war. Last night at about 11 P.M. while sleeping under the stars, my friend Donovan came down from the radio shack to tell me what happened. I must have answered him while asleep. I still don't remember talking to him. While on the 8 A.M. to 12 noon watch, he asked me if I saw the Press News and I said, "No, why do you ask?" Then he told me what had happened. I did not believe him until I picked up the Press News and read it myself. It was the first item in the Press News. I wrote a letter to him the first chance I had. This wasn't the first close call for my brother John. My brother Joe and he were both at Pearl Harbor, December 7, 1941, when the Japs pulled their sneak attack. Both of them were transferred from two ships that were sunk by the Japs. They were transferred only a couple of weeks before. Joe joined the Navy in 1936, John in 1938. The last letter I received from my sister Mary, reported that John had bumped into Joe out here somewhere. The carrier that was sunk is the U.S.S. Liscomb Bay.

## FRIDAY, JANUARY 21, 1943

We left this morning for maneuvers and gunnery. We fired star shells at night. A large sled that was towed by another ship, was our target. I received a letter from my sister Mary. After three months time from the time John's ship was sunk, I finally got to know what happened. John told Mary that he did not know what hit him on the head, knocking him unconscious and leaving him with a hole in his head. As his ship was sinking, a fellow sailor pushed him over the side. His life was saved by that action only. He was also cut over the eye. It later healed leaving a slight scar. His back and shoulders were also injured. A bad case of nerves later developed and he still wakes up with a cold sweat. I also received a letter from John. He was to have an operation performed on his head as it was still draining. His head was fractured and a plastic surgeon was to graft the opening and make it uniform. The doctor informed him that the only thing that saved his life was that his skull and bones are very hard. It would have killed an ordinary person. John is now located at a hospital in Corona, California. He wrote that it was a beautiful place, formerly being a country club. In the distance he can see the snowcapped mountains. He further wrote that his ship was sunk just before sunup. Nine hundred lost their lives including a three star admiral in those early morning hours. My sister Mary first learned of the tragedy upon returning from work by way of a newspaper that she had happened to buy. She was dumfounded. Finally receiving a telegram from John, she fell to her knees and thanked God for saving his life. Approximately 200 men were saved and of those numerous were wounded.

# PAUL GOLDMAN

Born in 1910, Paul Goldman was working as a chemist in the U.S Federal Service when called into the Navy. He had received his B.S. in Chemistry at City College of New York in 1930 and had taken post-graduate work at Brooklyn Polytechnic Institute.

At the time of the diary Goldman's rank was Pharmacist's Mate First Class in the Hospital Corps, his training geared toward the furnishing of first aid to casualties of the planned invasion of Europe.

One very appealing touch in these diary fragments is the compassion shown to a wounded German prisoner brought back from the D-Day beaches, especially in view of the fact that Mr. Goldman is jewish.

Following the war Mr. Goldman returned to his work as a chemist. Now living in Sarasota, Florida, with his second wife Esther, Mr. Goldman has no children of his own but is called Grandpa by 5 children born to his wife's two daughters. He is a member of the Jewish War Veterans of the U.S.A.

*******

FRIDAY, MARCH 3, 1944
Leave Boston at 1100 aboard LST 506. Destination-Halifax, N.S. Traveling with convoy of LST's & other ships.
MARCH 8 LST 506 ties up to dock-Halifax Harbor-on Dartmouth side. I have Shore Patrol duty tonite in Halifax. Visited Canadian minesweeper today.
FRI. MARCH 10 At Halifax. Volunteered for S.P. duty again in Halifax. Saw "Destination Tokyo" at Capitol Theatre.
SAT. MARCH 11 at Halifax. Liberty tonight. Telephone home from a small grocery store in Dartmouth, N.S., which is across the bay from Halifax.
MONDAY, MARCH 13 At Halifax-Taking on supplies.
TUESDAY, MARCH 14 Start moving out at 1100. Sleeping in our clothes. Life belt handy. Raft No. 6
WEDNESDAY, MARCH 15 Moving in convoy-1 day out of Halifax.
TUES. MARCH 21 7 days. Gave talk on chemistry to corpsmen on LST 506 this afternoon.

FRIDAY, MARCH 24 Moving in convoy 10 days out of Halifax. Cloudy. Moved watch ahead 1 hr. for the 4th time since leaving N.Y. Getting close to European territory. About 2 more days travel.
TUES. MARCH 28 14 days out of Halifax. First sight of land off starboard side. (N. tip of Ireland) About 1130 also saw first plane vapor trails. Ran into several heavy fogs on way south thru the North Channel and Irish Sea. Port & Stbd running lights left on tonite en route.
WED. MARCH 29 15 days out of Halifax. No general quarters practice this morning. Some English birds flew past ship this A.M. & one rested on railing for several minutes (size of bird-between sparrow & robin, colored like sparrow). Ships moving S.E. thru Irish Sea. Dropped anchor in Milford Haven Harbor, Wales at 1900.
THURSDAY, MARCH 30 Anchored in Milfordhaven Harbor-clear view possible of surrounding countryside with its farmland, small quaint-looking houses, abrupt cliffs (upturned rock strata), military establishments, airfield, barrage balloons flown by several ships-liberty party went ashore (4 hrs.) 25 per cent of personnel.
FRIDAY, MARCH 31 Left Milfordhaven at 0700 heading S. toward Plymouth or Southampton. Most of ships in group now flying barrage balloons, including our own. Watch condition 2, 4 hrs. on & 4 hrs. off. Saw some flashes of light off port side of ship at 2245—somewhere on English coast.
SAT., APRIL 1 Arrived at Plymouth, England at 1430 after a rough, rainy trip via English Channel. Many barrage balloons visible around waterfront of this old city. Saw some bombed buildings for first time. Getting close to the war now. We are tied up to a Plymouth pier.
SUNDAY, APRIL 2 LST moved out to center of bay and anchored there for launching of LCT 619 which has been carried on deck from the U.S. Unlashing took from 0700 to 1300. LST was listed on stbd side and LCT was slid off deck in to water at 1550 English War Time). The LCT is a 100 foot landing boat of about 100 tons & carries a 12 man crew. The LST rocked very slightly when LCT slid off deck. Expect to go ashore this evening on first liberty in England. Was ashore from 1830 to 2400. Evidence of past bombings can be seen all over this town. Empty shells of buildings, piles of bricks & cement blocks, altho most of the rubbish has been pretty well cleaned up. Had one small glass of bitters (beer) in a crowded pub (Continental Hotel). Cost 9d (about 15 cents) Very weak & watery tasting beer. Took a bus trip, round trip to outskirts of town for 6d. Trip took about 11/2 hrs. and found this to be a very good & restful way of sightseeing, especially after 3 hrs. of walking around Plymouth. The stores were all closed except for some restaurants which had long queues (lines) waiting out in the street. Met Van Wie in town. He is now stationed at a Navy dispensary just outside Plymouth along with 9 other

PhMs from Brooklyn Naval Hospital. He was part of the "narrow" unit which arrived here about 2 weeks ago.

MON. APRIL 3 Our LST has now been moved in & tied up to a pier near a long ramp which slopes down from land to our bow for unloading of our cargo of tractor cranes. After our almost nightly pinochle game (not for money, as we haven't been paid for 2 months and none of us has more than a few cents and most of what we have is borrowed) our group of 40 corpsmen packed up several things for a week's stay at a school of special instruction, located at a base at Fowey (about 50 miles west of Plymouth, on the Channel).

TUES. APRIL 4 Early breakfast (0630-0700) then we travelled by LCVP, truck & train to Fowey. Our quarters here are in Quonset huts (28 men to a hut). Showers and toilet facilities across a very muddy road. In fact this base being so new—all the roads are muddy. Visited Fowey & the equally ancient town of Polruan across the bay. A small motor boat ferry took us across for the sum of 3d (5 cents). The food at this base is excellent and the butter (imported from Australia) is especially delicious. There is a castle in Fowey that dates back to about the year 1100. The author Daphne du Maurier lives about 3 miles from town and this section of Cornwall was the setting for her novel "Frenchman's Creek". There is a creek of that name about 16 miles from here.

WED. APRIL 5- Lectures began this morning at 1000 & lasted until 1730 with time out for lunch. We learned what part our LST's are expected to play in the coming invasion & in evacuation of casualties. (11th Amphibious Force). Visited Fowey again this evening with Stewart M. Morris (PhM 2/c). Walked thru the ancient narrow winding streets, looking into store windows & at the old buildings. This town has about 2000 pop. Visited the American Red Cross here for some tea & cookies (11d) Talked to some Canadian sailors who came here on a minesweeper and some English soldiers (Royal Artillery) one of whom is a Londoner and was telling us what sections to visit for a pleasant evening. He also suggested a Sunday trolley-bus tour of London & suburbs-cost 1 shilling.

THURS. APRIL 6- More lectures today at USNAAB, Fowey, Cornwall. Very interesting talks by Dr. Reynolds of Beach Battalion on the subject of amph. operations & handling of casualties, including transfer from "Far Shore" to "Near Shore" via "Water Gap"(LST) Saw some movies re "Amph. Operations".

FRI. APRIL 7 More lecture & movies. First Aid, War Gasses, Prep. and Use of Blood Plasma. 3 mile hike this afternoon. Saw movies tonight at Fowey Naval Station. "Lost Angels."

SAT. APRIL 8 Lectures on chemical warfare by Cdr. Eeley.

SUN. APRIL 9 More lectures on chem. warfare. Saw "Pistol Packing

Mama" at base auditorium. Air raid alert this morning 0200-0220. We get dressed, put on helmets & gas mask holders & stand outside huts until all clear sounds.

MONDAY APRIL 10 Final lecture on chem. warfare by Cdr. Eeley. Tested our gas masks this evening in a chamber of tear gas.

TUES. APRIL 11 Pep talks by Capt. Dowling, Cdr. Bell, Lt. Smith & Capt. Goff at U.S. NAAT S.B., Fowey, Cornwall. Variety show at lecture hall this evening-given by Coast Guard band—M.C. Jumping Jack Brown PhM 1/c-who also played bass fiddle & sang-very good show.

WED. APRIL 12-Our last day at this muddy, dirty base (Fowey) Packed our gear at 0454—left Fowey station 1530—arrived Falmouth RR station at 1830. Went by navy truck 12 miles to King Harry Ferry & from there by small boat out to LST 506 & very glad to get back to comparatively clean quarters.

THURS. APRIL 13 Up at 0600—breakfast at 0700—did some laundry this morning. Helped to do a little cleaning of tank deck of LST & inspection of damaged litters in preparation for reception of invasion casualties. After supper a group of the crew & corpsmen went ashore to a nearby cow pasture and played a game of baseball (soft ball). Crew won 6-2. Drs. Saracco & Seifarth played part of game as pitcher & catcher respectively for the corpsmen.

FRIDAY, APRIL 14-Our liberty boat left ship at 1800 to make the 6 mile trip down the river Fal to the Prince of Wales landing at Falmouth. About 3/4 of the way out, developed engine trouble, anchoring near shore while the mechs tried to find the cause of the difficulty. Meanwhile, another small Navy boat pulled alongside and gave liberty party a lift the rest of the way to town. Reached Falmouth at 1900. This town seems to be a little livelier than Plymouth and contained a well developed shopping center, altho the only shops open at this hour were tobacco stores. After visiting the Red Cross Service Center and signing the State Register (N.Y.S. section contains too few pages as usual and was completely filled in with names of visiting New York Staters) walked back to main street again and ran into Jim Geiss, now MM 3/c who occupied the bunk over mine in our Boot company barracks. He told me he's been here some 6 weeks. Showed me his quarters in the King's Hotel, where he is temp. working as mess cook along with several other Navy men. Navy maintains quarters & mess hall at this hotel. We had some beer & sandwiches. Returned to ship at 2310 & in bed by 2330.

SAT. APRIL 15-General inspection of ship & personnel this morning by skipper of LST Lt. Downes. Had liberty again tonite. Went to Falmouth with Stewart M. Morris, PhM 2/c. Rained all evening, also going & back. We went to a movie at the Red Cross. Saw Errol Flynn in "Gentleman Jim".

SUN. APRIL 16-Considerable excitement on board among our group of 40 hospital corpsmen as we learned what the expected division into 2 groups of 20 is to consist of. 20 of us, including myself, are to be transferred to LST 346 with Dr. Seifarth as leader of our group. We also have 8 out of the original 12 rated men-2 first mates, 3 second mates & 3 third mates & 12 hospital apprentices, leaving 2 seconds, 2 thirds, 16 H.a.'s and a chief comprising the group which remains aboard the 506. This latter group is led by Dr. Saracco. The situation is fouled up somewhat by the fact that no one seems to know just where the LST 346 is located at present or how we are supposed to get there. Furthermore, the group remaining is to get their pay within a few days while the 346 group will not be paid now for another indefinite period and of course the mail situation is still a mess as most of us have not received a single letter in the last 6 weeks, that is since leaving the states. Dr. Seifarth came down to our quarters this evening to distribute a carton of cigarettes among the men and to tell us of the general situation. It will be his problem to try to get some information and find some of the answers. Also, the 506 is supposed to be out all day tomorrow on maneuvers and the 346 group is supposed to get all their gear packed and get ready to move--but no one knows where.

MONDAY, APRIL 17-20 of us finally reached our new home, the LST 346, stationed at Fowey harbor. We travelled from Falmouth with all our gear via two Navy trucks and were on board the 346 by 1900. This ship is a veteran of the invasions of Sicily and Salerno. The skipper is Lt. Howell, Exec.-Lt.(j.g.) Fisk. Conditions aboard the 346 are a considerable improvement over the 506—the officers being much more reasonable, the crew very agreeable, and food tastier and served much more generously. There is even a mid-evening snack of coffee & sandwiches at 2100. There are quite a few war trophies on board, I've seen an Italian (Roma) rifle, a German jeep (belonging to the skipper) and an English motorcycle so far.

TUESDAY, APRIL 18-We spent this day adjusting ourselves to routine on board the 346. Reveille is at 0630. This means that bunks must be vacated and in order by 0700 or else—there may be extra duty imposed. Heard rumors that we may get some pay tomorrow.

WED. APRIL 19-At last-pay day-after waiting some 2 1/2 months, at 1330 we reached the disbursing office in Fowey and filed in by 4's to receive varying amounts of pay—Dale didn't get anything due to some book mixup. He was almost in tears. Larson, one of our first mates, drew about $600 (in English pounds). I rate some liberty this evening but at this time am undecided whether or not to go into Fowey as the weather is damp and the amusement rate very low in this village of 2000 which I've seen several times before. P.S. Did not go ashore tonite.

THURS. APRIL 20 Still no mail, which is the one black cloud in my present existence. As far as our daily routine on board the LST 346-the medical group is just resting easy-coasting along and waiting for orders & further instructions from our immediate superior, Dr. W.J. Seifarth.
FRI. APRIL 21 Had a few hours liberty in Fowey this evening. As the weather was misty only 3 of us got on the small boat for the short ride to town. The coxswain allowed me to take over the controls from our LST to the pier. Handling the 36 ft. boat was fairly simple as all there is to maneuver is the steering wheel and the combination reversing gear & accelerator handle. Sheehan & I played some classical records at the local Red Cross and had some tea and buns.
SAT. APRIL 22 LST 346 & convoy left Fowey at 0800. Beautiful sunny day, blue sky & warm. Watched some practice firing on one of our 40 mm. anti-aircraft guns at 1145. Arrive at little town of Salcombe (on the Channel) at 1700. Drop anchor in cozy little bay-bathing beaches on right side, headed in, people already in wading due to warmth of day.
SUN. APRIL 23-We're still anchored in the Salcombe River which is very narrow at this point. There are several small, sandy bathing beaches on one side of the river and on other side are some public buildings and fine-looking homes. The sun is shining but a heavy fog keeps blowing in from the channel, at times hiding both shores from sight and at other times, one shore is hidden by the fog while the other is lit up by sunshine. Am bothered by a cough which is especially bad at night. Spent the time between breakfast & lunch by resting in bed. Read thru the "Sunday Dispatch" London paper which Sheehan bought in Salcombe this morning. This place is about 300 miles west of London. About 2130 Dale (HA 1/c) was running a temp of 104.2° P-120, R-42-Dr. Seifarth had him moved to a nearby empty compartment and ordered TPR every 2 hrs, also APC's and Sod Bicarb every 2 hrs. At 2230-TPR was 103.2-126-32. We decided to set an all nite watch over Dale as a precaution. Nicholas had the first 2 hr. watch from 2400 to 0200, then Cox, then myself.
MON. APRIL 24 I was awakened at 0200 by Cox who said he had been informed by Nicholas that the patient was not doing so well. We went to Dale and noticed extreme restlessness, difficulty in breathing, a fixed stare and dilated pupils which did not react to the direct light of a flashlight. We could get no response from Dale and immediately sent for Dr. Seifarth. By 0210, Dale was beginning to turn blue in the face due to a pulmonary edema. We began artificial respiration; Cox, I and Bud Roe took turns. There did not seem to be any improvement in Dale's color and his pulse was rapidly failing in spite of injections of adrenalin, followed by coramine and caffeine. At 0145 Dr. Seifarth could no longer detect any pulse beat using a stethoscope and sor-

rowfully pronounced the fatal words "he is dead". The purple hue was already spreading from the head down past the throat and over the chest. We were still in the dark as to the exact cause of this rapid demise and spent several hours discussing the possible reasons, as between disease or poison. Dr. Seifarth decided to take a sample of fluid and this was done at 0530. The fluid obtained was not a clear water white as it should have been but rather had a white hazy cloudiness which tended to settle out upon standing. This condition raised the possibility of the presence of some meningo disease germ. Dale's body and gear were shipped out to a nearby shore dispensary at 0930 at the order of the skipper as we were due to leave this place (Salcombe) this morning. The LSTs here immediately after this event moved out into the channel for the short run to Brixham, where we dropped anchor at 1300. There is a very large bay there with the town of Torquay on one side of the bay & Brixham on the other. Report on analysis of Dale's spinal fluid showed-meningitis.

TUES., APRIL 25-As a result of case of meningitis on board, entire crew is being given doses of 4 gms. Sulfathiazole daily as a preventive measure.

LST's in this area including our own start taking on load of Army personnel & materiel. We loaded 43 large Army trucks and about 300 soldiers and officers from miscellaneous units. Top deck and tank deck are now crammed to capacity with some soldiers in the spare bunks while the others sleep wherever they can. Weather very warm & clear.

WED. APRIL 26-Preparing for maneuvers. Large assembly of assorted ships in bay and in waters immediately outside bay. "Lightnings" (P-38's) patrolling sky overhead.

THURS. APRIL 27 Large group of misc. ships including our LST 346 set out this morning for a "dry run" along the English Channel. After a number of turns the convoy finally headed back and anchored off a beach near Dartmouth. Army personnel & trucks were "readied" several times for unloading and finally were unloaded onto LCT's which made contact with our LST thru the bow door—during the entire run along the channel we saw no sign of the enemy.

FRI. APRIL 28-This is the day we have been waiting for-"mail call" at last for mail-starved sailors. 6 bags of mail were brought on board at 2000 from Dartmouth Navy P.O. Received 9 letters from the Mrs. and several others.

Dartmouth's another pretty town in a beautiful setting. Saw quite a few ancient-looking forts & castles built along the water's edge of the harbor. LST 289 is anchored here and seems to have met with some sort of an accident. The stern end has been ripped open above the water line, with considerable force and the explosion has twisted and contorted the deck as far forward as the galley hatch. The rear gun turrets are standing in midair, upside down. "Whitey" Spoelma, PhM 2/c was brought to a shore hospital this morning with an elevated temperature and everyone on board was concerned over the possibility of another meningitis case. However, news was signalled from shore that it was not meningitis.

SAT. APRIL 29-We're still anchored in the River Dart between the towns of Dartmouth and Kingswear, between which run several ferries. On the Dartmouth side we can see along the waterfront a number of hotels like the Raleigh, Queens, etc., which have the typical old English half-timbered type of architecture, showing the wooden frame structures as part of the outer wall decoration. Had liberty tonight. Went to Dartmouth and walked around sightseeing with Sheehan. We were shown thru the ancient St. Saviors Church (Catholic-1373) by the young, good-humored priest who was in charge. Bought a number of picture postcards of Dartmouth and a lighter for Davis.

SUN. APRIL 30, 1944-We were awakened at 0230 by general quarters alarm. Dressed and put on my helmet & life jacket & gas mask carrier and went topside to see what was up. Apparently enemy planes had been sighted some miles to the east as we saw the searchlights sweeping the sky, AA fire and occasional bright flashes on the ground which may have been bomb bursts or heavy gun fire. Saw a plane picked up for an instant in one of the lights but it immediately escaped into darkness by a swift turn and dive. Heard the roar of a plane going into a power dive and it sounded as if it were headed straight for us. This alert lasted until 0415 with nothing coming close to our ship. Slept to 1100 and had lunch at 1200. Our LST and other ships pulled out of Dartmouth at 1000 heading for Portland. After lunch went up to the top deck and lay around soaking up some sunshine as this is another beautiful sunny day. Anchored in bay off Portland about 1900.

MON. MAY 1 We moved back to Dartmouth today after having picked up about 30 additional seamen at Portland.

TUES. MAY 2-Went into town this afternoon with the mail orderly. Cashed my $20 money order at the Navy P.O. which is at the Royal Naval College of Dartmouth (a red brick rambling set of buildings set on a hill overlooking the River Dart). Watched a blacksmith at work reshoeing a mare.

WED., MAY 3-Liberty tonite from 1630-2400. Took a train ride from Kingswear to nearby Torquay. 25 minutes each way. Torquay is a very popular peacetime seashore resort and is the most modern of any of the places we have visited.

THURS. MAY 4 Filled out pay receipts this a.m. for another small pay. 6 pounds. Received pay on board the 346. A.A. 2/c Joe T. Karg was taken ashore tonite due to swollen parotid glands-suspected mumps. Learned that Dr. Seifarth is being transferred to the LST 311. Our new med. off. is to be Dr. Richardson, formerly of the ill-fated LST 289, recently hit in the stern by an E-boat-launched torpedo.

FRI. MAY 5-Did a little manual labor today as part of a 4 man working party of hosp. corpsmen that went ashore to help load and unload supplies and food. Had a delicious cream puff as lunch dessert today. Received birthday package of Barton's chocolate-mailed by R.G. 2 months ago.

SAT. MAY 6-Bedding had its weekly airing. Inspection of ship this morning. Had liberty today-started at 1300. Rode up to Torquay again-walked around looking in the store windows, at the passersby. Bought a bag of hot freshly made chips (potato) and ate them on a nearby park bench, sharing with the pigeons. Had some tea and pastels in an English Woolworth store. Pastel filling was mostly potato with a trace of meat. Bought 2 packs of chewing gum in an Army PX in Torquay. Rode back to Kingswear about 1930. Then crossed Dartmouth harbor to the Dartmouth side by hitching a ride on an English small boat. Waited in Dartmouth about 45 minutes and rode back to the 346 in an LCVP. On board by 2115 in time for coffee and a Spam sandwich and to read my mail, one letter from R.G. and one rather old one from Gersen. Then continued reading of "A Tree Grows in Brooklyn".

SUN. MAY 7 Our new med. officer, Dr. Richardson, introduced himself to those of us HC's who were not ashore on liberty this afternoon. According to his few pertinent remarks, our new regime of work and discipline is to begin tomorrow morning as of 0900. Finished reading "A Tree Grows in Brooklyn" today. Some of the female characters particularly interested me as they reminded me of my own wife. Especially "Francie" in her self-confidence and "Aunt Sissy" in her big-heartedness and longing for a child of her own.

MON. MAY 8 Dr. R. is beginning to make his weight felt on board the 346, starting with a formal inspection of sick bay, crew quarters & head. Our new chief PhM came aboard today-name-Blette, A.J., also from the LST 289 which is now undergoing repairs to its rear end.

TUES, MAY 9-Had a few beers tonite with Cox & Larson at the Queen's Hotel, Dartmouth, and then we took in a movie at the Cinedrome. We saw Laurel & Hardy in "Pack Up Your Troubles" and Chester Morris in "Confessions". The major portion of the audience consisted of military personnel of U.S., Britain, Canada and a few French. Young male civilians are rare.

WED. MAY 10-We left Dartmouth at 0600 for a run to nearby Plymouth. The medical unit on board were assigned new battle stations and liferaft numbers, by Chief Blette. My station at present is the

forward battle dressing station, starboard side, just below top deck and life raft No. 1 is the one I'm to go to upon getting the order "abandon ship". We had 2 G.Q. drills and one abandon ship order today on the way to Plymouth. Also some practice firing of the 20 and 40 mm. anti-aircraft guns. I printed up a large copy of the Watch, Quarter, and Stations Bill of the Med Unit for Chief PhM Blette. In sight of Plymouth by 1500. Ship turned around and started back for Dartmouth at 1530. Another G.Q. practice alarm on the way. Arrived in Dartmouth about 2030.
THURSDAY, MAY 11 Lecture this a.m. by Dr. Richardson on treatment of hemorrhage. This was a lucky mail bag for me today. Rec'd 16 pieces of mail. Expect to put in a little time this evening answering correspondence.
SAT MAY 13 Usual Sat. inspection was held. Altho bedding was not brought up on deck for weekly airing because of slight rain falling. Went ashore this a.m. with work party and helped transfer 12 large (300 lb.) crates of field blankets back to the ship to be used later for casualties. Had liberty again today and went to Dartmouth for a few hours. Did not go to the movie this time, having seen the picture before.
MON. MAY 15-3 GQ's today—0330, 1300 & 1430. We practiced pulling up "casualties" in an army litter from a small boat alongside-up to our top deck. Played some poker tonite until 2400 & then to bed. Hope there will not be any more GQ alarms this nite.
TUES, MAY 16-Didn't take advantage of liberty tonite-instead stayed on board and played poker, which is the favorite method of passing time here.
WED. MAY 17 Another lecture to the med group this morning by Dr. Richardson on further treatment of wounds, shock, burns, blast & gas casualties. Practice this afternoon on artificial respiration.
THURS. MAY 18 Further practice (hard work, too) in hauling up litters from small boat alongside and carrying same (loaded with a patient) down the ladders (stairs) to the tank deck. We worked in groups of 3 men apiece.
FRI. MAY 19 Had a special night watch 0200 to 0600 on Coleman, who is ill with tonsilitis & infected throat. Slept thru breakfast-up at 1030. Went to a movie in Dartmouth this evening with Cox & Sheehan. Saw East Side Kids in "Smart Alecs" & an English picture "Women Aren't Angels", which latter was rather more a comedy than anything else.
SAT. MAY 20 Med unit did a little work today opening cases of med supplies & distributing over appropriate sections of our ship. Mailed a package home to R.G. containing 2 novelty crown pins.
SUN. MAY 21 We are still sitting here in Dartmouth Harbor with grass covered hills rising on both sides of the river. Saw a movie on the tank

deck this afternoon-title "Heavenly Bodies" with Wm. Powell & Hedy LaMarr-sort of a light comedy. Went back to my sack to find a batch of 9 letters. Played some Pinochle this evening and then wrote about 8 v-mail letters.

MON. MAY 22-Warm sunny day. Litter-carrying practice this a.m. Oral tests being held by Dr. & Chief for med. unit in connection with advance in ratings.

TUES. MAY 23 7 truckloads of food rations & extra blankets brought in and dumped on our tank deck by army trucks.

WED. MAY 24 Nicholas & I helped Dr. Richardson store some of his excess gear ashore in a med. whse. near the Naval College. First talk by our second med. off. Dr. Overstreet (strictly south). Weather warm & sunny.

FRI. MAY 26-Our LST 346 went up the River Dart about 1 mile to take on about 40,000 gal. of water from the water-tender, HMS GRYFEVALE, which originally had been used as a packet in the Indian service. The crew are East Indians, officers Scotch and the guncrew are Scotch enlisted men. Since we were tied up alongside about 6 hours from (1200 to 1800) a number of us took the opportunity to hop over to the English ship (built in Glasgow) and look around and get acquainted. I gave one of the Scotch crew a white hat and in exchange received an assortment of unusual foreign paper money (5 pieces). I also bought 4 Indian coins from one of the Indians in exchange for English money. The water tanker has 2 large stills which are capable of producing about 200 tons of distilled water per day (48,000 gallons). These stills are used only when the ship is in a section where no good fresh water can be obtained at a nearby port as the distilling operation consumes a tremendous amount of coal and makes the water produced very costly when used for purposes of drinking, cooking & washing. The Gryfevale appeared to be about ⅓ larger than we are in size-it being a little over 5000 tons. Had E.E. Cox PhM 1/c(Tampa, Fla) give me a haircut this evening-not exactly professional but passable considering the lack of proper tools. By 2000 we were back to our corner position in Dartmouth Harbor, tied up alongside the LST 371, with the 49 & 283 nearby.

SAT. MAY 27-Went up to a large grassy ball field near the Royal Naval College, Dartmouth, to watch a baseball game between crews of LST 346 & LST 311. Started reading one of M.R. Rinehart's mystery novels "The Album".

SUN, MAY 28 Liberty started at 1300. Took the train going to Torquay but got off one station before, at Painton, to visit the zoo & miniature circus show. Music at the circus was furnished by some cracked phonograph records but the show itself was interesting, consisting mostly of exhibition by trained horses, ponies, dogs, monkeys, elephants & llamas. In conclusion we watched the head trainer "Samson" put 3 young but wild-looking lions thru their act inside a small cage. Rode to Torquay by bus, had some beers & then took in a show, "Shadow of a Doubt". Went to bed about 1 a.m. & was just asleep when GQ sounded at 1:30 a.m.. Went to my battle station with full equipment which consists of life jacket (kapok), gas mask, helmet, medical first aid kit, and cartridge belt on which are hung canteen of water and a small pouch containing 2 gms. of sulfadiazine and a small battle dressing for personal use. Feel like a human clothes support with all this equipment slung around myself. All clear sounded at 3 a.m. We heard a lot of anti-air-craft fire but couldn't see anything as we are stationed in the stbd. forward compartment just at the foot of the stairway going up to the top deck. Dr. Overstreet, our new Navy med off. also stationed with us. There is now a third doctor aboard-an Army med off. rank—captain, and 3 enlisted Army men of the med. unit.

MONDAY, MAY 29 Very warm & sunny-no trace of coolness in breezes today. Learned that Torquay was bombed early this morning, the raid starting just 2 hrs after we had taken the train back to Kingswear. The Queens Hotel (Torquay) was one of the buildings hit. There were some casualties there and in other sections of the town.

WED. MAY 31 All liberties cancelled today. This evening about 30 Seabees with gear, rifles & ammunition came aboard from a "rhino" ferry.

THURS. JUNE 1. Am beginning to feel a little low in spirits because I've had no letter from the wife for the last 8 days and there remains apparently very few more days during which incoming mail will be obtainable. The LSTs and other craft in the harbor are already taking on their loads of personnel and equipment which may mean that the Day is very close at hand. We may even load our own ship tonight and move out immediately, which of course will mean no more mail for an indefinite period. We started loading up around 8:30 pm after our ship had run her bow up on a nearby "hard". 2 hr. delay caused by breakdown of elevator mechanism between tank deck and top deck. Work resumed at 11:30 pm after a swarm of various mechanical experts had all helped with repairs. Loading completed by 0300. Other LSTs moving in for their loads. We have Misc. Army units aboard-medical, airborne (going over via LST). The ship is now jammed with trucks and soldiers, the latter sleeping anywhere there is a vacant space, even on the deck and on the mess tables.

FRI. JUNE 2 Cool & sunny. About 12 LSTs now loaded & ready to go here at Dartmouth. Each LST flying 2 barrage balloons. In the heavy wind this morning & due to the close proximity of the ships, 4 of the balloons became tangled and were lost. They rose up several thousand feet & then exploded. New ratings of med. unit were posted today. Was advanced to second class pharmacist mate as of June 1. Rumors about when we shove off are now flying thick & fast thru this ship. No letter from the wife yet. Tomorrow may be the last chance to receive mail.

SAT. JUNE 3 We were given final instructions this evening at 7:30 by the skipper Lt. Howell as to date and destination of invasion. We are to leave Dartmouth at 0700 tomorrow, sailing out to meet convoy. Steady stream of LCMs, LCTs moving out towards the channel today. Our destination—northern coast of France near Cherbourg.

SUN. JUNE 4 Due to unfavorable weather conditions we are still at Dartmouth at this time, 5:30 pm. Ship is a bit crowded now with 500 aboard and normal compliment 150-200. Between meals every table is occupied by soldiers playing poker and using their newly issued paper French money in denominations of 5 fr. (10c)10,50,100,200, etc. francs. This currency is brand new dated 1944, is colorful and artistically engraved. The soldiers have rec'd their last pay in French money in anticipation of using it soon in France.

MON. JUNE 5 We finally pulled out of Dartmouth Harbor this morning around 10 am. Weather cool, cloudy & windy—We join large formation of LSTs, destroyers & some cruisers in the Channel, heading East. We've been joined by a half dozen battleships & some large transports. Still heading east 1530. Was issued impregnated clothing consisting of overalls, jacket with hood and long woolen gloves. To be used when working outside during gas attack or alert. Convoy still heading east, now joined by a group of transport ships. Traveling under regulations of Condition 2 (alert) with 1/2 of ships' crew on watch at all times, changing watch every four hours. Channel roughening up tonite and many of soldiers & sailors suffering from mal-de-mer.

TUESDAY, JUNE 6 This should be the day. I was on watch (med. station) from 8 pm to midnight last night-then slept in my clothes till 6 am. Went up on deck for some fresh air and to nose around. Sun was just rising-our group of ships now has turned its direction of travel to southeast. Plane formations seen passing us overhead going towards France. Our small escort vessel—DE's, sub chasers & PTs are busy on the outskirts, patrolling the water and there are several planes skimming the surface around us also looking for trouble. Water has quieted down somewhat, much to everyone's relief. Having nothing else to do this morning I read thru a little novel by the name of "Talk of the Town" by Ann Pinchot. Sighted the coastline of France at 1300-very faintly in the distance. We must be about 15 miles from our destination. At 1315 counted about 200 of our big bombers (Fortresses) speeding towards the French coast. About 16 P-38s in groups of 4 have been constantly patrolling the sky above our convoy. At 1345 the soldiers are getting their gear together as they will be getting off soon. As soon as we drop them and their trucks and pick up any casualties that may be waiting to be transferred back to England, the first part of our job will be done. Will probably be repeating this process for the next few weeks if we can keep out of trouble in the meantime. While the LSTs were laying off shore about 12 miles out, the fleet big guns opened up a barrage which began at 1500 and continued intermittently until 2400. Further masses of bombers continue to pour in over the coast here (Western shore of Cherbourg peninsula). After dark tonight we saw a striking display of anti-aircraft fire and saw several planes shot down in flames but we had no way of knowing at the time whose planes were being hit. The Sea Bees we picked up were transferred today back to their Rhino ferry which the ship had towed from Dartmouth.

WED. JUNE 7 Soldiers are still aboard. (Entries for Wed., Thurs, Fri, are being written on Fri. June 9 because of lack of time to make daily entries). More & still more bombers continue to pour in overhead for inland bombing missions. The Navy heavy guns are shelling the coast-continuously. We moved in & anchored abut 3 miles from the beach to start unloading soldiers & equipment about 6 p.m. First casualties from the shore start to arrive by means of "ducks" & LCT's. We received 160 wounded on 2 ducks and one LCT. There were 10 German prisoners included. These were handled just like the others except for being segregated in a compartment by themselves. Our Med. unit worked steadily from 6 pm to midnight hauling the patients aboard and carrying them below where bunks had been cleared for them. Some of the more serious cases were treated on the LCT by Dr. Overstreet & Richardson with plasma coramine before being taken aboard. There were all types of injuries except abdominal perforations. We (the med. unit aboard the LST 346) finally put into practice some of the teachings which had been drilled into us. The litters began piling up on the top deck long before the ship's cargo had been taken off and hauling up of cases had to be delayed a number of times until room had been made below to clear some working space.

While we were working we saw one of our planes chase & shoot down a German plane which had tried to strafe the beach in front of us. The German pilot jumped before his plane crashed & was one of those brought aboard as a wounded prisoner.

We also saw a great deal of AA fire both ours & the enemy's. Saw one of our planes drop 2 bombs on enemy position further up the coast. Also saw 2 planes shot down and fall, looking like comets.

We worked straight thru the night getting the wounded settled, comfortable and below decks, and treating for shock which seems to have been the greatest immediate danger. Helped Dr. Richardson administer pentothal sodian (an anesthetic) to a soldier who was having a perforating gunshot wound of the right hand being cleaned up by our army surgeon, Dr. Redmond (Capt.).

Among the casualties were paratroopers Airborne (Glider troops) who had gone in before the first landings for the purpose of knocking out heavy gun emplacements. Their job had been well done but at a heavy cost. Some of them had been dropped in the wrong places and had landed in the middle of German machine gun nests. The paratroopers were unanimous in their slogan "Take no prisoners". It can be readily understood why these men, working alone or in small groups behind enemy lines could not be burdened with prisoners and at the same time could not allow any contacted enemy to remain alive to report their presence. Nevertheless, prisoners were taken and I spoke to one of them, Erich Schubert, who told me he had been fighting for 5 years, had fought at Stalingrad, and now was very glad to be out of it. He showed me a picture of his wife and baby girl, about whose existence he was very uncertain as his home is Berlin.

THURS. JUNE 8 Mine sweeper had been busy cleaning up the water near the beach before we pulled in but they did not get all of the mines out because LST 499 hit one as well as several small landing craft which sank immediately. The 499 did not sink at once but there were quite a few injured (about 50) and some deaths. We pulled up alongside the 499 about 11 am and took on the injured as well as whatever medical supplies they could pass over to us in a short time. The 499 had a large hole in the stern and was gradually settling so we didn't stay tied up to her any longer than necessary to get the casualties and supplies. With the new cases, we now had about 200 to take care of. Knowing we were in mine-infested waters and knowing also the terrific damage that a mine could cause we were feeling a little jittery and were trying to get a little lunch when during the meal we heard a terrific explosion which rocked the ship and made the trays jump up on the table. We all jumped up and scrambled for the top deck to get ready to leave in a hurry as we were sure our ship had struck a mine. I reached the deck in time to see a smaller ship only a few hundred yards away settling rapidly in the water and come to rest on the bottom with just the top of the mast showing above the surface. It was the HMS Minster, a British net layer with a crew of 90 which had hit a mine and sunk in just 90 seconds. We thought no one had survived but sent some small boats over anyway to pick up possible survivors. Our boat picked up 5 men who we brought on board, swelling our number of casualties to 210. From this point until we reached Portland on the morning of the 9th we were really busy looking after the needs of our patients, some of whom needed almost constant attention. The three doctors also had their hands full as they had to check each man at least once. There were two minor operations performed by Dr. Redmond, both to clean up gunshot wounds on the hands of two men. One English sailor from the sunken netlayer had a severe compound fracture of the upper left arm with the broken ends of the bone projecting from both sides of the arm. This same fellow also had a fracture of the left leg and a cut on his skull. He must have had great resistance because he responded well to questions and was still going strong the next morning. I finally crawled into an empty bunk about 2:30, am still wearing all my clothes which had not come off for 3 nights.

FRI JUNE 9 Was awakened at 7 am by Cox after what seemed to me a very short nap but which really must have been a refreshing sleep. Our casualties were taken off by Army negro first aid men and put into waiting ambulances. We were all very grateful that we didn't have to move them ourselves as we were still sore and aching from the job of hauling over 200 men on board and distributing them. As soon as the injured were off we immediately began taking on the load for our second run. This time we are taking some 300 soldiers of the 2nd Armored Division & their vehicles—heavy half-tracks heavily armored & armed. Before we can leave our stern anchor motor is being repaired and one of our spare anchors (3000 lbs.) is being moved into position with the assistance of the repair ship, the USS Melville, which came alongside for the job. We had a fairly easy day and had a chance to rest & wash up and clean up the ship which had become quite messy due to the overcrowded condition of the past week, aggravated by the use as an emergency hospital for some 200 men crowded into the crews quarters, the port & starboard compartments, and spread over the tank deck. Wrote a couple of letters home to a few people who might be worried after reading about casualties connected with the invasion.

SAT JUNE 10 We pulled out of Portland at 0500 with about 300 soldiers of the 2nd Armored Division & headed E & S for the Omaha sector beachhead, which is slightly east of the Cherbourg Peninsula. Reached our destination & anchored 1000 yards off shore at 8:30 pm. The harbor here is simply jammed with our ships of all types, sizes & description including one British hospital ship. The French coast of Normandy is now very visible—we saw & heard minor explosions on shore where mines are being set off. We are due to beach our LST at 03:30 to unload and it may be 12 hrs. before we get off the shore. Did a little reading and went to bed about 11:20.

SUNDAY, JUNE 11 On French soil-Was awakened this morning about 4 am by the noise of a nearby exploding bomb & gun fire. Went to my battle station and watched the proceedings of the battle from deck while waiting possible casualties. Our first casualty was Moggerman, who was on the boat deck just outside the wheel house when a 20 mm shell dropped and exploded at his feet. He got several cuts in his leg from the flying metal plus a few scratches. After the planes had disappeared our ship was run onto the beach and the soldiers & their half-tracks were unloaded (6-8 am). The tide was rapidly receding and by 0930 we were completely dry. This gave us a chance to get off the ship and do a little exploring around the sands. The German fortifications, barricades & tunnels were still to be seen. The grass on the slopes just back of the beach was considerably charred. Army personnel & vehicles as soon as unloaded started on the road over the hill into the interior. The charred blackened remains of the LCT 91 was only a hundred yds away from us on the beach, a D-Day casualty. After the LST was unloaded, the med. unit got busy & cleaned up the tank deck as we were expecting another load of casualties. We intended bringing them directly onto the tank deck this time, instead of down to the crews quarters which we did the first time and which had been a back-breaking job.

While I was walking around the beach near our LST, picking up a few shells to take home, I heard two explosions on the nearby hill, and saw a cloud of white smoke from one and a cloud of grey-black smoke from the other. The wind was carrying these smokes away from land directly towards the water and our ship. Then someone on land yelled "Gas" and I made a dash of about 60 yds to my compartment to get my mask on. Everyone else had heard the shout and in a few minutes we all had on our masks while Chief Gobel (Bosun) showed up in a complete set of protective clothing (against blister gases). It turned out to be a false alarm but was a good lesson to most of us to carry our masks when straying any distance away as there would have been many casualties had this been a real gas attack. 2 men were brought aboard wounded by explosion of 20 mm. shells. 2 more came on later in the day wounded by shrapnel. This makes 5 patients so far.

Our LST moved off the beach at 2 pm when the tide had come in enough to float the ship. We are now anchored about a mile off shore. News is coming in about the sinking of 4 LSTs in the channel from E-boat torpedo attacks. One LST went down in the harbor from a mine explosion this afternoon. This evening a war correspondent (Los Angeles Times) and a USCG photographer came aboard for transportation back to England. We are all beginning to feel that our greatest danger lies in mines and torpedoes in that order, mines above all. And so to bed, fully dressed again & ready for a quick exit if necessary.

MONDAY, JUNE 12 Awoke this morning about 7 am surprised that there had been no alarm during the night. Perhaps the heavy clouds had something to do with it. We started back across the channel to

England at 0800 as part of a huge convoy. Passed ships coming in with fresh supplies. The Coast Guard photographer took a picture on top deck of our med. unit this afternoon. He also took a shot of the officers in a group.

After a quiet trip we dropped anchor in Southampton harbor. Saw the LST 506 lying at anchor in the channel on our way in, thus dispelling rumors that she had been sunk. The 506 was the LST we came over on from the States and at present carries 1/2 of our original med. group. The other 1/2 went to the 346.

TUES. JUNE 13 Loaded up this morning with English and Canadian troops who are to set up and operate airfields in France. We did not start moving till after midnight. The weather so far this month has been cold & rainy.

WED. JUNE 14 We arrived at the French coast about 11 am today at a point east of our previous two landings, near the town of St. Aubin. This is the "Juno" beachhead, being operated by the British. Will be unloading about 11 pm when the tide will have receded enough to enable the motor vehicles to run down the ramp thru the open bow doors onto dry sands. Had a sunny day but the air was still very brisk.

Some enemy planes came snooping around as it started getting dark and we were about to start unloading. Heavy AA fire from the shore & nearby ships drove them off without any damage being done that we could see.

The English & Canadians were safely ashore with their equipment by 1230 and I went to bed about 1 am.

THURS. JUNE 15 We remained beached until about 9 am and then joined a convoy headed back to England for our 4th load. Our destination this time appears to be a port on the Thames River some 30 miles below London. I doubt whether we will get a chance to see the big city this time. The trip so far (9 pm) has been uneventful. We are due to arrive 9 am tomorrow morning.

FRI JUNE 16 We travelled up the Thames as far as the city of London and anchored in an enclosed basin of the West India Dock Co., entering thru a water lock. Took on a load of English, Scotch & Canadians and their equipment. Read of the second bombing of Japan, this time by American Super Fortresses, the new B-29's. Some German robot planes have been shot down last night. We are still tied up to the hard where the load was taken aboard.

SAT. JUNE 17 Spent the day getting acquainted with the various groups of English & Canadian soldiers who are on board. We moved out to the mouth of the Thames & anchored there until 1930 when the entire convoy started moving toward our next beachhead in France, the "Gold" Beach.

SUN. JUNE 18 Sunny, quiet-convoy moving west & south. Swell roast chicken dinner today. We anchored off the French coast at 9:30 pm after an uneventful trip across the channel. Weather has turned cold, rainy & windy and the ship is rolling in the choppy water. Some of the English soldiers were having a heated discussion on the subject of the measly pay and unattractive food. We compared methods of preparing Yorkshire Pudding, rice pudding & other items as practised by the English with our own American methods. This discussion lasted quite late much to the annoyance of several of our fellows who would rather have slept.
MON. JUNE 19 We haven't been able to beach & unload due to continuous rough weather. We have been anchored all day off shore with the ship rolling & rocking most of the time, causing the soldiers to wish they were on terra firma.
TUES. JUNE 20 Third day we haven't been able to unload due to rough weather and rolling sea. We are having a difficult time just to stay anchored in a safe spot about a mile off shore.
WED. JUNE 21 Fourth day of rough weather. Everyone aboard is getting very tired of this setup, but any attempt to beach under present conditions would risk having the ship pound itself apart in the heavy surf.
THURS. JUNE 22 It was finally decided that the supplies laying out on all the LSTs, Liberty ships, etc., out in the harbor would have to be landed today at all costs. The unloading has already been delayed since Sunday due to rough weather and the people on shore have been clamoring for much needed reinforcements. Fortunately the wind and weather turned agreeable and we beached at 6:00 pm. Incidentally, the 346 came to rest on the stern anchor of the LST 537 which had gone in an hour before us and had its anchor out on a 150 yd. wire cable. The result was a 6" hole near the bottom of our ship. As the water entering at this point went directly in to one of our ballast tanks no immediate harm has resulted. Our ramp was no sooner down on the still wet sands when at least half of the crew went ashore and scattered—souvenir hunting and to look around. There were at least 20 LST's unloading side by side along the beach and it was a spectacle worth seeing. I believe the Germans were aware of the activities under way as we could see a number of vapor trails high up, probably made by their recon. and photographer's planes. We had sufficient planes of our own patrolling the sky to be safe from any air attack. I spent several hours ashore myself, accompanied by two young H.A 1/c-R. J. Sheehan of Franklin, N.H. & Rule C. Trout of Spartanburg, S.C. We inspected a number of the former German dugouts just behind the beach. These are now inhabited by English troops who are in charge of this particular beach. Many of the dugouts had been fitted out as quite comfortable living

quarters since the Germans had several years time to work on them. The larger dugouts and shelters had wooden frame bunks, brick fireplaces and large metal drinking water drums installed. A number of the smaller dugouts still have piles of assorted gear jumbled together & left behind by the fleeing Germans. We did not attempt to disturb any of this material for very good reasons. We saw several marshy & grassy areas which are still mined and unsafe. Their borders carried signs bearing the warning "Mines". Safe pathways have been marked out with strips of white tape. Our attention was drawn to a large 4 motor allied plane (fortress) circling slowly overhead from which men in parachutes were jumping. I saw 4 parachutes coming down and while trying to figure out what it was all about soon saw the reason. The plane, still circling, started coming down and while falling half of the stbd wing folded up as if it had been perforated. The plane fell more rapidly now and crashed behind a nearby ridge, throwing up a tremendous cloud of flame upon hitting the ground. The parachutists were still falling very slowly and drifting inland due to the prevailing wind. We returned to the ship about 9 pm as the tide was coming in fast and in fact passed our bow door about 9:30. Some of the crew had delayed getting aboard and we watched several of them wading thru 3 or 4ft. of water in order to reach the ramp. The ramp was finally pulled up and the bow doors closed. There were still a few of our men missing and the skipper was now getting angry about the whole thing. The last few missing members were brought alongside by some "ducks" and they had to climb up the cargo nets. The executive officer interviewed these latecomers who had held up the ship and the result was no more liberties for these until further notice. We were now ready to haul up our stern anchor & pull out to deeper water where we remained overnight. Incidentally, enemy planes came over around midnight dropping dozens of flares but I didn't see any bombs falling. They may have been sowing floating mines which is one of their favorite tricks.

FRI. JUNE 23 Instead of heading back to England as we had expected to do today, orders came thru for the LSTs, now unloaded, to put up alongside the big English merchant ships & take their loads ashore as apparently there haven't been enough Rhino ferries available to do this job. We are to beach again at 1600 today with trucks & more British troops from the Brit. merchant ships. It was 6 pm before the tide had rolled back far enough to enable the trucks we had on the tank deck to roll down the ramp to comparatively dry sands.

Due to last evening's escapade of some crew members returning late to the ship, the skipper issued an order restricting the entire crew from the beach. Nevertheless, after the unloading, we knew the ship couldn't pull out for several hours and many of us got itching feet so we annoyed

Mr. Feiss, the officer on watch at the bow door exit until he permitted us to walk around as long as we kept within his sight. He really had a hard job keeping all the wandering boys in view as they had a tendency to scatter in all directions once their feet touched dry land.

4 of the older crew members received special permission to watch a soccer game among the English on a beach nearby. Some time later I was sent out to round up these privileged characters & tell them it was time to return. I found only one, who was on his way back to the ship when I met him. Noticed the LCT 619 on the beach not far from us. This is the LCT we had carried across the Atlantic on the LST 506 and which was launched at Plymouth, right from the top deck of the 506.

After the tide came in we moved out to deep water and anchored for the night.

SAT. JUNE 24 We're on our way back to England again for the finish of our fourth trip to the invasion coast. We're due to spend a few days at the next port while the ship receives some attention. Hope I find a few letters waiting. We had an excellent lunch of baked Va. ham, sweet potatoes, spinach, canned sweet cherries & coffee & fresh baked bread. This is the traditional Sat. lunch menu but tasted particularly good today. Everyone seems to be in good spirits, perhaps at our luck so far. Conditions are normal enough for the order of "air bedding" to be given for the first time in about 4 weeks. We're moving along full speed, in the center of a huge number of ships, England bound.

SUN. JUNE 25 We were awakened at 5 a.m. by the GQ alarm. On reaching the top deck we discovered the reason for the alarm was a couple of motor torpedo boats speeding thru our convoy. They were soon identified as friendly, however, and we were back in bed by 5:15 am. We were going East, thru the Straits of Dover at the time of the alarm and were in easy sight of the English coast on our port side. Slept thru breakfast, rising at 10:30 and washed up and made ready for lunch. We were headed for a London dry dock but after going some distance up the Thames we rec'd orders to turn around and put in at Chatham. Finally tied up at the Royal Dry Dock of Chatham at 6 p.m. Liberty is being given to 1/2 the crew for the first time in 4 weeks. This is an overnight liberty—expiring at 0845 tomorrow and most of the "liberty hounds" are headed for London, which is only 45 minutes distance by train. Expect to have my turn tomorrow with the other half of the crew. Our sleeping compartment seems very dead tonight with 5 out of the 8 occupants gone for the night. Played a little pinochle and then to sleep. The boys started coming in from liberty at 0130 feeling more or less happy. The last of the liberty party from our compartment came in after 8 am Monday morning from London and all excited and talkative about the sights they had seen, especially at Piccadilly Circus, where the newpaper vendors also loudly advertised their rubber goods for sale and where women were plentiful & available.

MONDAY JUNE 26 Our ship is still laid up here in Lock 45, completely dry and the drydock workers are busy getting her in shape for more travelling. Had my first good view of the new German pilotless Robot plane or "Flying Bomb" when we heard and saw one flying east about 2000 ft. altitude at 1400. Heard another at 1600 but did not see it because of the heavy clouds. Left the ship at 1630 on my first liberty in 4 weeks. Went to the business sections of Chatham first in order to get a new crystal for my wrist watch. This was completed by 1730 and at 1800 A.S. Kirkland PhM 3/c and I took the train for London. We arrived at Charing Cross station about 90 minutes later and we spent the next 4 hours of daylight that remained sightseeing around the Westminister district of London. We had a bite to eat at the "Rainbow Corners" Red Cross—Saw the damage being done by the flying bombs, a number of which have hit various parts of the city. There were very few American sailors about but lots of soldiers. We decided to take the 11:42 train back to Chatham as we didn't care to wander about London for 5 or 6 hours in the dark. About 10 minutes after we had pulled out of the station we heard the air raid sirens and 15 minutes later we saw the flaming exhausts of two rocket planes headed for the city we had just left. (We learned later from some of the boys who had stayed in London thru the night that there were several hits in the Piccadilly area). Reached the ship in the midst of a heavy rain and we warmed up with some hot coffee at 0230, then to bed.

TUES. JUNE 27 Repair work still progressing on the 346. Learned today that our med group will probably be transferred from the ship very soon. This is not surprising news in view of the fact that we had no casualties to bring back in our last 3 trips, and other facilities for handling the wounded are increasing rapidly. These other facilities being, hospital ships, air transport and field hospitals in France. Liberty again tonight for the first section. We had a real treat for supper tonight—fresh milk—something we haven't tasted since leaving the States.

WED. JUNE 28 Rode up to London on the 4:45 train, getting off at London Bridge Station. We (Kirkland & I) walked across London Bridge into the original City of London—then down to see the Tower of London, a medieval-looking, sprawled-out fortress surrounded by a wide dry moat. Took a ride on the underground (old-fashioned London subway with door that opened while the train is moving) to Charing Cross. Then out to the street and to a small restaurant. I had some steak & kidney pie & green peas. Had a strawberry trifle (one strawberry) for dessert. Then rode around the city on the top deck of a double-decker bus for 1½ hours. We had a few beers at the American Bar (Piccadilly) and then took the 11:42 to Chatham. By taxi to the dry dock and back to our ship by 1:30 a.m. to find about 10 letters waiting and the med. group busy packing up as we are leaving the 346 tomorrow.

THURS. JUNE 29 We (2 med. off. & chief of 19 corpsmen) said goodbye to the LST 346 at 11 am after 10 weeks. One truck carried our baggage & 2 trucks divided up 22 men and we are on our way to Plymouth. Stopped at Deptford USNAAB at 12 for lunch. Saw another "doodle-bug" pass overhead, cut off & crash several seconds later. This happened just as we arrived at Deptford, which is on the outskirts of London. After lunch, our trucks continued on, straight thru London and we had a real sightseeing trip—We stopped at Salisbury at 5 pm for some sandwiches at a very modern-appearing Red Cross. I went over and spent a few minutes looking over the noted Salisbury Cathedral (12th Century) and bought a few picture postcards of this beautiful structure. Stonehenge is only 10 miles from here but we didn't get to see it. Salisbury has many modern-looking shops. We arrived at a "survivors" base (Quonset Huts) at Exeter at 9:30 p.m. and spent the night here, sleeping on bare springs with a few blankets under us.

FRIDAY, JUNE 30 Mailed bracelet to wife from the Navy P.O. here at the Exeter Amphibious Supply Base, at which place we have spent the night. At 11:30 we loaded our gear into trucks & started out for Plymouth, where we arrived at 2:30 p.m. We stopped at the Vicarage Receiving Base (Quonset huts and very muddy) just outside Plymouth. We had some lunch and settled down in one of the huts for an indefinite stay until further orders come thru. This base is now crammed with hospital corpsmen who have been taken off LSTs for other duties elsewhere. Some are going back to the States and if we are lucky we'll go back for a short leave at home at least. About twenty of us were pulled out of the hut at 11 pm for a working party—unloading food supplies at a warehouse. This kept us busy till 4 am. We had plenty to eat, however, including some fresh apples & oranges which have just come in from the States. This is the last day of a cold & rainy month.

SAT. JULY 1 Still raining here and the ground is getting muddier. Bought some new black shoes at the small stores on the base. Cost $4.95. Met some corpsmen from Bklyn Naval Hospital. Looked up Jack Fisher (PhM 2/c) of Bklyn N.Hosp. He is now doing temp duty in the Med. Records Off. here at Vicarage. He was on the LST 496 which was sunk by a mine after their first trip to Normandy. To bed about 11:30 after playing some cards in our hut.

SUNDAY, JULY 2 Still raining. Did a little galley duty for dinner & supper along with some others from our hut. Saw some short subjects, including invasion pictures of Anzio beachhead. As this is a temporary base we expect orders to move on any minute or day & I've tried not to unpack too much. Fortunately these bunks are supplied with good mattresses and having dug up a couple of blankets believe I can get along for at least a week living out of two small ditty bags.

MONDAY, JULY 3 Put in a 4 hr. watch duty at the O.D.'s office this morning from 0800 to 1200. The work was very light & consisted of checking new arrivals & departees into & out of the base's roster books, also in trying to answer all kinds of questions or directing inquiries to the proper source of information. Still lots of rain but there were a few short sunny periods during the day.

TUES. JULY 4 Officially this is the holiday celebrated in the U.S. in remembrance of "Independence" but was observed very quietly here in England. I took a trip down to the nearby Fleet P.O. at Plymouth & picked out some mail for our group from the bag addressed to the LST 346. Bought a $100 war bond with some extra cash I had on hand. Was going to send a money order home but noticed a July 4th special War Bond compaign sale notice at the Plymouth Base. Was able to negotiate this purchase only after going up to Shapters Field & hunting up the officer in charge of selling War Bonds.

As a special July 4 treat, a bottle of Pabst beer was issued to every man with the evening meal. Since quite a few of the younger fellows have not yet developed a taste for beer, some of us feasted on 2 or more bottles.

Went to the movies at the base after supper. The picture was "Around the World" with Kay Kyser.

WED. JULY 5 Went after mail again today down at the Fleet P.O. at Plymouth. Had lunch at the Plymouth Base & waited until 2 p.m. at the P.O. for the latest mail for our group. Since we are supposed to leave Vicarage tomorrow for Scotland, got my things ready for moving.

A large number of survivors from LCM's arrived here at Vicarage today.

THURS. JULY 6 At last we are moving out of this mud hole of Vicarage Red. Barracks.

Went down for mail again to the Plymouth F.P.O.

Back at Vicarage we packed all our gear and were ready to move out at 1500 along with 8 other med. groups. Had a truck ride to the RR station in Plymouth & boarded a train which pulled out at 1800, bound for Glasgow. We were issued some boxes of K rations to use on the 20 hour trip. There were 6 of us to each train compartment and we were supposed to make our own sleeping arrangements as well as we could. Built a fire inside my steel helmet, using the wax wrapper of a K ration box as fuel. Warmed up a canteen of water and we had some hot bouillon soup.

FRI. JULY 7 After a more or less sleepless night, no water except what a few of us had in our canteens, we breakfasted on K rations. Train stopped at Carlisle (10 am) where we were issued hot coffee, sandwiches, & cookies. Arrived at Glasgow at 1400 near the piers. Moved our baggage to the USS Core, a baby flattop which was tied up about a mile from the train. Then came the usual rush to get a bunk & locker, pack our gear up to our respective compartments, make our beds, have some supper, shower & get ready for bed. Weather raining, cold & miserable.
SAT. JULY 8 Woke up about 6:30 after an unusually sound sleep. Routine on our new home-mustering about 4 times on flight deck & hangar deck-Getting acquainted with the many passageways & ladders. Changed 4 lbs. of English money into unfamiliar American currency-$16.14. Took in a movie on the hangar deck 7:30-8:30 pm. Smoked a cigar afterwards on one of the lower decks & enjoyed the bright warm sunshine.

We moved out of Glasgow harbor down the river several miles & have anchored at the new location, waiting for the order to move in convoy back to the States.
SUN. JULY 9 Am meeting more & more fellows I knew either from Sampson or Bklyn who are aboard this USS Core on their way back to the States like myself. It's possible to wander around this ship for several weeks & not meet everyone here. The crew alone consists of over 700 E. Men & officers and there are also over 200 passengers. Some more statistics—Flight deck about 450 ft. long by 50 ft. wide.
MONDAY, JULY 10 We moved out about 11 pm last night, headed south thru the Irish Sea, I believe. As it has been cloudy & windy all day we couldn't determine our direction of travel from the sun.

Movies tonite—"The Voice of Terror" an up-to-date Sherlock Holmes picture. Moved our time back 1 hr., a process which will have been repeated 6 times by the time we reach the States. Convoy of about 50 large ships traveling at 14 knots.
FRIDAY, JULY 14 5th day out

No G.Q. Water getting rougher today. At 6:30 pm we saw something out of the ordinary run of things. One of our 6 destroyer escort ships pulled up alongside us, both keeping up their speed—a light line was shot over to the DE and a bag of medical supplies was passed over to the DE along a heavier line. This little operation made an interesting picture with the DE speeding alongside not over 30 feet away at one time. Saw another movie tonite—"International Lady" with George Brent, Ilona Massey & Basil Rathbone.
SAT. JULY 15 6th day out

Another beautiful sunny day. Time moved back another 1/2 hr. making 4 hrs. change so far. 2 more hrs. to move back to reach U.S. War

Time. We've been eating plenty of ice cream on this ship as it is made fresh every day & sold at the canteen for 10 cents per cup.

SUN JULY 17th 7th day out

The daily news bulletin issued on this ship, "Morning Sun", continues to feature the sensational advances being made by the Russian armies in their steady, uninterrupted drive towards Germany. This in itself point toward a quick collapse of Germany as it is the general opinion here that the Germans will surrender to the Allies once the Russian army has entered their territory. We transferred some more supplies to another DE early this evening by the same process described a few days ago. For entertainment we had the ship's band playing & various amateur volunteer singers & musicians putting on an amusing show tonite. Four of the officers even helped along by their quartet singing.

WED. JULY 19 10th day out

Our trip is coming to an end at last. We should be in Hampton Roads anchorage some time after midnight. We were wakened early this morning to bid farewell to the Commodore we had aboard. He was transferred to a DE and left with the convoy in the direction of N.Y. & Phila. We were left with two D.E.s & continued on towards Norfolk. Firing practice this morning. Each of the Core's two 5" guns shot one shell into the air and the 20's and 40's opened fire using the burst of the 5" shell as a target. The two DE's lined up in our wake carried on target practice at the same time. A PBY is still flying circles around us at sunrise & sunset looking for enemy subs.

THURS. JULY 20 (We land at Nor.)

Abandon ship—with all our luggage, 2 seabags per man at least. 1 bed roll & assorted ditty bags. After the usual maneuvering back & forth on the hangar deck moving our gear until the officials had come to some agreement (in undress blues & perspiring fiercely) carried our gear off the ship & loaded it in to waiting trucks on Pier 7 Norfolk Navy Yard. We were taken on busses to NOB (Naval Operating Base) & were settled into barracks. Then came the unbelievably good news—30 days leave for all the returned corpsmen. Some of the boys started home tonight. Most are staying to be paid tomorrow. Called home. R.G. located at the Hersons.

FRI. JULY 21

After a long hot day of waiting around we finally drew pay to July 15. At 4 pm & started for home. Bought tickets Norfolk-N.Y Penn RR $8.30 round trip. Route is by ferry from Norfolk to Cape Charles (3 hrs. trip) then by RR. Enjoying *this* boat trip.

# WALTER L. RHINEHART

Like the previous diarist, Walter L. Rhinehart now lives in Sarasota, Florida. He was born, however, in Philadelphia in 1909. though he spent most of his life in the District of Columbia when not overseas with the Navy or the Agency for International Development and its predecessor agencies.

A 1935 graduate of George Washington University, Rhinehart worked with the Bureau of Prisons, Dept. of Justice, before joining the Navy in 1942. On return to civilian life he worked first for the Veterans' Administration and then, from 1948 until his retirement in 1966, he held posts with the Economic Cooperation Administration and its successors in such far-flung locales as France, Spain, Portugal, Korea, Afghanistan, Libya and Taiwan.

In World War II Rhinehart was an officer on board LSD destroyer-type ships which were involved in 13 major engagements, rising to the rank of Lt. Commander. Called back to duty in the Korean War he held the rank of Commander. He retired from the Navy Reserve in 1963.

By his first marriage, Rhinehart has a son, Walter L. Rhinehart, Jr. (called "the Geefle" in the diary) who is employed by the Dept. of State. In 1958, while stationed in Afghanistan, he married his second wife, Helen Blaine Sofio, now sharing his Florida retirement.

Commander Rhinehart's diary tends to be much less graphic than some others in its description of shipboard life and of battle but what does come out of it is a pensiveness and melancholy that many men felt, perhaps especially those who, like him, were married men and fathers.

Because of the rather routine nature of the battle reports, this diary is much more heavily excised than others, at a certain cost of continuity.

*******

## TO MYSELF

This being my first effort in life to maintain a diary I am not expecting any great things. With the optimism of fools and realizing that it is always the other guy whose chips are in I am obsessed with the desire to record the daily events of these gruesome days so that when the softening hand of time has caressed my feeble memory I may find a reference as in a file so that I may not be left behind as greater liars rend the skies.

Perhaps my son at some far distant date may find in it something of interest regarding his father and the greatest adventure of his life.

**JANUARY 21, 1944**

Arrived La Haina Roads, fueled, took on supplies. Reflected on Hawaiian landscape wondering whether it would be the last piece of US I should ever see.

**JUNE 10 & 11**

Marines went on a Coral (Beer) party. Mahaffy brought me 25 lb. chunk of Coral as a souvenir. Doc brought me a bottle of beer. Sent out our last mail. Got none, which doesn't make me too happy. We will be underway in 24 hrs. Nights like this set men to thinking. Where will we be before another Sunday? Many are writing letters, some just roaming around wondering. It's a funny ole life.

**JUNE 12**

At 0550 left Kwajalein Atoll for Guam with Northern Attack Force 531 under Admiral Connolly 5th Phib. Again we try our luck. On board Co. A and ½ B 3rd Marine Div., 35 tanks LCT 945, 14 LCMs. Twilight was magnificent and peaceful. I would give anything for a picture of the convoy at sunset. Soft Easterly trades blowing continuously. Letter from Eve. The folks have decided to move in our home. It makes me very happy as it will be so good for the Geefle.

**SEPT. 13, 1944**

USS Franks sighted what appeared to be a floating mine. Maneuvered to avoid area while can exploded mine. Passed through large numbers of floating oil drums and debris. Evidently the resting place of part of the Jap fleet. Fueled cans from USS Millicoma and USS Pecos. Millicoma has her fantail sheared away, evidently due to collision. The old man is warming up with the invasion jitters. I suppose it is his lumbago again.

**SEPT. 14**

The inevitable D minus one. The same gorgeous sunset making one wonder about those for whom it is the last sunset. Two task groups of LSTs on horizon and 3 more CVE groups. Mine sweepers left formation at 1800 to go in on sweeping job. Planes and BB have been hitting it steady for 5 days. Reveille at 230 GQ at 400.

**OCT 19**

Another day before with all its foreboding, fears, and speculations. It seems like all life parades before you on days like this. I find myself always asking why I again. Screen located and apparently sunk a Jap sub this noon. Intelligence informs that Japs are aware of our landing date and place to be prepared to repulse air attack at dawn.

**OCT. 20**

Came the dawn and at 6:30 we were in the swept channel of San Pedro Bay. DD 563 Ross hit a mine. As did ARS 8. Neither sunk. At 727 Jap float planes attack formation dropped 4 bombs among LSTs and escaped. Cruisers shot down 3 other planes attempting attack. The day is clear with a haze hanging over shore line. The battle wagon and cruisers continued 3 day shellacking. The Harris picked up a mine in her paravanes but it did not explode. Came to anchor in 10 fathoms of water off Tacolaban and discharged LCMs at 8:45 without incident. First wave hit beach at 1017 and went 500 yards without hitting any opposition. Mortar fire increased and as usual harassed boats and unloading parties. 2 LCVPs sunk and 5 LSTs took heavy pounding. USS Nashville with Doug tossed the spud about 2500 yds on our port beam. Got a feeling of attainment from this job that has been lacking from the others. Gives one the realization of clearing one's conscience of a badly done job in the past. MacArthur & the Pres. of the Philippines landed and made a radio address at 1520. "I have returned," said Doug. How much better it would have been to say "we", particularly when at that moment men were dying that he could return. At 1630 several Jap planes pulled a sneak attack, hitting the cruiser Honolulu. Asleep at the switch. We pulled the spud at 1630 and stood out with the G. Hall, C. Hall, Oakhill and Rushmore for Hollandia. Nothing better illustrates the need of a single command than the news summaries by the Army & Navy on this historic day. Pure claptrap & bombast by both sides with a personal angle. For posterity I can say, yes, I realize that today I stood on the very threshold of history and it is every bit as exciting as I could expect or imagine. The Blue Goose is hit pretty bad and they were about to beach her as we pulled out.

OCT. 24

This A.M. hazy as we crept in under the 8000 ft. hills of New Guinea and anchored in Hollandia Bay. Mail at last and Ed Schroeder got his order to the states. I am now senior watch officer and most eligible prospect for transfer. 11 months today I reported aboard.

OCT 26

Full size naval battle raging off Philippines. USS Princeton sunk, Birmingham damaged. Fleet is running low on planes. Jap air & sea fleet out in force. Leyte support group steamed out in battle formation to meet enemy. This may prove to be show down fight. We leave for Biak tomorrow to load for return to Leyte. I am now Chief Censor.

NOV. 4

Squally and cooler, looks like we will get there this time, wither or no. I am breaking in Lt. Ernest Hunt on the top watch. Also hope to hand him this First Lieut. detail one of these days and the sooner the better.

NOV. 5

Arrived in San Pedro Bay, Leyte Gulf, at 1000, discharged LCTs at Dulagi Red Beach then steamed to White Beach at Tacaloban and provisioned LC1. Took aboard Ens. Muller, casualty from P.T. battle. Saw the Ammen Claxton and Killen, latter is down well by the head. Stood out under Condition Zebra as Japs raided harbor at 1700. Many "bum boats" in the harbor, a double out-rigger type, some with sails. Natives of Moro origin dressed in reg. skivvies and hats trading Jap invasion money for clothes. Some girls, built very well but of the advanced sunburn variety. After 10 months this looked like café society. Muller indicated that airport reconstruction was not proceeding in a very speedy manner. No CB's at this deal.

NOV. 8

Yesterday was one of those days they don't show on recruiting posters. We hit the tail end of a typhoon coupled with a 30 knot wind and a 20 foot sea. This leaping lena did some real rolling. A 46° roll was registered at one time. It was an awesome sight from the conn with the wind moaning in the rigging and the Eppie's deck vertical with Davy Jones and heaven. Just as she seemed doomed to turn her last flip she would shudder and plunge back in the other direction. The large hook and the metal broke loose and much small gear. Today hot weather has returned and we are about 100 miles behind schedule. The Gunston Hall will conduct burial services for a casualty at 1430. The West Virginia carried a whale over her bow for a day without discovering why she couldn't keep up with her task group.

NOV. 30

Today was Thanksgiving aboard with a monster dinner. Turkey, ham, ice cream, et al. It is awfully hard to be thankful for anything so far and so long from home but then that is a selfish attitude when one finds he is still alive when many have passed on. Operations Orders came aboard today. Luzon may be the next stop. Suicide divers caught the Colorado and St. Louis at Leyte. Fairly heavy damage and about 60 men killed. This next run may be an A 1 hot number.

DEC 3

Wave of dysentery broke out aboard from something in the Turkey Day dinner. So far I am lucky for once. Had first fresh fruit and vegetables in 2 months. The "Mama" would really have gotten a kick out of seeing me eat boiled cabbage. Was up most of last night due to our Exec and his confusion of orders and Swenson's stupidity in grounding No. 3 boat. Things are still tough at Leyte. 4 two man submarines got in and sunk a tanker. We got 4 two man submarines. Got some of the best pictures yet of the Geefle. Just makes me realize more what I am missing.

DEC 5

Arrived at Sorido Bay, Biak, yesterday at 1300. Dropped the hook and launched LCTs to load troops. LCTs returned at 0148 this morning.

Weighed anchor at 0600. Got underway for Leyte at 1000. This is a hell of a way to fight a war is all I can say today.
DEC. 6
Sea has calmed considerably in last 24 hours so we are not getting slapped around so much. Air opposition off Leyte has increased in numbers and effectiveness, which bodes no good for our daylight approach.
DEC. 7
Three years ago today while I was flying over the Grand Canyon in a TWA airliner, Pearl Harbor became a fact of history. Today, three years later, we are back over that long road almost to the place we were on that day and instead of riding airliners I am riding the "Eppie Marin" and proud that I have a bit in that long road to pass on to that son of mine and here's hoping because of that bit he may always ride airliners.
DEC. 25, 1944
It has been a big day with a good dinner and a heart full of memories of home and those who have made this life worthwhile living. '42 in Casablanca, '43 in Los Angeles, '44 in New Guinea, '45 my fervent prayer is it will be at home. Sub rosa we consumed 1 qt. gin, 1 pt. rum, 1 pt. alky and 2 qts. of brandy to keep the resistance up.
DEC. 26
Disembarked LCTs at 0600 with difficulty in swell. Received 213 men and 18 officers aboard for transport. LCT loaded with 5 medium tanks embarked (cancelled). LCT 1035 broached on beach. Egloff with salvage party went to get her off. All embarking ceased and we secure from rehearsal maneuvers scheduled for tomorrow. Jap task force shelled Mindoro last night.
DEC. 27
Finally reloaded LCTs with 5 medium tanks apiece and 6 Dukws. 1035 broached last night eliminating us from maneuvers. 1037 almost sank but in a garrison finish made the well deck in time. The "croakers" are still after me. Dr. Pierce put in my annual physical today stating my visual defect and saying that it renders me unfit for sea duty. What effect it will have is questionable and I find myself not giving a damn. This Luzon deal looks like it is going to be tough sledding. It is a question how far you can push your luck.
DEC. 28
The day is overcast and the spirit is tired and blue. I think the continued setback in Europe has some bearing on our feelings. It is tough and fretting to experience reversals. Guess that's the difference between soldiers and civilians and we are primarily civilians. There will be 100-odd ships in this backup and despite all efforts I find myself thinking the same old things faced with days of suspense, GQs and

endless ocean. Will this be the time? When will it all end? Stood out to sortie at 1230. Remainder of ships as usual got underway at about 1400.

DEC. 29

Speed 8 knots and the watch in the driving tropical rain. God bless those limeys for that open air navigation bridge and they know what they can do with it. This will be a long drag. We should hit Leyte on the 4th of Jan. Cigarettes have been rationed aboard 1 pk per man per day. My room-mate Barlow the Navigator smokes a pipe so I am getting 2 packs and find I am smoking every bit that much or more. I suppose I should cut down a bit. The Japs have started to put out the old "We are expecting you" stuff.

DEC. 31

Here it is the end of another year. It certainly will be the soberest New Years Eve I have spent in many years and I will admit celebrating them in the middle of the Pacific Ocean is not an everyday occurrence. This year, while bringing some of the greatest trials and unpleasantness I have ever known from personal contacts has been the most adventurous and lucky in my whole life. As Life is always a mixture of both I should be happy that my lot on the fortunate side of the ledger is the greater balance.

The New Year spreads before me the most promising of any the last three. Thinking of those at home who wait and hope I pray I may be just as fortunate again and with it all will come peace. This year comes to an end at Longitude 134°46 E, Latitude 4°02 N 650 miles from the Philippine Islands.

1945

JANUARY 1, 1945

Here in the middle of the Pacific Ocean I begin this 36th year of my life on the way to invade the island of Luzon in the Lingayen Gulf. This month will mark the 12th month of the 1st cruise of the Epping Forest and my 14th month aboard. 40,000 miles and six major invasions has been our lot to date. Luck has attended me throughout this period. It is my fervent hope she will continue to do so. Observed holiday routine yesterday with the usual abandon ship drill. Dear Hank, the moron from Sapulpa, must have his fun. Day headlined by 6 or 7 sub contacts with several good attacks, results possible. Found the crew had drained the alcohol from the magnetic compasses for Christmas celebration, replacing it with water.

JANUARY 13, 1945

One year ago today I watched the coast of Calif. fade away in the distance. A long road we have travelled and a still longer one ahead I am afraid. The best luck today was a sack of mail which was a big surprise and the best morale builder upper we could ever have hoped to get. Some transfers for enlisted men arrived but none for officers. Tension is much worse aboard but I think I can keep from blowing my top although there are times it gets pretty tough.

JAN. 16

Dropped the hook on southern side of Morotai Island at 0700 Place has been under regular air attack at night, particularly the airport. There are some nurses here but I don't expect it will mean anything to us. Went to the beach this PM for recreation, got 2 bottles of beer and enjoyed just feeling earth under my feet. We are provisioning which is good news also we will have a movie, the Japs permitting.

JAN 17

Went over to talk to Lt. Cmdr. Stumm, Skipper of the Casa Grande, LSD 13, regards vacancy as Exec. The old man recommended me for the job. He indicated at the end of an hour's talk he would ask the Flag for my transfer when we returned to Leyte. If I take the job it will probably mean another year out here at least. If I don't it will be a matter of passing up another rung on the ladder which is not a Rhinehart custom. The ship is new but is fouled up like firedrill on Sunday.

JAN. 18, 1945

Skipper of the Casa Grande chopped the fat with ours today and a dispatch was sent to Com. 3rd Fleet asking for my transfer. I expect this will be fait accompli when we get back to Leyte.

JAN. 20, 1945

After a welcome four days of recreation, beer parties and 105° heat we stood out of Morotai for Leyte at 1730. Had $2,830.30 taxable income last year.

JAN. 26

Through the Mindoro Straits into the South China Sea. Three GQ, no soap. Relieved of my duties as 1st Lieut. Ships Censor, Deck Court Officer & Sr. Watch Officer by Hunt & Egloff. Orders arrived from CTG 78.4. I am packed and ready. I finish my career on the "Eppie" by standing the Mid Watch. A fitting end to a bizarre experience with some queer people. Thirteen months to the day I will board the #13 and I hope I am not superstitious. Got my mess share back $18.21. That is 21¢ for the Geefle.

JAN. 27, 1945

Arrived in Lingayen Gulf at 0700 and at 0830 I reported aboard the LSD-13, USS Casa Grande as Executive Officer. My farewells included the Old Man, Barlow, Bosn Miles and Carpenter Graves and that was sufficient. It is like a bad dream and I am glad it has passed. The new ship is in fine shape, good crew and officers. The morale seems to be excellent. The Capt. has been damn considerate and helpful. Left Lingayen Gulf for Leyte at 1800. The "Eppie" caught a 10 day stretch as station ship. Now ain't that tough. To the sack and no watch-Boy this is the life!

JAN. 28

Officially took over duties as Exec. at 1200. There is plenty of work ahead and the going may be tough but I think I can make the grade. Anyway it is worth something to be doing something and feeling a sense of accomplishment. It helps take my mind off of home or at least makes the separation bearable. At 0230 GQ, no meat. Through the straits and into the Sulu Sea.

JAN. 29

The bets that I will last run from two weeks to two months. It will be interesting to see. I am going to give it the works. The ship Radio Press News greeted me with "Avec tout Bonne Chance". Let's hope so.

31 MARCH

It is that hour before once again. The storm and sea have subsided. No contacts to date probably due to bad weather. Doug is with the fleet on a carrier. Doc & I discussed our troubles over a brandy & coke. The weather is cool, just like spring at home. Sometimes this evening I could almost smell the fresh damp earth and the smoke from burning leaves. Again I find myself wondering if I shall ever see and smell them again. We are 40 miles from Okinawa.

1 APRIL

In a misty cool morning the mightiest invasion armada in history hit the western coast of Okinawa Jima. Entered transport area at 430 after 2 GQs, two Jap snoopers shot down in flames. After the most intense sea and air bombardment I have ever seen Marines and Army swarmed ashore over the tomb-spotted landscape practically unopposed. At the end of the first day the Marines had gained almost what they expected to gain in three days. We remained in for the night for small boat repairs. "Sewing Machine Charlie" made his regular visit at 1530 in the form of a suicide bomber which hit the bridge of the West Virginia, casualties unknown. Heavy calibre shell fire straddled transports during unloading but was quickly silenced by our big boys. This is #8 for me and it still gives me the jitters. What a way to spend Easter Sunday.

3 APRIL

Moved to Berth 87 after a snooper missed our mast by inches. Reinforcement group arrived. The Solace Relief stood in today. Japs tried a Banzai charge on the airfield last night. Today a lot of Samurai swords are hanging on leatherneck belts. Japs are trying to land paratroopers tonight. The night is aglow with star shells and heavy shell fire. We leave for Keramo Retta tomorrow.

## JUNE 13

Passed Eniwetok at 1100. Beachhead in France appears to be secured and the Nazis are on the run to Florence in Italy. Got a short spell of "War horrors" but listening to the Marines singing hymns on the bridge deck at twilight helped pull me up by the boot straps.

## JUNE 15

Carrier planes shot down Jap plane at 1030. Beachhead 6000 yds. secured on Saipan. This has been the hottest day since I arrived in these parts. I understand where ST Coleridge got the dope for the Ancient Mariner. Our 8th wedding anniversary will soon be here. I must write the Mama Lamb a very special letter for the occasion.

# WILLIAM D. ASKIN

War involves a great deal of paper work and record-keeping in addition to fighting. The diary of William D. Askin, Yeoman 2nd Class on the U.S.S. LST 246, reminds us that battle records must be typed up, the papers must be put through to advance, demote, transfer, and compensate the men and women in military service. It, like some of the other diaries, illustrates also that there are times in service when boredom seems the most immediate enemy.

William D. Askin, born in 1924, entered the Navy in 1942, shortly after graduation from high school. His brother had joined the Navy before Pearl Harbor and, ironically, his father had served in the Navy during World War I in the same arena where his sons would later serve in World War II, the Philippines.

Following demobilization, Askin took a Bachelor of Journalism at the University of Missouri, financed by the GI Bill which staked so many veterans to higher education. After some years in newspaper work in Denver, Colo., and Norman, Okla., he was hired to edit the monthly paper of the Shell Pipe Line Corporation (part of Shell Oil Co.) in Houston, Texas.

For over 20 years now he has edited various corporate publications and been in charge of public relations for Texasgulf. Now residing in Connecticut, he is divorced, the father of two children.

*******

MONDAY, JANUARY 1, 1945
   Aboard LST 246, some 5000 miles from Frisco out of Manus Island and on way to attack Luzon Island in the Philippines on the 9th. Rate Y 2/c-Skipper had talk at 1000 and told crew dope on invasion. Looks fairly tough but air superiority is expected all the way. Chow was usual lousy but this being New Years the cooks broke out a steak. Listened to "Tokyo Rose" in afternoon. Heard news broadcast from Tokyo and a Jap Lieut. is claimed to have downed *12* B-29's. Big laugh all around. Quite interesting to hear, though. Very good English spoken.
TUESDAY, JANUARY 2
   Up late in usual Askin custom. Folkers wasn't around and I was muey p.o. Wrote same a letter telling him all about it. Heard Radio Tokyo again. (Comes in loud and clear) Tokyo Rose played a symphony, POW's

sent home msges and others did a skit. Newscast was good. Claimed to have ruined 500 B 29s. I don't think we have that many. Read more of "George M. Cohan" by Ward Morehouse. Very good biography. Typed up log and did very little else. Hallock & Williamson found my "Penny" story so I heaved it over the side. No regrets—as yet. Had long talk in eve with Rockwell. Then he taught me cribbage and I "liked" very much. Sat around later and discussed college life and his life and then at 10 had last 2 bottles of beer from Espiritu. Ice cold and for once I really enjoyed a bottle.

### WEDNESDAY, JANUARY 3

Usual routine. Up 8:30 and walked in on Doc Williamson and gathered in my tetanus shot. Folkers damned near fainted and I heard about that all day. Did some log work and played cribbage with Williamson. Yours truly won. Chow was stinko both meals I had. I haven't eaten breakfast in over 2 months. Had a Flash Red in the morning (G.Q.) and everybody damned near fainted. All we sighted was a C-47 and 2 Hellcats.

### THURSDAY, JANUARY 4

We are in sight of Jap-held land now, the Philippines. Saw first land at 1235, a small mountain rising up. Must be Mindanao. Finished up monthly reports and Machinery Index and Folkers worked! Getting my autograph book Mom sent me filled up with all the lads. Douched in eve after giving out cokes with usual good profit. Bulled around in eve and sold shoes to Vernon for $3. Hah! 300 percent profit. But what the hell, I didn't even require a No. 18 coupon. Dat ole Black Market. Moving thru the straits now and may be bombed tomorrow.

### SATURDAY, JANUARY 6

Had G.Q. at 1 a.m. while still in Mindanao Straits. Short and back to rack. Another G.Q. at 5 and back to rack at 7. Slept until chow at 11:30. Learned troops have been on board for 30 days as of today. Got em on Bougainville. Chow-ug. What the hell. Radio reported one can sunk, REID, and a cruiser "COLUMBIA" hit by shore batteries in Linguen Gulf—our destination. In Sulu Sea now and was in sight of Panay Island most of day. Worked on log and got a little done. Bull session in eve and singing.

### SUNDAY, JANUARY 7

Up at nine and very happy on absence of G.Q. Moving into and through Sulu Sea. Could see Mindanao practically all day. Our planes bombed in morning. PT boats left convoy with some LST's and turned in there. Worked on log in afternoon and got caught up on Jan. Afternoon GQ and officers looked-and acted-like jellyfish. It's a pitiful circus on that bridge. Taylor and Moore are hopeless. Bull session until midnite. Rocky has a very warped point of view towards women. His wife hurts him bad I think.

**MONDAY, JANUARY 8**

Up at 4 a.m. for Flash Red and back to rack at 4:45 and up at 8 for another and a can shot one down. Two carriers off our stbd bow were really putting out trouble with some cans helping. Later on in the day 3 of our cans caught one of theirs and put it out of the way in a sea battle. News bulletin said suicide planes were knocking off more ships than expected. Now in the China Sea. No work at all. Completed CB's orders and Coast Guards for work of day. Had cokes and big feed in eve with CB's Rocky and Ralph Squires. Big day tomorrow. All ship had f.w. showers. Tomorrow some won't come back.

**TUESDAY, JANUARY 9 D-Day, Luzon, P.I.**

Today is D-Day Philippines. Up at 4 a.m. and had breakfast and on G.Q. from 6 until 9 p.m. at night. I am beat right down to the sod. Had about 9 separate air raids and this ship places hits on one zero and smoke was seen to come out. Followed planes with glasses and could see it very clearly. We were near Pennsy and planes were after that. We were off the Pennsy about 2 hundred yards when they fired broadsides with 16". I thought we were gonna fall apart. H-Hour was 0930 and landing was unopposed except for sniper fire. We beached at about 1580 on Orange 2. Lost stern anchor and cable. All troops off. Saw about 6 dames on beach and had glasses on 'em all the time. One in pink was groovy. All out in the tummy. Pulled off beach at about 9:30. I was dead in my rack. Had one helluva smoke screen up-couldn't see nuttin.

**WEDNESDAY, JANUARY 10**

Woke up at 7 and ship was full of smoke from the damned screen. About 5 guys went on sick list. One raid quick but we didn't fire. Then underway to the Pennsylvania (BB 38) to take off empties. On working party were "survivors" of APD 10 "Brooks". Plane crashed into them. While alongside port of Pennsy, DD 481 (Leutze) tied up on our stbd and unloaded more empties. Two LST's, 1028 & 925 were hit by Jap torpedo boats last night in fog. Another raid at sunset and we opened up but missed. Saw a plane crash, whether sea or ship he hit we couldn't tell. Big flash. 2 P-61's were catching hell from all batteries. Folkers got hit by splinters and is current hero. 1013 got 10 men hurt and Dr. Twyman transferred over. We were underway when all this happened. Nearly ran down about 4 ships in the smoke. What a helluva eve.

**THURSDAY, JANUARY 11**

It appears we are going to Leyte and run supplies to Luzon. Fairly large convoy with several cans and one CVE as escorts. Notices posted on board said that torpedo boats used by the Japs were like our LC-P's and that swimmers were sent out to attach explosives to the sides of vessels. It is believed that is what happened to the 925 and others. Did a lot of log work today and finished up on the Machinery Index. We have on the key locker now a "Cockroach Victory Table" with a drawn pic of a c.r. and under it hash marks for each c.r. Record is now 7. Ah for the life of a sailor. Brown informed me that I earned $1339.50 last year. Whereinell is it?

**FRIDAY, JANUARY 12**

Up at 8 after Butler's yell and after no chow. Went down into pea coat locker to hunt for sea bags. Found same very fast—minus my hammock. Like to know whoinell has it! Had a GQ while we were down there and we really made it up quick. Lasted nearly 2 hours and boys were nervous. Back down and brought up sea bag and tossed all "John L's" over the side. Wore my stocking hat and all the men gave me merry razzing. Worked on log and on Folkers to work harder. Read Omnibook "Leave Her to Heaven" by Ben Ames Williams. Good.

**SATURDAY, JANUARY 13**

Up at eight and put in a damned good morning's work. Log pages, machinery index, other McAbee stuff and—well, hell, man, I worked. Folkers worked in aft and he is so damned slow it hurts. Maybe I demand too much but it's a crime. How he ever passed typing is beyond me! Worked on rates in aft and I let Pappas type his own. They broke Butler to S 1/c and gave Valentine back his cox.

**MONDAY, JANUARY 15**

Up very early for me, had some chow. Typed like mad all morning on Action Report. Brown helping. Folkers sleeping. Finished up at noon, 9 copies of 4 pages. Anchored off Leyte, P.I., and natives began to come alongside. 0ne with 5 dames, 3 boys got most of attention. Dames, Marie, 13 and pregnant. Chiquita 15 one of the prettiest and others of no consequence. Quite modest but all knew what was going on. Then other boats came alongside all afternoon and we had around 8 boats around us once. Gave em canned goods, shirts, all. Got hats, purses, and Jap occupational money. I got some money. This went on all afternoon. Mail aboard and I got one Yank of 9 Sept. 1944 and 2 Xmas cards. Movie on tank deck. "Lady in a Jam" Irene Dunne. Good in places. With Stallone and Valentino after show and got a case of peanut butter. Gave can to Mack. Why, I don't know.

**TUESDAY, JANUARY 16**

Up fairly early and did some work and then to rail for much bargaining. Lotta natives alongside and salt water soap was all that was needed. I traded off damned near a case. Got "guerilla" money, Jap money, coins, every damned thing. Hula skirt and a purse. Corny but cheap so what the hell. Learned Fuller was sunk at Lingayen. Was sunk night of 10th. I saw plane that hit it. Huge flash. Wonder if Abrams got off okay? DuPage hit too and small boat officer we had on at Peleliu was killed. Report no air attacks at all in 3 days. Finished up December log in afternoon! Eureka!!!!! Tied up to fuel barge in eve and filled tanks to capacity. Folkers on working party. Tough! Had noon shower and water rationing again looms.

### WEDNESDAY, JANUARY 17

Up at nine after a nice sleep. Worked a little in office on log after stowing laundry. Usual natives alongside. Got some more Jap money and sea shells for soap. Talked to one gal Rosaline who told us how bad the Japs were. Sure, probably told Jap sailors the opposite. *Very* poor people in these boats lately. There is a dance Friday at some high school on the beach. Everyone in area is invited. One boat came along with one guy handling violin & another on a 1000 year old banjo (it looked like). Played all tunes, even "Pistol Packing Mama". Rose knew words to STARDUST. Put me on working party in afternoon and I wasn't very happy. Got nice red sunburn though. We prepared to beach in eve and finally did then retracted and tried again. We are now trying to get off again at 10:15. Had a flash red, control yellow and whole area went black. NO firing. At GQ learned ship Calloway got a plane at Lingayen and a lotta the boys got killed. Mack's cousin is on it.

### THURSDAY, JANUARY 18

Up at nine and up on foc'sle to look over beach. Helluva lot of traffic, dust and B 24's flying over all the time. An autogiro cruising around the bay. Lands on a big transport out from the beach. Some of the boys went into town and get the dope. Local brothel has long line and puts out for 10 pesos per ($5). No one has admitted a ride as yet. Yesterday Brown gave me a drink of some native whiskey he got. My God!! Take varnish off a chair. Geez, what stuff. Damned near went blind. No mail, as usual. No work at all during day. Walked about 30 yds. on beach. Tried to retract all afternoon with the help of 2 tugs. No go. We are really on. Pumped off fuel and everything. Had movie in eve. "Wintertime" Sonja Henie. Beautiful. Nice to see a movie now and then. Douched and racked at 10:30. Learned we floated off beach at high tide at 11:00. No tugs, no nuttin'.

### FRIDAY, JANUARY 19

Re-beached on White 9 early in the a.m. and started loading with troops in heavy downpour. I rose at (jes like a rose too!) 9 and took a quick gander and we were nearly all loaded then. Into office and no work. Tried to put Folkers to work but he went on beach with Brown for mail. As usual-nil. Slept in afternoon. Quite cool because of rain so no strain. Read Omnibook's presentation of "Excuse My Dust" by Partridge. Pretty good. Now have 23 c.r. on Victory Table. Rain broke and we had tug trying to get us off beach. Had to wait for tide again to do it.

SATURDAY, JANUARY 20

Up at nine as per usual and looked hard for work(?). Couldn't find any so read a little of this and a little of that and listened to the radio in between times. At anchor all day and did log work in afternoon, finishing up Dec. finally. Had an orange today! Egad, fresh too. First in months.

SUNDAY, JANUARY 21

Up at nine and to office to slave away at nothing. Got boy to do a little but he set out for mail again. Usual rain all day. LST 18 and LST 896 tied up on port & stbd respectively, one for water, one for fuel. We get water once a day now, 2 hrs in morn. No showers. No laundry.

MONDAY, JANUARY 22

Up at 0845, new record and got hair combed anyway. Up to office and got work started on entries in service records. Messed around most of morning. Had usual heavy rain. Fuel oil very heavy in the water now but I guess we'll live. Tough though. Read a 1 Jan issue of Time today and found out what's going on in the world.

TUESDAY, JANUARY 23

Up at 6:30. Don't faint, read on. It was our early reveille GQ and you'll probably see me up a helluva lot of other mornings too. Had breakfast and then proceeded to work my tail off. Failed to mention yesterday but we have a monkey on board, property of Holland. Cute as hell, about as big as a rat, soulful eyes, long tail, and fleas. They are delousing him now. Folkers worked in afternoon. Still sad but what the hell. Cut down my amphibious shoes to oxfords. Rained like heck all day.

WEDNESDAY, JANUARY 24

Up very early and shaved in a hurry and then there wasn't any condition I. What a mad boy I was! So stayed up, ate all my three meals. Worked hard all day on Fitness Reports and Log. Folkers still a bit dense but I have hopes. Finished "Lost in the Horse Latitudes" by H. Allen Smith and one of the funniest books I've read. Really had the stuff. No rain today and Panay was off our stbd side. On board we now have 365 enlisted men and 21 officers of the 271st Artillery, First Cavalry Division.

FRIDAY, JANUARY 26

Dawn GQ and started day early again. Worked fairly hard in a.m. Junior flaked out; I gotta crack down on same. Monkey fell or rather, jumped overboard at 13:15 and is no more. GQ in eve. A mine went thru the whole convoy before somebody spotted it. Had a shower, everyone, even troops, had one.

SATURDAY, JANUARY 27

Up early and dull morning except for finishing up on that damned Alteration Request. We have only one engine running. Flywheel on stbd cracked and no run. Port screw is loused up so I don't know what's gonna happen. Arrived in Lingayen Bay around noon. Passed the mast of a ship sticking up in the water. Beach looks quiet except for occasional dive bombing by planes. Sat around rest of day. Just read, bulled, ate, wrote Doris and discovered letter I'd written her Dec. 25 and forgot to mail. Mailed same. Vernon trans to PINKNEY (PH2) with appendicitis.

SUNDAY, JANUARY 28

Up at noon and what the hell's it to you! It was cool and L was sleepy and it was Sunday and—hell, I got up at noon. Still sitting off beach and looking pretty. Boys dove to look at port screw. Not too good. Learned also the "Fuller" wasn't sunk. In aft. did a little work. We beached on White Beach at about 6 on port engine. We are in San Fabian area now, up from Lingayen. Troops off tomorrow.

MONDAY, JANUARY 29

All troops and vehicles disembarked on beach in morning. Didn't have a chance to see any of them. I put my feet on the soil of Luzon at about 1000. Quite an occasion. Natives all over and ambulances full of casualties from the front lines, about 60 miles away. Joe McGough got a Jap pistol for $100. Good buy though. Saw some portraits of Jap officers. Quite interesting. Up and down beach a couple of times. Had one alert in a.m. and one in afternoon. No firing by us. Fully unloaded in afternoon and pulled off easily with our "one engine". Moved to anchorage and ship seems vacant with all doggies off. Listened to records in eve. Ogle had some native wine. I had 3 drags and *knew* it! Ships laying down smoke screen in eve and verra dark. Racked at 10:00 or 2200.

TUESDAY, JANUARY 30

At anchor and I got up at 9 and didn't do a damned thing all day. Read and read and talked and talked. Hot, very hot. Had cherry pie for lunch and I really went for it. Heard Jap radio today and same old bull. Read some more of "Dress Rehearsal: The Story of Dieppe" by Quentin Reynolds. Good but not excellent. Folkers seems to be improving—at least I keep telling myself so. Made fog again in eve and crew's quarters was a no-man's-land.

WEDNESDAY, JANUARY 31

Up at 10 and not much doing. Folkers doing monthly reports and various items. Vernon back on board minus his appendix. Pale but seemingly all right. Some mail on board but as per usual Mrs. Askin's boy dinna receive any. So goes life. Read the 8 Jan. issue of Time and caught up on life. We got a tow line fixed onto the LST 276 and got underway for sea at 1830. Went into Condition I and shackle parted and now we are doing our best on one engine. We turned back to Lingayen, us and the LST 222. Oh hell! I'm thoroughly sick of this ship, this life, and at times the people around me. I have no respect whatsoever for any officer aboard and don't expect to have any. Continue thinking Mr. Rivett is one of the lousiest humans I know—strictly a small-time rat!!

THURSDAY, FEBRUARY 1

New month and a GQ at 3 a.m. that lasted till 4. I hit old rack and rose again at 10 into a very, very hot day. Not much in what was left of a.m. Finished Reynolds book. Wrote Janet a V-mail-why, I honestly don't know—anything to use up time. Started on "Timberline" by Gene Fowler again. Still the best. Had one coke and put another in box; one I never got. These low-life so-and-so's would lift their mother's rings if they could. I hope I never again mix with a bunch like this-the majority anyway. We were at anchor all day with everybody slowly but surely going nuts. In eve had records on "G.I. Jive" with Jill. Good but accompanied by Joe Guenter and his Master Fog Machine. There is a machine! Like a Model A Ford, put, put, and always sounds like it is ready to blow up—*but* it makes the fog so who can kick?

FRIDAY, FEBRUARY 2

Up at 9:30 because of heat and some damn fool left the light on! Sat at anchorage the whole day and it was a hot day too. Folkers made out his Purple Heart recommendation and did all office work. Yours truly didn't do nothin, no how. Had chocolate cake for chow and I also found my coke. My, my, Askin, whatta temper—but I still don't like various people. Learned we are to be here from 4 to 40 days. Bet it is closer to 40 and bub I hate to think of it. Played a little ball on the main deck with Lavenberg, Eddie, Rigby and Bryer. Hand was really swollen when I quit. Oke now. This Rigby must have been a fair ball player. Played in Am. Legion finals in Denver against Laurie. Douched and racked at 2200.

SATURDAY, FEBRUARY 3

Up for breakfast because of rolls but had one and went back to the rack. It was heavy enough to sink this vessel of the sea. Up again at 10 and to usual wanderings. Read magazines all afternoon or wandered to and fro. Crew is now living on port side while crew's quarters is painted. Showered in eve and then usual gab session. Security watch shooting away in rain. This sec. watch is a deal. Guys with .30-06's and .45 cal. submachine guns on rail all night to "repel any Japs". These boys really have a field day and fire at any and everything. Small boat is pulled up every night and it isn't safe around here.

SUNDAY, FEBRUARY 4

Up very late at 11 and "twas nice in the rack. Rain had cooled it off. Had ice cream for noon chow on chocolate cake. Nothing much in afternoon—just read, loafed, did a log page and then on main deck to play catch for an hour and a half. Really nice to work up a sweat and then "douche" afterward, which I did: Tied up to the LST 925 that was blown up by the Japs on Jan 9 by fixing a charge to the port side by the boiler and letting go. The 925 got the Jap small boat and they have a Jap flag on the conn big enough to fly! Geez!! Whole port side blown out. We are supposed to get a flywheel from them and shove in a convoy the 10th. I'm afraid. Shoved off to a movie party on repair ship, the "Egeri". Movie was "Jane Eyre", the most morbid picture they could have. I was really mad. In small boat everyone expected to be machine-gunned but all was well.

## MONDAY, FEBRUARY 5

Working week started and I rose at an early 0830. Not much doing and we pulled away from the 925. The swells pounded hell out of both ships during the night, parting quite a few lines. Did a little log work in morning and read some. Played catch with Rigby in afternoon and lost Mongelluzzo's ball over the side. Mine is the only one left. Really sweated and enjoyed it. Going utsnay on this wagon. Afternoon dragged and after regular "scrub down" chowed on usual lousy Mulligan Stew. (I call it other things but why make this book sordid!). We had a talk with Doc Twyman during day on how a baby was born. It was decided; head first and then the talk went thru sexology to finally we ended with the topic of masturbation. (Doc said a survey showed 14 out of 100 had "muff-dived"). Hmm.

## TUESDAY, FEBRUARY 6

Little log work and then, yes, and then cherry pie—a la mode for lunch. Egad, is this life or merely a dream on ye olde 246? Reading a recent best-seller, "The Razor's Edge" by Somerset Maugham: Very good. Started on Y 1/c book but "RE" got me off the track. My, my, we must concentrate, Askin. Took my first swim in Philippine waters by dipping off the small boat. The last baseball was also lost this February day. Movie in eve in smoke-filled tank deck but I dinna attend. It was a had-seen. Pappas came thru with a whole cherry pie so all is well.

## WEDNESDAY, FEBRUARY 7

We tied up to a heavy-cruiser Portland (CA 33) and took on 25,000 gals. of water. Met a East Denver guy, Harold Neal S/4c (Y) and we had quite a time. Easthorne, Rodriguez and I took chow aboard and nearly got bounced. A helluva lot of Denver guys on board and it was a treat. Back aboard and we shoved about 5.

## THURSDAY, FEBRUARY 8

Up early to transfer Smith, Leroy E. BIM3/c to Rocky Mount. He's got the sh--s and everything's going out of him. Used a cork on him I guess. Did some morning work and otherwise waited for God knows what. Had ice cream again for lunch and I swooned with delight. The

chow stank otherwise. Finished "Razor's Edge" and enjoyed it thoroughly. Tried to sleep in afternoon but no go. Too hot.
SATURDAY, FEBRUARY 10
   Rougher 'n hell all night and I got a good 2 hours sleep. Up at 8, why I'll never know, but I was up. A little work on log, etc. and read some. Pint of red ink broke in the cabinet and made a beautiful mess of everything. Moved bedding back on port side and wondered what it is all about. Later made out Neptune certificates for some of the boys.
SUNDAY, FEBRUARY 11
   Up at ten and even ten it was too early. Did a *little* work in office but Folkers struggled away too so I didn't hinder him. Listened to records all morning-muey good. Bulled with Eddie Rodriguez in eve and really enjoyed myself. Really a good boy—can dance like a Romero. We played Casino and I won, my, my, and then we bulled in office.
MONDAY, FEBRUARY 12
   Up around 11 and dull a.m. A little work. Sat around reading most of afternoon. Bull session hither and yon. In eve gathered Rodriguez, Bevans, Sloan around and delved into a solid 4 hour session ending at 11:30 with Eddie, P.V. Williamson and yours truly discussing whore houses of Honolulu. During the eve we discussed—hockey, baseball, soccer, clothes, church, altar boys and the usual sex trimmings. It was a good session though and even campaign bars played their part. I still have the double with 2 stars so I exhibited to all interested hands.
TUESDAY, FEBRUARY 13
   Up late and hung over rail as we trudged into Leyte and passed LST 991, the one our new skipper's on. Anchored and boat for mail. McAbee's relief came aboard and the new skipper an ex-chief gunner. Looks all right. Played records for 4 hrs. with Eddie in aft. Mail in and 20 ltrs., magazines from Mom and an Esquire from Nancy. Eddie had a ltr. from his parents saying his brother was killed at Lingayen. He can't believe it. Started to write letters in eve and Norman brought in a lot of work and made me muey sore. Up until mid with work and then groped my way to rack. A rugged one tomorrow.
WEDNESDAY, FEBRUARY 14
   My last full day on LST 246 and what a day. It's the 15th as I write. Up at 8 and worked until I was sick. And then went back for more. Being transferred tomorrow to U.S.S. LEONARD WOOD APA 12) and hence to states and pom-pom-but plenty. Made out cards for all the guys, 9 of us, for bars, etc. We now rate a bar for the Philippine campaign for being here for over 30 days. Liberty party on beach for 2 beers each. Crabb only one who got stinko. Got Neptune certificate and will mail. Pay day and pulled down $391. Have $440 on me now. Should get me there and back. Big poker games all down port side.

## THURSDAY, FEBRUARY 15

Up at reveille and went like mad thru chow and last minute work. Finally shoved off at 0900 after goodbyes to all the boys. Didn't shake any officers' hands. Came alongside LEONARD WOOD and they directed us to WARREN (PA 53) where we came aboard. Put in forward troop compartment—hottern hell. Assigned to "C" Division with Mack and that is all we found out. Have to have a lifebelt to get in chow. Fresh spuds though. Tommy's ship is about 600 yds. off stbd of our ship in this convoy of 14 ships. Supposed to hit states one month from today. Chow and bulled with the boys. We can snow them all on here. I racked topside. Cold but comfortable.

## SATURDAY, FEBRUARY 17

Up again, cool though, and had another breakfast. Damn, had breakfast for 3 days straight now. So began my usual laying around routine and hit my rack and at 1100 they caught up to me (At 1020 Tommy's ship and a few others turned off. Going 15 knots and they couldn't hold speed). Wanted me in ship's office. Letters for all the boys to get ribbons, etc. in the states. So I really snowed the two chiefs and got all squared away. Came back in the afternoon and knocked out a sample letter. Chief took it to exec and he took it to the Captain. Oh, hell, Askin, you're really in. Lousy chow in eve and then session on foc'sle. No GQ so that made it nice. Wind beats hell out of a person on foc'sle. Supposed to have missed mine by 75 yds. today. I wonder.

## SUNDAY, FEBRUARY 18

Up early and had fresh eggs (scrambled) for breakfast. Sat around and then Mack and I went to church. Nice services and pretty good sermon on "Temptation". Oh, brother, that is one thing I'm gonna live with. Garrrr. To office after chow and letter was approved. We had a firing run in the a.m. Two runs and it was pretty poor. LST's have got the fire-power for this boy. Typed up stencil in afternoon after lousing one. We anchored at 1600 in Ulithi Island, one of the Carolines. Just a couple of rocks sticking up. Typical cold chow on Sunday eve. Had movie on boat deck. "Arabian Nights" again in Technicolor with Maria "Oh Those Boobies" Montez. All boys were satisfied.

## MONDAY, FEBRUARY 19

Up fairly late—on call of "Chow Down". Chow is pretty poor on this baby if they ask me. But as yet they haven't inquired so I'll suffer. Sat around all morning reading "Tarawa" by Sherrod of TIME MAGAZINE. Very well done. Got some stationery from ship's service and wrote YANK on change of address. Showered, noon chow and rumors were: Invaded Bonins, Warren is to lay here 9 days and to go Bonins to take marines off. We are to be transferred. What the hell—the chow was lousy anyway.

**TUESDAY, FEBRUARY 20**

Up at the call of chow and it was as lousy as usual. All the boys in the mess hall said we were leaving so we spent the morning lashing our gear. Came afternoon and nothing happened and nobody knew nothing. So we sat and cursed and did nothing but read and sleep. And so, dear reader, evening set upon us and we all retired below and unlashed our gear and proceeded to make ready for another evening. Movie "Show Business". Saw it on 246 once but it was pretty good the second time too. Back and I scrubbed a suit of dungarees and then I racked.

**WEDNESDAY, FEBRUARY 21**

Up early enough for chow and collected my "laundry". Started to read and then Wagner was called up and was told that we would leave at 10. So we proceed to lash our gear once more fully confident. Then at 10 they said "at 1400". So at 1400 nuttin' happened and nothing did happen for the rest of the day. The SM I met blinked to Tommy and told him I was aboard so that is taken care of. To movie on bridge of ship with Shope's buddy Dick Anders and it was "Coney Island" with Miss Betty Grable who still fails to arouse me like others. Maybe I'm wrong but she hides too much. Back to my rack on dirty canvas. Gear stayed lashed!!

**THURSDAY, FEBRUARY 22**

Missed breakfast and they told me I didn't miss a damned thing so I rolled over. Sat around all morn, "bulling" and reading Omnibook. No new dope. Tanker tied up alongside and this ship took on fuel and also began taking on stores. News bulletin said 3500 casualties on Bonin invasions already. That's a helluva lot of marines. Sat around all afternoon too and then at movie we got dope. We leave at 0800 tomorrow, officers and EM. Oh happy day.

**FRIDAY, FEBRUARY 23**

Up for our last breakfast and then took our sea bags topside to the boat deck. About 1100 we loaded it on the LCVP and left the U.S.S. Warren for the S.S. Sea Fiddler Army Transport. On board and it was jammed. 1700 men on. Found out we are only credited with 16 mos. overseas. Rat R.C.B.!! No fresh water except for drinking and 2 meals a day with a bowl of soup at noon. Rugged duty. Had our soup and then just sat and wondered. Lot of POW from Philippines on board. In eve tried to rack below but too damn many bed bugs and lice so took a blanket topside at 2230.

**SATURDAY, FEBRUARY 24**

Up early and breakfast was murder. All chows are lousy except noon soup. Like a damned prison. Played cribbage all day and wondered if my strength would hold out. Taylor got us all a carton of cigs so we're better off than a lot of the boys. Bed bugs are really murder. Put 2 padlocks on my sea bag and hoped. Good soup, thank God. Got my sense of humor left but that's about all. Slept topside with all gear. To hell with the bugs.

SUNDAY, FEBRUARY 25

Up late but early enough for chow. Carried bedding below. Still at anchor but soon made preparations to get underway. Underway for Eniwetok, Marshall Islands about 1300 with one DE escorting. We are only ship. Some 1800 men on board now. Mack went on scullery detail. Had drills explained and now we have to lug a life jacket around with us. A bitch. This baby rides rough and really pitches. Vibrates like hell on fantail. Slept topside after usual crib games. Coldern hell but we liked it.

FEBRUARY 29

Sorry, girls, last year was yours!

SATURDAY, MARCH 3

Up late and liked it. Chowed with usual lousy chow and then sat on our fannies and deliberated our fate. Once in afternoon they took in the anchor and everybody cheered. Five minutes later they dropped it again and everybody bitched. Showered and washed some clothes and wrote some of a story. Played crib and beat Marshall 3 straight. Lucky. Racked topside and boys read blinker saying we shove at 1700 tomorrow. Then it began to rain and everybody went below. Mack and I tried it again and lasted the night out.

SUNDAY, MARCH 4

Rain drove us below about 6:30 and so I took an early chow . Sat around and read some and waited for the afternoon. Had emergency drills and then at 5 everybody cheered and the anchor was aweigh once more and it was good because we moved out at 11½ with a PC fore and aft for escort. Flaked out on deck at night after usual crib farces.

WEDNESDAY, MARCH 7

Sat around on my dead posterior for a change (!) and did nuttin'. To sick bay and that unsympathetic so-and-so of a shanker damned near ruined my toe. Things are tough here and besides that, lad, there's a war going on. Sea still rough, chow still lousy, conversation still limited. A little crib and showered and scrubbed and that was a day gone by. Slept below. Getting coldern hell in my opinion.

SATURDAY, MARCH 10

Up at stand-to (hell, you haven't any choice) and started usual day's routine-which is: sit on your dead "arse" and read. I carried it out faithfully. Toe is still no damned good. Read more of "Rome Hanks". Gory but sex to a minimum. Got address book all up to date and in eve blabbed with a chief electrician about Frisco . This Hankla starts talking, and if you take half of what he's saying you're nearly right. He is a first class P-I-T-A (For our gentle readers that means "First Class Pain in the Arse")

## MONDAY, MARCH 12

Tankers crossed off our bow and it was something different. Slowed our speed so the merchants can make more money. I hope to hell they make enough. Showered or "douched" out of the tin can and felt a lot better. Maybe liberty in Pearl tomorrow and everybody is holding his breath hoping for it. Had a physical inspection in aft. that was a farce.

## TUESDAY, MARCH 13

Arrived in Pearl—and Dear Diary—today I saw a woman!! Looks nice, doesn't it, those words!! Well, anyway we pulled in about 1000 and tied up at ABLE 31 just below the Section Base. Liberty in dungarees was granted to A.M. in the Yard so we took off at 1400. Went to Sub Base and the women in the canteen were really the nuts. God, man, they were gorgeous. Then we saw the shift break and all women leave. Geez! Saw a dame marine and a WAVE and they looked all right from where I sat. We bought a lot of gedrink and stuff and back to the ship. The base has really been changed a lot since May.

## WEDNESDAY, MARCH 14

Up late, missing breakfast and up topside to figure on how to get liberty. Got a early yard pass, put my dungarees over my whites and shoved off. Changed in Rec. Sta. and left dungs with chaplain. Bus broke down just outside of town and hoofed. All the whorehouses are closed, all amusement centers are closed. Ciro's empty; got ticket from SP for not squaring hat and no rate. Sadie was very glad to see me and had few drinks. Met a buddy of Tommy's there at Broadway. Got a pr. of shoes, magazines, book, candy, calendar and stuff. Got looped by 4:30 and left to return to ship. Got pic taken with hula gal and back to yard. Got dungs and changed over. Ate at repair dock cafeteria and then caught bus back. Women all over town, Waves, Wacs, Marines. Not bad, not good. Hit rack early but thirsty as hell after all that rum.

## THURSDAY, MARCH 15

Up late as possible and still get chow. Sat around. Throat sore as hell from yesterday's rum. Read magazines and about 1500 we got underway and left Pearl Harbor. Helluva lot of patients came on plus food. Had oranges for evening chow and it was the first in about 6 months. Left Pearl with one PC for escort. Ship started bouncing and vibrating like an LST. Cold too, damned cold. No stand-to's in the eve anymore so hit the rack early.

## SUNDAY, MARCH 18

Stayed in rack thru S-T again and made chow line as it neared end. Then up shivering and shined new shoes. That's all we seem to do around here—shine shoes. Read Esquire and it was good. Sea flat, that is there are no whitecaps but the swells are big enough. Shined shoes again in eve and after chow racked early. Too cold to stay up.

WEDNESDAY, MARCH 21

Still too cold to take and spent most of day in rack. All the boys just took it easy, then late they announced we would get in about 11 and disembark in the morning. Was topside most of the evening and it was coldern hell but the lights of Frisco warmed me. Went under Golden Gate Bridge and the boys really cheered—long and loud. It was nice.

# IN THE AIR

# HARRY SCHLOSS

Brief as the entries are, the diary of Harry Schloss is one of the more openly emotional in the collection. His frank expression of fear, his grief over lost comrades, and even over the death of a dog who was the crew mascot, his reaction to receipt of pictures of his wife Bea, all show a man less inclined than most to freeze his emotions for the duration as insurance against the pain of loss. It is also a unique diary among those received from members of bombing crews in that it does not confine itself to the record of missions, dealing with a rest and recreation furlough and the convalescence and rehabilitation following repatriation. Though these last pages are inevitably a bit anti-climactic after the dangerous missions, I have retained them for what they show of a combatant's natural curiosity as to the later fate of men he served with and liked. Though not elsewhere documented in these diaries, it has to have been a common experience to wonder about the fate of buddies.

Harry Schloss served as Waist Gunner (Engineer), holding the rank of Tech. Sergt. in the 17th Bomb Group, 34th Bomb. Sqd. (Thunderbirds). Before the war he had tried show business then became a salesman, to which work he returned when demobilized, becoming eventually manager of a shoe store. Now living in Sunrise, Florida, he is still married to the Bea spoken of so fondly in the diary and in addition to the son Michael whom he mentions in these pages he has a younger son Richard.

*******

Reported to Fort Jay, New York on Aug. 4, '42. It was a dreary, cold day and the 12 hour physical, which I passed, didn't help my spirits any. Got 14 days to clean up my business then report to draft board.
AUG. 18
Reported to Grand Central Station. Lef for Camp Upton. Damp and cold. Only there 1½ days. Left for unknown destination. Rumors.
AUG. 23
Arrived in Miami Beach, was assigned to 574 Tech School Sq. Co. 841. Slept at Wm. Penn Hotel. Next day started basic training. PFC in charge. Holy terror, good actor. Passed I.Q. with 131. Very high. Given choice of schools. Took gunnery. Made two good friends, Manny Salters and Bernie Rosenthal. Left for unknown dest.

SEPT. 19

Arrived at Ft. Myers, Fla. Flexible Gunnery School. Met the swellest bunch of guys. Learned to fire and take apart and assemble 30 and 50 calibre machine guns. Shot skeet. Then flew in T-6. Not bad in air to air firing. Graduated as sergeant on Oct. 25. Memories. Tore up Morgan Hotel. Wally and his dice. Zeikus digging ditches. Left for unknown destination.

OCT. 30

Arrived Will Rogers Field, Oklahoma City. Attached to 38th Air Base Squadron. Awaited arrival of the 46th Bomb. Sq. Did nothing but eat and sleep. Finally given permission to send for Bea. The 46 arrived Nov. 21. Put into 53rd Bomb Sq. C.O. Major Huntington. Jerk.

NOV. 30

Transferred to 21 Observation Squad. Learned radio code. Took 7 to 8 words my first week.

JAN. 14

Transferred to hell hole called Shepard Field. Cold, dreary, gloomy. Men marching at all hours of the day and night. Told stripes don't count. Course is on air mechanics. Lasted for four dismal months, on B-26's and B-25. Passed as engineer. Average 86.

MAY 21

Transferred to Paradise. Barksdale Field. 2 days in A.C.R.C. Assigned to 335th Bomb Gp 475th Bomb. Squad. R.T.O. training until June 27. Got 11 day furlough. Bea gave birth to a son, Michael Robert, on Sept. 20. Put on crew with Lt. Gates, Zimmerly, Radin & Wingard. Later Schultz. Chas. McGonagle came in as radio man. He was in pretty bad breakup. OK now. Transferred to 477th to complete training.

NOV 28

Left Barksdale for Hunter Field. Crew split up. Four to fly over. Wingar and I to go over by boat. Put in guardhouse for not saluting a major.

DEC 5

Left Hunter for P of E. Arrived Camp Patrick Henry at Lee Hall, VA. Arr. Dec. 6. Got my first glimpse of Italian and German prisoners of war. Also different colors and styles of other allied uniforms. Dave still with me.

DEC. 16

Left camp Pat Henry for unknown destination. Sailed on "Empress of Scotland" formerly the "Empress of Japan".

DECEMBER 25

Christmas Day. Arrived safely in Casablanca, Africa. The trip across was dull. Thanks to the infantry officers in charge. Their main aim in life was to see how tough they could make it for the air corps men.

However, one noticed that after each meal (we got two a day, incidentally) it was the infantry men who beat a hasty retreat to the various latrines. We were hidden away in a cozy little trip on "D" deck. 2nd deck from the bottom of the ship. There was plenty of water. All the pipes leaked. Christmas Day lunch. Spam, bread and coffee. On debarking at Casablanca we were taken to Camp Marshall Lysantey about 16 miles north of the town. In town the natives were the dirtiest, poorest I've ever seen. They kept coming over to our truck and begging for bon-bons or cigarettes. A sight I won't soon forget. At our arrival in Marshall Lysantey, we were put in one building. 78 of us with no beds and inadequate blankets. We slept on stone floors, all huddled up for warmth. I had always believed that Africa was a hot place. That's only two hours a day, during the winter months. The nights were cold. We also got our first taste of rationing. The people back home would kick if they were allowed one chocolate bar, 1 pack of gum and 8 packs of cigarettes a week. On our first day here, we were told we were not considered part of the Air Corps. We were infantry as long as we were at this camp. Hikes, drills, etc. Oh, unhappy day. However, we were saved from all this by the arrival of our crews at Cazes Air Field about 2 miles outside of Casa. I was never so glad to see anyone in my life. Did nothing for 10 days waiting for 50 hour inspection to be finished. Then was told our emergency air brake bottle was out. Another wait. Won $600 in black jack while waiting. Flew for first time in over a month on Jan. 5. Tested ships and guns. Expect to leave on Jan. 6 for Algiers. Took off for Algiers on Jan. 7. On arrival saw Col. Elliott Roosevelt. Looks like father. Algiers is nice city. Built on steps or hills. Beautiful boulevard in center of town. Spend one cold night here.

JAN. 8

Arrived in Sardinia. Attached to 17 Bomb Gp 34 Bomb Sq. A very famous outfit. Yano is only 12½ miles from here. Met a host of old friends. Flew on transition hops.

JAN. 13

First mission. Ship No. 13. Target. Air Drome. Got a piece of glass in my hand from turret. Flak came through, landed in Bill Schaffenaker's hand. Funny to be flying first mission with Bill. Old friend. Came on target too suddenly to be scared, was gone before I realized it. Heard flak. Big and black.

JAN 19

Second mission. Milk run. Bombed hell out of an airport. Flew in lead ship. No excitement. Lost $200 of $600 I came here with. Went to visit Yano. Good to see him. Still the same great guy. Took me around and hugged me. The big lug was very depressed until I came along. Dave came here from the 319 on a visit. Bought coffee and sugar. I

cooked 3 chickens. Unanimous in their praise of it.
JAN. 25

Third mission. The 1st objective was 40 minutes past Rome. Heavy overcast, could not get through, so flew to 2nd target. Too cloudy. Dry Run. Heavy flak but inaccurate. 7 slight holes in plane. First mission with crew intact. Brought back bombs. 1000 lbs. Flew to Naples for fuel. Right engine eats too much. Saw the famous Mt. Vesuvius. Naples bombed to shambles. I don't think there is 20 houses standing. Had a delicious sandwich of salmon and onions. First I've had in almost two years. Got my first letter from Bea in 11 weeks. Very happy. Got glimpse of invasion fleet, at least 100 ships were there. It looks great from the air.
JAN. 29

Fourth mission. Target-bridge. No flak, no fighters, it's a pleasure. Shot hell out of target. Germans laid smoke screen, but it did not reach target. Cooked 3 chickens last night. Boiled and made soup. Delicious. Dave came over for visit. Brought coffee, sugar and milk. He has 6 missions. Not bad, for the short time he's here. Still a good Joe. Got 8 letters. Hicky brought them back from Telergma. Don't know how it got there. Gates down there now as instructor. Owes me $100. He'll be back next month. Michael weighs 14 lbs. according to Bea. Boy, he's growing up. I miss Bea & the kid terribly. Up to now, have refused to talk about women. Hard to believe I'm still a virgin in the army, but if you could see the faces and dirt on the women here, you'd never doubt it. Average of 10 v.d. cases a month. I'm thinking of Bea.
FEB. 5

Flew 5th mission. After 8 days of no flying, due to bad weather. I've been on spare for 9 days. Made the mission when 3 ships turned back. Supposed to be a tough target. Target. Marshalling yards. Blew it all to hell. 93 per cent accuracy. Lt. Fitzgerald could not use bomb sight as it was frozen. Toed the bombs out. Amount of accuracy is very amazing. Big write-up in "Stars & Gripes". Coldest day of my life. 23 below zero. Trouble with fuel transfer. Fuse blew. Reset button froze. Finally worked after 15 very anxious minutes. Only 30 gals. in each tank & 1½ hours of flying time. The ocean looked mighty cold. Saw Deanna Durbin in "His Butler's Sister". Best picture since I've been in Africa. She's terrific.
FEB. 7

Flew on 6th mission. Couldn't get to bomb target as the clouds were very heavy. Target-road junction where German replacements were. Ships the night before caught hell here. We made a 360 turn on coast of Italy near Anzio & came out. Dry run. Milk run. Sent Bea $400. Deposited $85 in soldiers deposit. Every night Wes Long, Mike Dearsdorff & sometimes Tip O'Neill & myself sing the old songs, cook eggs and have a bull session. It's the best part of the day for me. The weather cold & rainy. The rain sounds like someone is throwing rocks at our tent. Hicky and I bought a bottle of brandy for $8. Tonight I get drunk.

FEB. 15

Flew on 7th mission. Over land for half an hour. Target-Bridge at Marsciano. Missed it but hit railroad to it. Used 1000 lb. bomb. 20° below zero. No flak, no fighters. Next day get grounded for 4 days due to cold.

FEB. 20

Boy, today I hit the jackpot. Anzio Beachhead. Flak all over the sky. It was black. 9 holes in ship. Not bad. Dropped frags. Covered bridge area. On arrival back in camp Dave was waiting for me. Went to his camp for overnight stay. Also had chance to visit Yan. Both going to different outfits. Next day did guard duty. Cold, but really cold.

FEB. 28

6 days trying to make number 9. Bad weather. Gates came back from Telergma today.

FEB. 29

Made number 9 today. Slight flak but very inaccurate. One ship cracked up on takeoff. 7 fellows burned to death. I almost cried. Then over the target at Viterbo two planes shot down, 11 chutes opened. Two of the boys flew right by my window. I prayed for them. On way out we fell out of formation to escort a ship in trouble. Escorted it to Corsica, where two spits took over. Hear he belly-landed. Hope & pray I never see another mission like this.

MARCH 2

Made first mission as crew since return of Gates, without Chuck, No. 10. Target-Anzio Beachhead. First two formations caught most of the flak, however, there was enough for us. Dropped frags. Good job.

MARCH 3

Flew on mission No. 11 over Rome marshalling yards. Every formation but ours dropped their bombs. 500 lbs. Gates damn good, so is Chuck. Saw some beautiful sights. Ruins of Colosseum, palaces, etc. Boy, those babies go in for beauty.

No. 12 on March 7 My 28th birthday. Target-Rome marshalling yards. Boy, they kicked hell out of it. 500 lb. bombs. Rome still more beautiful than on first mission.

Two days later went with Chuck and Long to Orestano to get bricks for house that Chuck, Magida, Gates & McGuire were building, on return found out McGuire shot down. Good Joe. Lots of boys heartbroken for whole crew.

MARCH 10

Went on mission no. 13. Bridge at Orvieto. Flew over land for 50 minutes, but did not drop bombs. Target all covered. Flak was light but accurate. One large whoom. Looked around for crew. All O.K. Very close. On way back R.P.M. gauge broke. Thought engine failure. Just gauge out.

MARCH 13

Flew on Mission 14. Target past Leghorn broke 4:45 time. Can low on fuel. Came home without formation. Not a milk run, lot of flak, but thank God it was inaccurate. I'd hate to go back there next month. Hit target. Bridge. 1000 lbs. Saw coast of France.

MARCH 14

Made mission 15. Target-Rome marshalling yards. 100 per cent concentration of bombs. Good job. Made 5:05 time. Cook's tour of Italy.

MARCH 15

Made Mission 16. Flying almost every day is tough. Target-Cassino. Right on front line. We were only one of 16 Bomb Groups to hit the town. When we got over it, there was nothing left of Cassino. Only a hole in the ground. Loads & loads of trucks going to the front. It was a sight I'll never forget. The town was only dust. Captain Tate asked me to write up my impressions of the raid for the squadron book. I did so. Capt. Tate said I did swell. Tonight is my first broadcast on the group radio program. Made the broadcast. Quite successful except that I read the news too fast, but with a little experience might do right well.

MARCH 16

Flew spare. Saw two ships collide and explode. Chet Angell, V.E. Miller & Wise. My buddies all dead. Flew back to field. Sick. 13 good men dead. Can't stand it much more. Guess I'm a sissy.

MARCH 17

Went on Mission 17. Dropped 1000 lb. bombs on Orvatello marshalling yards. 34th did good job. On return we were given speech by Lt. General Baker. He can't get over our record. He says in England they say that if a B-26 does half as good as a 17 it's O.K. Here it's the reverse. He watched the Cassino run, says it amazed him. On mission today, piece of flak cracked window over Gates' head. If it had come through we'd all be in bad shape. Especially Gates. On primary target, couldn't make it. Overcast.

MARCH 21

Made mission 18 today. No flak, no fighters. We came in over Italy at 14,000 ft. Both my legs froze. They were paralyzed. I'll never forget the horrible thoughts that ran through my mind. We kicked the hell out of a viaduct at Avetta. Time 5:15. My combat hours are piling up. O'Neill left for rest camp tonight. Boy, he needed it. Had to short Charlie. He has epileptic. We all miss him.

MARCH 23

Up all night with Wes. In the morning he was taken to Cagliari hospital. Malaria. Fine country for it. Got a beautiful write-up in "Stars & Gripes" by Stowall. About my announcing. Made 3rd broadcast last night.

MARCH 24

Made mission 19. Orvieto north bridge. Forgot baby booties for 1st & last time. Heavy flak, plenty of fighters. One of our escorting 47's shot down. Watched him all the way. Got 15 small holes in both engines. Flak still in them. One outfit hit target. 500 lbs. at 11,400 ft.

MARCH 27

Went on 20th mission. Poggaboni bridge. Hit both ends but not bridge itself. Dropped 2000 lbs. No flak, no fighters. Not very cold for a change. Next day General Anderson, British General in charge of operations, spoke highly of our bombing. Made awards.

APRIL 1

Made 21st mission. Bridge at Signa near Florence. No flak, no fighters. Quite warm. Felt moody, no mail.

APRIL 3

Made 22nd mission. Over Italy for quite a bit, but could not drop bombs because of heavy overcast. Proceeded to second target. Leghorn. Couldn't get through but they shot up flak. Slight & inaccurate. Got grounded for 3 days. Dizzy spells. Can't understand it. But perhaps the rest will do me good.

APRIL 7

Back on flying status again. Plenty of rest did it. Got some lovely pictures of Bea, Ruth, Kappy & Pop. Bea looks lovely. Like her old self. Next day I received some pictures of Bea & the kid. On these she looks plump in the face. Hope it's not so.

APRIL 10

Flew spare. Did not get in. Two new crews in two days. Oh boy, what a relief. Replacements would boost morale terrifically. The more the merrier. Radin left for rest camp. Insists on meeting Ruth some day. O.K. with me. He's a good joe.

APRIL 11

Made my 23rd mission today. Did not see any land but we made a bomb run over target of opportunity on Cicina bridge. Got credit for a mission. Too overcast. Did not drop bomb. Milk run. 4:15 time. Played ball this evening. It's funny how you can forget your troubles in a ball game. Made my sixth broadcast. Fair. Boy, those Russians are really going places. What a people. Some more replacements. Ground personnel. I wish some more crews would come in.

APRIL 12

Went on Mission 24. San Remo Bridge. Only about 20 miles from

Nice, France. However, the day was too cloudy to see too far. We missed bridge after two bomb runs. I bet on Darsey. Think he came closest. Won't know until tomorrow. Terrible bombing. 10,600 ft. 1000 lbs. Time 3:50. No flak, no fighters. Milk run. Darsey lost. Saw Deanna Durbin in "Hers to Hold" with Joseph Cotten. Both very good.

APRIL 14

Made 25th mission. Viaduct at Arezzo. Did not see bombs land. Flew with Mike. He had trouble releasing bombs, had to salvo two into ocean. Made Cook's tour of Italy. Flew for 5 hours. 1000 lbs. Alt. 9800 ft. Slight flak at Elba. Inaccurate.

On Friday April 13 I got hit on the back of the head on landing. It didn't bother me until Sunday. Was taken to hospital in Cagliari. Slight concussion. Returned to squadron on April 22. Feel better. Probably start flying on Monday. Gates and Zimmerly in rest camp.

APRIL 24

Flew on 26th mission. Target Arezzo. Couldn't make it so we hit 3rd alternative. Railroad bridge, blew it sky high. Caught flak at Arezzo. Lt. Pickle made beautiful turn to get out. Flew with Hanna. His 2nd mission as 1st pilot. Very smooth. 2000 lbs. Time 4:30. Got pretty sick on home-coming but made it.

APRIL 25

Flew on 27th mission. Bridge at Bucini. The first three flights dropped their bombs on primary target. We tried to bomb the harbor at Leghorn. We got a terrific accurate barrage of flak. Came home with 30 holes in our plane. Generator shot out. One large hole under my seat. Lucky. Three ships damaged. Two wounded slightly. Dropped bombs 500 yards off shore. Rotten bombing.

APRIL 30

Made my 28th mission. Bridge at Cortona. Either a hit or near miss. 500 lbs. No flak or fighters. Flew in lead ship. Long & Deardorff going to rest camp in 2 days. Should be my chance soon. Won $100 in cards in our shack.

MAY 1

Made mission 29. Marshalling yards at Florence. Could not see it. Passed over secondary and over 3rd target. Did not drop bombs. Caught flak in two or three places. Inaccurate. Time 4:30-Told today that newsreel cameramen would take pictures to be shown in America. I will be in front row. Presentation by French of Croix-de-Guerre. Colonel Gilbert and Major Richter will get them.

MAY 4

Flew on transition with Lts. John and Lynn. Landed at Alghero. Ate at Y.M.C.A. Interesting town. On arrival back at camp, got package from Bea & Ma. Won $250 during week at poker. Next day Lt. John, Lynn,

Kilness and 4 other enlisted men flew down to Catania to get a load of oranges. Town amazed us. 450,000 people. You could buy almost anything. Scotch, cognac, champagne, Italian pastry & ice cream. Had a steak dinner with french fried potatoes. Stood there two days. Had swell time. Refused women. Didn't miss it either. Got back, felt sick. Had 101½ temperature. O.K. next morning.

Flew on 30th mission on May 10. Our target was a bridge at Bucini. If we missed it was very close. 500 lbs. Time 4:30. Lost $105 last night in poker. Oh well, can't always win. Went on Mission 31 on May 11. San Giovanni bridge. Hit or near miss. 500 lbs. Heavy clouds. At night we were told about an invasion starting at 11 p.m. Plan to take Cassino and drive on Rome. Big deal tomorrow. 12 ships. I'm flying with crew. Looks tough.

Made mission 32 on May 12. Our target was German headquarters on the road to Rome. Could not see where bombs fell as clouds obscured view. Don't think we hit it. We caught flak everywhere we turned. *Very good evasive action.* We saw the guns firing across the front lines. Maybe a harbinger of things to come. Time 4:05 Bombs 500 lbs.

MAY 14

Mission 33-Target Arezzo bridge. Clear day but did not drop bombs. Other flights hit bridge. Flak, but inaccurate. Time 4:15 500 lbs. 34th really screwing up.

Went on 34th mission on May 16th. Bridge at Pisa. Good job. Hit or near miss. Saw Leaning Tower of Pisa. Beautiful city. 500 lbs. Alt 10,400 feet. Hear that 319 & 320 are getting hell shot out of them. Must find out about Dave. Long time no see. Paid him a visit and had a swell time.

Found out today, May 17, that rest camp has been called off for a while. The Huns have mined the waters around Capri. Long & Mike stuck there. Whatta break.

Flew on 35th mission on May 18. Target-bridge at Arezzo. Moved plenty of flak guns in. 432nd led & caught holy hell. Two ships out, single engine & hydraulic system. We had it quite easy. Hit or near miss on target. 500 lbs. Time 4:25 One slight dent on ship.

Made 36th Mission on May 19. Bridge at Vergato, past Bologna. 860 miles in all. We did not drop bombs, bombardier's fault. First 18 ships hit bridge. Bad weather forced us down at Corsica. Boy, was I scared. Wind tossed us around like bag. Time 5:15 1000 lbs. Saw 17's and 24's demolish town of Spezia. Horrible. Town utterly destroyed.

MAY 23

Went on 37th mission. Road junction at Marino. Americans started drive at Anzio. We were supposed to bomb junction to prevent reinforcements or retreat. Alt. 12,000 ft. 500 lbs. Time 4:05. Did not drop bombs, too overcast. I dropped window. New silver stuff, supposed to throw radar machines off. Perhaps it worked as we got no flak, but we did meet fighters. One shot down, they damaged two ships, wounded one. Ground troops shot up rockets. Millions of them, while tracers from fighters were all around us. Too bad we couldn't help our side. Saw Rome again today. It looks like this drive is a determined one. Hope it makes Rome.

MAY 25

Went on 38th mission. Target-Valmontone-Road junction on Highway 6 Road to Rome. Hit. 500 lbs. Time 4:05. Saw lots of Nazi trucks & planes. Reported it. Looks like this drive to Rome will finally make it. Slight flak but accurate. Two small holes. Fighters too.

Went on 39th mission on May 27. Target a railroad junction at Rignano, 3 miles south of Florence. Hit with 1000 lbs. Time 4:30. Lt. Fitzgerald paid me nice compliment. Nothing do I overlook. Got burnt letter from Bea. Must have been in a plane that cracked up. She says she got letter that I gave Glover to deliver. He's O.K. Squadron flying two missions a day. Most fellows don't mind, either. Heard Lt. Ashmore, Birney's co-pilot, down. Good joe.

MAY 29

Flew on 40th mission. If this was the old days, today's would have been the last. Target-Bridge at Tiara. Time 4:10 Alt 10,000 ft. 1000 lbs. Hit or near miss. Milk run, although we did see German fighters. Told I go to Naples for day tomorrow. Will try to take pictures. Left for Naples. Spent the day there. Flew over Mt. Vesuvius and Isle of Capri. Ate ice cream at Red Cross-6 plates in fact. Had two delicious meals at Officers Transient Mess.

May 30

Flew on 41st mission on May 31. It was my 13th for the month. Right on front lines. Dropped frags on troops at Albano. Time 3:50 Alt-9,800 ft. Hit. They shot hell out of us. One very large hole in right main tank. Slight leakage. Governor on left prop out. No ships down, thank the Lord. One bombardier in other squadron wounded. Mike, our dog, was killed this morning. I'm going to miss those sad eyes of his. A real pal. It happened just before we went on mission.

JUNE 1

Made 42nd mission. Town of Palestrina. Time 4:00 Alt-10,400 ft. 1000 lbs. Hit. Right over front line. We caught plenty of flak. On all sides. Lt. Eastburn almost downed. Deep dive but pulled out O.K.

New theatre opened June 3. Acted as master of ceremonies. Not a bad show. Mike, Long & myself started developing pictures. Got some nice action shots.

Flew on 43rd mission on June 4. Railroad bridge at Narni. Hit or near miss. Flak, but inaccurate. Time 4:30 Alt. 10,500 ft. 1000 lbs. No fighters. Allied patrols in Rome. Good news. Maybe 2nd front will start now.

JUNE 6

Just before we took off for mission, the news was broken to us that the invasion of France had started. Oh, boy, the most glorious news I've ever heard. Everybody's morale got a shot in the arm. Made 44th mission. Target-Villatra. Secondary target-road & town. Hit. 500 lbs. Alt. 9,800 ft. Time 4:10. Slight flak, no fighters. Lots of spitfires covered roads. No escape for Germans.

JUNE 10

Left camp for the "Isle of Capri" rest camp. Flew from here to Naples. Took ferry over to Capri. On my arrival was sent to the "Metropolitan Hotel". It was, by far, the nicest hotel, on the bottom of the hill. Gene Wingard, Mike Bonchousky & Tommy Townsend and I were assigned to one room. It had a small balcony overlooking the sea. A glorious sight. Had a delicious steak dinner, then rode the funny car or "Funicular" to the town of Capri. The car rides up and down a steep hill. One car goes up the other down, acts as a balance. Visited Red Cross, shot pool & played ping-pong. Then went to a movie. After show, I got quite a bun on.

JUNE 11

Got all my shopping over with. After supper, the four of us took a horse and cart up to Capri. We serenaded the horse. The natives got a kick out of it, the horse didn't. Gene & I drank p38's & a drink called the Bronx. Why it's called that, I don't know. Got pretty drunk.

JUNE 12

Went on boat ride. Saw "Blue Grotto". Water is the bluest I've ever seen. Nice sight. Back in time for lunch. Slept all afternoon. At night went to Red Cross dance. Dull, so I left. Drunk again.

JUNE 13

Went fishing. Caught three small ones and a cold. The guide took us on quite a tour of the island. After dinner, went for a ride to Anacapri. Up long winding roads & very narrow. It didn't seem possible that two cars could squeeze past. We made the driver stop so that we could see the views and take pictures. Got some beauties. After supper went back to Anacapri to see grand fiesta. Fiesta of "St. Antonio". One of the natives said I looked like him. Went back to hotel and to bed.

JUNE 14

Went walking all day. At night saw a good show "Capri Commandoes". Permanent party. Very good. After show, four of us got tipsy. Stood in Luigi's until it closed. Then bought four extra bottles of champagne. Drank two on the "Funicular". Threw bottles out of window.

## JUNE 15

Went sail-boating, swimming, fishing. Had a most enjoyable day. Met Fred Yost again. Flak happy. Went to bed early. *Not* drunk.

## JUNE 16

Gene & I hired a boat & went fishing. Also visited "White Grotto". Very lovely. Caught four fish & a baby octopus. Boatman bit it on neck to kill it. Says it's "good eating". I'll take his word for it. Swimming in afternoon. At night went to Red Cross, met Butler, Ellsay, Gushock. Told me that Major Fast & Capt. Edgar had been killed in a crash. Also five American Red Cross girls & one Italian girl. Also Harris, our Red Cross worker. Did not know who else was on ship. Felt miserable. Capt. Edgar, my boss at Special Service. And speedball. Saw the show & went out and got drunk.

## JUNE 17

Left Capri. Spent two days at Naples. Mostly at Red Cross. Ate ice cream & cake all day. Saw Danny Kaye in "Up in Arms". Excellent. On June 19 was told there was a plane from our outfit at Pomigliano. On arrival found out by boys that Zimmersly, Leo & Fitzgerald were on board ship that went down. I'll miss Chuck. Terrible blow. No bodies were found. Fitz had 62 missions. Eyes were shot. All of them swell guys. Gates was pilot of ship going back to camp. Thank the Lord. I don't believe I care to fly anymore. Will try not to. After trying for seven days, finally made my 45th mission. The target-La Spezia. 500 lbs. Time 4:15. Did not hit target as French beat us to it. They did a darn good job, too. The ammo dump was really blown up. Light, moderate, inaccurate flak. NO fighters. Lt. King one darn good pilot. But I miss Chuck. Radin made squadron navigator of 95. Nice going.

## JULY 1

Went to Naples. Ate delicious steak, french fried potatoes & spaghetti supper. Got a little drunk & turned in early. Returned next day to see mission return. Boy, were they shot up. Molbreak wounded. Hanna had ship "Bunny J" shot up. Hydraulic line out. He made one swell landing with nose gear not locked. About 50 holes. It looks like our milk run days are over. Oh, unhappy day. Next day went to hospital for observation on headaches. Remained one week. Slight case of sinus trouble.

Lots of new crews are coming in. Five in 2 weeks. Lots of the old boys are due to go home.

Flew on 46th mission on July 15. Target-Marceria-Bridge. Hit or near miss. Time 4:50. 1000 lbs. First mission in July & I really felt good. Harrigan is a good pilot. Slight, inaccurate flak. No fighters. Escort of P47's. Next day went on 47th mission. Target-Bridge at Ferriberrata. Hit-2000 lbs. When the bomb hit, the back end of the ship lifted up from the concussion. Time 4:30. Slight, heavy flak at Genoa. Inaccurate. New crew came in, 6 in 3 weeks.

Went on 48th mission on July 18-Target-Bridge at Piacenza. Carried 2000 lb. bombs. Time 4:15. Made a 360° bank over land & came home. Too overcast. Wish a few more were like that. Bobby Bleekan left this morning. A good friend. Long & Mike left for Rome for 3 days. My turn soon, I hope.

Made 49th mission on July 19-Piacenza. Bridge. Hit or near miss. Our plane did not drop. Bombardier's fault, I think. 2000 lb. Alt 11,400. Time 4:45. No flak or fighters. Rough weather. Good job by Hanna.

It looks like Hanna is running in one of the toughest streaks any man ever had. On July 20 he had to belly-land number 15 in Corsica. It had 96 missions on it. But the most terrible news of all was what happened to the crew of No. 22-Lts. Baker & Lynd-Capts. Carlson & Elliott, Colonel Gilbert & the enlisted men "Red" Wilcox, O'Donovan & Russell all were shot down over Italy. It was supposed to be the last mission for O'D, Red & Russ. And they were low men. Colonel Gilbert had 91 missions. First Craig now Carlson, it looks like that operations office berth is jinxed. Lt. Boudreaux had to belly-land 06 in Corsica. No one hurt. We really took a beating yesterday. The 319th caught hell, too. Don't know how many ships they lost. Two ships collided, that I know of. I'm beginning to get up in missions and I'm really getting worried.

Went on 50th mission on July 23. First three flights dropped on primary. 34th dropped on bridge at Acqui. Secondary. Alt. 10,200 ft. 1000 lbs. Time 5:05. Light flak, no fighters. Nice job by Lt. Brewer.

JULY 25

Went on 51st mission. Primary target. Bridge at Fassano. 3 & 4 flights hit. We dropped on secondary target at Albengo. Hit. 1000 lbs. Alt. 10,600 ft. Time 4:45. Flew lead ship with Lt. Boudreaux & Gates. Lt. Smith did good job. Flew over primary target twice. Then made approach on 2nd target from sea. If there was flak guns, we'd have caught hell. Messed up affair by 95th. No flak, no fighters. New crew came in last night.

JULY 30

Flew on 52nd mission. It was terrible. We were briefed on milk run. Target-Bridge at Ronco Scrivia-Alt. 10,200 ft. 2000 lbs. Time 5:15. We caught slight inaccurate flak near Genoa. Made 3 passes at target, at third breakaway we caught heavy, accurate flak. Then the fun started. Two MG 109-s came in on us. 04 got hell shot out of it. Natkus & two others wounded. Ship crashed in Corsica. We escorted the plane. I got one beautiful burst in. Wingard & Schultz really looked good. Was not scared until after we hit coast. All the wounds are slight. Messed up mission. Did not drop bomb. 95th again.

Went on 53rd mission on August 2. Gates' first lead. Target-Bridge at

Taggio was our secondary. Primary was Leven France. We flew over first but could not get enough bomb run, because of mountains. Hit or near miss on secondary. 500 lbs. Alt. 10,500 ft. Time 4:15. No flak, no fighters. Shackle fell from one ship through No. 16. Made large hole. Hanna & Long. Hanna really gets the tough breaks. Gates did a good job at lead. Went on 54th mission on Aug. 4 Target-Bridge in Leven, France. Alt. 10,600 ft. 1000 lbs. Did not drop. Made three passes over target. One of these days that's going to be very costly. Heard on return that it's been cut to 62 missions. With the Lord's help I'll be done by the end of this coming month. Pray it's cut again.

Went on 55th mission on Aug 6 Target-Bridge at Tarascon, France-2,000 lbs. Alt. 9,600 ft. Time 5:00. Miss. Gates' second lead. Thomas seems nervous. Hanna again ran into tough luck. Short of gas. Landed at Alghero. His last one. Today I saw Marseilles and Toulon. Got up at 4 a.m. Wed. Aug. 9 for my 56th mission. Carried 250 lbs. while the last three flights carried frags. I was really unhappy. We went after an airfield in Bergamo, Italy. Time 5:30. Alt. 10,800 ft. No flak, no fighters. The three groups, 319, 320 & 17 hit the fleet in the most devastating manner. Excellent job. Got my first papers for the Air Medal. Thomas hot on bombing. 432 had one ship shot down No. 51. 5 chutes seen to open. Hope they all made it. Long hop, 940 miles. Only 35 to 40 miles to Switzerland. If we were in trouble we'd have gone there.

Flew on 57th mission on Aug. 14. Our target was gun emplacements on the coast of France at Giens. Dropped and hit target. Alt. 9,400 ft. Bomb 500 lb. Time 3:30. Beautiful job. No flak or fighters. Milk run.
AUG. 15

Invasion of France from Corsica. Got up at 1 a.m. for breakfast. Briefing at 3 a.m. Took off at 5:15. Target-gun emplacements at Cape Benat. Too cloudy. Made 180 & missed on 2nd try. 500 lbs. Time 3:55. Alt. 8,400 ft. Saw huge armada making landing parties ready. Every conceivable type of ship. Hundreds and hundreds of our fighters over a multitude of targets. Took pictures. Hope they come out. 58th mission. 320th had 3 ships blow up today. Lost one crew. You could see the vivid explosions. Two new crews came in yesterday. Hope it keeps up that way. Went on 2nd mission of day and 59th. It's been a long day. Weather was a lot better. Target-Bridge at Aramont. Alt. 7,400 ft. 500 lbs. Hit or near miss. Time 5:00. Heavy flak. Capt. King got a piece right through his window. It hit him on headset. Saved his life. No fighters. We saw almost entire armada. 9 flattops. Gorgeous sight. Went on 60th mission on Aug. 16. Definitely no milk run. Target-Gun emplacements at Cape Cepet off Toulon. About 1 or 2 miles. Alt. 10,400 ft. 2000 lbs. Hit. 3:45 Time. Heavy, intense flak, no fighters. Two single engine jobs. Messed up target pretty much. It doesn't look like they are going to let me finish in peace. But as long as the good Lord hears my prayers, it'll be O.K.

Went on 61st mission on Aug. 18. Gun emplacements at Cape Cepet. Were told not to expect too much flak as the Germans were withdrawing. I wish S2 had come along. We went in at 9400 ft. 2000. Time 3:45. Hit. Then they hit us with everyting in the books. Shot down 03 with Olson, Brewer, Meyers, Jennings, Rhodes, Palin & Grisles. Five chutes came out. The flak was heavy, intense, accurate. No fighters. It's going to seem funny not hearing Bill Rhodes play his horn. He's probably in enemy territory. Two hit the water. My last 3 so far were rugged. It doesn't look as if the Heinies are going to let me finish up in peace.

Flew on 62nd and (I hope) my last mission on Aug. 20. Brother, it was no milk run. We hit Cape Cepet, again. Every squadron but the 34th lost a ship. Heavy, intense, accurate flak from Toulon. 2000 lbs. Target. Gun emplacements. Time 3:25. Hit. Our fleet was shelling them at the same time. The Lord must have heard my prayers. I was scared. 62 is supposed to be all. We'll see. Gates did wonderful evasive action job. It did look bad for a while. Four tough ones in a row to finish up. But, thank the Lord, I'm finished.

AUG. 30

17 fellows going home today. Nice bunch of boys. Hope it's my turn soon. On Aug. 28 Crisler, Rhodes, Palin & Jennings turned up on the squadron. Interesting story to tell, but sworn to secrecy. It's a miracle. Jennings pretty badly burned. All are going home. Ralph Grossman will visit Bea for me. Know I could depend on him.

SEPT. 2

Got the air medal today, from General Webster. Very nice affair.

SEPT. 6

Long and Deardorff left today. All by myself in shack. Told we'd move to Italy by Sept. 22. My guess-Viterbo.

SEPT. 10

Made T/Sgt. today. Starts from 1st of month. Highest rank I can get. No idea of when orders will go through. Rumor, now, is that we will move to Corsica. One hole to another. I hope it's untrue. Sardo was bad enough. Moved to Corsica on Sept. 21. A little better than Sardo. Company streets. Lots of work. No idea when I'll go home. On Sept. 29 went to visit "Chuck" Munger. Also ran into Ricks and "Eld" Throop. This island of Corsica is a lot cleaner than Sardinia. Populated by French. Hateful people. Everything to relieve us of our money. Dave, Konap, two other fellows and myself were charged $18 for a four course dinner. Still no replacements or any sign of any. Very discouraging. Two more sailors killed in Bastia. Off Limits. A guy goes nuts around here. Am on next Rome trip.

OCT. 9

Did not go direct to Rome but got a three day pass. Caught the courier out of Borgo to Florence. What a city. Beautiful cathedrals, streets, hotels, etc. We (Schaffenaker) slept at the Hotel Patria. Room service and all. Really a beautiful place. Left next day. Got lift to Rome. Landed at Ciampiano Air Field. Scene of my first mission. Really a sight to see. Saw in person how much damage we had done to the field. Caught a ride to Naples on Highway 7. Saw all the famous battlefields—Anzio, Terracina, Gaeta, Caserta, etc. In Caserta, a nice-sized city, there was not a house left intact. A horrible, but fascinating sight. Saw the huge foxholes at Anzio. Destroyed planes and tanks all along the road. Finally got to Naples. Saw a show and ate well in Naples. Left in B-26 for Corsica. Heard from Morty Franz. He's in France.

OCT. 10

17th B.G. awarded Presidential Citation. Great honor. Proud as hell. Got it for Anzio raid in February. Read in "Stars & Stripes" where the Major Benedict who flew Schaff & I from Florence to Rome is a famous character. 200 missions. Shot down 14 times. Big, ugly redhead. Buzzed every airport from Flo. to Rome. Flew 500 ft. to 1000 ft. all the way down. In Ciampiano they shot flares to warn him not to land, but he did anyway. Crazy.

OCT. 16

J.C. Gates made Captain today. Boy, he was happy as a king. He invited Gene & I over for drinks and cigars. Got half lit. It couldn't have happened to a better guy. Never would have bet on it, a year ago.

OCT. 20

Got the Presidential Citation formally, today. The whole group had a parade. Won it for the Jan. 13 raid on Ciampiano Air Field, Rome. My first mission. Outstanding. Only fellows in squadron before Jan. 13 can wear it permanently. I was lucky. New crew came in yesterday. More expected soon. Sent Bea $25 for her birthday. No time to mail gift to her, as it would take too long.

Schaffenaker, Baker, Hickey, Cathey, and Rabita's orders have gone in. No one before our crew now.

NOV. 4

Schaff, Baker, Hickey, Rabita, and Cathey along with Kilness, Pickle, Hanna and Reinecke left today. Will be my time soon I hope.

NOV. 9

Orders back today. Oh, happy day. Supposed to leave Saturday the 11th. Terrific wind storm all night long. Blew many tents down. Scared all night long.

NOV. 11

Left 34th for Naples. Taken to 7 Repl. Depot. Remained there 3 days. Bitter cold. Left there for "Blockhouse" in Naples proper. Slept on hard wood bed, no mattress. Food was better there, tho. Heavy winds and rains. Dave is here.

Left Naples on No. 18 for "Home Sweet Home" on Mt. Vernon. Had a very nice time on board. Very good meals. Slept on hammocks. Won $1500 on board ship. Landed in Boston harbor. Went to Myles Standish Field. Called Bea. First time I've heard her voice in over a year. Got home on the evening of the 30th. Whatta son I've got. Received lovely welcome from everyone. Got reservations for Bea & myself at the Hotel Ambassador in Atlantic City after my 28 day furlough. While home I took in plenty of shows & good food. Ran into Ed Moskowitz. Invited him over to the house. He brought a lovely gift for Michael. Left home for A.C. on the morning of the 28th. Got a nice room on the 12th floor for Bea & myself. This hotel is very large. They have a Turkish bath, swimming pool, pool tables, ping-pong etc. Everything that one could wish for. I was told that I'd be busy only for one hour a day. A misconception, as I had very little time off on the 29th and 30th. But my hardest day is over now. Bought tickets for N.C.O. club on New Year's Eve. On Jan. 7 met Rabbit Brooks, Perrault, and a host of other fellows I hadn't seen for a long time. Rabbit shipped to Columbus, Ohio. Shipped to Convalescent Hosp. at Ft. Thomas, Ky. along with Perrault, Falzone. Met Ralph Grossman there. This place is only for Air Corps men. Mostly guys trying to get out. Got a 10 day furlough. On return home found letter from Bill Schaffenaker. He's at same place as Rabbit. And surprise, Wally Wajtkowski, too. Decided to pay them a visit on return to camp. Did so. Found Bill in hospital with flu. Almost better now. Finally saw Wally, after almost 2 years. Same old guy. Drunkard. But, a prince. Anne is pregnant. Hope they have luck on this one. Wally refused to fly so he's a truck driver now. Kept his rating too. Lucky break. Heard that Yav & Mucciano shot down. Boy, I am very lucky. Those were two good men. Also heard that Gadd had blown himself up, experimenting. Knew he would someday. Our outfit is in France. Must be catching plenty of hell. Left Ft. Thomas on Feb. 26 for Atlantic City for reclassification. Told dr. that I thought I needed another stay at Ft. Thomas so they sent me on a 21 day furlough. Met Ed Radin. He's a captain now. Told me our outfit had caught holy hell. Miller lost arm and Lt. Engesath killed. Gates & Dave home. Mucciano not killed but severely injured. Met Chase at Atlantic City. Still shooting off his mouth about how big a hero he is. Maybe he's right & I've misjudged him. Got a 21 day convalescent furlough. Still don't know what to do with me. Finally, after return to Atlantic City they sent me to Plattsburg, N.Y., Conv. Hosp. Met a bunch of old friends. Very nice camp. Got severe headache on my first night here. Complained and got help for the first time. Bringing Whitey home with me this weekend.

# KENNETH E. BOOKE

Like most diaries kept by members of bombing crews, the diary of 1st Lt. Kenneth E. Booke was kept on a basis of mission-by-mission rather than day-by-day.

Booke entered the Army in 1936 at the age of 18 and from then until 1942 served in Company B, 21st Infantry. In 1942 he transferred to the Army Air Corps, was commissioned, and served with the 407th Squadron, 92nd Bomb Group, 8th Air Force as pilot of a B-17 bomber

Following the war, he worked as a mechanical designer. A native of New York State, he divorced his first wife in 1949 and moved to Ohio, where he remarried, fathered a second family, and died in 1973.

His diary, kept in a hardbound diary book which Lt. Booke purchased in London, was submitted by Frank Booke, a justifiably proud son born of the first marriage.

*******

MISSION ONE        BREMEN, GERMANY        DEC. 20, 1943

This morning at 4 o'clock Lt. Smornel, our operations officer, woke us up for our first mission. Smornel always has some little crack to make, such as, make a noise like an aeroplane, are you ready to engage the Luftwaffe, etc. This is always topped off with breakfast at three, briefing at four, or whatever the appointed times are.

For breakfast we had fresh eggs. This is more or less common practice, having an egg breakfast the morning of a mission.

Our takeoff and assembly was uneventfull, as was our trip over. At the target it was fairly clear, so we made a visual bombing. We encountered flak over the target and were in for it for about ten minutes. Later I learned that it was considered to be quite heavy.

I seen three ME 109s come in below us and to the right, sticking together in a fairly loose formation. They hit on "17" and knocked him out of the formation. I think the crew would have been able to bail out safely, all though I couldn't be sure as the episode left my field of vision.

Shortly after this another "109" dove through our formation, trying to break us up so his buddies could take a crack at us individually. Fortunately he didn't succeed.

S 2 told us at briefing that we would run right out of flak after our turn following "bombs away". Things turned out as they predicted, which tends to increase my respect for that department.

On the trip home, we seen one "B 17" "dicth" in the North Sea. Three spitfires circled over him, and several of our ships radioed in his position.

We were pretty worried about our gas supply coming home and when we landed we only had thirty gallons in each tank.

I can't say yet that I have a true idea of what a fellow feels like in combat. Today I was curious as hell and don't believe I had time to get very scared.

The battle damage to our ship was light. Our wind shield on the pilot's side was cracked by flak, and we had one hole between no. 2 engine and the fuselage.

We put in just about eight and a half hours on this raid. The total losses were something like twenty-some bombers.

MISSION TWO    Kiel, Germany    JAN. 5, 1944

This morning Smornel woke us up again. More eggs for breakfast and then briefing followed by takeoff.

Our trip over was quiet and the weather was in our favor. The cloud cover over enemy territory was ten tenths.

When we reached the target we had a few breaks in the clouds but the flak was still pretty inaccurate.

Our group was pretty badly disorganized over the target and at one time we just missed a collision.

We never did bomb the target, but later dropped them on the coast as we were leaving enemy territory. The raid wasent too bad all in all, all though we had bad visibility landing.

I was pretty scared over the target today, but I am sure that my being scared won't interfere with anything I will have to do.

Battle damage was negligible consisting of a few small flak holes.

The raid was another eight hour trip. The total losses were reported as eighteen bombers.

THREE    Kiel, Germany    JAN. 5, 1944

Today was pretty much of a repetition of yesterday up to a certain point.

We were routed into the target and out again nearly opposite to yesterday's flight plan. Today we flew across Denmark, then skirted down the coast and into Kiel, leaving nearly straight west and back across the North Sea.

We flew right wing man off of Lt. Reed, who led the high squadron. He done a dam good job.

The weather was clear as a bell over enemy territory today, and there appeared to be a light snow on the ground.

I figured we'd cacth hell with it as clear as it was and we did.

We had quite heavy flak over the target plus several fighter attacks. The fighters were 210's and they came in from one o'clock, three to five at a time for five waves.

I seen one B 17 hit in the right wing, the wing blow up and fold over, and the whole thing spin down. I didn't see any chutes blossom out. The way that ship was spinning, I don't believe it would have been possible to get out.

Later I learned that a captured B 17 in German hands was flying near our formation. This ship had fired a rocket into the formation, hitting the ship I had seen spin down.

The action and excitement over the target lasted some thirty-five minutes. I was mighty glad when we ran out of it.

We were supposed to have fighter cover, but they weren't around when we were over the target.

The run home was uneventfull, but landing was really hell again. The fog was pretty bad at home, and we at one time nearly stalled out over the field.

The whole thing lasted over eight hours. Lossed were 23 bombers.

Battle damage consisted of several flak holes, doing no concrete damage to the ship or the crew.

Lt. Ralph Davidson, our navigator, had one piece of flak come up through his map table and skin his glove. He found the piece of flak.

FOUR    Target No. 72 (Near Aires, France)    Jan. 14, 1944

The raid today was a real milk run for our outfit. I was woke up at ten o'clock this morning and didn't expect a raid was possable as it was so late in the day.

We were briefed after dinner, took off, flew just over the coast of France into enemy territory, dumped our bombs, and then returned.

We seen no flak and no enemy fighters. The sky was full of our fighters.

No ships were lost in the whole operation and the whole trip lasted only three hours and fourty-five minutes.

FIVE    Target No. 51 Near Bellevue, France    JAN. 21, 1944

Today we had another "milk run", that we have been trying to put over for the last two days. Weather prevented this raid yesterday and the day before.

This mission was very similar to the last one, insofar as depth into enemy territory and location of target were concerned.

We did see flak about ten miles off to our left, but nothing close to us.

We made four runs over the target, but were unable to release our bombs, due to an eight tenths cloud cover. It is a policy of the eighth air force to be accurate when bombing targets in France. If we hit anything other than German military installations it would tend to decrease our popularity with the French people.

*NOTE: The ensuing page of diary would normally have been numbered 13 but Booke numbered it 12 ½, omitting the "unlucky" number 13)*

I flew with Flight Officer H.W. Smith today. This was his first flight as first pilot and he done one hell of a fine job.

The whole run lasted only three hours and forty-five minutes-the flight was at 14,000 feet. There was no battle damage to our ship and there were no ships lost in our group.

This mission, being no. 5, entitles me to the air meadle.

SIX        Wilhelmshaven, Germany       FEB. 3, 1944

Before writing up this mission, I will mention the raid we did not go on the other day. The one to Brunswick, Germany. We lost three of the boys in our bks., due to a mid air collision, and they were three of the finest fellows a person could hope to find. Lts. Larson (pilot) Bennett (Co-Pilot) Herb Blowers (Navigator) and Joe Ante (Bombardier). A fellow could take up a lot of space just writing about what swell fellows each one was, but what's the use now. We all sure felt pretty bad about them.

To get on with the present, we went on a mission to Wilhelmshaven today. According to all standards today's run should have been fairly easy. The only cacth is, that no raid is a milk run for everybody.

We had things O.K. for quite a ways, well into enemy territory, and then we had a little trouble.

Our no. 2 supercharger went out, and we couldn't develop enough power to stay with our formation.

Our only alternative was to turn back, and we had quite a good distance to go before running out of danger.

We were at 23,000 and the clouds were just below us, so we ducked into them in order to avoid perception by fighters.

Everything went well until we hit a break in the clouds. We came into the clear, and to our left six hundred yards was a German 109. He flew parallell to us for about a minute, then he come in. He made one attack from the left waist and three on the tail. He (thank Heaven) didn't hit us and we didn't hit him. He had our marking painted on him and had his wing tips painted to resemble a P 51. These Germans are pretty darn smart at this war business.

After we left this circumstance, we eventually came to the coast of Holland. There some little town contained a German Flak gunner, who I believe could outshoot Sgt. York-He was really putting them in there, right at our altitude and just off our right wing tip. Thank the good Lord, he didn't hit us. One piece of flak did hit our upper gun turrett, but that was all.

We dropped our bombs in the north sea and made it back to the base with no further excitement.

Tonight Lt. Ben Van Der Gellson and I went to the "Ki Wee" bar and drank a few beers. There is an alert tomorrow and a few beers sure help a fellow get a good night's sleep. We lost nine today.

SEVEN     Frankfurt, Germany     Feb. 4, 1944

Today we started out on what we knew would be a long haul and it proved to be just that.

We have been briefed for Frankfurt three or four times in the past few weeks but due to weather, the mission has been scrubbed or called back. We were hoping this morning that it would be scrubbed again.

The trip was uneventfull untill we, by a mistake in navigation, crossed the Ruhr Valley. We were to skirt to the south of the Ruhr, thereby missing the flak.

Lt. Reid was hit in one engine while we were going through this area but stayed behind the formation and dropped his bombs on the target. The flak was really heavy and darned accurate.

Things went smooth then, until we got to Frankfurt. Again we hit heavy accurate flak. This time we lost Lt. Cook's crew out of the low squadron. Cook was hit, then spun down with one wing broken off. I flew with him on a mission we started to Frankfurt last week, but they called us back. He was one heck of a nice fellow, as were the rest of the boys in his crew.

I saw one ship circle down into enemy territory just after we left the target, one engine knocked out, and no hopes of getting home. He wasn't far from our outfit though.

We had a good tail wind coming in, but we were really bucking it coming out. Our ground speed was just a little over a hundred, and it took us 2 hours to hit the coast.

At the coast, due to another mistake in navigation, we crossed over the "Pas de Calais" area or "Flak Alley" as we call it. One ship in our low group was hit in no. three engine; and the crew was seen to bail out. This flak was heavy and accurate also.

After getting out of this it didn't take us long to get home.

We found out at interrogation that Reid had crashed landed in England and that three men were dead, one dying, and three missing. Later we heard that they were all dead, and still later, that the officer and the engineer were badly hurt and in the hospital. Sure hope the latter is true. Will enter the truth tomorrow.

I was talking to Prior (the co-pilot on Reid's crew) last night. He expected today's mission to be rough, but he no doubt didn't think it would be that rough on his bunch.

Our bombardier, Lt. C.R. Watson, was knocked out of his turrett by flak. He was not injured, except for a small fragment of glass in one eye.

We are pretty sure that he will be awarded the Purple Heart for this injury, or more properly expressed, this close shave.

We had a few flak holes in the wings, rudder and fuselage. Outside of this we had no battle damage.

We went in and stayed at twenty-eight thousand feet until we were close to the coast coming out. We then let down to 21,000.

The trip lasted about seaven and a half hours. I started praying when we hit the flak at Happy Valley and didn't say Ah men untill we left the enemy coast.

We seen no enemy fighters and our fighter cover was splendid. Tomorrow will enter losses if they are published. Our sqd. lost 2 today.

There is a very good chance of another mission tomorrow. I spent this evening drinking a few beers and now to bed.

The losses on this raid were 29 bombers and three fighters.

All of Lt. Reid's crew were killed except the tail gunner. He is quite seriously injured.

We lost two crews out of our sqd. today, for a total of three out of the group. This makes five crews lost now in the past week out of our sqd. alone. We can't afford this any more. We should be due for a change of luck.

EIGHT      France    FEB. 5, 1944

Today for the third time in a row, we went on another mission. Today's run was quite easy, thank the good Lord.

Our target was in southern France, and was an airfield used by four engine bombers of the Luftwaffe. We really hit the place, right in the center hanger of a group of three hangers. Flak was light at the target and seemed to be much smaller bursts than usual.

We didn't lose a ship at the target, or on the whole raid for that matter. We hit one small flak area on the way back, and one burst was mighty close to home. It was the first burst that I have been able to hear above the noise of everything else. It made a visious, bursting, cracking sound, sort of a "Krumph". I thought for sure that the nose had been hit. Called up Charly, and he was O.K., as was the navigator. The bust was a little high, so all it did was spray the upper surface of our left wing.

We had a little "sweating out" trying to land as the haze was real bad tonight. Made it O.K., though, thank the good Lord, and we will continue to do so with his help.

Tonight our group is having a party, but the hell of it is, there is another alert on for tomorrow. If we go tomorrow we will be the record in this theatre of op's.

I went up to the party and had a bit of chicken salad, a beer, a scotch and soda, and a glass of punch then to bed again. This makes the third day in a row that I have not been to the mess hall to eat. Have been satisfied with four sandwiches that I had at interrogation after the raids.

Sure hope we don't go tomorrow but think we will as the weather is clear.

Oh, yes, today's raid was at 17,000 feet and we had a strange navigator as ours was sick. We also had a different ball turret man and waist gunner, as our regulars, Sgt's Krepp and Benson, were frozen yesterday. Their electric suits went out and Krepp froze his feet, and Benson I havent acertained the exact nature of his as yet.

NINE      Frankfurt, Germany     FEB. 8, 1943

Today we started out to Frankfurt again. We were darned apprehensive, as we knew it would be a rough mission.

Our position in the formation was left wing man, low sqd., which is reputed to be the worst place in the event of fighter attack.

Everything went well on tk. off, assembly, and up to a point very deep into France. There the lead ship of the lead sqd. aborted, no one took over, and they were badly disorganized.

Our sqd. stuck together fairly well, but we were forced to drop back quite a ways.

Just about this time several 109s hit the lead sqd. and high sqd. I saw four ships hit and start home and the rest of the two sqds. completely disintegrated.

We were left all by ourselves with seven ships and then the fighters hit us. Thank a kind Lord, they didn't get anyone.

We started home, with P 47 escort that we had called, and made it to the French coast O.K. There we had a prop run away on no. one engine and had to drop back quite a bit. We had taken lead in the second element, and our wing men stuck with us. We got the prop working O.K. at about five thousand feet.

Made it back to the base all right.

Lt. Shevicks crew went down today. He went through training with us and came into this group with us. Shev is another Pop who will never see his child.

Lt. Smith, another of our bunch, seen Shev's windshield hit, seen Shev try to stand up, then settle back down again. The ship seemed under controll so most of the crew should have bailed out, we hope.

We lost two other ships out of the group today, which makes a total of three for the day. Things have been going pretty rough for our outfit lately.

We did run into sparse inaccurate flak, both going in and out.

We flew at twenty three thousand feet. Our ship had no battle damage.

There is a mission alert for tomorrow and we are on it, so, to bed.

TEN      Leipzig, Germany     FEB. 20, 1944

We were awakened this morning for a four thirty breakfast and a five thirty briefing. I thought, as did everyone else, that the raid would be a fairly short one.

When we got to the briefing room what did they have on the board but Leipzig again.

This is a raid we have been dreading for some time. The target is some 547 miles from the base, through France and Germany and is located at the extreme end of our fighters endurance.

This morning we all knew we were going to get the whey knocked out of us and we really expected it to be rough.

We just had a series of miricles that made this mission fall short of a slaughter.

Our fighter cover was perfectly coordinated all the way in and back, and our navigation was excellent. We dodged all of the flak areas except that we had to run through at the target, and there the flak wasn't too heavy.

Fighters (enemy 109's) hit the group behind us pretty hard, but no one picked on us.

I saw a 109 make one pass at a straggler several thousand feet below us and then two P 51s promptly shot the 109 down.

We saw several ships (B17) go down under controll in enemy territory and saw one spin in.

We landed back at the base after a rather uneventfull return trip. Had to let down through a ten tenths overcast, but visibility was good benethe it.

Our battle damage consisted of about 12 flak holes throughout the ship. Our right wing tanks and Tokeyoe's were punctured and the ship will be out of commission for several days. We were darn lucky the ship didn't cacth fire, as the gas was leaking out only about a foot from no. 4 turbo.

We lost one ship out of the group today and the total day's losses were 24 ships.

The raid was conducted at 21,000 ft. and lasted 9:15 in the air.

This raid being no. ten, gives me a cluster to the air meadle, which is the same as getting the same meadle twice.

ELEVEN       Lipstadt, Germany     FEB. 21, 1944

Today's raid according to all previous indications, should have been a "milk run". It was a damn tough mission, which proves that you never can judge a mission befor hand.

We had breakfast at 5:45, briefing 6:45, and didn't take off until ten fifteen. We had pleanty of our own fighters scheduled and only nine flak guns at the target, which all made it appear like an easy mission.

Things went well untill we ran out of our P 47 escort. We were unescorted for about 25 minutes and "several" enemy fighters pounded at us every unescorted minute. They were all Me 210's. Two of them made a nose attack from one o'clock high, and passed over our lead sqd. The pilot in one of the fighters was evidently shot on the way in and he flew head on, right into the left wing of Lt. McEnboy's ship. There was one big burst of flame and then it all started down. It is a horrible sight to watch a ship blow up or spin in on fire, but I am getting enough sense to look away after something like that happens now.

Lt. Skoubo from our sqd. was hit in no. 4 engine during the fighter attacks. We heard his last s.o.s. from Holland and he evidently went down there under controll.

Skoubo arrived in this sqd. the same date we did, and he was a swell fellow, well liked by every one.

We never did hit the target we went after, due to ten/tenths cloud cover. We did, however, get to an air field that was in the clear in a different area.

We hit several light flak areas, but it didn't cause any trouble for any of us.

The raid was run off at 20,000 ft. and lasted 7 hrs. 30 minutes.

We had no battle damage to our ship and had no outstanding trouble.

We lost two ships out of our group today. The day's total losses were not broadcast.

The fighter, bomber, collision was so close off our left wing that a lot of fellows in our sqd. thought it was us. Thank the good Lord, they were wrong.

After these eleven mission, I am getting to the point where flak and fighters don't scare me nearly as bad as they used to, which just goes to prove that a person can get used to nearly anything.

I don't believe any one can go through one of these missions without getting scared, but familiarity does breed the ability to accept it all a little more cooley.

TWELVE     Stuttgart, Germany     FEB. 25, 1944

Today I was supposed to be on pass until noon. I made the mistake of staying on the base, and had to go on this mission.

Lt. Leavy, the pilot, was sick. They needed his crew so they got another pilot from the 326th and we flew the crew. The pilot's name was Lt. Upson and he done a good job. Enjoyed flying with him.

Stuttgart, by all indications, should have been a slaughter for us. It just turned out that things went our way, and we had a comparatively easy time of it.

We encountered light flak at the coast, causing three ships to turn back out of the group. There were also several flak areas on the way in.

Our lead navigator, however, done a good job of leading us around them. The navigator from my own crew, Lt. Davison, flew in the lead ship as co-navigator.

Our fighter support was good all the way in and at the target we had P38s and 51s.

There was moderate flak at the target but nothing too heavy.

Before the target a "110" made several passes at the formation, fireing his two rockets on one of them. He did hit a ship in the high sqd. (Lt. Beach) and we saw him head for Switzerland with no. 1 engine on fire.

Our tail gunner claimed the 110 and felt pretty sure he was the one that got him.

The fighter support on the way home was beautifull. The sky was literally filled with 38s and 47s.

The enemy fighters did pass at other groups and took quite a heavy toll but for some reason they didn't bother us.

We had no battle damage to our ship outside of a cracked windshield from a spent cartridge.

We lost two ships out of our group today and none out of the sqd. On the raid the day preceding this, our sqd. lost two ships, one of which was Lt. Scarborough's crew. This crew was quartered in our bks. and they were all a decent bunch of fellows.

The entire trip lasted nine hours and some odd minutes. We had to let down thru an overcast back at the base.

Lt. Upson drew an areil camera, and we got several pictures while on the mission, some showing bombs away, flak, and other features of interest.

Stuttgart is roughly five hundred air miles from England. We flew at 21,000 ft. to the target, then let down to fifteen thousand on the way out.

Our group had three men with moderate flak injuries from today's raid, but nothing serious.

The total losses for the day were not published but I think that they ran rather high.

*At this point Booke pasted in his diary a propaganda leaflet that was dropped over Germany by the allies. It says "Where is the Luftwaffe? "That is the question that your soldiers on the Eastern Front and in Italy have asked again and again. The Luftwaffe has deserted the Homeland, everyone is saying. Yesterday on a clear day American bombers flew en masse over Berlin. Today they were over the capital city five times. Naturally you ask yourselves, "Where is the Luftwaffe?" Ask Goering! Ask Hitler!)*

THIRTEEN        Frankfurt, Germany        March 2, 1944

Today I was a little leery of this mission, it being no. thirteen, and Frankfurt being a tough target anyway. Actually we had a reasonable time of it.

We saw a few fighters on the way in and out, but nothing bothered us. Our fighter cover was ample and well coordinated.

We did run through several light flak areas, but nothing hit the ship.

These missions are not getting any easier, but I am getting so I mind them less and less. I can be entirely at ease in the flak now.

We did encounter very heavy barrage type flak over the target but our formation was just off on the left of it. I saw what appeared to be a fort hit in the bomb bays and blow up. It looked as though some one had emptied a giant waste paper basket of confetti.

We flew at 23,000 and the trip lasted 8:15 min.

We lost two ships out of the group today and none out of our sqd.

The total losses again were not published.

This raid puts me over the hump, on the down hill way to home.

FOURTEEN     Berlin, Germany     MARCH 8, 1944

Today, for the second time, the Eighth Air Force raided Berlin, Germany.

The first raid took place on the sixth and was really a rough raid, our group losing four ships. That day we lost Cooper out of our sqd., another fellow who came over here with us. There are dam few of us left now.

We expected to get the whey knocked out of us again today, but didn't as the dunderheads in H.Q. gave us ample fighter protection for a change.

We only saw one enemy fighter on the way into Berlin. He tried for the ship behind us, but missed. At the target, which was a ball bearing factory on the outskirts of the big town, we had pretty fair flak that was just fair for accuracy.

On the way out we crossed a few spots that threw flak up at us, but nothing to write home about. All in all, it was remarkably easy for a Berlin raid.

We went in at 22,000 over the target at 26,000 and out at 19,000. We hit the hell out of the target. The battle damage to our ship was nil, lost none out of the group and the whole trip lasted over eight hours.

One new development that has us all highly peeved, is the fact that they have raised our missions from 25 to 30. It is the same as telling a man that he has to fly untill he gets shot down.

When we got here, they had 6 per cent finishing their missions. The percentage was then boosted to 25 per cent by fighter support. Now they are sending us on longer, deeper raids, which means that things aren't a dam bit easier, and we have five more missions to go.

Some of this old bull really try's a man's patriotism, or whatever it is that makes us fly.

FIFTEEN     Berlin, Germany     MARCH 9, 1944

Today we again raided Berlin, Germany. We expected a rough time of it but for our group it wasn't too bad.

We had a solid ten tenths overcast to climb through befor assembly, and it was solid all the way to Berlin and back. The overcast was so thick over the continent that not a single German fighter appeared during the whole raid.

Our group led the whole show, and we bombed through the clouds using P.F.F. The Berlin flax gunners didn't start shooting untill we had nearly passed over the target, probably hoping we wouldn't locate the city.

The outfits behind us caught one hell of a lot of flak, the smoke being so thick that we couldn't see the divisions coming up behind the target.

Our trip home was quiet, seeming more like a pleasure flight than a combat mission. We went in at 25,000, let down off the tgt to 14,000 and came home at that altitude.

We had no battle damage to our ship. The trip lasted eight and a half hours. Captain Sewall and Captain Smyrel complimented us on our formation flying, which should give us some better spots in the formation from now on.

The whole Air Force lost only seven planes on this mission, but the ironicle part of it is that three were from our group.

We lost Lt. Webb here at the field. The cloud base was only 400' off of the ground, and it is assumed that he stalled out and spun in.

The bombardier on his crew was a twin brother to one of the pilots in our sqd. These two brothers came over here together, were on the same crew together, and were just split up for this mission.

We also lost Lt. Payne's crew, probably due to mechanical failure deep in Germany. I flew with Payne when he first arrived here about a week ago. He had only four missions counting this last one. His navigator, Lt. McDowell, flew with us on three missions while our regular navigator was leading the grp.

This is my fifteenth mission and makes another cluster to the Air Meadl.

SIXTEEN     Leichfield, Germany     MARCH 18, 1944

Today they sort of surprised us, as we were not on the alert list for this mission. Yakel, our regular pilot, is grounded and we were not expecting to fly.

I flew today with a fellow from the 326th who has just been checked out. We split the first pilot time, which is something Yakel never does regardless of how much I fly.

This was a long haul today, being in darn near as far as Berlin but further south. Our target was only thirty minutes or so from Munich.

We had excellent fighter protection on the way in and back also. We have had darn good luck with fighter protection of late. Usually some outfit is left unprotected, while the rest are well covered. They consequently get the whey wailed out of them.

We ran through quite a bit of flak at the target and it was pretty good for accuracy.

After we turned off of the target and were apparently out of the excitement the fellow I flew with got out of his seat to take off his electric suit. Our crew was talking over the results of the bombing and more or less relaxing a bit.

All of a sudden I noticed emty brass comeing out of Leavy's tail and he started evasive action. That was enough for me, so I started taking up evasive action also.

Later I told the fellows that it was pretty poor on our part, as no one saw the fighters come in, and no one on our crew fired a shot. P 38s and P51s got those fighters after they peeled off under us.

I rather imagine a lot of crews get shot down this way, getting too cocksure and careless after a number of missions.

We passed over some of the Alps on the way home and also over Lake Constance. We were only 15 miles from Switzerland at one time.

I had a camera with me today and got some fairly good shots.

We went in at 20,000 and dropped down to 15,000 after we left the target. The trip lasted eight hours and five minutes. Our battle damage consists of several scattered flak holes, but nothing of consequence. We lost one out of the group today and none from the sqd. The total losses were 48 bombers and fifteen fighters.

The fellows from our group, Lt. Cappel's crew, were escorted into Switzerland by P 38s and landed at an air field at the southern end of Lk. Constance. The war is over for them, as they will be interned.

The Alps sure were pretty, really a magnificent sight. Imagine my grandmother would enjoy this picture I took as she was born in Switzerland.

APRIL 4, 1944

Today we had a visitor that we sure were glad to see. Lt. Shevick, that we were sure was gone, turned up after escaping from France—All of his crew bailed out safely but only four of them are back to date—It just goes to show that people back home should never give up hope—Shev told us that the fighters tried their damdest to shoot him down after they winged him, and even tried to shoot him as he was parachuting down, then ground strafed him on the ground—they make a habit of doing this over France because the French help our Airmen get out, and it is so easy to get away. They (enemy) won't shoot at parachutes in Germany, as it is very hard to evade capture in Germany.

Lt. McElroy's crew lost this same mission all bailed out safely and some of them are back now.

This sort of thing sure makes a fellow feel O.K. When you are sure a friend "had it" and then shows up in good shape, it makes your chances look a lot better.

SEVENTEEN    Kassel, Germany    April 19, 1944

Today I made my first raid since a month ago. Quite a long lay off, due to our first Pilot, J.J. Yakel, being grounded.

This was my first raid as first Pilot today. I flew with a new co-pilot who had never been on a mission before. He done a good job, though, and was a likable fellow. I had my regular crew excepting Lt. George, the afore mentioned co-pilot and Lt. Hallen the navigator.

Our target was an air field 26 miles from Kassel, Germany. This is not a short raid, and by the same token it is not a long one. Kassel lies about 500 miles from England.

I was scheduled to fly no. 2 second element of the lead sqd. which is a much better spot.

We flew in at 22,000 feet going in north of the Ruhr Valley then coming out south of same at 19,000. We passed several flak areas on the way in, but didn't get in any untill the target.

At the target we had a heavy barrage of flak, but it was of short duration and we ran out of it quickly. I heard a peice of flak hit the armor plating under my seat and I would have jumped right out if it had not been for the safety belt. This one hole was the only battle damage to our ship.

Our bomb load was 10 500 lb. demolition bombs.

After bombs away I slid out to the left about four or five wing lengths thereby avoiding the flak that was popping in the formation.

Our fighter support was very good today except for some twenty minutes on the way in, but fortunately there were no Jerries around at that time. We got through with no fighter attacks.

We lost no ship from our grp. and had no men injured all though we did have a few come in on three engines.

The trip lasted some six and a half hours. All in all it was a very satisfactory mission. We (92nd Grp) had no losses, we hit the target nicely, and the trip wasn't too tireing.

There is a definite added responsibility in being first pilot, and the strain is much greater, but I am confident that I can handle it all right.

With the help of God, I am serenely confident that I will get through all of these missions in good shape.

EIGHTEEN    Lingham, France    APRIL 20, 1944

Today was another very rare and infrequent "milk run", just inside of France.

The target was located about 15 miles inland, and was some kind of construction sight. We hit the target with one squadrons bombs but the other sqd. missed due to poor formation. We used an unusual formation today, consisting of two six ship sqds to compose a twelve ship group.

My co-pilot today was Lt. Martin from Lt. Baird's crew. A fine little flyer and I hope to fly with him again.

The whole trip lasted only four hours and we saw no enemy fighters or flak.

I, due to not knowing the tail wheel was locked, sheered a pin prior to takeoff. The proper thing would have been to have it fixed before taking off, but I didn't want to chance missing an easy raid like this so we went anyway. The takeoff and landing were O.K.

A raid like this now and then sure gives a definite boost in a fellows outlook towards this racket. May many more of the same follow.

NINETEEN          Nancy, France          APRIL 25, 1944

Today we went on a raid to an air field in Nancy, France, which is located about 30 miles from Switzerland. I took Lt. Williamson (Bombardier) on his last raid today. He sure was pleased to finish up.

Yesterday while I was on pass, they had a rough time of it on a raid to Munich. We lost five out of the group of which three were from this sqd, two of the crews from my bks (Lt. Parramore's crew and Campbell's entire crew less Campbell). The fellows on Parramore's crew were some of my best buddies, Lts. Sampson, Steichen, and also Garris.

Parramore was last reported going into Switzerland about 15 minutes away and they felt sure he made it O.K. The other two crews from our sqd. were able to bail out according to reports.

I wrote to Parramore's, Steichen's and Sampson's mothers telling them what happened even though it is against regulations. This crew owed me twenty pounds so loaning to your buddies is not sound proposition over here.

To get on with the present, I flew with Charley Comerford for co-pilot. He is a darn nice guy to fly with and darn good at formation.

We had a fairly easy time of it, seeing no fighters and a moderate flak barrage at the target. We had no battle damage to the ship, allthough we had one burst underneath us that lifted us about 20 feet.

We flew darn good formation today. All in all it was an easy mission. We lost none out of the group and we really hit the target. The whole trip lasted a little over seven hours.

TWENTY          Brunswick, Germany          APRIL 26, 1944

Charly Comerford and I flew togeather again today. I really like to fly with him. He is better than a lot of the first pilots we have around here.

We expected a tough raid today, as our target was in the worst part of the fighter belt. We had a solid overcast all the way and I think that heald them down as we did not see one enemy fighter. This was very fortunate as our fighter escort was not with us most of the way in and back, due to our being a little late and off course.

We crossed the Dummer Lake area by mistake and caught a pretty heavy flak barrage. We have so many new and green pilots, that the formation just went to hell when we got in the flak. We would have been an easy mark for fighters had they been around.

This is the first time I have ever seen a flak barrage bust up our formation.

We had another fairly good flak barrage at the target, and ran across moderate flak areas on the way out. We had no battle damage to our ship. Our group lost no ships. We flew at 22,000 feet and the trip lasted seven and fifteen.

It was easier than we expected, due to no fighters. Another cluster to the air meadle today.

TWENTY-ONE        Pas de Calais Area, France        APRIL 27, 1944

Today we were woke up early and expected to go on a long raid, but it turned out to be just inside the coast of France.

I broke in a new pilot on this mission, takeing him as my co-pilot for his first mission.

We had heavy accurate flak at the target and the first of it knocked out my no. 3 engine. I stayed with the formation O.K. but they didn't drop bombs as the bombardier lost the target.

About mid-channel I pulled out of formation to drop my bombs, as I didn't want to land a bomb load with three engines.

On returning to base, another ship ran off the runway so I had to land cross wind. Made a fair landing.

Flew at 20,000 feet, four hour trip, no losses.

Capt. Jones crew finished up today, which leaves me as the oldest crew in the sqd. Sure hope the Lord lets me finish next.

TWENTY-TWO        Nancy Essey, France        APRIL 27, 1944

This afternoon we went on another mission. The second time this group has ever flown two missions in one day, and the first time since last summer.

This makes me four missions in three days and I am the tiredest I have ever been in my life. I put nearly twelve hours in the air today, and most of it in formation.

On take off I got dizzy for a minute and ran off the runway, but got it back on with a lot of luck. We had a 90° cross wind at about 15 mph.

I led the second element today, but was just too darned tired to do a good job.

Our target was an air field in Nancy, France, where we were the other day.

We crossed a darned heavy flak area, and I saw two ships spin down in flames and no end of crippled ships.

We had no flak at the target and even then we missed it. Our formation was poor, just because everyone was so darned tired.

We ran across a few flak areas on the way out and caught heavy flak at the coast. I saw two more ships go down in flames spinning there, and saw one fall in the water. One bombardier saw eight blow up or spin down in all today.

Twice today I was forced to fly across the prop wash of the wing ahead. It was absolutely all I could do to keep the darned thing from turning over.

When we got half way across the channel I pulled out of formation and set up the automatic pilot, as I was too darned tired to stay with the thing.

We landed at the base at 9:35. It was a long rough day. Seven and a half hours on this afternoon raid at 21,000 feet. Lost none out of our group.

Several flak holes throughout my ship.

My navigator done a wonderfull job this afternoon. Have had a little trouble getting him on the beam but know he will be O.K. from now on.

My co-pilot this afternoon was Lt. Martin who flew with me the other day. He is a good little man.

TWENTY-THREE        Saarbrucken, Germany        May 11, 1944

Today we started out rather late for so long a raid, take off being at three o'clock.

Our target was an oil refinery near the edge of town, but we didn't drop our bombs due to poor vis.

I broke in another new pilot today. Sure is amazing how little formation time some of them have when they get here.

We had an uneventfull trip on the way in, good fighter support giving us swell protection. At the target we encountered one darned heavy accurate flak barrage about five minutes thick. Holbrook saw it first and called off (flak at 11 o'clock, that is, I think it's flak, say, that's flak isn't it). Holbrook was the new pilot.

We passed over the target without bombing due to haze. We then made a 360° for another run, the leader changed his mind and started for the secondary, and we ended up with the 92nd group coming out alone without fighter support, thirty minutes late and 60 miles off course. It is damned amazing that we didn't get intercepted by enemy fighters and have the whey kicked out of us. As it was we made it back uneventfully.

Prior to this raid my crew and I spent a week in the rest home at Southport, England. My gunners were just about too jumpy to fly, and I took a physical check which recommended a rest before return to duty, therefor we got it.

I have fond hopes of finishing my tour alive now, but don't dare think too much about it for fear that I will become too fond of life and lose a little efficiency when in combat.

It takes a lot of self bull shooting and fooling to build a satisfactory state of mind. I think I have this accomplished and don't care for any change of attitude.

TWENTY-FOUR            Paris, France       MAY 20, 1944

This morning we were woke up at three o'clock, briefed at four on a plan A to Paris and a plan B to Ludwigshaven, Germ. We flew plan A due to impossible meteorlogical conditions at Plan B.

Here at this base we had a dense fog to take off in, vis. being less than 250 feet to completely nil. We had three ships crash on the takeoff of which nine men escaped alive. Makes a person wonder if the army has any sense at all at times.

When I took off, I hit a wall of fog half way down the runway and had to go on instruments, then broke out for an instant then back on instruments again. If I had hit prop wash there just would have been no hopes whatsoever—Our C.O., Col. Griffith, who led today, said he would never take off again in similar conditions as it was just suicide.

Only about half of our ships got off, due to the crashes and bombs blowing holes in the runway. We rearranged the formation and flew the raid with only one grp. Before we left the field we could see the smoke billowing up to 10,000 ft.

The trip to the target was uneventfull all though difficult to fly as we were doing only 140 mph to stay near another wing formation.

At the target we hit a fair flak barrage but got out of it fairly quick. Got good bombing results on the target, which was an air field just outside of Paris.

Our trip back was also uneventfull and we only hit flak one time between the target and coast. The engineer on Ennis's crew was grazed on the head in this flak. We had bad vis. back across England due to haze.

I let Tony Cappello, who is flying with me as co-pilot, land, and he made a pretty fair one.

The man who came in behind us blew a tire and pretty well wrecked the ship all though no one was hurt.

We flew the raid at 26,000, duration about 5½ hours, none lost from Sqd. or grp. Battle damage, light flak holes in left wing.

All in all it was a very easy raid, all though the takeoff was difficult and dangerous.

TWENTY-FIVE          Saarbrucken, Germany       MAY 23, 1944

This morning we were woke up at 1:15, the earliest briefing since I have been here.

The target was the marshalling yards at Saarbrucken.

We flew the new type of formation we were experimenting with the other day.

This type formation makes it much easier to fly the wing in tight formation but considerably weakens each group.

We had two PFF ships leading, and a solid overcast all the way to the target and back.

We flew to the target without stirring up any flak or fighters. They usually won't put up flak through an overcast, in order to try and conceal the targets.

Us being the lead group, we crossed the target without stirring up any flak, but the ones behind us got a pretty heavy barrage.

The trip back was quite as on the way in.

My co-pilot was sick (stomach cramps) and I had to do all the flying. I thought my darned arm would drop off.

This completes my tour as I started out, the next five raids being free gratis for old Doolittle.

We flew at 23,000 to 26,000. The whole trip lasted about seven hours. We lost no ships from the group. No battle damage to our ship.

All in all, a pretty darn nice raid. Sure hope the rest are just nearly as easy.

TWENTY-SIX          Berlin, Germany          MAY 24, 1944

An early briefing this morning, being woke up at one fifteen. What did we see on the map but that old horror target, "Big B."

We had darn good fighter support scheduled and had it as briefed all the way.

I had a little trouble finding the formation this morning, but got in O.K. eventually.

We had terrible con trails all the way in and it was a wonder that we stayed in formation at all. Couldn't see a darn thing but the ship you flew off of, the rest being a blank shimmering white wall. Sure do get the darndest cases of vertigo in this stuff.

We hit flak one time on the way in, just north of the Frisian Islands.

At the target we were in flak for fifteen minutes, and it was typical Berlin flak, being thick and accurate. I saw several enemy fighters but they were picking on other outfits. Saw one enemy fighter get shot down by our support.

Saw one B 17 spin down and a few others blow up. Several left the target on three engines. Today I saw the first parachute going down since I have been in combat.

We left the target and our sqd. got lost in the con trails on the way out, and we were alone, separated from our group for 45 minutes. We were darn lucky the fighters didn't slaughter us all.

The trip back across the north sea was miserable, due to more dense haze.

I landed at the base completely pooped out. Was in the air about eight hours today and it was all darn tough flying.

I broke in a new pilot by the name of Pysak.

Had trouble with three engines today, one being pretty worthless in altitude.

We lost one out of this grp. today, total losses being 36 bombers. We hit the target, which was the industrial area of the city.

TWENTY-SEVEN     France     MAY 25, 1944

This morning another early briefing and takeoff. I don't believe I have had more than four hours sleep in the past three days.

They had a plan A and B again this morning, plan B being most favorable due to meteorology. We flew plan B.

This was a very easy raid as we saw no flak or fighters whatsoever. The only thing that made it bad and dangerous was the con trails and very dense haze again. Another wing flew through our wing on the way to the chanell and one ship came very close to hitting me. He didn't miss by more than ten or fifteen feet.

The target was a marshallinq yard. We didn't drop our bombs (our group) due to poor visibility, but the rest of the wing hit it O.K.

I salvoed my bombs over a wooded area, due to an engine going out. Got the engine operating O.K. some time later though.

This mission was another six hour trip and I am pretty tired still. Broke in another new pilot today, whose name was Duncan. I think he will make out O.K.

We didn't lose any in our group today. I am up on the list for tomorrow again. I sure dread it as know I will still be pooped but might as well fly it and get another one in.

I have strong hopes of finishing now, but will feel a lot better with two more in. They usually give an easy one on the last raid.

I sincerely believe that I wouldn't be worth much in combat after the next three. I am completely wore out and jittery now. They never should have raised the number of missions above twenty-five.

If the Lord is good enough to let my crew and myself finish, I think a rest will put me back in shape for flying again.

TWENTY-EIGHT     Manheim, Germany     MAY 27, 1944

Today we again flew the old type formation, as the raid was into Germany where we expect for fighter opposition.

We had a well planned route in and out and the best fighter support I have ever seen. This area has been pretty tough for fighters in the past, especially of the twin engine type. We had good navigation in and out, so we missed all of the flak areas except at the target, where we barreled right through as usual.

The flak at the target (which was a marshalling yards) was very heavy and accurate. Our bombs fell just a little too short, but other parts of the yards were hit by other outfits.

Just after the target I saw a strageling Fort from a group that crossed before us several thousand feet below us. Saw the Fort just turn over on his back, dive straight down for several thousand feet, and then blow all to hell.

The trip back was very uneventfull and quiet.

We flew with nine men crews today, useing only one waist gunner. This should effect a considerable saveing of lives in the future and we don't really need two waist gunners most of the time.

I had Tony Capello land tonight and logged all the time as first pilot for him and co-pilot for myself. Done this as it is Tony's 29th mission and he will now have one in as first pilot on the records. He has sure been a big help to me and have liked flying with him best of any of them.

I had engine trouble with my ship again today. She has lost a lot of soup lately and no. 4 is on her last legs. It doesn't seem possible but I think an awfull lot of that old ship and would rather fly her than any of the new ones. I have put most of my raids in with it, and know just about every sputter and cough she is going to make.

If I can test hop her with the crew chief, Frank Boyle, I think she will be O.K. for a few more missions.

If they would just change the engines on her, I know she could be the best ship in the sqd. again.

The ship my ground crew had before this one, old "Reddy Teddy" flew 42 missions and then she went down in a mid-air collision. This was no fault of the airplane.

My ship "Reddy Teddy II" now has about 24 on it, and a lot more left in her too. I rather expect she will be a 50 mission ship all though this group has never had one go that high before, as most of the 8th Air Force hasent eather.

Frank Boyle and I have hooked armour plateing from every salvage job on the field, and spare parts, to install in Reddy Teddy II and a fellow is a lot better off in it than in some of the new ones.

So much for the ship and this mission. Maybe the darn things are just inanimate hunks of tin, but it is hard to believe when you fly them in this racket.

TWENTY-NINE        Pas de Calais area, France

Woke up at six this morning to pull the easiest raid of them all.

Our IP was in mid-channel and we dropped our bombs right on the coast. We saw only 6 bursts of flak.

The entire raid only lasted about four hours.

We had a 90° cross wind for take off and landings.

I finished up three of my enlisted men on this mission.

THIRTY        Paris, France

After landing this morning, Maj. Ward met me at Sqd. operations and told me to go to briefing for another raid this afternoon. Sure didn't expect to finish up today, this morning.

The target was a marshalling yds. in Paris.

We hit heavy accurate flak at the target and several flak areas on the way home.

I saw one B 17 hit direct over Paris, blow up and spin down.

We had dense clouds to fly through on the way in. I flew well out from the formation as we had good fighter support. When the flak came up in the formation I would just pull out to the right and let her burst. Everyone got anywhere from 20 to 30 flak holes in their ship but mine wasent hit once—Just didn't feel like takeing any chances on this last raid.

This ends my tour of combat. 230 hours of combat time with pleanty of blood and sweat for every damn minute.

Since I have been here we have lost some 900 men of which a little over half are known to be alive, P.O.W.s, ect.

It was a damn rough racket and I am glad it's over.

JUNE 5, 1944

Tomorrow will be "D-Day" and tomorrow I am scheduled to leave this group for my casual station. The Long Range Heavy Bombing will probably be out of date for the theater in the future.

AUGUST 25, 1944

This is the last entry I hope to make in this diary, and am making it as an apology to whoever I might let read it. The things I have seen and the emotions and fears I have experienced seem so much smaller and inconsequential when I am in a position to look back on them.

I have spent the last two months in three hospitals here in England, have talked to the wounded dough boys back from France and have seen one hell of a bunch of sadly maimed fellows—fellows with legs gone, lost arms, deaf, blind, mentle crack ups and countless other pathetic cases. These are the boys who have paid the top price in this damned war. These are the boys that deserve the most, and if everything runs true to form, will get the least. These are the guys who have seen the worst of the dam war, and I hope to God, will remember enough to keep us out of another one for the next few generations.

# RALPH G. EDWARDS

Bombers flying from air bases in Italy were required to fly twice as many missions as those flying in the North, a fact that caused some resentment among the men in the crews, according to Ralph G. Edwards, of Ogdensburg, New York. There was also some feeling that journalists and photographers tended to document the exploits of the pilots based in England rather more, at least partly because the newsmen found England a more comfortable base of operations, though perhaps also because the public relations officers of the units based in the North were a bit more skilled at getting press coverage. One tends to forget that all branches of the service have professionals whose job it is to claim as much of the glory for their units as possible.

Whatever the truth of the matter may be, these feelings do not enter into the diary that Edwards kept of his missions. What does come into the diary is frank expression of a fear most men must have felt but which it takes a different kind of bravery to admit to.

Born in 1920, Edwards was 23 years old at the time his 50 missions were flown. A Staff Sergeant of the 717th Bomb Squadron, 449th Bomb Group, Army Air Corps, he was originally right waist gunner but took over as tail gunner when the original tail gunner was killed while on a mission over Rumania with another crew. Subsequent to World War II, Ralph Edwards was a police officer, retiring from the Ogdensburg Police Dept. after 23 years' service.

Strangely enough, Edwards does not reveal the superstitious dread of his 13th mission which was a commonplace in so many bombing mission diaries submitted for consideration for this book. Perhaps the fact that those flying from the South had 37 more missions to go reduced the importance of the 13th from the status it held in the Northern sector.

*******

## MISSION NO. 1 JANUARY 10, 1944

Took off 0310 A.M. this morning to bomb an important railroad center in Yugoslavia. Got about 50 or 75 miles from target and developed severe leak in oxygen system and had to turn back. We encountered heavy flax over enemy coastline but just got one hole in rear bombay door. Ship okay. We had P-38 for escort on way over and we met three "Spitfires" on return trip over Adriatic Sea and they escorted us back. No enemy fighters encountered either way. Landed at 12:30 P.M.

My first mission.
MISSION NO. 2 JANUARY 14, 1944

Took off at 8:15 A.M. to bomb an important railroad center in Northern Italy. We picked up P-38 escort at "Isle of Capri" and continued to target. Blew target all to hell and moved over to Adriatic Sea for return flight. No flax encountered or no enemy opposition either. Bombed target at 22,000 ft. and damn cold too. 26 degrees to be exact. Sighted a few enemy escorts north of Florence but received no fire. Landed at 15:15 and ship okay. All the crew okay also. My second mission and still "Sweating it out"

MISSION NO. 4 JANUARY 19, 1944

Took off at 8:45 to bomb an air field in North Italy. Picked up P-38 escort a few hundred miles up the East coast on Adriatic Sea. We bombed the runway and the 450th hit the hangars. Caught approximately a dozen planes on the ground and blew them all to hell and also runway. Ran up against intense inaccurate flax over target and also on return sweeps to coast. One plane shot down but crew bailed out okay. No enemy fighters encountered. Ship okay except for flax hole in No. 2 engine. Bombed at 20,000 ft. Landed at 1330 hours and everything under control. Crew okay also.

MISSION NO. 6 JANUARY 22, 1944

Took off at 7:30 A.M. to bomb a supply highway about 20 miles North of main lines on West coast. When we arrived there our naval invasion was in progress about 5 miles North of target. We drove a spearhead with bombs and blasted road all to hell. Encountered heavy flax over target but no damage to ships. Two ME104s attacked rear of formation but were successfully beaten off. A formation of B-17s were taking a crack at target as we left. Returned over same route and everything under control as usual. Landed ship at 1130 hours and ship and crew okay-No escorts today.

1/23/44 Learned today that the invasion was pulled 30 miles South of Rome by American rangers and British Commandos and they held 9 miles of coast. We destroyed supply road completely and stopped supplies to the Nazis.

MISSION NO. 7 JANUARY 24, 1944

Took off at 1015 hours to bomb an airfield at Sofia, Bulgaria, used for refueling and service center for enemy fighters. Approximately 70 bombers took part in raid. About 200 miles into Yugoslavia we received light and inaccurate flax and was attacked by about 30 Fock Wolfe 190s. They used aerial & parachute bombs and 20 millimeter cannons. They shot up a few of our ships but nothing serious. At least 4 were shot down-probably by the fire of our P-34 escorts. Seen one go down at 4 o'clock with smoke streaming from his engines. When we left they were dog-fighting. Visibility was poor over target so we bombed secondary target which was railroad center at Skopje. I guess we destroyed yards. Headed home and encountered no flax or enemy fighters. Landed at 1500 hours and all okay. (later learned that one B-24 was shot down during conflict.)

MISSION NO. 13 FEBRUARY 15, 1944

Took off at 0700 hours to bomb a marshalling yards that was a short distance from the target of yesterday. We made a few hits on target although overcast on target was bad. Sighted more ships heading for the beach head today. Was plenty cold today. 40° below zero. Dropped eggs through bombay doors today. No enemy fighters sighted and also received no flax. Bombed at 20,000 ft. Landed at 1330 hours and all okay. No escort.

MISSION NO. 14 FEBRUARY 16, 1944

Took off at 0800 hours to bomb same target of the 14th. Done plenty of damage to target today. Received no flax or encountered no enemy fighters. Temperature was 38° below zero. Bombed at 21,000 ft. Flew today with Capt. Lass and Major Tape and lead the formation. Noticed fierce fighting on the beachhead today by artillery on land and heavy guns from battleships in harbor. We had alternate target on beach-head today and didn't use it. Landed at 1430 hours and all okay. No escort.

MISSION NO. 15 FEBRUARY 20, 1944

Took off at 0800 hours to bomb a troop area at the new allied beachhead. Met no enemy fighters but seen more flax over target than I ever seen yet. They threw up everything but the gun. Blew target all to hell and P-44s were strafing the area during our bombing run. Was camera man today and didn't fly with my crew or my ship. Everything okay except for a few flax holes in the ship. Returned home at 1400 hours and weather closed in just after landing. No escort.

MISSION 16 FEB. 22, 1944

Took off at 0800 hours to bomb a ME 109 factory at Regensburg, Germany. Flew over Adriatic Sea into Yugoslavia and then into Germany. Met up with some flax in Yugoslavia and then more after we cross the Alps Mountains into Germany. After a little while in Germany we seen about 20 ME 109s but they were about 10,000 feet below us and didn't take a pass at us as they couldn't catch us. Got nearly to target but weather closed in and we turned back. Got nearly to German border when about 40 ME 109s attacked us. They kept diving out of the sun and making passes at us about 8 at a time. I seen one come in at 5 o'clock and when he peeled off I filled him full of lead and he went down smoking. I think I got him. We lost 9 planes in encounter and we salvoed our bombs during attack. Returned home at 1300 hours and ship okay. No escort and flew at 25,000 ft.

NOTE: We found later that some of our ships dropped bombs on target.

## MISSION 17 FEBRUARY 23, 1944

Took off at 0800 hours to bomb an engine factory where engines for MEs are made and target was also in Germany. Hit flax twice before we got to target and was also intercepted by ME 110s and 210s just before we dropped bombs. We hit flax over target and then fighters attacked again. The main enemy force attacked another group off our right wing and a small part of the enemy force took passes at us. I took a crack at a few of them but probably missed as they keep their distance. I seen one 24 go down in flames at 4 o'clock and 4 enemy fighters go down in flames. P-38 escort then came into the picture and saved the day. Met a little flax on the way home and no enemy fighters. Lost no ships during encounters. Arrived home safely at 1530 hours.

NOTE: Learned that one of our ships blew up a few minutes after takeoff and all aboard killed. A B-26 also blew up while landing and all aboard killed. One of the boys that flew over the ocean with us is missing also.

## MISSION 18 FEBRUARY 15, 1944

Took off to bomb the same target of the 22nd. Took same route across Adriatic Sea, Yugoslavia, Austria and then to Regensberg, Germany. Got heavy accurate flax three times before we got to target and then was attacked about ten minutes before dropping bombs by ME 109s, ME 110s, and ME 210s and J.U. 89s. They took a rest while the flax came up to meet us over target. We got flax in the bombay-left wing-tail turret and nose. Then fighters attacked again. They came in from 4 to 8 o'clock and shot 20 millimeter and rocket bombs and wing guns. Our ball turret man got a ME 110 and I think I got one but not sure. We had 12 ships left in our group. We got separated from the rest. About 40 fighters attacked our 12 ships for 1 hour & 20 minutes in a running battle. One of our 12 ships went down in flames and one exploded over target. Four ME 110s went down in flames. Received a little flax on the way home and nearly ran out of gas. Was ready to bail out but didn't. Arrived home okay and crew okay. Landed at 1720 hours and fought a storm for 30 minutes before landing. No escort.

## MISSION 19 MARCH 2, 1944

Left the ground at 0800 hours to make another bombing run at "flax alley". We carried "frag" bombs to bomb enemy ground positions. Approached target at 21,000 ft. and "Salvoed" bombs and flax was thicker than hair on a dog. One of our ships went down on account of flax but the rest of our ships proceeded home without trouble. Seen eight chutes come out of plane that went down. Landed okay at 1230 hours and all okay except flax holes in nose and ball turrets and left

inboard tank. No enemy fighters attacked although we seen five F.W. 190s. All okay.
NOTE: Ship that was knocked down today—pilot is in hospital at allied beach-head and five members of crew. Four members of crew in enemy hands.

MISSION 20 MARCH 29, 1944

Took off at 0830 hours to try and catch up with our group as we had mag trouble on No. 4 engine. We couldn't find our group so we fell in with 41st group but we turned back one hour from target on account of under-cast. When nearly home we fell out of formation and buzzed the rest of the way home. Arrived home okay with no trouble. Landed at 1300 hours. We lost another ship today on take-off and ball & tail gunner killed. Pilot hurt pretty bad and rest suffered minor injuries. Target was bombed all to hell. Plenty of flax but no enemy fighters encountered. P-38 escort. Target-North Italy-just five miles from Switzerland and a few miles from Brenner Pass. Marshalling yard.

3/24/44 Learned tonite that entire 15th Air Force is flying tomorrow and that there is an invasion expected also soon. Probably in Northern or Southern France. End of war looks awfully close to me and hope I'm right.

MISSION 21 MARCH 30, 1944

Took off at 0700 hours to bomb a railroad yard at Sofia, Bulgaria. Flew across Adriatic Sea into Yugoslavia, Albania, then Bulgaria. Everything went along okay on way to target and bombed it all to hell at 20,000 feet. Got some light accurate flax over target and was attacked by a few ME 109s and F.W. 190s. Tail gunner claims a ME 109. One B-24 went down and crashed over target but from another group-not ours- due to flax. Got some light accurate flax when nearly to coast and got a few holes in right and left wing. Landed at 1200 hours and ship and crew okay. P-38 escort.

MISSION 23 APRIL 2, 1944

Took off at 0700 hours to bomb an aircraft factory at Steyn, Austria. Was supposed to have P-47 and P-38 escort but they didn't show up. Only a few stray ones. Met a mess of ME 109s about an hour before the I.P. and they took passes at us all the way in. They knocked down quite a few ships from other groups before target. No chutes. We bombed the already burning target and then our leader and right wing man crashed into each other and went by our ship in pieces. No chutes. Ships behind us got hit with flying debris and crashed but boys bailed out first. After target we again were attacked by 109s and ME 110s but nobody went down. One ship had No. 3 engine shot out and feathered but he stayed with us. Not much flax over target and we used tin-foil to spoil radar. Arrived home at 3:30 P.M. and ship and crew okay. Our squadron lost 3 ships and group lost 5 ships. God is still with us.

MISSION 25 APRIL 3, 1944

Took off at 0630 to bomb railroad center & warehouses at Budapest, Hungary. Was supposed to have P-47 escort but we flew off course a hundred miles into Rumania and we missed our escort. No enemy fighters intercepted us on our way to target and we placed bombs in center of already burning target. They laid up a terrific barrage of flax over target but we got through okay. After target we seen a few fighters but they didn't attack. One of our ships went down but from 719th sqdrn and a ship went down burning before we went over target. Our tail guns were out as gunner froze his feet and legs and had to be removed. Upon landing he was removed to hospital. I was engineer today and top turret gunner. Nothing eventful happened on way home and landed okay at 1400 hours. One flax hole in astral dome but other ships shot up pretty bad. God is still with us.

NOTE: Got credit for mission of Mar. 29. That makes 26 missions to date

4/4/44 Didn't fly today but the ship flew and two of our boys flew. Our ship came back with Joe although badly shot up. Our tail gunner was shot down in ship No. 38 but bailed out. Target was Bucharest, Rumania, and was a marshalling yard and warehouses and factories. Flax wasn't bad but fighters attacked after flax. ME 109s—FW 190s—JU 88s and used 20 millimeter explosive cannon, aerial bombs and wing guns. Our squadron lost two ships and four chutes bailed out and ship crashed. Our group lost seven ships today. Group went over target alone with no escort—Was supposed to fly but didn't.

I noticed tonite that incendiaries were being loaded up so tomorrow's mission will be a tough one. I am afraid to go up again and wish I had the nerve to admit it openly. God in heaven, please keep "Old Ironsides" in the sky.

Three men gone from crew. Ponticelli—frozen feet and legs. Copley—up for General Court martial Cordeira—shot down over Rumania.

There is four ships left out of the original 16. They are rushing in replacement ships & men every day.

MISSION 27 APRIL 5, 1944

Took off at 1000 hours to bomb m/y oil fields at Ploesti, Rumania. This makes the second time this place has ever been bombed. We were the 13th group to go over target today and smoke was rising to a height of 3,000 ft. or more. We hit heavy flax over target although we threw out lead foil to throw the radar off. After target we were attacked by about 40 ME 109s & FW 190s but didn't lose any ships. A group with us lost about 6 ships due to flax and fighters and I seen a FW 190 go down and the German bail out. A B-24 went down to our left and four chutes got out okay.

MISSION 30 APRIL 12, 1944

Our wheels left the ground at 0700 hours to bomb an aircraft plant in Southern Germany. Got some accurate flax over Yugoslavia and a piece hit my right arm but nothing serious. Picked up 40 to 50 P 38s about an hour from the target and they took us over the target. Also a few P 47s. Got heavy accurate flax over target but blew target all to hell. After target about 6 ME 109s and FW 190s attacked front of group out of sun. A couple of the other boys and myself got a ME 109 in a cross fire and knocked him down and our top turret got one also. Then the enemy fighters and our P 38s tangled. I saw 3 B-24s go down as a result of 20 millimeter explosive cannon fire. P-38s took over then and we come on for home. Hit flax again over Yugoslavia and shot the hydraulic lines for our flaps away so we had to pump our flaps down. Landed okay at 1500 hours and everyone okay but ship shot up a little. God is still with us. Tail turret today.

NOTE: 4/12/44

A crew that bailed out over North Yugoslavia just got back as they fell into the hands of the partisans. That was the mission of Feb. 23, 1944 and they left for U.S.A. today. All okay except L.W. gunner who was killed instantly.

MISSION NO. 32 APRIL 13, 1944

Took off at 9000 hours to bomb an airfield at Budapest, Hungary. Everything okay on way there and picked up about 25 or 30 P-38s about 30 minutes before target but no passes at us so we blew target all to hell. Got some slight inaccurate flax but nothing serious. One 24 dropped his frags on another 24 and the ship blew up and went down in flames and no chutes. Immediately after target seen about 7 or 8 JU 88s and ME 210s. A J.U. took a pass at us but didn't hit pay dirt. A ME 210 came into my tail turret but I shot hell out of his right engine. His 20 millimeter burst under our ball turret but no harm done. The ME went down and crashed in flames. Continued on home with no trouble and landed at 1600 hours and all okay—thank God.

MISSION 34 APRIL 15, 1944

Took off at 0830 hours to take another crack at Bucharest, Rumania. Got P-38 escort about an hour before target. There was a dense undercast and the Germans thought we wouldn't be able to find the target so they kept the flax guns silenced. We fooled them as we were using the path-finder and dropped bombs through undercast right on the nose. They learned their mistake and sent up heavy flax but too late and we were already on our way home. Seen a few enemy fighters but no attack. Returned home with no difficulty and landed at 1500 hours. Lost no ships today. "Milk run". Thank God.

## MISSION 36 APRIL 15, 1944

Took off at 0710 hours to bomb a huge M/Y in Rumania, just north of Ploesti. Picked up P-38 escort just about an hour before target but they left us before target. Target was already burning when we got there and black smoke was rising about 3000 to 4000 feet in the air from center of target after we left. Received medium inaccurate flak over target but we used lead foil to throw radar off. Just after target about 25 to 30 ME 109s and ME 110s jumped the group off to our left but didn't attack us. They knocked down three 24's who were straggling but a 109 went down in the encounter. I took a crack at a 109 who got about 700 or 800 yds. from me but I probably missed. One ship in our squadron straggled and got knocked down but 10 chutes came out. We lost another ship in the 716th sqd. Arrived home safely at 1430 hours. A few ships shot up pretty badly with 20 millimeter but "Old Ironsides" okay. Encountered light flax over Yugoslavia on return trip home. The Lord is still watching over us.

4/17/44 A P-51, while buzzing the field just hit the hangar and busted the plane and the pilot up into little pieces.

## MISSION 37 APRIL 17, 1944

Wheels left the ground at 0845 hours to bomb a huge M/Y at Sofia, Bulgaria. Just as we hit the coast of Yugoslavia we picked up about 40 to 50 P-51s and also a few P-38s and P-47s. The formation didn't fly too good on account of undercast and overcast so we managed to get in front so we led the group over the target at 22,000 ft. Blasted that yard all to hell and received light accurate flax but no damage to ship. Was looking for enemy fighters but seen not a one. Landed at 1445 hours and all okay. Still "sweating it out" and the Lord still with us.

4/24/44 Took off to bomb a M/Y at North Italy but had to turn back an hour from target with gas leak. No mission.

4/21/44 Took off to bomb the Ploesti oil fields again but weather closed in and had to turn back. No mission.

## MISSION 39 April 23, 1944

Took off at 1000 hours to bomb an aircraft plant in Austria—just ten miles south of Vienna. No difficulty on way up and picked up from 40-50 P-38s about an hour from target. Bombed target at 23,000 feet but didn't hit target too good and received intense accurate flax in return. There was supposed to be 300 ack-ack guns down there and I believe it too. All of our ships got shot up pretty badly and only one got knocked down. A nose turret man bailed out for no reason at all from one of the ships. No enemy fighters encountered and returned home. Landed at 1545 hours and all okay except for a few flax holes. Still thanking God and still "sweating it out".

4/25/44 Not flying today as I am Cpl. of the Guard. A dirty deal!____ Have been flying as tail turret gunner since the mission of 4/12/44

MISSION 41 APRIL 24, 1944

Took off at 0815 hours to bomb a M/Y in Rumania—just 20 miles north of Bucharest. Was supposed to pick up escort on way to target but didn't see a trace of them. Made a wrong turn near target—flew over Bucharest and got heavy, intense, accurate flax of some type over target and a long ways after. Had P-51 coverage over target. Groups behind us was attacked by F.W. 190's but only a few and no ships went down. Picked up P-38's about an hour from target and they took us to the coast of Yugoslavia & Adriatic Sea.

MISSION 42 APRIL 28, 1944

Took off at 1045 hours to bomb a harbor installation and troops at North Italy. Picked up P-38's on way to target and let our eggs go at 25,000 ft. over target for which we received heavy-slight-accurate flax in return. Done a good job on target and returned home with no mishaps. A P-38 fell into our formation with his right engine feathered. My heated equipment went out and I near froze my a____ off. Landed at 1600 hours and all okay thanks to God. Seen no enemy fighters. A "milk run".

MISSION 44 APRIL 29, 1944

Took off at 0700 hours to bomb a submarine base and harbor installations at Toulon, France, just 150 miles from Spain. Proceeded to target via Corsica and picked up a mess of P-38's just before target. Bombed target at 25,000 ft. and received heavy, intense, accurate flax in return. Seen a few F.W. 190's but didn't get a shot at them as P-38's took care of the situation very well. Left the target burning like hell and tore for home. A few of our ships got hit by flax but feathered engines and proceeded home with us. One of our ships still isn't home but he probably landed at Corsica. Got home at 1630 hours but No. 1 engine cut out just when we came in to land so we made a second approach. On second approach No. 1 and No. 3 engines started to cut out so we landed on cross-feed system. There was no fuel in No. 1 and No. 3 engines. It's a miracle that we didn't crash. Mission was over 1300 miles in all and glad to be back, thanks to the Lord. Ship okay except for a few flax holes.

4/29/44 Learned tonight that our crew is grounded tomorrow, but "Old Ironsides" is flying just the same.

MISSION 45 May 5, 1944

Took off at 1000 hours today to bomb a marshalling yard and oil refineries at Ploesti, Rumania. Received heavy-intense-accurate flax over Yugoslavia but no damage. Picked up about 50 or 60 P-38s and 30 P-51s about an hour and a half from target. They left us just before target and then we got *plenty* of heavy flax over target. When nearly out of flax, a big mess of ME 109s attacked us out of the sun. Our ship and two others straggled to the right and they caught us right. A 20 millimeter hit the co-pilot in the head and blew his head nearly off and also hit the navigator in the body and killed him also. They knocked down one of our three ships and crippled our ship. A 20 millimeter tore a big hole just beside the tail turret but hit everything else but me—hit and broke control caller-hit my parachute-sprung a leak in my turret-tore a lot of holes in the horizontal and verticle stabilizer and hit the turret body. No escort—Got flax again over Yugoslavia on way back. We lost 2 ships today. We landed okay with the engineer as co-pilot and me as engineer. I think I knocked down 1 or 2 enemy planes during encounters. All of our ships were badly shot up and one made a crash landing on the field. One of my guns went out during attack and both top turret guns went out. I thank the Lord for bringing us back today and please help me to keep my nerve to go up again.

5/6/44 Learned today that our group lost 6 ships and our squadron two. The crew and I went to the funeral of Fiester and Brown at Bari. They received a military burial and the Lord rest their souls in peace. There was a mission today but no loss of planes.

MISSION 48 MAY 24, 1944

They got us up at 2:30 A.M. for a big deal mission at the Wiener-Neustadt ME 109 factory near Vienna again. We had an oxygen leak in the ball turret and took off late. We tried to catch the formation—followed them all the way into Austria but as we didn't care to go over target alone—we dropped bombs before the target and headed for home in a hurry. The boys say there was plenty of flax over the target and plenty of fighters after the target but we only lost a few ships. The 450th was hit bad and lost about 7 or 8 ships. We had P-51's and 38's for escort. Arrived home at 1430 hours and was the last ship to land. The boys thought we weren't coming back but we fooled them again. I done some *real hard* praying today though. Just one more mission to go. Hurra!!!!! I flew with Sam's crew today in ship No. 13. Their crew is the only crew left out of 18 crews. I believe we have 22 men left out of the original 180 and two ships from the original 15. We get replacement ships and crews nearly every day now.

MISSION 49 MAY 26, 1944

Took off at 0600 hours to bomb a m/y and bridge at a little town that is on the border of Italy and France. Took a course up through Corsica and then on to target. Bombed at 20,000 ft. and didn't get one puff of flax until after bombs away but then we got plenty of heavy, intense, accurate flax until we hit the coast again. We lost three ships over target due to flax. I seen one B-24 go down at 7 o'clock and a wing fell away from it during the downward plunge and then it disappeared into the sea. No chutes came out. We picked up a mess of P-38's over target and they escorted us back as far as Corsica, where they are based. Landed at 1425 hours and ship and crew okay except for a few holes in the ship. Again I flew tail gunner with Samuelson's crew in ship No. 43. Well-only one more to "sweat out" so will have to pray a little harder tonight____

5/26/44 Learned today that "Old Ironsides" was forced down in Yugoslavia with ship intact (for some strange reason) and crew are prisoners of war. We are ordered to shoot the ship down on sight if we see it.

MISSION 50 MAY 27, 1944

Took off at 0600 hours to bomb a m/y at Marseilles, France. We were supposed to pick up P-51 escort over Corsica but didn't see them as usual. Proceeded to the target and they threw up everything that they had and it was plenty too! The group behind us (the 450th) was attacked by F.W. 190's just before target but they fought them off and they didn't bother us at all. Even the ships in the harbor fired on us. They had smoke pots going to hide target but it didn't hide it good enough as we blasted target all to hell! Left target with ship and crew okay and tore for home in a hurry. Arrived at base and landed in a hurry as we were nearly out of fuel. Landed at 1510 hours and everything okay. Mission lasted 9 hours and ten minutes. My last mission (thank God).

And so ends my 50 combat missions completed from my base in Grattaghi, Italy, and in which we bombed eight countries-Germany, France, Italy, Austria, Hungary, Bulgaria, Rumania and Yugoslavia.

# CARROLL A. LEWIS, JR.

Now Commanding General of the Texas Army, Carroll A. Lewis, Jr., of Houston, was just a 20-year-old 1st Lieutenant at the time he kept the following wartime diary. He served as pilot or co-pilot and tailgunner on the missions recounted here, serving with the 379th Bomb Group (Heavy).

Lewis was like many others who kept records of their bombing missions in that he meticulously recorded departure time, altitude, temperature, gallons of gas used, objective, type of bombs. His record stops short of recounting all his missions and one can see his enthusiasm waning for the keeping of a diary as the entries grow shorter and more routine, but what there is of it has a youthful exuberance that is appealing.

After the war Carroll Lewis became a land developer and author. His latest book is THE TREASURES OF GALVESTON BAY, which grows out of research and exploration into lost treasures, an interest that began when he was in college, at Rice University and the University of Houston.

*******

At Lincoln we were issued .45 automatic, knives, etc. also a B-17, 6, better known as 44 6615-After swinging the flux gate compass we were briefed and took off at 20:45 for Grenier Field, N.H. It was instruments all the way, but we dropped below the overcast to see Chicago and the Great Lakes, also flew down to Niagara Falls. Both pilots navigated all the way by radio compass—we were saving the navigator for that "waterhop". Landed at Grenier late that evening-were given quarters and we stayed there until weather cleared us out—which was about three days. We finally took off for Goose Bay-which was in Labrador-instruments again-We found an opening and let down at Goose which was an ATC field-We were quartered there for about 3 days. It was cold and barren. We couldn't see the North Lights. Took off for Iceland-instruments again. Saw tip of Greenland and icebergs. At Iceland we slept for 7 hrs. As soon as we hit-then took off for Valley Whales. Instruments again-I slept the whole trip. At Whales they took 6615 away from us. It was a fair ship. I had cut some relief tubes from some P-43s that were at Lincoln and each station on the ship had a relief tube. It was quite handy-On the way a package of powder which I had brought in my B-4 bag was knocked apart and it was all over the ship-it really smelled good—and we hated to leave the ship. While parking it Donahoe was racing down the ramp and came so close to another ship that he knocked the air temperature gauge off the nose. He has never recovered from that "accident". We had 24 bottles of whiskey stolen from our plane in Iceland. Somebody's going to be disappointed!

At Valley we first unloaded then we ate at the officers mess, where we paid 2 shillings (90 cents). After 6 hours in Valley we hopped on a train—The Whales people nearly died when I played my $22.50 clarinet while we were in the station. All the little kids hopped on us and said "Any gum, chum?" or "Any chooey, looey?" They are really crazy about gum and make pests out of themselves. After riding all night on the train we arrived in Stone, England. Here we stayed for a week. Got all of our money changed into English notes. Then we all boarded a train for the 379th Bomb Group which was our new station. On the train we started singing and playing the clarinet—which was done in the baggage car. We passed the hat and made "thruppence" apiece. Ate "G" rations on the train. Also saw some of the bombed-out towns—whenever we would stop at a station the little English kids would start hollering for gum. Arrived at Kimbolton on train from Stone—hopped in truck and were brought to the 379th which was scattered around to the four winds—from one point you could see a beautiful English countryside with typical haystacks and bush fences and only a few feet away would be a bomber with its tents, etc. We were brought up to the 524th Squadron (there was 4 squadrons in the group-524th, 525th, 526th, 527th). Here we were assigned quarters and had to give up our .45s to be sent to the boys in the front lines. I was given a room with a pilot (R.C. Evans) who had just finished his missions. It had 3 beds-one stove (which didn't work because we only had coke to burn). The walls are papered with pin-ups. As are all the other rooms.

For 2 weeks we went to school, flew 2 practice missions. Slept until 11:00 each morning—even when we *did* have classes. They have inspections every Saturday if you don't fly—so far we haven't stood one. The C.O. of the field is Col. Lyle. C.O. of our squadron is Capt. Creo. This place is famous for no promotions so I expect I'll be sporting these gold bars forever.

This is one of the first bomb groups to be based in England and it has one of the best records-The discipline on the field is like it was in Cadets but an expert "F.O." can get by easy—Ahem! We have good food and free movies every night, walk a mile to the mess hall—unless you have a bike. Only 10 men can go to town (Bedford) a night from each squadron-the first ten to sign up. We have outdoor latrines-and we have never gotten our room warm. And then____!!!

FIRST MISSION (Tactical-Eschweiler) 16 NOV. 1944

Breakfast at 5:00 Briefing at 6:00 Left field at 10:12 30 260 lb. Frag bombs. 2400 gal. gas Temp-40°

Flew high squadron—low low flight—Diamond (Tail-end Charlie) Bomb bay doors open over channel at 22,000 No. 3 engine turbo out over target. Moderate but accurate flak. No fighters. One ship seen going down—All chutes out. Intervalometer failed and had to salvo bombs. Probably our bombs hit Berlin. On return ships in our squadron only peeled off on top of overcast and let down through 5000 ft. of overcast. Ceiling was estimated at 600 ft. but was really about ½ ft. Made two passes at the field and the tower talked us in-full power-no flaps, landed half way down runway. Radio operator said he looked out his window and saw a bird on a church steeple looking *down* at our ship while we were trying to find the field. Our altimeter read *below* field elevation and we were just clearing the trees—Had to jump over high tension wires—Danger of colliding with planes was great because the visibility was zero. Almost ran into three planes. General opionion of the crew was that the landing was worse than the flak. That type of weather shows the need for S.B.A. at each field.

Landed at 1520. Had a shot of rye that nearly knocked me over since we had been taking sulfadiazine tablets for colds.

Rest of the squadron landed at another field and we will have to ferry them over tomorrow to pick up their ships. I hit the sack early tonight!

SECOND MISSION (Strategic-"Gelsenkirchen") 20 NOV. 1944

Breakfast at 5:30 Briefing at 6:30 Left field at 11:00 20 250 G.P. bombs 2200 gals gas Temp-38 C

Flew No. 3 ship, high flight, Lead Squadron, "B" Lead Group. Gelsenkirchen is in "Flak Happy" Ruhr Valley. We expected flak but saw none. 20 minutes before target we ran into an overcast. Groups were going in all directions and danger of collision was terrific. Our flight leader lost lead and peeled off so fast that we soon lost him—There we were in complete overcast. No ships to fly with-and 160 B-17s also flying in it. It was close to our target when we were separated so when D.R. was up-we salvoed bombs and head West *alone*! In a visibility of zero! If there was flak we couldn't see it, altho there might have been. We hit the clear after about 15 minutes in the soup at 24,000 ft. We were alone and fighters swarmed all around us—They were unidentified so we hung close to the clouds so if they attacked we would hide. The Navigator got his bearings so we had easy going back home—except for sweating out fighters. One P-51 escorted us across channel. We identified ourselves over the English coast but tail gunner reported one burst of flak—those limeys again! Landed at 1400. Only three ships landed with original squadron. Not a bad mission-but we really sweated the fighters.

THIRD MISSION (Strategic-"Merseberg")

Breakfast at 0400 Briefing at 0500 Left field 0858 21 Nov. 44 10 550 lb. G.P. bombs 2700 gals. gas

Flew right wing, low, low flight-low squadron Lead Group-Big groan went up in briefing when they showed us the target. "Merseberg" is the roughest run outside of "Big B" (Berlin)-For the first time the sky was clear and we assembled without having to fly through about 15,000 ft. of overcast. Hit clouds over channel. Stayed at 27,000 ft. until over I.P. when we ran into thick overcast—Let down to 18,000 ft. but was still in slight soup. Flak was thick for about 15 minutes. Saw one ship (not in our group) go down at 1 o'clock low—one chute went out—wing burst into fire then fell off—ship started spinning then burst into flame. "That's all, Brother". Not a nice sight. Waist gunner said he saw 3 chutes but I only saw one. We lost our ship in the odiamond with two engines out. By the time we got back to England, our ship was the only one in the low flight. They were trying out a new overcast system of landing so after that long mission we had to go almost up to Scotland before we landed. Landed at 1700—had about 7 flak holes in ship's upper turret, tail, wing, rudder control, aileron. We were lucky this time. Fighters were thick today as the luftwaffe makes a stab at us.

48 hour pass tomorrow.

"Old Timers" said that this was the roughest mission-besides the one to "Big B".

FOURTH MISSION (Strategic "Merseberg") 25 NOV. 44

Breakfast at 4:00 Briefing at 4:45 Left field at 9:02 10 500 lb. G.P. bombs 2700 gals gas Temp-40°C

Flew left wing, high flight, lead squadron, lead group—4th in battle order. Again a groan went up as we saw the Merseberg area target. Assembled at 8000 ft., flew over at 25,000 ft. Had P-51 escorts-Our ship monitored the fighter frequency. We flew over the top all the way. As we neared the target we heard the navigator say, "My God! Are we going to go through all that flak?" So we looked ahead and saw the famous "Merseberg Wall" which looked to be about two miles square of solid flak. It looked solid black. Then all of us began wondering if we would ever make it. The lead ship opened its bomb bays but ours were frozen—we finally got them down—then we hit the flak. No one in our formation was hit except a ship behind us—got his engine hit. The R.O. were trying a new "jamming" system—besides throwing the usual "chaff" which is strips of metalized paper which are thrown out to jam the RADAR FLAK. We got back all right—but again flew the formation through ceiling zero weather at the field. The low flight was jumping trees—We ran right over a smokestack and couldn't see our flight leader for a minute because of the smoke. We landed all right—and were lucky to do that. One ship cracked up on the runway because it landed with only one wheel-The other was shot. Landed at 16:30. Group party tonight but too tired to go.

FIFTH MISSION (Strategic "Misburg" "Hanover") 29 NOV. 44

Breakfast 04:45 Briefing 05:45 Left field 0920 12 500 lb. bombs 2400 gals gas Temp-42 C

Flew right wing low low flight, low squadron lead group. Since the Luftwaffe had been coming up for the last three raids we expected to see fighters galore-So for *our* division we had 18 groups of fighters (about 900 aircraft) which is a lot in anybody's language (P51s & 38s). The day was exceedingly clear-except over the target which we bombed by instruments at 25,000 ft. Flak was meager and very inaccurate. We didn't see any fighters and the mission back home was uneventful. A nice mission but very tiresome—listened to the AFN radio all the way over and all the way back. Good music. Glenn Miller, etc. Also heard several German broadcasts—No savvy! No ships damaged-target hit. That's all, brother.

SIXTH MISSION (Strategic "Zoetz") 1 DEC. 44

Breakfast 0445 Briefing at 0545 Leave field 10:30 20 250 G.P. Bombs 2700 gals gas

Flew left wing, low flight, High squadron, Third group. Expected Luftwaffe again but they didn't show up. Left the channel at 10,000 ft. Flew *way* into Germany almost to "Bloody Merseberg" which was our P.F.F. target, *but* the primary was *visual* so we bombed with a bombsight for the first time. The targets were covered with smoke screens-Flak was fairly thick but it missed our squadron entirely. We flew in prop wash all the time from groups ahead of us-The lead squadron had to make another run over the target. We lost 6 ships. Several ships had wounded aboard—who fired red red flares upon landing—We had to salvo our bombs-malfunction of racks-No fighters but we had 2 groups of P-38s at target and 2 groups of P-51 escorts—landed contact for the first time—no flak holes-Listened to the radio up until I.P. and from bomb run back home, good music, etc. Got the Air Medal today. A rough mission was the opinion of all—we were just lucky we landed at 1705!

Ferried No. 337777 "Four of a Kind". A ship that was christened by the King & Queen of England.

SEVENTH MISSION (Strategic "Koblansk" "Oberlanstein") 2 DEC. 1944

Breakfast 0600 Briefing 0700 Left field 0930 12 250 G.P. bombs 2400 gals gas.-50°C

Flew right wing-Low low flight, lead squadron, Third group. Assembled at 15,000 ft. Ate our candy bars and gum ahead of time—escape kits were rationed out and we set off—it was instruments all the way. I listened to the radio all the time (good music—Glenn Miller, etc.) so I didn't know much what was going on until they opened the bomb bay doors-Saw only 8 or 10 bursts of flak before we went into a cloud—Then "Bombs Away"-turned back, came home. On the way across the channel Stickler and I had a contest to see who could fly the tightest formation—The waist gunners were about to jump out of the lead plane—so we quit—No flak damage—easy mission—landed 1700—P 51's escort-No enemy fighters seen. Engineer's "Mae West" accidently got inflated while he was in the turret so he was stuck in it-Hollering "Help!". We finally told him to release the valve—and so he got out. I almost laughed myself to death.

EIGHTH MISSION Strategic-"Mannheim" "Ludwigshaven & Bridge" 12 DEC. 44

Breakfast at 0445, Briefing 0545 Left field 0912 2 2000 lb. bombs 2 1000 lbs. 2400 gals gas-52°C

Flew right wing, low low flight, high squadron-3rd group. At briefing groans arose as the map was uncovered because we were to bomb a bridge next to Ludwigshaven which was a rough flak area. Assembled at 11,000 ft.-went over target at 22,000 ft. Moderate flak & some new kind of white spinning rocket flak. Four of them hit pretty near us. The flak missed us because they were tracking the lead squadron. After we bombed we looked back and there was a solid wall of flak. It looked like a raincloud it was so thick. They just missed us-Then we went into clouds—All the way back we were in and out of clouds—finally above Dunqerque we let down and buzzed the channel—We almost hit a big sea bird. He looked to me as if he were about 5 ft. long—Also saw a sunken ship. We lost a couple of planes. Bandits were in the area but none attacked us—had a good P-51 escort. Over England we flew into a cloud that was so thick that we couldn't see our lead ship although our wing was overlapping his—so we all got separated but got together again over the top. Peeled off, came down. A very tiring mission-almost 5 hours on oxygen. There were so many planes in the air that the sky was dark. It was really crowded. Landed at 1600.

NINTH MISSION (Tactical-Koblenz) 18 DEC. 1944

Breakfast at 0615 Briefing at 0715 Left field at 1049 10 500 lb. G.P. bombs 2400 gals.-39°C Flew tail gunner in the lead ship—lead squadron-second group. In order to grade pilots on the way they flew formation we were trying a new formation. It really worked fine although we went through clouds at target no one was lost—A really tight formation. I had to keep track of everything—practically ran a sideline description of the whole mission. Assembled at 13,000 ft., climbed at 28,000 ft. We were supposed to bomb Kall, a tactical target, to help the 1st Army but clouds were so thick we had to bomb Koblensk on PFF. A good bomb run—Only saw about 7 bursts of flak at about 0700 o'clock but there might have been more—couldn't see very far-Got one flak hole in ship. I didn't see any enemy fighters so natcherly I didn't get any. I had a lot of fun—being a Clark Gable, Jr. Landed at 1600. And a new formation is born!

TENTH MISSION (Tactical "Airport near Giessen" 24 DEC. 1944

Briefing at 0230 Breakfast 0330 T.O. 10:50 14 250 lb. bombs 4 500 lb. bombs 2700 gals.-33°C We had to go to Grafton Underwood by truck and picked up a ship—and flew with the 384th Gp. left wing, low low element, high squadron. We were to bomb an airfield on the largest mission ever flown. We made an instrument take-off. Flew visual over the target—One FW 190 started in at us—but our tail gunner scared him away—Our P-51 escort took over. Bombs hit target and we turned to go home. I had taken off my flak suit and equipment-and settled back to tune in some music—All of a sudden—Wham! Bam! Boom! I looked out the window and flak was crawling in our formation. Accurate and surprising! The formation was blown all to hell—it scattered us for miles-Two of our engines were shot out. I still didn't have my flak suit or anything. I wuz just lucky I didn't get hit. No. 1 engine was feathered, but No. 2 couldn't feather so it wind-milled—much worse is a wind-milling prop than a feathered—We called for fighter protection—none came—We were at 22,000 losing altitude—We made it alone to the lines-Then began looking for a field in France to land on—all of them were bombed out. We decided to cross the channel—our interphone was out—command radio didn't work. A fire started in the nose—Navigator put it out—At the channel we had gone down to 8,000 ft. at 110 MPH. Threw out ammo & flak suits, etc. to lighten plane—crossed over cliffs of Dover firing flares so the Limeys wouldn't shoot us. Headed toward Base but darkness overtook us also bad weather ahead so we looked for a field to land in—Natcherly since it was Xmas we didn't want to go to a B-17 base so we landed or started to land at an RAF field—Dusk overtook us and we couldn't see the field very good—No lights on it—We made two passes and missed the runway—On the third pass we just passed the field and No. 3 engine began to burn oil—fire!—we couldn't feather because we needed power to hit the field. Made a 180° turn and crashlanded down wind—feathered No. 3 on approach, landed long-skidded brakes all the way for about 200 yards—Hydraulic pressure went out, had to use emergency pump. We came within 5 ft. of hitting a house—skidded to stop in front of it—hit the roof of a bicycle shed-Very lucky landing! at 1730. No one hurt-spent 3 days at the base, which was RAF—were treated swell by the people there-were driven up to the sergeants' mess-where the enlisted men stayed—we went up the hill to an abandoned insane asylum where the officers stayed-A very beautiful house-here we were given a room—washed and shaved. Then we met "the gang", a group of about 14 RAF and WAF officers-A splendid group! From then on it was one big party for 3 days—These English found an excuse to have a drink in everything—we had drinks in the bar "to steady our nerves", went to the ante room to chat—Had drinks before tea—Had tea in Ante room. Had drinks before going down to the sergeants' party—went to party-played games—boogie woogie which the English enjoyed very much. Learned to play "blackbird". Had drinks at the Sergeants' mess—listened to bagpipes-had drinks—Danced. Ajax and I jitterbugged and did the sensational "Bomph!" Had drinks and went to officers' mess at 0400 here we had a party—drinks, tea-finally went to bed—wuz awakened in the morning by a Bat woman (enlisted WAF) who tapped my shoulder saying "Good morning, sir-0630—Here's your tea" whereupon I drank the tea-went to sleep again. She woke me again-at 0730-She shined my shoes—I got up-had a drink before breakfast-Ate breakfast-Had drinks after breakfast. Had tea. Had drinks-Had snack. Had drinks. Then we went to Sergeants' mess where the sergeants marched us-and we served them dinner—an old custom. After serving them we went over to our house-had drinks, had tea, had drinks—Ate Xmas dinner at 1500. Had drinks, had tea, had drinks-Then had a cocktail party-Had tea-Had drinks-Then Ajax and I got on cycles and went into the Village—called Ilford, a suburb of London. Here we were invited to a home for supper. Mr. and Mrs. Butcher & daughter. Had drinks-supper-drinks-Then we left for home-came into the bar, had drinks-Then we had party for the enlisted personnel-played games-danced—jolly good fun! SMASHING! RIPPING! CLEVER! "Cheers" (whenever a drink!) Lovely! Whizzo! We danced-then party broke up-some more drinks-Then went to bed about 0400-Same thing next morning except after lunch we celebrated Boxing Day—laid mats in ante room-wrestled-boxed-scuffled, etc. all afternoon having drinks between each bout-That night we went down to sergeants' mess for dance-Then after dance to our club-more drinks, games, finally went to bed about 0400-woke again at 0630, drinks, breakfast, drinks-Farewells. They gave us a bottle of Scotch as a farewell gift and we rode truck home—in the snow! A smashing jolly good mission!

ELEVENTH MISSION (Tactical: Witlich) 29 DEC. 44

Breakfast 0400 Briefing 0500 T.0. 0930 Left field 10:30 12 500 lb. bombs (G.P.) 2400 gals.-50° C Flew left wing, low low element-high squadron "B" group. To bomb depot at Witlich to stop supplies for the Jerry advance (or breakthrough). Mission at 23,000 ft. okay-visual-Accurate flak-Made three runs over target-bombed-came back-Landed in haze-Flak holes in ship missed waist gunner by inches-landed at 0430. A very easy mission.

TWELFTH MISSION (Tactical-Kaiserslautern) 30 DEC. 44

Breakfast 0400 Briefing 0500 Left field at 1027 12 250 G.P. 2 500 incend. 2400 gals gas-50°C Flew element lead, low low-high squadron "C" group. Bombed by instruments-P.F.F. at 26,500 ft. NO FLAK seen. Made two passes at target-Landed at 0430. No. 2 and No. 4 leaked oil-but didn't go bad.

*THIRTEENTH* MISSION (Tactical: "Daun") 2 JAN 45

Breakfast at 0400 Briefing at 0500 Left field 0830 12 500 lb. bombs 2400 gas-40°C Flew lead low element-lead squadron "B" group. Front line job—No. 4 went out (oil) On first target run—On second No. 3 went out (oil) other engines were rough-We bombed-left formation, started limping home—No fighter support-hit cloud bank-no maps-no navigation-Just by luck we found a field by firing flares at C-17 who led us to field. Visibility almost zero-landed O.K. on last ⅛ of field. Really had luck to find field. Happened to be Le Bourget where Lindbergh landed-large civilian airport-Had been used by Nazis-was bombed out by us-8 miles to Paris-Met Lt. McDonald, my basic instructor and Lt. Johnny Hawn (27th ATG) landed at 1530

FIFTEENTH MISSION (Manneheim-Ludwigshafen) 13th JAN. 45 "Bridge"

Breakfast at 0345 Briefing at 0445 T.0. 0800 5 1000 lb. bombs 2400 gals. gas-50°C

Flew high lead element-hit flak at front lines also over target whicn was visual between the two rough cities-A solid barrage of flak met us-really accurate-worst since Merseberg-that flak was rated with the flak of Merseberg-Molesworth had only 3 ships left out of its 12 ship squadron-lucky we followed right behind them and they just barely were able to swing their guns on us-we had several holes, a two foot hole in the elevator control-same size just behind the tail gunner-Many were wounded. We were diverted to Baldwell Bay-An RAF base-All night long the buzz bombs came over and they shot at them-We didn't get much sleep! Landed at dusk.

SEVENTEENTH MISSION (Mannheim-Ludwigshafen Bridge) 20 JAN 45

Breakfast 0400 Brfg 0500 Left Field 0800 6 1000 lb. bombs 2700 gals-55°C Again the bridge. Light flak. Flew low element led-lead squadron, 27,000 ft. 5 hours on oxygen. Land 1600 G.H. run.

EIGHTEENTH MISSION (Asherweden-Marshalling yards) 21 JAN 45 Breakfast 0400 Brfg 0500 Left field 0800 6 1000 lb. bombs 2 500 frag bombs-incendiary-53° C Flew Deputy lead-low squadron-lead group.

No flak. Two 303rd Gp. collided. What a drunken formation we had! Only two hours before breakfast we had come back from our squadron party-Everybody thought we were stood down—but they trumped one up during the night-What a formation. Everyone was drunk. You should've seen em staggering to the ships-bombed at 22,000 ft., landed at 1540

*(No diary kept for concluding seven missions.)*

# WILLIAM J. SULLIVAN

Less of the personality of the diarist shows in the diary of William J. Sullivan than in some included here. He does, however, give a very clear record of his thirty missions and as these include one on which the plane failed to make it back to the base, it has its differences from those that precede it here.

Born in 1917, William J. Sullivan attended parochial schools. In 1954 he graduated from Northeastern University, which he attended nights with the financial help of the G.I. Bill even as he brought up a family of four, all of whom have graduated from college.

Since retirement in 1977 from a job as claims adjuster for the Penn Central Railroad and Amtrak, Mr. Sullivan has worked as a substitute teacher in the Boston public school system. He lives in Readville, Massachusetts.

Sullivan's rank at the time of the diary was Staff Sergeant, serving as Ball Turret Gunner of a B-17 belonging to the 517th Squadron, 379th Bomb Group, 8th Air Force.

*******

(1) APRIL 10, 1944 Brussels, Belgium 24,000 Ft.-29 Light Flak Airfield

We were all glad when we found out that our first one wasn't to be too long or too deep in enemy territory. After we had formed and started across the Channel the number one engine started throwing oil and acted rough. Before we reached the target the oil pressure dropped so we attempted to feather the prop but were unsuccessful. While on the bomb run the prop ran away and we could not stay in formation. We managed to drop our bombs in the vicinity of the target but had to drop out of formation. Our luck was with us and although we were a straggler we met no fighter opposition and managed to get back home safely. Just after we hit the runway upon landing the prop which had been windmilling flew off, rolling underneath the plane and landed on the grass along side the runway. We had now been christened and although we were still green we felt that we had an idea of what combat was like.

(2) APRIL 11, 1944 Sorau, Germany 12,000 Ft.-15 11 Hrs. 20 Min. Medium Flak A/C Assembling

When they unveiled the target map we saw that this one was to be quite long but since it was at low altitude it wouldn't be too tiring. We took the northern route up by the Baltic Sea and saw little flak until we reached the target area. We were quite surprised that we met no fighter opposition after going so deep into enemy territory. Over the target our bombs would not release but we finally managed to get rid of them. We ran into a bit of prop-wash about that time but kept control over the ship. One B-17 from another group was seen to go down and our tail gunner counted eight chutes before the plane blew up after falling into a river. After leaving the target area the sky was filled with groups of 17's from other strikes and it really was an inspiring sight and show of air power. Even after this mission we knew we still had a lot more to expect but didn't know just when. After we returned to the base we were told that the ship we had used, a new one #261 was to be our own.

(3) APRIL 13, 1944 Schwienfurt, Germany 20,000 Ft.-25 6 Hrs. Heavy Flak (acc.) Ball Bearing Factory

The name of this target alone scared us, especially when we heard the low whistles from the old-timers when the map was uncovered. However, we were informed that we would receive strong fighter protection but we knew this wouldn't stop the flak. We met our first enemy action about an hour before the target when a gang of about thirty 109's and 190's made a pass at our formation. After seeing how tight we flew, they continued on to hit another group and this time they were successful. From my position I saw the 20 m.m. shells bursting one moment and the next second five 17's went down in flames, three of them flipping over on their back. Three others caught fire and continued for a while before spinning earthward. It was a sickening feeling to watch and I found myself saying prayers automatically. The swiftness of the attack was so surprising that we didn't even fire, although a few boys tried some long shots. From there on till the target we were all tense and watchful even though we saw friendly fighters in the vicinity. At the target the flak was intense and another Fort went down and to make matters worse, we couldn't release our bombs. After we closed our doors I saw that the door had been sprung by a bomb which had fallen on them so we opened our doors again and this time they fell out. The P-38 escort was a welcome sight on the way home and after landing we all quickly accepted the shot of scotch to help soothe our nerves. Battle damage was a hole in one prop, one engine and a hole through the waist.

(4) APRIL 18, 1944 Oranienburg, Germany 24,000 Ft.-32 9 Hrs. Mod. Flak Airfield

We had learned a good lesson on our last raid at another group's expense. For even though friendly fighters may be close, one still can't relax a moment because the "bandits" can jump a group and be gone while the escort covers another group fairly close. So we were prepared for anything this time but met no opposition and the flak over the target was only moderate. However we did see two 17's go down and our ship had the mixture control cable on #3 engine shot away and a few other small holes. There's usually a reason for sweating out each mission and our next one was to be number 5 which they say if you come through safely you'll make them all okay, so lets hope so.

(5) APRIL 19, 1944 Kassell, Germany 24,000 Ft.-30 7 Hrs. 35 Min. Heavy Flak Airfield

Our target today was another airfield and the hits looked fairly good. Again we met no fighter opposition which made us all happy although we had good fighter coverage throughout the entire trip. Flak over the target was quite intense and upon landing we found a few holes in the wing. Although we knew we still have a lot to learn we felt as though we weren't as green as in the beginning and we were no longer rookies. Today was Patriot's Day but I still wished I was back in the states working in a defense plant and buying bonds.

(6) APRIL 24, 1944 Landsberg, Germany 18,000 Ft.-21 9 Hrs. Light Flak Airfield

Today we had another deep penetration into Germany so we were expecting a little trouble. It came in the form of fighters, 109's just before we hit the target area. They first hit another group, knocking one Fort down, and then came at us. The tail gunner and myself met the first attack of three, coming in level at about five o'clock. Then the other boys got some shots at a plane that was chased through our formation by a P-51. Just as we turned on the bomb run, two "bandits" came in high at eleven o'clock but turned away when the navigator and top-turret started welcoming them. We couldn't stop to appreciate the view of the snow-capped Alps in the distance but were more pleased later on when we saw the sight that every Fort man loves, an escort of P-36 and P-47's, waiting to aid us safely home.

(7) APRIL 27, 1944 Mensil Au Val, France 22,000 Ft.-23 5 Hrs. Intense Flak Defense Installation

This one looked pretty good on the map, for we weren't to be over enemy territory long. But some of the boys told us of the accuracy of the flak there, and we found it out by a large hole in the horizontal Stabalizer. Unlike other targets, the only flak we saw were the bursts close to us for they seemed to track us a long time before firing, but when they did they had our range. Although all of our ships returned safely, they all had numerous holes in them.

(8) APRIL 28, 1944 St. Avord, France 14,000 Ft.-7 7 Hrs. Light Flak Airfield

The boys are starting to call trips like these "milk runs", especially when we meet no fighter opposition and can find no flak holes upon return. The altitude helped to improve the trip for us, and it didn't seem as long as shorter missions at higher altitudes. We all stated that we could stand a lot more like this one.

(9) APRIL 30, 1944 Lyon, France 20,000 Ft.-23 8 Hrs. No Flak Airfield

We figured something was wrong this trip when we didn't see a single burst of flak on the entire mission. With nothing to bother us on the bomb run, the hits looked pretty good. But to spoil an otherwise perfect trip, came about a hundred enemy fighters while on the way home. Again our tight formation saved the day, for after two attacks they left us, probably for another group, getting one Fort. All of our ships returned safely.

(10) MAY 7, 1944 Berlin, Germany 27,000 Ft.-45 9 Hrs. Heavy Flak(Inacc) Subway R.R. Terminal Cloud Cover $^{10}/_{10}$

Here it was at last, the target we were all expecting sooner or later. We were in the big leagues now and playing this one on their home grounds. Everything went well until just before the target when some of the boys had to abort. The high altitude and heavy bomb load seemed to be too much for a few, and they started to high tail it for home. The complete cloud cover kept down the enemy fighters, for we saw none all day. When we reached the target area the sky seemed covered with Forts and flak which, although all around us, was very inaccurate. When we returned to our base we learned that two of our ships that aborted were missing. This broke a string of thirty-three consecutive missions in which our group had flown without a single loss.

(11) MAY 8, 1944 Sottevast, France 24,000 Ft.-3 4 Hrs. 45 Min. Light Flak (Acc.) Defense Installation

This one was to be another to the area of the accurate guns and the only advantage was in the length of time. Just before the target, we saw one Fort go down, and on the bomb run we knew what to expect at any moment. It was just the same as ever, only this time they followed us out over the channel. We saw some dog fights in the distance, and another Fort hit the brink but Air Sea Rescue was soon sent to their aid, for another plane called them after seeing some chutes. We found a few small holes in the wing and stabalizer.

(12) MAY 11, 1944 Ehrang, Germany 17,000 Ft.-22 6 Hrs. 20 Min. No Flak Marshalling Yards

This one again proved to us that we can't be too cautious. At one moment just before the target someone was calling out friendly fighters and in the next instant two fighters jumped our formation, knocking down one Fort from our group. In fact, the only one that saw the attack was our pilot. The hits were excellent, for one group knocked out one end of the target and we got the other. After we turned towards home, the smoke from the fires we started almost reached our altitude. Many fires were seen all along the route home, the result of other groups.

(13) MAY 15, 1944 Marquis Mimoyecques, France (Pas De Calais Area) 25,000 Ft.-38, 4 Hrs. 20 Min. No Flak Defense Installation

This one sounded and looked real good and turned out to be our easiest yet. We opened our bomb bay doors while the tail gunner could still see England. The bomb run started out over the channel and we were over enemy territory for only about four minutes. Our bombs failed to release so we brought them back. As we turned off the bomb run we saw a few bursts of flak behind us but that was all. We were back at the base by ten-thirty.

(14) MAY 19, 1944 Berlin, Germany 27,000 Ft.-41 9 Hrs. 35 Min. Heavy Flak (Inacc.) Subway R.R. Terminal Cloud Cover $^{10}/_{10}$

This time our return trip to Big B as the boys call it, was via the northern route. The weather seemed very bad and we had trouble following, but again it helped to keep the opposition down. Again there were many abortions from our group, one of whom was our group leader, but the deputy leader took over and did a swell job. We seemed all alone compared to the groups over the target, the last trip especially, when a few of the boys became stragglers after being hit with flak. Coming back over the Baltic Sea we saw our P-38 escort chasing away the "bandits" that were in the vicinity. At one time I could see the 20 m.m. bursting like fire crackers. We fell in with another group and felt a bit more secure by their company. I spotted a ME210 about 2000 ft. below us, probably waiting for stragglers, but he was too far away to shoot at so I just kept my eye on him. We found about five flak holes this trip and counted about four feathered props in our group.

(15) MAY 21, 1944 Marquis Mimoyecques, France (Pas De Calais Area) 21,000 Ft.-28 4 Hrs. 25 Min. Light Flak (Accur.) Defense Installation Cloud Cover $^{10}/_{10}$

Today we returned to the same target that we hit on our number 13. This time there were only twelve ships in our group and we occupied the number 3 spot in the lead squadron. We left the field at about 12:50 after climbing to 14,000 ft. through the overcast. The formation formed quickly and we proceeded to the English coast, crossing it about 13:40. The lead ship in our squadron had an external bomb which lost its tail vane and fuse over the target. We reached our I.P. while over the channel and dropped our bombs at 14:08. Just before bombs away we were hit by some flak which hit the ball turret, one piece shattering the front view plate. We were carrying eight one thousand pounders, two of which were on the external works and all bombs were salvoed with no trouble. After turning for home we ran into the overcast and had to return to the base at about 500 ft. Everyone seemed glad to get this one under their belt, for from now on it's all down hill and half the battle is won.

(16) MAY 24, 1944 Berlin, Germany 26,000 Ft.-36 9 Hrs. Mod Flak (Inacc.) City Proper Cloud Cover 9/10

"Big B" was to be our target again for today and with the briefed fighter escort we didn't feel too badly. But unlike our other two trips this one was really rough. As usual, when we hit this target the weather is quite cloudy but it didn't help to keep the opposition down today. Everything went smoothly until we hit our I.P. The lead ship dropped its bombs upon opening the bomb bay doors and all planes followed suit. We dropped our newspapers. Then we continued across the city and into the flak bursts which were all around us. Just after turning off the target we picked up some P-38 and P-51's. But again all that Jerry needed was one sweep and his damage was done. Between 40 and 60 enemy fighters hit our low group, knocking down about twenty Forts. The sky was filled with flaming pyres and everywhere I looked I could see Forts or parts of them spinning earthward. It was a terrifying and depressing sight and I turned my turret away as I said a prayer for those boys. They went as quickly as they came and we saw no more opposition for the day. But again it made one stop and consider how careful we must all be or rather how well prepared we should always be, mentally and morally, at all times. As like Schwienfort, this raid will always be in my memory and never will I ever refer to a raid as a "milk run". We lost three ships from our group.

(17) MAY 27, 1944 Manheim, Germany 26,000 Ft.-26 7 Hrs. 40 Mins. Heavy Flak (Inacc.) Marshalling Yards

I think we were a bit more prepared for Jerry today than we have been. When we saw the map we remembered our Landsberg raid and the attacks over the Ural Mts. Things went along okay until we reached the particular range which is quite black and dreary looking. At this time I mentioned to the gang that this is where they usually hang. Then we saw a group of fighters which appeared too large to be friendly. They hit a group in front of ours, knocking down two Forts. Numerous dog-fights were then seen and we passed over about nine chutes going down. Our escort kept them away from then on although we could see them in the distance. We continued on to the target, dropping our nickels over it, but our group couldn't bomb because of a group passing underneath. They hit a secondary near by and we started for home. Immediately we picked up P-38's which stayed with us until we reached the channel. Flak over the target was heavy but inaccurate, most of it bursting to our left. No damage was found on landing.

(18) MAY 29, 1944 Kreising, Poland 23,000 Ft.-22 10 Hrs. 25 Min. No Flak Airfield

We all whistled when we looked at the map and saw where this one was to be. The target, in Poland, was only 400 miles from the Russian front so we knew it would be a long ride. We were waiting all the time for enemy attacks, for we knew we were in pretty deep to miss them entirely. Our escort was good, however, and it wasn't until after the bomb run that we saw any action. Flak over the target was negligible and we only saw a few bursts after we had passed. Just before the Pomeranian Bay a fighter went down in flames after making a pass at a straggler. Then we saw nine chutes come out of a Fort which hit the bay. Bandits were reported in the vicinity but it wasn't until we hit Denmark that we saw them. Some P-51's chased a couple by us and one fell in the water. About that time we saw our P-38 escort and started across the channel to finish a very tiring mission, All of our planes returned safely and we had no damage whatsoever.

(19) MAY 30, 1944 Halberstadt, Germany 23,000 Ft.-23 7 Hrs. 35 Mins. No Flak A/C Factory

After yesterday's raid this one looked easy, or at least short, even though it was central Germany. We picked up an escort just after crossing the Zuider Zee and had one practically during the entire trip. The route in was well chosen and we saw very little flak. Over the target we had a perfect bomb run and the hits were well placed. It seemed strange to encounter no flak at all and we knew something would give us trouble so we kept looking for fighters. We saw a large group of 190's pass us at a distance and one went down after some P-51's gave chase. They hit a group behind us, knocking down one Fort. From then on we were kept busy watching for them till we hit Holland again on our way out but we never did see any at a recognizable distance.

(20) MAY 31, 1944 Gilze Rijen, Holland 19,000 Ft.-17 5 Hrs. 25 Mins. No Flak Airfield

This one was a welcome mission for it brought us over another leg and from now on we're on the home stretch. As we started across the channel towards France we saw some cumulus clouds over the continent which looked quite rough. After going above them we finally saw the ground again but received word that our primary target was scrubbed and we were to pick a target of opportunity. We reached an I.P. and started on the bomb run when #4 prop ran away but we managed to get back in formation in time to drop our bombs on an airfield. It only took about ten minutes then to reach the Dutch coast on the way out and we started across but had to circle to wait for another group. We saw a little flak along the route but none over the target and the escort was very good.

(21) JUNE 2, 1944 Paris, France 19,000 Ft.-17 5 Hrs. 20 Mins. Light Flak Marshalling Yards

Although this one was just on the outskirts of the city, the guns from Paris were firing at us. The freight yards served southern France and vicinity connecting with the capital. It was a late afternoon raid and so we really had an "Evening in Paris". The escort was the best we ever had, meeting us just when we hit the continent and staying with us till out again over the channel. The P-38's came in so close at times that it was almost possible to see the pilot. Clouds partly obscured the target just as we hit it, but we got in a few good hits. It was beginning to get dark as we landed and the few flak holes were difficult to see.

(22) JUNE 5, 1944 Grandcamp, France (Cherbourg Peninsula) 25,000 Ft.-36 5 Hrs. Light Flak Defense Installations

   Being another short one, this mission was welcomed by all. As usual, the I.P. was over the channel and we weren't to go too far inland. We picked up our P-51 escort soon after we left the coast and they stayed with us all the while. It wasn't until after we dropped our bombs that we saw any flak and then it was negligible. We found one small hole in the wing to spoil an otherwise perfect mission.

(23) JUNE 6, 1944 D-Day Arromanches, France (Cherbourg Pen.) 14,000 Ft.-10 5 Hrs. No Flak Radar Station

   When we all found out that this was to be the day we were waiting for, a tremendous cheer filled the briefing room. Our target was a radar station on the coast, close to a spot where the boys were to land. After taking off, we noticed the largest number of Forts we had ever seen. Clouds covered the channel on the way out and we bombed through the clouds. Not a single burst of flak was seen and the absence of it created a strange feeling. But we dropped our bombs and started back, still wondering if it were real. Just before hitting the English coast a large number of ships were seen in the channel, including cruisers and battleships. From now on anything can be expected and we'll have to be on our toes every minute.

(24) JUNE 7, 1944 Flers, France (Cherbourg Pen.) 20,000 Ft.-23 6 Hrs. No Flak Marshalling Yards

   Another trip to the same area we hit yesterday with about the same condition. Clouds obscured any activity in the channel except for the movement of numerous boats in all directions. We met no opposition and again we saw no flak whatsoever. Our target was a marshalling yard which would be used to bring up supplies to the defending enemy forces.

(25) JUNE 8, 1944 Orleans, France 20,000 Ft.-15 7 Hrs. No Flak Marshalling Yards

   Since this one was a bit deeper into enemy occupied territory we expected trouble but met none. The absence of flak and fighters has everyone guessing but it's a welcome change. Contrails were quite heavy on the way in but the weather cleared enough on the way out to see some activity in the channel. Along the beaches could be seen hundreds of boats and numerous gliders just inside the landing area. Convoys

shuttling back and forth filled the channel, creating an impressive sight.
(26) JUNE 13, 1944 St. Andrew Leur, France 20,000 Ft.-15 5 Hrs. No Flak Airfield

Today we had as a target another airfield northwest of Paris. On the way in we saw a few bursts of flak which we avoided. P-51's were quite numerous around the target area and we dropped our bombs without any trouble and came home. After we hit the English coast on the way in, we ran into some bad weather and had to hedge-hop home at about 500 feet. The rain made it impossible to see but we managed to find the field and land safely.

(27) JUNE 14, 1944 Creil, France (Paris Area) 20,000 Ft.-22 6 Hrs. Light Flak(Acc.) Airfield

The worst thing we encountered today was weather which was quite bad over the continent. There was some flak over the target, an airfield, but not much damage was done to any of our group. Before the I.P. we ran into some clouds and we lost the top squadron of our group. We later heard that they ran into fighters and only one returned. However, the weather cleared over the target and we were able to bomb visually.

(28) JUNE 20, 1944 Hamburg, Germany 25,000 Ft.-22 7 Hrs. Heavy Flak (Acc.) Oil Refinery

The boys had been here a few days before, while we were on a pass, and told us about the flak. So we expected a rough time in that regard but not quite as much as we did receive. Procedure was normal until we turned on our I.P. and number one started to act up. We just about feathered it and started on the bomb run when all Hell broke loose. The flak was the severest we had ever encountered and each burst seemed to be aimed at our particular squadron. After a few close bursts number two started to burn and number three was knocked out. We tried to feather #3 but no soap, so we just had to let it windmill. The pilot told us to put on our chutes, for he thought it was all over for us. We fell out of formation after dropping our bombs and started in the general direction of home. The smoke had stopped coming out of number two but it was pouring oil. We were losing altitude but everything seemed to be under control. The pilot got in touch with Air Sea Rescue and told them of our plight. At about ten thousand we started throwing out equipment when the pilot informed us that we would probably have to ditch. The radio room was cleared of all unnecessary equipment and we prepared to take our stations. While still descending, we went over our duties and ditching procedure, each man making sure of what he was to do. The radioman remained on inter-phone, informing us of our altitude and distance from shore. When about six miles out the pilot told them that it would be any minute now. Everybody braced themselves as we could feel the plane slowing down for the attempted landing. The first crash was slight as it was only the tail hitting the water. Then in a few seconds the big impact came. Water came in from everywhere and we were tossed about like corks. I landed face down in the water, in the opposite direction from which I had been sitting. The floor of the radio room gave way and we all went down. When I regained my senses I was under water but soon came up as we all had half of our 'Mae West's' inflated. I grabbed for an oxygen hose and some wires on the right side and tried to pull myself up. I could feel someone's body underneath me as I started to climb out the hatch. The tail gunner was partly out and trying to pull the life raft release. He told me to step on his arm and when I did he gave another yank and the first raft popped out. The plane had broken in two at the ball turret and was sinking fast. The second raft appeared and I jumped into the water and grabbed a rope on it. The first one was washed away before anyone could get to it, so we all held on to the other one. A K-dingy floated into the pilot's arms and he inflated that. I kicked myself away from the wing of the plane as I thought there might be a suction created, but it just slid out of sight slowly. The bombardier was floundering around so we managed to get him in the large raft. Then the co-pilot and waist gunner climbed in, followed by the radioman. That left the engineer, the navigator and myself in the water, as the pilot had climbed in the one-man raft. By this time the sea had become quite rough and both rafts were shipping water. The ones in the raft attempted to bail out some of the water but each wave would seem to fill it again. With the pump in the raft, they tried to pump up the seats so that another man could enter, but the position of the bombardier made it difficult. We saw a buoy about fifty yards away and attempted to paddle towards it but were swept by too quickly. Between the swells we could see the top of a tower and a beacon on land, so we knew we weren't too far out. After about forty minutes someone spotted a launch heading our way and everyone felt better. My arms were quite tired from holding on and my body was shivering from the cold water but the sight of the boat seemed to give me strength and I knew it would only be a matter of minutes before we were picked up. As the boat came by, they threw over a net and lines and pulled us towards them. In no time we were all aboard, exhausted but happy, and shaking hands with all the crew who seemed almost as happy to see us.

(29) JUNE 25, 1944 Bremen, Germany 25,000 Ft.-29 7 Hrs. Med. Flak (Acc.) Oil Refinery

This being our first mission since we ditched, all of us were a bit nervous. Again most of the trip was over water and we wouldn't be over enemy territory too long. Just before we reached the target I began to feel a bit strange from lack of oxygen. My legs got heavy and I couldn't answer the navigator on a check. The radio-man opened the turret door and put a bottle on my hose, and in doing so, sprung the door. So I had to leave my position and go on oxygen in the radio room. The flak wasn't too heavy although we picked up a few holes in the wings. The escort was very good and we dropped our bombs and headed home without any trouble.

(30) JUNE 25, 1944 Toulouse, France 25,000 Ft.-30 11 Hrs. Light Flak Airfield

When we were awakened for this one we knew by the gas load that it would be a long trip but being our last mission and eager to finish up we didn't care. We started over the front lines at low altitude and ran into some of the most accurate flak we ever encountered. A piece hit my turret, breaking the glass by my head and showering my face with fragments. However my helmet and oxygen mask prevented my getting cut. Once over the lines it was just a long tiresome ride to the target area at the base of the Pyrenees. We made two runs over the target but the flak was inaccurate. Our trip home was all over water for we swung out to sea on our return. Our gas supply started running low so we had to land at the first field we came to which was at Land's End on the southernmost tip of England. While refueling we checked the ship and found holes in the wings, supercharges and one in the tail. Our home field looked really good when we returned, especially since we knew it was to be our last view from the air.

# PRISONERS OF WAR

# THEARL MESECHER

Serving as mortar and machine gunner of Company I, 168th Infantry, 34th Division, PFC Thearl Mesecher was captured on February 17, 1943, near Fiad Pass in Tunisia, North Africa. The diary of his prisoner of war experiences was kept at intervals rather than daily. It was kept in three small, easily concealed notebooks. The first he bought for three cigarettes and a chocolate bar from a German prison guard at Friedrichhoffen. The second he wheedled from the German postmistress at still another prison camp at Lauenberg and the third was given him by one of the daughters of his foreman on the great farm where he did forced labor, located near Jaskow, Poland.

Mr. Mesecher's diary is much more carefully written than most, somewhat expanded and polished after release perhaps, but though I have generally tried to avoid diaries tampered with subsequently, his avoids telltale hindsights and retains such a sense of immediacy that I wish I had space to include more of it.

The diary became an obsession, Mr. Mesecher says. Diaries have a way of doing that to those of us who have the habit. Though never told by his own army that the keeping of diaries was forbidden, the Germans did so instruct him. Some items were too risky to record originally but were included at the first opportunity after he was freed.

Before the war Mesecher's work involved mine explosives; after it he became Assistant Director, Central Accounting, Iowa State Tax Commission. Born in 1914, he was 28 years old when captured. He now resides in Des Moines.

*******

Since my experiences as a combat soldier were similar to all other combat soldiers of the 34th Infantry Division, I will write only a brief account of the events immediately prior to my being taken prisoner-of-war by the German Army.

The German Army, under the command of General Rommell, advanced on the lines of the American forces with heavy thrusts of panzer units supported by heavy artillery barrages. Our lines were overrun and the Germans succeeded in advancing through a pass which we were attempting to hold. This advance disorganized American troops and many units in more forward positions found themselves hopelessly trapped behind the German lines.

This was the case of fifteen men of the 168th Infantry Regiment, myself included. Naturally, there were many more, but one only knows the happenings in his immediate vicinity.

After much maneuvering in our desperate struggle to free ourselves, and becoming weak from lack of food and water, we came upon a lone arab who directed us toward a small peak in the Atlas Mountains which he claimed was occupied by American troops. We headed for this position as fast as our weakened condition would permit. Soon we could see an American truck spotted upon a high knoll. We were sure that it was to act as a guide for us to their position.

A brief sense of security swept over us as we traveled in deployed formation toward it. We almost forgot our hunger and thirst as we gradually grew more careless in our haste and anxiety. We were snapped back to realization by the staccato chatter of machine gun fire in front and on both sides of us. At the first burst of enemy fire, we flattened ourselves on the burning white sand. Our hearts pounding like hammers.

We had been betrayed. The American truck had been captured by the Germans and was spotted there as a decoy to lure disorganized small bands of American soldiers into this death trap. After twenty-two months of training and combat, to end up in a position of this kind did not seem possible.

Fifteen men in the open like ducks on a pond against untold numbers in fox holes and dug-in gun positions. We could not back out as we could hear many motors directly to the rear. Probably tanks or armored cars. No one dared look. We were too busy with the things at hand.

They expected us to do something, hopeless as it may be, as seasoned troops always do. We threw everything at them we had, which was very ineffective. The motors in the rear sounded pretty close now as the dreaded 88 millimeter shells began to burst around us. We would fire a few rounds, get up and run a short distance, dive to the ground and fire again, thus trying to spread out and not all be blown to Kingdom Come by one artillery shell. In our maneuvering, we managed to get into a small ravine. About out of ammunition, exhausted and weak from our marching with no food or water for over two days now, we sat down and waited for the artillery shell which will end it all. We felt we had done all that could be expected of us under present circumstances.

We had nearly forgotten the motors to our rear but are sharply reminded of their presence when an enemy light tank appears at the head of the ravine with heavy guns pointing directly at us in our crouched position. We had a last-minute decision to make. We can surrender and be prisoners of war for the duration, or die a hero's death by firing on that tank. Had there been a band, and had it struck up a patriotic military march, we probably would have fired. There was no band. We did not fire.

I am sorry for the man who does not realize defeat. His name is ever present on the casualty lists. We do not feel that we are mistreating the pledge we made to comrades previously wounded, or the one we made as unfortunate buddies were laid in shallow sandy graves in the past few days. We do not feel that we have betrayed the people at home who wait with bated breath before the radio to hear the news commentator give the highlights of the day's activity abroad, and wonder what part their son, husband, or sweetheart had played. . .All the while visioning him as a hero. We all cannot be heroes; everyone doesn't win.

Many thoughts race through our minds as we walk to the tank with the large, black cross on each side and hand over our rifles, daggers, and other battle equipment. It gives one a sickening feeling to hand one's life, liberty, and pursuit to the enemy unconditionally.

We are marched back to the enemy's Battalion Command Post where we find many comrades. There are more arriving steadily. There are Infantry men, Artillery men, men from armoured outfits, Engineers and Medical units. Looks like they had captured the entire American Army.

Is our Command to blame for this, or is it just a part of war? We are arranged in a column of fives and started marching deep into German territory. There are approximately one thousand of us.

Officers and enlisted men march in the same ranks. Officers and enlisted men alike fall out of the march to lie on the white sand more dead than alive, from exhaustion.

The guards in charge of our column are relieved every two or three hours by Comrades brought to our position by truck. It was evident that we were going to find out what rough going really was.

There was an almost continuous procession of tanks, armored cars, artillery and trucks going to the front. The amount of previously captured American equipment in this procession was amazing.

We marched from noon until very early morning of the next day before reaching another assembly area. After three or four hours' rest, we moved on. No food or water in sight.

One great advantage was that in all our training, we had carried heavy loads of battle equipment and now we carried nothing.

As we marched on and on, we passed many vehicles which had been burned as a result of their being attacked on their way to the front. This brought a trace of a smile to the faces of the dusty and very weary American soldiers.

As we passed the numerous graves of enemy soldiers who had, perhaps, been less fortunate than we, I am sure there were no smiles from my comrades or myself.

It probably sounds strange but one who is, or has been, engaged in this business of legal murder and does his very best while on the battle field, finds it impossible to look upon the grave of the unfortunate enemy with anything else in mind than pity.

He also was a son, husband, or sweetheart of someone. He will be missed when he doesn't return the same as any one of us would, or perhaps, will be.

He probably had no personal grievance with the United States or any of its soldiers. He was an instrument or tool, the same as we. He was just unfortunate. It is a game of chance. There are many losers; winners are few.

We march on and on. God, will it ever end? They are passing out and lying thick along the road now.

Someone spies water in a small ditch along the road. We all wade into it, trying to get a drink. It turns out to be Alkali water but many drank it in spite of the mud and brine. Many fell out of the column soon after, and I would not speak of their fate.

We swayed and stumbled as our pace grew slower by the hour.

I have seen endurance tests while with the British Commandos in Scotland. I thought I knew what an endurance test was like, but the American soldier was taking one now that he will never forget.

I glance occasionally at my buddy, a husky young man from Postville, Iowa. He seems to be taking it as well as any of us. He checks up on me at intervals but our smile of approval of each other's ability and stamina have gradually become a mere flick of an eyelash.

We both have a chance to trade our cigarette lighters for a small crust of dark Italian bread. Nothing will ever taste so good as it did. Since we had had no food at all for five days, these few crumbs really helped.

Shortly after dark, we stopped and were given all the clean, fresh water we could drink from a German tank truck. We then curled up together and though it was too cold to sleep, we rested the balance of the night.

We started marching very early the next morning. At noon we were given a small slice of German bread. This was the first food we had received from our captors.

Arabs flocked around selling cactus fried as hot cakes. They aren't at all palatable, but we were very hungry so business was good for the Arab peddlers.

We finally ended up in Sfax late that night.

We are placed in a wire enclosure near Sfax. There are no buildings, so we dig a hole to sleep in. This was because there was a strong and very cold wind. The ground was damp and cold, also. We could not sleep but did manage to rest a little. After marching all day, it becomes very tiresome to walk around most of the night to keep warm.

Again we receive a small piece of bread which only makes us more hungry.

We are next loaded into boxcars and sent from Sfax to Tunis. Here we are given a small helping of rice, two candied dates, and three cigarettes by the French Red Cross. May God bless the Red Cross workers of any nation.

## FEBRUARY 23, 1943

Today we left Tunis by plane for Italy. I hope I shall never see Africa again.

The airport was bombed heavily by allied bombers. Killed many of my comrades and did much damage.

We flew over Mt. Vesuvius and landed at Naples, Italy. We were hauled to prison camp outside of Naples in Italian trucks.

The civilian population gazed at us in wonder and cheered wildly as we passed. They weren't cheering us as the English, Irish, and Scotch people did when we arrived there. They were cheering the Italian soldiers who stood guard over us with fixed bayonets. Women and children stood on the streets and threw stones at us. They shouted at us in their native tongue. They were all true Italians at heart. They had been taught to hate us.

Children of three great countries had nearly worshipped us. Candy and chewing gum had been given to children all over the world by the American soldier. Children had followed him in the streets in great cities everywhere. He was a welcome guest in any home, large or small. He had had the admiration of women and children throughout his Army career. Here was his first realization that it was a serious business, not a game. He was among the common enemy. Hatred flashed in their eyes.

In the prison camp we slept on the ground. The nights seemed awfully cold, so we walked most of the time to keep warm.

The ration was about one-half cup of boiled cauliflower tops for lunch. About the same amount of macaroni each evening along with a small hard biscuit completed the meal. We were getting very hungry and losing much weight.

## MARCH 5, 1943

We were loaded into boxcars today and shipped to Germany. When a boxcar is loaded and sealed, it is not opened again until the destination is reached. The suffering on these trips is so great that one would nearly have to experience this sort of thing to realize its severity.

We arrived at Stalag 7A at Mooseburg near Munich, Germany, two days later.

Here we are put into barracks and the food is a little better. Very little, however. Here I meet soldiers of every nation who has opposed Germany. Prisoners all.

Just saw several Russian prisoners brought in from the Russian Front. They have been marching for seventeen days. I have never seen men in such condition. They are so starved that there is very little hope for them.

Prisoners are herded around by vicious Police dogs. We are being registered here and will probably be sent to different areas to work.

MARCH 29, 1943

Today we left Stalag 7A by boxcar and arrived two days later at Stalag 5B at Villigen, Germany. This is near the world famous Black Forest. The food isn't so good here, but we do not expect to be here very long.

APRIL 20, 1943

Left Stalag 5B today for a large construction job at Freiderichoffen where the Graf Zepplin was built. Here we live two hundred and fifty men in one barracks. The bunks are about two feet apart in double decks. We have mattresses of wood shavings.

At night our pants and shoes are taken from us. The shutters and doors are closed and locked. Police dogs prowl the area. There is no plumbing or no ventilation at all. The air becomes very foul. There are no facilities for bathing or laundry. Everyone has lice in abundance.

The work is hard construction labor. We work six days per week. At this date, our daily routine is as follows: Roll call and to work at 7 A.M. One half-hour rest at noon while the guards have lunch. We return to the barracks at 6 P.M. At 7 P.M. we are given our only food which consists of a slice of dark bread and a thin soup which is a barley concoction with a few leaves of spinach added. Sometimes we get about one pint; sometimes not so much. After this comes roll call and orders for the next day. Punishment for any misbehavior comes at this time also. Now to bed, to sleep if you can.

We have each lost twenty-five or thirty pounds of weight and are getting pretty weak.

MAY 9, 1943

Today is Mother's Day. It is the happiest day of my life—not necessarily because it is Mother's Day, but because today we received our first food parcels from the Red Cross. We have had all the food we dare eat at this time, and our first cigarette since March. I certainly hope the food parcels keep coming, as we were getting pretty weak.

JULY 26, 1943

It has been suggested that there has been too much sabotage committed here by American soldiers. For that reason, we are again loaded into boxcars and shipped to Stalag 2B at Hammerstien in northern Germany.

Four days in a boxcar so crowded there isn't room to sit down. Jolted and bounced, night and day. Sickness, vomiting, diarrhea, foul air, no water or food. God, what more are we expected to stand?

At Hammerstien we are rationed one loaf of bread and one-quarter pound of margarine for five men. We received this amount every day.

AUGUST 1, 1943

We were taken by truck today to Lauenburg, Germany, which is a base camp. From there to a farm where we will work. There are only eleven of us here. My buddy and I managed to stick together. I am so glad. I don't know how I could get along without him. We all live in two small rooms in a wire enclosure. It reminds me of a squirrel cage.

Since it is the harvest season, we work from early morning until dark. Every available person is connected in some capacity with the war effort. Nearly all the home work and common labor jobs in Germany are done by prisoners. Some are soldiers, some are civilian prisoners.

While Germany occupies a country, they are at liberty to work any or all of the population in any way they see fit. This is the first real slavery I have seen.

It is very cold and damp. The Baltic Sea is only about six miles away. We do not have adequate clothing for this climate. We only have one pair of trousers and one shirt. Also wooden shoes.

We have no razors or barber equipment. We have to keep ourselves as clean as possible. We have had no Red Cross parcels since leaving Friederichoffen, so that means very little food and no cigarettes or tobacco.

Polish men and women who are civilian prisoners work in the fields with us. They have no shoes and scarcely any other clothing. The older women do not seem to mind it so much, but I certainly feel sorry for the teen-age girls. They have hardly enough clothing to flap in the breeze.

I doubt if I shall ever forget how one little Polish girl cried when a make-shift strap of some sort gave way, exposing her in entirety to everyone present. The guard scolded her for taking time to repair it. They laughed as if it had been part of a cheap burlesque. I am proud to say that no American soldier smiled or even acted as if he had noticed her misfortune.

There are many German women and girls working with us. Dirty and unkempt as we are, I cannot help but notice the manner in which they compare us with their own soldiers. They associate themselves with us as closely as possible at every opportunity. This is strictly forbidden, however.

## AUGUST 15, 1943

Today is my birthday. Hope I am home before the next one. We have had no mail yet.

## AUGUST 22, 1943

We are working very hard now, trying to get the grain into the barns before the rains come. The food isn't substantial enough for us to work such long hours.

On the Sundays that we don't work, we are locked in our squirrel cage, and the guard goes home or to the nearest village. We are lucky to have enough water to drink, none to wash with. Some things one must endure are perhaps necessary, or in some cases unavoidable. But a lack of even sufficient drinking water looks very much to me that they either do not wish to be bothered with us, or just want us to realize that we are prisoners.

They do not have adequate equipment to operate a farm of this size. Everything possible is done by hand.

In our country, we would not hold a dangerous criminal subject to such living conditions as we have here. There are more flies in our quarters and in the shed where our scant supply of food is kept, than one usually sees around a decaying carcass. I have not seen a piece of screen wire in this country.

## AUGUST 29, 1943

Today we received our first Red Cross parcel since last June. Food, cigarettes and toilet articles. Boy, are we happy! My buddy received a food parcel from home which he shared with me. See what I mean by Buddy?

I also received my first mail from home, dated May 12th.

## SEPTEMBER 5, 1943

Sunday-we are not working today. We received another Red Cross food parcel. Our morale is very high as far as food is concerned. It rains or rather drizzles about all the time now. We have never had a chance to dry our clothing as they are taken from us and put into a small room near the guards at night. This is done so we will not try to escape. In the morning, they are brought to us still wet.

Our only pair of trousers and one shirt are pretty well worn out. Hope we can get a jacket of some kind before winter.

We hear no news of the war, but our hopes are high. Occasionally we hear some German propaganda from which we can make a few deductions and get a rough idea what is going on.

## SEPTEMBER 19, 1943

Today received new trousers, shirts and shoes from the Red Cross. Regular U.S. Army issue. This solves the clothing problem. We are all very happy and thankful.

SEPTEMBER 24, 1943

Any work project in Germany for prisoners is called a Kommando. Today we left this Kommando and were taken to another a few miles away. It is only two miles from the Baltic Sea on a point about thirty miles west of Danzig, Poland.

There are American prisoners here which brings our group to forty men in all. We live in one large room with a kitchen attached. One man remains in the Lager as a cook while the others do field work. His chore is keeping the place clean as there is very little to cook.

The work at this time is potato harvesting. It is the hardest work so far. Maybe it wouldn't be so bad if we had more to eat, and they didn't drive us so hard.

One of the American prisoners was shot by the guard a few days ago, so everyone of the rest is pretty much on the ball.

NOVEMBER 11, 1943

Armistice Day-The day marking the end of the last war. Wish it were marking the end of this one. Here I am twenty-five years later, a prisoner of the same people. I don't quite understand it. When any of the civilans of the village has work of his own, he is only allowed to do it on Sunday when he isn't at his regular duties. He grabs a few prisoners to help him. It is only a racket they are working, but the guards permit it so we are helpless to refuse.

According to the rules of the Geneva Committee governing prisoners of war, we are entitled to twenty-four hours per week to do our laundry or attend to things of a personal nature. The Jerries, however, recognize no rules other than those which they make themselves.

We go to work when it is still dark and return after it is again too dark to work. It is very cold and damp. The conditions are terrible. How the war can last so long I cannot understand.

All the German people I come in contact with fully realize that they have lost the war and are beaten. They know and admit that Germany cannot possibly win. Fear such as we have never known forces them to carry on. They are very despondent and look and act more like prisoners than we do.

NOVEMBER 25, 1943

Thanksgiving Day in Germany. Since this is only an American holiday, the Germans do not recognize it as being more than just another day. Things in general are anything but pleasant. But we are very thankful for any one of a million things which we have today. Things we never realized were so important until we were deprived of them. We have seen so many people who were, or are, less fortunate than we.

We are thankful to be alive and enjoying good health. We are thankful that we are not starving as many people in Europe are today. We are thankful that we have warm clothing for the coming winter, that even as a prisoner we live in very little more fear than the average person around us, that in our own country we are not driven to work, to hunger, to a miserable existence of slavery and deprivation for a very meager fee and skimpy rations doled out of the hands of mighty Lords and Masters.

Most of all, though, we are thankful that the people in the United States aren't suffering as are many in the world today. That they have enough to eat and enough clothing, that they aren't subject to heavy bombing, that mighty armies aren't struggling in fierce combat across the peaceful plains of the middle west, that bombs and artillery aren't leveling our great cities to smoldering ruins, taking thousands of lives and leaving many homeless as well as badly maimed and crippled.

NOVEMBER 29, 1943

Our mattresses, whether wood shavings or straw, are always full of fleas. At times they become very annoying. Many of the boys have had the flea bites become infected. They cause sores that spread rapidly, and are very hard to heal. Have had much trouble the past four days with an infected tooth. I have been promised by the guard that he will take me to the dentist in Lauenburg tomorrow. I have always accused the American Army dentists of being rough. Tomorrow I can make a comparison.

NOVEMBER 30, 1943

One tooth extracted today. It is a very simple operation; they just lift it out. They do not use a needle first. Perhaps the shortage of drugs has something to do with it. I am thoroughly convinced from this experience that there will be no more dental work for me in Germany.

DECEMBER 6, 1943

It is dark when we go to work and dark when we quit. We work from seven-thirty A.M. to four P.M. We have one hour off at noon. Last summer we started to work at six-thirty and worked until eight, and sometimes ten, at night. We were allowed a half-hour rest at nine A.M. and again at four P.M.

The work is not always so hard, but one dares not stop one minute for anything. When we worked so many hours, it was very tiresome, but now the daylight hours are shorter, and it isn't so bad.

One does not get interested in work being done for the enemy, and this causes it to become more of a drudgery.

It is cloudy and raining most of the time. It has snowed several times this fall, but not very much at each time. There is always a damp, cold wind coming off the Baltic Sea. It is awfully muddy, and working conditions are bad.

DECEMBER 17, 1943

A new experience today-a rabbit drive. About one hundred civilians and forty prisoners encircled a large area. As we gradually close the circle, the chefs or large land owners, shoot the rabbits, deer, or hogs we drive ahead of us. There are many rabbits deer, and wild timber hogs in Germany. After spending the day on this hunt, we are pretty well exhausted.

In counting the spoils, we have two hundred large, brown jack rabbits, one deer, and one hog. The greater percent of this game goes to the Army. The common civilian, as well as the prisoner, gets nothing. The chef gets some, but I'm not sure what percent.

A land owner is the only one permitted to shoot any kind of wild game in Germany.

On other parts of this country, the farms are small, but up in Pommern Province they are all very large. In fact, all of Northern Germany is this way.

This particular farm where I am working is about ten thousand acres. The adjoining ones are equally large and nearly all farms are five thousand or more acres. There is, however, much timber land.

The chef, or owner, has a large mansion surrounded by a small village. He owns every home in this village. The people work for him on this great farm and are about as much his property as the horses they work. They are rationed so much food and paid so much by him.

They are only allowed enough food to keep them alive and a place to sleep. Sometimes two or three families are crowded in one house. The living conditions are very unsanitary.

A few are selected as foremen and are forced to treat the others as slaves in order to hold their positions. If one wish to go to town for any reason, he must convince the chef that the trip is absolutely necessary. If one can manage to do this, he is then issued a permit to be absent from work. He must show this permit to authorities in order to be able to buy a railroad ticket to the nearest place where his particular business could be taken care of.

The chef seems to have very little to do with running his own farm. It is all done by a Government inspector who also lives on the farm. Every morning except Sunday, in most cases, there is a bell that rings. Work Call. The workers of the village gather. . .men, women, children, and the German guards with their prisoners.

The work orders of the day are issued to the Misters, or bosses. These orders come from the Inspector as one scarcely ever sees the chef. Each foreman then selects the amount of laborers to do the particular job of work he is assigned for the day. The Inspector then spends the day riding a horse around visiting the different labor groups. Everyone is afraid of this man, and the foreman produces all he possibly can. A prisoner does not rate very highly in the eyes of the Inspector, who is usually a wounded German officer who is not physically fit for front line duty.

We are, in this manner, forced to do our best at whatever task we are assigned to. The guard's bayonet helps with the persuading in some cases. We are kept always aware of the fact that we are prisoners and have no rights at all.

DECEMBER 25, 1943

Christmas Day, and indeed, a very strange one. Christmas Eve in the past has always been a night of nights. Last night I was surrounded by iron bars and a locked door. Somehow we do not seem to mind the bars or locks so much. After being out in the cold all day we are glad to stay indoors at night.

The German girls of the village singing "Silent Night" in the distance makes me a bit homesick or lonesome or something. I really thought I was too hardened by now to be affected by such things, but I guess that even a stone has tender spots.

Yesterday there arrived a special Christmas parcel from the American Red Cross. It was perfect in every detail. We gave some sugar, chocolate, and margarine to one of the German ladies, and she baked us many cakes. They were very good, and the boys appreciated this act on her part.

We have enough food and clothing now since the American Red Cross is in full swing. I also received eight letters from home yesterday. With everything we have had today and knowing that everyone was all right at home, the day has nearly been a happy one.

I know I shall long remember this Christmas. We have hopes that the next one will be better.

We all this day join in giving thanks to God for our good fortune. That we did survive our engagements in combat. That mentally and physically, we are in fair condition. That we still have the strength and courage to face each day's tasks as they come, until the final day we again join the ranks of our American buddies to go home to the places and people we love.

We have, in the past few months of our imprisonment, kept our hearts from becoming bitter with hatred for our captors. Let us all try to continue in this manner to the end. Hate is a terrible thing.

DECEMBER 29, 1943

Today the rabbits that were killed on the drive twelve days ago were skinned and dressed. For twelve days they have been hanging in a warm room before even their heads were taken off. The Germans say the meat is better when seasoned, or tempered, this way. The odor of them, in their not-too-early stage of deterioration, was offensive indeed.

We did not get any of them, anyway. This is only mentioned to show the quality of the food they have. One can guess from that what the prisoners' food would be like.

When a cow or hog dies from any cause, disease or otherwise, they are taken to another village and butchered. The meat is distributed amongst the prisoners. In a large camp at Friedrichoffen, we were issued a quarter of beef for five hundred men. The hoof had not been taken off. Neither had the horse shoe.

FEBRUARY 24, 1944

Have received one clothing package and two cigarette packages from home this past year. Cannot understand where the parcels mailed every sixty days are going. They are long overdue.

There were three packs of either "Raleigh" or "Old Gold" cigarettes in every Red Cross food parcel. The German authorities are taking them away from us. They claim it is because of the propaganda on the pack. The "Raleighs" have a war bond advertisement. The "Old Golds" have the following verse:

### Freedom

Our heritage has always been freedom
We cannot afford to relinquish it.
Our armed forces will safeguard that heritage
If we too do our share to preserve it.

I suppose the entire food parcel will be next. One certainly could not live long on the food the Germans issue with no help from the Red Cross. At least we could not do the work that is expected of us. We have received Red Cross food parcels regularly since December first, and the food situation isn't bad at all.

APRIL 2, 1944

There doesn't seem to be any news at all. We have been watching the Jerry civilians' morale get lower and lower. It has been very interesting to watch the attitude of the people around us. I have been told, and can well imagine, what it was like when they were winning the war.

It snows or rains almost continually and is very wet and muddy. We see the sun only a few minutes at a time. We worked outside all winter and never missed a day. It has not been so very cold, except a few days at a time. We have been fortunate to get through the winter with no serious illness. There is always a strong, damp wind, but thank God, the winter is about over. Maybe summer, with its long hard hours of work will bring better weather and higher hopes.

APRIL 9, 1944

Easter Sunday again in Germany.

One year ago today we were working about as hard as we are now, and nearly starving at the same time. Many did.

Today we have Red Cross food parcels and besides that, my buddy, DuWayne Bulman, and I have eggs, a lovely cake, and a number of other articles of food. This was a contribution from a love-sick German girl. I worked in a blacksmith shop with her father and allowed her to think I was in love with her and she was expecting to, some day, come to America with me. The entire family treat me as I were one of them, this being a very dangerous act on their part. The American prisoners seem as well satisfied at this time as one could expect prisoners to be.

I am thankful for our good fortune today, in the face of such hardships and suffering throughout Europe. May I continue to keep the good faith that perhaps has brought me this good fortune.

Today saw fifty or sixty American B-17 bombers returning Home after a daylight raid on Danzig. They were attacked by German Anti-Aircraft fore and fighter planes. Two of the planes were behind the formation, probably wounded from their previous engagement. At any rate, these two planes were attacked by the German fighters. There were several fighters, and though one was shot down, the action did not last long with the helpless bombers.

After part of their crews had hit the silk, they came down about a mile from where I was standing. One went into a power dive. As it went out of our sight behind the timber line to crash on the rocky Baltic coast, there was one sight a soldier always notices and never forgets. The tail guns were still blazing as she crashed with a part of her unfortunate crew. The guns still in action as she plunged to earth, too badly wounded to carry on, her mission completed, shows us, at least, American courage. The kind it will take to win this war.

We hated to see this, naturally, but as the oily black cloud of smoke drifted Heavenward carrying the souls, we hope, of our unfortunate comrades, our morale became higher in spite of the lump in our throats. We knew that we must have losses.

We also knew that good, courageous men, brother Americans, supporters of the Stars and Stripes, were still in this war. We were beginning to think that America had forgotten us over here. And still, on this quiet Easter Sunday, we were not prepared for this sight.

MAY 28, 1944

Today received six cartons of cigarettes and one food parcel from home. They were mailed in February. I guess all the others have been lost.

We went today, Sunday, to clean the grave of our unfortunate comrade, Jerome Donovan, who was shot last summer by a guard because he was too weak to work.

JULY 4, 1944

Would like to see some fireworks on this Independence Day, but was just another day's work. Sure hope we can get out of here before long. We have clothing and food. We aren't suffering for anything except freedom.

The working hours are long and hard. The boys quarrel a lot. Their morale slips a little at times when weather or working conditions get bad. A smile and a pleasant word now would be worth a million dollars.

Many of the fellows are looking forward to big things when this war is finally over—homes, wives, good jobs, automobiles, and many other things. I guess I have passed the stage where one plans on the future. I have, to a certain extent, now given up all hopes for anything more in life than a little more living comfort than I have here.

Above all, I want freedom. I have no wife, no home, no job, no auto or any of the things the fellows speak of. If I can once again have my freedom in my own country, I will be satisfied.

My buddy and I confide in each other. Somehow, we manage to keep each other from cracking up. I never thought any man's nerves could stand such a strain. There are many things I dare not write. To write anything in a diary is forbidden, so one must be careful.

JULY 22, 1944

Twelve cartons of cigarettes from home today. My buddy, Bulman, also got a good parcel. My parents had my address wrong, but everything seems to be o.k. now as my parcels are coming through.

The busy season is on now, and they are driving us like slaves. The work is very hard. The hours are long. Some of the boys around on the different Kommandos are cracking up and having to be returned to the Stalag. Nerves shot, or to us, stir happy. Bulman and I think we can sweat it out now, though the end really isn't in sight.

No man has really eaten until he has starved. No man has really been clean until he has felt lice nibbling and crawling upon him. No man has really lived until he has felt death near at hand.

Sometimes I'm afraid our parents, relatives, or friends will be disappointed in us when we get home because of the terrible disposition we are gradually adopting.

Right now I would venture to say that not more than ten per cent of us will get home. The war isn't over yet and we, as prisoners, are in for trouble in the last days. There will be no food. Maybe marching, maybe forced into heavy action unarmed.

AUGUST 15, 1944

Another birthday for me in Germany. Thirty years old. Sometimes feel twice this age. Have been running a binder cutting grain. A working day is from six A.M. until dark now during a grain harvest-about fifteen hours. Seven days a week.

I had a lovely birthday cake this evening from my lovesick German girl friend. Had an awful time smuggling it into the lager. It really was worth the trouble, however.

AUGUST 27, 1944

Sunday—One year ago our comrade, Jerome Donovan, was shot. Today we held memorial service at his grave. A short sermon, prayers, taps, and the National Anthem. One of the boys from the Stalag band furnished the music. Everything was conducted in a military manner. The entire civilian population turned out and were very impressed.

SEPTEMBER 17, 1944

Sunday—Today I helped my civilian foreman dig potatoes. This was not compulsory but purely voluntary. This family, consisting of the old man, his wife, and two daughters, treat me as if I were one of them. They befriend me in every possible way, and it is very dangerous because it is strictly forbidden. They give me bread, butter, eggs, fruit, cake, fish, anything they think I could use, and actually cannot spare it, as their ration isn't very much. They are afraid that I'm going hungry, when I actually have more food than they do at this time.

Before the war the old man was a minister but was ousted from the Church for Anti-Nazi activities. He treats all the American prisoners very well, but my working for him and being about to bring his lovely daughter back to "God's Country" with me, doesn't exactly go unnoticed by the rest of the family. Sometimes I'm a bit ashamed of myself, but when the Red Cross parcels don't come, and my buddy and I get a little hungry, I forget it and carry on. I have made no promises but have allowed them to take perhaps a little too much for granted.

This old couple have lost two sons so far in the war, and the third is reported missing. These people aren't allowed to even speak to prisoners. Above all, we weren't allowed to associate with their women. To go to one of their homes unaccompanied by a guard.

When I volunteer to help this old man with his homework on Sunday, it looks pretty good to the guard. Actually, there is scarcely any, if any, work done. It is merely an excuse to have me over for Sunday dinner. And what a dinner! It is a continuous barrage of questions about America.

The girls are very clever in getting me alone with them, while the old man and lady smile their approval. I have learned to speak their language pretty well, and my activities are certainly bringing in the groceries.

People at home would, perhaps, disapprove of this shady business on my part, but some day, perhaps, I can make up for all of it.

This young girl is so sincere and honest that even though she be

German, at times my conscience bothers me.

**NOVEMBER 11, 1944**

Armistice Day again. Still the war goes on. In the past few days the "volksstraum", or home guard, has been organized. Men from sixteen to sixty take training every Sunday and are sworn to do anything asked of them to defend their community from the hands of the advancing enemy. They are volunteers, but nearly at the point of a bayonet. They resent this regimentation very much. It looks very much to me as if Germany were beaten and just waiting or preparing a last stand against the knockout blow. Germany had an Army when we fought them in Africa, but by the looks of the soldiers coming on furlough from the front today, old men and young boys, I do not see how they can last much longer.

There have been continuous food parcels from the Red Cross throughout this past year, but now they are cut in half. We are told that they will probably stop entirely as the transportation for them is getting impossible.

We all realize that we will get very hungry before this thing is over, but we are never quite ready to start dieting. I am very glad now, that I have allowed my lovely German girl to build air castles. Maybe my buddy and myself will be able to take it. Wish I could get a girl for the rest of the fellows. Perhaps they are gentlemen and wouldn't stoop to such deceitfulness, at least until they had gone without food for several days.

The German civilians are starving in these bombed cities. Little consideration is shown for prisoners in a country that has elected to fight a losing battle to the last man.

The German civilian has a terrible fear of this Nazi party. There are stool pigeons amongst them always. They also fear the enemy soldiers as they grind across their country in large tanks and fly over their heads in untold numbers, spreading death and destruction throughout the land. They are all afraid of the Russian soldiers very much. Now their propaganda system tries, as the American troops get closer, to paint them as gangsters' murderers and anything that would instill fear of them into the hearts of the German public.

The propaganda points out now that the American soldiers will murder innocent women and children. He will rape, plunder for valuables, and burn everything inflammable. At first it was only the "Luft Gangsters" or Air Corps that were so bad. Now, as the ground troops draw closer, they become demons overnight.

With clothing from the Red Cross, we dress much nicer than any civilian or soldier around here. We are, even during working hours, as clean and neat as possible.

Sometimes one will slip us a bit of forbidden information about the war. We, in turn, will hand him a cigarette or if we are befriended by any of the ladies, we usually pay off with a bit of soap, or chocolate. We usually have a little candy or gum, and the children think we are quite all right. We have a terrible black market in operation and since we control the items in demand, we sometimes put them at a terrible disadvantage.

We never fail to respect the older ladies as we would in our own home town.

Our general good manners and cleanliness are known and respected in every part of Germany where American prisoners are held. When they read or hear their own propaganda, they look at us, and it all becomes very deceiving. We have planned it this way, along with fictitious tales of truck loads of food following the front with their orders to feed the hungry civilian population.

Not one man, woman, or child in this village are afraid of us or our comrades on the front. Perhaps they will be very surprised, but we will wait and see.

A very small percent deserve to be treated other than as enemy. A few of them have befriended us from the day we arrived. The balance, though, are of a very cruel nature. They cannot be singled out or separated so it would be impossible to show any leniency on their behalf.

When we work, we are too busy to talk. When we aren't working, we are locked in the lager. But, the average civilian starts a conversation at every opportunity.

I, personally, do not have a guard where I work. My civilian foreman has taken full responsibility for me.

There is not a possible chance of escape from here, and we aren't guarded very closely. We are out on a point in the Baltic Sea with three companies of guards besides Gestapo and civilian police behind us.

NOVEMBER 19, 1944

Winter again is here. The same cold, wet weather. We have just had our first snow.

We found out last winter that a pair of galoshes and a pair of gloves would be worth a million dollars. We did not have them then. By writing home, we could have had them sent. We were all too sure that the war would be over by now. We were entirely too optimistic. We will pay for it the balance of the winter. It looks like the Red Cross food parcels will be discontinued any time now. With winter coming, this will be a bit rough.

My foreman's wife just showed me a notice of the death of her third and last son on the Russian front. They invited me to dinner this evening, and sent all the food I could carry to the lager for my buddy.

DECEMBER 7, 1944

Three years ago today the Pearl Harbor attack. Since that day, the

United States has received many severe blows. She has also dealt many severe blows.

I never thought I would be here this long. A prisoner is always a bit anxious. I try to keep from thinking about the war too much. It is progressing so terribly slow that, at times, I wonder if there really is a war going on. Of course, five minutes on the front would thoroughly convince me, I'm sure.

We work all week from before daylight until way after dark and wash our clothing on Sunday. It is a very tiresome routine week after week, month after month, summer and winter.

Time is very heavy on our hands. Everyone is very irritable. Working conditions and weather could not possibly be worse. It rains continually. Mud is knee-deep. Rations are very poor.

We managed to get by last winter because we were so sure it would be the last one. Now we are going through another, and according to what news we can gather, it looks like we will see all of this one here.

The boys on the front are really toughing it. I have a brother out there, and I'm worried about him.

Some of the boys show signs of cracking up a little. I'm going to try hard to keep from letting it get me down. If one ever slips once, or gets in the rut, he is beaten and usually doesn't last long.

I have lost lots of weight and am very nervous—smoking too much, perhaps.

If the Jerry authorities ever find this diary, my worries will be over, as this sort of business would be strictly forbidden, along with many things I have previously mentioned. Perhaps I can continue to keep it hidden.

Nearly everyone can stand the work here, at least for a while. Nearly anyone can go hungry, at least half the time. But, to be locked in the same small room with thirty to fifty men. . .always the same men! We eat, sleep, bathe, chop wood, or wash clothes in this same room. There is some fighting and quarreling, as everyone is very irritable. We are always together, either working, or locked in this room.

We don't mind the bars on the windows, or lock on the door.

We don't mind being pretty hungry for a good meal.

We don't mind being a bit homesick or lonesome. A pleasant word would mean everything right now.

We don't mind doing our laundry in a rusty pail every Sunday.

We don't mind the working in a downpour all day, with no fuel for the lager stove when we return.

We don't mind an officer of the German Army coming around every few days and cursing everyone in the room, threatening to stop our rations completely unless we do more work, or kicking the boys around like dogs, or making a man work in the rain who is so sick he faints.

We don't mind listening to enemy propaganda or being called swine or being followed continually by a man in a green suit with a rifle and bayonet.

We don't mind any (one) thing forever, or all of them for a while. But, to have all of them over a period of weeks, months, years, it produces a mental strain that sometimes is nearly unbearable. It is unbearable for some.

In case some of us do get home again, I hope people will not hate us for the disposition we will have developed as a result of this lovely place.

### DECEMBER 25, 1944

Last night was Christmas Eve. It was not quite so lonely as the one last year. I really enjoyed myself. Nearly every one of the boys were at the home of one of the many girls in village.

I went over to see the foreman's daughter, Dora. Had a lovely meal. Heard some lovely music on the radio broadcast from London. The old folks went to bed very early. If the controller over this district had come around inspecting, we would all have gotten in very serious trouble, and the guard would have been court-martialed.

Today has been very enjoyable also. I have had the best of food, thanks to the Red Cross and Dora.

The lager is decorated just as we would a ballroom at home. We have a beautiful Christmas tree with real decorations from the Red Cross.

We are indeed fortunate because I know that there are prisoners whom the Red Cross cannot reach, who aren't registered with them, as a result of negligence on the part of the Germans. It really took us a long time to get things established this way.

Our buddies on the front aren't so well off as we. God, what I would give to divide all this with them.

Our guard is an old man who is in sympathy with us, and that is probably responsible for his letting us get away with some of the forbidden things we do. Things are too perfect. I'm afraid trouble is brewing.

### JANUARY 13, 1945

Another rabbit drive today. I became very ill and managed to miss this one. Collecting these rabbits feeds the German soldiers on the front. They got eighty-three. Not so well as last year. Hope the blasted Krauts get hungry and quit fighting.

### JANUARY 22, 1945

Transferred today to another working Kommando. It is directly on the Polish border, not far from Danzig. There are fewer men here, but everything else is generally the same as the last place.

I don't mind the change in work, but I sure miss my buddy. Also, Dora and her mother, to say the least of the groceries they supplied me with. Hope my buddy doesn't get too hungry, now that I'm not there to kiss the German girl and bring home the groceries. I'm certainly a dead duck if the Jerries ever find this diary.

JANUARY 28, 1945

Sunday again, and very cold. It has been snowing and blowing for days. I have been out with a snow shoveling crew today. The drifts are very deep. Railroad and highway transportation is nearly halted.

I certainly miss Bulman, my buddy. Somehow we managed to keep each other's morale up. We became as close as brothers since all our soldier days have been together. I also miss Dora and her mother and the good food.

One of the boys just attempted suicide by cutting both his wrists with razor blades. I will not mention his name, just in case this diary should get home. He would want it this way. At one time the Jerries kept our blades for us, to avoid this sort of thing. I suppose they will again now.

This sort of thing is common among prisoners. Some try one way, some try another. Usually successful. Others force the guard to shoot them, while others just crack up, or go stir crazy. A few feeble attempts to escape are made. It is nearly impossible from here. The terrible loneliness of prison life, or hunger, is generally the reason. Occasionally, family troubles at home prompts this sort of action.

We have been helping the civilians prepare wagons for evacuation before the advancing Russian front. Evacuees come through every day now, in wagons, sleds, or on foot. I am thankful that my people aren't having to do this in far-away America. The wind howls, the snow gets deeper and deeper. My God, when will it all end?

FEBRUARY 2, 1945

The roads are pretty clear now, and the evacuees are coming in droves. One must see it to realize the suffering—hungry men, women, and children. If they don't find feed for the horses, they aren't going far.

As I sit here tonight, it is so comforting to know that my loved ones in far-away America aren't preparing to flee their comfortable homes before a mighty, oncoming army, leaving all but a very few necessities behind, and having no place of safety to go.

No one who has not seen the front can realize the destruction and suffering, as the enemy blasts everything into submission.

I have seen some of the most beautiful places completely demolished in only a few minutes.

I see humanity in a much different way than I used to. I understand the German language very well, but I will be so glad to hear some English spoken again. I am with other Americans, but Army slang and English are very different.

This lonely life is so terribly depressing, but at that, I suppose we prisoners are fortunate.

**FEBRUARY 4, 1945**

We get no Red Cross food parcels now at all. The western front has the transportation cut off, or else the Jerry is too busy to bother with us. Our buddies out there are giving them something to think about. The war is coming home to them and they are having a hard time seeing the glory in war that is supposed to be there. It seems to be a little different when the other side fights back. This waiting, and hoping, is very tiresome. Wonder how my brother is doing out there. I don't want anything to happen to him, naturally, but he would probably never be registered in Switzerland or get any Red Cross aid. He would probably be marched for days without food, as the transportation problem is serious. I hope he is killed if capture is the alternative.

**FEBRUARY 11, 1945**

Sunday again, and a more beautiful day I have never seen. It is warm as spring. Last night the village was full of refugees from east Prussia. Ragged, dirty people, rickety wagons, and hungry horses. Men, women, and children. They don't know where they are going. They are just going, and are getting pretty hungry. Soon they will be starving as their journey is just starting. The mighty Russian front comes grinding forward.

We hear the distant rumble; occasionally the larger windows rattle. At night the eastern sky is very ruddy. The noise is a little more south than it was. For two years I have been patiently waiting to hear those sounds. They are comrades. Yes. But we are in front of those guns, too.

Yesterday a German girl twenty-four years old, escaped from a civilian concentration camp about five miles away, and came here. When she was questioned as to why she walked so stiffly, she explained that both lower limbs had been frozen. There was no fuel in the camp, and she was starving. The authorities do not feed the civilian prisoners enough to keep them alive very long. She was so weak she could hardly stand up. She went to the chef's kitchen, and asked for food. She was given no food, but was locked in a potato cellar, and the guard was called. She was dragged from this cellar by him, beaten until she could not stand up, and then shot. She was better off dead! A life of this kind is not worth enduring the hardships.

Today four more came and were likewise locked up. They were starving and when the guards came, they caught them trying to steal two or three raw potatoes apiece. This was a terrible crime in the eyes of the two well-fed, well-dressed Gestapo. For punishment they were beaten over the heads with heavy clubs and stomped into the barnyard mud and filth. Their screams could be heard for half a mile, at least. They looked longingly at our lager, but we could not help them against armed guards and besides, we were locked in. I am very proud to be an enemy of any government that inflicts such brutal punishment upon its people, German people. I can well imagine what they did in occupied countries. The suffering one must witness is so much greater than the suffering one must endure as a prisoner.

I have seen cruelty amongst men until I'm, to a certain extent, accustomed to it. But I'm sure I could never become accustomed to this brutality and cruelty with women. I wish every woman in the United States could see what I have seen today. As long as there is one American alive, they will never be mistreated as these women were. But I do wish there were some way for them to know what they have and appreciate those boys who worship them.

I have seen women slave laborers working with large picks on the railroads, driving oxen, barefooted in snow and ice, starving, victims of legal murder, bear children in the forest with no shelter, or fire in January.

I sometimes wonder if this will have a hardening or seasoning effect upon me, or will make me more tender toward women. I will not have to worry about that if the Jerry ever finds this diary.

News just came in that the main Stalag has been abandoned. It looks like the Russians have driven across from Danzig and up to Stettin. If that is the truth, we are surrounded, trapped on this point. We are out of contact with the rest of the world. Maybe it won't be long now. Seeing so much suffering is getting on my nerves a bit.

FEBRUARY 13, 1945

The steady roar of the front is much closer now. Many French prisoners have been liberated by the Russian Army. Many are evacuated with, or ahead of, the civilians.

We continue to work every day as if nothing were happening.

FEBRUARY 17, 1945

I became a prisoner two years ago today. Things sure have happened in my young life the past two years.

We brought all our tools in from the timber this Saturday evening and that is something we have never done before.

The Russian artillery has everything on the place vibrating and is getting closer by the hour.

Something is going to break, and very soon, too. Everyone is so tense. I sure miss my buddy.

FEBRUARY 18, 1945

Sunday. Three years ago today I sailed from New York. Three years overseas is a long time. Wonder what it is like back home. Sounds strange, back home. I have nearly forgotten home.

Awakened at four o'clock this morning. Packed only a little of our personal items and food, taken to Lauenburg, to our company headquarters thirty kilometers away. The entire company, consisting of sixteen hundred prisoners, all American, took only a blanket and what food we could carry, and started marching west, accompanied by nervous, heavily armed guards.

No one has any idea how far, or how long, we will be marching. It looks like the beginning of the end. The road is full of wagons and people walking. This is the dreaded march I have expected for so long.

### FEBRUARY 21, 1945

Have walked eighty kilometers so far. Sleeping in barns, very crowded. Eating from our packs. When the food we are carrying gives out, we are through, as I do not see where any more would come from.

The guards know no more of our destination than we do. They eat with the farmers where we stop at night. Their food isn't so good, either.

My buddy and I are together again. He brought me a roll of cooked sausage, a cake, bread and butter, also a souvenir, and love and best wishes from Dora and her mother.

### FEBRUARY 24, 1945

Saturday. We have hiked one hundred and forty-five kilometers. Our packs, containing food and a few cigarettes seem very heavy but are getting lighter entirely too fast.

We will certainly be hurting when this food gives out. The roads are packed to capacity. Horses, dead from starvation, are lying along the road. Every few minutes we pass one. I'm afraid we will see people the same way before long. It isn't too cold, but very wet and muddy. The boys' feet are getting in pretty bad shape. We are all carrying a little too much weight, but food is not to be had without carrying it with us. This, however, isn't half as bad as what will come when our food is gone.

### FEBRUARY 26, 1945

We have marched more than two hundred kilometers to date. It has been raining, and a terrific wind is blowing in off the Baltic Sea. We are marching west along the coast.

My feet are in terrible shape, and my buddy is having stomach trouble. I have nearly died several times the past two years from eating this soggy, black bread, and I know just how he feels.

Tonight we are soaking wet, cold, tired, and hungry, and the war goes on. God, give us strength to stand it. We must stand it now. We just refused the raw, and very bloody ground horse meat for our meal. I was expecting that, as they are thick along the road. I am sure that the next time we will be hungry enough to eat it.

Russian prisoners have been known to eat fellow prisoners when they died. So far I have never known of an American being hungry enough to do this. I hope I never shall.

We cannot steal food on these farms where we stop because there is nothing to steal. Besides, we are guarded too closely. They have nothing to give us, and we could not carry enough with us to last forever.

FEBRUARY 28, 1945

Have marched about two hundred and sixty kilometers to date. The roads are cobblestones and mud. It is terrible walking. We are getting a bit hungry. Our food is about all gone now. My feet are getting awfully sore. I have no extra sox. It is too cold to remove one's shoes at night and besides, our feet are so swollen we could never get them back on.

Horse flesh isn't so bad if it hasn't been dead too long. Would be better if we could cook, or even heat it a little, but fire is prohibited.

MARCH 6, 1945

Have walked about three hundred and fifteen kilometers. Have laid over a couple of times because the roads were too crowded with evacuees.

Have been issued a loaf of hard sour bread, also a pound of margarine for twenty-five men. We also had a small handful of raw horseflesh sausage. Blood sausage. Where they got live blood beats me because I know where the horse came from.

We slept in the open field on the frozen ground on one of the coldest nights we had.

We were issued a Red Cross food parcel for three men today. It did not last long because we were so darn hungry. It did help a little.

Someone occasionally trades a pack of cigarettes for a loaf of bread, but it is very hard to do. We are kept away from civilians and guarded closely. The average civilian has little more than we do.

Usually the bread comes from the guard who steals it from our bread ration and sells it to us for cigarettes. There are no cigarettes in Germany, and they are at a great premium. We could buy our way across this country with what few we have if there weren't so many of us. Naturally, the bread goes to the highest bidder.

Soap, tobacco, or coffee are the best trade items.

I hope this hike is over soon as my buddy and I are getting awfully weak. We have very little water. Warm food, or a warm drink, is something one could only dream of having. In summer it would not be quite so bad.

Another night in the open field would about finish me up. One hates to give up now, after sweating out two years in this place.

MARCH 16, 1945

Have come about 500 kilometers now. The measured distance is on the main roads, but we travel on the small, crooked, country roads, and actually walk much farther than this measured distance. The signs along the roads, especially direction signs at cross roads, enable me to tabulate the mileage.

We just got a very small loaf of hard bread for three men. It helped a little but certainly will not supply the energy we are burning up. We are getting so weak now that even the barns seem cold. We do, occasionally, get a chance to steal a raw potato or carrot on the farms where we stay overnight. One more time some horse flesh blood sausage. It was decayed badly this time.

Bulman and I have taken a Scotch lad and an English one with us. They were lost from another column. Bill and Scotty are swell fellows. Hope we can keep them with us.

MARCH 20, 1945

We marched forty kilometers today (twenty-five miles). We lay over a day now occasionally because the roads are so full. With a group this large, we stand for hours morning and night, waiting for our slice of sour bread, if we get any, usually don't, or waiting to be counted in or out of the large barns we sleep in.

We either stand in line or march from daylight until dark. We are getting awfully weak, and many of the boys cannot go much farther.

There are many marching columns such as ours, and all the barns in this section are full every night.

There is no water all day on the road. In the barns, there are only a couple of men allowed to carry water under guard. There is only half enough to drink, and none to wash or shave. We are very dirty, very tired, very hungry and weak. The lice which nearly everyone has in abundance are all but driving us mad. We certainly cannot carry on much farther at this rate.

MARCH 25, 1945

We hear bombing night and day and see lots of air activity. We walk around most large cities to avoid being caught in a raid.

I saw a B-17 bomber go down just now. There were two men bailed out and one chute didn't stay open. Perhaps flak got it.

The lice are eating us alive. God, such filth. I never dreamed I could get so dirty. Sure wish I knew how much longer this will last. I'm afraid I cannot go on much farther.

I just had a chunk of raw horse meat for dinner. It smelled pretty rough, as the sun has been very warm the past few days.

MARCH 30, 1945

We have covered a distance of seven hundred and eighty kilometers. We are in a camp now on a large airport. A very dangerous position with the air full of American bombers. We have no food here, or no beds, but we do have decent barracks.

APRIL 1, 1945

Easter Sunday again. Today we were issued one small loaf of bread for nine men for three days. We are locked inside a wire enclosure and are starving. The lice are making us so miserable we can hardly stand it.

My buddy and I are broken out all over with a rash that feels like poison ivy. Our diet, or the lice, is responsible for this. I'm afraid we cannot endure this combination of physical torture very much longer.

As we were sitting in our barracks a few hours ago, there came a loud roar of motors, the familiar clatter of fifty caliber machine gun fire and slugs started tearing through our barracks. We dived to the floor. The planes climbed and dove, and hell really broke loose. We had no trenches to go to, so we sweat it out here until they leave, but they are no more than out of hearing distance when the unmistakable moan of heavy bombers comes to our ears.

We knew they were going to bomb this airport because the straffing planes were setting the stage for it. We have no air raid shelters. Just flat ground and our barracks. The boys dash wildly here and there. There is no use running because there is no place to go.

As Bulman, Scotty, Bill and I stand in the doorway and watch the formation of tiny, silvery crosses come gliding smoothly along toward us, we know that by an Act of God only could we possibly escape the tons of explosives that would be hurled down upon us in the next few minutes.

As the Jerry flak guns opened up around us, the barracks shook and our ears rang.

Between barrages of the Ack-Ack we could hear only our hearts beating. As the formation got nearly over us, I was relieved because I thought they would surely have started bombing at the end of the runway. At this very instant came the tiny familiar whistle which we all recognized at the same time. We dove to the ground as this innocent whistle gradually developed into a blood-curdling scream, as the heavy bombs began rocking the world around us. Closer and closer they came, pounding harder and harder. The entire world seemed to be jumping and bouncing. Many of the boys' noses started bleeding, or the hands came off their wrist watches. All our heads pounded violently. It was done. The flak guns silent, the raid was over. Besides being weak from hunger, sick, dirty, and covered with lice, everyone is so nervous that, I'm sure, I have never seen men in such condition.

We all fully realize that we are sunk, but I certainly hate to give up now.

APRIL 6, 1945

They have promised us that we will move away from here before we get another raid. The last one certainly did a lot of damage.

I'm so weak that I cannot stand up any length of time now. My legs just won't take it. About everyone is in the same condition. I don't see how we will be strong enough to march out of here. At any time now, the boys are going to start blacking out (fainting from starvation) on a large scale. I would never have sweat out the past two years if I had known this. One man just asked another what he was going to do when he got home. That is about the most stupid question I could think of at this time. I do not think there is one man here who can take another week of this. Many are getting that horrible look on their faces. I have seen it on the faces of starving Russian prisoners.

Just had another air raid alert. I feel as if I had been drunk.

APRIL 9, 1945

We moved from this airport, which is about seventy kilometers from Hanover at Celle, and the next day it was bombed and straffed until it would have been impossible for any of us to live through it.

We have marched about forty kilometers back east. Where we go from here beats me. It seems that the American front is crowding hard.

The Jerries have no rations to give us, and it looks like the end is about here.

Filth, lice, and this terrible rash, along with hunger and forced marching, against the speed of our American buddies coming. Some race, but I don't want to bet on it.

APRIL 13, 1945

All night marching.

We were nearly liberated last night. The guards abandoned us, but came back again and forced us on.

It seems that the American troops have driven to the Elbe River on both sides of us and the Jerries are trying to get us across before they close the gap. There is plenty of war going on around us, and things are really popping.

They are marching us hard now every night, and I'm beginning to stagger very much. If I make it until morning, I'll be very lucky. One cannot fall out of the march because the S.S. troops are everywhere and one would be shot on sight.

With my buddies in about the same condition, we try every way imaginable to keep each other going. Just as we were about ready to drop and give up, we stopped for a few minutes, the entire column.

I think the commander is checking on possibilities of getting us across the river.

Bulman and I seize this opportunity and evade the guards. We slipped into a barn and soon the column left without us. We later heard that the commander and the guards abandoned the column and made a dash for the river. The guards were changed several times on the march, so they would naturally have strength enough for the dash to freedom.

The column of prisoners went back to a village about a half mile from the barn where my buddy and I were hiding.

When morning came, we made ourselves very much at home, keeping an eye open at all times for the S.S. troops that were in the timber around us. We must not be found here or we will be shot. A young German girl here has fed us a lovely breakfast and is already secretly dreaming of going home with me, providing she can keep us hidden and fed until the American comrades arrive. That is the surest hand I have, and I had better play it to the end. My buddy smiles his approval.

The battle is raging very hot all around us, but there is no activity at this spot. If we are found by the retreating troops, we will be shot at once.

I can see, from my hiding place, this village where the balance of the column have been hiding. They are, at this moment, lined up in the road at the point of the bayonet, in the hands of the S.S. troops. Tough luck, lads. They will now be marched, or shot. The column only numbers four to five hundred men at this time.

Well, look who is here! A tiny American artillery observation plane just flew over. He is dipping his wings in recognition. He has spotted the column in the hands of the S.S. troops. There will be no artillery shells land here. Boy! What a relief! Just like a cold drink on a very hot day. We were too weak to try a break through, and the past few hours looked like the finish for us at any time. Now, perhaps, we have a chance, providing we can avoid being discovered by the prowling S.S. troops.

The tiny plane swooped and dived over the column of American prisoners, and the S.S. guards scatter like rabbits. Two start toward the rear on a motorcycle. The plane flies low over them, firing at them with an army pistol. What kind of war is this, anyway? It seems that one rider has been hit, as they dive from the cycle and fire rifles at the plane. Things are happening fast and furious around here now. American planes are straffing heavily a short distance to our rear, but do not know just what it is.

I have just seen the sights of sights. In the center of this small village sets a tank the size of a battleship. I have never seen such a machine before in my life. On the side is a large white star. The helmeted figure climbing out of the open turret, as the American prisoners swarm around waving and yelling, is grinning like a school boy. It is too far to see all this, but I know it because a Yank just naturally grins at a time like this.

If this is a reconnisence tank, the others will be up quickly. It has drawn very little, if any, fire.

We run to the village as fast as our weakened condition will permit.

Two Yanks walk up the road to meet us, grinning as I knew they would be. To grasp the hands of our comrades, whom we had waited for for over two years, is something I shall never forget. They assured us that the village was full of tanks and half-tracks, and that trucks were on the way up after us. As we walked around smoking our first cigarette for weeks, and happily shaking hands, there were tears streaking their dusty, unshaven faces, as well as our own.

They forced the German ladies of the village to fry eggs for us while we were waiting for the trucks to arrive.

Soon the trucks arrive and we are loaded on. We wave a last goodbye to the boys who saved us, and face the west for the first time. Once again we are rolling—toward home—a three years' dream come true.

At another village, way behind the lines, we eat a good supper and sleep in a feather bed in a lovely home, after the civilians have been ousted. We are on the other end of the gun once again. We are next taken to a large airport near Hanover. The prisoners of all nations are coming in by thousands as the front gradually liberates them.

They are being shipped out by plane every day. It must have been a little too much for me because I have wound up in the hospital. They are treating me for an old wound. I thought it had healed up. I had forgotten about it. I don't know how long I'll be here. I really don't care now that I'm on this side again.

My nerves aren't very steady, and I'm very weak. I think I can take anything now, but it seems that I'm so tired. I'm not going to worry or plan anything.

My buddy and I will be separated here. Bulman will go on home. I sure wish I could stay with him, but perhaps it's better this way, as he worries about me too much. I certainly hope he can hold up until he gets home. No one can ever be closer to me than he has been. We have always been together. Training, fighting, on leave in foreign cities, in prison, working and starving. After four years, two fellows in good times and bad get pretty well acquainted.

APRIL 18, 1945

Four years ago today I became a soldier in the American Army. I set out to see what it was all about. Now, as I lay here in this hospital and look out the window on a battle-torn countryside, it isn't real, or doesn't seem real. I feel as if I were returned from the dead. In fact, I was "The Living Dead"

I am in no hurry to get home. I don't want to see any friends. I have no plans for the future, no hopes or desires. I am very tired, and about finished, I guess. When I am given food, it is all right. When no food is given, that is alright. When I was captured over two years ago, I weighed one hundred and sixty pounds. Today I weight one hundred, even.

Today Bulman went to France. I certainly feel all alone. I am contented to lie here any length of time, as the weather is beautiful here in western Germany. I am getting enough to eat most of the time. I will get more when my condition will stand it.

Have just been transferred from the 105th General Hospital to the 93rd Evacuation Hospital on the airport at Hanover. I will leave here soon for some place. The beginning of the painful, tiresome, but happy road back.

APRIL 19, 1945

Flew today from Hildershine, Germany, to Paris, France. Hundreds of the liberated prisoners need medical attention as well as wounded men just off the front. The hospitals are crowded and very busy.

I am in St. Marcel, the largest hospital in Paris. I can walk again, and have a few articles of clothing and have drawn a partial payment.

The ward surgeon insists that I take a pass and see Paris a bit. I do not care about seeing Paris. It's New York that I want to see. I suppose that I have a little too much time to think while I'm hanging around here. My nerves are very jumpy. Our own planes overhead make me very nervous.

In the past two years we learned to regard allied planes as enemy and never even noticed the German planes that flew over us.

Everything seems so noisy. A dropped tin tray, a sharp whistle, a rumble of food carts in the hall, the flap of a window blind, the click of a cigarette lighter, and thousands of sounds unnoticeable to nearly everyone else, paralyze me at times, as they are sharp reminders of various things that in the past spelled danger.

If I could quit comparing the click of a cigarette lighter with that of an angry guard releasing the safety on his rifle. The rumble in the halls with sounds made by distant bombing or artillery.

Instead of always being on the alert to jump and move fast at the first harsh command, if I could only relax. There will be no harsh command. The American nurses are so gentle, so kind. They are nearly as worn out as I am. They understand so well how we feel.

# MICHAEL MAZZA

Suffering from several bullet wounds, Michael Mazza, of Haverhill, Massachusetts, was sent to a hospital in Hoenstein, Germany, after capture. On recovery he was sent off to a prisoner of war camp and assigned to the labor force in roughly the same area where the preceding diarist, Thearl Mesecher, also worked in the fields.

Mazza's account is briefer and less detailed than Mesecher's and I have cut some of the duplication of experience but it seemed worth including because of the differences, as well as because the scene of reunion with his family is touching.

Mazza was a 19 year old private, serving as infantry rifleman when captured. A printer before the war, he entered the postal service afterward and is now retired, the father of five daughters who have given him three grandchildren.

*******

AUGUST 6, 1944

There were about 3000 other Americans at this camp waiting to be sent out to different work camps. I was called for examination on the 25th of June by the camp doctor. He gave me a slip of paper stating that I was only able to do light work. But I was still to be sent out to a farm to work. Our camp spokesman was trying until 9:30 at night to get me off of the work list but it was to no avail. I was to leave on the 28th for a farm in Rowen, Germany, with three other Yanks. We left at 6 a.m. and slept in a barn in Lauenburg that night. We reached our destination the next day around noon. It was a small shack attached to a pigpen. There were 20 other Americans at the farm and they were all glad to see new faces. We stayed up until late that night getting the low down on what to expect and getting acquainted with one another. They were taken prisoner about six months before we were in Africa. Everyone has their own details to take care of in the barracks. There was one guy who was the chef and he knew how to cook potatoes about 15 different ways, which made it better when you had to eat them every day. I guess I was starting to get used to everything because even the German black bread started to taste like bread.

I started out doing light work but the Kraut boss I had didn't like the idea because it wasn't long before I was out working along side of the other men. We worked right with the German men and women civilians. There were a few Russian girls who, I imagine, were prisoners also. The days seemed to pass pretty fast while working in the fields. But the nights, when one had time to think, seemed to drag by. Before the lights went out at 10 p.m. we played chess, checkers, or cards to pass the time away.

American bombers flew over today. The first I've seen since I left the hospital. They dropped empty auxiliary gas tanks in Rowen and their bombs about 30 or 40 miles from here. The rumbling could be heard off in the distance.

AUGUST 15

I guess the Russians must be making quite a bit of headway because the Krauts are sending civilians and P.O.W.'s up to East Prussia to build trenches for the retreating soldiers. Some of the women, who work practically as hard as the horses, also went along. We've been pretty fortunate so far, none of us have been selected to go.

AUGUST 31

I received my first letter from the States today, dated July 4th, from my brother and his wife. This is my first news from home since November in '43 when I left home for overseas.

SEPT. 7

The German inspector came around today to look over the horses. Twelve are being taken away to be eaten by the soldiers at the front to keep them going. They will probably tell them it is prime beef. Last week they rounded up all the dogs in the neighborhood. What next!

SEPT. 8

I felt kind of sick for the last couple of days so I'm not working today. The guard had some pills sent from the doctor in the next town. I hope they do some good.

SEPT. 9

Well, I finally got a couple of letters from home. I feel a lot better today so I got out of bed. My fever has gone down some so I'll probably be back to work Monday.

SEPT. 10

I had a good breakfast today. I traded some cigarettes for a couple of eggs and had spam and eggs. They really hit the spot. Well, with today being Sunday, it's washday again. Then after I get my haircut I'll take it easy for the rest of the day because we start digging potatoes tomorrow. It will take quite a while to get them all dug because that is practically all that is planted here.

SEPT. 28

Mail has seemed to slow down again. It's been a couple of weeks since the last letter from home. Right now, with the Yanks in Germany, I don't think it will be too long before we will be heading for home.

Tomorrow will make three weeks that we have been picking potatoes with about two more to go.

OCT. 4

Well, here it is (mittag) middle of the day and another five hours of work to go. With 2½ more days to go before we get our Red Cross boxes, all I have left is a little coffee and some powdered milk. One of the boys gave me five packs of cigarettes to hold me until a package arrives from home.

NOV. 2

I've been in bed with a cold for the past few days and I'm feeling pretty low. To top it off we got the news that starting next week we were going to be cut down from one Red Cross box a week to one every two weeks. I still haven't received a package from home but I hope they start coming soon. According to the letters I have received there are about a half dozen on the way.

NOV. 18

My first package finally arrived today. It was filled with stuff, that I hadn't seen since leaving the states. Boy, what a banquet there will be tomorrow (Sunday) after I get my washing done. I don't think there will be anything left for the next day.

NOV. 21

This is what you might call a red letter day. I got 10 letters in the mail today with news of more packages on the way. A few snapshots of the family and friends will also be enclosed. The packages will come in handy with only half of a Red Cross box a week being given us. It gets pretty tiresome eating potatoes three times a day seven days a week. I traded a couple of packs of butts for a chicken yesterday. When I cut it open it looked as though the chicken has some kind of a disease. So I was out a chicken and two packs of butts.

NOV. 30

"Thanksgiving" but just another working day here. We had a wonderful dinner of potatoes, black bread, and that lousy German coffee. Well, I shouldn't complain, at least I'm still alive and able to eat. We have been getting quite a bit of rumors to the effect that we will be leaving here soon because the Reds were making a big drive. The Germans want to get us to the American lines to be liberated rather than let the Reds retake us.

DEC. 5

Well, here it is another day, and another 25 cents earned. I also got another letter from home today letting me know that everyone was well and feeling fine. I had a piece of goose today and I expect to have pork chops tomorrow night if the deal goes through. You can get something good to eat once in a while if you have any spare cigarettes to trade.

I hope a cigarette package comes from home soon so that I can trade for some chicken for my Christmas dinner. I'm beginning to wonder if the Krauts are grabbing them for themselves.

DECEMBER 25

Christmas Day—This is my second Christmas away from home but I've managed to have turkey each time although it doesn't taste the same. The turkey came in cans out of our Red Cross boxes which arrived in the nick of time for the holidays. It was quite welcome to see them because we expected nothing at all.

JAN. 28, 1945

Well, it's been a year and six days since I was taken prisoner and I honestly believe that in a couple of months I will be on my way out of here. It snowed all day yesterday and we had to work inside. With but little that can be done inside, we had it fairly easy. We have a five week supply of Red Cross boxes on hand now with rumors of more on the way.

FEB. 11

I had to work on the straw detail today because of wet grounds. Eight wagons of refugees came into Rowen yesterday from East Prussia and about 80 ditch diggers. The Reds must be getting pretty close.

FEB. 14

We have been cut down to half rations again so I guess I'll lose a little more weight. We are beginning to hurt as much as the Germans now with but little to eat. Four 'Limeys' on their way to another Commando stopped overnight at our barracks. They said that with the Reds on one side and the Yanks on the other that we are practically cut off. That means that our rations are going to be cut down to the bone.

I earned about 14 marks last month. That's about $5.60 in American money. I hauled and delivered cabbage this afternoon and picked up three lard sandwiches from the civilians. I helped uncover two wagonloads of spuds this morning.

FEB. 16

I picked cow beets this morning and worked in the woods this afternoon. It was a cool and quiet day all around. I just can't wait for that half of a Red Cross box we get tomorrow so I can have something besides black bread and potatoes.

FEB 18

Well, it has finally come. We got word today that the Reds were making a big drive and that we were going to leave here tomorrow morning with everything that we own. We will go by wagon to a town not far from here.

MAR. 10

We have now been on the road almost three weeks and are in Stolp, about 500 miles from where we started. We travelled about 250 miles the first week we were out and it was pretty rough. We started out with all our clothes and four Red Cross boxes each. By the time we had gone about ten miles, everything we had seemed as though they weighed twice as much. We discarded most of the things that we figured were not going to be needed. Blankets, extra pants, shirts, canned powdered milk, and margarine. Later on we wished we were able to carry all the things we got rid of. There were about a thousand Frenchmen behind us in the march that were making good use of the stuff. At present the bread and oleo that we get for rations each day is what I am living on.

MARCH 24

Here it is over a month now and still no idea where we are headed. We were issued one Red Cross box for every nine men which gave us about a bite apiece. We marched about 25 miles yesterday; so, for a change, they gave us today off. Except for one night when we slept out in the rain, we have been sleeping in barns. It was used for the sheep during the day and we used them at night.

MARCH 29

We are now in Eversdorf, Germany. We are resting today but only because it is raining. Three days ago we received three Red Cross boxes for every five men. It didn't go very far, but it sure helped. All these Krauts are giving us is a piece of bread and potato soup once a day. I will be able to picture the wonderful dinner they will be having at home next Sunday (Easter).

There was a bombing raid three days ago not far from where we stayed and those American planes really looked good. They are over this section of the country almost every day now. We walked through Salswedel yesterday and it looked as if it had been hit just recently.

My ankles have been bothering me quite a bit lately and I have developed a few blisters on my feet, but my hopes are high and I think I'll make it to the end. Wherever that is?

APRIL 1

Easter Sunday 7:30 A.M. I am in Messdorf, what part of Germany that is in I don't know. Right now it is cloudy and windy so I guess today will probably be another wet one. I imagine the planes will be over again today but we won't be able to see them.

One of the boys managed to get a couple of buckets of spuds, so I guess we will have enough of something to fill our stomachs. I imagine the Krauts will put on quite a hunt for them but as usual they won't turn up.

Today marks the sixth week we have been on the march with no knowledge of where we are headed for.

APRIL 3

We are now six kilometers from Stendal. My buddy confiscated three dozen of eggs yesterday and while we were boiling them we had them covered with potatoes so that the Krauts wouldn't spot them. When they found out they were missing and started to look for them, they looked everywhere but under the spuds. And only yesterday morning they found out that about 400 pounds of spuds were missing. We will be here about six days so I guess that a lot of other things will be missing before we leave.

APRIL 11

About 400 people were killed in a big bombing raid in Stendal, the place we left a couple of days ago. We are now in a pretty good-sized town called Tangermunde. We walked bout 18 kilometers and my ankles are all swelled up so that I can hardly stand. We heard a rumor to the effect that starting tommorrow we are going to be working on the railroads. Our rations are getting so that it's just about enough to keep us going. We have been out of Red Cross boxes for so long that I am beginning to forget how good food is beginning to taste.

APRIL 12

We are supposed to leave here this morning but rumors are flying again. They say that the Yanks are making a big drive toward Tangermunde and that we are unable to move on. Boy, I sure hope so. We had our soup around noon and are waiting for word to move out. About 12:17 a shell landed close to the building we are staying in and we all headed for cover. The Americans had finally reached us. They kept up with the artillery, laying it in pretty heavy until about 3:30 and then everything got quiet. About 6:30 an American officer and a private came walking into the yard. The German captain immediately handed over his surrender papers, which he had been holding in his hand since the barrage started, to the American officer. Believe me, it was the happiest moment of my life. As we marched out we could see American soldiers everywhere. We got a few rations from the food trucks and ate them as though we had never eaten before. The white bread looked and tasted like sponge cake compared to what we had been eating.

The Yanks told us that President Roosevelt had died that day. It was such a shock that none of us believed it at first.

APRIL 14

They loaded us on trucks and took us to a town about 20 miles from here. While on the way we were strafed by German fighter planes and we had to stop and scatter. Luckily no one was shot. When we reached the town the people were good enough to move out and let us use their homes. For a late snack that night we had fried chicken, french fried potatoes, and a little wine to wash it down.

APRIL 20

We were loaded onto trucks this morning and headed out to the air field. We boarded a plane and were off to France This was my first plane ride. It took us about four hours to get here and when we arrived we were greeted by Red Cross workers with hot coffee and doughnuts. Real American coffee. We then boarded trucks at the field and went out to Camp Lucky Strike. After a good delousing and a change of clothes we all got ready to go out and do the town. But as we were all restricted we could not leave the camp at all.

About a week later the boat docked and we were loaded on. We reached port in Virginia and immediately went out to Camp Patrick Henry. We were marched in to a movie to listen to a talk from some officer. He said that we would have all the time we were there to ourselves but that we couldn't leave the camp. Then came our first meal back in the States. It was one of the best meals that I ever had or will ever have in the Army. Maybe it was because I hadn't had steak for so long, but it still tasted better than I've ever had before.

After about a week of knocking around, the guys from the New England area were shopped to Fort Devens. When we reached there we were immediately given a physical. They said that in a couple of days we would be going home and that when we returned we would be sent to some resort for recuperation. But, to my disappointment, I had to report to the hospital for a rest because I was suffering from malnutrition. I was only 30 miles from home now and I still couldn't get there. I sent a telegram telling them that I had arrived and that I couldn't get home right away. That Sunday, Mother's Day, practically the whole family came up to see me. I was asleep when they arrived and they were standing around the bed waiting for me to wake up. I guess they didn't want to disturb me. When I finally was awakened I was a much surprised man. After being away for so long they all seemed to be strangers to me. Boy, what a feeling you get when you look at your own parents and don't recognize them. After talking for a while though, everything came back to me. After bringing me up to date on all the news, I felt like one of the family again.

# MIKE HARKOVICH

A summary of events from capture on December 4, 1944 to date begins the prisoner-of-war diary kept by Mike Harkovich of Boise, Idaho. Once he caught up to the entry of January 2, 1945, Harkovich wrote day-by-day on cigarette paper, cardboard, Red Cross paper or anything that came to hand. His is a very full account from which, for space reasons, much excision has been necessary, to my regret.

The very minor touches of earthy language only emphasize how absent it is from most of these diaries. How chaste even this language is compared to the scatology and profanity used by both sexes today, though in all eras the mouth tends to be fouler than the pen.

Harkovich, born in 1920, worked as a pants presser before the war and he returned to that occupation on release from the service. Now self-employed, with his own company, he has 3 children and 8 grandchildren.

A bowler for over 30 years, he has also played softball for 25 years, an interest very evident in the pages of his P.O.W. diary. Though he never kept a diary before the war, he has done so since.

At the time of this diary Harkovich had the rank of Staff Sergeant in the 44th Bomb Group, 66th Squadron, 8th Air Force.

*******

DEC. 4, 1944

I'll start with my home journey from our target on this unforgettable day, Mon. Dec. 4, 1944. We no sooner hit the target when no. 2 engine went "Kaput". Ten miles out her "mate" joined her. Companionship is oh so wonderful. We lost our formation, lost altitude, before we knew it we were all by our lonesome. Anyhow we tried to get fighter protection, but no soap, the transmitter was also "Kaput". We had to throw out all our guns & ammo. By the way it was 33° below, but that was no sign it was cold. I for one honestly sweat to beat hell. Nothing left to do but pray. Went quite a way then suddenly no. 1 got competition, no. 3 decided to cut in. It was smoking and giving trouble. Pilot gave warning to be set to hit the silk. Drifted down to 12,000 ft. Bingo, hold your cards, out of nowhere 6 Jerries-109's-came at us. Ring! Ring! sounded the emergency alarm to abandon ship. We left in the following order, B. Speir hit the silk first, F. Misk, F. Miller,

A. Moir, Red Spencer, myself, then last of all the pilot W. Rogers. When time came to jump for me I couldn't think, completely forgot the procedure they gave me at lectures, looked out the hatch, said to myself, "What am I waiting for?" & then left. Went head first, did a half somersault, and pulled the ripcord. While suspended on midair, I was scared stiff. It didn't seem like I was going down. Seemed as if I was going to spend the duration right in that one spot. I started to pray, "God, please let me go down." I finally noticed I started to descend. Sure felt relieved. Only counted 8 chutes. Evidently our nav., Mac, stayed with the plane, or his chute failed to open. Haven't heard about him since. I'll never forget my last 20 feet before I hit the good old earth. I went down like a bat out of lightning & hit with an awfull thud, fell backward & hit my back & head soundly. Was slightly dazed, got up on my feet and had me a time trying to unbuckle my chest and leg straps, due to the fierce wind that was howling. Got my chest strap off, when suddenly I heard a kachow, turned my head and saw a soldier coming at me with a rifle. I didn't know what to expect, what to think, what to do. All I could see were distress lights blinking in my mind, Oh, my dying ass! I threw my right hand up in the air as high as I possibly could, in doing so, I had to ungrip my chute, unbalancing myself, causing the wind to knock me for a loop. It was a beautiful strike. Before I regained my feet, I had this character upon me. He started to feel me, I started to drool, all jokes aside, he was frisking me and shouting "Pistul, pistul". Out of nowhere I started to get hit from all sides, kicked in the head, kicked in the mouth, punched in the nose and all parts of the face. Don't know how I ever held consciousness. After that bloody ordeal I was picked up and astonished to see a group of civilians gathered around me. I gathered they were the ones that beat me up, but I can't swear to it. Their looks, their sneers, and minds were of evil toward me. Three Jerry soldiers then proceeded to march me to the big wheels, and I walked weary beyond expression, exulting like a conqueror, dazed, helpless, and entranced, after what seemed like a three mile hike. They put me in the Luftwaffe's care. I was treated much better. I had to strip, turn over what belongings I owned, and had to answer a few questions. They returned my belongings with the exception of the English currency, that amounted to 12 pounds and 6 shillings or $49.20. They showed me Speir's dog tags and asked me if I knew him. They then led me to a large room where I found the co-pilot. They locked us both in. He had both his fingers on his right hand broken. Claims he received it while trying to protect his head from being bashed in by an iron bar from a civvy. A trickle of blood came from his chin, otherwise he was okay. Naturally we had a session concerning our exper. He told me that

B. Speir was dead, so he heard while being questioned. I saw red flames, felt sick thruout my whole body, couldn't talk. Bob was the best liked on the crew-happy-go-lucky, witty, always jesting. He had us in stitches at all times. We'll never forget him.

Later Red hobbled in on one foot. He sprained his right ankle and it was up like a balloon, otherwise okay. Bomb. was next. He didn't have a scratch on him. Claims he was knocked out when he landed. Civies stole his watch. F. Misk was next. Claims he was hit a few times. His watch was also stolen. Rogers was practically carried in. He couldn't walk. Had both his feet hurt. It was some time before Miller came in. We're now sweating Bob & Mac out. Jerries brought in straw to sleep on, cold—it was freezing. No heat whatsoever. I couldn't sleep, spent my time pacing the cell. About 2 in the morn. we were told about tran. No Bob, no Mac, decided the worst. Two of us carried Rog, two of us carried Red. They put us in a truck & drove us to a station under guard of 10 Jerries. It was nasty weather, rain drizzled, the wind howled, it was very cold. Arrived at the station an hour later. It was jammed with people and children loaded with their most treasured things. They were evacuating that certain town. We boarded the train, were put in a special room. The windows were all broken, the train was a shamble. About 8 we were fed bread and coffee. By the way we had bread and coffee while back in the cell. I couldn't eat because of my upper lip. It was a mess. I also forgot to mention that they kept the money from all of us. F. Misk was the heavy loser in that deal. He had 24 lbs., that's equiv. to $96 bucks. We had to transfer at another station. We had to do a little walking, first chance we had to see Ger. The buildings were all bombed. They were a complete wreck. Again there were people evacuating.

Finally boarded the train. Darkness came fast, chow again. The usual, bread with a thin layer of butter & coffee. My lip had gone down, and I gobbled it as if I was starved. I was. Oh for a smoke! Finally managed to fall asleep. Awoke before I fell asleep, so it seemed, amid a big confusion. The train stopped, people were hurrying off and rushing for shelter. Sirens were sounding like mad all over. We were also taken to a shelter. When the people saw us they started gabbing in their Ger. lingo and pointed at us. We could hear the sound of the bombs, crashing like thunder. Evidently the R.A.F. was close by. After about an hour the "all clear" sounded. We were hurried aboard. The Jerry guards expected trouble from the civies. While proceeding to the train we were able to get a scoop of the results from the R.A.F. bombings. We could see flames lashing hungerly toward the sky for miles and miles. The section where the bombs fell was lit up like a beautiful afternoon. "Beauty and the Beast" Ah me! Lives being taken at wholesale prices and so it goes. Fell

asleep again for a few hours. With breakfast came bread and coffee. that was the last meal on the train. Hit our destination about mid-afternoon.
DEC. 6

Felt like I was about to bust, hungry, tired and dirty. We all had to strip again, and were thoroughly searched. They kept our flying clothes and put us in a cell all by our lonesome. It was a small room about 10 x 5 with a bed, two blankets and a stool. The bed was made of wood with straw spread on it for a mattress. Class huh! The room was made of wood also. There was one window with bars. Who would think of escaping with hospitality so good. That was home for God knows how long. Oh, yes, there was a guard outside each door. Before I had a chance to appreciate my cozy little room, I heard the clang of keys, my door screeched open, the guard said "Kum", and I followed him to a room where I found out I was to be interrogated. The Ger. seemed to be quite friendly, but that's his job, as it's news he's after. He spoke English in a broken accent, but was easy to understand. He said sit down, and then said what happened to my mug. I laughed, he knew the civies had beat me up. He then proceeded to ask me questions. Some I answered, some I didn't. I was then led to my room. Supper came, no, not bread and coffee, we had boiled potatoes and sauercrout, surprised, I almost keeled over. I ate every bite of it and was still starved. Lights went out, and being tired I went to sleep. It was very uncomfortable and cold. I didn't take my clothes off, and with both blankets, I was still cold, finally fell asleep, but after what seemed a few min. I awoke shivering. I started to pace the floor. I was going batty my first night there. Day break finally set in. Looked around the room and saw cross marks designating the no. of days the last guy was in this room. There were 8 of them. I sat on my bed and put my head in my hands and started to think, think, think. Relived my life. Thought of the days when I was a newsboy. I gambled most of the time. When I won I wouldn't sell papers, I'd have me some pie and milk and then go to the movies. I remember my grade school days, then good old high school. I couldn't wait to graduate, finally when I did, I wanted to take a P.G. course. I used to be a smooth dancer, thats all I needed because the women went for it in a big way. Parties and dates followed. I remember Pres. Roosevelt's invitation to the Army, Sept. 11, 1942. I was very happy about it. I only wish my best pal Marty Norton could have been with me. What a guy! I worshiped him. God bless his soul and take care of him. I remember when I told Mom I wouldn't marry until I got two years of traveling in. I wanted to see the world. My opportunity came upon being drafted. I traveled consistently and got to see about 40 of the states. I think of B. Speir constantly. I've thought of my wife thousands of times. The more I think of her, the more I love her. I thought of the great mistake I made of marrying her. You see Bob

Speir's wife was pregnant. I put us in their place. I thought of everything imaginable. All that in three nights and two days. I left there Dec. 9. We only went across the street where there was another camp outside of a town called Wenzler. There we went through the same procedure of stripping and being searched. I received my first big surprise there. We received a suitcase with all sorts of toilet articles donated by the Red Cross. We were issued an overcoat, gloves, knit cap, shoes, etc., sent by our army. We then proceeded to the shower room. They gave us 10 min. under the shower, that was the first one since I went down. I think I left about 121 lbs. behind me. After the shower we were fed. We had bread, butter, salmon, potatoes, and hot tea. The best chow thus far. It really hit the spot. We were assigned to our barracks. It was nice to put clean clothes on. The barracks room was quite large and held 24 to a room. Made a fire and went to bed for a few hours. The bed was again made of wooden structure with straw for a mattress, slept in pajamas, strictly class from now on. Enjoyed my best night's sleep. Awoke at 7:30, had chow at 8. Roll call at 9:15. Our C.O. was a Col. Jerries counted us & then our C.O. gave us the lowdown on whats cooking. Had an air raid about 11:30, marched down to the shelters until it was over. Heard stories that would make a person shiver. Another crew landed in Berlin, seven of them were beat up and then hung by the civies. The other two got away. They were the ones that told me about it. I then considered myself quite fortunate in getting only a beating. Another pilot landed on a shelter in Berlin. What a beating he got. His head was all bandaged, face was bruised in every spot. He was really messed up. Another crew hit the silk, the tail gunner was afraid to jump. He's now pushing up daisies. Sad part is that he was only 19—so it goes. The bomb., Red, and I shipped out Dec. 12. On our way to our new base we went through a few big German towns. They were all bombed to hell. Hanover, a big city, was a complete wreck. All we could see was people evacuating. Made it to our next dest. in record time-two days, usually takes a week. Arrived on the 24th. Had a shower right off the start, first since Dec. 9th. Had a bull session with the big wheels, Col. Kobresky, our C.O. and his assistants, a few majors. We were given our rooms and beds. The rooms held 24, was fairly large, with a stove, two tables, three benches, two cabinets. The room was damp and cold, so naturally we froze that night. This was to be our permanent home, *until*. Their system here was quite different. They formed compounds, with 12 in each compound. Meals were made by cooks selected by us from our own men. Naturally experience was a big factor. Food came from the Red Cross parcels and Jerry rations, when they gave them. After we got situated, things were okey dokey, cokey cola. I feel much better already, Xmas Day. Dinner, listen to this, we had plum pudding, delicious mashed potatoes, super duper tasting turkey, stuffing, bread, jam, coffee, candy and nuts. Excuse this million dollar smile, but boy do I feel good. I had to unfasten my belt. What a feeling! When supper came we were hardly hungry, so we didn't have much. Xmas night was spent in a galla of cheer and good feelings. Pass the drinks! Everybody sang Xmas carols until early morn. The boys may be down, but they are far from out.

By the way, when we were marching into camp, all the other veteran P.O.W.'s were running out to greet us and yelling "New Krieges". There were all sorts of questions like "How's the war progressing? When is it going to be over? Did little Abner get married? Who's in the Rose Bowl? What are the latest song hits?"

On the 26th we started to make our room look as good as possible. Made frying pans, ash trays, a calendar, fixed the stove and what not. We had light details, stood two formations each day, just a routine check to see if anyone escaped. Had two light meals a day and one big one. A small library for reading materials, cards for amusement, and a British Catholic Chaplain for church services.

A few days later the rest of the crew came in. Once again we were one big,happy family. If only Bob and Mac were with us. Came the New Year. Raised hell and on the min. sounded off with all sorts of noises. Sang till we were hoarse, finally hit the sack. Went to special mass. It was dedicated to us. Our resolutions, speedy victory and to our loved ones. Happy New Year my darling wife and may the future ones be better. Happy New Year Mom and Dad, family and everyone. Pass the drinks!

Rumors are that the Russians are going crazy making record drives. Famous saying out here is "Come on, Joe". Cook made up a delicious dinner, meat loaf with plenty of mashed potatoes. The wives of all the fellows here are going to have an advantage. They won't have much trouble satisfying us. If my wife can cook as good as Michael Gallo, I'll be happy and contented, yea man. Fellows raised hell again tonight.
JAN. 2nd

Almost caught up to date on my diary. Really cold. Feel sorry for the jokers on bottom bunks. Their bunks are always damp and wet. Can't be helped. Did some reading. most of my time is spent playing cards. Lost 20 packs of cigarettes. Better luck next time Mickey. Made a toaster, means our bread is toasted from now on. Washed my clothes this morning, reason for being so tired, ho hum. Slept sound as a baby last night. It was the best nights sleep I've had. Been having horrible dreams lately. Found a blanket of snow upon awakening. It looks beautiful. The scenery in Germany is beautiful.

A Capt. and 2nd Looey swung blows across the hall. The Looey got a gorgeous blinker. He had it coming. He also got his hand cut when he missed a swing and hit our window pane. It's quite warm out today.

Went for a trot with my buddy, Wally Xubic, around the camp. He's a good kid. From Brooklyn. Lost more cigarettes. More fun losing cig. A couple of guys lost them all. They are going in the laundry business, charging cig. to do laundry. So it goes! One guy went into the barber business. Uses a razor blade and comb, scalped four guys today. Slow but sure.

JAN. 4th

It drizzled last night, very nasty outside, mud up to our ankles. Think I'll stay in today. Joke, laugh! Finally hit for 40 packs. The deck must have been marked in my favor. New Krieges arrived. Went down Xmas Eve, tough, no kidding. Claim they are fighting like hell in Luxemburg. The kid brother is probably in the thick of it. God protect him. They claim the Russians are going great guns. Expect the European war to be over in a few months. Hope they are right. The warning lights just blinked. It's now 9:45, lights will be out in 15 min.

JAN. 5th

It really froze over night. Today the wind is howling. The camp is a regular ice capade. Bring on the ice skates. Saw a map, found out we were approx. 35 miles south of Switzerland, blast the luck. Could have been worse. Started a Pennsylvania Club. If it goes through, it will be a good deal. Kobesky is our Pres. He is from Oil City, a little way from Pitts. He's really a good joe. Lost 60 packs of cig. Cards must have been marked, *against me*. I think I'll stick to reading.

JAN. 6th

Bad news—heard the parcels will be cancelled. We'll just have to stretch what food we have stored up. Had a shower, spent exactly three min. under the shower, oh boy. Went for a trot with Wally. Think I'll do it daily if weather permits. Have a kid in our barracks that had it tough. He was roaming Germany at night for 55 days, eating turnips, pears, or whatever he could get his hands on. Weighed 90 lbs. when he was picked up. Both feet were frozen. He is alright now; always smiling and well liked by all. He was only 20, lived in Philly, name of Dobson.

JAN. 7th

Went to Mass, prayed for my wife, Mom, Dad, Johnny and rest of family. Prayed for all the boys and a speedy victory. Always feel good after attending church. It does something to me. Had a good dinner, our cook made bread pudding, was it ever good. Good old Mike has a magic touch. Weather is surprisingly wonderful. Snowed a little last night, just enough to sling snowballs. Getting old, ran around the camp a few times again and was puffing like an old dilapidated steam engine. Knocked off a good mystery, discovered the murderer easily. Down to my last cig., things are tough. Think of the civvies back home. Poor things, can't get them no how, so I hear. Visited one of the other compounds. Got a chance to see some of the veteran "krieges". Some of them have been here for years. They look like ghosts, pale and sickly, no vitamins, lack of food, staying indoors, I can readily see why. Hustle up, Joe! Played pinochle for fun. Didn't lose a game.

JAN. 8th

Food getting low. Jerry rations came in, turnips, cabbage, spuds & bread. Washed clothes. Mon. is wash day for me. Wally and I wash ours together. We have a pounder and a scrubbing board. We alternate in pounding and scrubbing. After washing I lay on my deck and spend the rest of the day reading.

JAN. 9th

Caught up to date on my diary. Had toast and coffee for breakfast, cheese sandwiches and tea for dinner. Last of the cheese. Soup with turnips, spuds and cabbage for supper. Hate turnips so I didn't eat mine. Gave them to Dobson, however I regretted it later in the evening (not the fact that I gave it to the kid), but I was starved. Oh, what I wouldn't do with a steak smothered with pork chops. Something to dream about anyway.

JAN 10th

A hash for dinner with t, c, and s. Ate it all. Turnips aren't too bad, ha, ha. Weather continued to be nice. Played football and enjoyed it immensely. Banged my right thumb, it's plenty sore and swollen like a balloon. Should sleep good tonight. Almost time for the lights to go out, guess I'll say my prayers and call it a day. I pray every night. Good night darling, I love you.

JAN. 11

Toast and coffee, last of the coffee. I took my good old time drinking it. I wanted to make it last. Slept good, but felt sore in all parts of my body. Oh, my broken back. Can't even do a knee bend. I guess I'll live. Stayed indoors except for the times when nature had to take its course. Helped peel the spuds for supper. Dinner was light, much too light, water to drink. Layed in bed and dreamed for the afternoon. I'm accustomed to that as I do it quite frequently. I'm always thinking about you, honey. Helps the time go by. Supper brought on hash with the usual. It was very good, only the darn turnips make a guy fart too much. They are hitting me from all angles, the aroma is terrible. Gallo just let loose and shook the room. Think I'll try and read a stinky story.

JAN 12th

A beautiful day. Still sore from the football game, but went out and played today. Got bruised up, but loved it. Played pinochle most of the afternoon. Had quite a discussion concerning sex. Nobody is bothered as far as having the pencil protrude mornings or during the day. However, "wet dreams" come up occasionally. I've had three since I've

been down. I'll knock on wood. May have one tonight.
JAN 13th
   Shower party. I always look forward to it. It makes a guy feel good. Toast and water for breakfast and dinner. The cook is working on bread pudding for tomorrow. I'm starved, had the same as usual for supper. New "krieges" arrived today. Slightly disgusted. Nothing to do but bat your brains playing cards. Time marches on.
JAN. 18th
   Received two good pieces of info, one I can't discuss, the other is that parcels are due. Happy day. It stopped snowing last night. It's really freezing weather. Everybody rejoiced the coming parcels. They sang for hours after the lights went out. Hope their not disappointed.
JAN. 20th
   Took a good shower this morning. Went to see *Andy Hardy Goes to College* this afternoon. Thought I was kidding yesterday, didn't you? It was sent from Switzerland. I dam near froze before the picture ended, but it was worth it. Got in a couple of parcels. We'll start eating good tomorrow. Hope they keep coming. Everyone feels sharp as a tack. Naturally everyone sang for hours after the lights went out.
JAN 22nd
   Barley for breakfast. Washed clothes this morning. New krieges came in last night. Claim the Russians are still going like hell. Lots of snow for amusement. Had a snow fight this afternoon, caught up on having my face washed, not willingly, of course. Made up a pool, costing each joker a fin. Closest date of when the war ends wins. One optimist joker picked Feb. 10. I'm for him, hope he wins. Latest date picked was June 18. The rest varied between those two dates. I picked March 28, Ann's birthday. More parcels came in. Good deal. Cook is making a special meal tomorrow. Mike is a swell guy. Knocked the evening off playing pinochle. Time for my beauty sleep.
JAN. 23
   Good news, can't discuss it. New krieges, consisting of 50 Yanks, 21 Limeys, some French and some Polish. We have some Russian prisoners around, but are forbidden to get acquainted with them. They do all the work around here. We sneak them cig. as often as possible. Started on a good western story "Range Hawk". Delicious meatloaf, with toast and coffee. Michael Gallo for pres., boy he sure has the knack for cooking good meals. Made a racket after lights went out. All at one time they'd sound off with a "Come on, Joe".
JAN. 24
   Had horrible dreams last night about goings on back in the states. They are due to the previous night's thoughts. More snow and plenty of fog. Can't see 10 ft. ahead of you. Had the usual roll call at 9:30, at 11:00

had another one, that was a surprise! Something cooking! Had the usual roll call this afternoon. Heard some good news. We have 1800 ground pounders heading this way. They had to evacuate their previous camp because the Russians were too close. They were located east of Berlin. We are 90 miles northwest of Berlin. Started a novena today. It's for a speedy victory. Plenty of noise after lights, "Come on, Joe"

JAN. 25

Slept like a log—for two hours, froze my balls off, coughed most of the night. Freezing today. Plenty of chatter from the boys about yesterday's news. Coughing like hell. Think I'll quit smoking. Went to confes-. sions. Received three more parcels. Heard they are supposed to stop coming next week. One of the guys made a map. Discussed Stalin's drives. Made the novena. Prayed for you dearest. Always do.

JAN. 28

Stayed awake until two this morning, coughing too much. Sunday mass at 1:00. Said a prayer for the ground pounders on the march, expect lots of them to kick the bucket before they get here what with the weather as it is. A fierce wind is blowing about 50 miles an hour, snow coming down in bushels. I haven't left my room except for roll calls and emergencies. you know nature's call to the crapper. Received some horse meat and spuds from the jerries. Cook is fixing up a cake for supper. One of the jokers is having a birthday. Happy birthday, Pop! Saw a gang of old Ger. civvies with rifles. Looks like the fall of Ger. is imminent. Should see you soon, my darling. Wow is it cold, my feet are freezing while writing. Killed the afternoon playing cards. When I leave this hole I should be a card shark, eh what? Cook made a soup and added the horse meat. It was sure good. Lets have more horse meat! He, haw! Had the cake about 8:00 with coffee. Made whipped cream and put happy birthday on it, with 35 candles. One of the jokers played a violin and we all joined in and sang. Boy, was old pop ever surprised. The wind is howling. It is still snowing. Made the novena this afternoon. I'm making up for the times I slipped up when I had the opportunities to go to church.

JAN. 29

Blue Monday, woke up with an awful headache, however my cold is much better, thank God. It was way below zero last night, and very cold today. Very light breakfast, coffee, period. Short on bread, expect more in today. Expect the arrival of those ground pounders any day now. Made a collection of smokes for them. The more I think of them the more I feel for them. May God protect them.

Letting my clothes go until next Mon. I declared a holiday today. Bread came in, had sandwiches for dinner. Quite a few of the jokers got sick lately. Must be the horse meat. Hasn't affected me in the least as yet.

Hope I haven't counted my chickens before they were hatched. Played cards for the evening.

JAN. 30

Feel good this morning, slightly restless last night. Had a delicious breakfast. Helped scrub the room this morning. It's really spic and span, nothing like a nice clean room, you know. Reminds you of "Home Sweet Home". A colonel from the other compound got himself in a jam. He was in a furious state of mind—told a Jerry what he thought of the Germans. He was put in solitair on bread and water. Rumors say his case was brought up before the big wheels and is now awaiting his sentence. Brace yourself—he's supposed to face the firing squad. Takes three months so Old Joe Stalin better not be delayed. "Come on, Joe!" Heard the Ger. are supposed to put all the Jews together, separate from the rest of us. They feel, as a last resort, to really make it rough on them. There is no question about it, the Ger. really hate the Jews. One of the old krieges said that the Ger. soap is made out of Jewish flesh, and so it goes! Supper was good, however everyone has been getting sick lately. About 50 guys from our barracks, 6 from our room, have been heaving their guts. Lots of them have the G "eyes", others are layed up with fevers and colds, too many coughing. We're in a bad state of affairs, eh, what? "Come on, Joe".

JAN. 31

Had horrible dreams last night. Shot off a terrific load. Forced to wash my clothes. Barley with raisins for breakfast. Heard some good rumors this morning. Kobesky's taking bets that the war ends by the end of Feb. Some of the guys who left Wenzler went to a camp near Brestler. They were supposed to have been liberated. If that's true they are on their way home. Happy journey, fellows. Dinner was eaten amid a big bull session, everybody talking about hitting the road. Jerries tried to put a stop to all the racket that's been going on, but no soap, we still sing and make noises of all sorts. Everybody is catching scabies that come from the lice formed on the filthy mattresses. Our room hasn't got them as yet. I've got athletes feet, I scratched until my feet bled last night. Nothing I can do except suffer with the damn thing and hope for the best. Received five onions this afternoon. Cut some up and put it in the soup for supper. It was delicious with a capital D. Scooped the goop with Wally after lights went out.

FEB. 1

Heard some real good news that came in from the German communique. They claim the Russians are 35 miles from Berlin and only 25 miles from Stetten. Stetten is only 60 miles from here. Water power is shut off completely. Also heard electricity was cut off. We will know for sure tonight. We are using water from melted snow for coffee. Plenty of chatter, Rah! Rah! Come on, Joe! Darkness set on, still no lights. Ate supper with light from a lamp we made. Naturally all we could do was shoot the malarky. Another rumor that came up was that we'll probably have to go on the march soon. Time will tell!

FEB. 3

Darkness came fast last night. Maybe we haven't paid our water & electric bill, but we sure eat steak occasionally. For supper we had fried horse meat with mashed spuds. Horse meat was like a steak to us. Rained most of the night. Put buckets outside and had them filled for the morning. Used it to wash, since we got a couple of buckets of clean water for coffee. I miss my shower, curses. Good news—heard we'll get parcels next week. Bad news—heard my ass will be in a jam if I get caught with this diary. Can hardly stop. Keep your fingers crossed, Mickey. Jerries put a joker in the brig for ten days on bread & water for not saluting a Ger. officer. Jerries are really pissed off with us. Kobesky warned us to smarten up for our own good and not to get overconfident. Don't take too much for granted. One of the jokers asked a Jerry how far the Ruskies were. He said they were so close it was foolish to put it in miles. We heard they were ten miles from Berlin. Some jokers think it will be over in a week, I give them the rest of this month. My personal opinion is that at this very moment a crisis had begun. We don't know whether those jerries guarding us will eventually point their machine guns at us and give us the works. I think we'll have paratroopers dropped here in camp for protection. I certainly hope so, because our lives are really at stake. Maybe we'll wake up one morning and find the gates open, the Jerries gone. I think we'll eventually have planes land here to transport us to France. Then I'll be relieved but honestly I won't be happy till I'm with my beloved. Then I hope to God I never have to leave her again, never-never-never. However, right now we'll have to sweat-sweat-sweat. Finished my mystery. I figured the murderer out again, as usual, ahem. Think I'll be a detective after the war.

FEB. 4

Had some awful dreams again. Saw Bob Speir in one of them. A most unusually beautiful day out today. Went to Mass, but the chaplain failed to show up, so we didn't have any. Water pipes are working, sure washed up good this morning. No sign of any Russian P.O.W. around. Don't know what happened to them. You can notice quite a tension in camp. Heard the Russians were on the outskirts of Berlin. Played some football and felt good to release some of this stiffness. Scratched my feet until they bled again last night. Can't help it.

Haven't heard anything about those ground pounders. Maybe the Russians caught up with them. Parcels came in. Will be handed out tomorrow. People are evacuating Barth. That's the town right outside of camp. No mail is to be sent out. No more is to come in. The big day is due! The Luftwaffe seems to be out in full strength today. Just witnessed four 109's dog-fighting. Wally and I went for a trot around the camp. Had a fiddle and banjo for entertainment tonight. Sang to our heart's content.

FEB. 5

Received 4 parcels. Good old parcels—as long as they keep coming, everything will be oaky doke cokey cola. Washed all my dirty clothes with Wally this morning. News continues to be good. Nature is calling, excuse please. With all this fluid we take in, we really keep the crapper busy. Heard the Col. and that other joker were pardoned and set free. The Col. aged, his hair turned gray, he lost a considerable amount of weight, what with being locked up on bread and water for a few months and then sweating his life on top of that.

FEB. 6

Nasty outside, mud up to our ankles. Been having roll call in our rooms the past few days. Played pinochle most of the morning. Started to make prune juice according to one who experienced it before, it's supposed to be powerful stuff. Looks like there is going to be a drunken bunch of G.I.'s here in a few days. Shoes and socks came in from the states. Received a pair of each. Lights went out about 8:00.

FEB. 7

Layed awake for a few hours and listened to the snores and farts of the other jokers. What a way to spend an evening. Oh, Franky boy, cut it out! Heard we have 1500 jokers in Barth, waiting to be here. They are not the ground pounders we expected. Will know more about them later. Still nasty outside, however, it's quite chilly and should freeze up. Sure hope so. A luscious dinner consisting of spuds with butter, cheese, spiced ham that comes with the parcel, toast & jam and a cracker with coffee. It was only a little of each but sure was delicious. Just heard the new krieges arrived in camp. Think I'll go down and take a scoop at them. God, what a pitiful-looking bunch of fellows. If their mothers saw them now, I swear they'd keel over and die. They were gunners, 1500 in all, and every one of them wounded, unshaven, pale, cheek bones protruding as if they were skeletons. Eyes of some of them bandaged, the rest all blood shot. Most of them limping, canes and crutches under their arms. They came in from Stetten. There were 10,000 in all, but being wounded they came over in boxcars. The rest are on the march. Two of them I recognized. I was stationed with them while in the states over a year ago. I corresponded with one of them. I had listed him as dead, because his mail was returned to me. I spoke with them for awhile. At the present time they are confined to their barracks. They have all been down from 6 months to 2 years. The more I think of the situation, the more I am grateful to God for caring for me. I consider myself very, very fortunate so far. Salmon loaf and spuds for supper. Lights went out about 6:30. We ate supper under the kriegy lamp. Had a little bull session and finally hit the hay.

FEB. 8

Awoke quite suddenly in the middle of the night and was in an awful daze. Arose, went to the crapper. It was a beautiful night with a nice breeze. On a few second intervals, the lights from the guards blazed across the camp and I fully realized I was a P.O.W. Big wheels had a meeting. We were told to conserve our water, because the Jerries are expected to cut our water supply. Tried to visit my friends, but they are still confined to their barracks. Medical Doc examined them and most of them are dosed up with crabs and lice. Had sandwiches and cocoa for dinner. Cocoa, mind you. It was sure good. Started to read "The Bishop's Jaegers" by Thorne Smith. "Where the hell is Joe?"

FEB. 9

Not allowed to mingle with the new krieges yet. Maybe tomorrow. Received three parcels. Just received writing materials. Two letters and three cards. Only allowed to send one piece of mail per 9 days. At that rate this F———— war will last another 45 days. Personally, I still have confidence that it will end this month. It would sure do my heart good to beat this mail home. All aboard, Harrisburg, Pittsburg, New York and Chicago, change trains and hot for good old Boise, Idaho. My imagination can sure play tricks on me. It sounds silly, but sure makes me feel good.

FEB. 10

Ate supper last night in darkness. No lights again. After supper, Wally and I had a bull session on what we are going to do when we hit the good old U.S.A. I'm going to show my wife the good part of the world, you know, back east. Let's see, I'll meet her in Chicago, spend a few days there, visit Bob Speir's wife in Detroit for a few days, hit for Brooklyn, I've never been there, then New York City, Newark, N.J., and then home sweet home, Scranton, Pa. That's what our session consisted of mostly. Finally hit the hay and received a surprise dream. Dreamt of a chick I went steady with back home. It was my first flame and it was also the first time I ever dreamed about her. Beats me, this dreaming business. Both my friends came in this morning to pay their respects. They looked much better after getting some good rest, a good feed, shower and shave. Talked about other friends of mine when we were together in Texas. They are all P.O.W., that is most of them. Some of them are kaput. They told me some ghastly stories. They have both been down over a year, and both spent a few months in the hosp. for wounds they received from 20 mm. We talked for hours until dinner came and we had to disperse our bull session. Dinner was light, sandwiches and coffee. Heard our mail will not go on. I sent my letter out regardless. Hope in some way it gets through. I still honestly believe I'll beat it home. *God I hope so.* Received four parcels, also cabbage and jam from Jerries. It is 3:50 and getting dark. We are going to have a jamboree tonight. Two guitars and a fiddle. Away beyond the hills of Idaho-Play, white boy, play, yea man!

FEB. 11

Had a full house in our room last night. The boys really beat it out. They were all Hill-billy numbers, but sure sweet music to my ears. Due to the hoe-down, we ate a late supper, about 8:30. Very nasty & muddy outside. I certainly hope it freezes soon. This is ideal weather for the Jerries and only helps prolong the war. Went to mass at 11:00, feel so good it's hard to put in words. Received a good bit of news from the chaplain. Started out by saying that he wanted us to attend mass regularly. He stressed to us about Ash Wed. and the coming Lent, to be sure to go to confessions and communion. Finished up by saying he expects us to leave here next month. Hello, New York, give my regards to Broadway. That's sweeter music to my ears than I had last night. Had a chat with Misk and Miller. We are going to make a little donation for Bob Speirs baby. It is so hard to believe he is kaput. Coal Ration cut down. All they have is a months coal supply for us. Maybe we won't need any more of their coal. Wally is attracting my attention. He is laughing to beat hell at the story, "Bishop's Jaegers". There is no question about it, it is a very witty novel. It is unusally quiet and very mysterious thus afternoon. Wonder if it is because it is Sunday. Then again it may be because of the racket we had last night, eh, what? Can't hold it any longer, so I guess I'll hit the crapper and get it out of my system. There, I feel much better. There is a couple of Jerry pilots putting on an exhibition. Reminds me, we had some Jerries, just kids that looked about 14 & 15, going out to practice mornings. When we first came here we had regular Jerry soldiers, then old men of 40, 50 and 60, now the kids. I guess they all left for the east front to show their talents to the Russians. Incidentally, the rumors about the Russians being on the outskirts of Berlin were a lot of malarky. Today I heard they were 23 miles from Big B. Straining my eyes in this darkness. Tomorrow is another day, and time is plenty free so will sign off.

FEB. 12

No lights again last night. After supper scooped the goop with Wally, then proceeded to listen to farts and snores. Once again it was quite a battle. When I awoke I could still hear the snores, so, the snorers won out over the farters. No news, just sweating. Everyone seems to be under a strain. Harsh words aren't rare, arguments galore, so it goes. Joe said he'd be in Big B. 30 days after the fall of Warsaw. He's got 5 days to go. Come on, Joe! Chow is running out. Toast and coffee for dinner. Went for a stroll with my buddy Joe. He was really shot up. Had 30 flak holes in him. Expected to have his right hand amputated but the fortune of God was with him. Claims he'll never be the same. Rough. Dam this war anyhow.

FEB. 15

Joe has three more days to go. Didn't sleep well last night. Very restless, thinking, going nuts, absolutely blowing my top. Tough Shitsky. Toast and crummy water for breakfast. Still no parcels, heard again there won't be any. Just been told that water and lights may be shut off for good. Also told that we should cut our bread thin because there was some glass found in it. Had a personal inspection by Kobesky this morning. The joint is getting military. Suddenly heard we may go on the march soon. More dam rumors and can't believe half of them.

FEB. 17

DRINK DRINK DRANK DRUNK last night, oh, my aching head. Sick as a dog this morning. Out of 25 men each and every one of us got drunk. What a kick to that stuff. Out of the 25, 20 of us heaved our guts. Went to bed with our clothes on. The room was a mess from p-u-ck. The odor was terrible, but we didn't give a dam. Opened the windows and slept like logs until roll call next morning. This is the first time I can honestly say I'm glad I'm sick from drinking in my life. We have a few planks we take out of the floor, we call it the bombay. Everybody took turns at it. What a joke. One joker fell off the top bunk and the only thing he got out of the fall was a laughing jag. We danced, sang and went crazy, and I'm not exaggerating when I say crazy. That stuff was really terrific! All in all we had one hell of a time!

FEB. 18

Went to Mass and heard a swell sermon. Formed a choir, they were very good, especially when they sang "Holy Mary" and "Mother Dear, Oh, Pray for Us." I prayed for you, my darling wife, Johnny, Mom, Dad, and family, all the boys on the front lines and for a speedy victory. Heard some good news, parcels came in. They are supposed to hand them out tomorrow. Sure hope that rumor is on the level. We're practically out of food and have been living on Jerry rations the past few days. When I get home I'm going to have you busy as a bee, honey, making me snacks. I'm going to eat at least 6 times a day, amen.

FEB. 19

My God, I almost froze last night. It will take all day to thaw me out. Fell in love with the stove. We are all gathered around it and scooping the goop. Jerries are making stew again, with horse meat this time. Happy day, we received two parcels, supposed to get four more this week. As a rule we are supposed to get one per person per week, but due to the fact that Jerry transportation is wrecked to hell our parcels haven't been coming in regularly. New krieges came in, they were 90 ground pounders that came in from near Stetten. Claim that the Russians are 3 miles from Stetten at one section. That's music to our ears. They told some rough stories. The RAF dropped a 400 pound bomb on one of their barracks, naturally all in that barracks were killed. On their way over they were put in box cars. With them, Jerries added their tanks and guns on other cars. Our fighters happened along and straffed them, killing 60. The fact remains that our lives are at peril at all times. They sent 65 to the other compounds, we took 25 of them. They were all hospital cases, under-nourished, weak and banged up.

FEB. 20

It was much warmer last night, slept very good. Had some pleasant dreams about you, honey, beautiful, you're a doll, and still the same old joker. Jerries loaded the cellar with spuds. Supposed to have enough for three weeks. Had some trouble this afternoon. One of the ground pounders demanded food, got nasty with the big wheels, and asked any one of them to step out and fight. He is up for court martial.

FEB. 21

That joker had his court case this morning. He was de-ranked from the grade of S/Sgt. to Pvt., was sent to the cooler for two weeks, and will have another c.m. when he hits the states. Personally I think that's going too far, but after all he is only an enlisted man. What was he fighting for? Beats me! It's a damn shame! We all have a meeting, only sgts., at 1:00. At the meeting we had a speech by the Col. and a few of the rations officers. The object of the meeting was to put a stop to wild rumors about the food rationing. Silly rumors going around that the wheels are getting more than we are. It is strickly blarney and comes from instigators trying to start trouble. My, but it is beautiful out today, the sun is shining and the sky is very clear. Went for a walk around the camp with Wally and took advantage of the beautiful weather.

FEB. 22

And it looks like another beautiful day coming up. We only have water for a few hrs. in the morning and then it is shut off for the rest of the day. Everybody is running around like mad scrubbing the room, shining their shoes, and shaving for an 11:00 inspection. Boy, everybody looks sharper than a razor. Inspection came off, the room got a merit. I go for the inspections here in a big way. Reminds me of the good old days in the states. Went for a walk again and heard one of the gunners took a swing at the major. His name is mud, his goose is cooked! There was a cat on the loose around here. A looey got hold of him. With some help from another looey they proceeded to kill it in this way. While one twisted its neck the other cut a vein. They skinned it, boiled it, and then fried it. Claim it tasted like rabbit.

FEB. 23

And another nice day as far as the weather is concerned. Cook is making up a cake. We have another joker cooking for us, A Russian from Chicago. He sure knows his stuff, but is very bull-headed. Jerries are making us another stew for today. That joker that made a pass at the major is now in the cooler on bread and water. Went for a walk to kill some time. Were told to prepare for a 50 mile hike. Jerries trans. is kaput. Where they can take us is beyond me, but it seems like they're determined not to let the Russians get us. The wounded may get to stay here. There was a carload of parcels sent here Jan. 9 but due to the fact that they couldn't get here, we heard the Ger. people got them. Plenty of horse meat in the soup for supper.

FEB. 24

And our few beautiful days are gone for awhile. Awoke this morning with the entire camp filled with water from last nights downpour. Oodles of mud, it's up to our ankles. Spent last night discussing our preparation for evacuation. Most of us don't think we'll leave here because there's nowhere they can take us, besides I think the Russians are cutting off all routes. Seems like they are surrounding us, so they say. Received a note book today. Will come in handy to continue my diary. Everyone running out of smokes. Sure would be nice to get a parcel from home or some mail. It takes about 6 months and I don't expect to be here that long.

FEB. 25

Went to Mass and received communion. Boys from the other compound put on a show for us this afternoon. My God, but it was good. Without a question of doubt, it would make a hit on Braodway. They had a band organized from professional players and boy were they terrific. Their version of "San Fernando Valley" had everybody dizzy. Good news poured in today. Bets are being made that this war will end within 30 days. Parcels are supposed to be given out tomorrow and the wheels wrote in complaints about Jerry rations, light and water situations and other minor riff-raffs to the legislatures or representatives of Switzerland. Seems like it brought results, because Jerries came through with more bread than usual, spuds, cheese, coffee and cabbage. Sure hope we start eating three meals a day again.

FEB. 26

God, how thin everybody looks, no belly, flat chest, even their "Pride and Joy" seems to have shrank. Soup with t.c.s. and horsemeat for supper. There is a beautiful moon out. Think I'll get romantic with my boy Wally. Chatter, it's strictly about food. How much we are going to eat and everything mentionable. So it goes.

**FEB. 27**

Every time I wake up my hands are still asleep, no feeling in them, same with my feet when I sit down. I presume that is from lack of vitamins. An idea of everyday happenings—Four jokers playing pinochle, a couple playing solitaire, most of them reading, the rest of them (the bright ones) debating the war situation. There are two sides, the optimists and the pessimists, and life goes on! Working on sidewalks to prevent ankle deep mud. Parcels were given out, 6 to each room, that's for this week. Heard they sent G.I. trucks to Switzerland to transport our parcels. Isn't that just too wonderful for words.

**FEB. 28**

Had quite a commotion last night. A plane buzzed the camp three times. Those that claim they saw it said it was a mosquito. We heard it fire over the Baltic, also heard plenty of flak beating like a drummer boy. Most of the older krieges hit the deck and tried to hide because they were afraid of being straffed, and so it goes. A big explosion sounded this afternoon, it shook every room in the camp. It evidently was a delayed action job. Went for a walk with Wally. It seemed that the whole camp was out. It reminded me of May Aug Park, when I used to play the Romeo and give a quail a break and take her for a stroll. Excuse me while I pat my back, all jokes aside there was a big gang out there.

**MARCH 1**

This is the month where the wind gets it's rep. Here in Ger. on the very first day it is howling to beat hell, with the slight drizzle it is really beastly weather. Inspection coming up so everyone is busy. Inspections came off, I got called down for not shaving. Gave me a funny feeling, but it was good. Jokers in here got a big bang out of it, because I don't have to shave but once a week. Of all in the room I have the honor of being the one that shaves the least. I take after my dad in that respect. Looks like we are going to have three meals today. Heard 7 trucks loaded with parcels came in. Dinner was extra delicious. The cook made up some eggs and bacon (from parcels) mixed it with spuds and added on the side we had diced turnips, and cabbage, wow! was that ever good. Thats the first taste of bacon and eggs I've had since I've been down. Just got some turnips and sugar from jerries. I got to love turnips. Rain changed to snow. What silly, dreadful weather. I'll take the good old Idaho sunshine! They've been sending most of the jerries from here to the east front. One of them was supposed to go but figured a way out. He committed suicide.

**MARCH 3**

Froze last night, no fire, because coal ration has been cut. It's surprising the way the cook can make some meals with what little he has.

Finally finished that mystery. Didn't guess the murderer, dam it. It was sure a good story. Broke the monotony and played some pinochle to kill time. I'm sick of the game. It's been an awful dragging long day today.

MARCH 4

Went to mass and heard a good sermon. The chaplain sure is lucky, he always gets a full house. The cards are with him, eh what? One of the boys passed out, revived him, he said he was okay, arose and keeled over again, revived him the second time, but to no avail, he keeled over again for the third time. I think he's going to the hospital. They said it was from being undernourished. No surprise to me, and so it goes! Went for a walk with Wally, gee but it's a nice day out. *If* only it was back home.

MARCH 6

Dream, Dream, Dream, that's all I did last night. The camp is all fixed up, no mud, finished making the walk out of bricks and had loud speakers installed. All set for the big game. Saw 8 of our fighters overhead today. I presume they were a scouting party for a raid, however didn't see any bombers. From now on we will eat at the mess hall. One meal a day unless parcels come in & then it will be two a day. No more coal for our rooms, its all going to the mess hall. That's bad and I'm not kidding. For cripes sake, "Come on, Joe!"

MARCH 7

Plenty of action last night. The noise of a gang of RAF planes awoke us about 11:30. We heard the crash of the bombs as they were released, heard the flack guns shooting at them, and also heard some Jerry planes firing at them when they went out to meet them, evidently they bombed Stettin again. Really froze up overnight. Awoke a few times because I was cold. Had two pieces of toast and coffee for b. Shortly after they came in and borrowed our table and benches for the mess hall. They will probably keep them now that we are going to eat over there. That's what we get for not paying our taxes, ha. We have a few hunks of coal we are trying to conserve and use only when necessary. Therefore the room is like an ice box and will be from now on. We have been busy all morning making benches and tables for our own convenience. The room looks funny so empty. Ate supper at the mess hall. Had an argument with a Jew bastard. If it happens again, one of us is going to wind up in the hospital. I despise him like poison.

MARCH 8

Very cold last night, hard to sleep. Had inspection and was prepared for it. Nix getting called down for not shaving again. Snowing outside, very pretty sighty and plenty coldy. Everybody bitter and hungry. All we get to eat is 5 slices of bread, stew and coffee each day. Sweated a line of about 150 in the cold and finally ate in a cold room standing up. We have had it. My fingers are so thin, my rings keep coming off. The identification bracelet is much too big for my wrist. Everyone is moaning and groaning about this cafeteria style. If they give to each room, rations for 24, we can get more out of it. Slept double last night with my bed mate and had four blankets instead of two. Our camp has been declared a battle zone and in accordance with the Geneva Conference, captains and on up will move out of here. Multy good rumors. More rumors about leaving for home soon. Can't be too soon for me.

MARCH 10

Awoke quote early, everyone gets up early because we are asleep about 9 every night. When we awoke we all discussed our dreams. The other jokers dreamt the war was over and they were in civvy clothes, and so it goes. Went for a shower at 8:30 this morning. Put on clean underclothes. Feels good to change. Now if I can get enough energy to wash the dirty clothes. Three jokers passed out at roll call this morning. Lack of food is starting to hit everyone but good. Read "Captains Courageous" in a few hrs., it stunk. The situation here is really snafu. No reading material, food is very low, no smokes, we live on rumors. I've got enough smokes to last. I passed some out, to those that didn't have any. The weather is nice and that's a good deal because of the shortage in coal. We had to take a typhoid shot this afternoon. It had a kick like a mule, and everyone is complaining of a sore arm. Had some Jerry music coming in over the loud speakers. Don't know what to do with myself.

MARCH 11

Went to mass and again I feel better. Expect to go to confessions this week. Must make my Easter duties by all means. Everyone talks about home and food, our two main subjects. Heard the lights will go on every night from now on. Also heard a Jerry remark that he expects the war to end any day now. My arm feels okay now. The loud speaker has been going all day with Jerry music. Wrote a letter to Mom (God Bless Her). Hope to beat it home. They started to ration 24 mens stew at one time. Much more convenient that way, no line to sweat & we eat it here in our room. The stew was very thin, ¾ of a bowl with bread. So ends today's meal. Rumor just came in that a notice was put up on the board in the other compound to be prepared to leave. That means we evacuate if true. Time will tell. Went for a walk after supper. Tired, weak, I really don't think I'd be able to go very far if we do have to leave. So it goes.

MARCH 12

Awoke at 6:30 and went on a spud cutting detail at 7:00. Ate some raw spuds while working. They tasted awful, but food is food. Finished up at 9:30 and had my usual few pieces of toast and coffee. God, when I think of the set-up I had at the base, slept till noon, except when I flew, and then arose at 3:30 in the morning. Had a hot delicious dinner, went to a few classes and then ate an extra delicious supper. Spent my evenings at the Red Cross club on the base, eating snacks and making money playing pinochle until 11:00. What could be sweeter. Was actually getting fat, weighed 153, now approx. 130 and will probably weight less in time to come. So it goes! Had lights last night. Dat iss good! Had an air raid this afternoon. Seemed like all of the 8th was out. Could hear the engines buzzing for hrs. Had our first death here. A Lt. died of a blood disease. Plenty of arguments in the barracks today. That Jew bastard was almost set on his ass by one of the jokers. It won't be long, he will get it.

MARCH 13

Awoke at 6:30 again and went on a turnip detail this time. Filled myself up with raw turnips. They were much better than the spuds. Everybody is busy making field packs to make our march more convenient. It seems like the rumor about marching is true. I hope not, but time will tell. Sick as a dog. Have the chills, layed down, but couldn't sleep. Wally and I aren't on speaking terms. Why? I honestly don't know, and don't intend to ask. Have a dreadful headache, feel very miserable. Think I'll hit the hay early.

MARCH 14

Feel much better today, thank God. They put up a list of names of all whose cablegrams went through when they sent them Dec. 23. Mine was on it. Today they got in an exceedingly large amt. of mail. I may possibly have one, due to the cable. It will take a week to ten days before it's handed out, because it has to be censored by the Jerries. I'm keeping my fingers crossed. Started to read "The Man Who Loved Lions", it's a mystery and should be good. Mysteries are my favorites. Had quite a nice bowl of pudding. It sure hit the spot but tasted like more. We are always hungry here. For Pete's sake, Come on, Joe!—and I mean on the double.

MARCH 15

Had American records coming over the loud speaker last night. They were all good but when they played "I Walk Alone" I thought I'd go crazy, I was utterly speechless, dazed and froze while Dinah Shore sang it. You'd have to pierce the heart to understand exactly how I felt, honey. Another day started peeling turnips most of the morning and filled up on them. They were sweet and exceptionally good. It is a marvelous day out. Everybody is walking around. Our windows are wide open for the first time. Had three pieces of toast at 6:00 and then went for a walk. Hear we are having oatmeal for tomorrow's b. That's a good deal.

MARCH 16

No news, no rumors. Something's cooking. Getting more discouraged, seems like I'm here to stay. Think I'll file for my citizenship papers, no joke, everyone keeps dreaming about home, can't be helped.

Sure wish they would discontinue morning roll calls so we could sleep until 11:00. The days are longer.

MARCH 17

Here it is Sat. again. The days keep rolling by. The strain keeps getting worse. Carried a guy out on a stretcher this morning. Wonder if it could be food, you know, eating too much, ha. Joke. A couple of Looey's had it out in our barracks. They are both walking around with a beautiful blinker. It broke the monotony, and was a good show while it lasted. 15,000 tons of spuds came in. That is swell and is supposed to last one month. Looks like some of the jokers in our room are due for a nervous breakdown. One can't ask them a question without a sarcastic reply in return. I'm keeping my nose clean and devote most of my time to reading. They are also forming awful habits—for instance, continually shaking their heads, biting the fingernails, making silly motions and noises. It is really awful, but so it goes!

MARCH 23

The boys started to plant yesterday. Personally I don't think they'll be here to get any benefit out of it, but it doesn't hurt to play it safe, besides we have the time to spare. One of the jokers in the next room has a bad dose of crabs. I feel for him. He had to shave every bit of hair on him. His room had to have all their clothes deloused. I only hope he gets over it soon, and that it doesn't spread. Went to a musical entertainment given by the other compound. Boy were they ever good. I thought the drummer was going to let the bats fly out of his belfry, when they gave out with "St. Looey Blues". I'd give anything to know how to play a trumpet. I'm going to (with God's help) give my little brats an opportunity to have what I wanted and couldn't get. They had a chorus that sang "Begin the Beguine". They had three vocalists singing. Two of them would put "the voice" to shame. Really that's not exaggerating. They sang a few nos. that were written by one of the krieges here, that I expect to see on the hit parade some day. All in all it was a very good show and all I can say is best of luck to them all. I only hope they get together when they are back home, and I think they will. For supper we had mashed spuds with toast and coffee. That's the first time in over a month that we had three meals. It sure takes the strain off everyone and makes one feel good. 'Twas a wonderful day.

MARCH 24

We had 35 new krieges come in. When asked as to when the war will end, one joker looked at his watch and said, "Any minute." They came down in a raid over Big B. last Sunday. As for parcels we are supposed to get one per four men for Easter. Big ball game going on, and quite a crowd. Started to read "Maltese Falcon". I was so engrossed with it that I couldn't pry myself from finishing it. Sat out in the sun and knocked it off in a few hrs. It was the best book I've read thus far. Jerries came in and took a list of names of those who couldn't walk. It looks like an evacuation is inevitable, but once again time will tell. Played a few games of pinochle and hit the hay.

MARCH 26

Yesterday was Palm Sunday, today is the first day of Holy Week. I expect I'll go to mass all week. Smokes are kaput, however I have two cartons, but I'm saving them in case we hit the road. The chatter is strictly about moving. Famous sayings are, "Are you all set to leave?" and "Do you have your bag packed?". Just heard a couple of jokers tried to escape a week ago. They got over the barbed wire fence and into the woods, but after the Jerries sent their dogs out, they were recaptured. They weren't harmed and got a week in the cooler. They are foolish for trying to make a break, but after spending a few months in a hole like this, a guy is apt to do anything. Played some softball, our team won 3-1, but not through my fault. I couldn't hit it past the pitcher. One of the jokers passed out in this afternoon's formation. He straightened up like an ironing board and fell flat on his kisser, wow!

MARCH 27

Had a roll call at 8:15 and received a pleasant suprise out there. Col. Kobesky made an announcement that Red Cross parcels were in & we'd get a quarter of a parcel per man this afternoon. Everyone let out a cheer or a whistle that could be heard for miles. Barley for b. and then went to mass. Rumors about the war situation are multy, multy good. Our morale is sky high. In all reality we underestimated the Jerries strength as the big shots found out, but at the present time, the end could come overnight. With dinner came a full bowl of stew, two pieces of toast, and coffee. I had an extra treat in my stew, *worms*, I threw them out and nonchalantly proceeded with my eating.

MARCH 28

Went to mass and then went over for a shower. Happy Day!! Happy Day!! 10,000 more parcels came in. We are supposed to get 18 more parcels this week. Wow! We start eating good again, thank God. Multy good war news. Everyone is jubilant and running around like mad. Move over, honey, I'm a coming. By the way, I lost two fingernails while taking a shower. They just completely fell off.

MARCH 29

There are 40,000 parcels in. Enough for full rations for 5 weeks and more coming. We are looking forward to Easter Day. We are sure going to eat like kings that day. Everyone is happier than words can express. Plenty of smokes, no hard feelings, and arguments have ceased. Plenty of singing tonight.

**MARCH 30**

The birds are chirping like mad. There wasn't any mass this morning. This is the one day in the year that mass is disbanded. However there were prayers said & the kissing of the cross. The chaplain read the passions of our Lord and clearly discussed the sufferings of Christ. Also stated plainly and clearly what we owe our Lord. It was really very touching and gave one a feeling he has never had before. Everyone is busy as a bee making cakes, pies, fudge, etc. for Easter. Starting Sun. we will be eating three meals a day, I mean square meals. I don't think we will be hungry from now on. Had two nice-sized salmon paddies with gravy, two cups of coffee, two slices of toast with jam, peanut butter and cheese. It was really filling. I think I'll start unbuckling my belt in a few days. Man alive, I sure hope so! I lost over 30 lbs. since I've been down. The same goes for the majority of jokers here. We all look like broomsticks.

**MARCH 31**

After b. went to mass and heard a very nice sermon. Cakes are starting to pour in the mess hall to be cooked. All sizes and shapes. Two jokers brought in a cake and looked like pall bearers. They had it on a bench, it was so large it took two of them to scoop it over. We made an enormous one. Had 35 new krieges come in today. They went down the 24th of March. All the Jerries did was ask them their name, rank and serial no. They were all from Eng. Claim it will be over in 6 weeks at the latest. The barber is busy as hell giving Easter haircuts. Everyone is very happy. They are all getting ready for tomorrow, shaving, shining their shoes, etc. Plenty of noise and songs.

**APRIL 1**

Easter Sunday. Happy Easter my dearest wife. Had quite a commotion at roll call. A bunch of jokers fell out with black sweaters with a big letter designating "Happy Easter". The bugler played "Easter Parade"— we cheered and whistled!!!! It was sure nice. Went to mass at 11:00 and heard a beautiful mass. Everyone is running around like mad showing off their cakes. New krieges came in. Since there wasn't any food in the mess hall and parcels are stored in the warehouse, the col. asked that we invite one in each room for supper. Multy parcels came in. There are now 90,000 parcels in. Can you imagine that? It's unbelievable. I'd go nuts trying to describe the actions of all the jokers here. At the present time everything is wonderful. Good war news keeps pouring in. Haven't mentioned anything about today's meals because I'm making out a menu I expect to frame. However I'll say a little about supper. About 15 min. before chow time the cooks kicked us out so they could set the table. Went out and washed up spic and span. Came in and went to our respective places, stood there while one of us said a prayer, then sat down and dug in. After eating, we all had to unbuckle our belts and honestly couldn't get up out of our seats. We scooped the goop with our guest. He told us about the false alarm they had in good old New York about the war being over. I can just picture it. Felt sick so I went for a walk. The latrine is jammed with fellows who have the G.I.'s. After an hr. I felt better and came back. Everyone is farting, burping and laughing. That's a good sign. Plenty of chatter and good feelings. Before—at one time, most of the fellows thought the best way to die was at the time when he was getting a thrill. No, not a ride on the merry-go-round, but when he was having his "pride and joy" in some quiff's "snatch"— However, now—they think the best way to die is from eating too much. Loads of us got sick, but no complaints what-so-ever. Good joke—When the cook asked if we wanted a snack before hitting the sack, we all yelled "Nix, nix, nix". All in all, it was one marvelous day, thank God.

APRIL 4

The mess hall in the next compound burned down. They lost quite a bit of Jerry bread, that hurts, their bowls, cups and silverware, all their instruments, musical, and other things. That's really tough luck. So it goes! Have to go! It's like a dance hall anymore. I remember when it was empty at all times, now there is always a standing line. Just heard Max Schmelling is dining at our mess hall. Everyone went over to get a gander at him. Wow, but he is big. Has paws on him like an elephant. He was in civies. They say he lost a leg. I thought he was killed. Jerry music screaming blue murder.

APRIL 6

Slept well again. Had a "wet dream", honey, and you are to blame. I dreamed about you and I, scooping the goop at a card party, with a lot of friends and I gave you the nod and we took a brody. All I did was embrace you and I had it. After b. I went out and threw the ball around. We have a game scheduled for 6:30 tonight. Just heard we are having an inspection tomorrow. Had a multy big supper. We should knock the ball all over the field tonight, eh, what? The cook, Joe Miller, is our manager. He is a good boy, besides being from Pennsy. He promised us a treat tonight if we win. That's reason enough, ha, win—we moidered the bums. It was a riot! More noise than the Jerries are making on the front lines. Final score-Sgts. 16, Officers 7. With the snack came cookies with grape jam and two cups of super delicious malt. Another "wet dream" coming up, Mickey.

APRIL 7

Awoke at 6:30 and had b. at 6:45. Reason for getting up so early is because we have to scrub the windows, floor and tables for the big show. It is a lot of nonsense as far as I am concerned. The Col. inspected and gave us the okay slip. Multy good war news. The way everyone is running around, you'd think it was over already. 10,000 letters came in. God, I hope I get one from you, honey. Make it two, one from you and one from home. Cook is making a cake for tomorrow. We get a snack if we win, half of the cake. It is swell out. I'm surprised at the beautiful weather here in Ger. this time of the year. Went out and played ball—naturally we won—All the boys really knocked the apple all over the lot with the exception of me, dam it. Final score 11-8. Lots of chatter about the game. Bring on the snack!

APRIL 8

Notice my fingernails are growing back in. Having trouble with my right ear. It is constantly ringing. More new krieges came in. I knew one of them from Lincoln, Neb. We both worked in the mail room there. What a joke! "Kreigyland", where you meet your friends and relatives. Went to mass. The chaplain complained about the drop in attendance during weekly masses. Multy good war news. We have a map in our room and everytime we turn our heads it is advanced. "Dat is goot", yah?

APRIL 9

When we hit the sack last night, one of the jokers said there was a prowler underneath the barracks. All you could hear was shouts—"Piss on the son-of-a-bitch". Rough talk, eh, what? Latest dope from new kriegys, Song hits-"Accentuate the Positive, Eliminate the Negative" and "You Can't Fence Me In". Best movie, "Here Come the Waves", with Betty Hutton and Bing Crosby. Heard Errol Flynn is in a jam again. "Stars and Stripes", a newspaper we had at the base, claims the war will be over April 15. And, oh yes, Lil Abner is still free, and playing "hard to get". Poor Daisy Mae. Spuds came in. That is a good lick. I love them. Got a game on this evening with the "big wheels". Made a check on all who need blouses and ties this afternoon. Col. orders everyone to put their rank on. Maybe the war is already over.

APRIL 10

Col. announced another inspection this afternoon, curses. The protective powers from Switzerland are coming in at noon time. They will accompany the Col. at inspection. There seems to be an epidemic of sickness here. Everyone is heaving their guts, coughing and whatnot. Many of them are restricted to their rooms. So it goes! Organized an American and National League team. There are ten men from each barracks. I made the team from our barracks. Practiced this afternoon.

APRIL 12

Went for a shower immed. after roll call. Played this morning and won a well played ball game 2-1. Our pitcher was really on the ball. Ordered to high ball officers and address them as Sir. Moan, I'll wind up taking a bust in a P.O.W. camp. That will sure take the cake with the icing. Wrote a letter to mom. It is sure sentimental. I mentioned a little about everyone in the family. Also put in that I'd be home to read it to them. I honestly meant everything I said, and it is strictly straight from the heart, Amen.

APRIL 13

And Friday at that. Hope we don't hit any bad news on this supposedly unlucky day. Fried bread with syrup for b., coffee to drink. I feel miserable, headache, and chills, make me feel like an old man. Some really terrible news just came in. According to Jerry rumors, Pres. Roosevelt died. It isn't exactly a surprise, because he's been in poor health a long time. I sure hope it is propaganda. We are all talking about it and from one and all he sure takes the prize. He was one good joker, and so it goes! Chatter is strictly about the big boy. Too bad he couldn't see victory day.

APRIL 14

Plenty of activity about 1:00 this morning. Heard a gang of planes, awoke and saw white flares being dropped not too far from us. The flares lit up the town and made it look like broad daylight. Then saw big flashes made from the bombs. It was one gorgeous sight and reminded me of fire works on the 4th of July at Lake Areal. Everyone happy and talking about going home. According to Jerry news, Simpson is only approx. 75 miles from here. I'm so excited I can hardly write. American records really giving out with jazz. Sounds terrific!

APRIL 16

Sick as a dog last night, didn't get a wink of sleep. Arose twice to heave my guts, four times to take a shissen. What's wrong? Everything, stomach pains that made me groan all night, had the chills and froze. Morning come, had a terrible headache. Everyone seems to be sick, God it is really awful. Gave my b. away and stayed in bed till dinner. New krieges keep pouring in. We are over our quota and have to park them out in the hall, that is their sleeping quarters. Nothing much in war news. What in hell is holding those Russians up? Forgot to mention that during yesterday afternoon's roll call the Col. had us in a brace for one minute in honor of our Pres. It was so quiet you could hear a pin drop, I'll never forget it.

APRIL 17

Feel much better, thank God. I hear the reason everyone has been ill lately, is because of moldy bread. Believe they are evacuating the airport that is close by. Expect our fighters to strafe it sometime this week. Played ball and lost 5-0. They were just too good for us. Played cards all afternoon. Have multy cig. and give many out to whom ever needs them.

APRIL 20

Didn't get to eat b. Right after roll call the search party came around, about a doz. Jerries. They have it every week and alternate at barracks. One man is left in each room and they then proceed by rifling thru our suitcases, mattresses, and the complete room. They take most everything they want. They finally finished at 1:00. Naturally we were all starved and immediately had dinner. Was tired so I hit the sack for a few hrs. Upon awakening, noticed about 10 other jokers dead to the world. That is the first time I ever noticed so many of them all fagged since I've been here. Wrote a letter to you, my dearest and once again I say I expect to beat it home.

APRIL 21

Expected to be out of here this month but now I doubt it. Just heard some sad sad news. P.O.W.'s that were being evacuated were straffed by our pilots. Oil tanks that were attached to their train were set on fire and the flames started to hit them. Naturally they tried to make a break for protection. As they did, the Jerries machine-gunned them. Out of 450, only 4 survived. They were ground pounders, para-troopers and air corps men. So it goes! We played the wheels in a league game tonight. Tomorrow the all star team plays an exhibition game. We have 14 men on the all star team. Two short stops. My competitor is a Capt. and will probably start. Forgetting rank, he's plenty good. I do hope I get to play a few innings anyway. At afternoon roll call we heard a constant rumbling quite clearly. Rumors have it, that it is the Russians heavy artillery playing cat and mouse with Stettin. Multy good news just came out from Jerries. The heat is on! The Russians are breaking through all lines. Nix stopping them now. Had salmon loaf and mashed spuds with coffee for supper. Went out and played a good game to beat the wheels 5-3.

APRIL 23

Had pre-mixed cereal with multy bugs for b. It was well boiled and couldn't harm us, so everyone said, however, I picked them out. Played cards most of the morning. Jerry news just came out with, street fighting in suburbs of Berlin. Map keeps changing. Wow, my stomach sure hurts. Wonder if those crummy bugs are playing ball inside me. Parcels just came in. They were Canadian parcels and according to the hot rocks, they exceed our American parcels. Nix mail in this room, dam it. Stomach pains went away after a few farts. Got some clippers and scissors in the barracks. Think I'll sign off and get me scalped. Got what we call a whiffle, all but ¼ of an in. cut off. Plenty of compliments came with it, and every one following suit. They tell me I look 5 years younger. Yea, hon, your hubby is still a good-looking joker, ahem, ha ha. Actually I believe I am going around the bend. So it goes! Started a calisthenics program for those who are eager. I get all I want playing ball occassionally and during morning roll calls.

APRIL 24

Shot a terrific load last night. Don't even remember what I dreamt about. Better get home soon, Mick. Funny, but we are all having them quite frequently lately. Water is getting scarce, I'd better wash my body before it is completely shut off. More news came in. According to the map, Berlin is cut completely in half. "Dat iss Goot!" Spent the afternoon watching the wheels from our compound and the wheels from the other compound playing ball. It was strictly a comedy and turned out a basketball score 11-10 in favor of our wheels. In mention to a return engagement, they figure they won't be here. Are they joking? I wonder. Turned chilly so I didn't wash.

APRIL 26

Today seems to be rumor day. I'll give out what I heard so far—Paratroopers and gliders are supposed to drop in the next few days. A new gov. is supposed to be set up. Jerry guards are restricted from Barth, only a few miles from here. A flak school located a few miles south of here is supposed to have evacuated. Heard Hitler was killed. Horse meat came in. Had it fried for supper with spuds and gravy. It was tender and just like steak. The best meal we have had so far.

APRIL 27

Plenty of activity last night. Didn't get much sleep. Sirens kept whaling all night. Had three air raids close by. Watched the ball game between the wheels and bks. 4. Back home we have rain to call the games off but out here it takes air raids. Had three more. Game started at 9:00 and finished at 12:30. Wheels won 3-1. That is 7 air raids within 24 hrs. and probably still more to come.

APRIL 28

More activity last night. Obviously the Reds are playing hell with the Krauts. Had fried spuds with salt, pepper, and butter for b. and plenty of them. Three more wagon loads came into the mess hall. All the rooms over there are filled with them. Probably get plenty more today. Fuel situation is kaput. Tearing flooring and boards from barracks for fire. Big inspections coming off. Everyone is busy shining shoes, shaving, scrubbing the room etc. The inspections were personal and in open ranks. What a joke! Everyone laughed and thought it very childish. Just heard a big rumble that shook all the barracks. We all ran out to see if we could see its results.

APRIL 30

Jerries claim Russians are only 40 miles from here. They evacuated Russian P.O.W.s from here today. BOOM! Just heard four terrific explosions in succession. The Jerries are dynamiting the flak school and their airport. Working like hell digging trenches. With what? Klem cans, knives, sticks, our fingers, etc. Civilians evacuating Barth. Where they can go is beyond me, only God knows. The explosions are terrific and plentiful, makes the barracks shake like hell. Counted 16 190's flying overhead. Evidently they are headed for the east fronts. Boy, they haven't far to go. Everybody is worried about being straffed. Painting in large print P.O.W. on all the barracks in white. BOOM! My God, they just let loose with one that shook the barracks and shattered some of the windows. The wood from the explosion poured all over the compound. Strict orders that we have a water reserve on hand. Have our brew barrel and every pitcher filled. Finished our trenches. I'm sure stiff all over.

MAY 1

Hap, hap, happy day! Packing my grip. Taking a trip, down Idaho way. Yea, man. Everybody going mad. Jerries left camp at 3:00 this morning. South compound played "The Star Spangled Banner" at 4:30. We had quite a commotion. We had our men take posts in the towers. The Jerries also left their machine guns in the towers. Haven't slept since, can't sleep. Expect to be out of here in a few days. Had some more new krieges come in last night. When they came thru Barth the civilians cheered them. Most of them were Limeys who have been down 3-4-5 years. One of them ate b. with us. He told us his story. He had been a prisoner 4½ yrs, 37 months were spent in solitaire. He pulled his drawers down and showed us where he was cut by a razor from SS men. On both legs right on his thigh were cuts about 15 inches long. Poor guy was a mess, nervous, smoked cigarette after cigarette and drank 5 cups of coffee in a few min. So it goes! Have all our parcels in our room, plenty for the week. Water is kaput. On hand, enough for three days. Bread enough for eight days. Have been hearing BBC broadcasts all day. Everyone is walking around with a feeling that can't be expressed. It is simply unbelievable. The Russians are only 20 miles away. Possibly expect them tonight, tomorrow for sure. The Burg-a-master of Barth surrendered the town to our C.O. here. Our men are riding motorcycles and whatever vehicles were left. Everything is in our hands. We have our own M.P.'s formed. What a day, the 1st of May. Too much excitement around to continue writing.

MAY 2

We were informed that the Russians did enter Barth, at 10:20. We cheered and cheered. Went mad in our rooms. A little later the radio announced Hitler being dead and we all cheered again. Expect to be out of here in a few days. Plenty of Russians in Barth. They didn't know we were here and fired upon us. We thought we had had it, but before anyone was hurt we contacted them. Our C.O., Col. Zemke got in contact with a Russian Col. and was given full control of Barth. The Col. then moved on, another Russian Col. came and told us to hit the road. We were all packed and ready to leave, but the misunderstanding was straightened out. The Russian Col. came down and apologized, so we stay. We tore down the fence and towers, ramsacked the Jerries quarters, and warehouses and started a collection of souveniers. Just heard we are allowed to go into Barth, so naturally will have to continue tomorrow. Before I sign off I'd better tell about the most ghastly thing I've ever seen. Three women and two infants all shot thru the brain. God, it was horrible! Undoubtedly it was suicide from fear of the Russians, so it goes!

MAY 3

Can't believe I've been to Barth of my own free will. Had quite a time. There were multy Russians there and I now can understand why it was so long before they arrived here. They came by wagon and horse, a few G.I. trucks and jeeps that were sure a sight for sore eyes. They had everything mentionable, tanks, cannons, machine guns, hand grenades, musical instruments, whiskey, food, etc. They were all drunker than hoot owls. I was surprised they didn't cause trouble. Rugged, they looked strong as an ox, and had paws like gorillas. With them were their own women, kids that looked about 12 to 15 yrs. old with medals galore, old men that looked to be 60 to 65. I can easily understand why they are winning this war. My Austrian lingo came in handy. I spoke and shook hands with many of them. We all shook hands, embraced, and saluted at all times. The Americans gave them multy cigarettes and soap. I talked them out of cigars and brandy. They were giving it to us all. There were quite a few civilian Germans around, but surprisingly enough, they weren't harmed. Naturally we all came back staggering. G.I.'s came back with horses, cars, motorcycles, bicycles and what not. Bad comes with the good. There were a few of our boys and Russians killed by booby traps, so it goes! Today we are restricted from Barth and are allowed around the area. Had a speech from Zemke and once again we were warned to be careful, because the Russians didn't know we were here. Can't tell whether we are friend or foe, because they are stinking from drinking. They shoot first and ask questions later, so it goes! Latest news that came out—We may possibly have to stay here 10 days. No worry as far as food, water and fuel is concerned. The Russians gave us plenty of meat, and getting us fuel and water from Barth. It was confirmed that Hitler and Goebels committed suicide. Berlin fell yesterday and all of Italy gave in. Heard Mussolini was killed. Guess we will see the end of the war here. Got me a job as interpreter with the Russians. Am seriously thinking of going to Poland. All in all there is plenty of excitement. The only thing left here are the barracks. They found the bodies of 85 Russian P.O.W.'s that were killed by the Jerries before they left here. Plenty of rifle fire. Jerry snipers are still around.

MAY 4

Had a hoe down last night. A fiddle and two guitars, played and sang until midnight, then scooped the goop. Looks like we are back in the army again. All moaning why we don't fly out. Seems our wheels are off the ball. The room is going mad. Been eating all day, sick as a dog. Strict orders are to stay around the camp area. Been scooping the goop with the Russians all afternoon. Got me some Russian money. Heard many stories about the atrocities the Jerries pulled while invading Poland and Russia. I asked about it out of curiosity and they told me. Nix writing it, it was too horrible. Talking about horror, I saw something worse than the bodies of those 5 women I mentioned. They had a concentration camp that held Polish, Russian, Siberian and other races of women. They were all in the nude and dead from starvation. There is more to it but it is too hard to write. So it goes.

MAY 5

Plenty of G.I.'s hitting the road of their own accord. They were forbidden to do so, but I can hardly blame them. If I was single, I think I would have joined them. Had a Russian general and a few other big wheels pay us a visit. Speeches and cheers followed. The General gave our Col. orders. He couldn't understand why we weren't mourning the death of our Pres. He gave us an order to wear a black band on our left arm. Personally, I think our big cheeses have their heads up and locked. The Russians were also peeved to see the towers and wire fence still up when they arrived. It was their orders to tear them down—And so it goes! Been eating too much. Really sick as a dog. Just heard that the airport is all fixed and ready to go. Col. made an announcement and said in two days we'll be off for the races. Seems to me I've heard that song before. More G.I.'s taking off. The rest of us are sweating. Been hearing the latest song hits, and we sleep here again tonight.

MAY 6

Everybody restless, taking off by the hundreds. Nix excitement this morning, just waiting, waiting, sweating. After dinner I got onery, talked to Wally and both decided to sneak into Barth to get drunk. Four other jokers wanted to come. We started off and discovered more M.P.'s than we could count to get by. When they stopped us, I started to talk Russian and shook hands with the M.P., saying, Americansky. We got by and into town we went. It was as dry as the state of Texas. We scooped the goop with the Russians guarding the town. They were very friendly. We spent the afternoon riding with a couple of them in a horse and buggy. Finally came back with two turkeys and toothpaste. I feel guilty as hell for not going to church this morning. I had no reason for missing. Had a couple of jokers clean the turkeys for tomorrow night. Word just came in saying 2,000 jokers hit the road. Rumors have it that we have to spend 3 more weeks of waiting. They are all going batty. We also heard the war is over. Tomorrow we are hitting for another section where we heard there was plenty of vodka. Plenty of food, water, and music, but everyone is moaning and crying, "They want to go home."

MAY 7

Awoke at 10:30, had b. & took off. Just got back and told the jokers our experiences. I think we covered about 20 miles today. Visited every refugee camp around. Some of them were really filthy. There were French, Italian, Polish, Russian men, women and children. Talked to many Russian soldiers. They gave us anythIng we wanted. Insisted that we take cows back, but we said nix. Nix whiskey or eggs, there just wasn't any. All in all we had one hell of a time. Once again I heard the war has ended. Tomorrow and Wed. are supposed to be days of celebration. Zemke said he will get us out of here if he possibly can. We're supposed to be first priority, ha. Had the turkey with dressing, gravy, and spuds for supper and plenty of it. Tomorrow we hit another section. By the way, if we're caught it's the cooler, but I can't sit still. I love adventure and excitement. More fun roaming Germany, and we sleep here again. Goodnight, honey, I sure love you loads-My buddies can prove it.

MAY 8

Seems very quiet. Everyone uneasy. I'd go nuts if I didn't go sightseeing. Today we covered another section of town. Had loads of fun. Picked up more souveniers. Have quite a bit of paper money. As usual scooped the goop with many Russians. Got some salve from a Russian Doc. for my feet. Got back from town about 7:30. Latest poop from the group! Heard that BBC made a broadcast announcing the liberation of the prisoners of Barth and that the next of kin was notified. I feel much better now, because they found our mail we wrote last Dec. in the warehouse. They also found a typewritten copy of our death sentence (each and every one of us here). They figured we in the air corps were the cause of most of the deaths of civilians. So it goes!

MAY 9

Ate b. and then again hit for town. Spent the morning playing dominoes with the Russians. All of them said, "Voyna skon chena", war is kaput. Also taught them how to shoot dice. Came back at 5:30 and had supper. Slept for a few hrs. Needed help at wing headquarters to translate American into Russian. They want a record of all here to take to Moscow. Worked until 12:30.

MAY 10

Jokers still hitting the road. Rumors have it that Zemke is going to try and court martial all who left here. Plenty of food and water, but you can't blame them for wanting to go home. I'm sorry I didn't leave the first day. I heard those jokers are now in England. Really pissed off. Some bastard stole my souveneirs. Ate dinner and went to town. Really had a swell time. Shot the baloney with the Russians. They really get a bang out of me. Feeling is mutual. They forced me and my buddies to eat. I couldn't refuse if I wanted to. Brought back multy souveneirs, money, Jerry pistol, boots, bayonet, also got them for my pals. Came back about 8:00 and had supper. Nix poop from the group and I sleep here again tonight.

MAY 11

More jokers hit the road early this morning. Day of rest, staying in. Heard the meat here is diseased—but we continue to eat it. Everyone is really mad, can't blame them—but so it goes! Layed in the sun and got me a slight burn. Spent the afternoon playing ball, then went for a shower. Heard the best news yet, after supper. A promise that we start leaving tomorrow, be it by plane or truck, but to leave is definite. God, I hope it's the real McCoy. Wounded first, then the bloomin Limeys, but they should be second priority, because they are veteran krieges, then us. What a difference! Everybody is really happy. Just the thought of going home makes me feel sharp as a tack.

MAY 12

Nix sleep last night. Col. Zemke made a speech last night at 11:30. Word came in that we may start leaving today, Sat., tomorrow for sure. Expects B-17's and C-47's to arrive at 2:00. We went mad and started to sing, dance, and cheer. This morning everyone is smiling and in high spirits. Bags are packed and preparation for evacuation is all set. Bring on the planes!! This afternoon at 2:00 sharp *two* B-17's came in and landed. They were the big clogs and explained the situation. They will evacuate 800 sick and wounded today, the rest of us will leave tomorrow and more cheers followed. Everyone is wild with joy. Trucks and jeeps came in from the front lines with books and thousands of copies of "Stars and Stripes". There they come!! All totaled, 40 I think. They landed, loaded and left with 900 for England. Tomorrow we all leave for France. Flares going up all over the place. They set fire to all the towers. We are really going mad. Nix sleeping tonight. God, but those planes look mighty fine.

MAY 13

My, what a beautiful day for evacuation. The roar of the motors awoke us this morning at 7:00 Happy, happy day. Goodby Germany forever. Sun. night—FRANCE—WAHOO!!! I'll bet they heard us back in the good old U.S.A. Left Germany at 5:25 and arrived in France 3 hrs. later. It's time to sign off, thank God. Before I quit I want to express my deepest regrets. I wish Bob and Mac were here with me—but so it goes. My sincerest thanks to God for having protected me and seeing me thru. Now to sweat shipment home. Pass the drinks, I'll have a double—Roger-Wilko-and out.

# BERNARD EPSTEIN

The prisoner-of-war diary of 1st Lt. Bernard Epstein, of Swampscott, Massachusetts, deals chiefly with the liberation experience, a bit different from that of the other P.O.W. diarists.

A photographer before the war and now the owner of his own lumber company and home center in the Greater Boston area, Lt. Epstein served as a Cannon Company Forward Observer with the 99th Infantry Division.

Past president of his local Rotary Club, a member of the Masonic Order and Disabled American Veterans, Mr. Epstein is the happily married father of twin boys and two girls.

The officer's prisoner-of-war camp in which he was detained after capture was Oflag 79, Brunswick, Germany.

*******

The night of January 9th, 1945
   Heard heavy artillery bombing about 10 or 15 miles away. They must be darn close now. All I have to sweat out is our own bombings and artillery again. Welcome on, Yanks, Let's go.
The night of April 10th
   Awoke this morning to hear artillery and bombing going on all around our camp. Were issued ⅓ American Parcel and all together morale is very high. Just issued statement from German Commandant of Camp that we will not be moved East and that he is going to give the Camp up to Allies intact without a struggle. He also stated that our German sentries were issued instructions not to fire at oncoming troops or at anyone inside of Camp for any reason whatsoever. He also promised to keep us supplied with enough food until our troops arrived. Two airports close by our Camp are burning planes on the ground, planes which they probably have no fuel to fly back into Eastern Germany with. Demolition explosions can be heard from every direction. I have been very excited all day and my only concern now was that we are not bombed or shelled by our own or Jerry guns and planes. Jerry planes overhead are now very rare. But I am still keeping my fingers crossed until our troops arrive and liberate us. Night is now closing in on us and

a terrific artillery barrage has just opened up from the South West. And Brother if you think I'm not scared, you're mistaken. The barrage keeps moving closer every minute. Well, I will close now hoping to awake in the morning and find our boys here. What I mean is, I will try to sleep. My bed just keeps rocking back and forth. After three attempts can't sleep at all with all this racket going on. Some boys are down in the Airraid shelter but I can't make up my mind, so I will take my chances here. Brunswick is burning. Awoke 6:00 morning of the 11th. The artillery has quit somewhat, but not altogether.

APRIL 11

Nice bright sunshiny day. Not much activity. Only distant rumbling. There was no German check parade this morning, for the first time since my arrival. No one knows what to make of the relative quiet. Rumors are that Hanover has fallen. Others that Brunswick has been passed by thrust heading for Magdeburg. Perhaps I'll catch a little nap while I can. Have not slept an average of two hours a night for past week. Well, I will pause now until something of importance comes up. Afternoon: German rumors around Camp are that Hanover has fallen and that Brunswick is almost completely surrounded. We can hear lots of shelling in Brunswick, but no air activity at present. Planes can be seen coming from the West towards Brunswick. Morale is very high. I hope we don't have too much shelling around here tonight or I'll be bomb happy.

Things are really happening now. Planes (Fighter Bombers) have just come in from the West and we can see them Dive Bombing. Brunswick artillery also has increased. Guess we will spend another sleepless night. Oh, oh, there comes a fighter low straffing about 2000 yards away from us on the auto bon.

12th APRIL

Awoke this morning after my first pretty good night's sleep to find relative quiet around our camp. Everyone is pretty excited, I especially, for early this morning I heard some small arms fire around our camp that definitely sounds like light machine guns which means our boys have finally arrived. By 9:00 o'clock everyone was up and around the wires watching, waiting and hoping to see some of our boys around and to know that we are finally liberated. At 9:15 the boys up in the attic (our spotters) began yelling like hell and everyone at the wires took up the yell although we can't see anything yet we can hear motors approaching and if I miss my guess I'll be darned if they aren't our jeeps coming down the road. At 9:21 the first American jeep drove up to our gate and brother all hell has broken loose here, everybody is yelling and jumping around like mad and banging everyone on the back and yelling "It's true, it's true, we're liberated". Some of the weaker boys who have been waiting for this for 3 and 4 years have actually broken down and are crying like babies. There's an American officer beside me with one leg amputated and he is so overcome he can't talk. He's blowing his nose and tears are just streaming down his cheeks. I have a big lump in my throat and am so excited I think my heart is going to burst. There goes one of the barbed wire fences under the pressure of some 500 men where I'm standing. They're mobbing the poor G.I.'s on the jeep. Everybody wants their autographs. More jeeps and vehicles coming in now, the German guards are just as excited as we are, guess they're about fed up. Now some light armoured vehicles are arriving, the gates have been thrown open and the camp is liberated officially. The men inside are running around like mad. Jeeps are scattered all around the camp, what a sight, now G.I.'s are climbing the Goon machine gun towers and dismounting the guns and smashing them against the cement pavement. It's hard to believe we're really free. Yanks are tossing rations to the boys and what a scramble these half starved boys are making. Here come a couple of newspaper correspondents from the New York Times and New York Mirror.

They just finished interviewing me after 15 min. I walked them around and introduced them to other Americans. What an exciting day, I've been running around like mad. Guess I'll settle down and try to sleep. But I doubt it very much. A Major General of 30th Inf. just arrived in camp to notify us that we would be moved back to rear as soon as Jerry pockets are cleaned up and so to bed.

FRIDAY-13th

Although this day is supposed to be an unlucky day I don't believe it as we are all still excited and the yanks are bringing in food, food, good old food. C rations, K rations and what have you. We were told we might have to remain here for a few days as thousands of prisoners being released all along the line have higher priority than us. But that plenty of food would arrive and we would be made as comfortable as possible. We were informed that the Town of Brunswick is in a chaotic state. Food supplies are moving in right this minute. Our camp Doctor has just made an announcement that the men should not over eat or they would suffer from all sorts of ailments but I don't think that will stop men from stuffing themselves as we've been under starvation rations for the past month and men are hungry. I've tried to contact someone who might know something about my Reg. and what happened to our boys after we were captured. I finally met Sgt. Jim Pollack of the 801st T.D. Bn. who gave me quite a bit of information about the 99 as he was in that same sector when the Germans started their counter offensive. Jim comes from Wash., D.C. and I've promised to contact his folks at my first opportunity. Jim's quite a guy, got himself the Silver Star for gallantry in action in knocking out 8 German Tanks with a basooka and holding the line when he could have taken off with his group to join up with others further back. Took Jim around camp on tour introducing him to all the Americans. Jim secured some fresh eggs and sugar for us and we'll have fresh eggs for breakfast, my first fresh eggs for some 6 months. Jim took some snapshots of the camp and of me and gave me the roll of film to have developed (send his folks 2 sets of film also 1 set to each man in my room). Everything is a little quieter in camp now, but we are all still very much excited. Well, guess I'll try to get a good night's sleep and finish another exciting day. I guess I'll never forget my experiences here at Oflag 79 as long as I live.

Got into bed and heard a low flying plane overhead which didn't sound like one of ours, later found out that it was a Jerry Recon. plane. But no damage done. Guess we're still subject to attack by Jerry planes until we're way back into France or England.

SAT. APRIL 14, 1945

Through some influence in being an American Officer I managed to get some cigs and distribute them amongst the boys in my room also some extra food rations. The S.B.O. just issued a statement saying we would be allowed to take a walk outside the wire if we all conducted ourselves in an orderly manner and so the first place I visited was the famous auto bon just 300 yds. away from camp and then to the airport just across the street. Found planes all over the place blown up by the retreating Jerries, guess that was the terrific demolition explosion we heard when our troops were moving up. It's a huge Airport and after looking from one hangar to another we found two German planes intact, one a 110 M.E. Messerschmidt. One Junker. Boy if only I had a camera to take pictures with. Climbed into one but was afraid to pull any of the gadgets, afraid of booby traps but did take a chance and pulled out the bomb release button for a souvenir. Then returned to camp and found I was very tired guess I'm not as strong as I thought I was. So I'll just take it easy and rest up a bit. Boy just can't put into words how I feel to have plenty of butter, sugar, bread, etc. to eat and not have to worry about our rations being cut from week to week until finally we had nothing to eat. The times I've sweat out our own bombers over our camp every night sitting in complete darkness hoping they wouldn't drop their bombs too close to us and let me tell you some of those we heard were darn close, rattled and shook our windows and doors and partially threw us from our beds, must have been pretty heavy stuff they dropped, but all thats over with now and I'll try to forget it all. I think all of this has affected me a little because whenever the boys begin talking a little too loud or rattle cans in the room I feel like jumping up and screaming shut up. I guess what I'll want most when I get out of here is peace and quiet for at least a month away from all noises and some good foods, mostly dairy foods as my old stomach has been on the bum ever since I was put in the bog.

APRIL 15, 1945 Sunday

Awoke this morning to find that my pal Kirk was being moved out with other hospital patients to Hildersheim whence they will be flown to England hope they pick us up soon. I'm impatient as all hell. 35th Div. pulled up this morning and relieved some boys from the T.D. Bn. Walked to main gate with one of our G.I.'s who was locked up in one of the cells and brother if I had spent 93 days in one of those cells I'd have gone nuts and I don't mean maybe. The cells are about 4 ft. by 8 ft. and have heavy steel doors (solid) and one little window near the ceiling about 12" x 2 ft. I then took a walk to the Airport again and we inspected building after building finding store rooms of food in each building imagine all that food no further than 800 yds. away and us boys made to live on starvation rations. We also found remains of hundreds of our Red Cross parcels in the Luftwof quarters. Parcels which we'd have given our right arm for a few weeks back. The more I walk around and see things the more I realize just what these Nazi B——Ds are. I hope to hell they get everything thats coming to them. Also found little huts in back of Airport where Russians peasants live in rags and were forced to live with some of the non-com luftwof. Went for another walk this afternoon and came across a dark room (photograph) it had been pretty well kicked up but found a beautiful enlarging lens, a zicon and it took a full hour getting it out of its container without scratching the lens. Also found a German pin ball machine intact and took out lots of German coins for souveniers for the kids. Went fooling around Airport climbed into German planes and had a little field day. Came back to barracks to find that there is still no news of when we'll move out of here except that they believe we'll move out by plane and fly us to England, and so another day but there remains the night. I won't feel safe until I'm back in France, England or the States.

APRIL 16, 1945 (Monday)

Before I forget last night the boys got hold of a chicken and out of the 15 men in our room 6 of us were lucky enough to draw the lucky numbers for a chicken supper prepared by some of our French officers. My first decent meal in 7 months of course I suffered some repercussions stomach pains but it was good while eating. Then I walked to Airport and found an L-5 cub plane there went up to the major piloting it and asked if he could take me up for a ride to see our prison camp and surrounding area from the air after finding out that I was a prisoner here he told me to hop in and I really enjoyed myself saw all the destruction around Brunswick (pop. 178,000) peace time population, war time about 500,000 and all the bomb craters sprinkled close around the perimeter of our camp which shows our Air Corps boys know their stuff for none of those bombs dropped inside (of course barring the accidental bombing when the Americans dropped about 7500 pounders and about 123 anti-personnel bombs and incendiaries probably mistaking the camp for a German Garrison this happened long before the American prisoners arrived Aug. 24, 1944. Total casualties 4 killed and 20 casualties among the prisoners in camp only 15 Germans and a few wounded). Heard that the 9th Army is setting up their headquarters in Brunswick today so guess we're pretty far behind the lines now. Met a G.I. name of Jeff Wren, (drives chauffeur for General Simpson) gave me cigarettes, soap, razor blades and etc. darn swell kid promised to send me a contact printer that I found in Luftwof developing room. Couldn't take it with me so he said for me to leave it with him and he'd mail it home for me. I promised to send him a set of art photos. Returned to camp to find a convoy of trucks had arrived with orders to move us out in morning. Result I couldn't sleep last night. Had a meeting at 10:30 P.M. and were told we'd pull out at 7:30 in morning for Hildershein where we would be flown in C 47 to Le Havre.

APRIL 16

Saw all kinds of destruction on the way to Hildershein am now writing this brief from Airport awaiting the arrival of our planes. There are thousands of liberated prisoners here wearing a conglamoration of uniform parts of Russian, French, Belgian and etc. to make a uniform for themselves. This scene here is unbelievable unless you actually see it with your own eyes. Officers meeting their own men after not seeing them since our capture. The sky is clouding over it looks like a thunder storm coming up. Les and I rigged ourselves up a bed out of Jerry camouflage nets and a canvas in an abandoned hangar and none too soon either as it's thundering, lightning and pouring out.

APRIL 17

Awoke this morning hoping to fly out today. Just met Mormak, Van Devordee and Carr, brother I was the happiest man alive to meet these men from my company whom I hadn't seen since my capture. Didn't have much time to talk to them as our planes just arrived to take us off. Took their home addresses and loaded into my plane. Am now writing this brief from the skies over Germany, there's planes all around us and what a feeling to be heading back towards home. They say we'll land at Le Havre in 3½ hours from there I guess we load into ships for good old U.S.A.

Landed at some Airport where there were large convoys of trucks awaiting our arrival. We were greeted by many high Army & Navy Officials, Red Cross girls, coffee and doughnuts and loaded into trucks and sent on our way to our new destination. After 2½ hours we arrived at Camp Lucky Strike a huge tent city camp set up for incoming liberated Prisoners of War, were processed, deloused and assigned to tents, lots of warm U.S. blankets and Toilet Kit. Met many of my men from Cannon Co. and exchanged our stories of what happened since our departure on that memorable day Dec. 18, 1944. None of them had seen, heard or know what happened to the rest of the officers.

APRIL 18, 1945

Awoke after a good night's rest and strolled around camp trying to locate other men whom I might know. Everybody here treats us like Kings, good meals with Egg Knogs and chocolate milk shakes between meals, guess they're trying to fatten us up.

APRIL 19, 1945

Met some more of my men today, they keep coming in all the time, beginning to put on weight myself can tell as my belt has been let out some since my arrival.

APRIL 21, 1945

Received an $80.00 partial payment, bought $75.00 worth of clothes and still haven't got enough for a new change. Moved to another area where we received a Typhus shot and answered some questions pertaining to our treatment by Germans.

APRIL 23, 1945

Still waiting for news of shipment home. Wrote 3 letters, they say we'll probably beat the letters home. Hope so. Got a pass and went to St. Valerie thence to Carnie, two small towns not far from camp. Not much doing there as people aren't very friendly to Americans, seems that people along French Coast dislike us for razing their homes to ground during invasion.

APRIL 24, 1945

Called to Headquarters and given orders putting me in charge of some 200 men to watch over until we hit Ft. Devens. Moved these men to an area by ourselves and now my headaches begin. Every man has a bitch of some nature or other as to mess, when we're going home, what they're allowed to take home, etc. In order to clear this Camp for shipment home I must have men medically checked for communicable diseases, convert all their foreign money to U.S. money, see that every man gets a PX ration and lots more headaches.

APRIL 25, 1945

Met a couple of Officers attached to some Port Battalion who were to help us in clearing these men for shipment. Lem Landis, Joe Nelms, both swell guys. Took care of all my incidentals such as lamps, bedding, coal, wood, etc.

APRIL 26, 1945

Almost ready for shipment got most of big work done and then will await orders to ship. Took a walk to Gift Shop bought some gifts for my family and friends.

APRIL 27, 1945

Awoke this morning to finish up my remaining work to clear my men. Most of men in my group came from Maine, New Hampshire, Vermont, Massachusetts, Connecticut, Rhode Island. Took walk and came back and had roll call of men to see how many were absent. Heard a voice outside which sounded rather familiar. The flaps of the tent spread open and there stood Lt. Palmer, what a feeling to find Palmer hadn't been killed and was actually here. After my excitement Palmer told me what happened after my capture. Said that Capt. Arnoldy had escaped back to our lines with Lt. Fisher, himself and Westy and Brown. Brown sent back to States with bad case of trench foot. Westbrook was later killed on patrol. Capt. Arnoldy had been wounded in leg and sent back to Hospital and then he (Palmer) had been wounded twice since last leaving me. One of our Platoon Sgts. (Perry) had received a battlefield commission. Also told me I was turned in together with Captain Arnoldy and Lt. Brown for a Bronze Star Medal. Palmer was not captured but sent here to Camp Lucky Strike on light duty to help with administrative work of clearing men for shipment home.

APRIL 28, 1945

Still waiting orders for shipment all my work cleaned up and found that my group was first to clean up all work prior to shipment and promised we would be first group out.

Took ride with Lem and Joe to "Dieppe" not much doing there lots of destruction and signs of a terrific struggle in liberating the Town.

APRIL 30, 1945

Meeting of all group commanders at Ramp Headquarters which probably means it's finally come. Told to have men ready for shipment 3:00 morning, given pile of records and etc. to turn over to Devens upon arrival. Returned to my area to inform men of good news and was given a rousing cheer, these men are all anxious to get home some have been in the bog for over 2 years or more.

APRIL 31, 1945

Didn't go to bed as I had a lot of work to be completed getting everyone ready and all my papers in order. Raining like H—L out got all men loaded into trucks, checked and unchecked, found 12 men absent. Given orders to scratch their names off list and take off. Got soaked to skin, caught sweet cold and sore throat. Arrived at Le Havre loaded Navy boat, given good breakfast and told that my responsibilities for trip were over as they wanted us all to have rest on way back. What a relief. My nerves are half shot and I certainly need a rest.

# GLOSSARY

ACK-ACK  British slang term for anti-aircraft fire.
BANDITS  Allied voice-radio term for unidentified aircraft.
BARRAGE BALLOONS  Unmanned balloons resembling small blimps, moored by heavy steel cables to protect ships, bases or other potential targets from low-flying air attack.
CON TRAILS  Thin cloudy lines left in the sky when the hot gases being exhausted by airplane engines hit cold air and turn into clouds.
C-RATIONS  Field ration kit designed for easy preparation by individual soldiers—it consisted of 2 cans, one containing stew, hash, or meat and beans, the other including candy, sugar, powdered fruit juice or coffee and C-ration biscuits.
DUCKS  Amphibious vehicles (official name DUKW) which could carry 25 men on land, 50 on water, or 5000 pounds of cargo. Used first in the invasion of Sicily.
DOODLE BUGS  German robot bombs.
D-RATIONS  A field ration consisting of a special chocolate bar designed to stay hard in hot climates and vitamin-fortified to furnish the nutritional equivalent of a meal when other food was not available.
ETO  European Theatre of Operations.
FLAK  An abbreviation of the German word for anti-aircraft gun but applied by American pilots to the fire from the guns.
GENERAL QUARTERS  A signal for all hands on a ship to go to batle stations.
GROUND POUNDERS  Infantrymen.
I.P.  Initial Point, that exact spot where the bomber groups turn into the bomb run, head directly for the target and take no further evasive action until bombs are released.
K-RATIONS  Originally developed for airborne troops but commonly used by troops in the field, especially in the Pacific, these consisted of three small boxes meant to serve as breakfast, dinner, and supper, containing a can of protein food, biscuits, candy or

fruit bar, instant coffee or powdered fruit juice concentrate, sugar, chewing gum and cigarettes.

LST   Landing Ship Tank-a big, flat-bottomed ship designed to transport tanks and other large vehicles across large ocean distances and land them directly on a beach. Also hauled troops and cargo.

LCT   Landing Craft Tank-a short range ship which could carry from 4 to 8 tanks or other carge. They could be carried empty on the upper deck of an LST and slid off sideways to be loaded for landing.

LCVP   Landing Craft Vehicle Personnel—could carry 36 fully equipped troops, a 6,000 pound vehicle or 8100 lbs. of cargo.

PFF   Path Finder Force, a specialized air unit that leads a mission when the target is obscured by weather and bombing must be done by radar.

RHINO FERRY   A pontoon barge powered by outboard engines. Could hold 30-40 vehicles and was designed to carry vehicles and cargo ashore from amphibious transports and large landing ships, at beaches where the slope was too gradual to let landing craft unload correctly.

SHELTER HALF   An issue of a piece of canvas 5 x 6 x 4, a tent pole in two sections, a rope and five stakes which made up a tent when combined with and buttoned to the shelter half of a serviceman's assigned tentmate.

SHORT ARM INSPECTION   A check by medical officers of the servicemen's penises for signs of venereal disease.

TIN CANS   Often just 'cans'. A slang term for destroyers.

# INDEX

(Places and fighting units only, with reference to diaries in which they figure)

| | | | | | |
|---|---|---|---|---|---|
| Alexandria, La. | Barton | Corsica | Schloss | | |
| Algiers, North Africa | Schloss | Coutances, France | McCaughey | | |
| Anzio, Italy | Sais, Schloss | Curacao | Bielik | | |
| Archangel, Russoa | Brummer | | | | |
| Armed Guard Receiving Station | Bielik | Dartmouth, England | Goldman | | |
| Aruba | Bielik | Dieppe, France | Epstein | | |
| Atlantic City, N.J. | Schloss | Dijon, France | Sais | | |
| Ayr, Scotland | McCaughey | Doagh, Ireland | Barton | | |
| | | | | | |
| Bahia, Brazil | Bielik | Efate Island, New Hebrides | McNamara | | |
| Ballymoney, Ireland | Barton | Emirau Island | McNamara | | |
| Bari, Italy | Edwards | El Guettar, N. Africa | Siegel | | |
| Barneville, France | McCaughey | Eniwetok, Marshall Islands | McNamara | | |
| Barth, Germany | Harkovich | Epinal, France | Sais | | |
| Belem, Brazil | Bielik | Espiritu Santo, New Hebrides | Fahey | | |
| Biak | Rhinehart | Eversdorf, Germany | Mazza | | |
| Bizerte, Tunisia | Lovell | Exeter, England | Goldman | | |
| Bokerettes, Russia | Brummer | | | | |
| Boston, Mass. | McNamara | Falmouth, England | Goldman | | |
| Bou Chebka, Tunisia | Lovell | Fiad Pass, Tunisia | Mesecher | | |
| Bougainville | McNamara | Flexible Gunnery Schl, Fla. | Schloss | | |
| Brooklyn Receiving Station | McNamara | Florence, Italy | Schloss | | |
| | | Fort Devens, Mass | Mazza | | |
| Cagliari, Sardinia | Schloss | Fort Dix | Barton | | |
| Calcutta, India | Brummer | Fort Thomas, Kentucky | Schloss | | |
| Camenera, Cuba | McNamara | Fowey, England | Goldman | | |
| Camp Barkley, Texas | Barton | Friedrichshafen, Germany | Mesecher | | |
| Camp Carson, Colo. | Christensen | 574 Technical School, Miami | Schloss | | |
| | McCaughey | | | | |
| Camp Claiborne, La. | Barton | Gibraltar | Siegel | | |
| Camp Kilmer, N.J. | Sais, Siegel | Glasgow, Scotland | McCaughey | | |
| Camp Lucky Strike | Mazza, Epstein | | Brummer | | |
| Camp Marshall Lysantey, Africa | Schloss | Gold Beach | Goldman | | |
| Camp Patrick Henry, Va. | Mazza, Schloss | Goose Bay, Labrador | Lewis | | |
| Cape Cod Canal | McNamara | Grattaghi, Italy | Edwards | | |
| Capetown, S. Africa | Brummer | Guadalcanal | Petr | | |
| Capri, Italy | Schloss | | McNamara | | |
| Carentan, France | McCaughey | Guam | McNamara | | |
| Carnie, France | Epstein | Guantanamo Bay, Cuba | McNamara | | |
| Catania, Italy | Schloss | | | | |
| Cazes Airfield, Casablanca | Schloss | Halifax, Nova Scotia | Goldman | | |
| Chatham, England | Goldman | Hanover, Germany | Mesecher | | |
| Cherbourg | McCaughey | Heianza | Ellis | | |
| Ciampiano Airfield, Rome | Schloss | Hollandia Bay, New Guinea | Rhinehart | | |
| Colombo, Ceylon | Brummer | Honolulu, Hi. | McNamara | | |
| Colorado Springs, Colo. | Christensen | | Askin | | |
| Commercy, France | McCaughey | | | | |

| | | | |
|---|---|---|---|
| Iceland | Lewis and Brummer | 92nd Bomb Group, 407th Sq. 8th AF | Booke |
| Iokanka, Russia | Brummer | 93rd Evacuation Hospital, Hanover | Mesecher |
| Iwo Jima | McNamara | 99th Infantry Div., Cannon Co. | Epstein |
| | | 132nd Infantry, Americal Division | Petr |
| Jersey City, N.J. | Bielik | 168th Inftry, 34th Div., Co. I | Mesecher |
| Juno Beach | Goldman | 201st Regt. H. Co. | Christensen |
| | | 271st Artillery, 1st Cav. Div. | Askin |
| Kasserine Pass, Tunisia | Lovell | 379th Bomb Group, 524th Sq. 8th AF | Lewis |
| Kaufbeuren, Germany | Sais | 379th Bómb Grp, 527th Sq. 8th AF | Sullivan |
| Kerama Retto | McNamara | 449th Bomb Grp, 717th Sq. | Edwards |
| | Rhinehart | | |
| Kilrea, Ireland | Barton | Morotai Island | Rhinehart |
| | | Murmansk, Russia | Brummer |
| | | | |
| | | Nagasaki, Japan | McNamara |
| Kimbolton, England | Lewis | Nancy, France | McCaughey |
| Kingswear, England | Goldman | | Sais |
| Kolie Point, Guadalcanal | Petr | Naples, Italy | Bielik |
| | | | Mesecher |
| La Calle, Algeria | Lovell | | Sais |
| Lagos, Nigeria | Bielik | | Schloss |
| | Brummer | Naumia | McNamara |
| La Haina Roads, Hi. | Rhinehart | Navy Task Force 39 | McNamara |
| Landon, England | Goldman | | Fahey |
| | McCaughey | Nettuno, Italy | Sais |
| Langres, France | Sais | Newport, R.I. | McNamara |
| Lauenberg, Germany | Mazza | New York City | Bielik |
| | Mesecher | | Siegel |
| Le Havre, France | Epstein | Norfolk, Va. | Brummer |
| Leghorn, Italy | Bielik | | McNamara |
| Lessiholly, Ireland | Barton | | Goldman |
| Leyte Gulf | Askin | Northern Attack Force 531 | Rhinehart |
| | McNamara | Noumea, New Caledonia | McNamara |
| | Rhinehart | Nova Zembia, Russia | Brummer |
| Lingayen Bay | Askin | | |
| Lisburn, Ireland | Barton | Oflag 79, Brunswick, Germany | Epstein |
| Luneville, France | Sais | Okinawa | Ellis |
| Lunga Point, Guadalcanal | Petr | | McNamara |
| Luxembourg | McCaughey | | Rhinehart |
| Luzon, Philippines | Askin | Omaha Beach | Goldman |
| Lyon, France | Sais | Oran, Algeria | Brummer |
| | | | Siegel |
| Madras, India | Brummer | Oulton Park, Chester, England | McCaughey |
| Maknassy, Tunisia | Lovell | | |
| Marseille, France | Sais | Paestum, Italy | Sais |
| Mateur, Tunisia | Lovell | Pago Pago, Samoa | McNamara |
| | Siegel | Painton, England | Goldman |
| Messdorf, Germany | Mazza | Paisley, Scotland | McCaughey |
| Milford Haven, Wales | Brummer | Panama Canal | McNamara |
| | Goldman | Paris, France | McCaughey |
| Military Units | | Pearl Harbor, Hi. | Askin |
| Seabees Group No. 1008 | McNamara | | McNamara |
| 2nd Armored Division | Goldman | Pisa, Italy | Bielik |
| 3rd Division, Marines | McNamara | Plattsburg, N.Y., Conv. Hospital | Schloss |
| | Rhinehart | Plymouth, England | Goldman |
| 4th Division, Marines | McNamara | | McCaughey |
| 17th Bomb Group, 34th Bomb Sq. | Schloss | Port of Spain, Trinidad | Bielik |
| 18th Infantry Division, Co. K | Siegel | Portland, England | Goldman |
| 37th Division | Epstein | Portland, Maine | McNamara |
| 44th Bomb Group, 66th Sq., 8th AF | Harkovich | Purvis Bay, Solomons | Fahey |
| 50th General Hospital | McCaughey | | McNamara |
| 53rd Medical Battalion, Co. D | Barton | | |
| 60th Fld Arty Battalion, 9th Inftry Division | Lovell | Recife, Brazil | Bielik |

# Index 429

| | | |
|---|---|---|
| Rio de Janeiro | Bielik | *Essex* | McNamara |
| Rome, Italy | Sais | *Fairfield City* | Brummer |
| | Schloss | *Florida* | Bielik |
| | | *Franks* | Rhinehart |
| St. Marcel Hospital, Paris | Mesecher | *Fuller* | Askin and Petr |
| St. Valerie, France | Epstein | *Fullum* | McNamara |
| Saipan, Marianas | McNamara | *Gryfevale* | Goldman |
| Salcombe, England | Goldman | *Guam* | McNamara |
| Samar Island | McNamara | *Guest* | McNamara |
| San Diego, California | McNamara | *Gyatt* | Brummer |
| San Francisco, Ca. | Askin | *Hamul* | McNamara |
| | McNamara | *Hazelwood* | McNamara |
| San Juan, Puerto Rico | McNamara | *Harris* | Rhinehart |
| San Raphael, France | Sais | *Hudson* | McNamara |
| Sardinia | Schloss | *Ironclad* | Brummer |
| Seaton Barracks, England | McCaughey | *Kidd* | McNamara |
| Sedjenane, Tunisia | Lovell | *Killen* | Rhinehart |
| Sened, Tunisia | Lovell | *Langdon* | Brummer |
| Sfax, Tunisia | Mesecher | *Leonard Wood* | Askin |
| Shepard Field, Colo. | Schloss | *Leutze* | Askin |
| Stalag 7 A, Mooseburg, Germany | Mesecher | *Lorentia* | Brummer |
| Stalag 5 B, Villigen, Germany | Mesecher | | |
| Stendal, Germany | Mazza | *LCT 91* | Goldman |
| Strasbourg, France | Sais | *LST 222* | Askin |
| Suez Canal | Brummer | *LST 246* | Askin |
| Swansea, Wales | Brummer | *LST 276* | Askin |
| Sydney, Australia | Fahey | *LST 346* | Goldman |
| | McNamara | *LST 499* | Goldman |
| | | *LST 506* | Goldman |
| Tacaloban, Phillippines | Rhinehart | *LST 537* | Goldman |
| Tarryall River, Colo. | Christensen | *LST 925* | Askin |
| Tebessa, Algeria | Lovell | *LST 991* | Askin |
| Thelepe, North Africa | Lovell | *LST 1028* | Askin |
| Tinian Island | McNamara | *Massachusetts* | McNamara |
| Torquay, England | Goldman | *Melville* | Goldman |
| Tulagi | Fahey | *Millicoma* | Rhinehart |
| Tunis, Tunisia | Mesecher | *Milwaukee* | Bielik |
| | | *Minneapolis* | McNamara |
| Ulithi, Caroline Islands | Askin | *Montpelier* | Fahey |
| | McNamara | *Mt. Vernon* | Schloss |
| Ulm, Germany | Sais | *Nathanael Greene* | Brummer |
| Utah Beach | McCaughey | *New Mexico* | McNamara |
| | | *North Carolina* | McNamara |
| Vessels | | *Ordronaux* | Brummer |
| | | *Oromor* | Brummer |
| *Anthony* | McNamara | *Patoka* | Bielik |
| *A.V. Fraser* | Brummer | *Paulis Potter* | Brummer |
| *Bennett* | McNamara | *Pecos* | Rhinehart |
| *Benjamin Harrison* | Brummer | *Pennsylvania* | Askin and McNamara |
| *Braine* | McNamara | *Portland* | Askin |
| *Calloway* | Askin | *President Hayes* | McNamara |
| *Casa Grande* | Rhinehart | *Princeton* | Rhinehart |
| *Chester Valley* | Brummer | *Prometheus* | Rhinehart |
| *Cincinnati* | Bielik | *Richard Bland* | Brummer |
| *Colorado* | Rhinehart | *Rocky Mount* | Askin |
| *Corbieser* | McNamara | *Rowe* | McNamara |
| *Core* | Goldman | *St. Louis* | Rhinehart |
| *Dailey* | McNamara | *San Mateo* | McNamara |
| *Danman* | Brummer | *Santa Helena* | Siegel |
| *Denver* | Fahey and McNamara | *Sea Fiddler* | Askin |
| *Dixie* | McNamara | *Sharpsburg* | Brummer |
| *Egeria* | Askin | *Silver Sword* | Brummer |
| *Empress of Scotland* | Schloss | *Troubador* | Brummer |
| *Epping Forest* | Rhinehart | *Uruguay* | Brummer |

| | | | |
|---|---|---|---|
| *Van Valkenburgh* | McNamara | *West Virginia* | Rhinehart |
| *Virginia Dare* | Brummer | *Winonia* | Bielik |
| *Wadsworth* | McNamara | *Yosemite* | McNamara |
| *Wainwright* | Brummer | Vicarage Rcvg. Base, England | Goldman |
| *Warren* | Askin | | |
| *Washington* | Brummer and McNamara | Waringsfield, Ireland | Barton |
| *Waskatomska* | Brummer | Wentworth Institute, Mass. | McNamara |
| *West Point* | McNamara | Will Rogers Field, Okla. | Schloss |